Modern Philosophy – From Descartes to Nietzsche

BLACKWELL PHILOSOPHY ANTHOLOGIES

Each volume in this outstanding series provides an authoritative and comprehensive collection of the essential primary readings from philosophy's main fields of study. Designed to complement the *Blackwell Companions to Philosophy* series, each volume represents an unparalleled resource in its own right, and will provide the ideal platform for course use.

Modern Philosophy – From Descartes to Nietzsche
An Anthology

Edited by *Steven M. Emmanuel and Patrick Goold*

Virginia Wesleyan College

BLACKWELL
Publishers

Copyright © Blackwell Publishers Ltd 2002
Editorial matter and organization copyright © Steven M. Emmanuel and Patrick Goold

First published 2002

2 4 6 8 10 9 7 5 3 1

Blackwell Publishers Inc.
350 Main Street
Malden, Massachusetts 02148
USA

Blackwell Publishers Ltd
108 Cowley Road
Oxford OX4 1JF
UK

Library of Congress Cataloging-in-Publication Data

Modern philosophy : from Descartes to Nietzsche : an anthology / edited by Steven M.
Emmanuel and Patrick Goold.
    p.cm. — (Blackwell philosophy anthologies; 17)
Includes bibliographical references and index.
ISBN 0-631-21420-8 (hardback : alk. paper) — ISBN 0-631-21421-6 (pbk. : alk. paper)
    1. Philosophy, Modern. I. Emmanuel, Steven M. II. Goold, Patrick Allen. III. Series.

B791 .M66 2002
190—dc21   2001043105

British Library Cataloguing in Publication Data
A CIP catalogue record for this book is available from the British Library.

Typeset in 9 on 11 pt Ehrhardt
by Kolam Information Services Pvt Ltd, Pondicherry, India

Printed in Great Britain by MPG Books Ltd, Bodmin, Cornwall

This book is printed on acid-free paper.

Contents

Contents

Contents

Part XV   Arthur Schopenhauer (1788–1860)

Part XVI   John Stuart Mill (1806–73)

Part XVII   Karl Marx (1818–83)

Contents

Part XVIII Friedrich Nietzsche (1844–1900)

Preface

An anthology of philosophical writings can be useful to at least three distinct audiences. First, it can serve as a textbook for teachers and students in college courses in the history of philosophy. Second, it can provide the raw material out of which autodidact readers form their own view of the history of philosophical thought, or provide themselves with crucial background to something else they are reading. Finally, it can be a reference work for professional philosophers, providing them with a source of interesting texts and contexts quite likely not contained in the focused libraries of their specialities. Whereas most anthologies are aimed at the first audience, we have designed the present volume with an eye to serving all three. To accomplish this goal, however, we have found it necessary to depart from the standard anthology format.

Every modern philosophy anthology includes landmark texts of canonical figures in the tradition. But while we have included representative samples from all the leading figures of the modern period, we have not reproduced some of their standard works. Descartes's *Meditations on First Philosophy*, for example, is not included, nor are there any selections from Hobbes's *Leviathan* or Kant's *Critique of Pure Reason*. These texts are readily available in inexpensive student editions (and so can be obtained separately), and they are already part of the intellectual equipment of the professional philosopher. These omissions are largely made good by the inclusion, often in their entirety, of shorter texts that briefly restate the results of the longer works. Omitting the longer works also allows us to include a greater range of writings from each author's intellectual work.

A second departure from the standard anthology format is the inclusion of texts that are not strictly speaking philosophical. In the early modern period, philosophy and the natural sciences had not yet separated so fully as they have in our own day. Philosophical problems often arose out of scientific work and vice versa. A similar point stands *mutatis mutandis* with respect to the modern philosophers and many other now distinct spheres of cultural production. We risk anachronism if we filter what has come down to us in order to bring it into line with a division of labor that was not yet in place in the era in which it was written. In the case of intellectual figures renowned for their contributions to scientific as well as philosophical literature, something of the former is included. For instance, Descartes's treatise on the nature of light will be found here, as well as selections from Berkeley's essay on motion. Alongside the more purely philosophical works we have reproduced a variety of important but seldom anthologized writings concerning psychology, mathematics, education, history, religion, and politics. Among the latter will be found selections from Hobbes's discussion of method, Berkeley's commentary on morality, Kant's political theory, Mill's reflections on logic and religion, and Kierkegaard's polemical writings.

In making our selections we have tried to place the modern thinkers in conversation with each other. Sometimes they comment directly on one another's work: Leibniz comments on Descartes, Reid on Locke and Hume, Kant on

Hobbes, Schopenhauer on Kant and Hegel, Nietzsche on Schopenhauer, and so on. Thematic patterns tie the readings together in other ways. We hope that this will enable readers to see the history of modern philosophy as the story of a succession of thinkers engaged in the rational discussion of a constellation of core ideas. In this regard, our aim may be considered wholly traditional.

We wish, however, to avoid any Whiggish assumptions about the necessity of the course of this conversation. Such assumptions falsify the historicity of philosophy and fetter thinking about its as yet unrealized possibilities. Accident has a hand in the course of philosophy as in any other human project. For one thing, changing intellectual fashion affects how the story is told. The case of Hegel is illustrative. Hegel dominated philosophy in his day as a systematic metaphysician. A later period, less confident of the metaphysics, took the *Philosophy of Right* for the lasting work, and based a communitarian ethic on it. Still later, with positivism advancing on all fronts, Hegel dropped from the conversation altogether. In our time, philosophers inspired by recent work in biology, neuroanatomy, and computer science have begun to rethink epistemology along more coherentist and evolutionary lines. This development has had a surprising consequence: more than one recent commentator has noted the relevance of Hegel's thought to contemporary epistemological discussion, claiming that the *Phenomenology of Spirit* illuminates central issues in the work of Quine, Davidson, and Putnam.

Intellectual fashion might have taken a different course, assigning Hegel an altogether different significance in the great conversation. The same could be said about all of the thinkers in this volume. No one knows what sense the work of future philosophers will give to what has already unfolded. As Borges has famously written, every author creates his own precursors. Nor can we predict the results of future historical inquiry. The history of philosophy is not an *a priori* discipline. Though there is considerable agreement among scholars concerning the development of modern philosophical thought – the important problems and seminal texts – we must bear in mind that the history of philosophy is an empirical study and, as such, can never be closed or completed.

The careful historian will attempt to situate earlier thinkers in the context of an intricate cul-

tural conversation in which they were drawing on, and responding to, the work of others. Recognizing that happenings quite outside philosophy may determine what seems reasonable or even possible within philosophy, the historian will inquire into the extra-philosophical context that set the original problematic and constrained the range of approaches philosophers thought it necessary to consider. The results of such inquiry can force us to revise substantially our interpretation of a philosopher's work; they can also give hitherto neglected figures and texts new prominence. Recent studies of Descartes, for example, have challenged long-standing assumptions about the significance of his philosophical writings. As Stephen Gaukroger has persuasively argued, Descartes wrote the *Meditations* for the chief purpose of providing a metaphysical justification for his Copernican natural philosophy – a justification Descartes felt was needed in light of the Roman Inquisition's condemnation of Galileo in 1633. Not surprisingly, scholars are now turning to Descartes's contributions in physics, as well as in physiology and psychology, to orient and augment their understanding of his philosophical thought.

Even if we in the present generation find ourselves completely satisfied with our picture of the past, we must acknowledge that there were other possibilities that vanished for sufficient causes but not necessarily good reasons. Perhaps some of them, like Hegel's epistemology, will be resurrected for a time and given new employment in a future philosophy. Keeping that option open is one valuable function of historical study. A good anthology will therefore include texts that help tell the story of modern philosophy as we now have it. But it will also include some material that has been overlooked for no better reason than that it did not serve a narrative purpose for earlier generations. If this material has no other value, its inclusion may at least in some small way help to dispel the constraining illusion of inevitability.

Accordingly, in making our selections for this volume we have tried to reflect some of the results of recent scholarship. But we have also gone off the beaten track in modest ways; in part to unsettle complacency, and in part to provide resources for those seeking alternative narratives.

The significance of the past is established anew by each generation. In defining our past, we define our present and declare our vision for the future. What are the possibilities that lie before us? Out of what shall we construct our sense of what philosophy has been and what it might become? We hope our anthology, without being idiosyncratic, supplies enough unusual material to be useful to anyone seeking answers to these questions.

Acknowledgments

Bentham, Jeremy, *An Introduction to the Principles of Morals and Legislation* (1789) (ed. Laurence J. Lafleur) (Hafner Publishing Co., New York, 1948).

Bentham, Jeremy, "The Panopticon, or the Inspection-House" (1791) from (ed. John Bowring) *The Works of Jeremy Bentham*, vol. 4 (Russell and Russell Inc., New York, 1962).

Bentham, Jeremy, "A Fragment on Government" (1776) from (ed. John Bowring) *The Works of Jeremy Bentham*, vol. 1 (Russell and Russell Inc., New York, 1962).

Bentham, Jeremy, "A Fragment on Ontology" from (ed. John Bowring) *The Works of Jeremy Bentham*, vol. 8 (Russell and Russell Inc., New York, 1962).

Bentham, Jeremy, "Essay on Logic" from (ed. John Bowring) *The Works of Jeremy Bentham*, vol. 8 (Russell and Russell Inc., New York, 1962).

Bentham, Jeremy, "Chrestomathia" from (ed. John Bowring) *The Works of Jeremy Bentham*, vol. 8 (Russell and Russell Inc., New York, 1962).

Berkeley, George, "An Essay Towards a New Theory of Vision" (1709) from (ed. Colin Murray Turbayne) *Works on Vision* (The Bobbs–Merrill Co. Inc., Indianapolis, 1963).

Berkeley, George, *A Treatise Concerning the Principles of Human Knowledge* (1710) (ed. Colin Murray Turbayne) (The Bobbs–Merrill Co. Inc., Indianapolis, 1957).

Berkeley, George, "Concerning Motion" (*De Motu*, 1721) from (ed. T. E. Jessop) *Berkeley: Philosophical Writings* (Greenwood Press, New York, 1969).

Berkeley, George, "Passive Obedience" (1712) from (ed. Alexander Campbell Fraser) *The Works of George Berkeley*, vol. 4 (Oxford University Press, Oxford, 1901).

Descartes, René, "Principles of Philosophy" (*Principia Philosophiae*, 1644: Part 1: The Principles of Human Knowledge) from (trans. John Cottingham, Robert Stoothoff, and Dugald Murdoch) *The Philosophical Writings of Descartes*, vol. 1 (Cambridge University Press, Cambridge, 1985, © Cambridge University Press).

Descartes, René, "The Passions of the Soul" (*Les Passions de l'Ame*, 1649: Part 1: The Passions in General) from (trans. John Cottingham, Robert Stoothoff, and Dugald Murdoch) *The Philosophical Writings of Descartes*, vol. 1 (Cambridge University Press, Cambridge, 1985, © Cambridge University Press).

Descartes, René, "The Treatise on Light" (*Le Monde de Mr Descartes ou le Traité de la Lumière*, 1664) from (trans. Stephen Gaukroger) *The World and Other Writings* (Cambridge University Press, Cambridge, 1998, © Cambridge University Press).

Hegel, G. W. F., "Who Thinks Abstractly?" from (trans. Walter Kaufmann) *Hegel: Texts and Commentary* (Anchor Books, New York, 1965. Copyright © Weidenfeld and Nicolson, London).

Hegel, G. W. F., *The Logic of Hegel* (trans. William Wallace (Oxford, 1873).

Hegel, G. W. F., *Phenomenology of Spirit* (trans. A. V. Miller) (Oxford University Press, Oxford, 1977, reprinted by permission of Oxford University Press).

Hobbes, Thomas, "Concerning Body" (*De Corpore*, 1655) from (ed. Sir William Molesworth) *The English Works of Thomas Hobbes of Malmesbury*, vol. 1 (Scientia Aalen, 1962: reprint of the 1839 edition).

Hobbes, Thomas, "The Citizen" (*De Cive*, 1642) from (trans. Thomas Hobbes, ed. Bernard Gert) *Man and Citizen* (Peter Smith, Gloucester, MA, 1978, reprinted by permission of Hackett Publishing Company Inc., Cambridge, MA).

Hobbes, Thomas, "On Man" (*De Homine*, 1658) from (ed. Charles T. Wood, T. S. K. Scott-Craig and Bernard Gert) *Man and Citizen* (Peter Smith, Gloucester, MA, 1978, reprinted by permission of Hackett Publishing Company Inc., Cambridge, MA).

Hume, David, "An Enquiry Concerning Human Understanding" (1748) from (ed. Thomas Hill Green and Thomas Hodge Grose) *David Hume: Philosophical Works*, vol. 4 (Scientia Verlag Aalen, Germany, 1964).

Hume, David, *An Enquiry Concerning the Principles of Morals* (1751) (ed. L. A. Selby-Brigge, rev. P. H. Nidditch) (Clarendon Press, Oxford, 1975, reprinted by permission of Oxford University Press).

Hume, David, "Of the Original Contract" (1748) from (ed. Charles W. Hendel) *David Hume's Political Essays* (The Bobbs-Merrill Co. Inc., Indianapolis, 1953).

Hume, David, "The Natural History of Religion" (1757) from (ed. Thomas Hill Green and Thomas Hodge Grose) *David Hume: Philosophical Works*, vol. 4 (Scientia Verlag Aalen, Germany, 1964).

Kant, Immanuel, *What Real Progress Has Metaphysics Made in Germany since the Time of Leibniz and Wolff?* (1804) (trans. Ted Humphrey) (Abaris Books, New York, 1983).

Kant, Immanuel, "The Metaphysics of Morals" (*Metaphysik der Sitten*, 1797) from (trans. John Ladd) *The Metaphysical Elements of Justice* (The Bobbs-Merrill Co. Inc., Indianapolis, 1965).

Kant, Immanuel, "Immanuel Kant's Logic: A Manual for Lectures" (1800) from (trans. Robert S. Hartman and Wolfgang Schwarz) *Logic* (The Bobbs-Merrill Co. Inc., Indianapolis, 1974).

Kant, Immanuel, "On the Common Saying..." (1793) from (ed. Hans Reiss, trans. H. B. Nisbet) *Kant's Political Writings* (Cambridge University Press, Cambridge, 1970, © Cambridge University Press).

Kant, Immanuel, *Lectures on Philosophical Theology* (*Vorlesungen über die philosophische Religionslehre*, 1830) (trans. Allen W. Wood and Gertrude M. Clark) (Cornell University Press, Ithaca and London, 1978).

Kierkegaard, Søren, *Fear and Trembling* (*Frygt og Bæven*, 1843) (trans. Alastair Hannay) (Penguin Books, 1985).

Kierkegaard, Søren, *Practice in Christianity*, trans. Howard V. Hong and Edna H. Hong (Princeton University Press, 1991).

Kierkegaard, Søren, *Purity of Heart Is To Will One Thing* (English translation copyright 1938 by Harper & Brothers, renewed © 1966 by Douglas V. Steere. Reprinted by permission of HarperCollins Publishers, Inc.).

Kierkegaard, Søren, "The Fatherland" (*Fædrelandet*, 1855) from (trans. Walter Lowrie) *Attack Upon "Christendom"* (Princeton University Press, 1968. Copyright © 1968 by Princeton University Press. Reprinted by permission of Princeton University Press).

Acknowledgments

Kierkegaard, Søren, "The Instant" (*Øjeblikket*, 1855) from (trans. Walter Lowrie) *Attack Upon "Christendom"* (Princeton University Press, 1968. Copyright © 1968 by Princeton University Press. Reprinted by permission of Princeton University Press).

Leibniz, G. W., "Meditations on Knowledge, Truth, and Ideas" (1684) from (trans. Roger Ariew and Daniel Garber) *G. W. Leibniz: Philosophical Essays* (Hackett Publishing Company, Inc., Indianapolis, 1989).

Leibniz, G. W., "On Nature Itself" from (trans. Roger Ariew and Daniel Garber) *G. W. Leibniz: Philosophical Essays* (Hackett Publishing Company, Inc., Indianapolis, 1989).

Leibniz, G. W, "The Principles of Nature and of Grace" (1714) from (trans. Leroy E. Loemker) *Gottfried Wilhelm Leibniz: Philosophical Papers and Letters* (2nd edn) (Reidel Publishing Co., Dordrecht, 1969; reprinted by permission of Kluwer Academic Publishers, Dordrecht, The Netherlands).

Leibniz, G. W, "A Vindication of God's Justice Reconciled with His Other Perfections and All His Actions" (1710) from (trans. Paul and Anne Martin Schrecker) *Monadology and Other Philosophical Essays* (The Bobbs-Merrill Co., Inc., New York, 1965).

Locke, John, "Essay Concerning Human Understanding" (1690) from *The Works of John Locke*, vol. 2 (Scientia Verlag Aalen, Germany, 1963).

Locke, John, "Of the Conduct of the Understanding" (1706) from *The Works of John Locke*, vol. 3 (Scientia Verlag Aalen, Germany, 1963).

Locke, John, "A Discourse of Miracles" (1706) from *The Works of John Locke*, vol. 9 (Scientia Verlag Aalen, Germany, 1963).

Locke, John, *Two Treatises of Government* (1690) (ed. Thomas P. Peardon) (The Bobbs-Merrill Co. Inc., Indianapolis, 1952).

Malebranche, Nicolas, *The Search After Truth* (1674–5) (trans. Thomas M. Lennon and Paul J. Olscamp) (Ohio State University Press, Columbus, 1980).

Malebranche, Nicolas, *Treatise on Nature and Grace* (1680) (trans. Patrick Riley) (Oxford University Press, New York, 1992).

Malebranche, Nicolas, *Dialogues on Metaphysics and on Religion* (ed. Nicholas Jolley, trans. David Scott) (Cambridge University Press, Cambridge, 1997, © Cambridge University Press).

Marx, Karl, excerpts from *Marx's Concept of Man* by Erich Fromm (copyright © 1961, 1966 by Erich Fromm. Copyright © renewed 1994 by The Estate of Erich Fromm. Reprinted by permission of The Continuum International Publishing Company, Inc.).

Marx, Karl, *Capital: A Critique of Political Economy*, vol. 1 (trans. Samuel Moore and Edward Aveling) (International Publishers, New York, 1967).

Marx, Karl, with Friedrich Engels, *The Communist Manifesto* (trans. David McLellan) (Oxford University Press, Oxford, 1992, reprinted by permission of Oxford University Press).

Mill, John Stuart, "Speech on Perfectibility" (delivered 1828) from *The Collected Works of John Stuart Mill*, vol. 26 (ed. John M. Robson) (University of Toronto Press, 1988).

Mill, John Stuart, "Utilitarianism" (1863) from *Dissertations and Discussions*, vol. 3 (Henry Holt and Co., New York, 1882).

Mill, John Stuart, "On Democracy" (1835) from (ed. J. M. Robson) *J. S. Mill: A Selection of His Works* (Odyssey Press, New York, 1966).

Mill, John Stuart, "A System of Logic" (1843) from (ed. Ernest Nagel) *J. S. Mill's Philosophy of Scientific Method* (Hafner Publishing Co., New York, 1950).

Mill, John Stuart, "The Utility of Religion" (1874) from *Three Essays on Religion: Nature, the Utility of Religion and Theism* by John Stuart Mill (Longmans, Green, Reader and Dyer, London, 1874).

Nietzsche, Friedrich, "Preface" from (trans. R. J. Hollingdale) *Daybreak* (Cambridge University Press, Cambridge, 1982, © Cambridge University Press).

Nietzsche, Friedrich, *Human, All Too Human* (trans. R. J. Hollingdale) (Cambridge University Press, Cambridge, 1986, © Cambridge University Press).

Nietzsche, Friedrich, *The Gay Science*, translated and edited, with commentary by Walter Kaufmann (copyright © 1974 by Random House, Inc. Used by permission of Random House, Inc.).

Reid, Thomas, *Essays on the Intellectual Powers of Man* (1785) (ed. Baruch A. Brody) (The MIT Press, Cambridge, MA, 1969).

Reid, Thomas, *Essays on the Active Powers of the Human Mind* (1788) (ed. Baruch A. Brody) (The MIT Press, Cambridge, MA, 1969).

Reid, Thomas, *Thomas Reid on the Animate Creation* (ed. Paul Wood) (The Pennsylvania State University Press, University Park, 1995. Copyright © 1995 by The Pennsylvania State University. Reproduced by permission of the publisher. UK and Commonwealth rights permission of Edinburgh University Press).

Rousseau, Jean-Jacques, "Discourse on the Arts and the Sciences" (1750) from (trans. G. D. H. Cole, rev. J. H. Brumfitt and John C. Hall) *The Social Contract and Discourses* (J. M. Dent & Sons Ltd, London, 1973).

Rousseau, Jean-Jacques, "A Note to the *Discourse on the Origin of Inequality*" (1754) from (trans. G. D. H. Cole, rev. J. H. Brumfitt and John C. Hall) *The Social Contract and Discourses* (J. M. Dent & Sons Ltd, London, 1973).

Rousseau, Jean-Jacques, *Émile* (trans. Barbara Foxley) (J. M. Dent & Sons Ltd, London, 1969).

Rousseau, Jean-Jacques, "The Social Contract" from (trans. G. D. H. Cole, rev. J. H. Brumfitt and John C. Hall) *The Social Contract and Discourses* (J. M. Dent & Sons Ltd, London, 1973).

Schopenhauer, Arthur, *The World as Will and Representation* (trans. E. F. J. Payne) (Dover Publications Inc., New York, 1958).

Spinoza, Benedict de, "Treatise on the Emendation of the Intellect" (posthumously 1677) from (trans. Edwin Curley) *The Collected Works of Spinoza* (Princeton University Press, 1985. Copyright © 1985 by Princeton University Press. Reprinted by permission of Princeton University Press).

Spinoza, Benedict de, "Ethics" (posthumously 1677) from (trans. Edwin Curley) *The Collected Works of Spinoza* (Princeton University Press, 1985. Copyright © 1985 by Princeton University Press. Reprinted by permission of Princeton University Press).

Spinoza, Benedict de, "A Theologico-Political Treatise" (1670) from (trans. R. H. M. Elwes) *The Chief Works of Benedict de Spinoza*, vol. 1 (Dover Publications, New York, 1951).

We wish to express our heartfelt thanks to Margaret Aherne for her careful reading and editing of the manuscript. Finally, we would like to dedicate this book to our students.

PART I

René Descartes (1596–1650)

Introduction

While Descartes's *Meditations on First Philosophy* (1641) has long served as a general introduction to his thought, current studies are re-evaluating the significance of that work in the light of his other writings. Our opening selection, *The World or Treatise on Light* (1664), was the first part of a larger (but not fully realized) project to develop a unified physical theory that would explain all natural phenomena. A significant feature of this early work (commenced *ca.* 1629) is its commitment to the controversial hypothesis that the Earth moves around the Sun. Fearful of incurring the censure of the Roman Church, Descartes did not allow the work to go into print during his own lifetime. He did, however, publish a summary of his central metaphysical and scientific ideas in a work entitled *Principles of Philosophy* (1644). The last three parts of this work correspond very closely to the discussion of natural philosophy found in *The Treatise on Light* – minus the controversial hypothesis. Part 1, from which we have taken our excerpt, contains a more precise formulation of the metaphysical arguments developed in the *Meditations*. In both design and content, *Principles of Philosophy* demonstrates the sense in which Descartes's metaphysics was intended to serve as a justification for his physical theory. Our concluding selection is from Descartes's last work, *The Passions of the Soul* (1649). This study was the result of a long correspondence with Princess Elizabeth of Bohemia concerning the nature of the interaction between mind and body. In the excerpt below, taken from Part 1, Descartes explains the nature of the passions in terms of his understanding of human physiology.

1

The Treatise on Light

Chapter 6: Description of a New World, and the Qualities of the Matter of Which It Is Composed

For a while, then, allow your thought to wander beyond this world to view another, wholly new, world, which I call forth in imaginary spaces before it. The Philosophers tell us that these spaces are infinite, and they should certainly be believed, since it is they themselves who invented them. But in order to keep this infinity from impeding and hampering us, let us not try to go all the way, but rather enter it only far enough to lose sight of all the creatures that God made five or six thousand years ago, and after stopping there in some definite place, let us suppose that God creates anew so much matter all around us that, in whatever direction our imagination may extend, it no longer perceives any place that is empty.

Even though the sea is not infinite, those who are on a vessel in the middle of it can extend their view seemingly to infinity, and nevertheless there is still water beyond what they see. Thus even though our imagination seems to be able to stretch to infinity, and we do not assume this new matter to be infinite, we can assume nevertheless that it fills spaces much greater than those we have imagined. And in order that there be nothing in this assumption that you find objectionable, let us not allow our imagination to extend as far as it could, but purposely confine it to a determinate space

The Treatise on Light (1664). From *The World and Other Writings,* tr. and ed. Stephen Gaukroger (Cambridge University Press, 1998). Selection: chs 6–7, pp. 21–32.

which is no greater, say, than the Earth and the principal stars in the firmament, and let us suppose that the matter which God has created extends indefinitely far beyond in all directions. For it is much more reasonable to – and we are much better able to – prescribe limits to the action of our mind than to the works of God.

Now since we are taking the liberty of imagining this matter as we fancy, let us attribute to it, if we may, a nature in which there is absolutely nothing that everyone cannot know as perfectly as possible. To this end, let us explicitly assume that it does not have the form of earth, fire, or air, or any other more specific form, like that of wood, stone, or metal; nor does it have the qualities of being hot or cold, dry or moist, light or heavy, or of having any taste, odour, sound, colour, light, or of any other quality in nature of which there might be said to be something which is not known clearly by everyone.

On the other hand, let us not think that this matter is the "prime matter" of the Philosophers, which they have stripped so thoroughly of all its forms and qualities that nothing remains in it which can be clearly understood. Let us rather conceive of it as a real, perfectly solid body, which uniformly fills the entire length, breadth, and depth of this great space in the midst of which we have brought our mind to rest. Thus, each of its parts is so proportional to its size that it could not fill a larger one nor squeeze itself into a smaller one; nor, while it remains there, could it allow another body to find a place there.

Let us add further that this matter may be divided into as many parts and shapes as we can imagine, and that each of its parts can take on as many motions as we can conceive. Let us also suppose that God does divide it into many such parts, some larger some smaller, some of one shape some of another, as it pleases us to imagine them. It is not that He separates these parts from one another so that there is some void in between them; rather, let us think of the differences that He creates within this matter as consisting wholly in the diversity of the motions He gives to its parts. From the first instant of their creation, He causes some to start moving in one direction and others in another, some faster and others slower (or even, if you wish, not at all); and He causes them to continue moving thereafter in accordance with the ordinary laws of nature. For God has established these laws in such a marvellous way that even if we suppose that He creates nothing more than what I have said, and even if He does not impose any order or proportion on it but makes it of the most confused and muddled chaos that any of the poets could describe, the laws of nature are sufficient to cause the parts of this chaos to disentangle themselves and arrange themselves in such a good order that they will have the form of a most perfect world, a world in which one will be able to see not only light, but all the other things as well, both general and particular, that appear in the actual world.

But before I explain this at greater length, pause again for a minute to consider this chaos, and note that it contains nothing which you do not know so perfectly that you could not even pretend to be ignorant of it. For the qualities that I have placed in it are only such as you could imagine. And as far as the matter from which I have composed it is concerned, there is nothing simpler or more easily grasped in inanimate creatures. The idea of that matter is such a part of all the ideas that our imagination can form that you must necessarily conceive of it, or you can never imagine anything at all.

Nevertheless, the Philosophers are so subtle that they can find problems in things that seem extremely clear to other men, and the memory of their "prime matter", which they acknowledge to be rather hard to conceive, may divert them from knowledge of the matter of which I speak. Thus I should say to them at this point that, unless I am mistaken, the whole difficulty they face with their matter derives only from their wanting to distinguish it from its own proper quantity and from its outward extension, that is, from the property it has of occupying space. In this, however, I am willing for them to think they are right, for I have no intention of pausing to contradict them. And they should not find it strange that the quantity of the matter that I have described does not differ from its substance any more than number differs from the things numbered. Nor should they find it strange if I conceive of its extension, or the property it has of occupying space, not as an accident, but as its true form and essence; for they cannot deny that it is quite easy to conceive of it in this way. And my purpose, unlike theirs, is not to explain the things that are in fact in the actual world, but only to make up as I please a world in which there is nothing that the dullest minds cannot conceive, and which nevertheless could not be created exactly the way I have imagined it.

Were I to put in this new world the least thing that is obscure, this obscurity might well conceal some hidden contradiction I had not perceived, and thus without thinking I might suppose something impossible. Instead, since everything I propose here can be imagined distinctly, it is certain that even if there were nothing of this sort in the old world, God can nevertheless create it in a new one; for it is certain that He can create everything we imagine.

Chapter 7: The Laws of Nature of This New World

But I do not want to delay any longer telling you the means by which Nature alone is able to untangle the confusion of the chaos which I have been speaking about, and what the Laws of Nature that God has imposed on it are.

Take it then, first, that by "Nature" here I do not mean some deity or other sort of imaginary power. Rather, I use the word to signify matter itself, in so far as I am considering it taken together with the totality of qualities I have attributed to it, and on the condition that God continues to preserve it in the same way that He created it. For it necessarily follows from the mere fact that He continues to preserve it thus that there may be many changes in its parts that cannot, it seems to me, properly be attributed to the action of God, because this action never changes, and which I therefore attribute to Nature. The rules by which these changes take place I call the Laws of Nature.

In order to understand this better, remember that among the various qualities of matter we have supposed that its parts have had various different motions since the moment they were created, and furthermore that they all touch one another on all sides, without there being any void in between any two of them. From this it follows necessarily that from the time they begin to move, they also begin to change and diversify their motions by colliding with one another. Thus, while God subsequently preserves them in the same way He created them, He does not preserve them in the same state. That is to say, if God always acts in the same way and consequently always produces substantially the same effect, many differences in this effect occur, as if by accident. And it is easy to accept that God, who is, as everyone must know, immutable, always acts in the same way. Without my going any further into these metaphysical considerations, however, I will set out here two or three of the principal rules by which we must believe God to cause the nature of this new world to act, and these will be enough, I believe, to acquaint you with all the others.

The first is that each particular part of matter always continues in the same state unless collision with others forces it to change its state. That is to say, if the part has some size, it will never become smaller unless others divide it; if it is round or square, it will never change that shape unless others force it to; if it is brought to rest in some place it will never depart from that place unless others drive it out; and if it has once begun to move, it will always continue with an equal force until others stop or retard it.

There is no one who does not believe that this same rule is observed in the old world as regards size, shape, rest, and a thousand other things. But the Philosophers have exempted motion from it, which is the one thing that I most explicitly wish to include. Do not think that I intend to contradict them, though: the motion that they speak of is so very different from that which I conceive that it can easily happen that what is true of the one is not true of the other.

They themselves admit that the nature of their motion is very little understood. And trying to make it more intelligible, they have still not been able to explain it more clearly than in these terms: *Motus est actus entis in potentia, prout in potentia est.* These terms are so obscure to me that I am compelled to leave them in Latin because I cannot interpret them. (And in fact the words "motion is the act of a being which is in potency, in so far as it is in potency" are no clearer for being in the vernacular.) By contrast, the nature of the motion that I mean to speak of here is so easily known that

even geometers, who among all men are the most concerned to conceive the things they study very distinctly, have judged it simpler and more intelligible than the nature of surfaces and lines, as is shown by the fact that they explain "line" as the motion of a point and "surface" as the motion of a line.

The Philosophers also posit many motions which they believe can occur without any body's changing place, such as those they call *motus ad formam*, *motus ad calorem*, *motus ad quantitatem* (motion with respect to form, motion with respect to heat, motion with respect to quantity) and countless others. For my own part, I know of no motion other than that which is easier to conceive of than the lines of geometers, by which bodies pass from one place to another and successively occupy all the spaces in between.

In addition, the Philosophers attribute to the least of these motions a being much more solid and real than they do to rest, which they say is merely a privation of motion. For my part, I conceive of rest as a quality also, which should be attributed to matter while it remains in one place, just as motion is a quality attributed to matter while it is changing place.

Finally, the motion of which they speak has a very strange nature in that all other things have as a goal their perfection, and strive only to preserve themselves, whereas it has no other end or goal than rest, and contrary to all laws of nature it strives of itself to destroy itself. By contrast, the motion I suppose follows the same laws of nature as do generally all the dispositions and qualities found in matter. This includes those that the Schoolmen call *modos et entia rationis cum fundamento in re* (modes and beings of thought based in the thing) as well as those they call *qualitates reales* (their real qualities), in which I frankly confess I cannot find any more reality than in the others.

I put forward as my second rule that when one of these bodies pushes another it cannot give the other any motion except by losing as much of its own motion at the same time; nor can it take away any of the other's motion unless its own is increased by the same amount. This rule, together with the preceding, accords very well with all those observations in which we see one body begin or cease to move because it is pushed or stopped by another. For, having assumed the previous rule, we are free from the difficulty in which the Schoolmen find themselves when they wish to explain why a stone continues to move for some time after leaving the hand of the person who threw it. For we should ask instead, why does the stone not continue to move forever? Yet the reason is easy to give. For who can deny that the air in which it is moving offers it some resistance? We hear it whistle when it divides the air, and if a fan, or some other very light and extended body, is moved through the air, we shall even be able to feel by the weight in our hand that the air is impeding its motion rather than keeping it moving, as some have wanted to say. Now suppose we refuse to explain the effects of the air's resistance in line with our second rule, thinking that the more a body can resist the more it is capable of stopping the motion of others, as we might initially be persuaded perhaps. We will then have great difficulty explaining why the motion of this stone is diminished more in colliding with a soft body which offers moderate resistance than when it collides with a harder body which resists it more. Likewise, we shall find it hard to explain why, as soon as it has exerted itself a little against the latter, it immediately turns around, rather than stopping or interrupting its motion. But if we accept this rule, there is no difficulty here at all. For it tells us that the motion of one body is not retarded by its collision with another in proportion to how much the latter resists it, but only in proportion to how much the latter's resistance is surmounted, and to the extent that, in obeying the law, it receives into itself the force of motion that the former gives up.

Now although, in most of the motions we see in the actual world, we cannot perceive that the bodies that begin or cease to move are pushed or stopped by some others, we have no reason to judge that these two rules are not being followed exactly. For it is certain that such bodies can often receive their agitation from the two elements of air and fire, which are always found among them without being perceptible (as has just been said), or that they may receive it from the ordinary air, which also cannot be perceived by the senses. It is certain too that they can transfer this agitation sometimes to the grosser air, and sometimes to the whole mass of the earth; and when dispersed therein, it also cannot be perceived.

But even if everything our senses ever experienced in the actual world seemed manifestly contrary to what is contained in these two rules, the reasoning that has taught me them seems so strong that I cannot help believing myself obliged to suppose them in the new world that I am describ-

ing to you, for what more firm and solid a foundation could one find to establish a truth, even if one wished to choose it at will, than the very firmness and immutability which is in God?

Now these two rules follow manifestly from the sole fact that God is immutable and that, acting always in the same way, He always produces the same effect. For on the assumption that He placed a certain amount of motion in matter in general at the first instant He created it, we must admit either that He preserves the same amount of motion in it, or not believe that He always acts in the same way. If we assume, in addition, that from this first instant the various parts of matter, in which these motions are found unequally dispersed, began to retain them or transfer them from one to another, according as they had the force to do so, then we must of necessity hold that God causes them to continue always doing so. And that is what these two rules specify.

I shall add as a third rule that, when a body is moving, even if its motion most often takes place along a curved line and, as we said above, it can never make any movement that is not in some way circular, nevertheless each of its parts individually tends always to continue moving along a straight line. And so the action of these parts, that is the inclination they have to move, is different from their motion.

For example, if we make a wheel turn on its axle, even though its parts go in a circle (because, being joined to one another, they cannot do otherwise), nevertheless their inclination is to go straight ahead, as appears clearly if one of them is accidentally detached from the others, for as soon as it is free its motion ceases to be circular and continues in a straight line.

By the same token, when a stone is swung in a sling, not only does it fly straight out when it leaves the sling, but while it is in the sling it presses against the middle of it and causes the cord to stretch. This shows clearly that it always has a tendency to go in a straight line and that it goes in a circle only under constraint.

This rule rests on the same foundation as the other two, and depends solely on God's conserving everything by a continuous action, and consequently on His conserving it not as it may have been some time earlier but precisely as it is at the very instant He conserves it. So, of all motions, only motion in a straight line is entirely simple and has a nature which may be grasped wholly in an instant. For in order to conceive of such motion it is enough to think that a body is in the process of moving in a certain direction, and that this is the case at each determinable instant during the time that it is moving. By contrast, to conceive of circular motion, or any other possible motion, it is necessary to consider at least two of its instants, or rather two of its parts, and the relation between them. But so that the Philosophers (or rather the Sophists) do not find the opportunity here to engage in their useless subtleties, note that I am not saying that rectilinear motion can take place in an instant; but only that all that is required to produce it is found in bodies in each instant that may be determined while they are moving, whereas not everything that is required to produce circular motion is present. [...]

According to this rule, then, we must say that God alone is the author of all the motions in the world in so far as they exist and in so far as they are straight, but that it is the various dispositions of matter that render the motions irregular and curved. Likewise, the theologians teach us that God is also the author of all our actions, in so far as they exist and in so far as they have some goodness, but that it is the various dispositions of our wills that can render them evil.

I could set out many further rules here for determining in detail when and how, and by how much, the motion of each body can be diverted and increased or decreased by colliding with others, that is, rules that comprise all the effects of nature in a summary way. But I shall be content to tell you that, apart from the three laws that I have explained, I wish to suppose no others but those that most certainly follow from the eternal truths on which mathematicians have generally supported their most certain and most evident demonstrations: the truths, I say, according to which God Himself has taught us He disposed all things in number, weight, and measure. The knowledge of these truths is so natural to our souls that we cannot but judge them infallible when we conceive them distinctly, nor doubt that if God had created many worlds, they would be as true in each of them as in this one. Thus those who know how to examine the consequences of these truths and of our rules sufficiently will be able to recognise effects by their causes. To express myself in scholastic terms, they will be able to have *a priori* demonstrations of everything that can be produced in this new world.

And so that there will be nothing to prevent this, we shall, if you please, assume in addition that God will never perform a miracle in the new world, and that the intelligences, or rational souls, which we might later suppose to be there, will not disrupt the ordinary course of nature in any way.

Nevertheless, after this, I do not promise to set out exact demonstrations of everything I say. It will be enough for me to open up the way for you to find them yourselves, when you take the trouble to look for them. Most minds lose interest when one makes things too easy for them. And so as to present a picture which pleases you here, I must use shading as well as bright colours. So I shall be content to continue with the description I have begun, as if my intention were simply to tell you a fable.

2

Principles of Philosophy

Part One: The Principles of Human Knowledge

1. *The seeker after truth must, once in the course of his life, doubt everything, as far as is possible.*

Since we began life as infants, and made various judgements concerning the things that can be perceived by the senses before we had the full use of our reason, there are many preconceived opinions that keep us from knowledge of the truth. It seems that the only way of freeing ourselves from these opinions is to make the effort, once in the course of our life, to doubt everything which we find to contain even the smallest suspicion of uncertainty.

2. *What is doubtful should even be considered as false.*
Indeed, it will even prove useful, once we have doubted these things, to consider them as false, so that our discovery of what is most certain and easy to know may be all the clearer.

3. *This doubt should not meanwhile be applied to ordinary life.*
This doubt, while it continues, should be kept in check and employed solely in connection with the contemplation of the truth. As far as ordinary life is concerned, the chance for action would frequently pass us by if we waited until we could

Principles of Philosophy (1644). From **The Philosophical Writings of Descartes**, vol. 1, tr. John Cottingham, Robert Stoothoff, and Dugald Murdoch (Cambridge University Press, 1985). Selection: Part 1: "The Principles of Human Knowledge," pp. 193–222. (Angled brackets contain material added from later editions approved by Descartes.)

free ourselves from our doubts, and so we are often compelled to accept what is merely probable. From time to time we may even have to make a choice between two alternatives, even though it is not apparent that one of the two is more probable than the other.

4. *The reasons for doubt concerning the things that can be perceived by the senses.*
Given, then, that our efforts are directed solely to the search for truth, our initial doubts will be about the existence of the objects of sense-perception and imagination. The first reason for such doubts is that from time to time we have caught out the senses when they were in error, and it is prudent never to place too much trust in those who have deceived us even once. The second reason is that in our sleep we regularly seem to have sensory perception of, or to imagine, countless things which do not exist anywhere; and if our doubts are on the scale just outlined, there seem to be no marks by means of which we can with certainty distinguish being asleep from being awake.

5. *The reasons for doubting even mathematical demonstrations.*
Our doubt will also apply to other matters which we previously regarded as most certain – even the demonstrations of mathematics and even the principles which we hitherto considered to be self-evident. One reason for this is that we have sometimes seen people make mistakes in such matters and accept as most certain and self-evident things which seemed false to us. Secondly, and most importantly, we have been told that there is an

omnipotent God who created us. Now we do not know whether he may have wished to make us beings of the sort who are always deceived even in those matters which seem to us supremely evident; for such constant deception seems no less a possibility than the occasional deception which, as we have noticed on previous occasions, does occur. We may of course suppose that our existence derives not from a supremely powerful God but either from ourselves or from some other source; but in that case, the less powerful we make the author of our coming into being, the more likely it will be that we are so imperfect as to be deceived all the time.

6. *We have free will, enabling us to withhold our assent in doubtful matters and hence avoid error.*

But whoever turns out to have created us, and however powerful and however deceitful he may be, in the meantime we nonetheless experience within us the kind of freedom which enables us always to refrain from believing things which are not completely certain and thoroughly examined. Hence we are able to take precautions against going wrong on any occasion. *Absolutely*

7. *It is not possible for us to doubt that we exist while we are doubting; and this is the first thing we come to know when we philosophize in an orderly way.*

In rejecting – and even imagining to be false – everything which we can in any way doubt, it is easy for us to suppose that there is no God and no heaven, and that there are no bodies, and even that we ourselves have no hands or feet, or indeed any body at all. But we cannot for all that suppose that we, who are having such thoughts, are nothing. For it is a contradiction to suppose that what thinks does not, at the very time when it is thinking, exist. Accordingly, this piece of knowledge – *I am thinking, therefore I exist* – is the first and most certain of all to occur to anyone who philosophizes in an orderly way.

8. *In this way we discover the distinction between soul and body, or between a thinking thing and a corporeal thing.*

This is the best way to discover the nature of the mind and the distinction between the mind and the body. For if we, who are supposing that everything which is distinct from us is false, examine what we are, we see very clearly that neither extension nor shape nor local motion, nor anything of this kind which is attributable to a body, belongs

to our nature, but that thought alone belongs to it. So our knowledge of our thought is prior to, and more certain than, our knowledge of any corporeal thing; for we have already perceived it, although we are still in doubt about other things.

9. *What is meant by "thought".*

By the term "thought", I understand everything which we are aware of as happening within us, in so far as we have awareness of it. Hence, *thinking* is to be identified here not merely with understanding, willing and imagining, but also with sensory awareness. For if I say "I am seeing, or I am walking, therefore I exist", and take this as applying to vision or walking as bodily activities, then the conclusion is not absolutely certain. This is because, as often happens during sleep, it is possible for me to think I am seeing or walking, though my eyes are closed and I am not moving about; such thoughts might even be possible if I had no body at all. But if I take "seeing" or "walking" to apply to the actual sense or awareness of seeing or walking, then the conclusion is quite certain, since it relates to the mind, which alone has the sensation or thought that it is seeing or walking. *But how do we know we are actually thinking?*

10. *Matters which are very simple and self-evident are only rendered more obscure by logical definitions, and should not be counted as items of knowledge which it takes effort to acquire.*

I shall not here explain many of the other terms which I have already used or will use in what follows, because they seem to me to be sufficiently self-evident. I have often noticed that philosophers make the mistake of employing logical definitions in an attempt to explain what was already very simple and self-evident; the result is that they only make matters more obscure. And when I said that the proposition *I am thinking, therefore I exist* is the first and most certain of all to occur to anyone who philosophizes in an orderly way, I did not in saying that deny that one must first know what thought, existence and certainty are, and that it is impossible that that which thinks should not exist, and so forth. But because these are very simple notions, and ones which on their own provide us with no knowledge of anything that exists, I did not think they needed to be listed.

11. *How our mind is better known than our body.*

In order to realize that the knowledge of our mind is not simply prior to and more certain than the

[handwritten margin notes: *But how do we know that we actually being? May deem at us depend ought on in reality perhaps we don't. Maybe none of my thoughts are real thoughts*]

[handwritten bottom note: *Emerson? Did this distinction influence him*] knowledge of our body, but also more evident, we should notice something very well known by the natural light: nothingness possesses no attributes or qualities. It follows that, wherever we find some attributes or qualities, there is necessarily some thing or substance to be found for them to belong to; and the more attributes we discover in the same thing or substance, the clearer is our knowledge of that substance. Now we find more attributes in our mind than in anything else, as is manifest from the fact that whatever enables us to know anything else cannot but lead us to a much surer knowledge of our own mind. For example, if I judge that the earth exists from the fact that I touch it or see it, this very fact undoubtedly gives even greater support for the judgement that my mind exists. For it may perhaps be the case that I judge that I am touching the earth even though the earth does not exist at all; but it cannot be that, when I make this judgement, my mind which is making the judgement does not exist. And the same applies in other cases <regarding all the things that come into our mind, namely that we who think of them exist, even if they are false or have no existence>.

12. *Why this fact does not come to be known to all alike.*
Disagreement on this point has come from those who have not done their philosophizing in an orderly way; and the reason for it is simply that they have never taken sufficient care to distinguish the mind from the body. Although they may have put the certainty of their own existence before that of anything else, they failed to realize that they should have taken "themselves" in this context to mean their minds alone. They were inclined instead to take "themselves" to mean only their bodies – the bodies which they saw with their eyes and touched with their hands, and to which they incorrectly attributed the power of sense-perception; and this is what prevented them from perceiving the nature of the mind.

13. *The sense in which knowledge of all other things depends on the knowledge of God.*
The mind, then, knowing itself, but still in doubt about all other things, looks around in all directions in order to extend its knowledge further. First of all, it finds within itself ideas of many things; and so long as it merely contemplates these ideas and does not affirm or deny the existence outside itself of anything resembling them, it cannot be mistaken. Next, it finds certain common notions from which

it constructs various proofs; and, for as long as it attends to them, it is completely convinced of their truth. For example, the mind has within itself ideas of numbers and shapes, and it also has such common notions as: *If you add equals to equals the results will be equal*; from these it is easy to demonstrate that the three angles of a triangle equal two right angles, and so on. And so the mind will be convinced of the truth of this and similar conclusions, so long as it attends to the premisses from which it deduced them. But it cannot attend to them all the time; and subsequently, recalling that it is still ignorant as to whether it may have been created with the kind of nature that makes it go wrong even in matters which appear most evident, the mind sees that it has just cause to doubt such conclusions, and that the possession of certain knowledge will not be possible until it has come to know the author of its being.

14. *The existence of God is validly inferred from the fact that necessary existence is included in our concept of God.*
The mind next considers the various ideas which it has within itself, and finds that there is one idea – the idea of a supremely intelligent, supremely powerful and supremely perfect being – which stands out from all the others. <And it readily judges from what it perceives in this idea, that God, who is the supremely perfect being, is, or exists. For although it has distinct ideas of many other things it does not observe anything in them to guarantee the existence of their object.> In this one idea the mind recognizes existence – not merely the possible and contingent existence which belongs to the ideas of all the other things which it distinctly perceives, but utterly necessary and external existence. Now on the basis of its perception that, for example, it is necessarily contained in the idea of a triangle that its three angles should equal two right angles, the mind is quite convinced that a triangle does have three angles equalling two right angles. In the same way, simply on the basis of its perception that necessary and eternal existence is contained in the idea of a supremely perfect being, the mind must clearly conclude that the supreme being does exist.

15. *Our concepts of other things do not similarly contain necessary existence, but merely contingent existence.*
The mind will be even more inclined to accept this if it considers that it cannot find within

itself an idea of any other thing such that necessary existence is seen to be contained in the idea in this way. And from this it understands that the idea of a supremely perfect being is not an idea which was invented by the mind, or which represents some chimera, but that it represents a true and immutable nature which cannot but exist, since necessary existence is contained within it.

16. *Preconceived opinions prevent the necessity of the existence of God from being clearly recognized by everyone.*

Our mind will, as I say, easily accept this, provided that it has first of all completely freed itself from preconceived opinions. But we have got into the habit of distinguishing essence from existence in the case of all other things; and we are also in the habit of making up at will various ideas of things which do not exist anywhere and have never done so. Hence, at times when we are not intent on the contemplation of the supremely perfect being, a doubt may easily arise as to whether the idea of God is not one of those which we made up at will, or at least one of those which do not include existence in their essence.

17. *The greater the objective perfection in any of our ideas, the greater its cause must be.*

When we reflect further on the ideas that we have within us, we see that some of them, in so far as they are merely modes of thinking, do not differ much one from another; but in so far as one idea represents one thing and another represents another, they differ widely; and the greater the amount of objective perfection they contain within themselves, the more perfect their cause must be. For example, if someone has within himself the idea of a highly intricate machine, it would be fair to ask what was the cause of his possession of the idea: did he somewhere see such a machine made by someone else; or did he make such a close study of mechanics, or is his own ingenuity so great, that he was able to think it up on his own, although he never saw it anywhere? All the intricacy which is contained in the idea merely objectively – as in a picture – must be contained in its cause, whatever kind of cause it turns out to be; and it must be contained not merely objectively or representatively, but in actual reality, either formally or eminently, at least in the case of the first and principal cause.

18. *This gives us a second reason for concluding that God exists.*

Since, then, we have within us the idea of God, or a supreme being, we may rightly inquire into the cause of our possession of this idea. Now we find in the idea such immeasurable greatness that we are quite certain that it could have been placed in us only by something which truly possesses the sum of all perfections, that is, by a God who really exists. For it is very evident by the natural light not only that nothing comes from nothing but also that what is more perfect cannot be produced by – that is, cannot have as its efficient and total cause – what is less perfect. Furthermore, we cannot have within us the idea or image of anything without there being somewhere, either within us or outside us, an original which contains in reality all the perfections belonging to the idea. And since the supreme perfections of which we have an idea are in no way to be found in us, we rightly conclude that they reside in something distinct from ourselves, namely God – or certainly that they once did so, from which it most evidently follows that they are still there.

19. *Even if we do not grasp the nature of God, his perfections are known to us more clearly than any other thing.*

This is sufficiently certain and manifest to those who are used to contemplating the idea of God and to considering his supreme perfections. Although we do not fully grasp these perfections, since it is in the nature of an infinite being not to be fully grasped by us, who are finite, nonetheless we are able to understand them more clearly and distinctly than any corporeal things. This is because they permeate our thought to a greater extent, being simpler and unobscured by any limitations. < Furthermore, there is no reflection which can better serve to perfect our understanding, or which is more important than this, in so far as the consideration of an object which has no limits to its perfections fills us with satisfaction and assurance. >

20. *We did not make ourselves, but were made by God; and consequently he exists.*

However, this is something that not everyone takes note of. When people have an idea of some intricate machine, they generally know where they got the idea from; but we do not in the same way have a recollection of the idea of God being sent to us from God, since we have always possessed it.

Accordingly, we should now go on to inquire into the source of our being, given that we have within us an idea of the supreme perfections of God. Now it is certainly very evident by the natural light that a thing which recognizes something more perfect than itself is not the source of its own being; for if so, it would have given itself all the perfections of which it has an idea. Hence, the source of its being can only be something which possesses within itself all these perfections – that is, God.

21. *The fact that our existence has duration is suffi-cient to demonstrate the existence of God.*
It will be impossible for anything to obscure the clarity of this proof, if we attend to the nature of time or of the duration of things. For the nature of time is such that its parts are not mutually depend-ent, and never coexist. Thus, from the fact that we now exist, it does not follow that we shall exist a moment from now, unless there is some cause – the same cause which originally produced us – which continually reproduces us, as it were, that is to say, which keeps us in existence. For we easily understand that there is no power in us enabling us to keep ourselves in existence. We also understand that he who has so great a power that he can keep us in existence, although we are distinct from him, must be all the more able to keep himself in exist-ence; or rather, he requires no other being to keep him in existence, and hence, in short, is God.

22. *Our method of recognizing the existence of God leads to the simultaneous recognition of all the other attributes of God, in so far as they can be known by the natural power of the mind.*
There is a great advantage in proving the existence of God by this method, that is to say, by means of the idea of God. For the method enables us at the same time to come to know the nature of God, in so far as the feebleness of our nature allows. For when we reflect on the idea of God which we were born with, we see that he is eternal, omniscient, omnipotent, the source of all goodness and truth, the creator of all things, and finally, that he pos-sesses within him everything in which we can clearly recognize some perfection that is infinite or unlimited by any imperfection.

23. *God is not corporeal, and does not perceive through the senses as we do; and he does not will the evil of sin.*
There are many things such that, although we recognize some perfection in them, we also find in them some imperfection or limitation, and these therefore cannot belong to God. For example, the nature of body includes divisibility along with extension in space, and since being divisible is an imperfection, it is certain that God is not a body. Again, the fact that we perceive through the senses is for us a perfection of a kind; but all sense-perception involves being acted upon, and to be acted upon is to be dependent on something else. Hence it cannot in any way be supposed that God perceives by means of the senses, but only that he understands and wills. And even his understand-ing and willing does not happen, as in our case, by means of operations that are in a certain sense distinct one from another; we must rather suppose that there is always a single identical and perfectly simple act by means of which he simultaneously understands, wills and accomplishes everything. When I say "everything" I mean all *things*: for God does not will the evil of sin, which is not a thing.

24. *We pass from knowledge of God to knowledge of his creatures by remembering that he is infinite and we are finite.*
Now since God alone is the true cause of every-thing which is or can be, it is very clear that the best path to follow when we philosophize will be to start from the knowledge of God himself and try to deduce an explanation of the things created by him. This is the way to acquire the most perfect scientific knowledge, that is, knowledge of effects through their causes. In order to tackle this task with a reasonable degree of safety and without risk of going wrong we must take the precaution of always bearing in mind as carefully as possible both that God, the creator of all things, is infinite, and that we are altogether finite.

25. *We must believe everything which God has revealed, even though it may be beyond our grasp.*
Hence, if God happens to reveal to us something about himself or others which is beyond the nat-ural reach of our mind – such as the mystery of the Incarnation or of the Trinity – we will not refuse to believe it, despite the fact that we do not clearly understand it. And we will not be at all surprised that there is much, both in the immeasurable nature of God and in the things created by him, which is beyond our mental capacity.

26. *We should never enter into arguments about the infinite. Things in which we observe no limits – such as*

the extension of the world, the division of the parts of matter, the number of the stars, and so on – should instead be regarded as indefinite.

Thus we will never be involved in tiresome arguments about the infinite. For since we are finite, it would be absurd for us to determine anything concerning the infinite; for this would be to attempt to limit it and grasp it. So we shall not bother to reply to those who ask if half an infinite line would itself be infinite, or whether an infinite number is odd or even, and so on. It seems that nobody has any business to think about such matters unless he regards his own mind as infinite. For our part, in the case of anything in which, from some point of view, we are unable to discover a limit, we shall avoid asserting that it is infinite, and instead regard it as indefinite. There is, for example, no imaginable extension which is so great that we cannot understand the possibility of an even greater one; and so we shall describe the size of possible things as indefinite. Again, however many parts a body is divided into, each of the parts can still be understood to be divisible and so we shall hold that quantity is indefinitely divisible. Or again, no matter how great we imagine the number of stars to be, we still think that God could have created even more; and so we will suppose the number of stars to be indefinite. And the same will apply in other cases.

27. *The difference between the indefinite and the infinite.* [...]

28. *It is not the final but the efficient causes of created things that we must inquire into.* [...]

29. *God is not the cause of our errors.*
The first attribute of God that comes under consideration here is that he is supremely truthful and the giver of all light. So it is a complete contradiction to suppose that he might deceive us or be, in the strict and positive sense, the cause of the errors to which we know by experience that we are prone. For although the ability to deceive may perhaps be regarded among us men as a sign of intelligence, the will to deceive must undoubtedly always come from malice, or from fear and weakness, and so cannot belong to God.

30. *It follows that everything that we clearly perceive is true; and this removes the doubts mentioned earlier.*

It follows from this that the light of nature or faculty of knowledge which God gave us can never encompass any object which is not true in so far as it is indeed encompassed by this faculty, that is, in so far as it is clearly and distinctly perceived. For God would deserve to be called a deceiver if the faculty which he gave us was so distorted that it mistook the false for the true <even when we were using it properly>. This disposes of the most serious doubt which arose from our ignorance about whether our nature might not be such as to make us go wrong even in matters which seemed to us utterly evident. Indeed, this argument easily demolishes all the other reasons for doubt which were mentioned earlier. Mathematical truths should no longer be suspect, since they are utterly clear to us. And as for our senses, if we notice anything here that is clear and distinct, no matter whether we are awake or asleep, then provided we separate it from what is confused and obscure we will easily recognize – whatever the thing in question – which are the aspects that may be regarded as true. There is no need for me to expand on this point here, since I have already dealt with it in the *Meditations on Metaphysics*; and a more precise explanation of the point requires knowledge of what I shall be saying later on.

31. *Our errors, if considered in relation to God, are merely negations; if considered in relation to ourselves they are privations.*
Yet although God is no deceiver, it often happens that we fall into error. In order to investigate the origin and cause of our errors and learn to guard against them, we should realize that they do not depend on our intellect so much as on our will. Moreover, errors are not things, requiring the real concurrence of God for their production. Considered in relation to God they are merely negations, and considered in relation to ourselves they are privations.

32. *We possess only two modes of thinking: the perception of the intellect and the operation of the will.*
All the modes of thinking that we experience within ourselves can be brought under two general headings: perception, or the operation of the intellect, and volition, or the operation of the will. Sensory perception, imagination and pure understanding are simply various modes of perception; desire, aversion, assertion, denial and doubt are various modes of willing.

33. *We fall into error only when we make judgements about things which we have not sufficiently perceived.*
Now when we perceive something, so long as we do not make any assertion or denial about it, we clearly avoid error. And we equally avoid error when we confine our assertions or denials to what we clearly and distinctly perceive should be asserted or denied. Error arises only when, as often happens, we make a judgement about something even though we do not have an accurate perception of it.

34. *Making a judgement requires not only the intellect but also the will.*
In order to make a judgement, the intellect is of course required since, in the case of something which we do not in any way perceive, there is no judgement we can make. But the will is also required so that, once something is perceived in some manner, our assent may then be given. Now a judgement – some kind of judgement at least – can be made without the need for a complete and exhaustive perception of the thing in question; for we can assent to many things which we know only in a very obscure and confused manner.

35. *The scope of the will is wider than that of the intellect, and this is the cause of error.*
Moreover, the perception of the intellect extends only to the few objects presented to it, and is always extremely limited. The will, on the other hand, can in a certain sense be called infinite, since we observe without exception that its scope extends to anything that can possibly be an object of any other will – even the immeasurable will of God. So it is easy for us to extend our will beyond what we clearly perceive; and when we do this it is no wonder that we may happen to go wrong.

36. *Our errors cannot be imputed to God.* [...]

37. *The supreme perfection of man is that he acts freely or voluntarily, and it is this which makes him deserve praise or blame.* [...]

38. *The fact that we fall into error is a defect in the way we act, not a defect in our nature. The faults of subordinates may often be attributed to their masters, but never to God.*
The fact that we fall into error is a defect in the way we act or in the use we make of our freedom, but not a defect in our nature. For our nature remains the same whether we judge correctly or incorrectly. And although God could have endowed our intellect with a discernment so acute as to prevent our ever going wrong, we have no right to demand this of him. Admittedly, when one of us men has the power to prevent some evil, but does not prevent it, we say that he is the cause of the evil; but we must not similarly suppose that because God could have brought it about that we never went wrong, this makes him the cause of our errors. The power which men have over each other was given them so that they might employ it in discouraging others from evil; but the power which God has over all men is both absolute and totally free. So we should give him the utmost thanks for the goods which he has so lavishly bestowed upon us, instead of unjustly complaining that he did not bestow on us all the gifts which it was in his power to bestow.

39. *The freedom of the will is self-evident.*
That there is freedom in our will, and that we have power in many cases to give or withhold our assent at will, is so evident that it must be counted among the first and most common notions that are innate in us. This was obvious earlier on when, in our attempt to doubt everything, we went so far as to make the supposition of some supremely powerful author of our being who was attempting to deceive us in every possible way. For in spite of that supposition, the freedom which we experienced within us was nonetheless so great as to enable us to abstain from believing whatever was not quite certain or fully examined. And what we saw to be beyond doubt even during the period of that supposition is as self-evident and as transparently clear as anything can be.

40. *It is also certain that everything was preordained by God.* [...]

41. *How to reconcile the freedom of our will with divine preordination.* [...]

42. *Although we do not want to go wrong, nevertheless we go wrong by our own will.* [...]

43. *We never go wrong when we assent only to what we clearly and distinctly perceive.*
It is certain, however, that we will never mistake the false for the true provided we give our assent only to what we clearly and distinctly perceive. I say that this is certain, because God is not a de-

ceiver, and so the faculty of perception which he has given us cannot incline to falsehood; and the same goes for the faculty of assent, provided its scope is limited to what is clearly perceived. And even if there were no way of proving this, the minds of all of us have been so moulded by nature that whenever we perceive something clearly, we spontaneously give our assent to it and are quite unable to doubt its truth.

44. *When we give our assent to something which is not clearly perceived, this is always a misuse of our judgement, even if by chance we stumble on the truth. The giving of our assent to something unclear happens because we imagine that we clearly perceived it on some previous occasion.*

It is also certain that when we assent to some piece of reasoning when our perception of it is lacking, then either we go wrong, or, if we do stumble on the truth, it is merely by accident, so that we cannot be sure that we are not in error. Of course it seldom happens that we assent to something when we are aware of not perceiving it, since the light of nature tells us that we should never make a judgement except about things we know. What does very often give rise to error is that there are many things which we think we perceived in the past; once these things are committed to memory, we give our assent to them just as we would if we had fully perceived them, whereas in reality we never perceived them at all.

45. *What is meant by a clear perception, and by a distinct perception.*

Indeed there are very many people who in their entire lives never perceive anything with sufficient accuracy to enable them to make a judgement about it with certainty. A perception which can serve as the basis for a certain and indubitable judgement needs to be not merely clear but also distinct. I call a perception "clear" when it is present and accessible to the attentive mind – just as we say that we see something clearly when it is present to the eye's gaze and stimulates it with a sufficient degree of strength and accessibility. I call a perception "distinct" if, as well as being clear, it is so sharply separated from all other perceptions that it contains within itself only what is clear.

46. *The example of pain shows that a perception can be clear without being distinct, but cannot be distinct without being clear.*

For example, when someone feels an intense pain, the perception he has of it is indeed very clear, but is not always distinct. For people commonly confuse this perception with an obscure judgement they make concerning the nature of something which they think exists in the painful spot and which they suppose to resemble the sensation of pain; but in fact it is the sensation alone which they perceive clearly. Hence a perception can be clear without being distinct, but not distinct without being clear.

47. *In order to correct the preconceived opinions of our early childhood we must consider the simple notions and what elements in each of them are clear.* [...]

48. *All the objects of our perception may be regarded either as things or affections of things, or as eternal truths. The former are listed here.*

All the objects of our perception we regard either as things, or affections of things, or else as eternal truths which have no existence outside our thought. The most general items which we regard as things are *substance, duration, order, number* and any other items of this kind which extend to all classes of things. But I recognize only two ultimate classes of things: first, intellectual or thinking things, i.e. those which pertain to mind or thinking substance; and secondly, material things, i.e. those which pertain to extended substance or body. Perception, volition and all the modes both of perceiving and of willing are referred to thinking substance; while to extended substance belong size (that is, extension in length, breadth and depth), shape, motion, position, divisibility of component parts and the like. But we also experience within ourselves certain other things which must not be referred either to the mind alone or to the body alone. These arise, as will be made clear later on, in the appropriate place, from the close and intimate union of our mind with the body. This list includes, first, appetites like hunger and thirst; secondly, the emotions or passions of the mind which do not consist of thought alone, such as the emotions of anger, joy, sadness and love; and finally, all the sensations, such as those of pain, pleasure, light, colours, sounds, smells, tastes, heat, hardness and the other tactile qualities.

49. *It is not possible – or indeed necessary – to give a similar list of eternal truths.* [...]

50. *Eternal truths are clearly perceived; but, because of preconceived opinions, not all of them are clearly perceived by everyone.* [...]

51. *What is meant by "substance" – a term which does not apply univocally to God and his creatures.*

In the case of those items which we regard as things or modes of things, it is worthwhile examining each of them separately. By *substance* we can understand nothing other than a thing which exists in such a way as to depend on no other thing for its existence. And there is only one substance which can be understood to depend on no other thing whatsoever, namely God. In the case of all other substances, we perceive that they can exist only with the help of God's concurrence. Hence the term "substance" does not apply *univocally*, as they say in the Schools, to God and to other things; that is, there is no distinctly intelligible meaning of the term which is common to God and his creatures. <In the case of created things, some are of such a nature that they cannot exist without other things, while some need only the ordinary concurrence of God in order to exist. We make this distinction by calling the latter "substances" and the former "qualities" or "attributes" of those substances.>

52. *The term "substance" applies univocally to mind and to body. How a substance itself is known.*

But as for corporeal substance and mind (or created thinking substance), these can be understood to fall under this common concept: things that need only the concurrence of God in order to exist. However, we cannot initially become aware of a substance merely through its being an existing thing, since this alone does not of itself have any effect on us. We can, however, easily come to know a substance by one of its attributes, in virtue of the common notion that nothingness possesses no attributes, that is to say, no properties or qualities. Thus, if we perceive the presence of some attribute, we can infer that there must also be present an existing thing or substance to which it may be attributed.

53. *To each substance there belongs one principal attribute; in the case of mind, this is thought, and in the case of body it is extension.*

A substance may indeed be known through any attribute at all; but each substance has one principal property which constitutes its nature and essence, and to which all its other properties are referred. Thus extension in length, breadth and depth constitutes the nature of corporeal substance; and thought constitutes the nature of thinking substance. Everything else which can be attributed to body presupposes extension, and is merely a mode of an extended thing; and similarly, whatever we find in the mind is simply one of the various modes of thinking. For example, shape is unintelligible except in an extended thing; and motion is unintelligible except as motion in an extended space; while imagination, sensation and will are intelligible only in a thinking thing. By contrast, it is possible to understand extension without shape or movement, and thought without imagination or sensation, and so on; and this is quite clear to anyone who gives the matter his attention.

54. *How we can have clear and distinct notions of thinking substance and of corporeal substance, and also of God.*

Thus we can easily have two clear and distinct notions or ideas, one of created thinking substance, and the other of corporeal substance, provided we are careful to distinguish all the attributes of thought from the attributes of extension. We can also have a clear and distinct idea of uncreated and independent thinking substance, that is of God. Here we must simply avoid supposing that the idea adequately represents everything which is to be found in God; and we must not invent any additional features, but concentrate only on what is really contained in the idea and on what we clearly perceive to belong to the nature of a supremely perfect being. And certainly no one can deny that we possess such an idea of God, unless he reckons that there is absolutely no knowledge of God to be found in the minds of men.

55. *How we can also have a distinct understanding of duration, order and number.*

We shall also have a very distinct understanding of *duration*, *order* and *number*, provided we do not mistakenly tack on to them any concept of substance. Instead, we should regard the duration of a thing simply as a mode under which we conceive the thing in so far as it continues to exist. And similarly we should not regard order or number as anything separate from the things which are ordered and numbered, but should think of them simply as modes under which we consider the things in question.

56. *What modes, qualities and attributes are.*

By *mode*, as used above, we understand exactly the same as what is elsewhere meant by an *attribute* or *quality*. But we employ the term *mode* when we are thinking of a substance as being affected or modified; when the modification enables the substance to be designated as a substance of such and such a kind, we use the term *quality*; and finally, when we are simply thinking in a more general way of what is in a substance, we use the term *attribute*. Hence we do not, strictly speaking, say that there are modes or qualities in God, but simply attributes, since in the case of God, any variation is unintelligible. And even in the case of created things, that which always remains unmodified – for example existence or duration in a thing which exists and endures – should be called not a quality or a mode but an attribute.

57. *Some attributes are in things and others in thought. What duration and time are.*

Now some attributes or modes are in the very things of which they are said to be attributes or modes, while others are only in our thought. For example, when time is distinguished from duration taken in the general sense and called the measure of movement, it is simply a mode of thought. For the duration which we understand to be involved in movement is certainly no different from the duration involved in things which do not move. This is clear from the fact that if there are two bodies moving for an hour, one slowly and the other quickly, we do not reckon the amount of time to be greater in the latter case than the former, even though the amount of movement may be much greater. But in order to measure the duration of all things, we compare their duration with the duration of the greatest and most regular motions which give rise to years and days, and we call this duration "time". Yet nothing is thereby added to duration, taken in its general sense, except for a mode of thought.

58. *Number and all universals are simply modes of thinking.* [...]

59. *How universals arise. The five common universals: genus, species, differentia, property, accident.*

These universals arise solely from the fact that we make use of one and the same idea for thinking of all individual items which resemble each other: we apply one and the same term to all the things which are represented by the idea in question, and this is the universal term. When we see two stones, for example, and direct our attention not to their nature but merely to the fact that there are two of them, we form the idea of the number which we call "two"; and when we later see two birds or two trees, and consider not their nature but merely the fact that there are two of them, we go back to the same idea as before. This, then, is the universal idea; and we always designate the number in question by the same universal term "two". In the same way, when we see a figure made up of three lines, we form an idea of it which we call the idea of a triangle; and we later make use of it as a universal idea, so as to represent to our mind all the other figures made up of three lines. Moreover, when we notice that some triangles have one right angle, and others do not, we form the universal idea of a right-angled triangle; since this idea is related to the preceding idea as a special case, it is termed a *species*. And the rectangularity is the universal *differentia* which distinguishes all right-angled triangles from other triangles. And the fact that the square on the hypotenuse is equal to the sum of the squares on the other two sides is a *property* belonging to all and only right-angled triangles. Finally, if we suppose that some right-angled triangles are in motion while others are not, this will be a universal *accident* of such triangles. Hence five universals are commonly listed: *genus, species, differentia, property* and *accident*.

60. *Three sorts of distinction: firstly, what is meant by a "real distinction".*

Now number, in things themselves, arises from the distinction between them. But *distinction* can be taken in three ways: as a *real* distinction, a *modal* distinction, or a *conceptual* distinction. Strictly speaking, a *real* distinction exists only between two or more substances; and we can perceive that two substances are really distinct simply from the fact that we can clearly and distinctly understand one apart from the other. For when we come to know God, we are certain that he can bring about anything of which we have a distinct understanding. For example, even though we may not yet know for certain that any extended or corporeal substance exists in reality, the mere fact that we have an idea of such a substance enables us to be certain that it is capable of existing. And we can also be certain that, if it exists, each and every part of it, as delimited by us in our thought, is really distinct from the other parts of the same substance. Similarly, from the mere fact that each of us understands himself to be a thinking thing and is capable, in thought, of excluding from himself every other substance, whether thinking or extended, it is certain that each of us, regarded in this way, is really distinct from every other thinking substance and from every corporeal substance. And even if we suppose that God has joined some corporeal substance to such a thinking substance so closely that they cannot be more closely conjoined, thus compounding them into a unity, they nonetheless remain really distinct. For no matter how closely God may have united them, the power which he previously had of separating them, or keeping one in being without the other, is something he could not lay aside; and things which God has the power to separate, or to keep in being separately, are really distinct.

61. *What is meant by a "modal distinction".*

A *modal distinction* can be taken in two ways: firstly, as a distinction between a mode, properly so called, and the substance of which it is a mode; and secondly, as a distinction between two modes of the same substance. The first kind of modal distinction can be recognized from the fact that we can clearly perceive a substance apart from the mode which we say differs from it, whereas we cannot, conversely, understand the mode apart from the substance. Thus there is a modal distinction between shape or motion and the corporeal substance in which they inhere; and similarly, there is a modal distinction between affirmation or recollection and the mind. The second kind of modal distinction is recognized from the fact that we are able to arrive at knowledge of one mode apart from another, and *vice versa*, whereas we cannot know either mode apart from the substance in which they both inhere. For example, if a stone is in motion and is square-shaped, I can understand the square shape without the motion and, conversely, the motion without the square shape; but I can understand neither the motion nor the shape apart from the substance of the stone. A different case, however, is the distinction by which the mode of one substance is distinct from another substance or from the mode of another substance. An example of this is the way in which the motion of one body is distinct from another body, or from the mind; or the way in which motion differs from doubt. It seems more appropriate to call this kind of distinction a real distinction, rather than a modal distinction, since

the modes in question cannot be clearly understood apart from the really distinct substances of which they are modes.

62. *What is meant by a "conceptual distinction".*

Finally, a *conceptual distinction* is a distinction between a substance and some attribute of that substance without which the substance is unintelligible; alternatively, it is a distinction between two such attributes of a single substance. Such a distinction is recognized by our inability to form a clear and distinct idea of the substance if we exclude from it the attribute in question, or, alternatively, by our inability to perceive clearly the idea of one of the two attributes if we separate it from the other. For example, since a substance cannot cease to endure without also ceasing to be, the distinction between the substance and its duration is merely a conceptual one. And in the case of all the modes of thought which we consider as being in objects, there is merely a conceptual distinction between the modes and the object which they are thought of as applying to; and the same is true of the distinction between the modes themselves when these are in one and the same object. I am aware that elsewhere I did lump this type of distinction with the modal distinction, namely at the end of my Replies to the First Set of Objections to the *Mediations on First Philosophy*; but that was not a suitable place for making a careful distinction between the two types; it was enough for my purposes to distinguish both from the real distinction.

63. *How thought and extension may be distinctly recognized as constituting the nature of mind and of body.*

Thought and extension can be regarded as constituting the natures of intelligent substance and corporeal substance; they must then be considered as nothing else but thinking substance itself and extended substance itself – that is, as mind and body. In this way we will have a very clear and distinct understanding of them. Indeed, it is much easier for us to have an understanding of extended substance or thinking substance than it is for us to understand substance on its own, leaving out the fact that it thinks or is extended. For we have some difficulty in abstracting the notion of substance from the notions of thought and extension, since the distinction between these notions and the notion of substance itself is merely a conceptual distinction. A concept is not any more distinct because we include less in it; its distinctness simply depends on our carefully distinguishing what we do include in it from everything else.

64. *How thought and extension may also be distinctly recognized as modes of a substance.*

Thought and extension may also be taken as modes of a substance, in so far as one and the same mind is capable of having many different thoughts; and one and the same body, with its quantity unchanged, may be extended in many different ways (for example, at one moment it may be greater in length and smaller in breadth or depth, and a little later, by contrast, it may be greater in breadth and smaller in length). The distinction between thought or extension and the substance will then be a modal one; and our understanding of them will be capable of being just as clear and distinct as our understanding of the substance itself, provided they are regarded not as substances (that is, things which are separate from other things) but simply as modes of things. By regarding them as being in the substances of which they are modes, we distinguish them from the substances in question and see them for what they really are. If, on the other hand, we attempted to consider them apart from the substances in which they inhere, we would be regarding them as things which subsisted in their own right, and would thus be confusing the ideas of a mode and a substance.

65. *How the modes of thought and extension are to be known.*

There are various modes of thought such as understanding, imagination, memory, volition, and so on; and there are various modes of extension, or modes which belong to extension, such as all shapes, the positions of parts and the motions of the parts. And, just as before, we shall arrive at the best perception of all these items if we regard them simply as modes of the things in which they are located. As far as motion is concerned, it will be best if we think simply of local motion, without inquiring into the force which produces it (though I shall attempt to explain this later in the appropriate place).

66. *How sensations, emotions and appetites may be clearly known, despite the fact that we are frequently wrong in our judgements concerning them.*

There remains sensations, emotions and appetites. These may be clearly perceived provided we take great care in our judgements concerning them to include no more than what is strictly contained in our perception – no more than that of which we have inner awareness. But this is a very difficult rule to observe, at least with regard to sensations. For all of us have, from our early childhood, judged that all the objects of our sense-perception are things existing outside our minds and closely resembling our sensations, i.e. the perceptions that we had of them. Thus, on seeing a colour, for example, we supposed we were seeing a thing located outside us which closely resembled the idea of colour that we experienced within us at the time. And this was something that, because of our habit of making such judgements, we thought we saw clearly and distinctly – so much so that we took it for something certain and indubitable.

67. *We frequently make mistakes, even in our judgements concerning pain.* [...]

75. *Summary of the rules to be observed in order to philosophize correctly.*

In order to philosophize seriously and search out the truth about all the things that are capable of being known, we must first of all lay aside all our preconceived opinions, or at least we must take the greatest care not to put our trust in any of the opinions accepted by us in the past until we have first scrutinized them afresh and confirmed their truth. Next, we must give our attention in an orderly way to the notions that we have within us, and we must judge to be true all and only those whose truth we clearly and distinctly recognize when we attend to them in this way. When we do this we shall realize, first of all, that we exist in so far as our nature consists in thinking; and we shall simultaneously realize both that there is a God, and that we depend on him, and also that a consideration of his attributes enables us to investigate the truth of other things, since he is their cause. Finally, we will see that besides the notions of God and of our mind, we have within us knowledge of many propositions which are eternally true, such as "Nothing comes from nothing". We shall also find that we have knowledge both of a corporeal or extended nature which is divisible, moveable, and so on, and also of certain sensations which affect us, such as the sensations of pain, colours, tastes and so on (though we do not yet know the cause of our being affected in this way). When we contrast all this knowledge with the confused thoughts we had before, we will acquire the habit of forming clear and distinct concepts of all the things that can be known. These few instructions seem to me to contain the most important principles of human knowledge.

76. *Divine authority must be put before our own perception; but, that aside, the philosopher should give his assent only to what he has perceived.*
But above all else we must impress on our memory the overriding rule that whatever God has revealed to us must be accepted as more certain than anything else. And although the light of reason may, with the utmost clarity and evidence, appear to suggest something different, we must still put our entire faith in divine authority rather than in our own judgement. But on matters where we are not instructed by divine faith, it is quite unworthy of a philosopher to accept anything as true if he has never established its truth by thorough scrutiny; and he should never rely on the senses, that is, on the ill-considered judgements of his childhood, in preference to his mature powers of reason.

3

The Passions of the Soul

Part One: The Passions in General, and Incidentally the Whole Nature of Man

1. *What is a passion with regard to one subject is always an action in some other regard.*

The defects of the sciences we have from the ancients are nowhere more apparent than in their writings on the passions. This topic, about which knowledge has always been keenly sought, does not seem to be one of the more difficult to investigate since everyone feels passions in himself and so has no need to look elsewhere for observations to establish their nature. And yet the teachings of the ancients about the passions are so meagre and for the most part so implausible that I cannot hope to approach the truth except by departing from the paths they have followed. That is why I shall be obliged to write just as if I were considering a topic that no one had dealt with before me. In the first place, I note that whatever takes place or occurs is generally called by philosophers a "passion" with regard to the subject to which it happens and an "action" with regard to that which makes it happen. Thus, although an agent and patient are often quite different, an action and passion must always be a single thing which has these two names on account of the two different subjects to which it may be related.

The Passions of the Soul (1649). From *The Philosophical Writings of Descartes*, vol. 1, tr. John Cottingham, Robert Stoothoff, and Dugald Murdoch (Cambridge University Press, 1985). Selection: Part 1: "The Passions in General," pp. 328–48.

2. *To understand the passions of the soul we must distinguish its functions from those of the body.*

Next I note that we are not aware of any subject which acts more directly upon our soul than the body to which it is joined. Consequently we should recognize that what is a passion in the soul is usually an action in the body. Hence there is no better way of coming to know about our passions than by examining the difference between the soul and the body, in order to learn to which of the two we should attribute each of the functions present in us.

3. *The rule we must follow in order to do this.*

We shall not find this very difficult if we bear in mind that anything we experience as being in us, and which we see can also exist in wholly inanimate bodies, must be attributed only to our body. On the other hand, anything in us which we cannot conceive in any way as capable of belonging to a body must be attributed to our soul.

4. *The heat and the movement of the limbs proceed from the body, and thoughts from the soul.*

Thus, because we have no conception of the body as thinking in any way at all, we have reason to believe that every kind of thought present in us belongs to the soul. And since we do not doubt that there are inanimate bodies which can move in as many different ways as our bodies, if not more, and which have as much heat or more (as experience shows in the case of a flame, which has in itself much more heat and movement than any of our limbs), we must believe that all the heat and all the movements present in us, in so far as they do not depend on thought, belong solely to the body.

5. *It is an error to believe that the soul gives movement and heat to the body.*

In this way we shall avoid a very serious error which many have fallen into, and which I regard as the primary cause of our failure up to now to give a satisfactory explanation of the passions and of everything else belonging to the soul. The error consists in supposing that since dead bodies are devoid of heat and movement, it is the absence of the soul which causes this cessation of movement and heat. Thus it has been believed, without justification, that our natural heat and all the movements of our bodies depend on the soul; whereas we ought to hold, on the contrary, that the soul takes its leave when we die only because this heat ceases and the organs which bring about bodily movement decay.

6. *The difference between a living body and a dead body.*

So as to avoid this error, let us note that death never occurs through the absence of the soul, but only because one of the principal parts of the body decays. And let us recognize that the difference between the body of a living man and that of a dead man is just like the difference between, on the one hand, a watch or other automaton (that is, a self-moving machine) when it is wound up and contains in itself the corporeal principle of the movements for which it is designed, together with everything else required for its operation; and, on the other hand, the same watch or machine when it is broken and the principle of its movement ceases to be active.

7. *A brief account of the parts of the body and of some of their functions.*

To make this more intelligible I shall explain in a few words the way in which the mechanism of our body is composed. Everyone knows that within us there is a heart, brain, stomach, muscles, nerves, arteries, veins, and similar things. We know too that the food we eat goes down to the stomach and bowels, and that its juice then flows into the liver and all the veins, where it mixes with the blood they contain, thus increasing its quantity. Those who have heard anything at all about medicine know in addition how the heart is constructed and how the blood in the veins can flow easily from the vena cava into its right-hand side, pass from there into the lungs through the vessel called the arterial vein, then return from the lungs into the left-hand side of the heart through the vessel

called the venous artery, and finally pass from there into the great artery, whose branches spread through the whole body. Likewise all those not completely blinded by the authority of the ancients, and willing to open their eyes to examine the opinion of Harvey regarding the circulation of the blood, do not doubt that the veins and arteries of the body are like streams through which the blood flows constantly and with great rapidity. It makes its way from the right-hand cavity of the heart through the arterial vein, whose branches are spread throughout the lungs and connected with those of the venous artery; and via this artery it passes from the lungs into the left-hand side of the heart. From there it goes into the great artery, whose branches are spread through the rest of the body and connected with the branches of the vena cava, which carries the same blood once again into the right-hand cavity of the heart. These two cavities are thus like sluices through which all the blood passes upon each complete circuit it makes through the body. It is known, moreover, that every movement of the limbs depends on the muscles, which are opposed to each other in such a way that when one of them becomes shorter it draws towards itself the part of the body to which it is attached, which simultaneously causes the muscle opposed to it to lengthen. Then, if the latter happens to shorten at some other time, it makes the former lengthen again, and draws towards itself the part to which they are attached. Finally, it is known that all these movements of the muscles, and likewise all sensations, depend on the nerves, which are like little threads or tubes coming from the brain and containing, like the brain itself, a certain very fine air or wind which is called the "animal spirits".

8. *The principle underlying all these functions.*

But it is not commonly known how these animal spirits and nerves help to produce movements and sensations, or what corporeal principle makes them act. That is why, although I have already touched upon this question in other writings, I intend to speak briefly about it here. While we are alive there is a continual heat in our hearts, which is a kind of fire that the blood of the veins maintains there. This fire is the corporeal principle underlying all the movements of our limbs.

9. *How the movement of the heart takes place.*

Its first effect is that it makes the blood which fills the cavities of the heart expand. This causes the blood, now needing to occupy a larger space, to rush from the right-hand cavity into the arterial vein and from the left-hand cavity into the great artery. Then, when this expansion ceases, fresh blood immediately enters the right-hand cavity of the heart from the vena cava, and the left-hand cavity from the venous artery. For there are tiny membranes at the entrances to these four vessels which are so arranged that the blood can enter the heart only through the latter two and leave it only through the former two. When the new blood has entered the heart it is immediately rarefied in the same way as before. This and this alone is what the pulse or beating of the heart and arteries consists in, and it explains why the beating is repeated each time new blood enters the heart. It is also the sole cause of the movement of the blood, making it flow constantly and very rapidly in all the arteries and veins, so that it carries the heat it acquires in the heart to all the other parts of the body, and provides them with nourishment.

10. *How the animal spirits are produced in the brain.*
What is, however, more worthy of consideration here is that all the most lively and finest parts of the blood, which have been rarefied by the heat in the heart, constantly enter the cavities of the brain in large numbers. What makes them go there rather than elsewhere is that all the blood leaving the heart through the great artery follows a direct route towards this place, and since not all this blood can enter there because the passages are too narrow, only the most active and finest parts pass into it while the rest spread out into the other regions of the body. Now these very fine parts of the blood make up the animal spirits. For them to do this the only change they need to undergo in the brain is to be separated from the other less fine parts of the blood. For what I am calling "spirits" here are merely bodies: they have no property other than that of being extremely small bodies which move very quickly, like the jets of flame that come from a torch. They never stop in any place, and as some of them enter the brain's cavities, others leave it through the pores in its substance. These pores conduct them into the nerves, and then to the muscles. In this way the animal spirits move the body in all the various ways it can be moved.

11. *How the movements of the muscles take place.*
For, as already mentioned, the sole cause of all the movements of the limbs is the shortening of certain muscles and the lengthening of the opposed muscles. What causes one muscle to become shorter rather than its opposite is simply that fractionally more spirits from the brain come to it than to the other. Not that the spirits which come directly from the brain are sufficient by themselves to move the muscles; but they cause the other spirits already in the two muscles to leave one of them very suddenly and pass into the other. In this way the one they leave becomes longer and more relaxed, and the one they enter, being suddenly swollen by them, becomes shorter and pulls the limb to which it is attached. This is easy to understand, provided one knows that very few animal spirits come continually from the brain to each muscle, and that any muscle always contains a quantity of its own spirits. These move very quickly, sometimes merely eddying in the place where they are located (that is, when they find no passages open for them to leave from), and sometimes flowing into the opposed muscle. In each of the muscles there are small openings through which the spirits may flow from one into the other, and which are so arranged that when the spirits coming from the brain to one of the muscles are slightly more forceful than those going to the other, they open all the passages through which the spirits in the latter can pass into the former, and at the same time they close all the passages through which the spirits in the former can pass into the latter. In this way all the spirits previously contained in the two muscles are gathered very rapidly in one of them, thus making it swell and become shorter, while the other lengthens and relaxes.

12. *How external objects act upon the sense organs.*
We still have to know what causes the spirits not to flow always in the same way from the brain to the muscles, but to come sometimes more to some muscles than to others. In our case, indeed, one of these causes is the activity of the soul (as I shall explain further on). But in addition we must note two other causes, which depend solely on the body. The first consists in differences in the movements produced in the sense organs by their objects. I have already explained this quite fully in the *Optics*. But in order that readers of this work should not need to consult any other, I shall say once again that there are three things to consider in the nerves. First, there is the marrow, or internal substance, which extends in the form of tiny fibres from the brain, where they originate, to the

extremities of the parts of the body to which they are attached. Next, there are the membranes surrounding the fibres, which are continuous with those surrounding the brain and form little tubes in which the fibres are enclosed. Finally, there are the animal spirits which, being carried by these tubes from the brain to the muscles, cause the fibres to remain so completely free and extended that if anything causes the lightest motion in the part of the body where one of the fibres terminates, it thereby causes a movement in the part of the brain where the fibre originates, just as we make one end of a cord move by pulling the other end.

13. *This action of external objects may direct the spirits into the muscles in various different ways.*

I explained in the *Optics* how the objects of sight make themselves known to us simply by producing, through the medium of the intervening transparent bodies, local motions in the optic nerve-fibres at the back of our eyes, and then in the regions of the brain where these nerves originate. I explained too that the objects produce as much variety in these motions as they cause us to see in the things, and that it is not the motions occurring in the eye, but those occurring in the brain, which directly represent these objects to the soul. By this example, it is easy to conceive how sounds, smells, tastes, heat, pain, hunger, thirst and, in general, all the objects both of our external senses and of our internal appetites, also produce some movement in our nerves, which passes through them into the brain. Besides causing our soul to have various different sensations, these various movements in the brain can also act without the soul, causing the spirits to make their way to certain muscles rather than others, and so causing them to move our limbs. I shall prove this here by one example only. If someone suddenly thrusts his hand in front of our eyes as if to strike us, then even if we know that he is our friend, that he is doing this only in fun, and that he will take care not to harm us, we still find it difficult to prevent ourselves from closing our eyes. This shows that it is not through the mediation of our soul that they close, since this action is contrary to our volition, which is the only, or at least the principal, activity of the soul. They close rather because the mechanism of our body is so composed that the movement of the hand towards our eyes produces another movement in our brain, which directs the animal spirits into the muscles that make our eyelids drop.

14. *Differences among the spirits may also cause them to take various different courses.*

The other cause which serves to direct the animal spirits to the muscles in various different ways is the unequal agitation of the spirits and differences in their parts. For when some of their parts are coarser and more agitated than others, they penetrate more deeply in a straight line into the cavities and pores of the brain, and in this way they are directed to muscles other than those to which they would go if they had less force.

15. *The causes of these differences.*

And this inequality may arise from the different materials of which the spirits are composed. One sees this in the case of those who have drunk a lot of wine: the vapours of the wine enter the blood rapidly and rise from the heart to the brain, where they turn into spirits which, being stronger and more abundant than those normally present there, are capable of moving the body in many strange ways. Such an inequality of the spirits may also arise from various conditions of the heart, liver, stomach, spleen and all the other organs that help to produce them. In this connection we must first note certain small nerves embedded in the base of the heart, which serve to enlarge and contract the openings to its cavities, thus causing the blood, according to the strength of its expansion, to produce spirits having various different dispositions. It must also be observed that even though the blood entering the heart comes there from every other place in the body, it often happens nevertheless that it is driven there more from some parts than from others, because the nerves and muscles responsible for these parts exert more pressure on it or make it more agitated. And differences in these parts are matched by corresponding differences in the expansion of the blood in the heart, which results in the production of spirits having different qualities. Thus, for example, the blood coming from the lower part of the liver, where the gall is located, expands in the heart in a different manner from the blood coming from the spleen; the latter expands differently from the blood coming from the veins of the arms or legs; and this expands differently again from the alimentary juices when, just after leaving the stomach and bowels, they pass rapidly to the heart through the liver.

16. *How all the limbs can be moved by the objects of the senses and by the spirits without the help of the soul.*
Finally it must be observed that the mechanism of our body is so composed that all the changes occurring in the movement of the spirits may cause them to open some pores in the brain more than others. Conversely, when one of the pores is opened somewhat more or less than usual by an action of the sensory nerves, this brings about a change in the movement of the spirits and directs them to the muscles which serve to move the body in the way it is usually moved on the occasion of such an action. Thus every movement we make without any contribution from our will – as often happens when we breathe, walk, eat and, indeed, when we perform any action which is common to us and the beasts – depends solely on the arrangement of our limbs and on the route which the spirits, produced by the heat of the heart, follow naturally in the brain, nerves and muscles. This occurs in the same way as the movement of a watch is produced merely by the strength of its spring and the configuration of its wheels.

17. *The functions of the soul.*
Having thus considered all the functions belonging solely to the body, it is easy to recognize that there is nothing in us which we must attribute to our soul except our thoughts. These are of two principal kinds, some being actions of the soul and others its passions. Those I call its actions are all our volitions, for we experience them as proceeding directly from our soul and as seeming to depend on it alone. On the other hand, the various perceptions or modes of knowledge present in us may be called its passions, in a general sense, for it is often not our soul which makes them such as they are, and the soul always receives them from the things that are represented by them.

18. *The will.*
Our volitions, in turn, are of two sorts. One consists of the actions of the soul which terminate in the soul itself, as when we will to love God or, generally speaking, to apply our mind to some object which is not material. The other consists of actions which terminate in our body, as when our merely willing to walk has the consequence that our legs move and we walk.

19. *Perception.*
Our perceptions are likewise of two sorts: some have the soul as their cause, others the body. Those having the soul as their cause are the perceptions of our volitions and of all the imaginings or other thoughts which depend on them. For it is certain that we cannot will anything without thereby perceiving that we are willing it. And although willing something is an action with respect to our soul, the perception of such willing may be said to be a passion in the soul. But because this perception is really one and the same thing as the volition, and names are always determined by whatever is most noble, we do not normally call it a "passion", but solely an "action".

20. *Imaginings and other thoughts formed by the soul.*
When our soul applies itself to imagine something non-existent – as in thinking about an enchanted palace or a chimera – and also when it applies itself to consider something that is purely intelligible and not imaginable – for example, in considering its own nature – the perceptions it has of these things depend chiefly on the volition which makes it aware of them. That is why we usually regard these perceptions as actions rather than passions.

21. *Imaginings which are caused solely by the body.*
Among the perceptions caused by the body, most of them depend on the nerves. But there are some which do not and which, like those I have just described, are called "imaginings". These differ from the others, however, in that our will is not used in forming them. Accordingly they cannot be numbered among the actions of the soul, for they arise simply from the fact that the spirits, being agitated in various different ways and coming upon the traces of various impressions which have preceded them in the brain, make their way by chance through certain pores rather than others. Such are the illusions of our dreams and also the daydreams we often have when we are awake and our mind wanders idly without applying itself to anything of its own accord. Now some of these imaginings are passions of the soul, taking the word "passion" in its proper and more exact sense, and all may be regarded as such if the word is understood in a more general sense. Nonetheless, their cause is not so conspicuous and determinate as that of the perceptions which the soul receives by means of the nerves, and they seem to be mere shadows and pictures of these perceptions. So before we can characterize them satisfactorily we must consider how these other perceptions differ from one another.

22. How these other perceptions differ from one another.

All the perceptions which I have not yet explained come to the soul by means of the nerves. They differ from one another in so far as we refer some to external objects which strike our senses, others to our body or to certain of its parts, and still others to our soul.

23. The perceptions we refer to objects outside us.

The perceptions we refer to things outside us, namely to the objects of our senses, are caused by these objects, at least when our judgements are not false. For in that case the objects produce certain movements in the organs of the external senses and, by means of the nerves, produce other movements in the brain, which cause the soul to have sensory perception of the objects. Thus, when we see the light of a torch and hear the sound of a bell, the sound and the light are two different actions which, simply by producing two different movements in some of our nerves, and through them in our brain, give to the soul two different sensations. And we refer these sensations to the subjects we suppose to be their causes in such a way that we think that we see the torch itself and hear the bell, and not that we have sensory perception merely of movements coming from these objects.

24. The perceptions we refer to our body.

The perceptions we refer to our body or to certain of its parts are those of hunger, thirst and other natural appetites. To these we may add pain, heat and the other states we feel as being in our limbs, and not as being in objects outside us. Thus, at the same time and by means of the same nerves we can feel the cold of our hand and the heat of a nearby flame or, on the other hand, the heat of our hand and the cold of the air to which it is exposed. This happens without there being any difference between the actions which make us feel the heat or cold in our hand and those which make us feel the heat or cold outside us, except that since one of these actions succeeds the other, we judge that the first is already in us, and that its successor is not yet there but in the object which causes it.

25. The perceptions we refer to our soul.

The perceptions we refer only to the soul are those whose effects we feel as being in the soul itself, and for which we do not normally know any proximate cause to which we can refer them. Such are the feelings of joy, anger and the like, which are aroused in us sometimes by the objects which stimulate our nerves and sometimes also by other causes. Now all our perceptions, both those we refer to objects outside us and those we refer to the various states of our body, are indeed passions with respect to our soul, so long as we use the term "passion" in its most general sense; nevertheless we usually restrict the term to signify only perceptions which refer to the soul itself. And it is only the latter that I have undertaken to explain here under the title "passions of the soul".

26. The imaginings which depend solely on the fortuitous movement of the spirits may be passions just as truly as the perceptions which depend on the nerves.

It remains to be noted that everything the soul perceives by means of the nerves may also be represented to it through the fortuitous course of the spirits. The sole difference is that the impressions which come into the brain through the nerves are normally more lively and more definite than those produced there by the spirits – a fact that led me to say in article 21 that the latter are, as it were, a shadow or picture of the former. We must also note that this picture is sometimes so similar to the thing it represents that it may mislead us regarding the perceptions which refer to objects outside us, or even regarding those which refer to certain parts of our body. But we cannot be misled in the same way regarding the passions, in that they are so close and so internal to our soul that it cannot possibly feel them unless they are truly as it feels them to be. Thus often when we sleep, and sometimes even when we are awake, we imagine certain things so vividly that we think we see them before us, or feel them in our body, although they are not there at all. But even if we are asleep and dreaming, we cannot feel sad, or moved by any other passion, unless the soul truly has this passion within it.

27. Definition of the passions of the soul.

After having considered in what respects the passions of the soul differ from all its other thoughts, it seems to me that we may define them generally as those perceptions, sensations or emotions of the soul which we refer particularly to it, and which are caused, maintained and strengthened by some movement of the spirits.

28. Explanation of the first part of this definition.

We may call them "perceptions" if we use this term generally to signify all the thoughts which are not actions of the soul or volitions, but not if we use it to signify only evident knowledge. For experience shows that those who are the most strongly agitated by their passions are not those who know them best, and that the passions are to be numbered among the perceptions which the close alliance between the soul and the body renders confused and obscure. We may also call them "sensations", because they are received into the soul in the same way as the objects of the external senses, and they are not known by the soul any differently. But it is even better to call them "emotions" of the soul, not only because this term may be applied to all the changes which occur in the soul – that is, to all the various thoughts which come to it – but more particularly because, of all the kinds of thought which the soul may have, there are none that agitate and disturb it so strongly as the passions.

29. *Explanation of the other part of the definition.*
I add that they refer particularly to the soul, in order to distinguish them from other sensations, some referred to external objects (e.g. smells, sounds and colours) and others to our body (e.g. hunger, thirst and pain). I also add that they are caused, maintained and strengthened by some movement of the spirits, both in order to distinguish them from our volitions (for these too may be called "emotions of the soul which refer to it", but they are caused by the soul itself), and also in order to explain their ultimate and most proximate cause, which distinguishes them once again from other sensations.

30. *The soul is united to all the parts of the body conjointly.*
But in order to understand all these things more perfectly, we need to recognize that the soul is really joined to the whole body, and that we cannot properly say that it exists in any one part of the body to the exclusion of the others. For the body is a unity which is in a sense indivisible because of the arrangement of its organs, these being so related to one another that the removal of any one of them renders the whole body defective. And the soul is of such a nature that it has no relation to extension, or to the dimensions or other properties of the matter of which the body is composed: it is related solely to the whole assemblage of the body's organs. This is obvious from our inability to conceive of a half or a third of a soul, or of the extension which a soul occupies. Nor does the soul become any smaller if

we cut off some part of the body, but it becomes completely separate from the body when we break up the assemblage of the body's organs.

31. *There is a little gland in the brain where the soul exercises its functions more particularly than in the other parts of the body.*
We need to recognize also that although the soul is joined to the whole body, nevertheless there is a certain part of the body where it exercises its functions more particularly than in all the others. It is commonly held that this part is the brain, or perhaps the heart – the brain because the sense organs are related to it, and the heart because we feel the passions as if they were in it. But on carefully examining the matter I think I have clearly established that the part of the body in which the soul directly exercises its functions is not the heart at all, or the whole of the brain. It is rather the innermost part of the brain, which is a certain very small gland situated in the middle of the brain's substance and suspended above the passage through which the spirits in the brain's anterior cavities communicate with those in its posterior cavities. The slightest movements on the part of this gland may alter very greatly the course of these spirits, and conversely any change, however slight, taking place in the course of the spirits may do much to change the movements of the gland.

32. *How we know that this gland is the principal seat of the soul.*
Apart from this gland, there cannot be any other place in the whole body where the soul directly exercises its functions. I am convinced of this by the observation that all the other parts of our brain are double, as also are all the organs of our external senses – eyes, hands, ears and so on. But in so far as we have only one simple thought about a given object at any one time, there must necessarily be some place where the two images coming through the two eyes, or the two impressions coming from a single object through the double organs of any other sense, can come together in a single image or impression before reaching the soul, so that they do not present to it two objects instead of one. We can easily understand that these images or other impressions are unified in this gland by means of the spirits which fill the cavities of the brain. But they cannot exist united in this way in any other place in the body except as a result of their being united in this gland.

33. The seat of the passions is not in the heart.

As for the opinion of those who think that the soul receives its passions in the heart, this is not worth serious consideration, since it is based solely on the fact that the passions make us feel some change in the heart. It is easy to see that the only reason why this change is felt as occurring in the heart is that there is a small nerve which descends to it from the brain – just as pain is felt as in the foot by means of the nerves in the foot, and the stars are perceived as in the sky by means of their light and the optic nerves. Thus it is no more necessary that our soul should exercise its functions directly in the heart in order to feel its passions there, than that it should be in the sky in order to see the stars there.

34. How the soul and the body act on each other.

Let us therefore take it that the soul has its principal seat in the small gland located in the middle of the brain. From there it radiates through the rest of the body by means of the animal spirits, the nerves, and even the blood, which can take on the impressions of the spirits and carry them through the arteries to all the limbs. Let us recall what we said previously about the mechanism of our body. The nerve-fibres are so distributed in all the parts of the body that when the objects of the senses produce various different movements in these parts, the fibres are occasioned to open the pores of the brain in various different ways. This, in turn, causes the animal spirits contained in these cavities to enter the muscles in various different ways. In this manner the spirits can move the limbs in all the different ways they are capable of being moved. And all the other causes that can move the spirits in different ways are sufficient to direct them into different muscles. To this we may now add that the small gland which is the principal seat of the soul is suspended within the cavities containing these spirits, so that it can be moved by them in as many different ways as there are perceptible differences in the objects. But it can also be moved in various different ways by the soul, whose nature is such that it receives as many different impressions – that is, it has as many different perceptions as there occur different movements in this gland. And conversely, the mechanism of our body is so constructed that simply by this gland's being moved in any way by the soul or by any other cause, it drives the surrounding spirits towards the pores of the brain, which direct them through the nerves to the muscles; and in this way the gland makes the spirits move the limbs.

35. Example of the way in which the impressions of objects are united in the gland in the middle of the brain.

Thus, for example, if we see some animal approaching us, the light reflected from its body forms two images, one in each of our eyes; and these images form two others, by means of the optic nerves, on the internal surface of the brain facing its cavities. Then, by means of the spirits that fill these cavities, the images radiate towards the little gland which the spirits surround: the movement forming each point of one of the images tends towards the same point on the gland as the movement forming the corresponding point of the other image, which represents the same part of the animal. In this way, the two images in the brain form only one image on the gland, which acts directly upon the soul and makes it see the shape of the animal.

36. Example of the way in which the passions are aroused in the soul.

If, in addition, this shape is very strange and terrifying – that is, if it has a close relation to things which have previously been harmful to the body – this arouses the passion of anxiety in the soul, and then that of courage or perhaps fear and terror, depending upon the particular temperament of the body or the strength of the soul, and upon whether we have protected ourselves previously by defence or by flight against the harmful things to which the present impression is related. Thus in certain persons these factors dispose their brain in such a way that some of the spirits reflected from the image formed on the gland proceed from there to the nerves which serve to turn the back and move the legs in order to flee. The rest of the spirits go to nerves which expand or constrict the orifices of the heart, or else to nerves which agitate other parts of the body from which blood is sent to the heart, so that the blood is rarefied in a different manner from usual and spirits are sent to the brain which are adapted for maintaining and strengthening the passion of fear – that is, for holding open or re-opening the pores of the brain which direct the spirits into these same nerves. For merely by entering into these pores they produce in the gland a particular movement which is obtained by nature to make the soul feel this passion. And since these pores are related mainly to the little nerves which serve to contract or expand the orifices of the heart, this makes the soul feel the passion chiefly as if it were in the heart.

37. *How all the passions appear to be caused by some movement of the spirits.*

Something similar happens with all the other passions. That is, they are caused chiefly by the spirits contained in the cavities of the brain making their way to nerves which serve to expand or constrict the orifices of the heart, or to drive blood towards the heart in a distinctive way from other parts of the body, or to maintain the passion in some other way. This makes it clear why I included in my definition of the passions that they are caused by some particular movement of the spirits.

38. *Example of movements of the body which accompany the passions and do not depend on the soul.*

Moreover, just as the course which the spirits take to the nerves of the heart suffices to induce a movement in the gland through which fear enters the soul, so too the mere fact that some spirits at the same time proceed to the nerves which serve to move the legs in flight causes another movement in the gland through which the soul feels and perceives this action. In this way, then, the body may be moved to take flight by the mere disposition of the organs, without any contribution from the soul.

39. *How one and the same cause may excite different passions in different people.*

The same impression which the presence of a terrifying object forms on the gland, and which causes fear in some people, may excite courage and boldness in others. The reason for this is that brains are not all constituted in the same way. Thus the very same movement of the gland which in some excites fear, in others causes the spirits to enter the pores of the brain which direct them partly into nerves which serve to move the hands in self-defence and partly into those which agitate the blood and drive it towards the heart in the manner required to produce spirits appropriate for continuing this defence and for maintaining the will to do so.

40. *The principal effect of the passions.*

For it must be observed that the principal effect of all the human passions is that they move and dispose the soul to want the things for which they prepare the body. Thus the feeling of fear moves the soul to want to flee, that of courage to want to fight, and similarly with the others.

41. *The power of the soul with respect to the body.*

But the will is by its nature so free that it can never be constrained. Of the two kinds of thought I have distinguished in the soul – the first its actions, i.e. its volitions, and the second its passions, taking this word in its most general sense to include every kind of perception – the former are absolutely within its power and can be changed only indirectly by the body, whereas the latter are absolutely dependent on the actions which produce them, and can be changed by the soul only indirectly, except when it is itself their cause. And the activity of the soul consists entirely in the fact that simply by willing something it brings it about that the little gland to which it is closely joined moves in the manner required to produce the effect corresponding to this volition.

42. *How we find in our memory the things we want to remember.*

Thus, when the soul wants to remember something, this volition makes the gland lean first to one side and then to another, thus driving the spirits towards different regions of the brain until they come upon the one containing traces left by the object we want to remember. These traces consist simply in the fact that the pores of the brain through which the spirits previously made their way owing to the presence of this object have thereby become more apt than the others to be opened in the same way when the spirits again flow towards them. And so the spirits enter into these pores more easily when they come upon them, thereby producing in the gland that special movement which represents the same object to the soul, and makes it recognize the object as the one it wanted to remember.

43. *How the soul can imagine, be attentive, and move the body.*

When we want to imagine something we have never seen, this volition has the power to make the gland move in the way required for driving the spirits towards the pores of the brain whose opening enables the thing to be represented. Again, when we want to fix our attention for some time on some particular object, this volition keeps the gland leaning in one particular direction during that time. And finally, when we want to walk or move our body in some other way, this volition makes the gland drive the spirits to the muscles which serve to bring about this effect.

44. *Each volition is naturally joined to some movement of the gland, but through effort or habit we may join it to others.*

Yet our volition to produce some particular movement or other effect does not always result in our producing it; for that depends on the various ways in which nature or habit has joined certain movements of the gland to certain thoughts. For example, if we want to adjust our eyes to look at a far-distant object, this volition causes the pupils to grow larger; and if we want to adjust them to look at a very near object, this volition makes the pupils contract. But if we think only of enlarging the pupils, we may indeed have such a volition, but we do not thereby enlarge them. For the movement of the gland, whereby the spirits are driven to the optic nerve in the way required for enlarging or contracting the pupils, has been joined by nature with the volition to look at distant or nearby objects, rather than with the volition to enlarge or contract the pupils. Again, when we speak, we think only of the meaning of what we want to say, and this makes us move our tongue and lips much more readily and effectively than if we thought of moving them in all the ways required for uttering the same words. For the habits acquired in learning to speak have made us join the action of the soul (which, by means of the gland, can move the tongue and lips) with the meaning of the words which follow upon these movements, rather than with the movements themselves.

45. *The power of the soul with respect to its passions.*

Our passions, too, cannot be directly aroused or suppressed by the action of our will, but only indirectly through the representation of things which are usually joined with the passions we wish to have and opposed to the passions we wish to reject. For example, in order to arouse boldness and suppress fear in ourselves, it is not sufficient to have the volition to do so. We must apply ourselves to consider the reasons, objects, or precedents which persuade us that the danger is not great; that there is always more security in defence than in flight; that we shall gain glory and joy if we conquer, whereas we can expect nothing but regret and shame if we flee; and so on.

46. *What prevents the soul from having full control over its passions.*

There is one special reason why the soul cannot readily change or suspend its passions, which is what led me to say in my definition that the passions are not only caused but also maintained and strengthened by some particular movement of the spirits. The reason is that they are nearly all accompanied by some disturbance which takes place in the heart and consequently also throughout the blood and the animal spirits. Until this disturbance ceases they remain present to our mind in the same way as the objects of the senses are present to it while they are acting upon our sense organs. The soul can prevent itself from hearing a slight noise or feeling a slight pain by attending very closely to some other thing, but it cannot in the same way prevent itself from hearing thunder or feeling a fire that burns the hand. Likewise it can easily overcome the lesser passions, but not the stronger and more violent ones, except after the disturbance of the blood and spirits has died down. The most the will can do while this disturbance is at its full strength is not to yield to its effects and to inhibit many of the movements to which it disposes the body. For example, if anger causes the hand to rise to strike a blow, the will can usually restrain it; if fear moves the legs in flight, the will can stop them; and similarly in other cases.

47. *The conflicts that are usually supposed to occur between the lower part and the higher part of the soul.*

All the conflicts usually supposed to occur between the lower part of the soul, which we call "sensitive", and the higher or "rational" part of the soul – or between the natural appetites and the will – consist simply in the opposition between the movements which the body (by means of its spirits) and the soul (by means of its will) tend to produce at the same time in the gland. For there is within us but one soul, and this soul has within it no diversity of parts: it is at once sensitive and rational too, and all its appetites are volitions. It is an error to identify the different functions of the soul with persons who play different, usually mutually opposed roles – an error which arises simply from our failure to distinguish properly the functions of the soul from those of the body. It is to the body alone that we should attribute everything that can be observed in us to oppose our reason. So there is no conflict here except in so far as the little gland in the middle of the brain can be pushed to one side by the soul and to the other side by the animal spirits (which, as I said above, are nothing but bodies), and these two impulses often happen to be opposed, the stronger cancelling the effect of the weaker. Now we may distinguish two kinds of movement produced in the gland by the spirits. Movements of the first kind represent to the soul the objects which stimulate the senses, or the impressions occurring in the brain; and these have no influence on the will. Movements of the second kind, which do have an influence on the will, cause the passions or the bodily movements which accompany the passions. As to the first, although they often hinder the actions of the soul, or are hindered by them, yet since they are not directly opposed to these actions, we observe no conflict between them. We observe conflict only between movements of the second kind and the volitions which oppose them – for example, between the force with which the spirits push the gland so as to cause the soul to desire something, and the force with which the soul, by its volition to avoid this thing, pushes the gland in a contrary direction. Such a conflict is revealed chiefly through the fact that the will, lacking the power to produce the passions directly (as I have already said), is compelled to make an effort to consider a series of different things, and if one of them happens to have the power to change for a moment the course of the spirits, the next one may happen to lack this power, whereupon the spirits will immediately revert to the same course because no change has occurred in the state of the nerves, heart and blood. This makes the soul feel itself impelled, almost at one and the same time, to desire and not to desire one and the same thing; and that is why it has been thought that the soul has within it two conflicting powers. We may, however, acknowledge a kind of conflict, in so far as the same cause that produces a certain passion in the soul often also produces certain movements in the body, to which the soul makes no contribution and which the soul stops or tries to stop as soon as it perceives them. We experience this when an object that excites fear also causes the spirits to enter the muscles which serve to move our legs in flight, while the will to be bold stops them from moving.

48. *How we recognize the strength or weakness of souls, and what is wrong with the weakest souls.*
It is by success in these conflicts that each person can recognize the strength or weakness of his soul. For undoubtedly the strongest souls belong to those in whom the will by nature can most easily conquer the passions and stop the bodily move-

ments which accompany them. But there are some who can never test the strength of their will because they never equip it to fight with its proper weapons, giving it instead only the weapons which some passions provide for resisting other passions. What I call its "proper" weapons are firm and determinate judgements bearing upon the knowledge of good and evil, which the soul has resolved to follow in guiding its conduct. The weakest souls of all are those whose will is not determined in this way to follow such judgements, but constantly allows itself to be carried away by present passions. The latter, being often opposed to one another, pull the will first to one side and then to the other, thus making it battle against itself and so putting the soul in the most deplorable state possible. Thus, when fear represents death as an extreme evil which can be avoided only by flight, while ambition on the other hand depicts the dishonour of flight as an evil worse than death, these two passions jostle the will in opposite ways; and since the will obeys first the one and then the other, it is continually opposed to itself, and so it renders the soul enslaved and miserable.

49. *The strength of the soul is inadequate without knowledge of the truth.*
It is true that very few people are so weak and irresolute that they choose only what their passion dictates. Most have some determinate judgements which they follow in regulating some of their actions. Often these judgements are false and based on passions by which the will has previously allowed itself to be conquered or led astray; but because the will continues to follow them when the passion which caused them is absent, they may be considered its proper weapons, and we may judge souls to be stronger or weaker according to their ability to follow these judgements more or less closely and resist the present passions which are opposed to them. There is, however, a great difference between the resolutions which proceed from some false opinion and those which are based solely on knowledge of the truth. For, anyone who follows the latter is assured of never regretting or repenting, whereas we always regret having followed the former when we discover our error.

50. *There is no soul so weak that it cannot, if well-directed, acquire an absolute power over its passions.*
It is useful to note here, as already mentioned above [Art. 44], that although nature seems to have joined every movement of the gland to certain

of our thoughts from the beginning of our life, yet we may join them to others through habit. Experience shows this in the case of language. Words produce in the gland movements which are ordained by nature to represent to the soul only the sounds of their syllables when they are spoken or the shape of their letters when they are written, because we have acquired the habit of thinking of this meaning when we hear them spoken or see them written. It is also useful to note that although the movements (both of the gland and of the spirits and the brain) which represent certain objects to the soul are naturally joined to the movements which produce certain passions in it, yet through habit the former can be separated from the latter and joined to others which are very different. Indeed this habit can be acquired by a single action and does not require long practice. Thus, when we unexpectedly come upon something very foul in a dish we are eating with relish, our surprise may so change the disposition of our brain that we cannot afterwards look upon any such food without repulsion, whereas previously we ate it with pleasure. And the same may be observed in animals. For

although they lack reason, and perhaps even thought, all the movements of the spirits and of the gland which produce passions in us are nevertheless present in them too, though in them they serve to maintain and strengthen only the movements of the nerves and the muscles which usually accompany the passions and not, as in us, the passions themselves. So when a dog sees a partridge, it is naturally disposed to run towards it; and when it hears a gun fired, the noise naturally impels it to run away. Nevertheless, setters are commonly trained so that the sight of a partridge makes them stop, and the noise they hear afterwards, when someone fires at the bird, makes them run towards it. These things are worth noting in order to encourage each of us to make a point of controlling our passions. For since we are able, with a little effort, to change the movements of the brain in animals devoid of reason, it is evident that we can do so still more effectively in the case of men. Even those who have the weakest souls could acquire absolute mastery over all their passions if we employed sufficient ingenuity in training and guiding them.

PART II

Thomas Hobbes (1588–1679)

Introduction

Students are typically introduced to Hobbes by way of his *magnum opus*, *Leviathan* (1651). Though the latter work contains many of the leading themes in Hobbes's philosophy, he wrote much else including tracts on law and history, mathematics and physics, as well as translations of Thucydides, Aristotle, and Homer. The ideas presented in *Leviathan* were also elaborated in various other writings. The following selections are drawn from a trilogy of works that were intended to be a comprehensive statement of Hobbes's philosophical system: *The Citizen* (*De Cive*, 1642), *Concerning Body* (*De Corpore*, 1655), and *On Man* (*De Homine*, 1658). Departing from the chronological order of publication, we begin

with the opening section of *Concerning Body*. In addition to presenting Hobbes's views on the nature of scientific method, this text provides a useful framework for understanding the differences between Hobbes and Descartes. The next selection is from *The Citizen*, a work which would later form the basis of Hobbes's discussion of government in *Leviathan*. We have included the entirety of chapter V, in which Hobbes presents his views on the causes and origin of government. The final selection is drawn from *On Man*. Though this work purports to be about human nature, a large part of it is actually devoted to a discussion of optics. We have included here those sections in which Hobbes presents his views on language, morality, and religion.

Concerning Body

Chapter VI: Of Method

1. Method and science defined. 2. It is more easily known concerning singular, than universal things, that they are; and contrarily, it is more easily known concerning universal, than singular things, why they are, or what are their causes. 3. What it is philosophers seek to know. 4. The first part, by which principles are found out, is purely analytical. 5. The highest causes, and most universal in every kind, are known by themselves. 6. Method from principles found out, tending to science simply, what it is. 7. That method of civil and natural science, which proceeds from sense to principles, is analytical; and again, that, which begins at principles, is synthetical. 8. The method of searching out, whether any thing propounded be matter or accident. 9. The method of seeking whether any accident be in this, or in that subject. [...]

1. For the understanding of *method*, it will be necessary for me to repeat the definition of philosophy, delivered above (Chap. I, art. 2.) in this manner, *Philosophy is the knowledge we acquire, by true ratiocination, of appearances, or apparent effects, from the knowledge we have of some possible production or generation of the same; and of such production, as has been or may be, from the knowledge we have of the effects.* METHOD, therefore, in the study of

Concerning Body (*De Corpore*, 1655). From *The English Works of Thomas Hobbes of Malmesbury*, vol. 1, ed. Sir William Molesworth (Scientia Aalen, 1962). Reprint of the 1839 edition. Selection: Part 1, ch. 6, "Of Method," pp. 65–77.

philosophy, *is the shortest way of finding out effects by their known causes, or of causes by their known effects.* But we are then said to know any effect, when we know *that there be causes of the same*, and *in what subject those causes are*, and *in what subject they produce that effect*, and *in what manner they work the same*. And this is the science of causes, or, as they call it, of the διότι. All other science, which is called the ὅτι, is either perception by sense, or the imagination, or memory remaining after such perception.

The first beginnings, therefore, of knowledge, are the phantasms of sense and imagination; and that there be such phantasms we know well enough by nature; but to know why they be, or from what causes they proceed, is the work of ratiocination; which consists (as is said above, in the 1st Chapter, Art. 2) in *composition*, and *division* or *resolution*. There is therefore no method, by which we find out the causes of things, but is either *compositive* or *resolutive*, or *partly compositive*, and *partly resolutive*. And the resolutive is commonly called *analytical* method, as the compositive is called *synthetical*.

2. It is common to all sorts of method, to proceed from known things to unknown; and this is manifest from the cited definition of philosophy. But in knowledge by sense, the whole object is more known, than any part thereof; as when we see a man, the conception or whole idea of that man is first or more known, than the particular ideas of his being *figurate*, *animate*, and *rational*; that is, we first see the whole man, and take notice of his being, before we observe in him those other particulars. And therefore in any knowledge of the ὅτι, or that any thing *is*, the beginning of our

search is from the whole idea; and contrarily, in our knowledge of the διότι, or of the causes of any thing, that is, in the sciences, we have more knowledge of the causes of the parts than of the whole. For the cause of the whole is compounded of the causes of the parts; but it is necessary that we know the things that are to be compounded, before we can know the whole compound. Now, by parts, I do not here mean parts of the thing itself, but parts of its nature; as, by the parts of man, I do not understand his head, his shoulders, his arms, &c. but his figure, quantity, motion, sense, reason, and the like; which accidents being compounded or put together, constitute the whole nature of man, but not the man himself. And this is the meaning of that common saying, namely, that some things are more known to us, others more known to nature; for I do not think that they, which so distinguish, mean that something is known to nature, which is known to no man; and therefore, by those things, that are more known to us, we are to understand things we take notice of by our senses, and, by more known to nature, those we acquire the knowledge of by reason; for in this sense it is, that the *whole*, that is, those things that have universal names, (which, for brevity's sake, I call *universal*) are more known to us than the *parts*, that is, such things as have names less universal, (which I therefore call *singular*); and the causes of the parts are more known to nature than the cause of the whole; that is, universals than singulars.

3. In the study of philosophy, men search after science either simply or indefinitely; that is, to know as much as they can, without propounding to themselves any limited question; or they enquire into the cause of some determined appearance, or endeavour to find out the certainty of something in question, as what is the cause of *light*, of *heat*, of *gravity*, of a *figure* propounded, and the like; or in what *subject* any propounded *accident* is inherent; or what may conduce most to the *generation* of some propounded *effect* from many *accidents*; or in what manner particular causes ought to be compounded for the production of some certain effect. Now, according to this variety of things in question, sometimes the *analytical method* is to be used, and sometimes the *synthetical*.

4. But to those that search after science indefinitely, which consists in the knowledge of the causes of all things, as far forth as it may be attained, (and the causes of singular things are compounded of the causes of universal or simple things) it is necessary that they know the causes of universal things, or of such accidents as are common to all bodies, that is, to all matter, before they can know the causes of singular things, that is, of those accidents by which one thing is distinguished from another. And, again, they must know what those universal things are, before they can know their causes. Moreover, seeing universal things are contained in the nature of singular things, the knowledge of them is to be acquired by reason, that is, by resolution. For example, if there be propounded a conception or *idea* of some singular thing, as of a *square*, this square is to be resolved into a *plain, terminated with a certain number of equal and straight lines and right angles*. For by this resolution we have these things universal or agreeable to all matter, namely, *line, plain*, (which contains *superficies*) *terminated, angle, straightness, rectitude*, and *equality*; and if we can find out the causes of these, we may compound them altogether into the cause of a square. Again, if any man propound to himself the conception of *gold*, he may, by resolving, come to the ideas of *solid, visible, heavy*, (that is, tending to the centre of the earth, or downwards) and many other more universal than gold itself; and these he may resolve again, till he come to such things as are most universal. And in this manner, by resolving continually, we may come to know what those things are, whose causes being first known severally, and afterwards compounded, bring us to the knowledge of singular things. I conclude, therefore, that the method of attaining to the universal knowledge of things, is purely *analytical*.

5. But the causes of universal things (of those, at least, that have any cause) are manifest of themselves, or (as they say commonly) known to nature; so that they need no method at all; for they have all but one universal cause, which is motion. For the variety of all figures arises out of the variety of those motions by which they are made; and motion cannot be understood to have any other cause besides motion; nor has the variety of those things we perceive by sense, as of *colours, sounds, savours*, &c. any other cause than motion, residing partly in the objects that work upon our senses, and partly in ourselves, in such manner, as that it is manifestly some kind of motion, though we cannot, without ratiocination, come to know what kind. For though many cannot understand till it be in some sort demonstrated to them, that all mutation consists in motion; yet this happens not from any obscurity in the thing itself, (for it is not intelli-

gible that anything can depart either from rest, or from the motion it has, except by motion), but either by having their natural discourse corrupted with former opinions received from their masters, or else for this, that they do not at all bend their mind to the enquiring out of truth.

6. By the knowledge therefore of universals, and of their causes (which are the first principles by which we know the διότι of things) we have in the first place their definitions, (which are nothing but the explication of our simple conceptions.) For example, he that has a true conception of *place*, cannot be ignorant of this definition, *place is that space which is possessed or filled adequately by some body*; and so, he that conceives *motion* aright, cannot but know that *motion is the privation of one place, and the acquisition of another*. In the next place, we have their generations or descriptions; as (for example) that *a line is made by the motion of a point, superficies by the motion of a line*, and *one motion by another motion*, &c. It remains, that we enquire what motion begets such and such effects; as, what motion makes a straight line, and what a circular; what motion thrusts, what draws, and by what way; what makes a thing which is seen or heard, to be seen or heard sometimes in one manner, sometimes in another. Now the method of this kind of enquiry, is *compositive*. For first we are to observe what effect a body moved produceth, when we consider nothing in it besides its motion; and we see presently that this makes a line, or length; next, what the motion of a long body produces, which we find to be superficies; and so forwards, till we see what the effects of simple motion are; and then, in like manner, we are to observe what proceeds from the addition, multiplication, subtraction, and division, of these motions, and what effects, what figures, and what properties, they produce; from which kind of contemplation sprung that part of philosophy which is called *geometry*.

From this consideration of what is produced by simple motion, we are to pass to the consideration of what effects one body moved worketh upon another; and because there may be motion in all the several parts of a body, yet so as that the whole body remain still in the same place, we must enquire first, what motion causeth such and such motion in the whole, that is, when one body invades another body which is either at rest or in motion, what way, and with what swiftness, the invaded body shall move; and, again, what motion this second body will generate in a third, and so

forwards. From which contemplation shall be drawn that part of philosophy which treats of motion.

In the third place we must proceed to the enquiry of such effects as are made by the motion of the parts of any body, as, how it comes to pass, that things when they are the same, yet seem not to be the same, but changed. And here the things we search after are sensible qualities, such as *light, colour, transparency, opacity, sound, odour, savour, heat, cold*, and the like; which because they cannot be known till we know the causes of sense itself, therefore the consideration of the causes of *seeing, hearing, smelling, tasting*, and *touching*, belongs to this third place; and all those qualities and changes, above mentioned, are to be referred to the fourth place; which two considerations comprehend that part of philosophy which is called *physics*. And in these four parts is contained whatsoever in natural philosophy may be explicated by demonstration, properly so called. For if a cause were to be rendered of natural appearances in special, as, what are the motions and influences of the heavenly bodies, and of their parts, the reason hereof must either be drawn from the parts of the sciences above mentioned, or no reason at all will be given, but all left to uncertain conjecture.

After *physics* we must come to *moral philosophy*; in which we are to consider the motions of the mind, namely, *appetite, aversion, love, benevolence, hope, fear, anger, emulation, envy, &c.*; what causes they have, and of what they be causes. And the reason why these are to be considered after *physics* is, that they have their causes in sense and imagination, which are the subject of *physical* contemplation. Also the reason, why all these things are to be searched after in the order above-said, is, that physics cannot be understood, except we know first what motions are in the smallest parts of bodies; nor such motion of parts, till we know what it is that makes another body move; nor this, till we know what simple motion will effect. And because all appearance of things to sense is determined, and made to be of such and such quality and quantity by compounded motions, every one of which has a certain degree of velocity, and a certain and determined way; therefore, in the first place, we are to search out the ways of motion simply (in which geometry consists); next the ways of such generated motions as are manifest; and, lastly, the ways of internal and invisible motions (which is the enquiry of natural philosophers).

And, therefore, they that study natural philosophy, study in vain, except they begin at geometry; and such writers or disputers thereof, as are ignorant of geometry, do but make their readers and hearers lose their time.

7. *Civil* and *moral philosophy* do not so adhere to one another, but that they may be severed. For the causes of the motions of the mind are known, not only by ratiocination, but also by the experience of every man that takes the pains to observe those motions within himself. And, therefore, not only they that have attained the knowledge of the passions and perturbations of the mind, by the *synthetical method*, and from the very first principles of philosophy, may by proceeding in the same way, come to the causes and necessity of constituting commonwealths, and to get the knowledge of what is natural right, and what are civil duties; and, in every kind of government, what are the rights of the commonwealth, and all other knowledge appertaining to civil philosophy; for this reason, that the principles of the politics consist in the knowledge of the motions of the mind, and the knowledge of these motions from the knowledge of sense and imagination; but even they also that have not learned the first part of philosophy, namely, *geometry* and *physics*, may, notwithstanding, attain the principles of civil philosophy, by the *analytical method*. For if a question be propounded, as, *whether such an action be just or unjust*; if that *unjust* be resolved into *fact against law*, and that notion *law* into the *command* of him or them that have *coercive power*; and that *power* be derived from the *wills* of men that constitute such power, to the end they may live in peace, they may at last come to this, that the appetites of men and the passions of their minds are such, that, unless they be restrained by some power, they will always be making war upon one another; which may be known to be so by any man's experience, that will but examine his own mind. And, therefore, from hence he may proceed, by compounding, to the determination of the justice or injustice of any propounded action. So that it is manifest, by what has been said, that the method of philosophy, to such as seek science simply, without propounding to themselves the solution of any particular question, is partly analytical, and partly synthetical; namely, that which proceeds from sense to the invention of principles, analytical; and the rest synthetical.

8. To those that seek the cause of some certain and propounded appearance or effect, it happens, sometimes, that they know not whether the thing, whose cause is sought after, be matter or body, or some accident of a body. For though in geometry, when the cause is sought of magnitude, or proportion, or figure, it be certainly known that these things, namely magnitude, proportion, and figure, are accidents; yet in natural philosophy, where all questions are concerning the causes of the phantasms of sensible things, it is not so easy to discern between the things themselves, from which those phantasms proceed, and the appearances of those things to the sense; which have deceived many, especially when the phantasms have been made by light. For example, a man that looks upon the sun, has a certain shining idea of the magnitude of about a foot over, and this he calls the sun, though he know the sun to be truly a great deal bigger; and, in like manner, the phantasm of the same thing appears sometimes round, by being seen afar off, and sometimes square, by being nearer. Whereupon it may well be doubted, whether that phantasm be matter, or some body natural, or only some accident of a body; in the examination of which doubt we may use this method. The properties of matter and accidents already found out by us, by the synthetical method, from their definitions, are to be compared with the idea we have before us; and if it agree with the properties of matter or body, then it is a body; otherwise it is an accident. Seeing, therefore, matter cannot by any endeavour of ours be either made or destroyed, or increased, or diminished, or moved out of its place, whereas that idea appears, vanishes, is increased and diminished, and moved hither and thither at pleasure; we may certainly conclude that it is not a body, but an accident only. And this method is *synthetical*.

9. But if there be a doubt made concerning the subject of any known accident (for this may be doubted sometimes, as in the precedent example, doubt may be made in what subject that splendour and apparent magnitude of the sun is), then our enquiry must proceed in this manner. First, matter in general must be divided into parts, as, into object, medium, and the sentient itself, or such other parts as seem most conformable to the thing propounded. Next, these parts are severally to be examined how they agree with the definition of the subject; and such of them as are not capable of that accident are to be rejected. For example, if by any true ratiocination the sun be found to be greater than its apparent magnitude, then that magnitude is not in the sun; if the sun be in one determined

straight line, and one determined distance, and the magnitude and splendour be seen in more lines and distances than one, as it is in reflection or refraction, then neither that splendour nor apparent magnitude are in the sun itself, and, therefore, the body of the sun cannot be the subject of that splendour and magnitude. And for the same reasons the air and other parts will be rejected, till at last nothing remain which can be the subject of that splendour and magnitude but the sentient itself. And this method, in regard the subject is divided into parts, is analytical; and in regard the properties, both of the subject and accident, are compared with the accident concerning whose subject the enquiry is made, it is synthetical. [...]

The Citizen

V: Of the Causes and First Beginning of Civil Government

1. That the laws of nature are not sufficient to preserve peace. 2. That the laws of nature, in the state of nature, are silent. 3. That the security of living according to the laws of nature, consists in the concord of many persons. 4. That the concord of many persons is not constant enough for a lasting peace. 5. The reason why the government of certain brute creatures stands firm in concord only, and why not of men. 6. That not only consent, but union also, is required to establish the peace of men. 7. What union is. 8. In union, the right of all men is conveyed to one. 9. What civil society is. 10. What a civil person is. 11. What it is to have the supreme power, and what to be a subject. 12. Two kinds of cities, natural, and by institution.

1. It is of itself manifest that the actions of men proceed from the will, and the will from hope and fear, insomuch as when they shall see a greater good or less evil likely to happen to them by the breach than observation of the laws, they will wittingly violate them. The hope therefore which each man hath of his security and self-preservation, consists in this, that by force or craft he may disappoint his neighbour, either openly or by

The Citizen (*De Cive*, 1642). From *Man and Citizen*, tr. Thomas Hobbes, ed. Bernard Gert (Gloucester, MA: Peter Smith, 1978). Selection: Part 2, ch. 5, "Of the Causes and First Beginning of Civil Government," pp. 165–72.

stratagem. Whence we may understand, that the natural laws, though well understood, do not instantly secure any man in their practice; and consequently, that as long as there is no caution had from the invasion of others, there remains to every man that same primitive right of self-defence by such means as either he can or will make use of, that is, a right to all things, or the right of war. And it is sufficient for the fulfilling of the natural law, that a man be prepared in mind to embrace peace when it may be had.

2. It is a fond saying, that all laws are silent in the time of war, and it is a true one, not only if we speak of the civil, but also of the natural laws, provided they be referred not to the mind, but to the actions of men, by chap. iii. art. 27. And we mean such a war, as is of all men against all men; such as is the mere state of nature; although in the war of nation against nation, a certain mean was wont to be observed. And therefore in old time, there was a manner of living, and as it were a certain economy, which they called λησ τρικὴν, living by rapine; which was neither against the law of nature (things then so standing), nor void of glory to those who exercised it with valour, not with cruelty. Their custom was, taking away the rest, to spare life, and abstain from oxen fit for plough, and every instrument serviceable to husbandry. Which yet is not so to be taken, as if they were bound to do thus by the law of nature; but that they had regard to their own glory herein, lest by too much cruelty they might be suspected guilty of fear.

3. Since therefore the exercise of the natural law is necessary for the preservation of peace, and that for the exercise of the natural law security

is no less necessary; it is worth the considering what that is which affords such a security. For this matter nothing else can be imagined, but that each man provide himself of such meet helps, as the invasion of one on the other may be rendered so dangerous, as either of them may think it better to refrain than to meddle. But first, it is plain that the consent of two or three cannot make good such a security; because that the addition but of one, or some few on the other side, is sufficient to make the victory undoubtedly sure, and heartens the enemy to attack us. It is therefore necessary, to the end the security sought for may be obtained, that the number of them who conspire in a mutual assistance be so great, that the accession of some few to the enemy's party may not prove to them a matter of moment sufficient to assure the victory.

4. Furthermore, how great soever the number of them is who meet on self-defence, if yet they agree not among themselves of some excellent means whereby to compass this, but every man after his own manner shall make use of his endeavours, nothing will be done; because that, divided in their opinions, they will be a hinderance to each other; or if they agree well enough to some one action, through hope of victory, spoil, or revenge, yet afterward, through diversity of wits and counsels, or emulation and envy, with which men naturally contend, they will be so torn and rent, as they will neither give mutual help nor desire peace, except they be constrained to it by some common fear. Whence it follows that the consent of many (which consists in this only, as we have already defined in the foregoing section, that they direct all their actions to the same end and the common good), that is to say, that the society proceeding from mutual help only, yields not that security which they seek for, who meet and agree in the exercise of the above-named laws of nature; but that somewhat else must be done, that those who have once consented for the common good to peace and mutual help, may by fear be restrained lest afterwards they again dissent, when their private interest shall appear discrepant from the common good.

5. Aristotle reckons among those animals which he calls politic, not man only, but divers others, as the ant, the bee, &c.; which, though they be destitute of reason, by which they may contract and submit to government, notwithstanding by consenting, that is to say, ensuing or eschewing the same things, they so direct their actions to a common end, that their meetings are not obnoxious unto any seditions. Yet is not their gathering together a civil government, and therefore those animals not to be termed political; because their government is only a consent, or many wills concurring in one object, not (as is necessary in civil government) one will. It is very true, that in those creatures living only by sense and appetite, their consent of minds is so durable, as there is no need of anything more to secure it, and by consequence to preserve peace among them, than barely their natural inclination. But among men the case is otherwise. For, first, among them there is a contestation of honour and preferment; among beasts there is none: whence hatred and envy, out of which arise sedition and war, is among men; among beasts no such matter. Next, the natural appetite of bees, and the like creatures, is conformable; and they desire the common good, which among them differs not from their private. But man scarce esteems anything good, which hath not somewhat of eminence in the enjoyment, more than that which others do possess. Thirdly, those creatures which are void of reason, see no defect, or think they see none, in the administration of their commonweals; but in a multitude of men there are many who, supposing themselves wiser than others, endeavour to innovate, and divers innovators innovate divers ways; which is a mere distraction and civil war. Fourthly, these brute creatures, howsoever they may have the use of their voice to signify their affections to each other, yet want they that same art of words which is necessarily required to those motions in the mind, whereby good is represented to it as being better, and evil as worse than in truth it is. But the tongue of man is a trumpet of war and sedition: and it is reported of Pericles, that he sometimes by his elegant speeches thundered and lightened, and confounded whole Greece itself. Fifthly, they cannot distinguish between *injury* and *harm*; thence it happens that as long as it is well with them, they blame not their fellows. But those men are of most trouble to the republic, who have most leisure to be idle; for they use not to contend for public places, before they have gotten the victory over hunger and cold. Last of all, the consent of those brutal creatures is natural; that of men by compact only, that is to say, artificial. It is therefore no matter of wonder, if somewhat more be needful for men to the end they may live in peace. Wherefore consent or contracted society, without some common power whereby particular men may be ruled through fear of punishment,

doth not suffice to make up that security, which is requisite to the exercise of natural justice.

6. Since therefore the conspiring of many wills to the same end doth not suffice to preserve peace, and to make a lasting defence, it is requisite that, in those necessary matters which concern peace and self-defence, there be but one will of all men. But this cannot be done, unless every man will so subject his will to some other one, to wit, either man or council, that whatsoever his will is in those things which are necessary to the common peace, it be received for the wills of all men in general, and of every one in particular. Now the gathering together of many men, who deliberate of what is to be done or not to be done for the common good of all men, is that which I call a *council*.

7. This submission of the wills of all those men to the will of one man or one council, is then made, when each one of them obligeth himself by contract to every one of the rest, not to resist the will of that one man or council, to which he hath submitted himself; that is, that he refuse him not the use of his wealth and strength against any others whatsoever; for he is supposed still to retain a right of defending himself against violence: and this is called *union*. But we understand that to be the will of the council, which is the will of the major part of those men of whom the council consists.

8. But though the will itself be not voluntary, but only the beginning of voluntary actions (for we will not to will, but to act); and therefore falls least of all under deliberation and compact; yet he who submits his will to the will of another, conveys to that other the right of his strength and faculties. Insomuch as when the rest have done the same, he to whom they have submitted, hath so much power, as by the terror of it he can conform the wills of particular men unto unity and concord.

9. Now union thus made is called a city or civil society; and also a civil person. For when there is one will of all men, it is to be esteemed for one person; and by the word *one*, it is to be known and distinguished from all particular men, as having its own rights and properties. Insomuch as neither any one citizen, nor all of them together (if we except him, whose will stands for the will of all), is to be accounted the city. A *city* therefore (that we may define it), is *one person*, whose will, by the compact of many men, is to be received for the will of them all; so as he may use all the power and faculties of each particular person to the maintenance of peace, and for common defence.

10. But although every city be a civil person, yet every civil person is not a city; for it may happen that many citizens, by the permission of the city, may join together in one person, for the doing of certain things. These now will be civil persons; as the companies of merchants, and many other convents. But cities they are not, because they have not submitted themselves to the will of the company simply and in all things, but in certain things only determined by the city, and on such terms as it is lawful for any one of them to contend in judgment against the body itself of the sodality; which is by no means allowable to a citizen against the city. Such like societies, therefore, are civil persons subordinate to the city.

11. In every city, that man or council to whose will each particular man hath subjected his will so as hath been declared, is said to have the *supreme power*, or *chief command*, or *dominion*. Which power and right of commanding consists in this, that each citizen hath conveyed all his strength and power to that man or council; which to have done, because no man can transfer his power in a natural manner, is nothing else than to have parted with his right of resisting. Each citizen, as also every subordinate civil person, is called the *subject* of him who hath the chief command.

12. By what hath been said, it is sufficiently showed in what manner and by what degrees many natural persons, through desire of preserving themselves and by mutual fear, have grown together into a civil person, whom we have called a *city*. But they who submit themselves to another for fear, either submit to him whom they fear, or some other whom they confide in for protection. They act according to the first manner, who are vanquished in war, that they may not be slain; they according to the second, who are not yet overcome, that they may not be overcome. The first manner receives its beginning from natural power, and may be called the natural beginning of a city; the latter from the council and constitution of those who meet together, which is a beginning by institution. Hence it is that there are two kinds of cities: the one natural, such as is the paternal and despotical; the other institutive, which may be also called political. In the first, the lord acquires to himself such citizens as he will; in the other, the citizens by their own wills appoint a lord over themselves, whether he be one man or one company of men, endued with the command in chief. But we will speak, in the first place, of a city political or by institution; and next, of a city natural.

6

On Man

X: On Speech and Sciences

1. Definition of speech: peculiar to man. 2. The origin of speech. 3. The advantages and disadvantages of speech. 4. Science and demonstration arise from the knowledge of causes. 5. Theorems are demonstrable for things only insofar as their causes are in our power; in other cases it can be demonstrated only that such and such is possible.

1. Speech or language is the connexion of names constituted by the will of men to stand for the series of conceptions of the things about which we think. Therefore, as a name is to an idea or conception of a thing, so is speech to the discourse of the mind. And it seems to be peculiar to man. For even if some brute animals, taught by practice, grasp what we wish and command in words, they do so not through words as words, but as signs; for animals do not know that words are constituted by the will of men for the purpose of signification.

Moreover the signification that does occur when animals of the same kind call to one another, is not on that account speech, since not by their will, but out of the necessity of nature, these calls by which hope, fear, joy, and the like are signified, are forced out by the strength of these passions. And since

On Man (*De Homine*, 1658). From *Man and Citizen*, tr. Charles T. Wood, T. S. K. Scott-Craig, and Bernard Gert (Gloucester, MA: Peter Smith, 1978). Selections: Bk 10, "On Speech and Sciences," pp. 37–43; Bk 11, "On Appetite and Aversion, Pleasure and Displeasure and Their Causes," pp. 45–54; Bk 14, "On Religion," pp. 71–82.

among animals there is a limited variety of calls, by changing from one call to another, it comes about that they are warned of danger so that they may flee, are summoned to feeding, aroused to song, solicited to love; yet these calls are not speech since they are not constituted by the will of these animals, but burst forth by the strength of nature from the peculiar fears, joys, desires, and other passions of each of them; and this is not to speak, which is manifest in this, that the calls of animals of the same species are in all lands whatsoever the same, while those of men are diverse.

Therefore other animals also lack understanding. For understanding is a kind of imagination, but one that ariseth from the signification constituted by words.

2. Because, however, I would say that names have arisen from human invention, someone might possibly ask how a human invention could avail so much as to confer on mankind the benefit speech appears to us to have. For it is incredible that men once came together to take counsel to constitute by decree what all words and all connexions of words would signify. It is more credible, however, that at first there were few names and only of those things that were the most familiar. Thus the first man by his own will imposed names on just a few animals, namely, the ones that God led before him to look at; then on other things, as one or another species of things offered itself to his senses; these names, having been accepted, were handed down from fathers to their sons, who also devised others. But when, in the second chapter of Genesis, God is said to have prohibited the eating of the fruit of the tree of knowledge of good and evil before Adam had

given names to anything, in what manner could Adam have understood that command of God, when he did not as yet know what was meant by *eating*, *fruit*, *tree*, *knowledge*, and lastly, *good* or *evil*? It must be, therefore, that Adam understood that divine prohibition not from the meaning of the words, but in some supernatural manner, as is made manifest a little later from this: that God asked him who had told him that he was naked. Similarly, how could Adam, the first mortal, have understood the serpent speaking of death, whereof he could have had no idea? Hence these things could not have been understood in any natural way; and as a consequence, speech could not have had a natural origin except by the will of man himself. This is made even clearer by the confusion of languages at Babel. For from that time the origins of language are diverse and have been brought by single men to single peoples. What others say, however – that names have been imposed on single things according to the nature of those things – is childish. For who could have it so when the nature of things is everywhere the same while languages are diverse? And what relationship hath a *call* (that is, a sound) with an *animal* (that is, a body)?

3. Of the advantages related to language the following are pre-eminent. *First*, that the power of numeral words enables man not only to count things, but also to measure them, whatsoever they may be; so with bodies (insofar as they have any dimensions), whether they be long, or long and wide, or long, wide, and thick; and similarly he can add, subtract, multiply, divide, and compare them with one another; similarly he can also subject times, motion, weight, and degrees of increase and decrease to calculation. From these things the enormous advantages of human life have far surpassed the condition of other animals. For there is no one that doth not know how much these arts are used in measuring bodies, calculating times, computing celestial motions, describing the face of the earth, navigating, erecting buildings, making engines, and in other necessary things. All of these proceed from numbering, but numbering proceeds from speech. *Secondly*, one may teach another, that is, communicate his knowledge to another, he can warn, he can advise, all these he hath from speech also; so that a good, great in itself, through communication becomes even greater. *Thirdly*, that we can command and understand commands is a benefit of speech, and truly the greatest. For without this there would be no society among men, no peace, and consequently no disciplines; but first savagery, then solitude, and for dwellings, caves. For though among certain animals there are seeming polities, these are not of sufficiently great moment for living well; hence they merit not our consideration; and they are largely found among defenseless animals, not in need of many things; in which number man is not included; for just as swords and guns, the weapons of men, surpass the weapons of brute animals (horns, teeth, and stings), so man surpasseth in rapacity and cruelty the wolves, bears, and snakes that are not rapacious unless hungry and not cruel unless provoked, whereas man is famished even by future hunger. From this it is easily understood how much we owe to language, by which we, having been drawn together and agreeing to covenants, live securely, happily, and elegantly; we can so live, I insist, if we so will. But language also hath its disadvantages; namely because man, alone among the animals, on account of the universal signification of names, can create general rules for himself in the art of living just as in the other arts; and so he alone can devise errors and pass them on for the use of others. Therefore man errs more widely and dangerously than can other animals. Also, man if it please him (and it will please him as often as it seems to advance his plans), can teach what he knows to be false from works that he hath inherited; that is, he can lie and render the minds of men hostile to the conditions of society and peace; something that cannot happen in the societies of other animals, since they judge what things are good and bad for them by their senses, not on the basis of the complaints of others, the causes whereof, unless they be seen, they cannot understand. Moreover, it sometimes happens to those that listen to philosophers and Schoolmen that listening becomes a habit, and the words that they hear they accept rashly, even though no sense can be had from them (for such are the kind of words invented by teachers to hide their own ignorance), and they use them, believing that they are saying something when they say nothing. Finally, on account of the ease of speech, the man who truly doth not think, speaks; and what he says, he believes to be true, and he can deceive himself; a beast cannot deceive itself. Therefore by speech man is not made better, but only given greater possibilities.

4. *Science* is understood as being concerned with theorems, that is, with the truth of general propositions, that is, with the truth of conse-

quences. Indeed, when one is dealing with the truth of fact, it is not properly called *science*, but simply *knowledge*. Therefore it is science when we know a certain proposed theorem to be true, either by knowledge derived from the causes, or from the generation of the subject by right reasoning. On the other hand, when we know (insofar as possible) that such and such a theorem may be true, it is knowledge derived by legitimate reasoning from the experience of effects. Both of these methods of proof are usually called demonstrations; the former kind is, however, preferable to the latter; and rightly so; for it is better to know how we can best use present causes than to know the irrevocable past, whatsoever its nature. Therefore science is allowed to men through the former kind of *a priori* demonstration only of those things whose generation depends on the will of men themselves.

5. Therefore many theorems are demonstrable about quantity, the science whereof is called geometry. Since the causes of the properties that individual figures have belong to them because we ourselves draw the lines; and since the generation of the figures depends on our will; nothing more is required to know the phenomenon peculiar to any figure whatsoever, than that we consider everything that follows from the construction that we ourselves make in the figure to be described. Therefore, because of this fact (that is, that we ourselves create the figures), it happens that geometry hath been and is demonstrable. On the other hand, since the causes of natural things are not in our power, but in the divine will, and since the greatest part of them, namely the ether, is invisible; we, that do not see them, cannot deduce their qualities from their causes. Of course, we can, by deducing as far as possible the consequences of those qualities that we do see, demonstrate that such and such *could* have been their causes. This kind of demonstration is called *a posteriori*, and its science, physics. And since one cannot proceed in reasoning about natural things that are brought about by motion from the effects to the causes without a knowledge of those things that follow from that kind of motion; and since one cannot proceed to the consequences of motions without a knowledge of quantity, which is geometry; nothing can be demonstrated by physics without something also being demonstrated *a priori*. Therefore physics (I mean true physics), that depends on geometry, is usually numbered among the mixed mathematics. For those sciences are usually called mathematical that are learned not from use and

experience, but from teachers and rules. Therefore those mathematics are pure which (like geometry and arithmetic) revolve around quantities in the abstract so that work in the subject requires no knowledge of fact; those mathematics are mixed, in truth, which in their reasoning also consider any quality of the subject, as is the case with astronomy, music, physics, and the parts of physics that can vary on account of the variety of species and the parts of the universe.

Finally, politics and ethics (that is, the sciences of *just* and *unjust*, of *equity* and *inequity*) can be demonstrated *a priori*; because we ourselves make the principles – that is, the causes of justice (namely laws and covenants) – whereby it is known what *justice* and *equity*, and their opposites *injustice* and *inequity*, are. For before covenants and laws were drawn up, neither justice nor injustice, neither public good nor public evil, was natural among men any more than it was among beasts.

XI: On Appetite and Aversion, Pleasure and Displeasure and Their Causes

1. What appetite and aversion are, and their causes. 2. They are not dependent on our will. 3. Appetite is born of experience. 4. Till now, good and evil have been diversely named. 5. The various names for good: *pulchrum*, pleasant, useful. 6. The greatest good to each is his own preservation; the greatest evil, with respect to nature, is his own destruction. 7. Riches. 8. Wisdom. 9. The arts. 10. Letters. 11. Work. 12. What pleasures are. 13. What *pulchra* are. 14. Goods compared. 15. The greatest good.

1. Appetite and aversion do not differ from delight and annoyance otherwise than desire from satisfaction of desire, that is, than the future differs from the present. For appetite is delight, and aversion, annoyance; but the former differs from pleasure, the latter from displeasure, as being not yet present, but foreseen or expected. Moreover, delight and annoyance, although they are not called senses, nevertheless differ only in this: that the sense of an object, as external, comes from the reaction or resistance that is made by an organ; and hence it consists in the endeavour of an organ to push outward; delight, however, consists in the passion made by the action of an object, and is an endeavour inwards.

2. Therefore the causes, as of sense, so of appetite and aversion, delight and annoyance, are these same objects of the senses. From this it can be understood that neither our appetite nor our aversion causeth us to desire or shun this or that; that is, we do not desire because we will. For will itself is an appetite; and we do not shun something because we will not to do it, but because now appetite, then aversion, is generated by those things desired or shunned, and a preconception of future pleasure and displeasure necessarily follows from those same objects. What then: Do we desire food and the other necessities of nature because we will? Are hunger, thirst, and desires voluntary? When desiring, one can, in truth, be free *to act*; one cannot, however, be free *to desire*; a fact that is made so obvious to anyone by his own experience that I cannot but be amazed that there are so many people who do not understand how this can be. Whenever we say that someone hath free-will to do this or that, or not to do it, it must always be understood with this necessary condition: *if he wills*. For to talk of having free-will to do this or that whether one wills or not is absurd.

Whenever it is asked of someone whether he ought to do a certain proposed thing or to let it pass, he is said to *deliberate*, that is, he hath the liberty of putting aside either choice. In this deliberation, accordingly as advantages and disadvantages show themselves this way and that, so appetite and aversion will alternate, until the thing demands that a decision be made. The last appetite (either of doing or omitting), the one that leads immediately to action or omission, is properly called the *will*.

3. According to the method of nature, sense is prior to *appetite*. For it cannot be known whether or not what we see as a pleasure would have been so, except by experience, that is, by feeling it. Therefore it is commonly said that there is no desire for the unknown. In truth, however, there can be a desire to experience the unknown. Whence it is that infants desire few things while youths try many new things, and with increasing age, mature men (especially educated ones) experiment with innumerable things, even with those that are unnecessary; experienced people know what every pleasure is, and, by drawing on memory, they afterwards desire more often. Even if first experiences of something be sometimes displeasing, especially when new or rare, by habit they are rendered not displeasing, and afterwards pleasing; that much can habit change the nature of single men.

4. The common name for all things that are desired, insofar as they are desired, is *good*; and for all things we shun, *evil*. Therefore Aristotle hath well defined *good* as that which all men desire. But, since different men desire and shun different things, there must needs be many things that are *good* to some and *evil* to others; so that which is *good* to us is *evil* to our enemies. Therefore *good* and *evil* are correlated with desiring and shunning. There can be a common *good*, and it can rightly be said of something, *it is commonly a good*, that is, useful to many, or good for the state. At times one can also talk of a good for everyone, like health: but this way of speaking is relative; therefore one cannot speak of something as being *simply good*; since whatsoever is good, is good for someone or other. In the beginning everything that God created was good. Why? Because all His works pleased Him. It is also said that God is good to all who invoke His name, but not to those who blaspheme His name. Therefore good is said to be relative to person, place, and time. What pleaseth one man now, will displease another later; and the same holds true for everyone else. For the nature of good and evil follows from the nature of circumstances (συντυχίαν).

5. The names of *good* and *evil* also vary in a number of different ways. For the same thing that, as desired, is said to be good, is said to be *pleasing* as acquired; the thing that, as desired, is said to be good, is said to be *pulchrum* when contemplated. For *pulchritudo* is that quality in an object that makes one expect good from it. For whatsoever things are seen as similar to those that have pleased, seem as though they would please. Therefore *pulchritudo* is an indication of future good. This, when it is viewed in action, is called honesty; when it dwells in a form, it is called *beauty*; and it pleaseth by imagination, even before the good of which it is a sign is acquired. For the same reason *evil* and *turpe* are spoken about in the same way. Furthermore, the thing that, when desired, is called good, is, if desired for its own sake, called pleasing; and if for some other thing, it is called useful. For the good that we desire for its own sake we do not *use*, since *usefulness* is applied to means and instruments, while *enjoyment* applies to something proposed as an end. Moreover, good (like evil) is divided into *real* and *apparent*. Not because any apparent good may not truly be good in itself, without considering the other things that follow from it; but in many things, whereof part is good and part evil, there is sometimes such a necessary

connexion between the parts that they cannot be separated. Therefore, though in each one of them there be so much good, or so much evil; nevertheless the chain as a whole is partly good and partly evil. And whenever the major part be good, the series is said to be good, and is desired; on the contrary, if the major part be evil, and, moreover, if it be known to be so, the whole is rejected. Whence it happens that inexperienced men that do not look closely enough at the long-term consequences of things, accept what appears to be good, not seeing the evil annexed to it; afterwards they experience damage. And this is what is meant by those who distinguish good and evil as *real* and *apparent*.

6. Moreover, the greatest of goods for each is his own preservation. For nature is so arranged that all desire good for themselves. Insofar as it is within their capacities, it is necessary to desire life, health, and further, insofar as it can be done, security of future time. On the other hand, though death is the greatest of all evils (especially when accompanied by torture), the pains of life can be so great that, unless their quick end is foreseen, they may lead men to number death among the goods.

Power, if it be extraordinary, is good, because it is useful for protection; and protection provides security. If it be not extraordinary, it is useless; for what all have equally is nothing.

Friendships are good, certainly useful. For friendships, among many other things, confer protection. Therefore enemies are evil, as they bring dangers and remove security.

7. Riches, if immense – certainly as Lucullus defined the wealthy man as one that can support an army on his own – are useful. For they are almost certain protection. Moderate wealth, to those willing to use it for protection, is also useful; for it acquires friendships; friendships, moreover, are protection. Those unwilling to use riches for protection, however, provoke envy. Therefore to that extent they are an *apparent good*.

Riches that are not inherited, but acquired by one's own industry, are good; for they are pleasing. For they seem to everyone an argument for his own prudence. Destitution or even poverty, lacking necessities, is evil, since to need necessities is evil. Poverty without need is good; it delivers its owner from envy, calumny, and plots.

8. Wisdom is useful. For some protection is to be had from it. It is also desirable for its own sake, that is, pleasing. It is also *pulchrum* because it is

difficult to acquire. Ignorance is bad; as in it there is no protection, or foresight of approaching evil.

The love of riches is greater than wisdom. For commonly the latter is not sought except for the sake of the former. And if men have the former, they wish to seem to have the latter also. For it is not as the Stoics say, that he who is wise is rich; but, rather, it must be said that he who is rich is wise.

The glory of wisdom is greater than riches. For the latter are usually had as a sign of the former. Want is less a disgrace than stupidity; for the former can be attributed to the inequity of fortune; the latter is attributable to nature alone. Stupidity is, however, more bearable than want; for the former, as they say, is not characteristically a burden.

9. The sciences and arts are good. For they are pleasing. For nature hath made man an admirer of all new things, that is, avid to know the causes of everything. So it is that science is the food for so many minds, and is related to the mind as food is to the body; and as food is to the famished, so are curious phenomena to the mind. They differ in this, however, that the body can become satiated with food while the mind cannot be filled up by knowledge.

Again, every art is useful insofar as it is possible to apply it to matter. They are also of the greatest public utility, since it is to them that we owe nearly all the useful tools and trappings of mankind. It ought to be understood, however, that not all men have the science whereunto they profess; for those that discuss the causes of things on the basis of others' writings, and those that make discoveries by copying others' sentences, are utterly worthless. For to do what hath been done, hath nothing good about it in itself; but on the contrary, this is sometimes evil, since by confirming ancient errors they obstruct the path of truth.

10. Letters are also good, especially languages and histories; for they are pleasing. They are useful, too, especially histories; for these supply in abundance the evidence on which rests the science of causes; in truth, natural history for physics and also civil histories for civil and moral science; and this is so whether they be true or false, provided that they are not impossible. For in the sciences causes are sought not only of those things that were, but also of those things that can be. The languages that are in use among neighbouring peoples are also useful, for commerce and

negotiations. Also Latin and Greek, assuredly the languages of the sciences, for science.

11. Work is good; it is truly a motive for life. Therefore unless you walk for the sake of walking, you do so for your work. *Where shall I turn, what shall I do?* are the voices of people grieving. Idleness is torture. In all times and places, nature abhors a vacuum.

12. To progress is pleasing; for it is an approach to an end, that is, to what is more pleasing. To see evil done to another is pleasing; but it pleaseth not because it is evil, but because it is another's. Whence it is that men are accustomed to hasten to the spectacle of the death and danger of others. In the same way, it is displeasing to see another's good; not because it is good, but because it is another's. Imitation is pleasing; for it recalls the past. It is pleasing to represent the past, if it was good, because it was good; and if it was evil, because it is past. Therefore music, poetry, and painting are pleasing.

Novelties are pleasing; for they are desired as food for the mind. To think well of one's own power, whether rightly or wrongly, is pleasing. For if one judgeth oneself truly, one seems to have provided for one's own protection; and if falsely, it is still pleasing; for those things that please when true will also please when false.

Therefore victory is pleasing; for it makes one think well of himself; and all games and contests are pleasing; since those that compete always imagine victory. Especially pleasing, however, are contests of talents; as in them everyone thinks that first place will be assigned to him. Therefore, to be vanquished in a contest of talents is displeasing.

To be praised is pleasing; for it makes us think well of ourselves.

13. Signs or indications of good are *pulchrum*. Therefore a sign of extraordinary power is *pulchrum*. Also, therefore, to do what is both good and difficult is *pulchrum*; for it is an indication of uncommon power. Extraordinary form is *pulchrum*; for it is a sign in all things of the extraordinary execution of the work whereunto one was born. That is finely formed, moreover, that hath the form of that thing which we have proved to be the best of its kind.

To be praised, loved, and magnified is *pulchrum*; for they are testimonies to virtue and power. To be summoned to public office is *pulchrum*; for it is a public testimony to virtue.

In the arts, new inventions, if useful, are *pulchrum*: for they are a sign of extraordinary power.

Trifles, on the other hand, though more difficult, are less *pulchrum*: they are indeed signs of power, but useless, and at the same time indicate a mind of no great will and purpose.

To have learned the arts from others, that is, to have been taught, is certainly useful, but not *pulchrum*; as there is nothing extraordinary about it. For few are those who cannot be taught.

To be bold in danger when the situation demands it is *pulchrum*: for it is not common. If the situation doth not demand it, it is stupidity, that is, *turpe*. To act everywhere according to one's disposition and profession is *pulchrum* in conspicuous men; as it is an indication of a free disposition. To do the contrary in conspicuous persons is *turpe* and is the sign of a servile mind and of having something to hide: for no one hides a thing that is *pulchrum*. To find fault with things that are right, a sign of ignorance, is *turpe*: for knowledge is power. Moreover, to taunt is more *turpe*, a sign of lack of education. To err is not *turpe*, since it is common to all. For a teacher, to err too often is *turpe*, since it is contrary to his profession.

Self-confidence is *pulchrum*: being a certain sign of one conscious of his own virtue. Ostentation is *turpe*: for it ariseth from a need for praise.

Contempt for all but the greatest riches is *pulchrum*: for it is an indication of a person who has no need of small amounts. The love of money is *turpe*: it is the sign of one that can be led anywhere by a bribe. Furthermore, it is a sign of need, even in wealthy men.

To ignore a favour-seeker, is *pulchrum*; for it is an indication of self-confidence. To placate enemies with gifts is *turpe*. For it is a ransoming of oneself, or a purchasing of peace, a sign of need; for men are not accustomed to purchase, except those things that they need.

14. If good and evil be compared, other things being equal, the greater is that which lasts longer, as the whole is to the part.

And, other things being equal, that which is stronger, for the same reason. For larger and smaller differ as greater and less.

And, other things being equal, what is good for more is greater than what is good for fewer. For the more general and the more particular differ as greater and less.

To regain a good is better than not to have lost it. For it is more rightly esteemed because of the memory of evil. Therefore it is better to recover one's health than not to have been sick.

15. Concerning the pleasurable things whereof there be satiation, such as the pleasures of the flesh, I shall say nothing, because they are excessively well known, their pleasure is balanced by loathing, and because some of them are offensive. The greatest good, or as it is called, felicity and the final end, cannot be attained in the present life. For if the end be final, there would be nothing to long for, nothing to desire; whence it follows not only that nothing would itself be a good from that time on, but also that man would not even feel. For all sense is conjoined with some appetite or aversion; and not to feel is not to live.

For of goods, the greatest is always progressing towards ever further ends with the least hindrance. Even the enjoyment of a desire, when we are enjoying it, is an appetite, namely the motion of the mind to enjoy by parts, the thing that it is enjoying. For life is perpetual motion that, when it cannot progress in a straight line, is converted into circular motion.

XIV: On Religion

1. Definition of religion. 2. What it is to love and fear God. 3. What faith is. 4. Faith depends on laws. 5. Justice is inscribed in the heart by God. 6. God can remit sins without injustice, with no punishment exacted. 7. No one's just works are sins. 8. Definition and subdivisions of worship. 9. What public worship is. 10. The parts of worship: prayers, thanksgiving, public fasts, offerings. 11. Various superstitious cults. 12. The end of worship is to allay anxieties about the future. 13. What things there are that change religions.

1. Religion is the external worship (*cultus*) of men who sincerely honour God. Moreover, they sincerely honour God who believe not only that He exists, but also that He is the omnipotent and omniscient creator and ruler of all things, and, further, that He is by His own will the distributor of prosperity and adversity. Therefore religion as such (that is, natural) consists of two parts; whereof one is *faith* (or the belief that God exists and that He governs all things), the other is *worship*. Moreover, the first part, which concerns faith in God, is usually called *piety* toward God. For he who believes the above cannot not endeavour to obey Him in all things; neither can he not endeavour to give thanks in prosperity nor to utter supplications in adversity; for these things are the most characteristic works of piety; in them are contained the love and fear wherewith we are commanded to love and fear God.

2. But God is not to be loved by man, as man is by man. For we always understand by the love of man toward man either the desire for embraces or benevolence, both whereof would be unsuitable for understanding love toward God. To love God is to keep His commandments gladly. To fear God is to watch lest we fall into sin, in the same way as we are accustomed to fear the laws.

3. Moreover, faith, save for our belief that God hath made and rules all things, because it concerns things that are placed beyond the grasp of human nature, is opinion which ariseth from the authority of the speakers. So unless there hath been an antecedent opinion that he who speaks, learned what he saith by some supernatural means, there can be no reason why we ought to believe him. Therefore we believe no one about supernatural things, unless we believe that he hath previously done some supernatural deed. Moreover, how can someone be believed who saith that the things he saith or teacheth are confirmed by miracles unless he himself hath worked miracles? For if a private person is to be believed without a miracle, why should the various teachings of one man be any better than those of another? Therefore the greatest part of our religion and most gratifying faith in God must not depend on private persons, unless they work miracles.

4. If religion, beyond what consists in natural piety, doth not depend on private persons, miracles now having ceased, it must depend on the laws of the state. And so religion be not philosophy, but rather in all states law; and on that account it is not to be disputed but observed. For it can neither be doubted that God must be thought of with honour, nor that He ought to be loved, feared, and worshipped. For these things are common to religions among all peoples. Only those things are to be disputed wherein one man disagrees with another; which, because of this, do not concern faith in God. In these disputations, moreover, while we are seeking scientific knowledge of those things that do not belong to science, we are destroying faith in God, as much as we have any in us. For such knowledge bears the same relationship to faith as success doth to hope; for, as the apostle teacheth of the three virtues, *faith*, *hope*, and *charity*, when the kingdom of God is at hand, *faith* and *hope* will no longer exist, and

charity alone will abide. Therefore questions about the nature of God, the creator of nature, are excessively inquisitive and do not increase the works of piety; those moreover which dispute about God, wish to win people over not so much to faith in God (in whom all believe already) as to faith in themselves.

5. Since, however, to love God is the same as to keep His commandments, and to fear God is the same as to fear lest we do something against His commandments, it can further be asked how one can know what things God hath commanded. To this question it can be replied, God himself, because He hath made men rational, hath enjoined the following law on them, and hath inscribed it in all hearts: that no one should do unto another that which he would consider inequitable for the other to do unto him. In this precept are contained both universal justice and civil obedience. For who would not judge it inequitable, if he were constituted by the people with the highest sovereignty in the state, in order to rule and to issue laws, for his laws to be spurned, or his authority overlooked, not to mention disputed, by any subject whatsoever? Therefore, if, when you were a king, you judged this to be inequitable, would you not have, in law, a most certain rule for your actions? Moreover, that law is also divine, which orders obedience to supreme powers, that is, to the laws of those in supreme command.

6. But since men now violate the commandments of God and sin daily, how can it be consistent with divine justice, someone may ask, that God doth not require punishment of them for their sins? But do we consider a man to be unjust or more holy if he never punisheth the harms done him, and if he be so forgiving that he demands no revenge of any kind nor, indeed, any repentance? Therefore, unless we say that God be less compassionate than men, there is no reason why God cannot forgive sinners, at least the repentant, without any punishment having been received by them or by others in their place. Though God formerly demanded sacrifices for the people's sins, those sacrifices did not have punishment as their purpose, but were constituted as *signs* that those sinning were by themselves turning back to God and were returning to their former obedience. And so the death of our Saviour was not a punishment for sins, but a sacrifice for sins. And although He is said to bear our sins, this is not to be understood as a punishment any more than were the sacrifices of old, which did not consist in the punishments of

animals for the sins that the Jews committed, but in the offerings of thankful men. Every year God required two he-goats of the Israelites; of these, one, which was for an offering, was burned, and the other, which was burdened with the sins of the people, was driven into the wilderness as though it were about to bear away the people's sins. Similarly Christ, insofar as He was offered on the cross, was killed; but insofar as He was burdened with our sins, He rose again. For, as the apostle saith, unless Christ be risen again, our sins remain.

7. Therefore, since piety consists of faith, justice, and charity, and since justice and charity are, moreover, moral virtues, I cannot agree with those who call them splendid sins. For if, indeed, they were sins, insofar as a man be holier than others, by that much less ought he to be believed as less just. What is it, therefore, that displeaseth God in those who do justice? For the most part, that which is displeasing to faith, (that is, to piety) is the simulation of justice by those lacking in it. For those who do just works and give alms only for glory or for the acquiring of riches or for the avoidance of punishment are unjust, even though their works are very frequently just. Therefore, God is said to have hated the sacrifices of His people, which, however, because they had been commanded by God, could not have been sins. But, as just works without faith are an abomination to God, so also are sacrifices and all worship without justice and charity.

8. We are properly said to cultivate (*colere*) that thing, whatsoever it is, that we strive by services and labour to make as beneficial for us as we can. Thus we cultivate (*colimus*) the land so that it may be more fruitful for us; we cultivate or worship (*colimus*) powerful men for the sake of the power or protection that may accrue to us; so also we worship (*colimus*) God, that we may have His favour for ourselves. Therefore cultivation (*cultus*) of the divine, or divine worship, is to perform those actions that are signs of piety toward God. For these are pleasing to God, and by them alone can His favour be returned to us. Moreover, these actions are for the most part of the same kind as those we perform whenever we cultivate (*colimus*) men, but also in each way the best; for by our nature we are unable to show any other signs of piety. One kind of worship (*cultus*), however, is *private*, another *public*. It is private when men exhibit it according to their own individual will. It is public when the same is exhibited by the command of the state. Private worship is exhibited

either by one person in secret or by many collectively; it is a sign of their sincere piety; for of what use is simulation that is seen by no one save Him who also sees the simulation? Such simulation can only be vain. In secret worship there are no ceremonies. I call ceremonies those signs of the act of piety that arise not from the nature of the act, but from the will of the state; for nature hath given everyone, to whom it hath given the belief that God exists, to fall prostrate and to genuflect when praying or adoring, as a sign of humility and subjection in the presence of God. In the private worship of many together, there can be ceremonies, since men can jointly decide among themselves about the fittingness of common performance; only provided that they do nothing contrary to the laws of the state. But such a situation is an invitation to simulation, which is, however, sometimes without fault. For men, if many be gathered together in one place at the same time, are so possessed by the nature of a crowd that individuals conceal their timidity and demand that no one speak scurrilously, inconsiderately, boorishly, or in a disorganized manner to them or in their presence; but rather most elegantly as far as they understand that; and they demand a fitting seriousness of gesture, such as no one useth in his own home. Wherefore, he who speaks to a crowd or in their presence when all others are silent, must adopt a role graver and holier than he otherwise might; this is, indeed, a kind of play-acting, but without fault, since when a crowd demands something, the many are more powerful than the one.

9. There can be no public worship without ceremonies; for public worship is what the state hath commanded to be exhibited by all citizens at constituted places and times, as a sign of the honour had by God. Therefore the right to judge what is fitting and what is not, in the public worship of God is within the power of the state. Ceremonies are signs of the acts of piety, not so much those that are commanded by the nature of the act (which is rational worship), but rather those that are commanded by the will of the state. And on that account, when considering many peoples it necessarily follows that there may be many things in the worship of God among one people that do not exist among another; and that the worship of some people will often be laughed at by others. No worship hath at any time been directly ordained by God save among the Jews, when He Himself was reigning. The ceremonies of other peoples were rational (some, indeed, more than others); but

among all it was rational to use ceremonies established by civil law.

10. The parts of worship are either rational or superstitious, if not fantastic. The rational parts are, first, *prayers*; for by them we signify that we believe that all future goods that are to be hoped for come from God, and from Him alone. Secondly, *thanksgiving*; for by this we signify that we believe that all past goods were given to us by God, and through His grace alone. Moreover, pious men are sometimes said to prevail on God, or even to overcome Him, with prayers; not that they at any time compelled God to change His mind or His eternal decrees; rather, God, the ruler of all things, wishes His gifts at some times to precede men's prayers, and at others, to follow them. Hence it is not improper that both prayers and thanksgiving are called by one name, *supplications*. Thirdly, *public fasts*, and other acts of those lamenting sins. For they are a sign of repentance, that is, of one's shame about one's sins; thereafter, being conscious of past failings, we rely less on our own strength, and wish to be cautious in the future so that we shall not again fall into sin. Moreover, we are accustomed to signify our humility and grief by ashes, sackcloth, and prostration; not that shame and humility are not genuine without them; but because nature herself teaches us to worship God (who sees into our hearts), in the same ways that we see cultivated or worshipped, men who cannot judge whether repentance is genuine save by such signs. In truth, those who savour their sins as soon as they know for a certainty that they are forgiven, know that they will savour them again, and are unable to grieve further about them, unless the grief be of a kind that also includes shame: for if they grieve, it is manifestly a sign that they grieve because they see themselves reduced to such misery that either they themselves or the sins they love must be abandoned; just as the merchant grieves at sea, whenever he sees that either himself or his merchandise is about to be lost. And so in divine worship sadness after sins is fitting and natural, but that sadness must not be of a contrary mind, but of one that is ashamed and humble. Fourthly, *offerings*, that is, sacrifices and oblations, are a rational part of public worship of the divine. For it is not rational that those from whom we have accepted everything should get nothing in return, that is, that we should consecrate nothing to God, that is, that we should set aside no portion from public worship of the divine for the support of ministers, for the honour of that ministry. For

so it was in the Church that the ministers of Christ were supported by the Gospels, that is, by those things that were freely given by men because of the Good News; and so it was among the Jews and many other peoples that priests were supported by oblations and sacrifices; hence it is rational that in all states ministers of divine worship are supported by things consecrated to God, which on that account ought to be the most perfect of each kind.

11. On account of the different opinions held by those men who believed that there were many gods (especially those who thought that there once was a heavenly people, more or less a state of aerial men), superstitious worship hath greater variety than can be told. They also believed that those deities had a tongue of their own in heaven, and what was named one thing by men was named another by the deities; so that the man who was called Romulus on earth was in heaven named Quirinus; a similar thing is seen with other names, both among the Greek poets and the Fathers of the heathen church; in almost the same way, what we call the *state*, the clergy call the *church*, what in the state is called a *law* is in the church called a *canon*, and what in a kingdom is called *majesty* is in the church called *holiness*. And not content with a single state for the gods, they established another for the sea gods under the rule of Neptune, and a third in hell under Pluto. As a result, there was almost no creature that they did not invoke as a god or goddess; there was almost no virtue without altar or temple, save labour and industry, divine powers that are in and of themselves propitious. Finally, whatsoever was nameable was by the same token deifiable. There is no man who doth not understand that all of this is inconsistent with natural reason. Nevertheless, local law was able to have this superstition called religion, and all other worship, superstition.

12. The end that all states allege for divine worship is this, that by it their god or deities may be made favourable, sometimes to the state itself, sometimes to individual citizens. For many, however, divine favour by itself is not enough. For, they think, *God is about to give me certain gifts, but perhaps other than I myself wish; He turns away evil, but only through my own prudence. Would that I might know, therefore, which of the things He prepares to give me – and that are about to come to me – are good, and which of them evil, as it may be necessary to ward them off.* Therefore they so worship that they always seem to be doubting either divine wisdom or divine kindness. And this is why

almost all mortals, anxious about the future, turn to more kinds of prophecies than can be easily enumerated. There is, however, only one kind of prophecy that is certain, namely the voice of a prophet, but only if that prophet shall have performed a miracle; other prophecies are false. Astrology which dares by contemplating the stars, to predict about chance future events or to pronounce either way is not a science; it is, rather, the stratagem of a man to steal money from stupid people in order to escape poverty. Those who pretend that they are prophets, when they have performed no miracles, have the same purpose. That dreamers who have produced no miracle hold their own dreams to be prophecies of the future is stupidity; that they demand to be believed is insane; that they rashly predict evil for the state is a crime. It is not true, as many believe, that malicious people harm those to whom they wish evil; rather, when the evils that they call down actually happen as they wish, then they themselves assert – confessing as though they had at some time done these things themselves – that those evils were done as a result of their own prayers by a demon they have seen while dreaming and employed by a covenant for their work. Therefore these people do not know the future; rather, what they select, they hope the future will be. Nevertheless, both because of their wish to harm and because of their impious worship, not undeservedly are they punished. Further, forebodings of the mind, that is, hope and fear, and even each and every dream, are held as prophecies. In the same way, the chance flight of birds was an augury. Men gaped at the entrails of cattle as predictions of the future. Unintentional words in speaking were believed an omen of the future. Everything unusual was said to be a portent and prodigy because through them the deities seemed to be showing what was about to happen. They even used various kinds of lots, that is, they put their luck to the test in all chance things. For the rest, I pass by the innumerable other kinds of divination lest I linger overlong on men's stupidity.

13. There are two things, usually, that change religions, both to be found in priests: absurd dogmas, and manners contrary to the religion that they teach. For the prudent men of the Roman Church erred when they decided that they could take advantage of the people's ignorance to such an extent that they might hope not only then, but always to be able to make the people believe contradictory language. Little by little the people became

educated, and at last sometimes came to understand the meaning of the words that they used. Whence it happened, that when they saw not only that the doctors of religion themselves said contradictory things, but also that they religiously ordered others so to speak, the latter were first inclined sometimes to contemn themselves as ignorant and then to suspect their religion to be false, and either to correct it or to expel it from the state. Therefore doctors of religion must especially take care lest they mix anything from the teachings of physics into the rules for worshipping God. For, since they have no scientific knowledge of natural things, at times they can hardly avoid falling into absurd propositions; afterwards such men make everything that they teach to be contemned, especially when detected by the untaught; just as the ignorance of Roman doctors, detected by Luther, not only abolished a great part of the Roman religion both in our nation and among other peoples, but also separated those same peoples from their Roman dependency. If, however, they had kept silent about transubstantiation (that is, about the nature of body and place), about free-will (that is, about the nature of will and understanding), and about other things that I pass over for the sake of brevity, they could have retained what they had acquired. As for what concerns the other cause for change in religions, namely manners, it is manifest that no one from

the people is so stupid as not to think one an imposter (who doth not believe what he orders to be believed) when he sees that one ordering him to believe things otherwise difficult to believe, living as though he himself did not believe; especially if his believing is useful to the one ordering him to believe. If, therefore, they teach, as they do everywhere, that it needs be believed that one should be less covetous than others, less ambitious, less proud, less indulgent of the senses, less mixed up in worldly business (that is, in secular affairs), less insulting, less envious, more simple in heart (that is, more open), more compassionate, more truthful – and yet do not themselves behave in such a manner – they should not complain if after them people do not join the faith. Truly, I believe that the Christian religion grew remarkably at the time of the Holy Apostles in large part because the lives of the heathen priests were not holy. That is to say, over and beyond the vices that they shared with the people, they embroiled themselves in the controversies that states had with each other; and they watched over the gods, just as nurses are wont to watch over children, especially so that no one save whom they wished might approach the gods, or so that the gods might love no one save those that they themselves had commended. Moreover, these covetous men commended only those from whom they received favours.

PART III

Benedict de Spinoza (1632–77)

Introduction

The young Spinoza entered philosophy through the study of medieval Jewish thinkers such as Ibn Ezra and Maimonides. It is said, however, that he often told people he had all his philosophical knowledge from Descartes. The first selection is taken from an early work, *Treatise on the Emendation of the Intellect* (published posthumously in 1677). In it Spinoza presents his solution to the problem of the criterion. The second, from the *Ethics* (also published posthumously in 1677),

shows how the intellect is free with respect to "the affections of the Body" and how, if properly trained, it leads the wise to a love of God. In these two selections one sees Spinoza in his most Cartesian mode. The final selections, from *A Theologico-Political Treatise* (1670), contain Spinoza's influential discussions of the nature of the state, and of the right to freedom of thought and expression in speculative matters. Spinoza had an enormous influence on nineteenth-century German philosophy. Schelling and Hegel were especially moved by the speculative grandeur of his writings.

7

Treatise on the Emendation of the Intellect

[Of Method]

[50] Let us begin, therefore, from the first part of the Method, which is, as we have said, to distinguish and separate true ideas from all other perceptions, and to restrain the mind from confusing false, fictitious, and doubtful ideas with true ones. It is my intention to explain this fully here, so as to engage my Readers in the thought of a thing so necessary, and also because there are many who doubt even true ideas, from not attending to the distinction between a true perception and all others. So they are like men who, when they were awake, used not to doubt that they were awake, but who, after they once thought in a dream that they were certainly awake (as often happens), and later found that to be false, doubted even of their waking states. This happens because they have never distinguished between the dream and the waking state.

[51] In the meantime, I warn the reader that I shall not discuss the essence of each perception, and explain it by its proximate cause, because that pertains to Philosophy, but shall discuss only what the Method demands, i.e., what false, fictitious and doubtful ideas are concerned with, and how we shall be freed from each of them. Let the first inquiry, therefore, be about the fictitious idea.

[52] Since every perception is either of a thing considered as existing, or of an essence alone, and since fictions occur more frequently concerning

Treatise on the Emendation of the Intellect (posthumously, 1677). From *The Collected Works of Spinoza*, ed. and tr. Edwin Curley (Princeton University Press, 1985). Selection: sects 50–86, pp. 23–37.

things considered as existing, I shall speak first of them – i.e., where existence alone is feigned, and the thing which is feigned in such an act is understood, *or* assumed to be understood. E.g., I feign that Peter, whom I know, is going home, that he is coming to visit me, and the like.[1] Here I ask, what does such an idea concern? I see that it concerns only possible, and not necessary or impossible things.

[53] I call a thing impossible whose nature implies that it would be contradictory for it to exist; necessary whose nature implies that it would be contradictory for it not to exist; and possible whose existence, by its very nature, does not imply a contradiction – either for it to exist or for it not to exist – but whose necessity or impossibility of existence depends on causes unknown to us, so long as we feign its existence. So if its necessity or impossibility, which depends on external causes, were known to us, we would have been able to feign nothing concerning it.

[54] From this it follows that, if there is a God, or something omniscient, he can feign nothing at all. For as far as We are concerned, after I know that I exist,[2] I cannot feign either that I exist or that I do not exist; nor can I feign an elephant which passes through the eye of a needle; nor, after I know the nature of God, can I feign either that he exists or that he does not exist.[3] The same must be understood of the Chimera, whose nature implies that it would be contradictory for it to exist. From this what I have said is evident: that the fiction of which we are speaking here does not occur concerning eternal truths.[4] I shall also show immediately that no fiction is concerned with eternal truths.

[55] But before proceeding further, I must note here in passing that the same difference that exists between the essence of one thing and the essence of another also exists between the actuality or existence of the one thing and the actuality or existence of the other. So if we wished to conceive the existence of Adam, for example, through existence in general, it would be the same as if, to conceive his essence, we attended to the nature of being, so that in the end we defined him by saying that Adam is a being. Therefore, the more generally existence is conceived, the more confusedly also it is conceived, and the more easily it can be ascribed fictitiously to anything. Conversely, the more particularly it is conceived, then the more clearly it is understood, and the more difficult it is for us, [even] when we do not attend to the order of Nature, to ascribe it fictitiously to anything other than the thing itself. This is worth nothing.

[56] Now we must consider those things that are commonly said to be feigned, although we understood clearly that the thing is not really as we feign it. E.g., although I know that the earth is round, nothing prevents me from saying to someone that the earth is a hemisphere and like half an orange on a plate, or that the sun moves around the earth, and the like. If we attend to these things, we shall see nothing that is not compatible with what we have already said, provided we note first that we have sometimes been able to err, and now are conscious of our errors; and then, we can feign, or at least allow, that other men are in the same error, or can fall into it, as we did previously.

We can feign this, I say, so long as we see no impossibility and no necessity. Therefore, when I say to someone that the earth is not round, etc., I am doing nothing but recalling the error which I, perhaps, made, or into which I could have fallen, and afterwards feigning, or allowing, that he to whom I say this is still in the same error, or can fall into it. As I have said, I feign this so long as I see no impossibility and no necessity. For if I had understood this, I could have feigned nothing at all, and it would have had to be said only that I had done something.

[57] It remains now to note also those things that are supposed in Problems. This sometimes happens even concerning impossible things. E.g., when we say "Let us suppose that this burning candle is not now burning, or let us suppose that it is burning in some imaginary space, *or* where there are no bodies." Things like this are sometimes supposed, although this last is clearly understood

to be impossible. But when this happens, nothing at all is feigned. For in the first case I have done nothing but recall to memory[5] another candle that was not burning (or I have conceived this candle without the flame), and what I think about that candle, I understand concerning this one, so long as I do not attend to the flame.

In the second case, nothing is done except to abstract the thoughts from the surrounding bodies so that the mind directs itself toward the sole contemplation of the candle, considered in itself alone, so that afterwards it infers that the candle has no cause for its destruction. So if there were no surrounding bodies, this candle, and its flame, would remain immutable, or the like. Here, then, there is no fiction, but[6] true and sheer assertions.

[58] Let us pass now to fictions that concern either essences alone or essences together with some actuality *or* existence. The most important consideration regarding them is that the less the mind understands and the more things it perceives, the greater its power of feigning is; and the more things it understands, the more that power is diminished.

For example, as we have seen above, we cannot feign, so long as we are thinking, that we are thinking and are not thinking; in the same way, after we know the nature of body, we cannot feign an infinite fly, or after we know the nature of the soul,[7] we cannot feign that it is square, though there is nothing that cannot be put into words.

But as we have said, the less men know Nature, the more easily they can feign many things, such as, that trees speak, that men are changed in a moment into stones and into springs, that nothing becomes something, that even Gods are changed into beasts and into men, and infinitely many other things of that kind.

[59] Someone, perhaps, will think that fiction is limited by fiction, but not by intellection. That is, after I have feigned something, and willed by a certain freedom to assent that it exists in nature in this way, this has the consequence that I cannot afterwards think it in any other way. For example, after I have feigned (to speak as they do) that body has such a nature, and willed, from my freedom, to be convinced that it really exists in this way, I can no longer feign an infinite fly; and after I have feigned the essence of the soul, I can no longer feign that it is square.

[60] But this needs to be examined. First, either they deny or they grant that we can understand something. If they grant it, then necessarily what

they say about fiction will also have to be said about intellection. But if they deny it, let us – who know that we know something – see what they say.

Evidently, they say that the soul can sense and perceive in many ways, not itself, nor the things that exist, but only those things that are neither in itself nor anywhere; that is, the soul can, by its own force alone, create sensations or ideas, which are not of things; so they consider it, to some extent, as like God.

Next, they say that we, or our soul, has such a freedom that it compels us, or itself, indeed its own freedom. For after it has feigned something, and offered its assent to it, it cannot think or feign it in any other way, and is also compelled by that fiction so that even other things are thought in such a way as not to conflict with the first fiction. As they are here forced to admit the absurdities which I review here, because of their own fiction, we shall not bother to refute them with any demonstrations.

[61] Rather, leaving them to their madness, we shall take care to draw from the words we have exchanged with them something true and to our purpose, viz.:[8] when the mind attends to a fictitious thing which is false by its very nature, so that it considers it carefully, and understands it, and deduces from it in good order the things to be deduced, it will easily bring its falsity to light. And if the fictitious thing is true by its nature, then when the mind attends to it, so that it understands it, and begins to deduce from it in good order the things that follow from it, it will proceed successfully, without any interruption – just as we have seen that, from the false fiction just mentioned, the intellect immediately applies itself to show its absurdity, and the other things deduced from that.

[62] So we ought not to fear in any way that we are feigning something, if only we perceive the thing clearly and distinctly. For if by chance we should say that men are changed in a moment into beasts, that is said very generally, so that there is in the mind no concept, i.e., idea, or connection of subject and predicate. For if there were any concept, the mind would see together the means and causes, how and why such a thing was done. And one does not attend to the nature of the subject and of the predicate.

[63] Next, provided the first idea is not fictitious, and all the other ideas are deduced from it, the haste to feign things will gradually disappear. And since a fictitious idea cannot be clear and distinct, but only confused, and since all confusion results from the fact that the mind knows only in part a thing that is a whole, or composed of many things, and does not distinguish the known from the unknown (and besides, attends at once, without making any distinction, to the many things that are contained in each thing), from this it follows, first, that if an idea is of some most simple thing, it can only be clear and distinct. For that thing will have to become known, not in part, but either as a whole or not at all.

[64] Secondly, it follows that if, in thought, we divide a thing that is composed of many things into all its most simple parts, and attend to each of these separately, all confusion will disappear.

Thirdly, it follows that a fiction cannot be simple, but that it is made from the composition of different confused ideas, which are different things and actions existing in nature; or rather, from attending at once,[9] without assent, to such different ideas. For if it were simple, it would be clear and distinct, and consequently true. And if it were made from the composition of distinct ideas, their composition would also be clear and distinct, and therefore true. For example, once we know the nature of the circle, and also the nature of the square, we cannot then compound these two and make a square circle, or a square soul, and the like.

[65] Let us sum up again briefly, and see why we do not need to fear that the fiction will in any way be confused with true ideas. For as for the first [fiction] of which we spoke before, viz. where the thing is clearly conceived, we saw that if that thing that is clearly conceived (and also its existence) is, through itself, an eternal truth, we can feign nothing concerning such a thing. But if the existence of the thing conceived is not an eternal truth, we need only to take care to compare the existence of the thing with its essence, and at the same time attend to the order of Nature.

As for the second fiction, we said that it consists in attending at once, without assent, to different confused ideas, which are of different things and actions existing in Nature. We saw also that a most simple thing cannot be feigned, but [only] understood, and also that a composite thing can be understood, provided that we attend to the most simple parts of which it is composed. Indeed we also cannot feign from them any actions that are not true; for at the same time we will be forced to consider how and why such a thing happened.

[66] With these matters thus understood, let us pass now to the investigation of the false idea so

that we may see what it is concerned with, and how we can take care not to fall into false perceptions. Neither of these will be difficult for us now, after our investigation of the fictitious idea. For between fictitious and false ideas there is no other difference except that the latter suppose assent; i.e. (as we have already noted), while the presentations appear to him [who has the false idea], there appear no causes from which he can infer (as he who is feigning can) that they do not arise from things outside him. And this is hardly anything but dreaming with open eyes, *or* while we are awake. Therefore the false idea is concerned with, or (to put it better) is related to the existence of a thing whose essence is known, *or* to an essence, in the same way as a fictitious idea.

[67] [The false idea] that is related to existence is emended in the same way as the fiction. For if the nature of the thing known presupposes necessary existence, it is impossible for us to be deceived concerning the existence of that thing. But if the existence of the thing is not an eternal truth (as its essence is), so that its necessity or impossibility of existing depends on external causes, then take everything in the same way as we said when we were speaking of fictions. For it may be emended in the same way.

[68] As for the other kind of false idea, which is related to essences, or also to actions, such perceptions must always be confused, composed of different confused perceptions of things existing in nature – as when men are persuaded that there are divinities in the woods, in images, in animals, etc.; or that there are bodies from whose composition alone the intellect is made; or that corpses reason, walk, and speak; or that God is deceived, and the like. But ideas that are clear and distinct can never be false. For the ideas of things that are conceived clearly and distinctly, are either most simple, or composed of most simple ideas, i.e., deduced from most simple ideas. But that a most simple idea cannot be false, anyone can see – provided that he knows what the true is, *or* the intellect, and at the same time, what the false is.

[69] As for what constitutes the form of the true, it is certain that a true thought is distinguished from a false one not only by an extrinsic, but chiefly by an intrinsic denomination. For if some architect conceives a building in an orderly fashion, then although such a building never existed, and even never will exist, still the thought of it is true, and the thought is the same, whether the building exists or not. On the other hand, if

someone says, for example, that Peter exists, and nevertheless does not know that Peter exists, that thought, in respect to him is false, or, if you prefer, is not true, even though Peter really exists. Nor is this statement, Peter exists, true, except in respect to him who knows certainly that Peter exists.

[70] From this it follows that there is something real in ideas, through which the true are distinguished from the false. This will now have to be investigated, so that we may have the best standard of truth (for we have said that we must determine our thoughts from the given standard of a true idea, and that method is reflexive knowledge), and may know the properties of the intellect. Nor must we say that this difference arises from the fact that the true thought is knowing things through their first causes. In this, indeed, it differs greatly from the false, as I have explained it above. For that Thought is also called true which involves objectively the essence of some principle that does not have a cause, and is known through itself and in itself.

[71] So the form of the true thought must be placed in the same thought itself without relation to other things, nor does it recognize the object as its cause, but must depend on the very power and nature of the intellect. For if we should suppose that the intellect had perceived some new being, which has never existed (as some conceive God's intellect, before he created things – for that perception, of course, could not have arisen from any object), and that from such a perception it deduced others legitimately, all those thoughts would be true, and determined by no external object, but would depend only on the power and nature of the intellect. So what constitutes the form of the true thought must be sought in the same thought itself, and must be deduced from the nature of the intellect.

[72] To investigate this, therefore, let us consider some true idea, of which we know most certainly that its object depends on our power of thinking, and that it has no object in nature. For it is clear from what has already been said that we shall be able more easily to investigate what we wish to in such an idea. E.g., to form the concept of a sphere, I feign a cause at will, say that a semicircle is rotated around a center, and that the sphere is, as it were, produced by this rotation. This idea, of course, is true, and even though we may know that no sphere in nature was ever produced in this way, nevertheless, this perception is

true, and a very easy way of forming the concept of a sphere.

Now it must be noted that this perception affirms that the semicircle is rotated, which affirmation would be false if it were not joined to the concept of a sphere, or to a cause determining such a motion, *or* absolutely, if this affirmation were isolated. For then the mind would only tend to affirm of the semicircle nothing but motion, which neither is contained in the concept of the semicircle nor arises from the concept of the cause determining the motion. So falsity consists only in this: that something is affirmed of a thing that is not contained in the concept we have formed of the thing, as motion or rest of the semicircle.

From this it follows that simple thoughts cannot but be true; for example, the simple idea of a semicircle, or of motion, or of quantity, etc. Whatever they contain of affirmation matches their concept, and does not extend itself beyond [the concept]. So we may form simple ideas at will, without fear of error.

[73] It only remains, then, to ask by what power our mind can form these [simple ideas] and how far this power extends. For once this is discovered, we shall easily see the highest knowledge we can reach. It is certain that this power does not extend to infinity. For when we affirm of a thing something not contained in the concept we form of it, that indicates a defect of our perception, *or* that we have thoughts, *or* ideas, which are, as it were, mutilated and maimed. For we saw that the motion of a semicircle is false when it is in the mind in isolation, but true if it is joined to the concept of a sphere, or to the concept of some cause determining such a motion. But if it is – as it seems at first – of the nature of a thinking being to form true, *or* adequate, thoughts, it is certain that inadequate ideas arise in us only from the fact that we are a part of a thinking being, of which some thoughts wholly constitute our mind, while others do so only in part.

[74] But we still need to consider something which was not worth the trouble of noting concerning fictions, and which gives rise to the greatest deception – viz. when it happens that certain things that appear in the imagination are also in the intellect, i.e., that they are conceived clearly and distinctly. For then, so long as the distinct is not distinguished from the confused, certainty, i.e., a true idea, is mixed up with what is not distinct.

For example, some of the Stoics heard, perhaps, the word *soul*, and also that the soul is immortal,

which they only imagined confusedly; they also both imagined and at the same time understood that the most subtle bodies penetrate all others, and are not penetrated by any. Since they imagined all these things at once – while remaining certain of this axiom – they immediately became certain that the mind was those most subtle bodies and that those most subtle bodies were not divided, etc.

[75] But we are freed from this also, as long as we strive to consider all our perceptions according to the standard of a given true idea, being on guard, as we said in the beginning, against those we have from report or from random experience. Moreover, such a deception arises from the fact that they conceive things too abstractly. For it is sufficiently clear through itself that I cannot apply what I conceive in its true object to something else. Finally, it arises also from the fact that they do not understand the first elements of the whole of Nature; so proceeding without order, and confusing Nature with abstractions (although they are true axioms), they confuse themselves and overturn the order of Nature. But we shall not need to fear any such deception, if we proceed as far as we can in a manner that is not abstract, and begin as soon as possible from the first elements, i.e., from the source and origin of Nature.

[76] But as for knowledge of the origin of Nature, we need not have any fear of confusing it with abstractions. For when things are conceived abstractly (as all universals are), they always have a wider extension in our intellect than their particulars can really have in nature. And then, since there are many things in nature whose difference is so slight that it almost escapes the intellect, it can easily happen, if they are conceived abstractly, that they are confused. But since, as we shall see later, the origin of Nature can neither be conceived abstractly, *or* universally, nor be extended more widely in the intellect than it really is, and since it has no likeness to changeable things, we need fear no confusion concerning its idea, provided that we have the standard of truth (which we have already shown). For it is a unique and infinite[10] being, beyond which there is no being.[11]

[77] So far we have been speaking of the false idea. It remains now to investigate the doubtful idea – i.e., to ask what are the things that can lead us into doubt, and at the same time, how doubt is removed. I am speaking of true doubt in the mind, and not of what we commonly see happen, when someone says in words that he doubts, although

his mind does not doubt. For it is not the business of the Method to emend that. That belongs rather to the investigation of stubbornness, and its emendation.

[78] There is no doubt in the soul, therefore, through the thing itself concerning which one doubts. That is, if there should be only one idea in the soul, then, whether it is true or false, there will be neither doubt nor certainty, but only a sensation of a certain sort. For in itself [this idea] is nothing but a sensation of a certain sort.

But doubt will arise through another idea which is not so clear and distinct that we can infer from it something certain about the thing concerning which there is doubt. That is, the idea that puts us in doubt is not clear and distinct. For example, if someone has never been led, either by experience or by anything else, to think about the deceptiveness of the senses, he will never doubt whether the sun is larger or smaller than it appears to be. So Country People are generally surprised when they hear that the sun is much larger than the earth. But in thinking about the deceptiveness of the senses, doubt arises. I.e., [the person] knows that his senses have sometimes deceived him, but he knows this only confusedly; for he does not know how the senses deceive. And if someone, after doubting, acquires a true knowledge of the senses and of how, by their means, things at a distance are presented, then the doubt is again removed.

[79] From this it follows that, only so long as we have no clear and distinct idea of God, can we call true ideas in doubt by supposing that perhaps some deceiving God exists, who misleads us even in the things most certain. I.e., if we attend to the knowledge we have concerning the origin of all things and do not discover – by the same knowledge we have when, attending to the nature of the triangle, we discover that its three angles equal two right angles – anything that teaches us that he is not a deceiver [then the doubt remains]. But if we have the kind of knowledge of God that we have of the triangle, then all doubt is removed. And just as we can arrive at such a knowledge of the triangle, even though we may not know certainly whether some supreme deceiver misleads us, so we can arrive at such a knowledge of God, even though we may not know whether there is some supreme deceiver. Provided we have that knowledge, it will suffice, as I have said, to remove every doubt that we can have concerning clear and distinct ideas.

[80] Further, if someone proceeds rightly, by investigating [first] those things which ought to be investigated first, with no interruption in the connection of things, and knows how to define problems precisely, before striving for knowledge of them, he will never have anything but the most certain ideas – i.e., clear and distinct ideas. For doubt is nothing but the suspension of the mind concerning some affirmation or negation, which it would affirm or deny if something did not occur to it, the ignorance of which must render its knowledge of the thing imperfect. From this it is [to be] inferred that doubt always arises from the fact that things are investigated without order.

[81] These are the matters I promised to discuss in this first part of the Method. But to omit nothing that can lead to knowledge of the intellect and its powers, I shall say a few words about memory and forgetting. The most important consideration is that memory is strengthened both with the aid of the intellect and also without its aid. For regarding the first, the more intelligible a thing is, the more easily it is retained; and conversely, the less intelligible, the more easily forgotten. E.g., if I give someone a large number of disconnected words, he will retain them with much more difficulty than if I give him the same words in the form of a story.

[82] It is also strengthened without the aid of the intellect, by the force with which the imagination, or what they call the common sense, is affected by some singular corporeal thing. I say singular, for the imagination is affected only by singular things. If someone, e.g., has read only one Comedy, he will retain it best so long as he does not read several others of that kind, for then it will flourish in isolation in the imagination. But if there are several of the same kind, we imagine them all together and they are easily confused. I say also corporeal, for the imagination is affected only by bodies. Therefore since the memory is strengthened both by the intellect and also without the intellect, we may infer that it is something different from the intellect, and that concerning the intellect considered in itself there is neither memory nor forgetting.

[83] What, then, will memory be? Nothing but a sensation of impressions on the brain, together with the thought of a determinate duration[12] of the sensation, which recollection also shows. For there the soul thinks of that sensation, but not under a continuous duration. And so the idea of that sensation is not the duration itself of the sensation,

i.e., the memory itself. But whether the ideas themselves undergo some corruption, we shall see in [my] Philosophy.

If this seems quite absurd to anyone, it will suffice for our purpose if he thinks that the more singular a thing is, the more easily it may be retained, as the example of the Comedy just mentioned makes clear. Further, the more intelligible a thing is, the more easily it too is retained. So we cannot but retain a thing that is most singular if only it is also intelligible.

[84] In this way, then, we have distinguished between a true idea and other perceptions, and shown that the fictitious, the false, and the other ideas have their origin in the imagination, i.e., in certain sensations that are fortuitous, and (as it were) disconnected; since they do not arise from the very power of the mind, but from external causes, as the body (whether waking or dreaming) receives various motions.

But if you wish, take imagination any way you like here, provided it is something different from the intellect, and in which the soul has the nature of something acted on. For it is all the same, however you take it, after we know that it is something random, by which the soul is acted on, and at the same time know how we are freed from it with the help of the intellect. So let no one be surprised that here, where I have not yet proved that there is a body, and other necessary things, I speak of the imagination, the body and its constitution. For as I have said, it does not matter what I take it to be, after I know that it is something random, etc.

[85] We have shown that a true idea is simple, or composed of simple ideas; that it shows how and why something is, or has been done; and that its objective effects proceed in the soul according to the formal nature of its object. This is the same as what the ancients said, i.e., that true knowledge proceeds from cause to effect – except that so far as I know they never conceived the soul (as we do here) as acting according to certain laws, like a spiritual automaton.

[86] From this we have acquired as much knowledge of our intellect as was possible in the beginning, and such a standard of the true idea that now we do not fear confusing true ideas with false or fictitious ones. Nor will we wonder why we understand certain things that do not fall in any way under the imagination, why there are some things in the imagination which are completely opposed to the intellect, and finally why there are others that agree with the intellect; for we know that those activities by which imaginations are produced happen according to other laws, wholly different from the laws of the intellect, and that in imagination the soul only has the nature of something acted on.

Notes

1 See further what we shall note concerning hypotheses that we clearly understand; but the fiction consists in our saying that such as these exist in the heavenly bodies.

2 Because the thing makes itself evident, provided it is understood, we require only an example, without other proof. The same is true of its contradictory – it need only be examined for its falsity to be clear. This will be plain immediately, when we speak of fictions concerning essence.

3 Note. Although many say that they doubt whether God exists, nevertheless they have nothing but the name, or they feign something which they call God; this does not agree with the nature of God, as I shall show later in the proper place.

4 By an eternal truth I mean one, which, if it is affirmative, will never be able to be negative. Thus it is a first and eternal truth *that God is*; but *that Adam thinks* is not an eternal truth. *That there is no Chimera* is an eternal truth; but not *that Adam does not think.*

5 Afterwards, when we speak of fiction that concerns essences, it will be clear that the fiction never makes, or presents to the mind, anything new, but that only things which are in the brain or the imagination are recalled to memory, and that the mind attends confusedly to all of them at once. Speech and a tree, for example, are recalled to memory, and since the mind attends confusedly, without distinction, it allows that the tree speaks. The same is understood concerning existence, especially, as we have said, when it is conceived so generally, as being. Then it is easily applied to all things which occur in the mind together. This is very much worth noting.

6 The same must also be understood concerning the hypotheses that are made to explain certain motions, which agree with the phenomena of the heavens; except that when people apply them to the celestial motions, they infer the nature of the heavens from them. But that nature can be different, especially

since many other causes can be conceived to explain such motions.

7   It often happens that a man recalls this term *soul* to his memory, and at the same time forms some corporeal image. But since these two things are represented together, he easily allows that he imagines and feigns a corporeal soul: because he does not distinguish the name from the thing itself. Here I ask my readers not to hasten to refute this, which, as I hope, they will not do, provided that they attend as accurately as possible to the examples, and at the same time, to the things that follow.

8   Although I seem to infer this from experience, and someone may say that this is nothing, because a demonstration is lacking, he may have one, if he wishes; since there can be nothing in nature that is contrary to its laws, but since all things happen according to certain laws of nature, so that they produce their certain effects, by certain laws, in an unbreakable connection, it follows from this that when the soul conceives a thing truly, it proceeds to form the same effects objectively. See below, where I speak of the false idea.

9   Note that the fiction, considered in itself, does not differ much from the dream, except that the causes which appear to the waking by the aid of the senses, and from which they infer that those presentations are not presented at that time by things placed outside them, do not appear in dreams. But error, as will be evident immediately, is dreaming while awake. And if it is very obvious, it is called madness.

10 These are not attributes of God that show his essence, as I shall show in [my] Philosophy.

11 This has already been demonstrated above. For if such a being did not exist, it could never be produced; and therefore the mind would be able to understand more things than Nature could bring about – which we have shown above to be false.

12 But if the duration is indeterminate, the memory of the thing is imperfect, as each of us also seems to have learned from nature. For often, to believe someone better in what he says, we ask when and where it happened. Although the ideas themselves also have their own duration in the mind, nevertheless, since we have become accustomed to determine duration with the aid of some measure of motion, which is also done with the aid of the imagination, we still observe no memory that belongs to the pure mind.

Ethics

Fifth Part of the Ethics: On the Power of the Intellect, or on Human Freedom

Preface

I pass, finally, to the remaining Part of the Ethics, which concerns the means, or way, leading to Freedom. Here, then, I shall treat of the power of reason, showing what it can do against the affects, and what Freedom of Mind, *or* blessedness, is. From this we shall see how much more the wise man can do than the ignorant. But it does not pertain to this investigation to show how the intellect must be perfected, or in what way the Body must be cared for, so that it can perform its function properly. The former is the concern of Logic, and the latter of Medicine.

Here, then, as I have said, I shall treat only of the power of the Mind, *or* of reason, and shall show, above all, how great its dominion over the affects is, and what kind of dominion it has for restraining and moderating them. For we have already demonstrated above that it does not have an absolute dominion over them. Nevertheless, the Stoics thought that they depend entirely on our will, and that we can command them absolutely. But experience cries out against this, and has forced them, in spite of their principles, to confess that much practice and application are required to restrain and moderate them. If I remember rightly, someone tried to show this by the example of two

Ethics (posthumously, 1677). From *The Collected Works of Spinoza*, ed. and tr. Edwin Curley (Princeton University Press, 1985). Selection: Part 5, pp. 594–606.

dogs, one a house dog, the other a hunting dog. For by practice he was finally able to bring it about that the house dog was accustomed to hunt, and the hunting dog to refrain from chasing hares.

Descartes was rather inclined to this opinion. For he maintained that the Soul, *or* Mind, was especially united to a certain part of the brain, called the pineal gland, by whose aid the Mind is aware of all the motions aroused in the body and of external objects, and which the Mind can move in various ways simply by willing. He contended that this gland was suspended in the middle of the brain in such a way that it could be moved by the least motion of the animal spirits. He maintained further that this gland is suspended in the middle of the brain in as many varying ways as there are varying ways that the animal spirits strike against it, and moreover, that as many varying traces are impressed upon it as there are varying external objects which drive the animal spirits against it. That is why, if the Soul's will afterwards moves the gland so that it is suspended as it once was by the motion of the animal spirits, the gland will drive and determine the animal spirits in the same way as when they were driven back before by a similar placement of the gland.

Furthermore, he maintained that each will of the Mind is united by nature to a certain fixed motion of this gland. For example, if someone has a will to look at a distant object, this will brings it about that the pupil is dilated. But if he thinks only of the pupil which is to be dilated, nothing will be accomplished by having a will for this, because nature has not joined the motion of the gland which serves to drive the animal spirits against the Optic nerve in a way suitable for dilating or contracting the pupil with the will to dilate or contract it. Instead, it has joined that motion with the will to look at distant or near objects.

Finally, he maintained that even though each motion of this gland seems to have been connected by nature from the beginning of our life with a particular one of our thoughts, they can still be joined by habit to others. He tries to prove this in *The Passions of the Soul* I, 50.

From these claims, he infers that there is no Soul so weak that it cannot – when it is well directed – acquire an absolute power over its Passions. For as he defines them, these are

> ... perceptions, or feelings, or emotions of the soul, which are particularly related to the soul, and which [NB] are produced, preserved, and strengthened by some motion of the spirits (see *The Passions of the Soul* I, 27).

But since to any will we can join any motion of the gland (and consequently any motion of the spirits), and since the determination of the will depends only on our power, we shall acquire an absolute dominion over our Passions, if we determine our will by firm and certain judgments according to which we will to direct the actions of our life, and if we join to these judgments the motions of the passions we will to have.

Such is the opinion of that most distinguished Man – as far as I can gather it from his words. I would hardly have believed it had been propounded by so great a Man, had it not been so subtle. Indeed, I cannot wonder enough that a Philosopher of his caliber – one who had firmly decided to deduce nothing except from principles known through themselves, and to affirm nothing which he did not perceive clearly and distinctly, one who had so often censured the Scholastics for wishing to explain obscure things by occult qualities – that such a Philosopher should assume a Hypothesis more occult than any occult quality.

What, I ask, does he understand by the union of Mind and Body? What clear and distinct concept does he have of a thought so closely united to some little portion of quantity? Indeed, I wish he had explained this union by its proximate cause. But he had conceived the Mind to be so distinct from the Body that he could not assign any singular cause, either of this union or of the Mind itself. Instead, it was necessary for him to have recourse to the cause of the whole Universe, i.e., to God.

Again, I should like very much to know how many degrees of motion the Mind can give to that pineal gland, and how great a force is required to hold it in suspense. For I do not know whether this gland is driven about more slowly by the Mind than by the animal spirits, or more quickly; nor do I know whether the motions of the Passions which we have joined closely to firm judgments can be separated from them again by corporeal causes. If so, it would follow that although the Mind had firmly resolved to face dangers, and had joined the motions of daring to this decision, nevertheless, once the danger had been seen, the gland might be so suspended that the Mind could think only of flight. And of course, since there is no common measure between the will and motion, there is also no comparison between the power, *or* forces, of the Mind and those of the Body. Consequently, the forces of the Body cannot in any way be determined by those of the Mind.

To this we may add that this gland is not found to be so placed in the middle of the brain that it can be driven about so easily and in so many ways, and that not all the nerves extend to the cavities of the brain.

Finally, I pass over all those things he claimed about the will and its freedom, since I have already shown, more than adequately, that they are false.

Therefore, because the power of the Mind is defined only by understanding, as I have shown above, we shall determine, by the Mind's knowledge alone, the remedies for the affects. I believe everyone in fact knows them by experience, though they neither observe them accurately, nor see them distinctly. From that we shall deduce all those things which concern the Mind's blessedness.

Axioms

A1: If two contrary actions are aroused in the same subject, a change will have to occur, either in both of them, or in one only, until they cease to be contrary.

A2: The power of an effect is defined by the power of its cause, insofar as its essence is explained or defined by the essence of its cause.

This axiom is evident from Part III P7.

Proposition 1: *In just the same way as thoughts and ideas of things are ordered and connected in the Mind, so the affections of the body, or images of things are ordered and connected in the body.*

Demonstration: The order and connection of ideas is the same as the order and connection of things (by IIP7), and vice versa, the order and connection of things is the same as the order and connection of ideas (by IIP6C and P7). So just as the order and connection of ideas happens in the Mind according to the order and connection of affections of the Body (by IIP18), so vice versa (by IIIP2), the order and connection of affections of the Body happens as thoughts and ideas of things are ordered and connected in the Mind, q.e.d.

P2: *If we separate emotions, or affects, from the thought of an external cause, and join them to other thoughts, then the Love, or Hate, toward the external cause is destroyed, as are the vacillations of mind arising from these affects.*

Dem.: For what constitutes the form of Love, or Hate, is Joy, or Sadness, accompanied by the idea of an external cause (by Defs. Aff. [Definitions of the Emotions] VI, VII). So if this is taken away, the form of Love or Hate is taken away at the same time. Hence, these affects, and those arising from them, are destroyed, q.e.d.

P3: *An affect which is a passion ceases to be a passion as soon as we form a clear and distinct idea of it.*

Dem.: An affect which is a passion is a confused idea (by General Def. Aff.). Therefore, if we should form a clear and distinct idea of the affect itself, this idea will only be distinguished by reason from the affect itself, insofar as it is related only to the Mind (by IIP21 and P21S). Therefore (by IIIP3), the affect will cease to be a passion, q.e.d.

Corollary: The more an affect is known to us, then, the more it is in our power, and the less the Mind is acted on by it.

P4: *There is no affection of the Body of which we cannot form a clear and distinct concept.*

Dem.: Those things that are common to all can only be conceived adequately (by IIP38), and so (by IIP12 and L2 [II/98]) there is no affection of the Body of which we cannot form some clear and distinct concept, q.e.d.

Cor.: From this it follows that there is no affect of which we cannot form some clear and distinct concept. For an affect is an idea of an affection of the Body (by Gen. Def. Aff.), which therefore (by P4) must involve some clear and distinct concept.

Scholium: There is nothing from which some effect does not follow (by IP36), and we understand clearly and distinctly whatever follows from an idea which is adequate in us (by IIP40); hence, each of us has – in part, at least, if not absolutely – the power to understand himself and his affects, and consequently, the power to bring it about that he is less acted on by them.

We must, therefore, take special care to know each affect clearly and distinctly (as far as this is possible), so that in this way the Mind may be determined from an affect to thinking those things which it perceives clearly and distinctly, and with which it is fully satisfied, and so that the affect itself may be separated from the thought of an external cause and joined to true thoughts. The result will be not only that Love, Hate, etc., are destroyed (by P2), but also that the appetites, *or* Desires, which usually arise from such an affect, cannot be excessive (by IVP61).

For it must particularly be noted that the appetite by which a man is said to act, and that by which he is said to be acted on, are one and the same. For example, we have shown that human nature is so constituted that each of us wants the others to live according to his temperament (see IIIP31S). And indeed, in a man who is not led by reason this appetite is the passion called Ambition, which does not differ much from Pride. On the other hand, in a man who lives according to the dictate of reason it is the action, *or* virtue, called Morality (see IVP37S1 and P37 Alternate dem.).

In this way, all the appetites, *or* Desires, are passions only insofar as they arise from inadequate ideas, and are counted as virtues when they are aroused or generated by adequate ideas. For all the Desires by which we are determined to do something can arise as much from adequate ideas as from inadequate ones (by IVP59). And – to return to the point from which I have digressed – we can devise no other remedy for the affects which depends on our power and is more excellent than this, which consists in a true knowledge of them. For the Mind has no other power than that of thinking and forming adequate ideas, as we have shown (by IIIP3) above.

P5: *The greatest affect of all, other things equal, is one toward a thing we imagine simply, and neither as necessary, nor as possible, nor as contingent.*

Dem.: An affect toward a thing we imagine to be free is greater than that toward a thing we imagine to be necessary (by IIIP49), and consequently is still greater than that toward a thing we imagine as possible or contingent (by IVP11). But imagining a thing as free can be nothing but simply imagining it while we are ignorant of the causes by which it has been determined to act (by what we have shown in IIP35S). Therefore, an affect toward a thing we imagine simply is, other things equal, greater than that toward a thing we imagine as necessary, possible, or contingent. Hence, it is the greatest of all, q.e.d.

P6: *Insofar as the Mind understands all things as necessary, it has a greater power over the affects, or is less acted on by them.*

Dem.: The Mind understands all things to be necessary (by IP29), and to be determined by an infinite connection of causes to exist and produce effects (by IP28). And so (by P5) to that extent [the mind] brings it about that it is less acted on by the affects springing from these things, and (by IIIP48) is less affected toward them, q.e.d.

Schol.: The more this knowledge that things are necessary is concerned with singular things, which we imagine more distinctly and vividly, the greater is this power of the Mind over the affects, as experience itself also testifies. For we see that Sadness over some good which has perished is lessened as soon as the man who has lost it realizes that this good could not, in any way, have been kept. Similarly, we see that no one pities infants because of their inability to speak, to walk, or to reason, or because they live so many years, as it were, unconscious of themselves. But if most people were born grown up, and only one or two were born infants, then everyone would pity the infants, because they would regard infancy itself, not as a natural and necessary thing, but as a vice of nature, *or* a sin. We could point out many other things along this line.

P7: *Affects that arise from, or are aroused by, reason are, if we take account of time, more powerful than those that are related to singular things which we regard as absent.*

Dem.: We regard a thing as absent, not because of the affect by which we imagine it, but because the Body is affected by another affect which excludes the thing's existence (by IIP17). So an affect which is related to a thing we regard as absent is not of such a nature that it surpasses men's other actions and power (see IVP6); on the contrary, its nature is such that it can, in some measure, be restrained by those affections which exclude the existence of its

external cause (by IVP9). But an affect that arises from reason is necessarily related to the common properties of things (see the Def. of reason in IIP40S2), which we always regard as present (for there can be nothing which excludes their present existence) and which we always imagine in the same way (by IIP38). So such an affect will always remain the same, and hence (by A1), the affects that are contrary to it, and that are not encouraged by their external causes, will have to accommodate themselves to it more and more, until they are no longer contrary to it. To that extent, an affect arising from reason is more powerful, q.e.d.

P8: *The more an affect arises from a number of causes concurring together, the greater it is.*

Dem.: A number of causes together can do more than if they were fewer (by IIIP7). And so (by IVP5), the more an affect is aroused by a number of causes together, the stronger it is, q.e.d.

Schol.: This proposition is also evident from A2.

P9: *If an affect is related to more and different causes which the Mind considers together with the affect itself, it is less harmful, we are less acted on by it, and we are affected less toward each cause, than is the case with another, equally great affect, which is related only to one cause, or to fewer causes.*

Dem.: An affect is only evil, *or* harmful, insofar as it prevents the Mind from being able to think (by IVP26 and P27). And so that affect which determines the Mind to consider many objects together is less harmful than another, equally great affect which engages the Mind solely in considering one, or a few objects, so that it cannot think of others. This was the first point.

Next, because the Mind's essence, i.e., power (by IIIP7), consists only in thought (by IIP11), the Mind is less acted on by an affect which determines it to consider many things together than by an equally great affect which keeps the Mind engaged solely in considering one or a few objects. This was the second point.

Finally (by IIIP48), insofar as this affect is related to many external causes, it is also less toward each one, q.e.d.

P10: *So long as we are not torn by affects contrary to our nature, we have the power of ordering and connecting the affections of the Body according to the order of the intellect.*

Dem.: Affects which are contrary to our nature, i.e. (by IVP30), which are evil, are evil insofar as they prevent the Mind from understanding (by IVP27). Therefore, so long as we are not torn by affects contrary to our nature, the power of the Mind by which it strives to understand things (by IVP26) is not hindered. So long, then, the Mind has the power of forming clear and distinct ideas, and of deducing some from others (see IIP40S2 and P47S). And hence, so long do we have (by P1) the power of ordering and connecting the affections of the Body according to the order of the intellect, q.e.d.

Schol.: By this power of rightly ordering and connecting the affections of the Body, we can bring it about that we are not easily affected with evil affects. For (by P7) a greater force is required for restraining Affects ordered and connected according to the order of the intellect than for restraining those which are uncertain and random. The best thing, then, that we can do, so long as we do not have perfect knowledge of our affects, is to conceive a correct principle of living, *or* sure maxims of life, to commit them to memory, and to apply them constantly to the particular cases frequently encountered in life. In this way our imagination will be extensively affected by them, and we shall always have them ready.

For example, we have laid it down as a maxim of life (see IVP46 and P46S) that Hate is to be conquered by Love, *or* Nobility, not by repaying it with Hate in return. But in order that we may always have this rule of reason ready when it is needed, we ought to think about and meditate frequently on the common wrongs of men, and how they may be warded off best by Nobility. For if we join the image of a wrong to the imagination of this maxim, it will always be ready for us (by IIP18) when a wrong is done to us. If we have ready also the principle of our own true advantage, and also of the good which follows from mutual friendship and common society, and keep in mind, moreover, that the highest satisfaction of mind stems from the right principle of living (by IVP52), and that men, like other things, act from the necessity of nature, then the wrong, *or* the Hate usually arising from it, will occupy a very small part of the imagination, and will easily be overcome.

Or if the Anger which usually arises from the greatest wrongs is not so easily overcome, it will still be overcome, though not without some vacillation. And it will be overcome in far less time than if we had not considered these things beforehand in this way (as is evident from P6, P7, and P8).

To put aside Fear, we must think in the same way of Tenacity: i.e., we must recount and frequently imagine the common dangers of life, and how they can be best avoided and overcome by presence of mind and strength of character.

But it should be noted that in ordering our thoughts and images, we must always (by IVP63C and IIIP59) attend to those things which are good in each thing so that in this way we are always determined to acting from an affect of Joy. For example, if someone sees that he pursues esteem too much, he should think of its correct use, the end for which it ought be pursued, and the means by which it can be acquired, not of its misuse and emptiness, and men's inconstancy, or other things of this kind, which only someone sick of mind thinks of. For those who are most ambitious are most upset by such thoughts when they despair of attaining the honor they strive for; while they spew forth their Anger, they wish to seem wise. So it is certain that they most desire esteem who cry out most against its misuse, and the emptiness of the world.

Nor is this peculiar to the ambitious – it is common to everyone whose luck is bad and whose mind is weak. For the poor man, when he is also greedy, will not stop talking about the misuse of money and the vices of the rich. In doing this he only distresses himself, and shows others that he cannot bear calmly either his own poverty, or the wealth of others.

So also, one who has been badly received by a lover thinks of nothing but the inconstancy and deceptiveness of women, and their other, often sung vices. All of these he immediately forgets as soon as his lover receives him again.

One, therefore, who is anxious to moderate his affects and appetites from the love of Freedom alone will strive, as far as he can, to come to know the virtues and their causes, and to fill his mind with the gladness which arises from the true knowledge of them, but not at all to consider men's vices, or to disparage men, or to enjoy a false appearance of freedom. And he who will observe these [rules] carefully – for they are not difficult – and practice them, will soon be able to direct most of his actions according to the command of reason.

P11: *As an image is related to more things, the more frequent it is,* or *the more often it flourishes, and the more it engages the Mind.*

Dem.: For as an image, *or* affect, is related to more things, there are more causes by which it can be aroused and encouraged, all of which the Mind (by Hypothesis) considers together with the affect. And so the affect is the more frequent, *or* flourishes more often, and (by P8) engages the Mind more, q.e.d.

P12: *The images of things are more easily joined to images related to things we understand clearly and distinctly than to other images.*

Dem.: Things we understand clearly and distinctly are either common properties of things or deduced from them (see the Def. of reason in IIP40S2), and consequently (by P11) are aroused in us more often. And so it can more easily happen that we consider other things together with them rather than with [things we do not understand clearly and distinctly]. Hence (by IIP18), [images of things] are more easily joined with [things we understand clearly and distinctly] than with others, q.e.d.

P13: *The more an image is joined with other images, the more often it flourishes.*

Dem.: For the more an image is joined with other images, the more causes there are (by IIP18) by which it can be aroused, q.e.d.

P14: *The Mind can bring it about that all the Body's affections,* or *images of things, are related to the idea of God.*

Dem.: There is no affection of the Body of which the Mind cannot form some clear and distinct concept (by P4). And so it can bring it about (by IP15) that they are related to the idea of God, q.e.d.

P15: *He who understands himself and his affects clearly and distinctly loves God, and does so the more, the more he understands himself and his affects.*

Dem.: He who understands himself and his affects clearly and distinctly rejoices (by IIIP53), and this Joy is accompanied by the idea of God (by P14). Hence (by Def. Aff. VI), he loves God, and (by the same reasoning) does so the more, the more he understands himself and his affects, q.e.d.

P16: *This Love toward God must engage the Mind most.*

Dem.: For this Love is joined to all the affections of the Body (by P14), which all encourage it (by P15). And so (by P11), it must engage the Mind most, q.e.d.

P17: *God is without passions, and is not affected with any affect of Joy or Sadness.*

Dem.: All ideas, insofar as they are related to God, are true (by IIP32), i.e. (by IID4), adequate. And so (by Gen. Def. Aff.), God is without passions.

Next, God can pass neither to a greater nor a lesser perfection, (by IP20C2); hence (by Defs. Aff. II, III) he is not affected with any affect of Joy or Sadness, q.e.d.

Cor.: Strictly speaking, God loves no one, and hates no one. For God (by P17) is not affected with any affect of Joy or Sadness. Consequently (by Defs. Aff. VI, VII), he also loves no one and hates no one.

P18: *No one can hate God.*

Dem.: The idea of God which is in us is adequate and perfect (by IIP46, P47). So insofar as we consider God, we act (by IIIP3). Consequently (by IIIP59), there can be no Sadness accompanied by the idea of God, i.e. (by Def. Aff. VII), no one can hate God, q.e.d.

Cor.: Love toward God cannot be turned into hate.

Schol.: But, it can be objected, while we understand God to be the cause of all things, we thereby consider God to be the cause of Sadness. To this I reply that insofar as we understand the causes of Sadness, it ceases (by P3) to be a passion, i.e. (by IIIP59), to that extent it ceases to be Sadness. And so, insofar as we understand God to be the cause of Sadness, we rejoice.

P19: *He who loves God cannot strive that God should love him in return.*

Dem.: If a man were to strive for this, he would desire (by P17C) that God, whom he loves, not be God. Consequently (by IIIP19), he would desire to be saddened, which is absurd (by IIIP28). Therefore, he who loves God, etc., q.e.d.

P20: *This Love toward God cannot be tainted by an affect of Envy or Jealousy: instead, the more men we imagine to be joined to God by the same bond of Love, the more it is encouraged.*

Dem.: This Love toward God is the highest good which we can want from the dictate of reason (by IVP28), and is common to all men (by IVP36); we desire that all should enjoy it (by IVP37). And so (by Def. Aff. XXIII), it cannot be stained by an affect of Envy, nor (by P18 and the Def. of Jealousy, see IIIP35S) by an affect of Jealousy. On the contrary (by IIIP31), the more men we imagine to enjoy it, the more it must be encouraged, q.e.d.

Schol.: Similarly we can show that there is no affect which is directly contrary to this Love and by which it can be destroyed. So we can conclude that this Love is the most constant of all the affects, and insofar as it is related to the Body, cannot be destroyed, unless it is destroyed with the Body itself. What the nature of this Love is insofar as it is related only to the Mind, we shall see later.

And with this, I have covered all the remedies for the affects, *or* all that the Mind, considered only in itself, can do against the affects. From this it is clear that the power of the Mind over the affects consists:

I. In the knowledge itself of the affects (see P4S);

II. In the fact that it separates the affects from the thought of an external cause, which we imagine confusedly (see P2 and P4S);

III. In the time by which the affections related to things we understand surpass those related to things we conceive confusedly, *or* in a mutilated way (see P7);

IV. In the multiplicity of causes by which affections related to common properties or to God are encouraged (see P9 and P11);

V. Finally, in the order by which the Mind can order its affects and connect them to one another (see P10, and in addition, P12, P13, and P14).

But to understand better this power of the Mind over the affects, the most important thing to note is that we call affects great when we compare the affect of one man with that of another, and see that the same affect troubles one more than the other, or when we compare the affects of one and the same man with each other, and find that he is affected, *or* moved, more by one affect than by another. For (by IVP5) the force of each affect is defined by the power of the external cause compared with our own. But the power of the Mind is defined by knowledge alone, whereas lack of power, *or* passion, is judged solely by the privation of knowledge, i.e., by that through which ideas are called inadequate.

From this it follows that that Mind is most acted on, of which inadequate ideas constitute the greatest part, so that it is distinguished more by what it undergoes than by what it does. On the other hand, that Mind acts most, of which adequate ideas constitute the greatest part, so that though it may have as many inadequate ideas as the other, it is still distinguished more by those which are attributed to human virtue than by those which betray man's lack of power.

Next, it should be noted that sickness of the mind and misfortunes take their origin especially from too much Love toward a thing which is liable to many variations and which we can never fully possess. For no one is disturbed or anxious concerning anything unless he loves it, nor do wrongs, suspicions, and enmities arise except from Love for a thing which no one can really fully possess.

From what we have said, we easily conceive what clear and distinct knowledge – and especially that third kind of knowledge (see IIP47S), whose foundation is the knowledge of God itself – can accomplish against the affects. Insofar as the affects are passions, if clear and distinct knowledge does not absolutely remove them (see P3 and P4S), at least it brings it about that they constitute the smallest part of the Mind (see P14). And then it begets a Love toward a thing immutable and eternal (see P15), which we really fully possess (see IIP45), and which therefore cannot be tainted by any of the vices which are in ordinary Love, but can always be greater and greater (by P15), and occupy the greatest part of the Mind (by P16), and affect it extensively.

With this I have completed everything which concerns this present life. Anyone who attends to what we have said in this Scholium, and at the same time, to the definitions of the Mind and its affects, and finally to IIIP1 and P3, will easily be able to see what I said at the beginning of this Scholium, viz. that in these few words I have covered all the remedies for the affects. So it is time now to pass to those things which pertain to the Mind's duration without relation to the body. [. . .]

9

A Theologico-Political Treatise

Chapter XVI: Of the Foundations of a State; of the Natural and Civil Rights of Individuals; and of the Rights of the Sovereign Power

Hitherto our care has been to separate philosophy from theology, and to show the freedom of thought which such separation insures to both. It is now time to determine the limits to which such freedom of thought and discussion may extend itself in the ideal state. For the due consideration of this question we must examine the foundations of a state, first turning our attention to the natural rights of individuals, and afterwards to religion and the state as a whole.

By the right and ordinance of nature, I merely mean those natural laws wherewith we conceive every individual to be conditioned by nature, so as to live and act in a given way. For instance, fishes are naturally conditioned for swimming, and the greater for devouring the less; therefore fishes enjoy the water, and the greater devour the less by sovereign natural right. For it is certain that nature, taken in the abstract, has sovereign right to do anything she can; in other words, her right is co-extensive with her power. The power of nature is the power of God, which has sovereign right over all things; and, inasmuch as the power of nature is

A Theologico-Political Treatise (1670). From *The Chief Works of Benedict de Spinoza*, vol. 1, tr. R. H. M. Elwes (New York: Dover Publications, Inc., 1951). Selections: ch. 16 (excerpt), "Of the Foundations of a State," pp. 200–7; ch. 20, "That in a Free State Every Man May Think What He Likes, and Say What He Thinks," pp. 257–66.

simply the aggregate of the powers of all her individual components, it follows that every individual has sovereign right to do all that he can; in other words, the rights of an individual extend to the utmost limits of his power as it has been conditioned. Now it is the sovereign law and right of nature that each individual should endeavour to preserve itself as it is, without regard to anything but itself; therefore this sovereign law and right belongs to every individual, namely, to exist and act according to its natural conditions. We do not here acknowledge any difference between mankind and other individual natural entities, nor between men endowed with reason and those to whom reason is unknown; nor between fools, madmen, and sane men. Whatsoever an individual does by the laws of its nature it has a sovereign right to do, inasmuch as it acts as it was conditioned by nature, and cannot act otherwise. Wherefore among men, so long as they are considered as living under the sway of nature, he who does not yet know reason, or who has not yet acquired the habit of virtue, acts solely according to the laws of his desire with as sovereign a right as he who orders his life entirely by the laws of reason.

That is, as the wise man has sovereign right to do all that reason dictates, or to live according to the laws of reason, so also the ignorant and foolish man has sovereign right to do all that desire dictates, or to live according to the laws of desire. This is identical with the teaching of Paul, who acknowledges that previous to the law – that is, so long as men are considered of as living under the sway of nature, there is no sin.

The natural right of the individual man is thus determined, not by sound reason, but by desire and power. All are not naturally conditioned so as to act according to the laws and rules of reason; nay, on the contrary, all men are born ignorant, and before they can learn the right way of life and acquire the habit of virtue, the greater part of their life, even if they have been well brought up, has passed away. Nevertheless, they are in the meanwhile bound to live and preserve themselves as far as they can by the unaided impulses of desire. Nature has given them no other guide, and has denied them the present power of living according to sound reason; so that they are no more bound to live by the dictates of an enlightened mind, than a cat is bound to live by the laws of the nature of a lion.

Whatsoever, therefore, an individual (considered as under the sway of nature) thinks useful for himself, whether led by sound reason or impelled by the passions, that he has a sovereign right to seek and to take for himself as he best can, whether by force, cunning, entreaty, or any other means; consequently he may regard as an enemy anyone who hinders the accomplishment of his purpose.

It follows from what we have said that the right and ordinance of nature, under which all men are born, and under which they mostly live, only prohibits such things as no one desires, and no one can attain: it does not forbid strife, nor hatred, nor anger, nor deceit, nor, indeed, any of the means suggested by desire.

This we need not wonder at, for nature is not bounded by the laws of human reason, which aims only at man's true benefit and preservation; her limits are infinitely wider, and have reference to the eternal order of nature, wherein man is but a speck; it is by the necessity of this alone that all individuals are conditioned for living and acting in a particular way. If anything, therefore, in nature seems to us ridiculous, absurd, or evil, it is because we only know in part, and are almost entirely ignorant of the order and interdependence of nature as a whole, and also because we want everything to be arranged according to the dictates of our human reason; in reality that which reason considers evil, is not evil in respect to the order and laws of nature as a whole, but only in respect to the laws of our reason.

Nevertheless, no one can doubt that it is much better for us to live according to the laws and assured dictates of reason, for, as we said, they have men's true good for their object. Moreover, everyone wishes to live as far as possible securely beyond the reach of fear, and this would be quite impossible so long as everyone did everything he liked, and reason's claim was lowered to a par with those of hatred and anger; there is no one who is not ill at ease in the midst of enmity, hatred, anger, and deceit, and who does not seek to avoid them as much as he can. When we reflect that men without mutual help, or the aid of reason, must needs live most miserably, as we clearly proved in Chap. V., we shall plainly see that men must necessarily come to an agreement to live together as securely and well as possible if they are to enjoy as a whole the rights which naturally belong to them as individuals, and their life should be no more conditioned by the force and desire of individuals, but by the power and will of the whole body. This end they will be unable to attain if desire be their only guide (for by the laws of desire each man is drawn in a different direction); they must, therefore, most firmly decree and establish that they will be guided in everything by reason (which nobody will dare openly to repudiate lest he should be taken for a madman), and will restrain any desire which is injurious to a man's fellows, that they will do to all as they would be done by, and that they will defend their neighbour's rights as their own.

How such a compact as this should be entered into, how ratified and established, we will now inquire.

Now it is a universal law of human nature that no one ever neglects anything which he judges to be good, except with the hope of gaining a greater good, or from the fear of a greater evil; nor does anyone endure an evil except for the sake of avoiding a greater evil, or gaining a greater good. That is, everyone will, of two goods, choose that which he thinks the greatest; and, of two evils, that which he thinks the least. I say advisedly that which he thinks the greatest or the least, for it does not necessarily follow that he judges right. This law is so deeply implanted in the human mind that it ought to be counted among eternal truths and axioms.

As a necessary consequence of the principle just enunciated, no one can honestly promise to forego the right which he has over all things,[1] and in general no one will abide by his promises, unless under the fear of a greater evil, or the hope of a greater good. An example will make the matter clearer. Suppose that a robber forces me to promise that I will give him my goods at his will and pleasure. It is plain (inasmuch as my natural right is, as I have shown, co-extensive with my power)

that if I can free myself from this robber by stratagem, by assenting to his demands, I have the
natural right to do so, and to pretend to accept
his conditions. Or again, suppose I have genuinely
promised someone that for the space of twenty
days I will not taste food or any nourishment;
and suppose I afterwards find that my promise
was foolish, and cannot be kept without very
great injury to myself; as I am bound by natural
law and right to choose the least of two evils, I have
complete right to break my compact, and act as if
my promise had never been uttered. I say that I
should have perfect natural right to do so, whether
I was actuated by true and evident reason, or
whether I was actuated by mere opinion in thinking I had promised rashly; whether my reasons
were true or false, I should be in fear of a greater
evil, which, by the ordinance of nature, I should
strive to avoid by every means in my power.

We may, therefore, conclude that a compact is
only made valid by its utility, without which it
becomes null and void. It is, therefore, foolish to
ask a man to keep his faith with us for ever, unless
we also endeavour that the violation of the compact we enter into shall involve for the violator
more harm than good. This consideration should
have very great weight in forming a state. However, if all men could be easily led by reason alone,
and could recognize what is best and most useful
for a state, there would be no one who would not
forswear deceit, for everyone would keep most
religiously to their compact in their desire for the
chief good, namely, the preservation of the state,
and would cherish good faith above all things as
the shield and buckler of the commonwealth.
However, it is far from being the case that all
men can always be easily led by reason alone;
everyone is drawn away by his pleasure, while
avarice, ambition, envy, hatred, and the like so
engross the mind that reason has no place therein.
Hence, though men make promises with all the
appearances of good faith, and agree that they will
keep to their engagement, no one can absolutely
rely on another man's promise unless there is
something behind it. Everyone has by nature a
right to act deceitfully, and to break his compacts,
unless he be restrained by the hope of some greater
good, or the fear of some greater evil.

However, as we have shown that the natural
right of the individual is only limited by
his power, it is clear that by transferring, either
willingly or under compulsion, this power into the
hands of another, he in so doing necessarily

cedes also a part of his right; and further, that
the sovereign right over all men belongs to him
who has sovereign power, wherewith he can compel men by force, or restrain them by threats of the
universally feared punishment of death; such sovereign right he will retain only so long as he can
maintain his power of enforcing his will; otherwise
he will totter on his throne, and no one who is
stronger than he will be bound unwillingly to obey
him.

In this manner a society can be formed without
any violation of natural right, and the covenant can
always be strictly kept – that is, if each individual
hands over the whole of his power to the body
politic, the latter will then possess sovereign natural right over all things; that is, it will have sole
and unquestioned dominion, and everyone will be
bound to obey, under pain of the severest punishment. A body politic of this kind is called a Democracy, which may be defined as a society which
wields all its power as a whole. The sovereign
power is not restrained by any laws, but everyone
is bound to obey it in all things; such is the state of
things implied when men either tacitly or expressly handed over to it all their power of self-
defence, or in other words, all their right. For if
they had wished to retain any right for themselves,
they ought to have taken precautions for its defence and preservation; as they have not done so,
and indeed could not have done so without dividing and consequently ruining the state, they placed
themselves absolutely at the mercy of the sovereign power; and, therefore, having acted (as we
have shown) as reason and necessity demanded,
they are obliged to fulfil the commands of the
sovereign power, however absurd these may be,
else they will be public enemies, and will act
against reason, which urges the preservation of
the state as a primary duty. For reason bids us
choose the least of two evils.

Furthermore, this danger of submitting absolutely to the dominion and will of another, is one
which may be incurred with a light heart: for we
have shown that sovereigns only possess this right
of imposing their will, so long as they have the full
power to enforce it: if such power be lost their
right to command is lost also, or lapses to those
who have assumed it and can keep it. Thus it is
very rare for sovereigns to impose thoroughly irrational commands, for they are bound to consult
their own interests, and retain their power by
consulting the public good and acting according
to the dictates of reason, as Seneca says, "violenta

imperia nemo continuit diu." No one can long retain a tyrant's sway.

In a democracy, irrational commands are still less to be feared: for it is almost impossible that the majority of a people, especially if it be a large one, should agree in an irrational design: and, moreover, the basis and aim of a democracy is to avoid the desires as irrational, and to bring men as far as possible under the control of reason, so that they may live in peace and harmony: if this basis be removed the whole fabric falls to ruin.

Such being the ends in view for the sovereign power, the duty of subjects is, as I have said, to obey its commands, and to recognize no right save that which it sanctions.

It will, perhaps, be thought that we are turning subjects into slaves: for slaves obey commands and free men live as they like; but this idea is based on a misconception, for the true slave is he who is led away by his pleasures and can neither see what is good for him nor act accordingly: he alone is free who lives with free consent under the entire guidance of reason.

Action in obedience to orders does take away freedom in a certain sense, but it does not, therefore, make a man a slave, all depends on the object of the action. If the object of the action be the good of the state, and not the good of the agent, the latter is a slave and does himself no good: but in a state or kingdom where the weal of the whole people, and not that of the ruler, is the supreme law, obedience to the sovereign power does not make a man a slave, of no use to himself, but a subject. Therefore, that state is the freest whose laws are founded on sound reason, so that every member of it may, if he will, be free;[2] that is, live with full consent under the entire guidance of reason.

Children, though they are bound to obey all the commands of their parents, are yet not slaves: for the commands of parents look generally to the children's benefit.

We must, therefore, acknowledge a great difference between a slave, a son, and a subject; their positions may be thus defined. A slave is one who is bound to obey his master's orders, though they are given solely in the master's interest: a son is one who obeys his father's orders, given in his own interest; a subject obeys the orders of the sovereign power, given for the common interest, wherein he is included.

I think I have now shown sufficiently clearly the basis of a democracy: I have especially desired to do so, for I believe it to be of all forms of government the most natural, and the most consonant with individual liberty. In it no one transfers his natural right so absolutely that he has no further voice in affairs, he only hands it over to the majority of a society, whereof he is a unit. Thus all men remain, as they were in the state of nature, equals.

This is the only form of government which I have treated of at length, for it is the one most akin to my purpose of showing the benefits of freedom in a state.

I may pass over the fundamental principles of other forms of government, for we may gather from what has been said whence their right arises without going into its origin. The possessor of sovereign power, whether he be one, or many, or the whole body politic, has the sovereign right of imposing any commands he pleases: and he who has either voluntarily, or under compulsion, transferred the right to defend him to another, has, in so doing, renounced his natural right and is therefore bound to obey, in all things, the commands of the sovereign power; and will be bound so to do so long as the king, or nobles, or the people preserve the sovereign power which formed the basis of the original transfer. I need add no more. [...]

Chapter XX: That in a Free State Every Man May Think What He Likes, and Say What He Thinks

If men's minds were as easily controlled as their tongues, every king would sit safely on his throne, and government by compulsion would cease; for every subject would shape his life according to the intentions of his rulers, and would esteem a thing true or false, good or evil, just or unjust, in obedience to their dictates. However, we have shown already (Chapter XVII.) that no man's mind can possibly lie wholly at the disposition of another, for no one can willingly transfer his natural right of free reason and judgment, or be compelled so to do. For this reason government which attempts to control minds is accounted tyrannical, and it is considered an abuse of sovereignty and a usurpation of the rights of subjects, to seek to prescribe what shall be accepted as true, or rejected as false, or what opinions should actuate men in their worship of God. All these questions fall within a man's natural right, which he cannot abdicate even with his own consent.

I admit that the judgment can be biassed in many ways, and to an almost incredible degree, so that while exempt from direct external control it may be so dependent on another man's words, that it may fitly be said to be ruled by him; but although this influence is carried to great lengths, it has never gone so far as to invalidate the statement, that every man's understanding is his own, and that brains are as diverse as palates.

Moses, not by fraud, but by Divine virtue, gained such a hold over the popular judgment that he was accounted superhuman, and believed to speak and act through the inspiration of the Deity; nevertheless, even he could not escape murmurs and evil interpretations. How much less then can other monarchs avoid them! Yet such unlimited power, if it exists at all, must belong to a monarch, and least of all to a democracy, where the whole or a great part of the people wield authority collectively. This is a fact which I think everyone can explain for himself.

However unlimited, therefore, the power of a sovereign may be, however implicitly it is trusted as the exponent of law and religion, it can never prevent men from forming judgments according to their intellect, or being influenced by any given emotion. It is true that it has the right to treat as enemies all men whose opinions do not, on all subjects, entirely coincide with its own; but we are not discussing its strict rights, but its proper course of action. I grant that it has the right to rule in the most violent manner, and to put citizens to death for very trivial causes, but no one supposes it can do this with the approval of sound judgment. Nay, inasmuch as such things cannot be done without extreme peril to itself, we may even deny that it has the absolute power to do them, or, consequently, the absolute right; for the rights of the sovereign are limited by his power.

Since, therefore, no one can abdicate his freedom of judgment and feeling; since every man is by indefeasible natural right the master of his own thoughts, it follows that men thinking in diverse and contradictory fashions, cannot, without disastrous results, be compelled to speak only according to the dictates of the supreme power. Not even the most experienced, to say nothing of the multitude, know how to keep silence. Men's common failing is to confide their plans to others, though there be need for secrecy, so that a government would be most harsh which deprived the individual of his freedom of saying and teaching what he thought; and would be moderate if such freedom were granted. Still we cannot deny that authority may be as much injured by words as by actions; hence, although the freedom we are discussing cannot be entirely denied to subjects, its unlimited concession would be most baneful; we must, therefore, now inquire, how far such freedom can and ought to be conceded without danger to the peace of the state, or the power of the rulers; and this, as I said at the beginning of Chapter XVI., is my principal object.

It follows, plainly, from the explanation given above, of the foundations of a state, that the ultimate aim of government is not to rule, or restrain, by fear, nor to exact obedience, but contrariwise, to free every man from fear, that he may live in all possible security; in other words, to strengthen his natural right to exist and work without injury to himself or others.

No, the object of government is not to change men from rational beings into beasts or puppets, but to enable them to develope their minds and bodies in security, and to employ their reason unshackled; neither showing hatred, anger, or deceit, nor watched with the eyes of jealousy and injustice. In fact, the true aim of government is liberty.

Now we have seen that in forming a state the power of making laws must either be vested in the body of the citizens, or in a portion of them, or in one man. For, although men's free judgments are very diverse, each one thinking that he alone knows everything, and although complete unanimity of feeling and speech is out of the question, it is impossible to preserve peace, unless individuals abdicate their right of acting entirely on their own judgment. Therefore, the individual justly cedes the right of free action, though not of free reason and judgment; no one can act against the authorities without danger to the state, though his feelings and judgment may be at variance therewith; he may even speak against them, provided that he does so from rational conviction, not from fraud, anger, or hatred, and provided that he does not attempt to introduce any change on his private authority.

For instance, supposing a man shows that a law is repugnant to sound reason, and should therefore be repealed; if he submits his opinion to the judgment of the authorities (who, alone, have the right of making and repealing laws), and meanwhile acts in nowise contrary to that law, he has deserved well of the state, and has behaved as a good citizen should; but if he accuses the authorities of injustice, and stirs up the people against them, or if he seditiously strives to abrogate the law without their consent, he is a mere agitator and rebel.

Thus we see how an individual may declare and teach what he believes, without injury to the authority of his rulers, or to the public peace; namely, by leaving in their hands the entire power of legislation as it affects action, and by doing nothing against their laws, though he be compelled often to act in contradiction to what he believes, and openly feels, to be best.

Such a course can be taken without detriment to justice and dutifulness, nay, it is the one which a just and dutiful man would adopt. We have shown that justice is dependent on the laws of the authorities, so that no one who contravenes their accepted decrees can be just, while the highest regard for duty, as we have pointed out in the preceding chapter, is exercised in maintaining public peace and tranquillity; these could not be preserved if every man were to live as he pleased; therefore it is no less than undutiful for a man to act contrary to his country's laws, for it the practice became universal the ruin of states would necessarily follow.

Hence, so long as a man acts in obedience to the laws of his rulers, he in nowise contravenes his reason, for in obedience to reason he transferred the right of controlling his actions from his own hands to theirs. This doctrine we can confirm from actual custom, for in a conference of great and small powers, schemes are seldom carried unanimously, yet all unite in carrying out what is decided on, whether they voted for or against. But I return to my proposition.

From the fundamental notions of a state, we have discovered how a man may exercise free judgment without detriment to the supreme power: from the same premises we can no less easily determine what opinions would be seditious. Evidently those which by their very nature nullify the compact by which the right of free action was ceded. For instance, a man who holds that the supreme power has no rights over him, or that promises ought not to be kept, or that everyone should live as he pleases, or other doctrines of this nature in direct opposition to the above-mentioned contract, is seditious, not so much from his actual opinions and judgment, as from the deeds which they involve; for he who maintains such theories abrogates the contract which tacitly, or openly, he made with his rulers. Other opinions which do not involve acts violating the contract, such as revenge,

anger, and the like, are not seditious, unless it be in some corrupt state, where superstitious and ambitious persons, unable to endure men of learning, are so popular with the multitude that their word is more valued than the law.

However, I do not deny that there are some doctrines which, while they are apparently only concerned with abstract truths and falsehoods, are yet propounded and published with unworthy motives. This question we have discussed in Chapter XV., and shown that reason should nevertheless remain unshackled. If we hold to the principle that a man's loyalty to the state should be judged, like his loyalty to God, from his actions only – namely, from his charity towards his neighbours; we cannot doubt that the best government will allow freedom of philosophical speculation no less than of religious belief. I confess that from such freedom inconveniences may sometimes arise, but what question was ever settled so wisely that no abuses could possibly spring therefrom? He who seeks to regulate everything by law, is more likely to arouse vices than to reform them. It is best to grant what cannot be abolished, even though it be in itself harmful. How many evils spring from luxury, envy, avarice, drunkenness, and the like, yet these are tolerated – vices as they are – because they cannot be prevented by legal enactments. How much more then should free thought be granted, seeing that it is in itself a virtue and that it cannot be crushed! Besides, the evil results can easily be checked, as I will show, by the secular authorities, not to mention that such freedom is absolutely necessary for progress in science and the liberal arts: for no man follows such pursuits to advantage unless his judgment be entirely free and unhampered.

But let it be granted that freedom may be crushed, and men be so bound down, that they do not dare to utter a whisper, save at the bidding of their rulers; nevertheless this can never be carried to the pitch of making them think according to authority, so that the necessary consequences would be that men would daily be thinking one thing and saying another, to the corruption of good faith, that mainstay of government, and to the fostering of hateful flattery and perfidy, whence spring stratagems, and the corruption of every good art.

It is far from possible to impose uniformity of speech, for the more rulers strive to curtail freedom of speech, the more obstinately are they resisted; not indeed by the avaricious, the flatterers, and other numskulls, who think supreme salvation consists in filling their stomachs and gloating over their money-bags, but by those whom good education, sound morality, and virtue have rendered more free. Men, as generally constituted, are most prone to resent the branding as criminal of opinions which they believe to be true, and the proscription as wicked of that which inspires them with piety towards God and man; hence they are ready to forswear the laws and conspire against the authorities, thinking it not shameful but honourable to stir up seditions and perpetuate any sort of crime with this end in view. Such being the constitution of human nature, we see that laws directed against opinions affect the generous-minded rather than the wicked, and are adapted less for coercing criminals than for irritating the upright; so that they cannot be maintained without great peril to the state.

Moreover, such laws are almost always useless, for those who hold that the opinions proscribed are sound, cannot possibly obey the law; whereas those who already reject them as false, accept the law as a kind of privilege, and make such boast of it, that authority is powerless to repeal it, even if such a course be subsequently desired.

To these considerations may be added what we said in Chapter XVIII. in treating of the history of the Hebrews. And, lastly, how many schisms have arisen in the Church from the attempt of the authorities to decide by law the intricacies of theological controversy! If men were not allured by the hope of getting the law and the authorities on their side, of triumphing over their adversaries in the sight of an applauding multitude, and of acquiring honourable distinctions, they would not strive so maliciously, nor would such fury sway their minds. This is taught not only by reason but by daily examples, for laws of this kind prescribing what every man shall believe and forbidding anyone to speak or write to the contrary, have often been passed, as sops or concessions to the anger of those who cannot tolerate men of enlightenment, and who, by such harsh and crooked enactments, can easily turn the devotion of the masses into fury and direct it against whom they will.

How much better would it be to restrain popular anger and fury, instead of passing useless laws, which can only be broken by those who love virtue and the liberal arts, thus paring down the state till it is too small to harbour men of talent. What greater misfortune for a state can be conceived than that honourable men should be sent like criminals into exile, because they hold diverse opinions which they cannot disguise? What, I say, can be more hurtful than that men who have committed no crime or wickedness should, simply because they are enlightened, be treated as enemies and put to death, and that the scaffold, the terror of evil-doers, should become the arena where the highest examples of tolerance and virtue are displayed to the people with all the marks of ignominy that authority can devise?

He that knows himself to be upright does not fear the death of a criminal, and shrinks from no punishment; his mind is not wrung with remorse for any disgraceful deed: he holds that death in a good cause is no punishment, but an honour, and that death for freedom is glory.

What purpose then is served by the death of such men, what example is proclaimed? The cause for which they die is unknown to the idle and the foolish, hateful to the turbulent, loved by the upright. The only lesson we can draw from such scenes is to flatter the persecutor, or else to imitate the victim.

If formal assent is not to be esteemed above conviction, and if governments are to retain a firm hold of authority and not be compelled to yield to agitators, it is imperative that freedom of judgment should be granted, so that men may live together in harmony, however diverse, or even openly contradictory their opinions may be. We cannot doubt that such is the best system of government and open to the fewest objections, since it is the one most in harmony with human nature. In a democracy (the most natural form of government, as we have shown in Chapter XVI.) everyone submits to the control of authority over his actions, but not over his judgment and reason; that is, seeing that all cannot think alike, the voice of the majority has the force of law, subject to repeal if circumstances bring about a change of opinion. In proportion as the power of free judgment is withheld we depart from the natural condition of mankind, and consequently the government becomes more tyrannical.

In order to prove that from such freedom no inconvenience arises, which cannot easily be checked by the exercise of the sovereign power, and that men's actions can easily be kept in bounds, though their opinions be at open variance, it will be well to cite an example. Such an one is not very far to seek. The city of Amsterdam reaps the fruit of this freedom in its own great prosperity and in the admiration of all other people. For in this most flourishing state, and most splendid city, men of every nation and religion live together in the greatest harmony, and ask no questions before trusting their goods to a fellow-citizen, save whether he be rich or poor, and whether he generally acts honestly, or the reverse. His religion and sect is considered of no importance: for it has no effect before the judges in gaining or losing a cause, and there is no sect so despised that its followers, provided that they harm no one, pay every man his due, and live uprightly, are deprived of the protection of the magisterial authority.

On the other hand, when the religious controversy between Remonstrants and Counter-Remonstrants began to be taken up by politicians and the States, it grew into a schism, and abundantly showed that laws dealing with religion and seeking to settle its controversies are much more calculated to irritate than to reform, and that they give rise to extreme licence: further, it was seen that schisms do not originate in a love of truth, which is a source of courtesy and gentleness, but rather in an inordinate desire for supremacy. From all these considerations it is clearer than the sun at noonday, that the true schismatics are those who condemn other men's writings, and seditiously stir up the quarrelsome masses against their authors, rather than those authors themselves, who generally write only for the learned, and appeal solely to reason. In fact, the real disturbers of the peace are those who, in a free state, seek to curtail the liberty of judgment which they are unable to tyrannize over.

I have thus shown: – I. That it is impossible to deprive men of the liberty of saying what they think. II. That such liberty can be conceded to every man without injury to the rights and authority of the sovereign power, and that every man may retain it without injury to such rights, provided that he does not presume upon it to the extent of introducing any new rights into the state, or acting in any way contrary to the existing laws. III. That every man may enjoy this liberty without detriment to the public peace, and that no inconveniences arise therefrom which cannot easily be checked. IV. That every man may enjoy it without injury to his allegiance. V. That laws dealing with speculative problems are entirely useless. VI. Lastly, that not only may such liberty be granted without prejudice to the public peace, to loyalty, and to the rights of rulers, but that it is even necessary for their preservation. For when people try to take it away, and bring to trial, not only the acts which alone are capable of offending, but also the opinions of mankind, they only succeed in surrounding their victims with an appearance of martyrdom, and raise feelings of pity and revenge rather than of terror. Uprightness and good faith are thus corrupted, flatterers and traitors are encouraged, and sectarians triumph, inasmuch as concessions have been made to their animosity, and they have gained the state sanction for the doctrines of which they are the interpreters. Hence they arrogate to themselves the state authority and rights, and do not scruple to assert that they have been directly chosen by God, and that their laws are Divine, whereas the laws of the state are human, and should therefore yield obedience to the laws of God – in other words, to their own laws. Everyone must see that this is not a state of affairs conducive to public welfare. Wherefore, as we have shown in Chapter XVIII., the safest way for a state is to lay down the rule that religion is comprised solely in the exercise of charity and justice, and that the rights of rulers in sacred, no less than in secular matters, should merely have to do with actions, but that every man should think what he likes and say what he thinks.

I have thus fulfilled the task I set myself in this treatise. It remains only to call attention to the fact that I have written nothing which I do not most willingly submit to the examination and approval of my country's rulers; and that I am willing to retract anything which they shall decide to be repugnant to the laws, or prejudicial to the public good. I know that I am a man, and as a man liable to error, but against error I have taken scrupulous care, and have striven to keep in entire accordance with the laws of my country, with loyalty, and with morality.

Notes

1 "*No one can honestly promise to forego the right which he has over all things.*" In the state of social life, where general right determines what is good or evil, stratagem is rightly distinguished as of two kinds, good and evil. But in the state of Nature, where every man is his own judge, possessing the absolute right to lay down laws for himself, to interpret them as he pleases, or to abrogate them if he

thinks it convenient, it is not conceivable that stratagem should be evil.

2   "*Every member of it may, if he will, be free.*" Whatever be the social state a man finds himself in, he may be free. For certainly a man is free, in so far as he is led by reason. Now reason (though Hobbes thinks otherwise) is always on the side of peace, which cannot be attained unless the general laws of the state be respected. Therefore the more a man is led by reason – in other words, the more he is free, the more constantly will he respect the laws of his country, and obey the commands of the sovereign power to which he is subject.

PART IV

Nicolas Malebranche (1638–1715)

Introduction

Malebranche studied philosophy at the Collége de la Marche and theology at the Sorbonne, but it was his discovery in 1664 of Descartes's *Treatise on Man* (*L'Homme de René Descartes*) that bound him to philosophy. He would spend the next ten years working out the implications of this new mechanistic science for his Catholic philosophy. Our selections are taken from *The Search After Truth* (1674), *Treatise on Nature and Grace* (1680), and *Dialogues on Metaphysics and on Religion* (1688). In them Malebranche takes up many of the problems that concerned Descartes in the *Meditations* – the nature of ideas, perception of material objects, the possibility of avoiding error, God's existence and our knowledge of him – elaborating on Descartes's solutions and developing them in his own distinctive way.

10

The Search After Truth

The Pure Understanding. The Nature of Ideas

Chapter One

I. What is meant by ideas. That they really exist and are necessary in order to perceive any material object. II. A classification of all the ways external objects can be seen.

I. What is meant by ideas

I think everyone agrees that we do not perceive objects external to us by themselves. We see the sun, the stars, and an infinity of objects external to us; and it is not likely that the soul should leave the body to stroll about the heavens, as it were, in order to behold all these objects. Thus, it does not see them by themselves, and our mind's immediate object when it sees the sun, for example, is not the sun, but something that is intimately joined to our soul, and this is what I call an *idea*. Thus, by the word *idea*, I mean here nothing other than the immediate object, or the object closest to the mind, when it perceives something, i.e., that which affects and modifies the mind with the perception it has of an object.

It should be carefully noted that for the mind to perceive an object, it is absolutely necessary for the idea of that object to be actually present to it – and about this there can be no doubt; but there need

The Search After Truth (1674–5), tr. Thomas M. Lennon and Paul J. Olscamp (Columbus: Ohio State University Press, 1980). Selection: "The Pure Understanding. The Nature of Ideas," Bk 3, Part 2, chs 1–7, pp. 217–40.

not be any external thing like that idea. For it often happens that we perceive things that do not exist, and that even have never existed – thus our mind often has real ideas of things that have never existed. When, for example, a man imagines a golden mountain, it is absolutely necessary that the idea of this mountain really be present to his mind. When a madman or someone asleep or in a high fever sees some animal before his eyes, it is certain that what he sees is not nothing, and that therefore the idea of this animal really does exist, though the golden mountain and the animal have never existed.

Yet given that men are naturally led, as it were, to believe that only corporeal objects exist, they judge of the reality and existence of things other than as they should. For as soon as they perceive an object, they would have it as quite certain that it exists, although it often happens that there is nothing external. In addition, they would have the object be exactly as they see it, which never happens. But as for the idea that necessarily exists, and that cannot be other than as it is seen, they ordinarily judge unreflectingly that it is nothing – as if ideas did not have a great number of properties, as if the idea of a square, for example, were not different from that of a circle or a number, and did not represent completely different things, which can never be the case for nonbeing, since nonbeing has no properties. It is therefore indubitable that ideas have a very real existence. But now let us examine their nature and essence, and let us see what there can be in the soul that might represent all things to it.

Everything the soul perceives belongs to either one of two sorts: either it is in the soul, or outside the soul. The things that are in the soul are its own thoughts, i.e., all its various modifications – for by the words *thought, mode of thinking,* or *modification of the soul,* I generally understand all those things that cannot be in the soul without the soul being aware of them through the inner sensation it has of itself – such as its sensations, imaginings, pure intellections, or simply conceptions, as well as its passions and natural inclinations. Now, our soul has no need of ideas in order to perceive these things in the way it does, because these things are in the soul, or rather because they are but the soul itself existing in this or that way – just as the actual roundness and motion of a body are but that body shaped and moved in this or that way.

But as for things outside the soul, we can perceive them only by means of ideas, given that these things cannot be intimately joined to the soul. Of these, there are two sorts: spiritual and material. As for the spiritual, there is reason to believe they can be revealed to the soul by themselves and without ideas. For although experience teaches us that we cannot communicate our thoughts to one another immediately and by ourselves, but only through speech or some other sensible sign to which we have attached our ideas, still it might be said that God has established this state of affairs only for the duration of this life in order to prevent the disorder that would now prevail if men could communicate as they pleased. But when order and justice reign, and we are delivered from the captivity of our body, we shall perhaps be able to communicate through the intimate union among ourselves, as the angels seem to be able to do in heaven. Accordingly, it does not seem to be absolutely necessary to have ideas in order to represent spiritual things to the soul, because they might be seen through themselves, though in imperfect fashion.

I shall not inquire[1] here how two minds can be united, or whether they can in this way reveal their thoughts to each other. I believe, however, that the only purely intelligible substance is God's, that nothing can be revealed with clarity except in the light of this substance, and that a union of minds cannot make them visible to each other. For although we may be closely joined together, we are and shall be unintelligible to each other until we see each other in God, and until He presents us with the perfectly intelligible idea He has of our being contained in His being. Thus, although I may seem to allow that angels can by themselves show to each other both what they are and what they are thinking (which I really do not

believe), I warn that it is only because I have no desire to dispute the point – provided that you grant me what cannot be disputed, to wit, that you cannot see material things by themselves and without ideas.

In the seventh chapter I shall explain my view on how we know minds, and I shall show that for the moment we cannot know them entirely by themselves, although they might be capable of union with us. But here I am speaking mainly about material things, which certainly cannot be joined to our soul in the way necessary for it to perceive them, because with them extended and the soul unextended, there is no relation between them. Besides which, our souls do not leave the body to measure the heavens, and as a result, they can see bodies outside only through the ideas representing them. In this everyone must agree.

II. A classification of all the ways external objects can be seen

We assert the absolute necessity, then, of the following: either (a) the ideas we have of bodies and of all other objects we do not perceive by themselves come from these bodies or objects; or (b) our soul has the power of producing these ideas; or (c) God has produced them in us while creating the soul or produces them every time we think about a given object; or (d) the soul has in itself all the perfections it sees in bodies; or else (e) the soul is joined to a completely perfect being that contains all intelligible perfections, or all the ideas of created beings.

We can know objects in only one of these ways. Let us examine, without prejudice, and without fear of the difficulty of the question, which is the likeliest way. Perhaps we can resolve the question with some clarity though we do not pretend to give demonstrations that will seem incontrovertible to everyone; rather, we merely give proofs that will seem very persuasive to those who consider them carefully, for one would appear presumptuous were one to speak otherwise.

Chapter Two

That material objects do not transmit species resembling them

The most commonly held opinion is that of the Peripatetics, who hold that external objects transmit species that resemble them, and that these species are carried to the common sense by the external senses. They call these species *impressed*, because objects impress them on the external senses. These impressed species, being material and sensible, are made intelligible by the *agent*, or *active intellect*, and can then be received in the *passive intellect*. These species, thus spiritualized, are called *expressed* species, because they are expressed from the impressed species, and through them the *passive intellect* knows material things.

We shall not pause here to further investigate these lovely things and the different ways different philosophers conceive of them. For although they disagree about the number of faculties they attribute to the interior sense and to the understanding, and although there are many of them who doubt whether an *agent intellect* is needed in order to know sensible objects, still they practically all agree that external objects transmit species or images that resemble them, and with only this as their basis, they multiply their faculties and defend their *agent intellect*. As this basis has no solidity, as will be shown, it is not necessary to pause further in order to overthrow everything that has been built upon it.

We assert, then, that it is unlikely that objects transmit images, or species, that resemble them, and here are some reasons why. The first is drawn from the impenetrability of bodies. All objects (such as the sun, the stars, as well as those closer to our eyes) are unable to transmit species of a nature other than their own. This is why philosophers commonly say that these species are gross and material as opposed to the expressed species, which are spiritualized. These impressed species are therefore little bodies. They therefore cannot penetrate each other or the whole of the space between the earth and the heavens, which must be full of them. From this it is easy to conclude that they must run against and batter each other from all directions, and that hence they cannot make objects visible.

Furthermore, a great number of objects located in the sky and on earth can be seen from the same place or the same point; the species of all these objects would then have to be capable of being reduced to a point. Now since they are extended they are impenetrable; therefore, . . . and so on.

But not only can a great number of very large objects be seen from the same point; there is no point in the universe's vast stretches from which an almost infinite number of objects cannot be discovered, and even objects as large as the sun, moon, and heavens. In the entire world there is no point where the species of all these things ought not meet – which is contrary to all indications of the truth.

The second reason is based on the change that occurs in the species. It is certain that the closer an object is, the larger its species must be, since we see the object as larger. Now, I do not see what can make this species diminish or what can become of the parts composing it when it was larger. But what is even harder to understand on their view is how, if we look at this object with magnifying glasses or a microscope, the species suddenly becomes five or six hundred times larger than it was before, for still less do we see with what parts it can so greatly increase its size in an instant.

The third reason is that when we look at a perfect cube, all the species of its sides are unequal, and yet we see all its sides as equally square. And likewise when we look at a picture of ovals and parallelograms, which can transmit only species of the same shape, we see in it only circles and squares. This clearly shows that the object we are looking at need not produce species that resemble it in order for us to see it.

Finally, it is inconceivable how a body that does not sensibly diminish could continually emit species in all directions, or how it could continually fill the vast spaces around it with them – and all this with inconceivable speed. For a hidden object can be seen at the very moment of its discovery from several million leagues away and from every direction. And, what seems stranger still, very active bodies, such as air and a few others, lack the force to emit images resembling them – as coarser and less active bodies, such as earth, stones, and almost all hard bodies do.

But I do not wish to linger to adduce all the reasons opposed to this view, since it would be an endless task and the least mental effort will yield an inexhaustible number of them. Those we have just given are enough, and even they are not necessary after what was said about this subject in the first book, where the errors of the senses were explained. But so many philosophers hold this view that I thought it necessary to say something about it in order to provoke them to reflect on their thoughts.

Chapter Three

That the soul does not have the power to produce ideas. The cause of our error in this matter

The second view belongs to those who believe that our souls have the power of producing the ideas of the things they wish to think about, and that our souls are moved to produce them by the impressions that objects make on the body, though these impressions are not images resembling the objects causing them. According to them, it is in this that man is made after the image of God and shares in His power. Further, just as God created all things from nothing, and can annihilate them and create new things in their place, so man can create and annihilate ideas of anything he pleases. But there is good reason to distrust all these views that elevate man. These are generally thoughts that come from his pride and vanity, and not from the Father of lights.

This share in God's power that men boast of for representing objects to themselves and for several other particular actions is a share that seems to involve a certain independence (as it is generally explained). But it is also an illusory share, which men's ignorance and vanity makes them imagine. Their dependence upon the power and goodness of God is much greater than they think, but this is not the place to explain the matter. Let us try only to show that men do not have the power to form ideas of the things they perceive.

Since ideas have real properties, no one can doubt that they are real beings, or that they differ from one another, and that they represent altogether different things. Nor can it be reasonably doubted that they are spiritual and are very different from the bodies they represent. This seems to raise a doubt whether the ideas by means of which bodies are seen are not more noble than the bodies themselves. Indeed, the intelligible world must be more perfect than the material, terrestrial world, as we shall see in what follows. Thus, when it is claimed that men have the power to form such ideas as please them, one runs the risk of claiming that men have the power of creating beings worthier and more perfect than the world God has created. Yet this is never thought about, because an idea is fancied to be nothing since it cannot be sensed — or if it is considered as a being, it is only as a meager and insignificant being, because it is thought to be annihilated as soon as it is no longer present to the mind.

But even if it were true that ideas were only lesser and insignificant beings, still they are beings, and spiritual beings at that, and given that men do not have the power of creation, it follows that they are unable to produce them. For the production of ideas in the way they explain it is a true creation, and although they may try to palliate the temerity and soften the harshness of this view by saying that the production of ideas presupposes something whereas creation presupposes nothing, still they have not resolved the fundamental difficulty.

For it ought to be carefully noted that it is no more difficult to produce something from nothing than to produce it by positing another thing from which it cannot be made and which can contribute nothing to its production. For example, it is no more difficult to create an angel than to produce it from a stone, because given that a stone is of a totally contrary kind of being, it can contribute nothing to the production of an angel. But it can contribute to the production of bread, of gold, and such, because stone, gold, and bread are but the same extension differently configured, and they are all material things.

It is even more difficult to produce an angel from a stone than to produce it from nothing, because to make an angel from a stone (insofar as it can be done), the stone must first be annihilated and then the angel must be created, whereas simply creating an angel does not require anything to be annihilated. If, then, the mind produces its own ideas from the material impressions the brain receives from objects, it continuously does the same thing, or something as difficult, or even more difficult, as if it created them. Since ideas are spiritual, they cannot be produced from material images in the brain, with which they are incommensurable.

But if it be said that an idea is not a substance, I would agree — but it is still a spiritual thing, and as it is impossible to make a square out of a mind, though a square is not a substance, so a spiritual idea cannot be formed from a material substance, even though an idea is not a substance.

But even if the mind of man were granted a sovereign power of annihilating and creating the ideas of things, still it would never use it to produce them. For just as a painter, no matter how good he is at his art, cannot represent an animal he has never seen and of which he has no idea — so that the painting he would be required to produce could not be like this unknown animal — so a man could not form the idea of an object unless he knew it beforehand, i.e., unless he already had the idea of it, which idea does not depend on his will. But if he already has an idea of it, he knows the object, and it is useless for him to form another idea of it.

It is therefore useless to attribute to the mind of man the power of producing its ideas.

It might be said that the mind has general and confused ideas that it does not produce, and that those of its own making are clearer, more distinct, particular ideas. But this amounts to the same thing. For just as an artist cannot draw the portrait of an individual in such fashion that he could be certain of having done a proper job unless he had a distinct idea of the individual, and indeed unless the subject were to sit for it – so a mind that, for example, has only the idea of being or of animal in general cannot represent a horse to itself, or form a very distinct idea of it, or be sure that the idea exactly resembles a horse, unless it already has an initial idea against which it compares the second. Now if it already has one idea, it is useless to form a second, and therefore the question about the first idea, . . . , and so on.

It is true that when we conceive of a square through pure intellection, we can still imagine it, i.e., perceive it by tracing an image of it for ourselves in the brain. But it should be noted, first, that we are neither the true nor the principal cause of the image (but this is too long a matter to be explained here), and second, that far from being more distinct and more accurate than the first idea, the second idea accompanying the image is accurate only because it resembles the first, which serves as a model [regle] for the second. For ultimately, the imagination and the senses themselves should not be taken as representing objects to us more distinctly than does the pure understanding, but only as affecting and moving the mind more. For the ideas of the senses and of the imagination are distinct only to the extent that they conform to the ideas of pure intellection. The image of a square that the imagination traces in the brain, for example, is accurate and well formed only to the extent that it conforms to the idea of a square we conceive through pure intellection. It is this idea that governs the image. It is the mind that conducts the imagination and requires it, as it were, to consider occasionally whether the image it depicts is a figure composed of four straight and equal lines, and exactly right-angled – in a word, whether what one is imagining is like what one conceives.

After what has been said, I do not think anyone can doubt that those who claim the mind can form its own ideas of objects are mistaken, since they attribute to the mind the power of creating, and even of creating wisely and with order, although it has no knowledge of what it does – which is inconceivable. But the cause of their error is that men never fail to judge that a thing is the cause of a given effect when the two are conjoined, given that the true cause of the effect is unknown to them. This is why everyone concludes that a moving ball which strikes another is the true and principal cause of the motion it communicates to the other, and that the soul's will is the true and principal cause of movement in the arms, and other such prejudices – because it always happens that a ball moves when struck by another, that our arms move almost every time we want them to, and that we do not sensibly perceive what else could be the cause of these movements.

But when an effect does not so frequently follow something not its cause, there are still people who believe it to be caused by that thing, though not everyone falls into this error. For example, a comet appears and a prince dies, stones are exposed to the moon and are eaten by worms, the sun is in conjunction with Mars at the birth of a child and something extraordinary happens to the child. This is enough to convince many people that the comet, the moon, and the conjunction of the sun and Mars are the causes of the effects just noted and others like them; and the reason why not everyone is of the same belief is that these effects are not always observed to follow these things.

But given that all men generally have ideas of things present to the mind as soon as they want them, and that this occurs many times daily, practically everyone concludes that the will attending the production, or rather, the presence of ideas is their true cause, because at the time they see nothing they can assign as their cause, and because they believe that ideas cease to exist as soon as the mind ceases to perceive them and begin to exist again when they are represented to the mind. This is also why some people judge that external objects transmit images resembling them, as we have just pointed out in the preceding chapter. Unable to see objects by themselves, but only through their ideas, they judge that the object produces the idea – because as soon as it is present, they see it; as soon as it is absent, they no longer see it; and because the presence of the object almost always attends the idea representing it to us.

Yet if men were not so rash in their judgments, they would conclude from the fact that the ideas of things are present to their mind as soon as they wish, only this, that in the order of nature their will is generally necessary for them to have these ideas, but not that the will is the true and principal cause that presents ideas to their mind, and still less that the will produces them from nothing or in the way they explain it. They should conclude not that objects transmit species resembling them because the soul ordinarily perceives them only when they are present, but only that the object is ordinarily necessary for the idea to be present to the mind. Finally, because a ball does not have the power to move itself, they should not judge that a ball in motion is the true and principal cause of the movement of the ball it finds in its path. They can judge only that the collision of the two balls is the occasion for the Author of all motion in matter to carry out the decree of His will, which is the universal cause of all things. He does so by communicating to the second ball part of the motion of the first, i.e., to speak more clearly, by willing that the latter ball should acquire as much motion in the same direction as the former loses, for the motor force of bodies can only be the will of Him who preserves them, as we shall show elsewhere.

Chapter Four

That we do not perceive objects by means of ideas created with us. That God does not produce ideas in us each time we need them

The third view is held by those who would have it that all ideas are innate or created with us.

To see the implausibility of this view, it should be considered that there are in the world many totally different things of which we have ideas. But to mention only simple figures, it is certain that their number is infinite, and even if we fix upon only one, such as the ellipse, the mind undoubtedly conceives of an infinite number of different kinds of them when it conceives that one of its diameters may be infinitely lengthened while the other remains constant.

Likewise, an infinite number of different kinds of triangles can be conceived, given that the altitude can be infinitely increased or decreased while the base remains the same; moreover, and this is what I ask be noted here, the mind to some extent perceives this infinite number of triangles, although we can imagine very few of them and cannot simultaneously have particular and distinct ideas of many triangles of different kinds. But it should be especially noted that the mind's general idea of this infinite number of different kinds of

triangles suffices to prove that if we do not conceive of all these different triangles by means of particular ideas, in short, if we do not comprehend the infinite, the fault does not lie with our ideas, and that our failure to grasp the infinite is only for lack of capacity and scope of mind. If a man were to apply himself to an investigation of the properties of all the different kinds of triangles, and even if he should continue his investigation forever, he would never want for further particular ideas. But his mind would exhaust itself for no purpose.

What I have just said about triangles is applicable to figures of five, six, a hundred, a thousand, of ten thousand sides, and so on to infinity. And if the sides of a triangle can have infinite relations with each other, making an infinity of different kinds of triangles, it is easy to see that figures of four, five, or a million sides can have even greater differences, since they can have a greater number of relations and combinations of their sides than can simple triangles.

The mind, then, perceives all these things; it has ideas of them; it is certain that it will never want for ideas should it spend countless centuries investigating even a single figure, and that if it does not perceive these figures in an instant, or if it does not comprehend the infinite, this is only because of its very limited scope. It has, then, an infinite number of ideas – what am I saying? – it has as many infinite numbers of ideas as there are different figures; consequently, since there is an infinite number of different figures, the mind must have an infinity of infinite numbers of ideas just to know the figures.

Now, I ask whether it is likely that God created so many things along with the mind of man. My own view is that such is not the case, especially since all this could be done in another, much simpler and easier way, as we shall see shortly. For as God always acts in the simplest ways, it does not seem reasonable to explain how we know objects by assuming the creation of an infinity of beings, since the difficulty can be resolved in an easier and more straightforward fashion.

But even if the mind had a store of all the ideas necessary for it to perceive objects, yet it would be impossible to explain how the soul could choose them to represent them to itself, how, for example, the soul could make itself instantly perceive all the different objects whose size, figure, distance and motion it discovers when it opens its eyes in the countryside. Through this means it could not even perceive a single object such as the sun when it is before the body's eyes. For, since the image the sun imprints in the brain does not resemble the idea we have of it (as we have proved elsewhere), and as the soul does not perceive the motion the sun produces in the brain and in the fundus of the eyes, it is inconceivable that it should be able to determine precisely which among the infinite number of its ideas it would have to represent to itself in order to imagine or see the sun and to see it as having a given size. It cannot be said, then, that ideas of things are created with us, or that this suffices for us to see the objects surrounding us.

Nor can it be said that God constantly produces as many new ideas as there are different things we perceive. This view is refuted well enough by what has just been said in this chapter. Furthermore, we must at all times actually have in us the ideas of all things, since we can at all times will to think about anything – which we could not do unless we had already perceived them confusedly, i.e., unless an infinite number of ideas were present to the mind; for after all, one cannot will to think about objects of which one has no idea. Furthermore, it is clear that the idea, or immediate object of our mind, when we think about limitless space, or a circle in general, or indeterminate being, is nothing created. For no created reality can be either infinite or even general, as is what we perceive in these cases. But all this will be seen more clearly in what follows.

Chapter Five

That the mind sees neither the essence nor the existence of objects by considering its own perfections. That only God sees them in this way

The fourth view is that the mind needs only itself in order to see objects, and that by considering itself and its own perfections, it can discover all external things.

It is certain that the soul sees in itself, and without ideas, all the sensations and passions that affect it at the moment – pleasure, pain, cold, heat, colors, sounds, odors, tastes, its love and hatred, its joy and sadness, and all the rest – because none of the soul's sensations and passions represent anything resembling them outside the soul, and are but modifications of which a mind is capable. But the difficulty lies in knowing whether the ideas representing something outside the soul and resembling them to some extent (such as the ideas of the sun, of a house, a horse, a river, etc.) are merely modifications of the soul, as a result of which the mind would need only itself to represent external things to itself.

There are some people who do not hesitate to affirm that with the soul made for thinking, it has within itself all that it needs to perceive objects, i.e., by considering its own perfections, because given that the soul is indeed more noble than anything it distinctly conceives of, it can to some extent be said to contain them *eminently*, as the School would put it, i.e., in a way more noble and sublime than they are in themselves. They would have it that higher things contain the perfections of lower things in this way. Thus, given that they are the noblest creature they know of, these people claim to have within themselves in a spiritual way all that exists in the visible world, and to be able to modify themselves in such fashion as to perceive all that the human mind is capable of knowing. In a word, they would have the soul be like an intelligible world, which contains in itself all that the material and sensible world contains, and indeed, infinitely more.

But it seems to me rash to wish to maintain this view. Unless I am mistaken, it is natural vanity, love of independence, and the desire to be like Him who contains in Himself all beings that confound the mind and lead us to fancy that we possess what in fact we do not. "Say not that you are a light unto yourself," says Saint Augustine [Serm. 8, *De verbis Domini*], for only God is a light unto Himself and can see all that He has produced and might produce by considering Himself.

It cannot be doubted that only God existed before the world was created and that He could not have produced it without knowledge or ideas; consequently, the ideas He had of the world are not different from Himself, so that all creatures, even the most material and terrestrial, are in God, though in a completely spiritual way that is incomprehensible to us. God therefore sees within Himself all beings by considering His own perfections, which represent them to Him. He also knows their existence perfectly, because given that they depend for their existence on His will, and given that He cannot be ignorant of his own volitions, it follows that He cannot be ignorant of their existence, and consequently, God sees in Himself not only the essence of things but also their existence.

But such is not the case with created minds, which can see in themselves neither the essence nor the existence of things. They cannot see the essence of things within themselves since, given their own limitations, created minds cannot contain all beings as does God, who might be termed universal being, or simply, *He Who is* [Exod. 3:14], as He calls Himself. Therefore, since the human mind can know all beings, including infinite beings, and since it does not contain them, we have a sure proof that it does not see their essence in itself. For the mind not only sees things one after another in temporal succession, but it also perceives the infinite, though it does not comprehend it, as we have said in the preceding chapter. Consequently, being neither actually infinite nor capable of infinite modifications simultaneously, it is absolutely impossible for the mind to see in itself what is not there. It does not see the essence of things, therefore, by considering its own perfections or by modifying itself in different ways.

Nor does it see their existence in itself, because they do not depend for their existence upon its will, and because the ideas of things can be present to the mind though the things themselves might not exist. For everyone can have the idea of a golden mountain without there being a golden mountain in nature, and although one may rely on the reports of the senses to judge the existence of objects, nevertheless reason does not assure us that we should always believe our senses, since we clearly detect that they deceive us. When a man's blood is heated, for example, or simply when he is asleep, he sometimes sees country scenes, battles, and other such things before his eyes that are not present nor perhaps ever were. Undoubtedly, then, it is not in itself or though itself that the mind sees the existence of things, but rather it depends on something else for this.

Chapter Six

That we see all things in God

In the preceding chapters we have examined four different ways in which the soul might see external objects, all of which seem to us very unlikely. There remains only the fifth, which alone seems to conform to reason and to be most appropriate for exhibiting the dependence that minds have on God in all their thoughts.

To understand this fifth way, we must remember what was just said in the preceding chapter – that God must have within Himself the ideas of all the beings He has created (since otherwise he could not have created them), and thus He sees all these beings by considering the perfections He contains to which they are related. We should know, furthermore, that through His presence God is in close union with our minds, such that He might be said to be the place of minds as space is, in a sense, the place of bodies. Given these two things, the mind surely can see what in God represents created beings, since what in God represents created beings is very spiritual, intelligible, and present to the mind. Thus, the mind can see God's works in Him, provided that God wills to reveal to it what in Him represents them. The following are the reasons that seem to prove that He wills this rather than the creation of an infinite number of ideas in each mind.

Not only does it strictly conform to reason, but it is also apparent from the economy found throughout nature that God never does in very complicated fashion what can be done in a very simple and straightforward way. For God never does anything uselessly and without reason. His power and wisdom are not shown by doing lesser things with greater means – this is contrary to reason and indicates a limited intelligence. Rather, they are shown by doing greater things with very simple and straightforward means. Thus, it was with extension alone that He produced everything admirable we see in nature and even what gives life and movement to animals. For those who absolutely insist on substantial forms, faculties, and souls in animals (different from their blood and bodily organs) to perform their functions, at the same time would have it that God lacks intelligence, or that He cannot make all these remarkable things with extension alone. They measure the power and sovereign wisdom of God by the pettiness of their own mind. Thus, since God can reveal everything to minds simply by willing that they see what is in their midst, i.e., what in Him is related to and represents these things, there is no likelihood that He does otherwise, or that He does so by producing as many infinities of infinite numbers of ideas as there are created minds.

But it should be carefully noted that we cannot conclude from their seeing all things in God in this way that our minds see the essence of God. God's essence is His own absolute being, and minds do not see the divine substance taken absolutely but only as relative to creatures and to the degree that they can participate in it. What they see in God is very imperfect, whereas God is most perfect. They see matter that is shaped, divisible, and so on, but there is nothing divisible or shaped in God, for

God is all being, since He is infinite and comprehends everything; but He is not being in particular. Yet what we see is but one or more particular beings, and we do not understand this perfect simplicity of God, which includes all beings. In addition, it might be said that we do not so much see the ideas of things as the things themselves that are represented by ideas, for when we see a square, for example, we do not say that we see the idea of the square, which is joined to the mind, but only the square that is external to it.

The second reason for thinking that we see beings because God wills that what in Him representing them should be revealed to us (and not because there are as many ideas created with us as there are things we can perceive) is that this view places created minds in a position of complete dependence on God – the most complete there can be. For on this view, not only could we see nothing but what He wills that we see, but we could see nothing but what He makes us see. "Non sumus sufficientes cogitare aliquid a nobis, tamquam ex nobis, sed sufficientia nostra ex Deo est" [2 Cor. 3:5]. It is God Himself who enlightens philosophers in the knowledge that ungrateful men call natural though they receive it only from heaven. "Deus enim illis manifestavit" [Rom. 1:19]. He is truly the mind's light and the father of lights. "Pater luminum" [James 1:17] – it is He who teaches men knowledge – "Qui docet hominem scientiam" [Ps 93:10]. In a word, He is the true light that illumines everyone who comes into the world: "Lux vera quae illuminat omnem hominem venientem in hunc mundum" [John 1:9].

For after all, it is difficult enough to understand distinctly the dependence our minds have on God in all their particular actions, given that they have everything we distinctly know to be necessary for them to act, or all the ideas of things present to their mind. And that general and confused term concourse, by means of which we would explain creatures' dependence on God, rouses not a single distinct idea in an attentive mind; and yet it is good that men should distinctly know that they are capable of nothing without God.

But the strongest argument of all is the mind's way of perceiving anything. It is certain, and everyone knows this from experience, that when we want to think about some particular thing, we first glance over all beings and then apply ourselves to the consideration of the object we wish to think about. Now, it is indubitable that we could desire to see a particular object only if we had

already seen it, though in a general and confused fashion. As a result of this, given that we can desire to see all beings, now one, now another, it is certain that all beings are present to our mind; and it seems that all beings can be present to our mind only because God, i.e., He who includes all things in the simplicity of His being, is present to it.

It even seems that the mind would be incapable of representing universal ideas of genus, species, and so on, to itself had it not seen all beings contained in one. For, given that every creature is a particular being, we cannot say that we see a created thing when, for example, we see a triangle in general. Finally, I think that sense can be made of the way the mind knows certain abstract and general truths only through the presence of Him who can enlighten the mind in an infinity of different ways.

Finally, of the proofs of God's existence, the loftiest and most beautiful, the primary and most solid (or the one that assumes the least) is the idea we have of the infinite. For it is certain that (a) the mind perceives the infinite, though it does not comprehend it, and (b) it has a very distinct idea of God, which it can have only by means of its union with Him, since it is inconceivable that the idea of an infinitely perfect being (which is what we have of God) should be something created.

But not only does the mind have the idea of the infinite, it even has it before that of the finite. For we conceive of infinite being simply because we conceive of being, without thinking whether it is finite or infinite. In order for us to conceive of a finite being, something must necessarily be eliminated from this general notion of being, which consequently must come first. Thus, the mind perceives nothing except in the idea it has of the infinite, and far from this idea being formed from the confused collection of all our ideas of particular beings (as philosophers think), all these particular ideas are in fact but participations in the general idea of the infinite; just as God does not draw His being from creatures, while every creature is but an imperfect participation in the divine being.

Here is an argument that may prove demonstrative for those accustomed to abstract reasoning. It is certain that ideas are efficacious, since they act upon the mind and enlighten it, and since they make it happy or unhappy through the pleasant or unpleasant perceptions by which they affect it. Now nothing can act immediately upon the mind unless it is superior to it – nothing but God alone;

for only the Author of our being can change its modifications. All our ideas, therefore, must be located in the efficacious substance of the Divinity, which alone is intelligible or capable of enlightening us, because it alone can affect intelligences. "Insinuavit nobis Christus," says Saint Augustine [*Tract. 23 on St John*], "animam humanam & mentem rationalem non vegetari, non beatificari, NON ILLUMINARI NISI AB IPSA SUBSTANTIA DEI."

Finally, God can have no other special end for His actions than Himself. This is a notion common to all men capable of a little reflection, and Sacred Scripture allows no doubt that God made all things for Himself. Therefore, not only must our natural love, i.e., the impulse He produces in our mind, tend toward Him but also the knowledge and light He gives it must reveal to us something in Him, for everything coming from God can be only for God. If God had made a mind and had given the sun to it as an idea, or immediate object of knowledge, it seems to me God would have made this mind and its idea for the sun and not for Himself.

God can make a mind in order for it to know His works, then, only if that mind to some extent sees God in seeing His works. As a result, it might be said that if we do not to some extent see God, we see nothing, just as if we do not love God, i.e., if God were not continuously impressing upon us the love of good in general, we would love nothing. For, given that this love is our will, we could neither love nor will anything without it, since we can love particular goods only by directing toward these goods the impulse of love that God gives us for Himself. Thus, as we love something only through our necessary love for God, we see something only through our natural knowledge of God; and all our particular ideas of creatures are but limitations of the idea of the Creator, as all the impulses of the will toward creatures are only determinations of its impulse toward the Creator.

I do not think there are any theologians who will disagree that the impious love God with this natural love I am speaking about, and Saint Augustine and several other Fathers maintain as indubitable that the impious see eternal truths and moral rules in God. Accordingly, the view I am expounding should upset no one. Here is how Saint Augustine expresses it:

Ab illa incommutabilis luce veritatis etiam impius, dam ab ea avertitur, quodammodo tangitur. Hinc est quod etiam impii cogitant aeternitatem, & multa recte reprehendunt, recteque laudant in hominum moribus. Quibus ea tandem regulis judicant, nisi in quibus vident, quemadmodum quisque vivere debeat, etiam si nec ipsi eodem modo vivant? Ubi autem eas vident? Neque enim in sua natura. Nam cum procul dubio mente ista videantur, eorumque mentes constet esse mutabiles, has vero regulas immutabiles videat, quisquis in eis & hoc videre potuerit . . . ubinam ergo sunt istae regulae scriptae, nisi in libro lucis illius, quae veritas dicitur, unde lex omnis justa describitur . . . in qua videt quid operandum sit, etiam qui operatur injustitiam, & ipse est qui ab illa luce avertitur a qua tamen tangitur. [Book 14, *De Trin.* ch. 15]

Saint Augustine has an infinity of such passages by which he proves that we already see God in this life through the knowledge we have of eternal truths. The truth is uncreated, immutable, immense, eternal, and above all things. It is true by itself. It draws its perfection from no other thing. It renders creatures more perfect, and all minds naturally seek to know it. Only God can have all these perfections. Therefore, truth is God. We see some of these immutable, eternal truths. Therefore, we see God. These are the arguments of Saint Augustine – ours are somewhat different, and we have no wish to make improper use of the authority of so great a man in order to support our own view.

We are of the opinion, then, that truths (and even those that are eternal, such as that twice two is four) are not absolute beings, much less that they are God Himself. For clearly, this truth consists only in the relation of equality between twice two and four. Thus, we do not claim, as does Saint Augustine, that we see God in seeing truths, but in seeing the *ideas* of these truths – for the ideas are real, whereas the equality between the ideas, which is the truth, is nothing real. When we say, for example, that the cloth we are measuring is three ells long, the cloth and the ells are real. But the equality between them is not a real being – it is only a relation found between the three ells and the cloth. When we say that twice two is four, the ideas of the numbers are real, but the equality between them is only a relation. Thus, our view is that we see God when we see eternal truths, and not that these truths are God, because the ideas on which these truths depend are in God – it might even be that this was Saint Augustine's meaning. We further believe that changeable and corruptible things are known in God, though Saint Augustine speaks only of immutable and incorruptible things, because for this to be so, no imperfection need be placed in God, since, as we have already said, it is enough that God should reveal to us what in Him is related to these things.

But although I may say that we see material and sensible things in God, it must be carefully noted that I am not saying we have sensations of them in God, but only that it is God who acts in us; for God surely knows sensible things, but He does not sense them. When we perceive something sensible, two things are found in our perception: *sensation* and pure *idea*. The sensation is a modification of our soul, and it is God who causes it in us. He can cause this modification even though He does not have it Himself, because He sees in the idea He has of our soul that it is capable of it. As for the idea found in conjunction with the sensation, it is in God, and we see it because it pleases God to reveal it to us. God joins the sensation to the idea when objects are present so that we may believe them to be present and that we may have all the feelings and passions that we should have in relation to them.

We believe, finally, that all minds see eternal laws, as well as other things, in God, but with a certain difference. They know order and eternal truths, and even the beings that God has made according to these truths or according to order, through the union these minds necessarily have with the Word, or the wisdom of God, which enlightens them, as has just been explained. But it is through the impression they constantly receive from the will of God, who leads them toward Him and who tries, as it were, to make their will entirely like His own, that they realize that the immutable order is their own indispensable law, an order which thus includes all eternal laws, such as that we ought to love good and avoid evil, that justice should be prized more than all riches, that it is better to obey God than to command men, and an infinity of other natural laws. For the knowledge of all these laws, or of the obligation minds are under to conform to the immutable order, is not different from the knowledge of this impression, which they always feel in themselves, though they do not always follow it through the free choice of their will, and which they know to be common to all minds, though it is not equally strong in all minds.

It is through this dependence, this relation, this union of our mind with the Word of God, and of our will with His love, that we are made in the image and likeness of God. And though this image may be greatly effaced through sin, yet it must subsist as long as we do. But if we bear the image of the Word humiliated upon earth, and if we follow the impulses of the Holy Ghost, this union of our mind with the Word of the Father, and with the love of the Father and the Son, will be reestablished and made indelible. We shall be like God if we are like the God-man. Finally, God will be entirely in us, and we in Him in a way much more perfect than that by which we must be in Him and He in us that we might subsist.

These are some of the reasons that might lead one to believe that minds perceive everything through the intimate presence of Him who comprehends all in the simplicity of His being. Each of us will judge the matter according to the inner conviction he receives after seriously considering it. But I do not think there is any plausibility in any of the other ways of explaining these things, and this last way seems more than plausible. Thus, our souls depend on God in all ways. For just as it is He who makes them feel pain, pleasure, and all the other sensations, through the natural union He has established between them and our bodies, which is but His decree and general will, so it is He who makes them know all that they know through the natural union He has also established between the will of man and the representation of ideas contained in the immensity of the Divine being, which union is also but His general will. As a result of this, only He can enlighten us, by representing everything to us – just as only He can make us happy by making us enjoy all sorts of pleasures.

Let us hold this view, then, that God is the intelligible world or the place of minds, as the material world is the place of bodies; that from His power minds receive their modifications; that in His wisdom they find all their ideas; that through His love they receive their orderly impulses, and because His power and love are but Himself, let us believe with Saint Paul, that He is not far from any of us, and that in Him we live and move and have our being. "Non longe est ab unoquoque nostrum, in ipso enim vivimus, movemus, & sumus" [Acts 17:28].

Chapter Seven

I. The four different ways of perceiving things. II. How we know God. III. How we know bodies. IV.

How we know our own souls. V. How we know pure spirits and the souls of other men

In order to clarify and simplify the view I have just laid out concerning the way in which the mind perceives all the various objects of its knowledge, I must distinguish its four ways of knowing.

I. The four ways of perceiving things
The first is to know things by themselves.

The second is to know them through their ideas, i.e., as I mean it here, through something different from themselves.

The third is to know them through *consciousness*, or inner sensation.

The fourth is to know them through conjecture.

We know things by themselves and without ideas when they are intelligible by themselves, i.e., when they can act on the mind and thereby reveal themselves to it. For the understanding is a purely passive faculty of the soul, whereas activity is found only in the will. Even its desires are not the true causes of ideas – they are but the occasional or natural causes of their presence as a result of the natural laws concerning the union of our soul with universal Reason, as I have explained elsewhere. We know things through their ideas when they are not intelligible by themselves, whether because they are corporeal or because they cannot affect the mind or reveal themselves to it. Through consciousness we know everything that is not distinct from ourselves. Finally, through conjecture we know those things that are different both from ourselves and from what we know either in itself or through ideas, such as when we believe that certain things are like certain others we know.

II. How we know God
Only God do we know through Himself, for though there are other spiritual beings besides Him, which seem intelligible by their nature, only He can act on our mind and reveal Himself to it. Only God do we perceive by a direct and immediate perception. Only He can enlighten our mind with His own substance. Finally, only through the union we have with Him are we capable in this life of knowing what we know, as we have explained in the preceding chapter; for He is the only master, according to Saint Augustine, ruling our mind without the mediation of any creature.

I cannot conceive how a created thing can represent the infinite, how being that is without re-

striction, immense and universal, can be perceived through an idea, i.e., through a particular being different from universal and infinite being. But as far as particular beings are concerned, there is no difficulty in conceiving how they can be represented by the infinite being that contains them in His most efficacious and, consequently, most intelligible substance. Thus, it must be said that (a) we know God through Himself, though our knowledge of Him in this life is very imperfect, and (b) we know corporeal things through their ideas, i.e., in God, since only God contains the intelligible world, where the ideas of all things are located.

But while we can see all things in God, it does not follow that we in fact do so – we see in God only the things of which we have ideas, and there are things we perceive without ideas, or know only through sensation.

III. How we know bodies
Everything in this world of which we have some knowledge is either a mind or a body, a property of a mind or a property of a body. Undoubtedly, we know bodies with their properties through their ideas, because given that they are not intelligible by themselves, we can perceive them only in that being which contains them in an intelligible way. Thus, it is in God and through their ideas that we perceive bodies and their properties, and for this reason, the knowledge we have of them is quite perfect – i.e., our idea of extension suffices to inform us of all the properties of which extension is capable, and we could not wish for an idea of extension, figure, or motion more distinct or more fruitful than the one God gives us.

As the ideas of things in God include all their properties, whoever sees their ideas can also see all their properties successively; for when we see things as they are in God, we always see them in perfect fashion, and the way we see them would be infinitely perfect if the mind seeing them were infinite. What is lacking to our knowledge of extension, figures, and motion is the shortcoming not of the idea representing it but of our mind considering it.

IV. How we know our own soul
Such is not the case with the soul, [which] we do not know through its idea – we do not see it in God; we know it only through *consciousness*, and because of this, our knowledge of it is imperfect. Our knowledge of our soul is limited to what we sense taking place in us. If we had never sensed

pain, heat, light, and such, we would be unable to know whether the soul was capable of sensing these things, because we do not know it through its idea. But if we saw in God the idea corresponding to our soul, we would at the same time know, or at least could know all the properties of which it is capable – as we know, or at least can know, all the properties of which extension is capable, because we know extension through its idea.

It is true that we know well enough through our consciousness, or the inner sensation we have of ourselves, that our soul is something of importance. But what we know of it might be almost nothing compared to what it is in itself. If all we knew about matter were some twenty or thirty figures it had been modified by, we certainly would know almost nothing about it in comparison with what we can know about it through the idea representing it. To know the soul perfectly, then, it is not enough to know only what we know through inner sensation – since the consciousness we have of ourselves perhaps shows us only the least part of our being.

From what we have just said it might be concluded that although we know the existence of our soul more distinctly than the existence of both our own body and those surrounding us, still our knowledge of the soul's nature is not as perfect as our knowledge of the nature of bodies, and this might serve to reconcile the differing views of those who say that nothing is known better than the soul, and those who claim to know nothing less.

This might also serve to prove that the ideas which represent to us things outside us are not modifications of our soul. For if the soul saw all things by considering its own modifications, it would have to know its own nature or essence more clearly than that of bodies, and all the sensations or modifications of which it is capable more clearly than the figures or modifications of which bodies are capable. However, it knows itself capable of a given sensation not through the perception it has of itself in consulting its idea but only through experience, whereas it knows that extension is capable of an infinite number of figures through the idea it has of extension. There are even certain sensations like colors and sounds which are such that most people cannot tell whether or not they are modifications of the soul, but there is no figure that everyone, through the idea he has of extension, does not recognize as the modification of a body.

What I have just said also shows why the modifications of the soul cannot be made known through definition; for since we know neither the soul nor its modifications through ideas but only through sensation, and since such sensations as, for example, pleasure, pain, heat, and so on, are not attached to any words, it is clear that if someone had never seen color or felt heat, he could not be made to know these sensations through any definition of them that might be given him. Now, given that men have their sensations only on account of their body, and given that their bodies are not all disposed in the same way, it often happens that words are equivocal, that the words we use to express the modifications of our soul mean just the opposite of what we intend, and that we often make people think of bitterness, for example, when we believe we are making them think of sweetness.

Although our knowledge of our soul is not complete, what we do know of it through consciousness or inner sensation is enough to demonstrate its immortality, spirituality, freedom, and several other attributes we need to know. And this seems to be why God does not cause us to know the soul, as He causes us to know bodies, through its idea. The knowledge that we have of our soul through consciousness is imperfect, granted; but it is not false. On the other hand, that knowledge we have of bodies through sensation or consciousness, if the confused sensation we have of what takes place in our body can be called consciousness, is not only imperfect, but also false. We therefore needed an idea of the body to correct our sensations of it – but we need no idea of our soul, since our consciousness of it does not involve us in error, and since to avoid being mistaken in our knowledge of it, it is enough not to confuse it with the body – and reason enables us to do this since our idea of the body reveals to us that the modalities of which it is capable are quite different from those we sense. Finally, if we had an idea of the soul as clear as that which we have of the body, that idea would have inclined us too much to view the soul as separated from the body. It would have thus diminished the union between our soul and body by preventing us from regarding it as dispersed through all our members, though I shall not further explain the matter here.

V. How we know other men's souls
Of all the objects of our knowledge, only the souls of other men and pure intelligences remain; and

clearly we know them only through conjecture. At present we do not know them either in themselves or through their ideas, and as they are different from ourselves, we cannot know them through consciousness. We conjecture that the souls of other men are of the same sort as our own. We suppose them to feel what we feel in ourselves, and even when these sensations have no relation to the body, we are certain we are not mistaken because we see in God certain ideas and immutable laws from which we know with certainty that God acts uniformly in all minds.

I know that twice two is four, that it is better to be just than rich, and I am not mistaken in believing that others know these truths as well as I do. I love pleasure and good, I abhor pain and evil, I want to be happy, and I am not mistaken in believing that all men, the angels, and even demons have these same inclinations. I even know that God will never make a mind that does not desire to be happy, or that can desire to be unhappy. But I know this with evidence and certainty because it is God who teaches it to me – for

who else but God could reveal to me His designs and volitions? But when the body plays a part in what happens in me, I am almost always mistaken in judging others by myself. I feel heat, I see something of a certain size, a certain color, I taste such and such a flavor upon the approach of certain bodies – but I am mistaken if I judge others by myself. I am subject to certain passions, I have a liking or an aversion for such and such things, and I judge that others are like me – but my conjecture is often false. Thus, the knowledge we have of other men is very liable to error if we judge them only by the sensations we have of ourselves.

If there are beings different from God and ourselves, as well as from bodies and pure spirits, they are unknown to us. I can hardly persuade myself of their existence, and after examining the arguments of certain philosophers holding that there are these things, I have found them unsound. This reinforces our view that since all men have the same nature, we all have the same ideas, because we all need to know the same things.

Note

1 This paragraph is italicized because you may omit it as being too difficult to understand unless you know my views about the soul and the nature of ideas.

11

Treatise on Nature and Grace

Illustration: What It Is to Act by General Wills, and by Particular Wills

I

I say that God acts by general wills, when he acts in consequence of general laws which he has established. For example, I say that God acts in me by general wills when he makes me feel pain at the time I am pricked; because in consequence of the general and efficacious laws of the union of the soul and the body which he has established, he makes me feel pain when my body is ill-disposed.

In the same way, when a ball strikes a second one, I say that God moves the second by a general will, because he moves it in consequence of the general and efficacious laws of the communication of motion – God having generally established that at the moment that two bodies strike, the motion is divided between the two according to certain proportions; and it is through the efficacy of this general will that bodies have the power to move each other.

II

I say on the contrary that God acts by particular wills when the efficacy of his will is not determined at all by some general law to produce

Treatise on Nature and Grace (1680), tr. Patrick Riley (New York: Oxford University Press, 1992). Selection: "Illustration: What It Is to Act by General Wills, and by Particular Wills," pp. 195–6.

some effect. Thus, supposing that God makes me feel the pain of pinching without there happening in my body, or in any creature whatsoever, any changes which determine him to act in me according to general laws – I say then that God acts by particular wills.

In the same way, supposing that a body begins to move itself without being struck by another, or without any change in the will of minds, or in any other creature that determines the efficacy of some general laws, I say then that God moves this body by a particular will.

III

According to these definitions, one sees that, far from denying Providence, I suppose on the contrary that it is God who does all in all things; that the nature of the pagan philosophers is a chimera; and that, properly speaking, what is called *nature* is nothing other than the general laws which God has established to construct or to preserve his work by very simple means, by an action which is uniform, constant, perfectly worthy of an infinite wisdom and of a universal cause. But that which I suppose here, though certain for reasons which I have given elsewhere, is not absolutely necessary to what I plan to prove. For if one will have it that God has communicated his power to creatures, in such a way that the bodies which surround us have a real and veritable power by which they can act upon our soul and make it happy or unhappy through pleasure and pain, and that bodies, in moving, have in themselves a certain entity which is called *impressed quality* which they can diffuse in those that they meet with, and diffuse it with that promptitude and that uniformity which we observe – it will still be equally easy for me to prove what I claim. For then the efficacy of the action of the concourse of the general cause will be necessarily determined by the action of the particular cause. God, for example, will be obliged, according to these principles, to lend his concourse to a body at the moment that it strikes others, in order that this body can communicate motion to them – which is always to act in virtue of a general law. I do not, none the less, reason according to this supposition, because I believe it false in every way, as I have made clear in the third chapter of the second part of the sixth book of *Recherche de la vérité*, in the illustration of this same chapter, and elsewhere. These truths supposed, here are the marks by which one can recognize whether an effect is produced by a general will, or by a particular will.

12

Dialogues on Metaphysics and on Religion

Dialogue VI

Proofs of the existence of bodies drawn from revelation. Two kinds of revelation. How it happens that the natural revelations of sensations are an occasion for error for us

ARISTES. What a difficult question you have given me to solve, Theodore! I was quite right to tell you that it was up to you, who know the strengths and weaknesses of the sciences and the utility and fecundity of their principles, to direct my steps in that intelligible world to which you transported me. For I confess I do not know where I should turn. What you have taught me can indeed aid me in preventing me from straying in that unknown land. To this end I need simply follow the light, step by step, and yield only to the evidence attending clear ideas. But it is not enough to advance; we also have to know where we are going. It is not enough constantly to discover new truths; we must know the location of these fertile truths which bestow on the mind all the perfection of which it is now capable, these truths which should regulate the judgments we must make concerning God and His admirable works, and should regulate the movements of our heart

Dialogues on Metaphysics and on Religion (1688), ed. Nicholas Jolley, tr. David Scott (Cambridge University Press, 1997). Selection: Dialogue 6, "Proofs of the existence of bodies drawn from revelation. Two kinds of revelation. How it happens that the natural revelations of sensations are an occasion for error for us," pp. 89–103.

and give us a taste, or at least a foretaste, of the sovereign good we desire.

If, in choosing from the sciences, we had to adhere to evidence alone without considering utility, arithmetic would be preferable to all the others. Numerical truths are the clearest of all, since all other relations are clearly known only insofar as they can be expressed through measures common to all the exact relations measured by unity. And this science is so fertile and profound that, were I to spend ten thousand centuries penetrating its depths, I would still discover an inexhaustible store of clear and luminous truths. However, I do not think you will find it very appropriate that, being charmed by the evidence radiating there from all sides, we go in that direction. For, after all, how would delving into the most hidden mysteries of arithmetic and algebra help us? It is not enough to race through many countries, to penetrate deeply into sterile lands, to discover places where no one ever was. We must proceed straight to those happy countries where we find fruits in abundance, solid foods capable of nourishing us.

Thus, when I compared the sciences to each other according to my lights, their various advantages either in terms of their evidence or their utility, I found myself in an odd predicament. Sometimes the fear of falling into error gave preference to the exact sciences, like arithmetic and geometry, the demonstrations of which admirably satisfy our vain curiosity. And sometimes the desire to know not the relations of ideas among themselves, but the relations of the works of God, among which we live, both among themselves and to us, involved me in physics, morality, and the other sciences which often depend on experiences and fairly uncertain phenomena. It is a strange thing, Theodore, that the most useful sciences are full of impenetrable obscurities, and that we find a sure and rather easy and single path in those which are not so necessary! Now, please tell me how to evaluate fairly the relation between the easiness of the former and utility of the latter, in order to given preference to the science that deserves it. And how can we be sure that those very sciences which seem the most useful are so in fact, and that those which seem merely evident do not have great uses which go unnoticed? I admit, Theodore, that after having thought a lot about this, I still do not know how to decide.

I. THEODORE. You have not wasted your time, my dear Aristes, in the reflections you have made. For although you do not exactly know what you should apply yourself to, I am already well assured you will not engage in a number of false studies, in which half the world is seriously involved. Indeed I am certain that were I to make a mistake in choosing the subject of our conversation, you would be able to set me aright. When people raise their head and look in all directions, they do not always follow those who go in front. They follow them only when they go where they must go or want to go themselves. And when the leader of the pack imprudently sets out on routes which are dangerous and end up nowhere, the others force him back. Thus, continue your reflections on your steps and on mine. Do not rely too much on me. Observe carefully whether I lead you where we both should go.

Thus, take note, Aristes. There are two kinds of sciences. Some consider the relations between ideas, others the relations between things by means of their ideas. The former are evident in every way, the latter can be so only by assuming that things are similar to the ideas we have of them, on the basis of which we reason about them. These latter sciences are quite useful, but they are shrouded in great obscurity, because they assume facts whose truth it is very difficult to know exactly. But if we were able to find some means of assuring ourselves of the fairness of our assumptions, we would be able to avoid error and at the same time discover those truths which closely concern us. For, once again, the truths or relations of ideas among themselves concern us when they represent the relations which obtain between the things that have some connection to us.

Hence, it seems to me evident that the best use we can make of our mind is to examine what the things are which have some connection to us, what the various kinds of connections are, what their cause is, what their effects are; and all of this in conformity with clear ideas and irrefutable experiences, the former of which assure us of the nature and properties of things, the latter of which assure us of the relation and connection they have to us. However, in order not to become trivial and useless, our entire examination must be directed only toward what renders us happy and perfect. Thus, to reduce all this to a few words, it seems evident to me that the best use we could make of our mind is to attempt to acquire an understanding of the truths we believe through faith, and of everything that leads to their confirmation. For no comparison can be made between the utility of these truths and the advantage to be derived from the knowledge of other truths. True, we believe these great truths. But faith does not exempt those who can from filling their mind with such truths and convincing themselves of them in all possible ways. For, on the contrary, faith is given to us to regulate, on its basis, all the steps of our mind as well as all the movements of our heart. It is given to us to guide us to the understanding of the very truths it teaches us. There are so many people who scandalize the faithful by means of an extravagant metaphysics and who insultingly require proofs of what they should believe on the infallible authority of the church, that although the solidity of your faith renders you impervious to their attacks, your charity should lead you to remedy the disorder and confusion they wreak everywhere. Do you approve then, Aristes, of the plan I am proposing for the course of our discussions?

ARISTES. Yes, I certainly do. But I did not think you would want to give up metaphysics. Had I thought that, it seems to me I would have indeed resolved the question of preference in the sciences. For it is clear that no discovery is comparable to an understanding of the truths of faith. I believed you simply wanted to make me something of a philosopher and a good metaphysician.

II. THEODORE. That is still all I am thinking of and I do not plan to abandon metaphysics, although in what follows I shall perhaps take the liberty of going beyond its usual limits. This general science rules over all the others. It can draw examples from them and a little detail which is necessary to render its general principles sensible.

For by metaphysics I do not mean those abstract considerations of certain imaginary properties, the principal use of which is to furnish the wherewithal for endless dispute to those who want to dispute. By this science I mean the general truths which can serve as principles for the particular sciences.

I am persuaded, Aristes, that it is necessary to be a good philosopher to gain understanding of the truths of faith; and that the stronger we are in the true principles of metaphysics, the stronger we are in the truths of religion. I am assuming, you may well think, what is necessary to make this proposition admissible. But no, I shall never believe that the true philosophy is opposed to faith and that good philosophers can have different opinions from good Christians. For whether Jesus Christ in His divinity speaks to philosophers in their innermost being or instructs Christians through the visible authority of the church, it is impossible that He contradict Himself, although it is quite possible to imagine contradictions in His pronouncements or take our own decisions for His pronouncements. Truth speaks to us in various ways, but it certainly always says the same thing. Therefore, we must not oppose philosophy and religion, unless it is the false philosophy of the pagans, the philosophy founded on human authority, in short, all those non-revealed opinions which do not bear the character of truth, that invincible evidence which compels attentive minds to submit. By the metaphysical truths we have discovered in our foregoing discussions you can judge whether the true philosophy contradicts religion. On my part I am convinced it does not. For were I to present you with several propositions contrary to the truths Jesus Christ teaches us through the visible authority of His church, as these propositions are based solely in me and do not bear that character of invincible evidence, they in no way belong to the true and sound philosophy. But I do not know why I forbear telling you truths which are impossible to doubt, however little attention we have given them.

ARISTES. Allow me to tell you, Theodore, that I was delighted to see a wonderful relation between what you taught me, or rather between what reason taught me through you, and those great and necessary truths which the authority of the church makes the simple and ignorant believe, whom God desires to save as much as philosophers. For instance, you have convinced me of the corruption of my nature and of the necessity

of a savior. I know that all intellects have only one single and unique master, the divine Word, and that only Reason, incarnate and rendered sensible, can deliver carnal people from the blindness into which we are all born. I grant you, with an extreme satisfaction, that these fundamental truths of our faith and many others I would be too long telling you are the necessary consequences of the principles you have demonstrated to me. Please continue. I shall try to follow you wherever you lead me.

THEODORE. Ah, my dear Aristes, take care once again that I do not go astray. I fear you are too easy on me, and that your approval prompts me into a certain negligence and causes me to fall into error. Fear for me, and mistrust everything someone subject to illusion can tell you. Moreover, you will learn nothing unless your reflections put you in possession of the truths I shall try to demonstrate to you.

III. There are only three kinds of beings about which we have any knowledge and to which we can have any connection: God, or the infinitely perfect Being who is the principle or cause of all things; minds, which we know only through the inner feeling we have of our nature; and bodies, of the existence of which we are assured by the revelation we have of them. Now what we call a human being is but a composite . . .

ARISTES. Easy, Theodore. I know there is a God or an infinitely perfect Being [Dialogue II]. For if I think of it – and I certainly do think of it – it must exist, for nothing finite can represent the infinite. I also know that minds exist, assuming there are beings resembling me [Dialogue I]. For I cannot doubt that I think, and I know that whatever thinks is something different from extension or matter. You have proved these truths to me. But what do you mean, that we are assured of the existence of bodies "by the revelation we have of them"? What! Do we not see them, do we not sense them? We do not need "revelation" to teach us that we have a body when we are pricked; we sense it quite clearly.

THEODORE. Yes, undoubtedly, we do sense it. But that sensation of pain we have is a kind of "revelation." This expression strikes you. But it is for just this reason that I use it. For you always forget that it is God Himself who produces in our soul all those various sensations by which it is affected on the occasion of the changes that happen to our body, as a result of the general laws of the union of the two substances composing humans; laws which are simply the efficacious and continual volitions of the creator, as I shall explain to you in the following. The point which pricks our hand does not cause pain by the hole it makes in the body. Nor is it the soul which produces this uncomfortable sensation in itself, since it suffers the pain despite itself. Assuredly it is a superior power. It is therefore God Himself, who through the sensations with which He affects us reveals to us what is happening outside us – I mean in our body and in those bodies surrounding us. Remember, please, what I have already told you so often.

IV. ARISTES. I was wrong, Theodore. But what you are saying evokes a very strange thought in my mind. I almost dare not suggest it to you, for I fear you will consider me a visionary. It is that I am beginning to doubt that bodies exist. The reason is that the revelation God gives us of their existence is not sure. For, after all, it is certain we sometimes see things that do not exist, as when we sleep or when fever causes some disturbance in the brain. If, as you say, God can sometimes give us deceptive sensations in consequence of His general laws, if He can reveal false things to us through our senses, why could He not do this constantly, and how could we discern truth from falsehood in the obscure and confused testimony of our senses? It seems to me that prudence obliges me to suspend my judgment concerning the existence of bodies. Please give me an exact demonstration of their existence.

THEODORE. "An exact demonstration"! That is a little too much, Aristes. I confess I do not have one. On the contrary, it seems to me that I have an "exact demonstration" of the impossibility of such a demonstration. However, be reassured. I am not lacking in proofs which are certain and capable of dispelling your doubt, and I am pleased such a doubt has occurred to you. For, after all, doubting that bodies exist for reasons which make it impossible to doubt God's existence and the incorporeality of the soul is a certain sign that we have risen above our prejudices and that, instead of subjecting reason to the senses, as most people do, we acknowledge its right to sovereign judgment in us. Unless I am deceived, here is a demonstrative proof that it is impossible to provide an exact demonstration of the existence of bodies.

V. The notion of the infinitely perfect Being does not contain a necessary relation to any creature. God is completely self-sufficient. Matter, therefore, is not a necessary emanation of the divinity. At least – and this is enough for the present – it is not evident that it is a necessary emanation of it. Now, we can give an "exact demonstration" of a truth only when we show that it has a necessary connection with its principle, only when we show that there is a necessary relation contained in the ideas we are comparing. Thus, it is not possible to demonstrate rigorously that bodies exist.

Actually, the existence of bodies is arbitrary. If there are any, it is because God willed to create them. Now, the same does not hold true of that volition to create bodies as holds true of the volitions to punish crimes and reward good deeds, to require love and fear from us, and so on. These and a thousand other similar volitions of God are necessarily contained in divine Reason, in that substantial law which is the inviolable rule of the volitions of the infinitely perfect Being, and generally of all intellects. But the volition to create bodies is not necessarily contained in the notion of the infinitely perfect Being, of the Being which is fully self-sufficient. Far from it; that notion seems to exclude such a volition from God. Thus, there is no way apart from revelation by which we can be assured that God has indeed willed to create bodies, as long as you assume what you no longer doubt, namely that bodies are not visible by themselves, that they can neither act on our mind nor be represented to it, and that our mind itself can know them only in the ideas representing them and sense them only through its modalities or sensations, and that it can be the cause of these only as a result of the arbitrary laws of the union of the soul and body.

VI. ARISTES. I quite understand, Theodore, that we cannot demonstratively deduce the existence of bodies from the notion of the infinitely perfect and self-sufficient Being, because the volitions of God relating to the world are not contained in the notion we have of Him. Now, as only these volitions can give existence to creatures it is clear that we cannot demonstrate that bodies exist. For we can demonstrate only those truths which have a necessary connection to their principle. Thus, since we cannot be assured of the existence of bodies through the evidence of a demonstration, there is no further way but through the authority of revelation. But this way does not seem sure to me. For although in the notion of the infinitely perfect Being I clearly discover that He cannot will to deceive me, experience teaches me that His revelations are deceptive. These are two truths which I cannot reconcile. For, after all, we often have sensations which reveal falsehoods to us. People feel pain in an arm they no longer have. All those whom we call mad see objects before them that do not exist. And perhaps there is no one who in sleep has not often been thoroughly unsettled and distressed by mere phantoms. God is not a deceiver. He cannot will to deceive anyone, neither the mad nor the wise. Yet nonetheless we are completely seduced by the sensations by which He affects us and through which He reveals the existence of bodies to us. Thus, it is quite certain that we are frequently deceived. But it seems less certain to me that we are not always deceived. Let us see, therefore, on what foundation you are basing the certainty you claim to possess that bodies exist.

VII. THEODORE. In general there are two kinds of revelations. Some are natural, others supernatural. I mean that some occur as a consequence of certain general laws which are known to us, according to which the author of nature acts in our mind on the occasion of what happens to our body. Others occur through general laws which are unknown to us, or through particular volitions added to the general laws to remedy the disagreeable effects they have because of the sin which has disordered everything. Now the former and the latter revelations, the natural and the supernatural, are true in themselves. But the former are now an occasion for error, not because they are false by themselves but because we do not put them to the use for which they were given to us, and because sin has corrupted nature and introduced a kind of contradiction into the relation the general laws have to us. Certainly the general laws of the union of the soul and the body, as a consequence of which God reveals to us that we have a body and that we exist in the midst of many other bodies, are very wisely established. Recall our previous discussions. They are not deceptive by themselves, in their institution, considered as they were before sin and in the design of their author. For we must realize that before his sin, before his blindness and the turmoil that the rebellion of his body caused in his mind, man clearly knew by the light of Reason:

1. That God alone can act in him, render him happy or unhappy through pleasure or pain, in short, modify or affect him.

2. He knew by experience that God always affected him in the same way in the same circumstances.

3. Thus, he recognized by experience as well as by Reason that the action of God was and had to be uniform.

4. Hence, he was determined to believe that there were beings which were the occasional causes of the general laws according to which he sensed that God acted on him. For, once again, he knew very well that God alone acted on him.

5. Whenever he wanted, he was able to prevent himself from sensing the action of sensible objects.

6. The inner feeling he had of his own volitions and of the respectful and submissive action of these objects taught him, therefore, that they were inferior to him, because they were subordinate to him, for then everything was perfectly in accordance with the divine order.

7. Thus, consulting the clear idea joined to the sensation by which he was affected on the occasion of these objects, he saw clearly that they were only bodies, since this idea represents only bodies.

8. He concluded, therefore, that the various sensations by which God affected him were simply revelations by which God taught him that he had a body and was surrounded by many other bodies.

9. But, knowing by Reason that God's action had to be uniform, and knowing by experience that the laws of the union of the soul and body were always the same; seeing indeed that these laws were established simply to inform him of what he had to do to preserve his life, he easily discovered that he must not judge the nature of bodies by the sensations he had of them, nor let himself be persuaded of their existence by these same sensations, except when his brain was agitated by an external cause and not by a movement of animal spirits excited by an internal cause. He was able to recognize when it was that external cause which produced actual traces in his brain, because the course of animal spirits was perfectly subject to his volitions. Thus, he was not like mad or feverish people, nor like us when we are asleep, subject to taking phantoms for reality; because he could discern whether the traces in his brain were produced by the internal and involuntary course of the animal spirits, or by the action of objects, the former course being voluntary in him and dependent on his practical desires. All this seems evident to me and a necessary consequence of two incontestable truths: first, that before sin man had very clear ideas and his mind was free from prejudices; second, that his body, or at least the principal part of his brain, was perfectly subordinated to him.

If this is granted, Aristes, you can indeed see that the general laws, as a result of which God gives us these sensations or natural revelations which assure us of the existence of bodies and of the relation they have to us, are very wisely established; you see that these revelations are in no way deceptive by themselves. Nothing could have been done better, for the reasons I have already stated. How is it, then, that they now cast us into an infinity of errors? Surely it is because our mind is dimmed, because we are full of prejudices from childhood, because we do not know how to put our senses to the use for which they were given to us. And all this is so, take note, precisely because through our own fault we have lost the power we should have over the principal part of the brain, over that part in which every change is always followed by some new thought. For our union with universal Reason is extremely weakened by our dependence on our body. For, after all, our mind is so situated between God who enlightens us and the body which blinds us, that the more it is united to the one, of necessity the less it is united to the other.

As God exactly follows and must exactly follow the laws He has established of the union of the two substances of which we are composed, and because we have lost the power to prevent the traces which the rebellious animal spirits effect in the brain, we take phantoms for realities. But the cause of our error does not come precisely from the falsity of our natural revelations, but from the imprudence and temerity of our judgments, from our ignorance of the path God must take, from the disorder which, in short, sin has caused in all our faculties, and from the confusion it has introduced into our ideas, not by changing the laws of the union of the soul and body, but by elevating our body and through its rebellion depriving us of the power to put these laws to the use for which they were established. You will understand all this more clearly in our following discussions, or when you have meditated on it. However, Aristes, notwithstanding everything I have just said, I do not see that there can be any good reason to doubt that bodies exist generally. For if I am deceived in respect of the existence of a particular body, I see very well that this is because God follows exactly the laws of the union of the soul and body; I see that it is because the uniformity of God's action cannot be disturbed by the irregularity of ours, and because the loss we suffered through our own fault of the power we had over our body need not have

changed anything in the laws of its union with our soul. This reason suffices to prevent me from being deceived about the existence of a particular body. I am not invincibly led to believe that it exists. But I do not have this reason, and I do not see it is possible to find any other reason to prevent me from believing generally that bodies exist despite all the various sensations I have of them, sensations so consistent, so linked together, so well ordered, that it seems to me certain that God would be deceiving us if there were nothing in everything we see.

VIII. But to deliver you completely from your speculative doubt, faith furnishes us with a demonstration which is impossible to resist. For whether bodies do or do not exist it is certain that we see them and that only God can give us sensations of them. Thus, it is God who presents to my mind the appearances of the people with whom I live, of the books I study, of the preachers I hear. Now, in the appearance of the New Testament I read of the miracles of a Man–God, His Resurrection, His Ascension into heaven, the preaching of the apostles, His joyful success, the establishment of the church. I compare all this with what I know from history, with the law of the Jews, with the prophets of the Old Testament. These are still only appearances. Yet once again I am certain that it is God alone who gives them to me, and that He is not a deceiver. I then compare anew all the appearances I just mentioned with the idea of God, the beauty of religion, the sanctity of morality, the necessity of a creed, and finally I find myself led to believe what faith teaches us. In short, I believe it without needing completely rigorous, demonstrative proof. For nothing seems more irrational to me than lack of faith, nothing more imprudent than not submitting to the greatest authority possible concerning those matters which we cannot examine with geometrical precision, either because we lack the time or for a thousand other reasons. People need an authority to teach them necessary truths, truths which should lead them to their end, and to reject the authority of the church is to overturn providence. This seems evident to me and I shall prove it in what follows [Dialogue XIII]. Now, faith teaches me that God has created heaven and earth. It teaches me that Scripture is a divine book. And this book, or its appearance, teaches me clearly and positively that there are thousands and thousands of creatures. Thus, all my appearances are hereby changed into reality. Bodies exist; that is demonstrated in complete rigor, given faith. Thus, I am assured that bodies exist, not only by the natural revelation of the sensations of them which God gives me, but even more by the supernatural revelation of faith. Here, my dear Aristes, are the main arguments against a doubt which comes to mind hardly in a natural way. There are few people who are philosophers enough to propose it. And although we can, against the existence of bodies, formulate difficulties which appear insurmountable mainly to those who do not know that God must act in us by general laws, still I do not believe anyone can ever seriously doubt it. Thus, it was not really necessary to detain ourselves dispelling a doubt so minimally dangerous. For I am quite certain that you yourself did not need everything I just told you to be assured you are here with Theodore.

ARISTES. I am not very certain of this. I am certain that you are here. But this is because you are telling me things which another would not tell me and which I would never tell myself. Moreover, the friendship I have for Theodore is such that I encounter him everywhere. Do I know whether I shall always be able to distinguish properly between the true and the false Theodore, as this friendship increases even more, though that hardly seems possible?

THEODORE. You are not wise, my dear Aristes. Will you never desist from these flattering ways? It is unworthy of a philosopher.

ARISTES. How severe you are! I did not expect this reply.

THEODORE. Nor did I yours. I thought you were following my reasoning. But your answer gives me some reason to fear that you have made me address your doubt well nigh in vain. Most people raise difficulties without reflection, and instead of being seriously attentive to the answers they are given, they think only of some rejoinder which would make people admire the subtlety of their imagination. Far from being mutually instructed, they think only of flattering each other. Together they are corrupted by the hidden expectations of the most criminal passions, and instead of quelling all those feelings which the passion of pride excites in them, instead of sharing the true goods which Reason imparts to them, they heap praise upon one another, which goes to their head and confuses them.

ARISTES. Ah, Theodore, how keenly aware I am of what you are saying! But what is this! Are you reading my heart?

THEODORE. No, Aristes. It is in mine that I read what I am telling you. It is in mine that I find that source of lust and vanity which makes me speak ill of humankind. I know nothing of what happens in your heart, except in relation to what I feel in my own. I fear for you what I am afraid of for myself. But I am not so rash as to judge of your actual dispositions. My manners surprise you. They are harsh and awkward – rustic, if you will. But what is this! Do you think that true friendship, based on Reason, seeks subterfuge and disguise? You do not know the privileges of the "meditators." They have the right unceremoniously to tell their friends what they find fault with in their conduct. I would like, my dear Aristes, to see a little more simplicity and much more attention in your replies. I would like Reason always to have the superior position in you and your imagination to be silenced. But if it is now too tired of its silence, let us leave metaphysics. We shall take it up another time. Do you know that the meditator of whom I spoke to you a couple of days ago wishes to come here?

ARISTES. Who? Theotimus?

THEODORE. Yes indeed, Theotimus himself.

ARISTES. Ah, that virtuous man! What a joy! What an honor!

THEODORE. He has learned somehow that I was here and that we were philosophizing together. For when Aristes is about, it is soon known. That is because everyone wants him. See what it is to have a fine mind and such brilliant qualities. He must be everywhere in order not to disappoint anyone. He is no longer his own man.

ARISTES. What slavery!

THEODORE. Do you wish to be freed from it? Become meditative, and soon the whole world will let you be. The great secret of delivering oneself from the importunity of many people is to speak reasonably to them. This language, which they do not understand, gets rid of them forever, without their having reason to complain.

ARISTES. That is true. But when will Theotimus be here?

IX. THEODORE. Whenever it suits you.

ARISTES. Well, please advise him straight away that we are expecting him, and above all assure him I am no longer what I was once. But let this not upset the course of our discussion. I renounce my doubt, Theodore. But I do not regret having suggested it to you. For by the things you have told me I discern the resolution of a number of apparent contradictions which I was unable to reconcile with the notion we have of the divinity. When we sleep God makes us see thousands of objects which do not exist. This is because He follows and must follow the general laws of the union of the soul and body. It is not because He wills to deceive us. If He acted on us by particular volitions we would not see all these phantoms while asleep. I am no longer surprised to see monsters and all these irregularities of nature. I see their cause in the simplicity of God's ways. Oppressed innocence no longer surprises me; if the stronger ordinarily prevail over it, this is because God governs the world by general laws and defers the punishment of crimes to another time. He is just notwithstanding the joyous success of the impious, notwithstanding the prosperity of the forces of the most unjust conquerors. He is wise, although the universe is full of works in which there are a thousand defects. He is immutable, although He seems constantly to contradict Himself, although with hail He ravages the earth He covered with fruit through an abundance of rain. All these contradictory effects indicate neither contradiction nor change in the cause which produces them. On the contrary, God inviolably follows the same laws, and His conduct bears no relation to ours. If someone suffers pain in an arm they no longer have, it is not because God plans to deceive them. It is solely because God does not change His plans and because He strictly obeys His own laws. It is because He approves them and will never condemn them; it is because nothing can upset the uniformity of His conduct, nothing can oblige Him to deviate from what He has done. It seems to me, Theodore, I can discern that this principle of general laws has an infinity of consequences of very great utility.

THEODORE. That is good, my dear Aristes. You give me much joy. I did not think you had been attentive enough to grasp properly the principles on which my answers to you depend. That is quite good. But we must examine these principles thoroughly, in order for you to know more clearly their solidity and wonderful fecundity. For do not imagine that it is enough for you to catch sight of them and even to have understood them, to be able to apply them to all the difficulties which depend on them. Through practice you must make yourself master of them and acquire the ability to refer to them everything they can explain. But I am inclined to postpone the examination of these great principles until Theotimus has arrived. Nevertheless, try to discover by yourself what the things are which have some connection to us, what the causes of these connections are, and what their effects are. For it is good that your mind be prepared for the topic of our discussions, in order that you can more easily correct me if I go astray or follow me if I lead you directly to where we should proceed with all our might.

PART V

G. W. Leibniz (1646–1716)

Introduction

Much of Leibniz's own thinking was sharpened by his critical responses to the work of others. Hobbes, Arnauld, Malebranche, Huygens, and Clarke were among his correspondents; and he wrote critical commentaries on major works by Descartes, Spinoza, and Locke. In our first two selections, *Meditations on Knowledge, Truth, and Ideas* (1684) and *On Nature Itself* (1698), Leibniz clarifies his early metaphysical and scientific theories in critical opposition to the positions of Descartes, Spinoza, Malebranche, and others. Our next selection, "A Vindication of God's Justice Reconciled with His Other Perfections and All His Actions" (1710), is from the appendix to the *Theodicy*. In it Leibniz offers a concise statement of his positions on freedom of the will, evil, and the nature of divine justice. We close the chapter with one of Leibniz's last essays, *The Principles of Nature and of Grace* (1714). Written in the same year as the *Monadology* – and covering much of the same ground as the better-known work – *Principles* provides the reader with a retrospective overview of Leibniz's philosophy.

13

Meditations on Knowledge, Truth, and Ideas

Since controversies rage today among distinguished persons over true and false ideas and since this is an issue of great importance for recognizing truth, an issue on which Descartes himself is not altogether satisfactory, I would like to explain briefly what I think can be established about the distinctions and criteria that relate to ideas and knowledge [*cognitio*]. Thus, knowledge is either obscure or *clear*, and again, clear knowledge is either confused or *distinct*, and distinct knowledge either inadequate or *adequate*, and adequate knowledge either symbolic or *intuitive*: and, indeed, if knowledge were, at the same time, both adequate and intuitive, it would be absolutely perfect.

A notion which is not sufficient for recognizing the thing represented is *obscure*, as, for example, if whenever I remember some flower or animal I once saw, I cannot do so sufficiently well for me to recognize that flower or animal when presented and to distinguish it from other nearby flowers or animals, or, for example, if I were to consider some term insufficiently explained in the schools, like Aristotle's entelechy, or his notion of a cause insofar as it is something common to material, formal, efficient and final causes, or if I were to consider other terms of that sort, for which we have no settled definition. Whence, a proposition which involves such a notion is also obscure. Therefore, knowledge is *clear* when I have the means for recognizing the thing represented. Clear knowledge, again, is either confused or distinct. It is

Meditations on Knowledge, Truth, and Ideas (1684). From *G. W. Leibniz: Philosophical Essays*, ed. and tr. Roger Ariew and Daniel Garber (Indianapolis, IN: Hackett Publishing Co., 1989). Selection: pp. 23–7.

confused when I cannot enumerate one by one marks [*nota*] sufficient for differentiating a thing from others, even though the thing does indeed have such marks and requisites into which its notion can be resolved. And so we recognize colors, smells, tastes, and other particular objects of the senses clearly enough, and we distinguish them from one another, but only through the simple testimony of the senses, not by way of explicit marks. Thus we cannot explain what red is to a blind man, nor can we make such things clear to others except by leading them into the presence of the thing and making them see, smell, or taste the same thing we do, or, at very least, by reminding them of some past perception that is similar. This is so even though it is certain that the notions of these qualities are composite and can be resolved because, of course, they do have causes. Similarly, we see that painters and other artists correctly know [*cognosco*] what is done properly and what is done poorly, though they are often unable to explain their judgments and reply to questioning by saying that the things that displease them lack an unknown something. But a *distinct notion* is like the notion an assayer has of gold, that is, a notion connected with marks and tests sufficient to distinguish a thing from all other similar bodies. Notions common to several senses, like the notions of number, magnitude, shape are usually of such a kind, as are those pertaining to many states of mind, such as hope or fear, in a word, those that pertain to everything for which we have a *nominal definition* (which is nothing but an enumeration of sufficient marks). Also, one has distinct knowledge of an indefinable notion, since it is *primitive*, or its own mark, that is, since it is irresolvable and is understood only through itself and therefore lacks requisites. But in composite notions, since, again, the individual marks composing them are sometimes understood clearly but confusedly, like heaviness, color, solubility in *aqua fortis*, and others, which are among the marks of gold, such knowledge of gold may be distinct, yet *inadequate*. When everything that enters into a distinct notion is, again, distinctly known, or when analysis has been carried to completion, then knowledge is *adequate* (I don't know whether humans can provide a perfect example of this, although the knowledge of numbers certainly approaches it). However, we don't usually grasp the entire nature of a thing all at once, especially in a more lengthy analysis, but in place of the things themselves we make use of signs, whose explicit explanation we usually omit for the sake of brevity, knowing or believing that we have the ability to produce it at will. And so when I think about a chiliagon, that is, a polygon with a thousand equal sides, I don't always consider the nature of a side, or of equality, or of thousandfoldedness (that is, of the cube of tenfoldedness), but in my mind I use these words (whose sense appears only obscurely and imperfectly to the mind) in place of the ideas I have of these things, since I remember that I know the meaning of those words, and I decide that explanation is not necessary at this time. I usually call such thinking, which is found both in algebra and in arithmetic and, indeed, almost everywhere, *blind* or *symbolic*. And indeed, when a notion is very complex, we cannot consider all of its component notions at the same time. When we can, or indeed insofar as we can, I call knowledge *intuitive*. There is no knowledge of a distinct primitive notion except intuitive, just as our thinking about composites is for the most part symbolic.

From this it already follows that we don't perceive ideas of even those things we know distinctly, unless we make use of intuitive thinking. And, indeed, it happens that we often mistakenly believe that we have *ideas* of things in mind when we mistakenly suppose that we have already explained some of the terms we use. Furthermore, what some maintain, that we cannot say anything about a thing and understand what we say unless we have an idea of it, is either false or at least ambiguous. For, often, we do understand in one way or another the words in question individually or remember that we understood them previously. But since we are content with this blind thinking and don't pursue the resolution of notions far

enough, it happens that a contradiction that might be included in a very complex notion is concealed from us. An argument for the existence of God, celebrated among the Scholastics long ago and revived by Descartes, once led me to consider this point more distinctly. The argument goes: whatever follows from the idea or definition of anything can be predicated of that thing. Since the most perfect being includes all perfections, among which is existence, existence follows from the idea of God (or the idea of the most perfect being, or the idea of that than which nothing greater can be thought). Therefore existence can be predicated of God. But one must realize that from this argument we can conclude only that, if God is possible, then it follows that he exists. For we cannot safely use definitions for drawing conclusions unless we know first that they are real definitions, that is, that they include no contradictions, because we can draw contradictory conclusions from notions that include contradictions, which is absurd. To clarify this I usually use the example of the fastest motion, which entails an absurdity. For let us suppose some wheel turning with the fastest motion. Everyone can see that any spoke of the wheel extended beyond the edge would move faster than a nail on the rim of the wheel. Therefore the nail's motion is not the fastest, contrary to the hypothesis. However, at first glance we might seem to have the idea of a fastest motion, for we certainly understand what we say; but yet we certainly have no idea of impossible things. And so, in the same way, the fact that we think about a most perfect being is not sufficient for us to assert that we have an idea of it. And so, in the demonstration given a bit earlier, either we must show or we must assume the possibility of a most perfect being in order properly to draw the conclusion. However, nothing is truer than that we have an idea of God and that a most perfect being is possible, indeed, necessary; yet the argument is not sufficient for drawing the conclusion and was long ago rejected by Aquinas.

And so we also have a distinction between *nominal definitions*, which contain only marks of a thing to be distinguished from other things, and *real definitions*, from which one establishes that a thing is possible. And with this we give our due to Hobbes, who claimed that truths are arbitrary, since they depend on nominal definitions, without considering the fact that the reality of a definition is not a matter of decision and that not just any notions can be joined to one another. Nominal definitions are insufficient for perfect knowledge [*scientia*] except when one establishes in another way that the thing defined is possible. It is also obvious, at last, what *true* and *false ideas* are; namely, an idea is true when its notion is possible and false when it includes a contradiction. Moreover, we can know the *possibility* of a thing either *a priori* or *a posteriori*. The possibility of a thing is known *a priori* when we resolve a notion into its requisites, that is, into other notions known to be possible, and we know that there is nothing incompatible among them. This happens, among other cases, when we understand the way in which a thing can be produced, whence *causal definitions* are more useful than others. The possibility of a thing is known *a posteriori* when we know through experience that a thing actually exists, for what actually exists or existed is at very least possible. And, indeed, whenever we have adequate knowledge, we also have *a priori* knowledge of possibility, for having carried an analysis to completion, if no contradiction appears, then certainly the notion is at least possible. I won't now venture to determine whether people can ever produce a perfect analysis of their notions or whether they can ever reduce their thoughts to *primitive possibilities* or to irresolvable notions or (what comes to the same thing) to the absolute attributes of God, indeed to the first causes and the ultimate reason for things. For the most part we are content to have learned the reality of certain notions through experience, from which we then compose others following the example of nature.

From this I think that we can finally understand that one cannot always appeal safely to an idea and that many use this splendid honorific improperly to prop up certain creatures of their imagination, for we don't always have an idea corresponding to every thing we consciously think of, as I showed a while ago with the example of the greatest speed. Nor do I see that the people of our day have abused any less the principle that they have laid down, that *whatever I clearly and distinctly perceive about a thing is true or is assertable of the thing in question*. For, often, what is obscure and confused seems clear and distinct to people careless in judgment. Therefore, this axiom is useless unless we use criteria for the clear and distinct, criteria which we have made explicit, and unless we have established the truth of the ideas. Furthermore, the rules of *common logic*, which even the geometers use, are not to be despised as criteria for the truth of assertions, as, for example, the rule that nothing

is to be admitted as certain, unless it is shown by careful testing or sound demonstration. Moreover, a sound demonstration is one that follows the form prescribed by logic. Not that we always need syllogisms ordered in the manner of the schools (in the way that Christian Herlinus and Conrad Dasypodius presented the first six books of Euclid); but at very least the argument must reach its conclusion by virtue of its form. Any correct calculation can also be considered an example of such an argument conceived in proper form. And so, one should not omit any necessary premise, and all premises should have been either previously demonstrated or at least assumed as hypotheses, in which case the conclusion is also hypothetical. Those who carefully observe these rules will easily protect themselves against deceptive ideas. Pascal, a most talented man, largely agrees with this in his excellent essay "On the Geometrical Mind" (a fragment of which appears in the admirable book of the distinguished Antoine Arnauld on the art of thinking well). The geometer, he says, must define all terms which are even a bit obscure and prove all truths which are even a bit dubious. But I wish that he had defined the limits beyond which a notion or statement is no longer even a bit obscure or dubious. Nevertheless, what belongs here can be gathered from an attentive consideration of what we have said above, for we are now trying to be brief.

As to the controversy over whether we see everything in God (which is certainly an old opinion and should not be rejected completely, if it is understood properly) or whether we have our own ideas, one must understand that, even if we were to see everything in God, it would nevertheless be necessary that we also have our own ideas, that is, not little copies of God's, as it were, but affections or modifications of our mind corresponding to that very thing we perceived in God. For certainly there must be some change in our mind when we have some thoughts and then others, and, in fact, the ideas of things that we are not actually thinking about are in our mind as the shape of Hercules is in rough marble. Moreover, it is necessary not only that there actually be in God an idea of absolute and infinite extension but also that there be an idea of each shape, which is nothing but a modification of absolute extension. Furthermore, when we perceive colors or smells, we certainly have no perception other than that of shapes and of motions, though so very numerous and so very small that our mind cannot distinctly consider each individual one in this, its present state, and thus does not notice that its perception is composed of perceptions of minute shapes and motions alone, just as when we perceive the color green in a mixture of yellow and blue powder, we sense only yellow and blue finely mixed, even though we do not notice this, but rather fashion some new thing for ourselves.

14

On Nature Itself

(1) Recently I received a defense of his dissertation, *De Idolo Naturae* (published in Altdorf), from Johann Christopher Sturm, that celebrated gentleman, distinguished in mathematics and physics; it had been challenged by that excellent and most accomplished physician of Kiel, Gunther Christopher Schelhammer in his book, *De Natura*. Now, I too once pondered the same question, and there was something of a dispute in letters that passed between me and the distinguished author of the dissertation, a dispute which he recently mentioned in a respectful way, publishing several of the transactions that passed between us in his *Physica Electiva* (vol. I, bk. 1, chap. 3, epilogue, sec. 5, pp. 119, 120). So, all the more willingly I applied my mind and attention to that question, important in and of itself, judging it necessary to present both my own view as well as the entire matter a bit more distinctly in terms of those principles which I have already made known on several occasions. Sturm's apologetic dissertation seemed to provide an appropriate occasion for undertaking this project, since one might judge that the author has presented there, in a few words and in summary, what is most important to the matter. But I am not entering into other aspects of that controversy between these distinguished gentlemen.

(2) Above all, I think that we should investigate two questions: first, what constitutes the nature we customarily attribute to things, whose generally accepted properties the celebrated Sturm thinks reek of something pagan; and second, whether there is any *energeia* in created things, which he seems to deny. As to the first question, *on nature itself* (if we may reflect on what it is not, as well as what it is), I certainly agree that there is no such thing as the soul of the universe. I also agree that those wonders which present themselves daily, and about which we customarily say (quite rightly) that the work of nature is the work of intelligence, should not be ascribed to certain created intelligences endowed with wisdom and power [*virtus*] only in proportion to the task at hand, but rather that the whole of *nature* is, so to speak, the *workmanship of God*, indeed, so much so that any natural machine you may choose consists of a completely infinite number of organs (which is the true and insufficiently appreciated distinction between the natural and the artifical), and therefore requires the infinite wisdom and power of the author and ruler. And so, I think that the omniscient heat of Hippocrates, and Avicenna's Cholcodean giver of souls, the exceedingly wise plastic virtue of Scaliger and others, and the hylarchic principle of Henry More are in part impossible, and in part unnecessary. I hold that it is enough for the machine of things to have been constructed with such wisdom that, through its very development, those very wonders come to pass, chiefly (as I believe) by means of organisms unfolding themselves through some predetermined plan. And so I approve of the fact that the distinguished gentleman rejects the fiction of any sort of created, wise nature, fashioning and governing the mechanisms of bodies. But I do not think that it follows from this, nor do I think that it is in agreement with

On Nature Itself (1698). From *G. W. Leibniz: Philosophical Essays*, ed. and tr. Roger Ariew and Daniel Garber (Indianapolis, IN: Hackett Publishing Co., 1989). Selection: pp. 155–67.

reason to deny all created, active force inherent in things.

(3) We have spoken of what isn't the case. Now let us examine a bit more directly what that nature is, that nature which Aristotle not inappropriately called the *principle of motion and rest*; though, having taken the phrase rather broadly, that philosopher seems to me to understand not only local motion or rest in a place, but *change* in general and stasis or persistence. From this it also follows, as I might note in passing, that the definition of motion he gives, though more obscure than it ought to be, is not, however, as silly as it appears to those who understand it as if he wanted only to define local motion. But on to the matters at hand. Robert Boyle, a distinguished gentleman well versed in the careful observation of nature, wrote a little book called *On Nature Itself*, whose main point was, if I remember rightly, that we ought to judge that nature is the very mechanism of bodies itself. This can, indeed, be approved of in a broad sense. But investigating the matter with greater care, we must distinguish the ultimate causes [*principia*] in this mechanism from that which is derived from them. So, for example, in explaining a clock, it is not sufficient to say that it is driven by a mechanical principle [*ratio*] unless you distinguish whether it is driven by a weight or by a spring. And I have already said a number of times that the source of the mechanism itself flows, not from material principles and mathematical reasons alone, but from some higher and, so to speak, metaphysical source, something that I think will be of use in preventing the mechanical explanation of natural things from being extended too far, to the detriment of piety, as if matter can stand by itself and as if mechanism required no intelligence or spiritual substance.

(4) *The foundation of the laws of nature*, among other things, provides a notable indication of this. That foundation should not be sought in the conservation of the same quantity of motion, as it has seemed to most, but rather in the fact that it is necessary that *the same quantity of active power be preserved*, indeed (something I discovered happens for a most beautiful reason) that the *same quantity of motive action* also be conserved, a quantity whose measure is far different from that which the Cartesians understand as quantity of motion. And when two mathematicians, who are clearly among the most talented, fought with me about this matter, in part through letters, in part in public, one came over entirely into my camp, and the

other came to the point of abandoning all his objections after much careful airing and candidly confessed that he did not yet have a response to one of my arguments. For that reason, I was very surprised that the distinguished gentleman [Sturm], explaining the laws of motion in the published part of his *Physica Electiva*, took the common view of them for granted, as if they were untouched by any objection (though he himself acknowledged that this view rests on no demonstration, but only on a certain probability [*verisimilitudo*], something he also repeats in his latest dissertation, chap. 3, sec. 2.). Perhaps he wrote before my work came out, and then either did not have the leisure to review what he had written, or it did not cross his mind to review it, especially since he believed that the laws of motion are arbitrary, a view that seems to me not to be altogether coherent. For I believe that God came to decree those laws observed in nature through considerations of wisdom and reasons of order. And I think that it is apparent from this (something that I once noted, using an opportunity afforded by the laws of optics, something that was afterwards greatly applauded by the distinguished Molyneux in his *Dioptrics*) that final causes not only advance virtue and piety in ethics and natural theology, but also help us to find and lay bare hidden truths in physics itself. And so, when the most celebrated Sturm listed my view among the hypotheses during his treatment of the final cause in his *Physica Eclectica*, I wish that he had considered it sufficiently in his discussion, for it can scarcely be doubted that in such a discussion he would have taken the occasion to assert many things in favor of the excellence of the argument, things both remarkable for their fruitfulness and also beneficial for piety.

(5) But now we must consider what he himself says about the notion of a nature in his apologetic dissertation, and what seems yet to be lacking in what he says. He grants, in chapter 4, sec. 2, 3 and in other places throughout the work, that the motions now existing happen *by virtue of the eternal law* God once set up, a law he then calls a volition and *command*. He also grants that there is no need for a new divine command, a new volition, not to speak of a new effort [*conatus*], or for any other labors (sec. 3), and Sturm rejects the view that God moves a thing like a woodcutter moves an ax, or like a miller operates a mill, either by holding back the water or diverting it to the wheel, a view he rejects as having been wrongly imputed to

him by his opponent. But yet, it certainly seems to me that this explanation is insufficient. For, I ask, has that volition or command, or, if you prefer, divine law that was once laid down, bestowed a mere *extrinsic denomination*, as it were, on things? Or, on the other hand, has it conferred some kind of enduring impression produced in the thing itself, that is, as that gentleman Schelhammer (as admirable in judgment as he is in experience) puts it, quite nicely, has it conferred an inherent law [*lex insita*] (even if it is not known to the creatures in which it exists), from which both actions and passions follow? The first seems to be the doctrine of the inventors of the system of occasional causes, principally that of that very acute Malebranche, while the latter is the received view, and, as I judge, the one that contains the most truth.

(6) For, since that past command does not now exist, it cannot now bring anything about unless it left behind some subsistent effect at the time, an effect which even now endures and is now at work. Whoever thinks otherwise, in my judgment, renounces all distinct explanation of things; anything could equally well be said to follow from anything else if something absent in place or time could be at work here and now, without an intermediary. And so, it is not sufficient to say that God, creating things in the beginning, willed that they follow a certain definite law in their change [*progressus*] if we imagine his will to have been so ineffective that things were not affected by it and no lasting effect was produced in them. And indeed, it contradicts the notion of that pure and absolute divine power and will to suppose that God wills and yet produces or changes nothing through willing, to suppose that he always acts but never accomplishes anything and leaves behind no work or accomplishment at all. Certainly, if nothing had been impressed on creatures by the divine words, "let the earth be fruitful and let the animals multiply," if things were disposed after that command just as if no command had intervened, then, since there must be some connection between cause and effect, either immediate or through some intermediary, it follows that either nothing now obeys that command or that the command held only at the time it was given and must always be renewed in the future, something the distinguished author correctly rejects. But if, indeed, the law God laid down left some trace of itself impressed on things, if by his command things were formed in such a way that they were rendered appropriate for fulfil-

ling the will of the command then already we must admit that a certain efficacy has been placed in things, a form or a force, something like what we usually call by the name "nature," something from which the series of phenomena follow in accordance with the prescript of the first command.

(7) Now, this inherent force can indeed be understood distinctly, but it cannot be explained through the imagination, nor, of course, should it be explained in that way, any more than the nature of the soul should be. For *force* is among those things which are reached, not by the imagination, but by the intellect. And so, when that distinguished gentleman (in chap. 4, sec. 6 of his apologetic dissertation) seeks an explanation in terms of the imagination for the way in which an inherent law works in bodies ignorant of that law, I interpret him to mean that he wants it to be explained through the intellect, for one certainly cannot believe that he requires us to picture sounds or hear colors. Furthermore, if difficulty in explaining things were a sufficient reason for rejecting them, then something he complains is wrongly imputed to him (chap. 1, sec. 2) would follow, namely, that he would rather hold that everything is moved by divine power [*virtus*] alone, than admit anything called a nature, of whose nature he is ignorant. Indeed, even Hobbes and others who want everything to be corporeal could depend on this principle with equal right since they persuade themselves that nothing can be explained distinctly and through the imagination, except body. But they are correctly refuted by the very fact that there is a force for acting in things, a force which is not derived from things that can be imagined. And simply to thrust this force back into a command of God's, given once in the past, affecting things in no way nor leaving an effect after itself, is so far from making the matter more easily explicable that it is, rather, to set aside the role of the philosopher altogether and cut the Gordian knot with a sword. But a more distinct and more correct explanation of active force than has yet been attained can be derived from our dynamics and from the account of the laws of nature and motion it contains, which is both true and in accordance with the facts.

(8) But if some defender of the new philosophy which introduces inertness [*inertia*] and inactivity [*torpor*] into things were to go so far as to deprive God's commands of all lasting effects and the ability to produce things in the future, and didn't even care that he required new labors of God all

the time (which Sturm prudently professes to be foreign to his meaning), he himself may judge how worthy he thinks this is of God. But we cannot exempt him from criticism unless he can explain how it is that things themselves can endure through time, even while those attributes of things, which we call by the name "nature" in them, cannot endure, since it is fitting that just as the words "let there be" [*fiat*] leave something behind, indeed, the very thing that persists, so should the no less *wonderful* word "*blessing*" have left something behind in things, a fecundity or a nisus for producing their actions and for being effectual, something from which a result follows if nothing prevents it. To this I can add something which I have already explained elsewhere, even if, perhaps, I have not yet made it sufficiently obvious to all, namely, that the very substance of things consists in a force for acting and being acted upon. From this it follows that persisting things cannot be produced if no force lasting through time can be imprinted on them by the divine power. Were that so, it would follow that no created substance, no soul would remain numerically the same, and thus, nothing would be conserved by God, and consequently everything would merely be certain vanishing or unstable modifications and phantasms, so to speak, of one permanent divine substance. Or, what comes to the same thing, God would be the very nature or substance of all things, the sort of doctrine of ill repute which a recent writer, subtle indeed, though profane, either introduced to the world or revived. Indeed, if corporeal things contained nothing but that which is material, they could quite rightly be said to be in constant change, but they would not have anything substantial, as the Platonists also once correctly recognized.

(9) The *other question* is whether creatures can properly and truly be said to act. Once we understand that the inherent nature is no different from the force of acting and being acted upon, this question reduces to the earlier one. For there can be no action [*actio*] without a force for acting, and, conversely, a power [*potentia*] which can never be exercised is empty. Since, nevertheless, action and power are different things, the former successive, the latter persisting, let us look then at action. Here, I confess, I find some difficulty in explaining the views of the celebrated Sturm. For he denies that created things, properly speaking, act in and of themselves, but then, however, he admits that they do act, insofar as he disavows, in a certain

sense, the comparison between creatures and an ax moved by a woodcutter. From this I can't infer anything with certainty, nor do I see him explain with sufficient clarity just how far he departs from the received views, or what distinct notion of action he might have had in mind; as it is well known from the debates of the metaphysicians, this is no clear or easy matter. To the extent that I have made the notion of action clear to myself, I believe that the widely received doctrine of philosophy, that *actions pertain to supposita*, follows from that notion and is grounded in it. Furthermore, I believe that we must grasp the fact that this also holds reciprocally, so that not only is it the case that everything that acts is an individual substance [*substantia singularis*], but also that every individual substance acts without interruption, including even body itself, in which one never finds absolute rest.

(10) But now we must consider a bit more closely the view of those who deny true and proper action to created things, as Robert Fludd, author of the Mosaic Philosophy, did long ago, and as now do certain of the Cartesians, who think that things do not act, but that God acts directly on things [*in rerum praesentiam*] in accordance with what is appropriate for them, and who thus think that things are occasions, not causes, and that things receive but do not bring anything about or produce anything. Although Cordemoy, de la Forge, and other Cartesians had proposed this doctrine, Malebranche, above all, adorned it with a certain rhetorical luster, commensurate with his acumen. But no one, so far as I know, has brought forward any solid reasons. Indeed, if this view were extended so far as to eliminate even the *immanent actions* of substances (something which Sturm rightly rejects in his *Physica Electiva*, book I, chap. 4, epilogue, sec. 11, p. 176, and in this he shows his circumspection quite nicely), then it would be as distant as it could possibly be from reason. For who would call into doubt that the mind thinks and wills, that we elicit in ourselves many thoughts and volitions, and that there is a spontaneity that belongs to us? If this were called into doubt, then not only would human liberty be denied and the cause of evil things be thrust into God, but it would also fly in the face of the testimony of our innermost experience and consciousness, testimony by which we ourselves sense that the things my opponents have transferred to God, without even a pretense of reason, are ours. But if we were to attribute an inherent force to our

mind, a force for producing immanent actions, or to put it another way, a force for acting immanently, then nothing forbids, in fact, it is reasonable to suppose that the same force would be found in other souls or forms, or, if you prefer, in the natures of substances – unless someone were to think that, in the natural world accessible to us, our minds alone are active, or that all power for acting immanently, and further, as I put it, all power for acting *vitally* is joined to an intellect, assertions that are neither confirmed by any rational arguments, nor can they be defended except by distorting the truth. In another place I shall give a better account of what can be said about the *transeunt actions of created things*. Indeed, elsewhere I have already explained a part of it, namely, that the *interaction* between *substances* or monads arises not from an influx, but through an agreement derived from divine preformation, accommodating each thing to things outside of itself while each follows the inherent force and laws of its own nature; in this also consists the *union of the soul and the body*.

(11) Moreover, it is indeed true that bodies are in and of themselves inert [*inertia*], if this is properly understood, namely, in the sense that what is assumed to be at rest at some time and in some respect cannot put itself into motion in that respect, nor will it allow itself to be put into motion by another thing without resistance – any more than it can spontaneously change either its degree of velocity or direction at any given time, or any more than it can allow itself to be changed by another thing easily and without resistance. And furthermore, we must admit that extension, or that which is geometrical in bodies, if taken by itself, has nothing in itself from which action and motion can arise. Indeed, we must admit, rather, that matter resists being moved through a certain *natural inertia* it has (as Kepler nicely named it), so that it is not indifferent to motion and rest, as is commonly believed, but requires more active force for motion in proportion to its size. Hence it is in this very passive force of resisting (which includes impenetrability and something more) that I locate the notion of primary matter or bulk [*moles*], which is everywhere the same in a body and proportional to its size, and I show that from this follow laws of motion far different than they would be if only impenetrability and extension were in bodies and their matter. And just as there is natural *inertia* opposed to *motion* in matter, so too in body itself, indeed in all substance, there is a natural *constancy* opposed to *change*. Indeed, this doctrine does not support, but rather opposes those who deny activity [*actio*] to things. For, as certain as it is that matter cannot initiate motion through itself, it is just as certain that a body conceived in and of itself retains an impetus once it is imparted, and remains constant in its mobility [*levitas*], that is, it has the tendency to persevere in that series of its changes, which it has once entered upon, as admirable experiments on motion impressed by a mover in motion also show. And since these activities and entelechies certainly cannot be modifications of primary matter or bulk [*moles*], something essentially passive, as the most judicious Sturm has clearly acknowledged (how he did this we shall discuss in the following paragraph), we must judge even from this that a *first entelechy* must be found in corporeal substance, a first subject of activity, namely a primitive motive force which, added over and above extension (or that which is merely geometrical), and over and above bulk (or that which is merely material), always acts but yet is modified in various ways in the collision of bodies through conatus and impetus. And this substantial principle itself is what is called *the soul* in living things and *the substantial form* in other things; insofar as, together with matter, it constitutes a substance that is truly one, or something one *per se*, it makes up what I call a monad, since, if these true and real unities were eliminated, only entities through aggregation, indeed (it follows from this), no true entities at all would be left in bodies. For, although there are atoms of substance, namely monads, which lack parts, there are no atoms of bulk [*moles*], that is, atoms of the least possible extension, nor are there any ultimate elements, since a continuum cannot be composed out of points. In just the same way, there is nothing greatest in bulk nor infinite in extension, even if there is always something bigger than anything else, though there is a being greatest in the intensity [*intensio*] of its perfection, that is, a being infinite in power [*virtus*].

(12) However, I see that in this apologetic dissertation (chap. 4, sec. 7 and following) the celebrated Sturm has attempted to attack the motive force inherent in bodies through certain arguments. "From numerous considerations," he says, "I shall here show that corporeal substance is indeed incapable of any *actively* motive power" (though I don't understand what a power non-actively motive might be). He also says that he will use two similar arguments, one from the nature of

matter and body, the other from the nature of motion. The former reduces to this: that matter is, in its nature, an essentially passive substance, and so it is no more possible for it to be given an active force than it would be for God to will a stone to be alive and rational, that is, to be a nonstone, while it remains a stone. Thus the things that are in body are only modifications of matter, and a modification of a thing that is essentially passive cannot render a thing active (this, I grant, is nicely put). But one can give an appropriate reply from the philosophy which is commonly received, no less than it is true. I understand matter as either secondary or primary. Secondary matter is, indeed, a complete substance, but it is not merely passive; primary matter is merely passive, but it is not a complete substance. And so, we must add a soul or a form analogous to a soul, or a first entelechy, that is, a certain urge [*nisus*] or primitive force of acting, which itself is an inherent law, impressed by divine decree. I do not think that the celebrated and ingenious gentleman who recently defended the view that body is made up of matter and spirit shrinks from this view. But spirit is to be understood, not as an intelligent being (as he usually does elsewhere), but as a soul or as a form analogous to a soul, not as a simple modification, but as something constitutive, substantial, enduring, what I usually call a *monad*, in which there is something like perception and appetite. This received doctrine, which is also consistent with the doctrine of the schoolmen, properly interpreted, must first be refuted, in order for the argument of the distinguished gentleman to have force. And in the same way, it follows from this that one cannot concede his assumption that whatever is in corporeal substance is a modification of matter. For it has been noted that, according to the received philosophy, there are souls in the bodies of living things which are certainly not modifications of matter. For despite the fact that the outstanding gentleman has settled on the opposite view, and seems to deny all true sensation and all soul, properly speaking, to brute animals, one cannot assume this opinion as a basis for demonstration before it itself is demonstrated. On the contrary, I believe that it is consistent with neither order nor with the beauty or reasonableness of things for there to be something living, that is, acting from within itself, in only the smallest portion of matter, when it would contribute to greater perfection for such things to be everywhere. Nor is there any reason why souls or things analogous to souls should not be everywhere, even if dominant and consequently intelligent souls, like human souls, cannot be everywhere.

(13) It seems to me that the second argument, which the distinguished gentleman derives from motion, does not have any greater necessity in its conclusion. He says that *motion* is only the successive existence of the moving thing in different places. Let us grant this for the moment, even if it is not entirely satisfactory, and even if it expresses what results from motion better than it expresses its formal definition [*formalis ratio*], as it is called. But motive force is not excluded on these grounds. For in the present moment of its motion, not only is a body in a place commensurate to itself, but it also has a conatus or nisus for changing its place, so that the state following from the present one results *per se* from the force of its nature. If things were otherwise, then at the present moment (and furthermore, at any moment whatsoever) a body A in motion would differ not at all from a resulting body B, and the view of that distinguished gentleman (if his view of the matter is different from mine) would entail that there is no clear criterion in bodies for distinguishing them, since in a plenum, the only criterion for distinguishing between masses uniform in themselves is connected with motion. From this view it would also follow, finally, that absolutely nothing would change in bodies, and that everything would always remain the same. For if no portion of matter whatsoever were to differ from equal and congruent portions of matter (something that the distinguished gentleman should admit, since he has eliminated active forces or impetus, and with them all other qualities and modifications except "existing in this place" and "successively coming to exist in some other place"), and furthermore, if one momentary state were to differ from another in virtue of the transposition of equal and interchangeable portions of matter alone, portions of matter in every way identical, then, on account of this perpetual substitution of indistinguishables, it obviously follows that in the corporeal world there can be no way of distinguishing different momentary states from one another. For the *denomination* by which one part of matter would be distinguished from another would be only *extrinsic*, indeed, it would derive from what will happen, namely from the fact that the part of matter in question will later be some other place or another. But in the present there is no distinguishing criterion. Indeed, we cannot even get such a criterion,

properly grounded, from the future, since even later on one will never arrive at any true criterion of distinction for the present. This is because, under the assumption of perfect uniformity in matter itself, one cannot in any way distinguish one place from another, or one bit of matter from another bit of matter in the same place. It is also useless to turn to *shape* over and above motion. For in a mass that is perfectly homogeneous, undivided, and full, no shape, that is, no boundary or distinction between its different parts arises, except through motion itself. But if motion contains no mark for distinguishing things from one another, then it likewise bestows no mark with respect to shape. And since everything substituted for something prior would be perfectly equivalent, no observer, not even an omniscient one, would detect even the slightest indication of change. And thus, everything would be just as if there were no change or discrimination in bodies, nor could we ever explain the different appearances we sense. Things would be just as they would were we to imagine two perfect and concentric spheres, perfectly similar to one another both in whole and in part, the one enclosed in the other in such a way that there is not even the smallest gap. Let us then assume that the enclosed sphere either revolves or is at rest, and, to say nothing more, not even an angel could find any difference between its states at different times, nor have any evidence for discerning whether the enclosed sphere is at rest or revolves, and what law of motion it follows. Indeed, because we lack both a *gap* and a criterion of distinction, we cannot even define the boundaries of the spheres, in much the same way as we cannot determine motion because we lack a *criterion of distinction* alone. Even if those who have not penetrated these matters deeply enough may not have noticed this, it ought to be accepted as certain that such consequences are alien to the nature and order of things, and that *nowhere are there things perfectly similar* (which is among my new and more important axioms). Another consequence of this is that, in nature, there are neither corpuscles of maximal hardness, nor a fluid of maximal thinness, nor a subtle matter universally diffused, nor ultimate elements which certain people call by the names "primary" and "secondary". Because, I think, Aristotle (more profound in my view than many think) saw several of these principles, he judged that, over and above change in place, one must have alteration, and that matter is not everywhere similar to itself, or else it would remain unchangeable. However, dissimilarity or qualitative difference, and also *alloiosis* or alteration, which Aristotle explained insufficiently, derive from different degrees and directions of nisus, and thus derive from modifications of the monads existing in things. From this I think it can be understood that we must necessarily place something in bodies over and above uniform mass and its transposition, which, at any rate, would change nothing. Those who accept *atoms* and the *void* do diversify matter, to be sure, insofar as they make some of it divisible, some indivisible, one place full, another empty. But having overthrown the prejudices of youth, I have realized for a long time now that atoms should be rejected, along with the void. The celebrated gentleman adds that the existence of matter through different moments should be attributed to the will of God. Thus, he asks, why not attribute the fact that it exists here and now to that same cause? I respond: it can scarcely be doubted that this very thing is due to God, as is everything else that involves perfection. But just as that first and universal cause conserving everything does not destroy, but rather causes the natural subsistence of a thing beginning to exist, or its perseverance in existence, once existence is granted, so in the same way he will not destroy, but will rather support the natural efficacy of a thing incited to motion or its perseverance in acting, once it is impressed.

(14) There are also many other things in that apologetic dissertation that are problematic, such as what he says in chapter 4, sec. 11, namely, assuming that motion is transferred from one ball through several intermediaries into another ball, the last ball is moved *by the same force* as the first. However, it seems to me that it is moved with equivalent force, but not by the same force. This might seem astonishing, but this happens because each and every thing pushed by a neighboring body pressing on it is put into motion by *its very own force*, namely by elastic force (I am not now discussing the cause of this elasticity, and I do not deny that it ought to be explained mechanically through the motion of a fluid existing in bodies and flowing through them). Also, what he says in sec. 12 will seem truly astonishing, that something that cannot begin motion in itself cannot continue that motion of its own accord. For, quite the contrary, it is well known that, just as force is necessary for producing motion, so too, once an impetus is given, far from requiring a new force for continuing the motion, one needs a force to stop it.

For conservation by a universal cause necessary to things is not at issue here – a conservation which, as we have already warned, if it removed the efficacy of things, would also remove their existence.

(15) From this it again follows that the doctrine of occasional causes defended by several persons can lead to dangerous consequences (unless it is explained in such a way that certain moderating changes are brought to bear, as the distinguished Sturm admitted in part, and in part seems to be on the verge of admitting), though these consequences are, doubtless, unintended by its most learned defenders. For this view is so far from increasing the glory of God by removing the idol of nature that, quite the contrary, it seems with Spinoza to make of God the very nature of things, while created things disappear into mere modifications of the one divine substance, since that which does not act, which lacks active force, which is robbed of discriminability, robbed finally of all reason and basis for existing, can in no way be a substance. I am most firmly persuaded that the distinguished Sturm, a gentleman outstanding in both piety and his teachings, is very far from conveying such thoughts. And so, there is no doubt that he will either show clearly how some substance or even some change remains in things on his doctrine, or he will surrender to the truth.

(16) Certainly many things make me suspect all the more that his views are not sufficiently clear to me, nor mine to him. Somewhere he confessed to me that a certain *small part of the divine power* (that is, I should think, an expression, likeness, proximate effect of the divine power, since the divine force certainly cannot be divided into parts) can, and in fact in a certain way even ought, to be understood as belonging to things and attributed to things. (The material sent to me which he repeated in his *Physica Electiva* can be seen in the passage I cited above near the beginning of this essay.) If, as would appear from his words, this is to be understood in the sense in which we speak of the soul as a small part of the divine breath, then the disagreement between us up to this point is already removed. But the fact that I see him relate such a view hardly anywhere else, and I do not see him set forth its consequences, makes me less willing to attribute it to him. On the other hand, I observe that what he writes in numerous places is hardly consistent with this view, and also that the apologetic dissertation leads to things altogether different. To be sure, when, in certain letters, he first objected to my views on the inherent force, as expressed in the *Acta Eruditorum* of Leipzig in March 1694 (further illustrated by a specimen of my dynamics in the same Journal, April 1695), but having received my response, he soon judged kindly that we differ only in the way we express ourselves. But when, taking note of this, I cautioned him about a few other things, he immediately turned in the other direction and cited many differences between us, differences which I acknowledge. But, having only just discounted these differences, he quite recently returned to writing, again, that any differences between us are only verbal, something that would have been most gratifying to me. Therefore, on the occasion of this latest apologetic dissertation, I wanted to set the matter out so that we can finally get clear about our views and their truth with greater ease. For, in general, this distinguished gentleman has both skill in perceiving and perceptiveness in setting things out, and so I might expect that no small light could be brought to bear on such an important issue through his application to it. Furthermore, I might expect that my labors would not therefore be useless to the extent that or because they might perhaps give him an opportunity to weigh and illuminate with his usual industriousness and power of judgment, several things of some importance in the present matter missed up until now by many authors, things, if I am not mistaken, I have filled out with new, more profound, and more broadly grounded axioms. From this, it seems, there could arise a restored and corrected system of philosophy, a philosophy midway between the formal and the material, a system that correctly joins and preserves both.

15

The Theodicy: Appendix

A Vindication of God's Justice Reconciled with His Other Perfections and All His Actions

1. The apologetic examination of the cause of God not only enhances the divine glory, but also serves our own advantage. It may move us to honor his greatness, that is, his power and wisdom, as well as to love his goodness and the perfections which derive from it, namely, his justice and holiness, and to imitate them as much as it is in our power. This apology contains two parts, of which the first may be considered as rather preparatory and the second as the principal. The first part studies, separately, *the greatness and the goodness of God*; the second, what pertains to these two perfections taken together, including the *providence* which he extends to all creatures, and the *government* which he exercises over the creatures endowed with intelligence, particularly in all matters concerning piety and salvation.

2. Theologians of excessive rigor have taken into account his greatness at the expense of his goodness, while those of greater laxity have done the opposite. True orthodoxy would consist in paying equal respect to both perfections. One may designate as *anthropomorphism* the error of those who neglect his greatness, and as *despotism* the error of those who disregard his goodness.

"A Vindication of God's Justice Reconciled with His Other Perfections and All His Actions" (1710). From *Monadology and Other Philosophical Essays*, tr. by Paul and Anne Martin Schrecker (New York: The Bobbs-Merrill Co., Inc., 1965). Selection: pp. 114–28.

3. The *greatness of God* has to be studiously defended, particularly against the Socinians and some semi-Socinians, among whom Conrad Vorst is in this respect the most reprehensible. This greatness can be considered under two main headings, God's omnipotence and his omniscience.

4. The *omnipotence* implies God's independence from everything else, as well as the dependence of everything upon him.

5. The *independence of God* manifests itself in his existence as well as in his actions: in his existence since he is a necessary and eternal being and, as it is commonly expressed, an *Ens a se*. Hence it follows also that he is beyond measure.

6. In his actions he is independent both naturally and morally. He is naturally independent, since he is absolutely free, and determined to action only by himself. He is morally independent since he is ἀνυπεύθυνος [*anupeuthunos*], that is, has no superior.

7. The *dependence of everything on God* extends to all that is possible, that is, to all that does not imply contradiction, as well as to all that is actual.

8. The *possibility* of things, even of those that have no actual existence, has itself a reality founded in the divine existence. For if God did not exist, nothing would be possible, and the possibles are from eternity in the ideas of the divine intellect.

9. *Actual* beings depend upon God for their existence as well as for their actions, and depend not only upon his intellect but also upon his will. Their existence depends upon God, since all things have been freely created by God and are maintained in existence by him. There is a sound doctrine which teaches that this divine

preservation in existence is a continued creation – comparable to the rays continually emitted by the sun – although the creatures do not emanate from the divine essence nor emanate necessarily.

10. *In their actions* all things depend upon God, since God concurs in their actions in so far as these actions have some degree of perfection, which must always come from God.

11. God's *concurrence* (even the ordinary, non-miraculous, concurrence) is at the same time immediate and special. It is *immediate* since the effect depends upon God not only for the reason that its cause originates in God, but also for this other reason, that God concurs no less nor more indirectly in producing this effect than in producing its cause.

12. The concurrence is *special* because it aims not only at the existence of the thing and its actions, but also at the mode and qualities of this existence in so far as there is inherent in them some degree of perfection, which always flows from God, the father of light and dispenser of all good.

13. So far we have dealt with the divine power. Let us now proceed to his wisdom, which, because of its immensity, is called *omniscience*. Since this wisdom is the most perfect possible (just as is his omnipotence), it comprehends every idea and every truth, that is, everything, simple or complex, which can be an object of the understanding. It comprehends equally everything possible and everything actual.

14. His knowledge of the *possibles* constitutes what is called the *science of simple intelligence*. Its objects are the things as well as their relationships, and, in respect to both, their necessity or contingency.

15. *Contingent possibles* can be considered either separately or as all correlated in an infinity of entire possible worlds, each of which is perfectly known to God, though only one among them has been produced into existence. It is indeed useless to invent a plurality of actual worlds since a single universe comprehends for us the totality of created things in all times and places; in this sense we use here the term *world*.

16. His knowledge of actual things, that is, of the world produced into existence and of all past, present, and future states of the world, is called *science of vision*. It differs from the science of simple intelligence of this same world considered as merely possible only in that it contains, added to the latter, the reflexive knowledge whereby God knows his decree to produce it into actual existence. Nothing more is needed as a foundation for the divine foreknowledge.

17. The *science* commonly called intermediate is contained in the science of simple intelligence if the latter is taken in the sense we have expounded above. If, however, one wants a science midway between the science of simple intelligence and the science of vision one could conceive both the science of simple intelligence and the intermediate science differently from the common usage. In this case one could assign to the intermediate science not only the knowledge of conditional future events but, generally, the knowledge of all contingent possibles. Thus the science of simple intelligence would be taken in a more restricted sense, namely, as dealing with possible and necessary truths, while the science of vision would deal with contingent and actual truths. The intermediate science and the science of simple intelligence would have this in common, that they both deal with possible truths, while the intermediate science and the science of vision would both deal with contingent truths.

18. So far we have considered the divine greatness; now we shall deal with the *divine goodness*. Just as wisdom or knowledge of truth is a perfection of the understanding, so goodness or striving for the good is a perfection of the will. All will, indeed, has as its object the good, be it but an apparent good; but the divine will has no object which would not be both good and true.

19. We shall study, therefore, both the will and its object, namely, good and evil, which provide the reasons for willing and rejecting. As to the will, we will study its nature and its species.

20. The *nature* of the will requires *freedom*, which consists in this: that the voluntary action be spontaneous and deliberate, and therefore exclude that necessity which suppresses deliberation.

21. Freedom excludes *metaphysical necessity*, the opposite of which is impossible, that is, implies contradiction. However, it does not exclude *moral* necessity, the opposite of which is unfit. For although God cannot fall into error in choosing, and therefore always chooses what is most fitting, this is so little opposed to his freedom that it rather renders it more perfect. It would be incompatible with his freedom if there were only one possible objective of the will, that is, if only one aspect of the universe were possible. For in this case there would no longer be any choice nor any possibility of praising the wisdom and goodness of Him who acts.

22. Therefore, those who maintain that only the actual – what God actually has chosen – is possible are mistaken, or at least express themselves awkwardly. This was the error of Diodorus the Stoic, according to Cicero, and among Christian thinkers that of Abelard, Wycliff, and Hobbes. I shall deal with freedom more elaborately later on, when human freedom will have to be defended.

23. So much about the nature of will. We come now to the *division of will*. For our present purpose we must introduce two divisions: on the one hand, the distinction of antecedent will and consequent will, and, on the other hand, the distinction between productive and permissive will.

24. The *first division* distinguishes between acts of will which are antecedent or prior and those which are consequent or final; or, which comes to the same, the will either inclines or decrees. In the first case it is incomplete; in the second, complete or absolute. Some authors, however, explain differently this division (at least the first). They maintain that the antecedent will of God (for instance, that all men be saved) precedes the consideration of the actions of the creatures, while the consequent will (for instance, that some be damned) is posterior to this consideration. But the first also precedes and the second also follows other acts of the divine will. For the very consideration of the actions of the creatures is not only presupposed by certain acts of the divine will, but also presupposes in its turn certain acts of the divine will without which actions of the creatures could not occur. This is why St. Thomas, Scotus, and others understand this division in the same sense in which we do, namely, that the antecedent will is directed toward some particular good in itself, in proportion to its degree of goodness, so that this will is only a relative will (*secundum quid*). The consequent will, on the contrary, aims at the whole and contains the ultimate determination whence it issues in an absolute decree. Since we are speaking of the divine will, it always obtains its full effect. For the rest, if anyone refuses to accept our explanation, we will not quarrel with him about words and if he prefers he may substitute for *antecedent* and *consequent*, *prior* and *final*.

25. The *antecedent will* is entirely serious and pure and ought not to be confused with velleity (which consists in this: that one would will if one were able, and would wish to be able), which does not exist in God; nor is it to be confused with conditional will, with which we do not deal here. The antecedent will of God tends toward actualizing all good and repelling all evil, as such, and in proportion to the degree of goodness and evil. How serious this will is, God himself confirmed when he so firmly asserted that he did not want the death of the sinner, that he wanted all men to be saved, and that he hated sin.

26. The *consequent will* arises from the concurrence of all antecedent acts of will. When the effects of all antecedent acts of will cannot be carried out together, the maximum effect which can be obtained by wisdom and power will be obtained. This will is also commonly called *decree*.

27. Hence it is evident that even the antecedent acts of will are not altogether vain, but have their own kind of efficacy. For though they produce effects, these effects are not always full, but are restricted by the concurrence of other antecedent acts of will. However, the decisive act of will, which results from all inclining acts of will, always produces its full effect, provided the power is adequate to the will, which it certainly is in the case of God. Only with regard to this decisive act of will is this axiom valid: who has the power and the will does what he wills. For since this power is supposed to imply also the knowledge required for action, nothing intrinsic or extrinsic can be thought of as lacking for action. And it can not be said that the felicity and perfection of God *qua* will is in any way diminished by the fact that not all his acts of will produce their full effects. For he wills what is good only according to the degree of goodness which is inherent in it, and his will is the more satisfied the better the result obtained.

28. According to the *second division*, the will is either *productive* when it determines the actions of the agent himself, or *permissive* when it regards the actions of others. Sometimes one may permit (that is, not prevent) actions which one has not the right to commit, as for instance, acts of sin; on this, more later. The proper object of permissive will is not the permitted action but the permission itself.

29. So far we have dealt with the will; now we shall study the *reasons for willing*, namely, *good* and *evil*. Either of these is of three kinds: metaphysical, physical, and moral.

30. *Metaphysical* good or evil, in general, consists in the perfection or imperfection of all creatures, even those not endowed with intelligence. The heavenly Father, according to Christ's own words, takes care of the lilies of the field and of the sparrows; and according to Jonah, God watches over the animals [Matthew 6:28–30, Matthew 10:29; Luke 12:6; Jonah 4:11].

31. *Physical* good or evil is understood as applying especially to the advantage or disadvantage of intelligent substances. An example of this is the *evil of punishment*.

32. *Moral* good or evil is attributed to the virtuous or vicious actions of these substances, for example, the evil of guilt. In this sense physical evil ordinarily is the effect of moral evil, although the two do not always occur in the same subjects. This may seem to be devious, but the deviation is later redressed with such profit that even the innocents would not wish not to have suffered. See also below, article 55.

33. God wills what is good *per se*, at least antecedently. He wills in general the perfection of all things and particularly the felicity and virtue of all intelligent substances; and as has already been pointed out, he wills each good according to its degree of goodness.

34. Evils are not the object of God's antecedent will unless this will tends to suppress them. They are, however, though indirectly, the objects of his consequent will. For sometimes greater goods could not be obtained if these evils were eliminated. In this case the removal of the evil would evidently not produce the desired effect. Thus, though the suppression is consistent with the antecedent will, it is not taken over into the consequent will. This is why Thomas Aquinas, following St. Augustine, was right in saying that God permits certain evils to occur lest many goods be prevented.

35. Sometimes metaphysical and physical evils (e.g., imperfections in things and the evils of punishment in persons) become subsidiary goods, namely as means for greater goods.

36. Moral evil or the evil of guilt has never, however, the function of a means. For, as the Apostle admonishes, evil ought not to be done so that good may ensue [Romans 3:8]. At the most, moral evil sometimes has the function of the kind of condition called *sine qua non*, that is, of an indispensable and concomitant condition without which the desired good could not be obtained. For the desired good implies also the desired suppression of the evil. At any rate, the admission of some evil does not follow from the principle of absolute necessity, but from the principle of fitness. There must, indeed, be a reason for God to permit the evil rather than not to permit it; but no reason of the divine will can be determined by anything but the good.

37. Moreover, the evil of guilt is never the object of God's productive will, but only sometimes of his permissive will, since he himself never commits a sin, but, at the most, in certain cases permits it to be committed.

38. Concerning the permission to sin, there is a general rule common to God and man, namely, that nobody ought to permit another man to sin unless by preventing it he would himself commit an evil action. In one word, it is always *illicit* to permit another man to sin unless duty demands this permission. We shall elaborate on this below in article 66.

39. Thus, among the objectives of the divine will, the ultimate end is the best, while any good may be a subaltern end, and indifferent events, such as the evil of punishment, may often be means. But the evil of guilt is an end only as the condition *sine qua non* for something which for other reasons ought to be. In this sense, as Christ has said, "It is impossible but that offences will come" [Matthew 18:7; Luke 17:1].

40. So far we have dealt with the divine greatness and goodness separately, as far as is necessary for the preparatory part of this apology. Now we shall study what pertains to the two perfections taken together. Now, *common to greatness and goodness* is everything which presupposes not goodness alone, but also greatness (that is, wisdom and power). For greatness makes it possible for goodness to attain its effect. Goodness, in its turn, refers either to all created things or especially to intelligences. Joined to greatness, goodness constitutes, in the first case, providence in the creation and government of the universe, and in the second case, justice in ruling, particularly over the substances which are endowed with reason.

41. The divine wisdom directs the divine goodness which extends to the totality of created things. Therefore the *divine providence* manifests itself in the total series of the universe. It follows that among the infinite number of possible series God has selected the best, and that consequently this best universe is that which actually exists. For all things in the universe are in mutual harmony and the truly wise will therefore never decide without having taken the whole into consideration, nor will his judgment bear on anything but the whole. With regard to the parts taken separately, the divine will may have been antecedent; with regard to the whole, it must be understood as a decree.

42. Hence, to speak rigorously, there is no necessity for a succession of divine decrees, but one may say that there has been one decree of God only, which decree has produced into existence the

present series of the universe, all the elements of this series having been considered beforehand and compared with the elements entering into other series.

43. This is why the divine decree is also immutable, since all reasons which might be opposed to it have already been considered. But therefrom no other *necessity* arises than the necessity of the consequence, or the so-called *hypothetical* necessity. This is the kind of necessity which arises from the prevision and preordination attributed to God. This necessity is not absolute; it does not make that which follows (*consequens*) absolutely necessary, since another order of the universe was equally possible, both as to the parts and as to the whole, and since God by his choice of this contingent series has not abolished its contingency.

44. Despite the certainty of the events in this universe, our prayers and labors are not useless for the obtaining of those future goods which we desire. For when God contemplated in his mind the representation of this actual series before deciding to create it, this representation contained also the prayers which, if this series were chosen, would figure in it, just as the representation contained all the other causes of all the effects which the series would comprehend. These prayers and these other causes, therefore, have contributed their due weight to the choice of this series and of the events figuring in it. And the reasons which now move God to action or permission had already moved him at that time to decide how he would act and what he would permit.

45. We have already remarked above that events, though determined by the divine foreknowledge and providence, are not thereby determined absolutely to occur whatever you do or do not do, but that they are determined by their causes and reasons. Therefore, if one called prayers or effort and labor useless, he would indulge in that *Sophism* which the ancients already called *lazy*.

46. Thus the infinite wisdom of the Almighty allied with his boundless goodness has brought it about that nothing better could have been created, everything taken into account, than what God has created. As a consequence all things are in perfect harmony and conspire in the most beautiful way: the formal causes or souls with the material causes or bodies, the efficient or natural causes with the final or moral causes, and the realm of grace with the realm of nature.

47. Whenever, therefore, some detail of the work of God appears to us reprehensible, we should judge that we do not know enough about it and that according to the wise who would understand it, nothing better could even be desired.

48. Hence it follows, furthermore, that there is no greater felicity than to serve so good a master, and that we should therefore love God above everything else and trust him without reservation.

49. The strongest reason for the choice of the best series of events (namely, our world) was Jesus Christ, God become Man, who as a creature represents the highest degree of perfection. He had, therefore, to be contained in that series, noblest among all, as a part, indeed the head, of the created universe. To him also all power has been granted in heaven and on earth, in him all the peoples were to be blessed, and through him every creature will be freed from servitude and corruption to enjoy the liberty and glory of the children of God.

50. So far we have dealt with general providence. Goodness, with special reference to intelligent creatures, together with wisdom, constitutes *justice*, of which the highest degree is *holiness*. Taken in this very wide sense, justice comprehends not only strict law but also equity, and therefore also laudable mercy.

51. Justice, taken in a general sense, can be divided into justice in a more *special* sense and holiness. *Justice in the special sense* is concerned with physical good and evil, namely, that of intelligent beings; holiness, with moral good and evil.

52. *Physical good and evil* occur in this life as well as in life hereafter. There is much complaint that *in this life* human nature is exposed to so many evils. Those who feel this way fail to consider that a great part of this evil is the effect of human guilt. In fact, they do not recognize with sufficient gratitude the divine goods of which we are the beneficiaries, and pay more attention to our sufferings than to our blessings.

53. Others are particularly dissatisfied with the fact that physical good and evil are not distributed in proportion to moral good and evil, or in other words, that frequently the just are miserable while the unrighteous prosper.

54. To these complaints there are two answers: the first, given by the Apostle, namely, that the afflictions of this life are nothing compared with the future glory, which will be revealed to us [II Corinthians 4:17]. The second, which Christ Himself has suggested, in an admirable parable: If the grain falling to the soil did not die, it would not bear fruit [John 12:24].

55. Thus our afflictions not only will be largely compensated, but they will serve to increase our felicity. These evils are not only profitable, but indispensable. See also article 32.

56. A still greater difficulty arises with regard to *future life*. For there, too, it is objected, evil by far prevails over good, since few are elected. It is true that Origen has absolutely denied the eternity of damnation; some of the ancient authors, among them Prudentius, have believed that only few would be damned for eternity. Some others have thought that eventually all Christians would be saved, and Jerome seems sometimes to have shared this opinion.

57. But there is no reason to resort to these paradoxes which are to be rejected. The true answer is that the whole amplitude of the celestial realm must not be evaluated according to our inadequate knowledge. For the Vision of God can give to the blessed such a glory that the sufferings of all the damned cannot be compared to such a good. Moreover, the scripture acknowledges an incredible multitude of *blessed Angels*, and nature itself shows us a great *variety of creatures*, as new inventions bring to evidence. Thus it is easier for us than it was for St. Augustine and other ancients to defend the predominance of good over evil.

58. Our earth, indeed, is but a satellite of one sun, and there are as many suns as there are fixed stars. Moreover, there is probably an immense space beyond all fixed stars. Nothing, therefore, prevents those suns and particularly the region beyond all suns, from being inhabited by blessed creatures. The planets themselves may be or become happy as Paradise. In our Father's house are many mansions, as Christ himself has rightly said of the heaven of the blessed [John 14:2]. Some theologians call that region the Empyreum and place it beyond the stars or suns, although nothing certain can be affirmed concerning the region of the blessed. Yet it may be affirmed that even in the visible world there are likely to be many mansions for rational creatures, without limitation of happiness.

59. Thus the argument drawn from the multitude of the damned is founded only on our ignorance and could be destroyed by one single answer, as hinted before: if all things were well known to us, it would clearly appear that a better world than that made by God could not even be desired. As to the penalties of the damned, they last on because the malice of the damned lasts on. An eminent theologian, Johann Fechtius, in his excellent book on the state of the damned, has very well refuted those who deny that sins committed in the hereafter deserve punishment, as though the justice essential to God could ever cease.

60. The most serious difficulties, however, arise apropos of the *divine holiness*, that is, apropos of the perfection which refers to the moral good and evil of others. This perfection makes him love virtue and hate vice even in others and removes him as far as possible from pollution and contamination by sin. And yet, it is objected, crime is frequently triumphant in the midst of the realm of God Almighty. Yet, however great this difficulty, with the help of the divine light, it can be overcome even in this life so that the pious who love God can be satisfied in this respect as much as need be.

61. The *objection* points out, indeed, that God concurs too much in sin and man not enough. *God, it is said, concurs too much in moral evil*, both physically and morally, by his will, which produces and permits sin.

62. Those who hold this opinion observe that moral concurrence would take place even if God did not actively contribute to sin, since he permits or does not prevent it, though he could.

63. But, they add, God in fact concurs at the same time morally and physically because he does not only not prevent the sinners, but even helps them in a certain manner by providing for them forces and occasions. Hence the passages in the sacred Scriptures which say that God hardens and incites the evildoers.

64. This is the reason why certain authors even dare to infer that God is morally and physically, or certainly in at least one of the two ways, an accomplice, even the author, of sin. By this means they destroy the divine holiness as well as his justice and goodness.

65. Others prefer to tear down the divine omniscience and omnipotence or, in one word, his greatness. According to them, God either does not foresee the evil, or is not concerned with it at all, or is unable to resist its torrential flood. This was the opinion of the Epicureans and of the Manichaeans. Something similar is taught, although in a less crude way, by the Socinians, who rightly wish to protect the divine holiness from pollution, but wrongly abandon the other divine perfections.

66. To respond first to the argument that *permission* is equivalent to *moral concurrence* we need only come back to what we have started to point

out before, namely, that the permission to sin is legitimate (that is, morally possible) when it turns out to be a duty (that is, morally necessary). This is the case whenever another's sin cannot be prevented unless one commits an offense oneself, that is, unless one violates what one owes to oneself or to others. A soldier on duty, for instance, particularly in times of danger, ought not to desert his post with the purpose of preventing two friends preparing for a duel from fighting it out. See also article 38. If we speak of divine duties we understand this not in a human sense but Θεοπρεπῶς [*theoprepōs*] (as it is proper to God), namely, that otherwise he would act contrary to his perfections.

67. Furthermore, if God had not selected for creation the best series of the universe (in which sin does occur), he would have admitted something worse than all sin committed by creatures. For, in this case, he would have acted contrary to his own perfections, and thereby also to all other perfection. For divine perfection can never fail to select the most perfect, since what is less good implies some evil. God himself and with him all things would be abolished if God either lacked power, or erred in his intellect, or failed in his will. [...]

The Principles of Nature and of Grace, Based on Reason

1. *Substance* is a being capable of action. It is simple or compound. *Simple substance* is that which has no parts. *Compound substance* is a collection of simple substances, or *monads*. *Monas* is a Greek word signifying unity or that which is one. Compounds, or bodies, are pluralities, and simple substances – lives, souls, and spirits – are unities. There must of necessity be simple substances everywhere, for without simple substances there would be no compounds. As a result, the whole of nature is full of life.

2. *Monads*, having no parts, can neither be formed nor unmade. They can neither begin nor end naturally, and therefore they last as long as the universe, which will change but will not be destroyed. They cannot have shapes, for then they would have parts. It follows that one monad by itself and at a single moment cannot be distinguished from another except by its internal qualities and actions, and these can only be its *perceptions* – that is to say, the representations of the compound, or of that which is without, in the simple – and its *appetitions* – that is to say, its tendencies from one perception to another – which are the principles of change. For the simplicity of a substance does not prevent the plurality of modifications which must necessarily be found together in the same simple substance; and these modifications must consist of the variety of relations of correspondence which the substance has with things outside. In the same way there may be

The Principles of Nature and of Grace, Based on Reason (1714). From *Philosophical Papers and Letters*, tr. and ed. Leroy E. Loemker (Dordrecht: Reidel, 1969). Selection: pp. 636–41.

found, in one *center* or point, though it is perfectly simple, an infinity of angles formed by the lines which meet in it.

3. Everything is a plenum in nature. Everywhere there are simple substances actually separated from each other by their own actions, which continually change their relations. And each outstanding simple substance or monad which forms the center of a compound substance (such as an animal, for example), and is the principle of its uniqueness, is surrounded by a mass composed of an infinity of other monads which constitute the body belonging to this central monad, corresponding to the affections by which it represents, as in a kind of center, the things which are outside of it. This body is *organic* when it forms a kind of automaton or natural machine, which is a machine not only as a whole but also in its smallest observable parts. And since everything is connected because of the plenitude of the world, and each body acts on every other one more or less, depending on the distance, and is affected by its reaction, it follows that each monad is a living mirror, or a mirror endowed with an internal action, and that it represents the universe according to its point of view and is regulated as completely as is the universe itself. The perceptions in the monad arise from each other according to the laws of the appetites or of the *final causes of good and of evil*, which consist in observable perceptions, whether regulated or unregulated, in the same way that bodily changes and external phenomena arise from each other according to the laws of *efficient causality*, that is, of motions. Thus there is a perfect *harmony* between the perceptions of the monad and the motions of the body, pre-established from the

beginning between the system of efficient causes and that of final causes. It is in this that the accord and the physical union of soul and body consist, without either one being able to change the laws of the other.

4. Together with a particular body, each monad makes a living substance. Thus not only is there life everywhere, joined to members or organs, but there are also infinite degrees of it in the monads, some of which dominate more or less over others. But when the monad has organs so adjusted that by means of them the impressions which are received, and consequently also the perceptions which represent these impressions, are heightened and distinguished (as, for example, when rays of light are concentrated by means of the shape of the humors of the eye and act with greater force), then this may amount to *sentiment*, that is to say, to a perception accompanied by *memory* – a perception of which there remains a kind of echo for a long time, which makes itself heard on occasion. Such a living being is called an *animal*, as its monad is called a *soul*. When this soul is raised to the level of *reason*, it is something more sublime and is counted among the *spirits*, as will be explained presently.

It is true that animals are sometimes in the condition of simple living beings, and their souls in the condition of simple monads, namely, when their perceptions are not distinct enough so that they can be remembered. This happens in a deep sleep without dreams or in a swoon. But perceptions which have become completely confused must be developed again in animals, for reasons which I shall give below in Section 12. So it is well to make a distinction between perception, which is the inner state of the monad representing external things, and *apperception*, which is consciousness or the reflective knowledge of this inner state itself and which is not given to all souls or to any soul all the time. It is for lack of this distinction that the Cartesians have made the mistake of disregarding perceptions which are not themselves perceived, just as people commonly disregard imperceptible bodies. It it this too which has made these same Cartesians think that only spirits are monads and that there is no soul in beasts, still less other *principles of life*. And after having defied the everyday opinion of men too much in denying that beasts have feeling, they adjusted their views too far to popular prejudices, on the other hand, when they confused a *long stupor* coming from a great confusion of perceptions with *death* in the *rigorous*

sense, in which all perception would cease. This has confirmed the poorly grounded opinion that certain souls are destroyed and has supported the pernicious view of certain so-called free-thinkers who have denied the immortality of our souls.

5. There is a connection between the perceptions of animals which has some resemblance to reason, but it is grounded only on the memory of *facts* or effects and not on the knowledge of *causes*. Thus a dog runs away from the stick with which he has been beaten, because his memory represents to him the pain which the stick had caused him. Men too, insofar as they are empiricists, that is to say, in three-fourths of their actions, act only like beasts. For example, we expect day to dawn tomorrow because we have always experienced this to be so; only the astronomer predicts it with reason, and even his prediction will ultimately fail when the cause of daylight, which is by no means eternal, stops. But *reasoning* in the *true* sense depends on necessary or eternal truths, as are those of logic, number, and geometry, which make the connection of ideas indubitable and their conclusions infallible. Animals in which such consequences cannot be observed are called *beasts*, but those who know these necessary truths are the ones properly called *rational animals*, and their souls are called *spirits*. These souls are capable of performing acts of reflection and of considering what is called "I", "substance", "soul", "spirit" – in a word, things and truths which are immaterial. It is this which makes us capable of the sciences or of demonstrative knowledge.

6. The investigations of the moderns have taught us, and reason confirms them, that the living beings whose organs are known to us, that is, plants and animals, do not come from putrefaction or chaos, as the ancients believed, but from *preformed* seeds, and therefore from the transformation of living beings existing prior to them. There are little animals in the seeds of large animals, which assume a new vesture in conception, which they appropriate and which provides them with a method of nourishment and growth, so that they may emerge into a greater stage and propagate the large animal. It is true that the souls of human spermatic animals are not rational and become so only when conception determines them for human nature. Just as animals in general are not completely born in conception or *generation*, moreover, neither do they completely perish in what we call *death*, for it is reasonable that what has no natural beginning also has no end within the order of

nature. Thus, abandoning their masks or their rags, they merely return, but to a finer stage, on which, however, they can be as sensitive and as well ordered as on the larger one. And what has been said about grosser animals takes place also in the generation and death of spermatic animals themselves, that is, they are the enlargements of other smaller spermatic animals, in proportion to which they may be considered large, for everything in nature proceeds to infinity.

Not only souls, therefore, but animals as well, cannot be generated or perish; they are only developed, enveloped, reclothed, stripped, transformed. Souls never leave the whole of their bodies and do not pass from one body to another entirely new to them. Thus there is no *metempsychosis*, though there is *metamorphosis*. Animals change, take on, and put off, only parts; in nutrition this takes place little by little and through minute, insensible particles, but continually, while in conception or in death, where much is acquired or lost all at once, it occurs suddenly and noticeably but infrequently.

7. So far we have been speaking simply as *natural scientists*; now we must rise to *metaphysics* and make use of the great, but not commonly used, *principle* that *nothing takes place without a sufficient reason*; in other words, that nothing occurs for which it would be impossible for someone who has enough knowledge of things to give a reason adequate to determine why the thing is as it is and not otherwise. This principle having been stated, the first question which we have a right to ask will be, "Why is there something rather than nothing?" For nothing is simpler and easier than something. Further, assuming that things must exist, it must be possible to give a reason *why they should exist as they do* and not otherwise.

8. Now this sufficient reason for the existence of the universe cannot be found in the series of contingent things, that is to say, of bodies and their representations in souls. For since matter is in itself indifferent to motion or rest, and to one motion rather than to another, one cannot find in it a reason for motion and still less for some particular motion. Although the present motion in matter arises from preceding motion, and that in turn from motion which preceded it, we do not get further however far we may go, for the same question always remains. The sufficient reason, therefore, which needs no further reason, must be outside of this series of contingent things and is found in a substance which is the cause of this

series or which is a necessary being bearing the reason for its existence within itself; otherwise we should not yet have a sufficient reason with which to stop. This final reason for things is called *God*.

9. This simple primary substance must include eminently the perfections contained in the derivative substances which are its effects. Thus it will have perfect power, knowledge, and will; that is to say, it will have omnipotence, omniscience, and sovereign goodness. And since justice, taken in its most general sense, is nothing but goodness conforming with wisdom, there is also necessarily a sovereign justice in God. The reason which has made things exist through him has also made them depend on him for their existence and operation, and they are continually receiving from him that which causes them to have some perfection. But whatever imperfection remains with them comes from the essential and original limitation of the created beings.

10. It follows from the supreme perfection of God that he has chosen the best possible plan in producing the universe, a plan which combines the greatest variety together with the greatest order; with situation, place, and time arranged in the best way possible; with the greatest effect produced by the simplest means; with the most power, the most knowledge, the greatest happiness and goodness in created things which the universe could allow. For as all possible things have a claim to existence in God's understanding in proportion to their perfections, the result of all these claims must be the most perfect actual world which is possible. Without this it would be impossible to give a reason why things have gone as they have rather than otherwise.

11. The supreme wisdom of God has made him choose especially those *laws of motion* which are best adjusted and most fitted to abstract or metaphysical reasons. There is conserved the same quantity of total and absolute force or of action, also the same quantity of relative force or of reaction, and finally, the same quantity of directive force. Furthermore, action is always equal to reaction, and the entire effect is always equal to its full cause. It is surprising that no reason can be given for the laws of motion which have been discovered in our own time, and part of which I myself have discovered, by a consideration of *efficient causes* or of matter alone. For I have found that we must have recourse to *final causes* and that these laws do not depend upon the *principle of necessity*, as do the truths of logic, arithmetic, and geometry, but upon

the *principle of fitness*, that is to say, upon the choice of wisdom. This is one of the most effective and obvious proofs of the existence of God for those who can probe into these matters thoroughly.

12. It follows also from the perfection of the supreme Author, not only that the order of the entire universe is the most perfect possible, but also that each living mirror which represents the universe according to its own point of view, that is, each *monad* or each substantial center, must have its perceptions and its appetites regulated in the best way compatible with all the rest. From this it also follows that souls, that is to say, the most dominant monads, or rather animals themselves, cannot fail to awake from the state of stupor into which death or some other accident may place them.

13. For everything has been regulated in things, once for all, with as much order and agreement as possible; the supreme wisdom and goodness cannot act except with perfect harmony. The present is great with the future; the future could be read in the past; the distant is expressed in the near. One could learn the beauty of the universe in each soul if one could unravel all that is rolled up in it but that develops perceptibly only with time. But since each distinct perception of the soul includes an infinity of confused perceptions which envelop the entire universe, the soul itself does not know the things which it perceives until it has perceptions which are distinct and heightened. And it has perfection in proportion to the distinctness of its perceptions.

Each soul knows the infinite, knows everything, but confusedly. Thus when I walk along the seashore and hear the great noise of the sea, I hear the separate sounds of each wave but do not distinguish them; our confused perceptions are the result of the impressions made on us by the whole universe. It is the same with each monad. Only God has a distinct knowledge of everything, for he is the source of everything. It has been very well said that he is everywhere as a center but that his circumference is nowhere, since everything is immediately present to him without being withdrawn at all from this center.

14. As for the reasonable soul or *spirit*, there is something more in it than in monads or even in simple souls. It is not only a mirror of the universe of creatures but also an image of divinity. The spirit not only has a perception of the works of God but is even capable of producing something which resembles them, though in miniature. For not to mention the wonders of dreams in which we invent, without effort but also without will, things which we should have to think a long time to discover when awake, our soul is architectonic also in its voluntary actions and in discovering the sciences according to which God has regulated things (by weight, measure, number, etc.). In its own realm and in the small world in which it is allowed to act, the soul imitates what God performs in the great world.

15. For this reason all spirits, whether of men or of higher beings [*genies*], enter by virtue of reason and the eternal truths into a kind of society with God and are members of the City of God, that is to say, the most perfect state, formed and governed by the greatest and best of monarchs. Here there is no crime without punishment, no good action without a proportionate reward, and finally, as much virtue and happiness as is possible. And this takes place, not by a dislocation of nature, as if what God has planned for souls could disturb the laws of bodies, but by the very order of natural things itself, by virtue of the harmony pre-established from all time between the realms of nature and of grace, between God as architect and God as monarch, in such a way that nature leads to grace, and grace perfects nature by using it.

16. Thus, though reason cannot teach us the details of the great future, these being reserved for revelation, we can be assured by this same reason that things are arranged in a way which surpasses our desires. God being also the most perfect, the happiest, and therefore the most lovable of substances, and *true pure love* consisting in the state which causes pleasure to be taken in the perfections and the felicity of the beloved, this love must give us the greatest pleasure of which one is capable, since God is its object.

17. And it is easy to love him as we ought if we know him as I have said. For though God is not visible to our external senses, he is nonetheless most love-worthy and gives very great pleasure. We see how much pleasure honors give to men, although they do not consist of qualities which appear to the external senses. Martyrs and fanatics, though the affection of the latter is not well ordered, show what power the pleasure of the spirit has. What is more, even the pleasures of sense are reducible to intellectual pleasures, known confusedly. Music charms us, although its beauty consists only in the agreement of numbers and in the counting, which we do not perceive but

which the soul nevertheless continues to carry out, of the beats or vibrations of sounding bodies which coincide at certain intervals. The pleasures which the eye finds in proportions are of the same nature, and those caused by other senses amount to something similar, although we may not be able to explain them so distinctly.

18. It may even be said that the love of God already gives us, here and now, a foretaste of future felicity. And although it is disinterested, by itself it constitutes our greatest good and interest, even when we do not seek these in it and when we consider only the pleasure it gives and disregard the utility it produces. For it gives us a perfect confidence in the goodness of our Author and Master, and this produces a true tranquillity of spirit, not such as the Stoics have who resolutely force themselves to be patient, but by a present contentment which itself assures us of future happiness. And apart from the present pleasure, nothing could be more useful for the future, for the love of God also fulfils our hopes and leads us in the way of supreme happiness, since, by virtue of the perfect order established in the universe, everything is done in the best possible way, as much for the general good as for the greatest particular good of those who are convinced of it and are satisfied by the divine government. This cannot fail to be true of those who know how to love the source of all good. It is true that the supreme happiness (with whatever *beatific vision* or knowledge of God it may be accompanied) cannot ever be full, because God, being infinite, cannot ever be known entirely. Thus our happiness will never consist, and ought never to consist, in complete joy, which leaves nothing to be desired and which would stupefy our spirit, but in a perpetual progress to new pleasures and new perfections.

PART VI

John Locke (1632–1704)

Introduction

Like Spinoza, Locke by his own admission was attracted to philosophy through his reading of Descartes. How much did the differences in their character and education have to do with the very different directions in which these two men took their common inspiration? Spinoza, the solitary ascetic, whose training began with study of the Torah and Jewish mystics, practiced the solitary craft of lens grinding. Locke, a man of affairs and friend of famous and powerful persons, learned experimental philosophy at Oxford and trained to be a physician. It is as if each took a portion of the complex character of Descartes and developed it hypertrophically.

Our opening selections come from Locke's *magnum opus, An Essay Concerning Human Understanding*, first published in 1690. Together they provide an overview of Locke's empiricism about the formation of ideas and the extent of human knowledge. Three sections from *Of the Conduct of the Understanding* (posthumously published in 1706) alert us to the fallacies that arise when loose and "insinuating" ways of writing are used. Locke proposes a technique of critical reading that first of all cuts through the wordplay to get at "the clear and distinct ideas of the question," and at the author's "train of argumentation," and then "bottoms" all proposed disputes on certain "fundamental verities." Newton's law of gravitation and the injunction to love our neighbors as ourselves are given as two examples of such verities. In *A Discourse of Miracles* (also 1706), Locke uses the method of the *Conduct* to clarify a discussion of miracles. The final Locke selection is the chapter "Of the Beginning of Political Societies" from *The Second Treatise of Government* (1690). This is Locke's great statement of contract theory and his philosophical justification for the overthrow of King James II.

17

Essay Concerning Human Understanding

Of Ideas in General, and Their Original

1. Every man being conscious to himself that he thinks; and that which his mind is applied about whilst thinking being the *ideas* that are there, it is past doubt that men have in their minds several ideas, – such as are those expressed by the words *whiteness, hardness, sweetness, thinking, motion, man, elephant, army*, drunkenness, and others: it is in the first place to be inquired, *How he comes by them?*

I know it is a received doctrine, that men have native ideas, and original characters, stamped upon their minds in their very first being. This opinion I have at large examined already; and, I suppose what I have said in the foregoing Book will be much more easily admitted, when I have shown whence the understanding may get all the ideas it has; and by what ways and degrees they may come into the mind; – for which I shall appeal to every one's own observation and experience.

2. Let us then suppose the mind to be, as we say, white paper, void of all characters, without

Essay Concerning Human Understanding (1690; 2nd edn. 1694), 2 vols. From *The Works of John Locke*, vol. 2 (Germany: Scientia Verlag Aalen, 1963). Selections: Book II (in vol. 1), ch. 1, "Of Ideas in General, and Their Original," sects 1–5, pp. 121–5; ch. 2, "Of Simple Ideas," sects 1–3, pp. 144–7; ch. 8, "[Of the Qualities and Powers of Bodies,]" sects 7–15, pp. 168–73; ch. 9, "Of Perception," sects 1–15, pp. 183–92; ch. 12, "Of Complex Ideas," sects 1–7, pp. 213–16. Book IV (in vol. 2): ch. 3, "Of the Extent of Human Knowledge," sects 1–6, pp. 190–8; ch. 10, "Of Our Knowledge of the Existence of a God," sects 1–6, pp. 306–10.

any ideas: – How comes it to be furnished? Whence comes it by that vast store which the busy and boundless fancy of man has painted on it with an almost endless variety? Whence has it all the *materials* of reason and knowledge? To this I answer, in one word, from EXPERIENCE. In that all our knowledge is founded; and from that it ultimately derives itself. Our observation employed either, about external sensible objects, or about the internal operations of our minds perceived and reflected on by ourselves, is that which supplies our understandings with all the *materials* of thinking. These two are the fountains of knowledge, from whence all the ideas we have, or can naturally have, do spring.

3. First, our Senses, conversant about particular sensible objects, do convey into the mind several distinct perceptions of things, according to those various ways wherein those objects do affect them. And thus we come by those *ideas* we have of *yellow, white, heat, cold, soft, hard, bitter, sweet*, and all those which we call sensible qualities; which when I say the senses convey into the mind, I mean, they from external objects convey into the mind what produces there those perceptions. This great source of most of the ideas we have, depending wholly upon our senses, and derived by them to the understanding, I call SENSATION.

4. Secondly, the other fountain from which experience furnisheth the understanding with ideas is, – the perception of the operations of our own mind within us, as it is employed about the ideas it has got; – which operations, when the soul comes to reflect on and consider, do furnish the understanding with another set of ideas, which could not be had from things without. And such

are *perception, thinking, doubting, believing, reasoning, knowing, willing,* and all the different actings of our own minds; – which we being conscious of, and observing in ourselves, do from these receive into our understandings as distinct ideas as we do from bodies affecting our senses. This source of ideas every man has wholly in himself; and though it be not sense, as having nothing to do with external objects, yet it is very like it, and might properly enough be called *internal sense.* But as I call the other Sensation, so I call this REFLECTION, the ideas it affords being such only as the mind gets by reflecting on its own operations within itself. By reflection then, in the following part of this discourse, I would be understood to mean, that notice which the mind takes of its own operations, and the manner of them, by reason whereof there come to be ideas of these operations in the understanding. These two, I say, viz. external material things, as the objects of SENSATION, and the operations of our own minds within, as the objects of REFLECTION, are to me the only originals from whence all our ideas take their beginnings. The term *operations* here I use in a large sense, as comprehending not barely the actions of the mind about its ideas, but some sort of passions arising sometimes from them, such as is the satisfaction or uneasiness arising from any thought.

5. The understanding seems to me not to have the least glimmering of any ideas which it doth not receive from one of these two. *External objects* furnish the mind with the ideas of sensible qualities, which are all those different perceptions they produce in us; and *the mind* furnishes the understanding with ideas of its own operations.

These, when we have taken a full survey of them, and their several modes, combinations, and relations, we shall find to contain all our whole stock of ideas; and that we have nothing in our minds which did not come in one of these two ways. Let any one examine his own thoughts, and thoroughly search into his understanding; and then let him tell me, whether all the original ideas he has there, are any other than of the objects of his senses, or of the operations of his mind, considered as objects of his reflection. And how great a mass of knowledge soever he imagines to be lodged there, he will, upon taking a strict view, see that he has not any idea in his mind but what one of these two have imprinted; – though perhaps, with infinite variety compounded and enlarged by the understanding, as we shall see hereafter. [. . .]

Of Simple Ideas

1. The better to understand the nature, manner, and extent of our knowledge, one thing is carefully to be observed concerning the ideas we have; and that is, that some of them are *simple* and some *complex*.

Though the qualities that affect our senses are, in the things themselves, so united and blended, that there is no separation, no distance between them; yet it is plain, the ideas they produce in the mind enter by the senses simple and unmixed. For, though the sight and touch often take in from the same object, at the same time, different ideas; – as a man sees at once motion and colour; the hand feels softness and warmth in the same piece of wax: yet the simple ideas thus united in the same subject, are as perfectly distinct as those that come in by different senses. The coldness and hardness which a man feels in a piece of ice being as distinct ideas in the mind as the smell and whiteness of a lily; or as the taste of sugar, and smell of a rose. And there is nothing can be plainer to a man than the clear and distinct perception he has of those simple ideas; which, being each in itself uncompounded, contains in it nothing but *one uniform appearance, or conception in the mind*, and is not distinguishable into different ideas.

2. These simple ideas, the materials of all our knowledge, are suggested and furnished to the mind only by those two ways above mentioned, viz. sensation and reflection. When the understanding is once stored with these simple ideas, it has the power to repeat, compare, and unite them, even to an almost infinite variety, and so can make at pleasure new complex ideas. But it is not in the power of the most exalted wit, or enlarged understanding, by any quickness or variety of thought, to *invent* or *frame* one new simple idea in the mind, not taken in by the ways before mentioned: nor can any force of the understanding *destroy* those that are there. The dominion of man, in this little world of his own understanding being muchwhat the same as it is in the great world of visible things; wherein his power, however managed by art and skill, reaches no farther than to compound and divide the materials that are made to his hand; but can do nothing towards the making the least particle of new matter, or destroying one atom of what is already in being. The same inability will every one find in himself, who shall go about to

fashion in his understanding one simple idea, not received in by his senses from external objects, or by reflection from the operations of his own mind about them. I would have any one try to fancy any taste which had never affected his palate; or frame the idea of a scent he had never smelt: and when he can do this, I will also conclude that a blind man hath ideas of colours, and a deaf man true distinct notions of sounds.

3. This is the reason why – though we cannot believe it impossible to God to make a creature with other organs, and more ways to convey into the understanding the notice of corporeal things than those five, as they are usually counted, which he has given to man – yet I think it is not possible for any *man* to imagine any other qualities in bodies, howsoever constituted, whereby they can be taken notice of, besides sounds, tastes, smells, visible and tangible qualities. And had mankind been made but with four senses, the qualities then which are the objects of the fifth sense had been as far from our notice, imagination, and conception, as now any belonging to a sixth, seventh, or eighth sense can possibly be; – which, whether yet some other creatures, in some other parts of this vast and stupendous universe, may not have, will be a great presumption to deny. He that will not set himself proudly at the top of all things, but will consider the immensity of this fabric, and the great variety that is to be found in this little and inconsiderable part of it which he has to do with, may be apt to think that, in other mansions of it, there may be other and different intelligent beings, of whose faculties he has as little knowledge or apprehension as a worm shut up in one drawer of a cabinet hath of the senses or understanding of a man; such variety and excellency being suitable to the wisdom and power of the Maker. I have here followed the common opinion of man's having but five senses; though, perhaps, there may be justly counted more; – but either supposition serves equally to my present purpose.

Of the Qualities and Powers of Bodies

[...] 7. To discover the nature of our *ideas* the better, and to discourse of them intelligibly, it will be convenient to distinguish them *as they are ideas or perceptions in our minds*; and *as they are modifications of matter in the bodies that cause such perceptions in us*: that so we may not think (as perhaps usually is done) that they are exactly the images and re-semblances of something inherent in the subject; most of those of sensation being in the mind no more the likeness of something existing without us, than the names that stand for them are the likeness of our ideas, which yet upon hearing they are apt to excite in us.

8. Whatsoever the mind perceives *in itself*, or is the immediate object of perception, thought, or understanding, that I call *idea*; and the power to produce any idea in our mind, I call *quality* of the subject wherein that power is. Thus a snowball having the power to produce in us the ideas of white, cold, and round, – the power to produce those ideas in us, as they are in the snowball, I call qualities; and as they are sensations or perceptions in our understandings, I call them ideas; which *ideas*, if I speak of sometimes as in the things themselves, I would be understood to mean those qualities in the objects which produce them in us.

9. Qualities thus considered in bodies are,

First, such as are utterly inseparable from the body, in what state soever it be; and such as in all the alterations and changes it suffers, all the force can be used upon it, it constantly keeps; and such as sense constantly finds in every particle of matter which has bulk enough to be perceived; and the mind finds inseparable from every particle of matter, though less than to make itself singly be perceived by our senses: v.g. Take a grain of wheat, divide it into two parts; each part has still solidity, extension, figure, and mobility: divide it again, and it retains still the same qualities; and so divide it on, till the parts become insensible; they must retain still each of them all those qualities. For division (which is all that a mill, or pestle, or any other body, does upon another, in reducing it to insensible parts) can never take away either solidity, extension, figure, or mobility from any body, but only makes two or more distinct separate masses of matter, of that which was but one before; all which distinct masses, reckoned as so many distinct bodies, after division, make a certain number. These I call *original* or *primary qualities* of body, which I think we may observe to produce simple ideas in us, viz. solidity, extension, figure, motion or rest, and number.

10. *Secondly*, such qualities which in truth are nothing in the objects themselves but powers to produce various sensations in us by their primary qualities, i.e. by the bulk, figure, texture, and motion of their insensible parts, as colours, sounds, tastes, &c. These I call *secondary qualities*. To these might be added a *third* sort, which are

allowed to be barely powers; though they are as much real qualities in the subject as those which I, to comply with the common way of speaking, call qualities, but for distinction, secondary qualities. For the power in fire to produce a new colour, or consistency, in *wax* or *clay*, – by its primary qualities, is as much a quality in fire, as the power it has to produce in *me* a new idea or sensation of warmth or burning, which I felt not before, – by the same primary qualities, viz. the bulk, texture, and motion of its insensible parts.

11. The next thing to be considered is, how bodies produce ideas in us; and that is manifestly by impulse, the only way which we can conceive bodies to operate in.

12. If then external objects be not united to our minds when they produce ideas therein; and yet we perceive these *original* qualities in such of them as singly fall under our senses, it is evident that some motion must be thence continued by our nerves, or animal spirits, by some parts of our bodies, to the brains or the seat of sensation, there to produce in our minds the particular ideas we have of them. And since the extension, figure, number, and motion of bodies of an observable bigness, may be perceived at a distance by the sight, it is evident some singly imperceptible bodies must come from them to the eyes, and thereby convey to the brain some motion; which produces these ideas which we have of them in us.

13. After the same manner that the ideas of these original qualities are produced in us, we may conceive that the ideas of *secondary* qualities are also produced, viz. by the operation of insensible particles on our senses. For, it being manifest that there are bodies and good store of bodies, each whereof are so small, that we cannot by any of our senses discover either their bulk, figure, or motion, – as is evident in the particles of the air and water, and others extremely smaller than those; perhaps as much smaller than the particles of air and water, as the particles of air and water are smaller than peas or hail-stones; – let us suppose at present that the different motions and figures, bulk and number, of such particles, affecting the several organs of our senses, produce in us those different sensations which we have from the colours and smells of bodies; v.g. that a violet, by the impulse of such insensible particles of matter, of peculiar figures and bulks, and in different degrees and modifications of their motions, causes the ideas of the blue colour, and sweet scent of that flower to be produced in our minds. It being no more

impossible to conceive that God should annex such ideas to such motions, with which they have no similitude, than that he should annex the idea of pain to the motion of a piece of steel dividing our flesh, with which that idea hath no resemblance.

14. What I have said concerning colours and smells may be understood also of tastes and sounds, and other the like sensible qualities; which, whatever reality we by mistake attribute to them, are in truth nothing in the objects themselves, but powers to produce various sensations in us; and depend on those primary qualities, viz. bulk, figure, texture, and motion of parts as I have said.

15. From whence I think it easy to draw this observation, – that the ideas of primary qualities of bodies are resemblances of them, and their patterns do really exist in the bodies themselves, but the ideas produced in us by these secondary qualities have no resemblance of them at all. There is nothing like our ideas, existing in the bodies themselves. They are, in the bodies we denominate from them, only a power to produce those sensations in us: and what is sweet, blue, or warm in idea, is but the certain bulk, figure, and motion of the insensible parts, in the bodies themselves, which we call so. [...]

Of Perception

1. Perception, as it is the first faculty of the mind, exercised about our ideas; so it is the first and simplest idea we have from reflection, and is by some called thinking in general. Though thinking, in the propriety of the English tongue, signifies that sort of operation in the mind about its ideas, wherein the mind is active; where it, with some degree of voluntary attention, considers any thing. For in bare naked perception, the mind is, for the most part, only passive; and what it perceives, it cannot avoid perceiving.

2. What perception is, every one will know better by reflecting on what he does himself, what he sees, hears, feels, &c. or thinks, than by any discourse of mine. Whoever reflects on what passes in his own mind, cannot miss it: and if he does not reflect, all the words in the world cannot make him have any notion of it.

3. This is certain, that whatever alterations are made in the body, if they reach not the mind; whatever impressions are made on the outward

parts, if they are not taken notice of within; there is no perception. Fire may burn our bodies, with no other effect than it does a billet, unless the motion be continued to the brain, and there the sense of heat, or idea of pain, be produced in the mind, wherein consists actual perception.

4. How often may a man observe in himself, that whilst his mind is intently employed in the contemplation of some objects, and curiously surveying some ideas that are there, it takes no notice of impressions of sounding bodies made upon the organ of hearing, with the same alteration that uses to be for the producing the idea of sound? A sufficient impulse there may be on the organ; but if not reaching the observation of the mind, there follows no perception; and though the motion that uses to produce the idea of sound be made in the ear, yet no sound is heard. Want of sensation, in this case, is not through any defect in the organ, or that the man's ears are less affected than at other times when he does hear: but that which uses to produce the idea, though conveyed in by the usual organ, not being taken notice of in the understanding, and so imprinting no idea in the mind, there follows no sensation. So that wherever there is sense, or perception, there some idea is actually produced, and present in the understanding.

5. Therefore I doubt not but children, by the exercise of their senses about objects that affect them in the womb, receive some few ideas before they are born; as the unavoidable effects, either of the bodies that environ them, or else of those wants or diseases they suffer: amongst which (if one may conjecture concerning things not very capable of examination) I think the ideas of hunger and warmth are two; which probably are some of the first that children have, and which they scarce ever part with again.

6. But though it be reasonable to imagine that children receive some ideas before they come into the world, yet those simple ideas are far from those innate principles which some contend for, and we above have rejected. These here mentioned being the effects of sensation, are only from some affections of the body, which happen to them there, and so depend on something exterior to the mind; no otherwise differing in their manner of production from other ideas derived from sense, but only in the precedency of time; whereas those innate principles are supposed to be quite of another nature, not coming into the mind by any accidental alterations in, or operations on, the body, but, as it were, original characters impressed upon it in the very first moment of its being and constitution.

7. As there are some ideas which we may reasonably suppose may be introduced into the minds of children in the womb, subservient to the necessities of their life and being there; so, after they are born, those ideas are the earliest imprinted which happen to be the sensible qualities which first occur to them: amongst which, light is not the least considerable, nor of the weakest efficacy. And how covetous the mind is to be furnished with all such ideas as have no pain accompanying them, may be a little guessed by what is observable in children new-born, who always turn their eyes to that part from whence the light comes, lay them how you please. But the ideas that are most familiar at first being various, according to the divers circumstances of children's first entertainment in the world, the order wherein the several ideas come at first into the mind is very various and uncertain also; neither is it much material to know it.

8. We are further to consider concerning perception, that the ideas we receive by sensation are often in grown people altered by the judgment, without our taking notice of it. When we set before our eyes a round globe, of any uniform colour, v.g. gold, alabaster, or jet, it is certain that the idea thereby imprinted in our mind is of a flat circle variously shadowed, with several degrees of light and brightness coming to our eyes: but we having by use been accustomed to perceive what kind of appearance convex bodies are wont to make in us, what alterations are made in the reflections of light by the difference of the sensible figures of bodies, the judgment presently, by an habitual custom, alters the appearances into their causes; so that from that which is truly variety of shadow or colour, collecting the figure, it makes it pass for a mark of figure, and frames to itself the perception of a convex figure and an uniform colour; when the idea we receive from thence is only a plane variously coloured, as is evident in painting. To which purpose I shall here insert a problem of that very ingenious and studious promoter of real knowledge, the learned and worthy Mr. Molineaux, which he was pleased to send me in a letter some months since; and it is this: Suppose a man born blind and now adult, and taught by his touch to distinguish between a cube and a sphere of the same metal, and nighly of the same bigness, so as to tell, when he felt one and the other, which is the cube, which the sphere. Suppose then the cube

and sphere placed on a table, and the blind man be made to see: quære, "whether by his sight, before he touched them, he could now distinguish and tell which is the globe, which the cube?" to which the acute and judicious proposer answers: Not. For though he has obtained the experience of how a globe, how a cube affects his touch; yet he has not yet obtained the experience, that what affects his touch so or so, must affect his sight so or so; or that a protuberant angle in the cube, that pressed his hand unequally, shall appear to his eye as it does in the cube. I agree with this thinking gentleman, whom I am proud to call my friend, in his answer to this his problem; and am of opinion, that the blind man, at first sight, would not be able with certainty to say which was the globe, which the cube, whilst he only saw them: though he could unerringly name them by his touch, and certainly distinguish them by the difference of their figures felt. This I have set down, and leave with my reader, as an occasion for him to consider how much he may be beholden to experience, improvement, and acquired notions, where he thinks he had not the least use of or help from them: and the rather, because this observing gentleman further adds, that having, upon the occasion of my book, proposed this to divers very ingenious men, he hardly ever met with one, that at first gave the answer to it which he thinks true, till by hearing his reasons they were convinced.

9. But this is not, I think, usual in any of our ideas but those received by sight: because sight, the most comprehensive of all our senses, conveying to our minds the ideas of light and colours, which are peculiar only to that sense; and also the far different ideas of space, figure, and motion, the several varieties whereof change the appearances of its proper object, viz. light and colours; we bring ourselves by use to judge of the one by the other. This, in many cases, by a settled habit, in things whereof we have frequent experience, is performed so constantly and so quick, that we take that for the perception of our sensation which is an idea formed by our judgment; so that one, viz. that of sensation, serves only to excite the other, and is scarce taken notice of itself: as a man who reads or hears with attention and understanding, takes little notice of the characters or sounds, but of the ideas that are excited in him by them.

10. Nor need we wonder that this is done with so little notice, if we consider how very quick the actions of the mind are performed: for as itself is thought to take up no space, to have no extension; so its actions seem to require no time, but many of them seem to be crowded into an instant. I speak this in comparison to the actions of the body. Any one may easily observe this in his own thoughts, who will take the pains to reflect on them. How, as it were in an instant, do our minds with one glance see all the parts of a demonstration, which may very well be called a long one, if we consider the time it will require to put it into words, and step by step show it another! Secondly, we shall not be so much surprised that this is done in us with so little notice, if we consider how the facility which we get of doing things, by a custom of doing, makes them often pass in us without our notice. Habits, especially such as are begun very early, come at last to produce actions in us which often escape our observation. How frequently do we, in a day, cover our eyes with our eyelids, without perceiving that we are at all in the dark! Men that by custom have got the use of a by-word, do almost in every sentence pronounce sounds which, though taken notice of by others, they themselves neither hear nor observe: and therefore it is not so strange that our mind should often change the idea of its sensation into that of its judgment, and make one serve only to excite the other, without our taking notice of it.

11. This faculty of perception seems to me to be that which puts the distinction betwixt the animal kingdom and the inferior parts of nature. For however vegetables have, many of them, some degrees of motion, and upon the different application of other bodies to them, do very briskly alter their figures and motions, and so have obtained the name of sensitive plants, from a motion which has some resemblance to that which in animals follows upon sensation; yet I suppose it is all bare mechanism, and no otherwise produced than the turning of a wild oat-beard, by the insinuation of the particles of moisture, or the shortening of a rope, by the affusion of water: all which is done without any sensation in the subject, or the having or receiving any ideas.

12. Perception, I believe, is in some degree in all sorts of animals; though in some, possibly, the avenues provided by nature for the reception of sensations are so few, and the perception they are received with so obscure and dull, that it comes extremely short of the quickness and variety of sensation which are in other animals; but yet it is sufficient for, and wisely adapted to, the state and condition of that sort of animals who are thus made: so that the wisdom and goodness of the

Maker plainly appear in all the parts of this stupendous fabric, and all the several degrees and ranks of creatures in it.

13. We may, I think, from the make of an oyster or cockle, reasonably conclude that it has not so many nor so quick senses as a man, or several other animals; nor if it had, would it, in that state and incapacity of transferring itself from one place to another, be bettered by them. What good would sight and hearing do to a creature that cannot move itself to or from the objects wherein at a distance it perceives good or evil? And would not quickness of sensation be an inconvenience to an animal that must lie still, where chance has once placed it; and there receive the afflux of colder or warmer, clean or foul water, as it happens to come to it?

14. But yet I cannot but think there is some small dull perception, whereby they are distinguished from perfect insensibility. And that this may be so, we have plain instances even in mankind itself. Take one, in whom decrepit old age has blotted out the memory of his past knowledge, and clearly wiped out the ideas his mind was formerly stored with; and has, by destroying his sight, hearing, and smell quite, and his taste to a great degree, stopped up almost all the passages for new ones to enter; or, if there be some of the inlets yet half open, the impressions made are scarce perceived, or not at all retained. How far such an one (notwithstanding all that is boasted of innate principles) is in his knowledge and intellectual faculties above the condition of a cockle or an oyster, I leave to be considered. And if a man had passed sixty years in such a state, as it is possible he might, as well as three days, I wonder what difference there would have been, in any intellectual perfections, between him and the lowest degree of animals.

15. Perception then being the first step and degree towards knowledge, and the inlet of all the materials of it, the fewer senses any man, as well as any other creature, hath, and the fewer and duller the impressions are that are made by them, and the duller the faculties are that are employed about them, the more remote are they from that knowledge which is to be found in some men. But this being in great variety of degrees (as may be perceived amongst men) cannot certainly be discovered in the several species of animals, much less in their particular individuals. It suffices me only to have remarked here, that perception is the first operation of all our intellectual faculties,

and the inlet of all knowledge in our minds: and I am apt too to imagine, that it is perception, in the lowest degree of it, which puts the boundaries between animals and the inferior ranks of creatures. But this I mention only as my conjecture by the by; it being indifferent to the matter in hand which way the learned shall determine of it.

Of Complex Ideas

1. We have hitherto considered those ideas, in the reception whereof the mind is only passive, which are those simple ones received from sensation and reflection before mentioned, whereof the mind cannot make one to itself, nor have any idea which does not wholly consist of them. But as the mind is wholly passive in the reception of all its simple ideas, so it exerts several acts of its own, whereby out of its simple ideas, as the materials and foundations of the rest, the others are framed. The acts of the mind, wherein it exerts its power over its simple ideas, are chiefly these three: (1) Combining several simple ideas into one compound one; and thus all *complex ideas* are made. (2) The second is bringing two ideas, whether simple or complex, together, and setting them by one another, so as to take a view of them at once, without uniting them into one; by which way it gets all its *ideas of relations*. (3) The third is separating them from all other ideas that accompany them in their real existence: this is called abstraction: and thus all its *general ideas* are made. This shows man's power, and its ways of operation, to be much the same in the material and intellectual world. For the materials in both being such as he has no power over, either to make or destroy, all that man can do is either to unite them together, or to set them by one another, or wholly separate them. I shall here begin with the first of these in the consideration of complex ideas, and come to the other two in their due places. As simple ideas are observed to exist in several combinations united together, so the mind has a power to consider several of them united together as one idea; and that not only as they are united in external objects, but as itself has joined them together. Ideas thus made up of several simple ones put together, I call *complex*; – such as are beauty, gratitude, a man, an army, the universe; which, though complicated of various simple ideas, or complex ideas made up of simple ones, yet are,

when the mind pleases, considered each by itself, as one entire thing, and signified by one name.

2. In this faculty of repeating and joining together its ideas, the mind has great power in varying and multiplying the objects of its thoughts, infinitely beyond what sensation or reflection furnished it with: but all this still confined to those simple ideas which it received from those two sources, and which are the ultimate materials of all its compositions. For simple ideas are all from things themselves, and of these the mind *can* have no more, nor other than what are suggested to it. It can have no other ideas of sensible qualities than what come from without by the senses; nor any ideas of other kind of operations of a thinking substance, than what it finds in itself. But when it has once got these simple ideas, it is not confined barely to observation, and what offers itself from without; it can, by its own power, put together those ideas it has, and make new complex ones, which it never received so united.

3. *Complex ideas*, however compounded and decompounded, though their number be infinite, and the variety endless, wherewith they fill and entertain the thoughts of men; yet I think they may be all reduced under these three heads: –

1. MODES.
2. SUBSTANCES.
3. RELATIONS.

4. First, *Modes* I call such complex ideas which, however compounded, contain not in them the supposition of subsisting by themselves, but are considered as dependences on, or affections of substances; – such as are the ideas signified by the words triangle, gratitude, murder, &c. And if in this I use the word mode in somewhat a different sense from its ordinary signification, I beg pardon; it being unavoidable in discourses, differing from the ordinary received notions, either to make new words, or to use old words in somewhat a new signification; the later whereof, in our present case, is perhaps the more tolerable of the two.

5. Of these *modes*, there are two sorts which deserve distinct consideration: –

First, there are some which are only variations, or different combinations of the same simple idea, without the mixture of any other; – as a dozen, or score; which are nothing but the ideas of so many distinct units added together, and these I call *simple modes* as being contained within the bounds of one simple idea.

Secondly, there are others compounded of simple ideas of several kinds, put together to make one complex one; – v.g. beauty, consisting of a certain composition of colour and figure, causing delight to the beholder; theft, which being the concealed change of the possession of anything, without the consent of the proprietor, contains, as is visible, a combination of several ideas of several kinds: and these I call *mixed modes*.

6. Secondly, the ideas of *substances* are such combinations of simple ideas as are taken to represent distinct *particular* things subsisting by themselves; in which the supposed or confused idea of substance, such as it is, is always the first and chief. Thus if to substance be joined the simple idea of a certain dull whitish colour, with certain degrees of weight, hardness, ductility, and fusibility, we have the idea of lead; and a combination of the ideas of a certain sort of figure, with the powers of motion, thought and reasoning, joined to substance, make the ordinary idea of a man. Now of substances also, there are two sorts of ideas: – one of *single* substances, as they exist separately, as of a man or a sheep; the other of several of those put together, as an army of men, or flock of sheep – which *collective* ideas of several substances thus put together are as much each of them one single idea as that of a man or an unit.

7. Thirdly, the last sort of complex ideas is that we call *relation*, which consists in the consideration and comparing one idea with another. [. . .]

Of the Extent of Human Knowledge

1. Knowledge, as has been said, lying in the perception of the agreement or disagreement of any of our ideas, it follows from hence, That,

First, we can have knowledge no further than we have *ideas*.

2. Secondly, That we can have no knowledge further than we can have *perception* of that agreement or disagreement. Which perception being: 1. Either by *intuition*, or the immediate comparing any two ideas; or, 2. By *reason*, examining the agreement or disagreement of two ideas, by the intervention of some others; or, 3. By *sensation*, perceiving the existence of particular things: hence it also follows:

3. Thirdly, That we cannot have an *intuitive knowledge* that shall extend itself to all our ideas, and all that we would know about them; because we cannot examine and perceive all the relations they

have one to another, by juxta-position, or an immediate comparison one with another. Thus, having
the ideas of an obtuse and an acute angled triangle,
both drawn from equal bases, and between parallels,
I can, by intuitive knowledge, perceive the one not
to be the other, but cannot that way know whether
they be equal or no; because their agreement or
disagreement in equality can never be perceived
by an immediate comparing them: the difference
of figure makes their parts incapable of an exact
immediate application; and therefore there is need
of some intervening qualities to measure them by,
which is demonstration, or rational knowledge.

4. Fourthly, It follows, also, from what is above
observed, that our *rational knowledge* cannot reach
to the whole extent of our ideas: because between
two different ideas we would examine, we cannot
always find such mediums as we can connect one
to another with an intuitive knowledge in all the
parts of the deduction; and wherever that fails, we
come short of knowledge and demonstration.

5. Fifthly, *Sensitive knowledge* reaching no further than the existence of things actually present to
our senses, is yet much narrower than either of the
former.

6. Sixthly, From all which it is evident, that the
extent of our knowledge comes not only short of the
reality of things, but even of the extent of our own
ideas. Though our knowledge be limited to our
ideas, and cannot exceed them either in extent or
perfection; and though these be very narrow
bounds, in respect of the extent of All-being, and
far short of what we may justly imagine to be in
some even created understandings, not tied down
to the dull and narrow information that is to be
received from some few, and not very acute, ways
of perception, such as are our senses; yet it would
be well with us if our knowledge were but as large
as our ideas, and there were not many doubts and
inquiries *concerning the ideas we have*, whereof we
are not, nor I believe ever shall be in this world
resolved. Nevertheless, I do not question but that
human knowledge, under the present circumstances of our beings and constitutions, may be
carried much further than it has hitherto been, if
men would sincerely, and with freedom of mind,
employ all that industry and labour of thought, in
improving the means of discovering truth, which
they do for the colouring or support of falsehood,
to maintain a system, interest, or party they are
once engaged in. But yet after all, I think I may,
without injury to human perfection, be confident,
that our knowledge would never reach to all we

might desire to know concerning those ideas we
have; nor be able to surmount all the difficulties,
and resolve all the questions that might arise concerning any of them. We have the ideas of a *square*,
a *circle*, and *equality*; and yet, perhaps, shall never
be able to find a circle equal to a square, and
certainly know that it is so. We have the ideas of
matter and *thinking*, but possibly shall never be
able to know whether any mere material being
thinks or no; it being impossible for us, by the
contemplation of our own ideas, without revelation, to discover whether Omnipotency has not
given to some systems of matter, fitly disposed, a
power to perceive and think, or else joined and
fixed to matter, so disposed, a thinking immaterial
substance: it being, in respect of our notions, not
much more remote from our comprehension to
conceive that GOD can, if he pleases, superadd
to matter *a faculty of thinking*, than that he should
superadd to it *another substance with a faculty of
thinking*; since we know not wherein thinking consists, nor to what sort of substances the Almighty
has been pleased to give that power, which cannot
be in any created being, but merely by the good
pleasure and bounty of the Creator. For I see no
contradiction in it, that the first Eternal thinking
Being, or Omnipotent Spirit, should, if he pleased,
give to certain systems of created senseless matter,
put together as he thinks fit, some degrees of
sense, perception, and thought: though, as I
think I have proved, lib. iv. ch. 10, § 14, &c., it is
no less than a contradiction to suppose matter
(which is evidently in its own nature void of
sense and thought) should be that Eternal first-
thinking Being. What certainty of knowledge can
any one have, that some perceptions, such as, v.g.,
pleasure and pain, should not be in some bodies
themselves, after a certain manner modified and
moved, as well as that they should be in an immaterial substance, upon the motion of the parts of
body: Body, as far as we can conceive, being able
only to strike and affect body, and motion,
according to the utmost reach of our ideas, being
able to produce nothing but motion; so that when
we allow it to produce pleasure or pain, or the idea
of a colour or sound, we are fain to quit our reason,
go beyond our ideas, and attribute it wholly to the
good pleasure of our Maker. For, since we must
allow He has annexed effects to motion which we
can no way conceive motion able to produce, what
reason have we to conclude that He could not
order them as well to be produced in a subject
we cannot conceive capable of them, as well as in

a subject we cannot conceive the motion of matter can any way operate upon? I say not this, that I would any way lessen the belief of the soul's immateriality: I am not here speaking of probability, but knowledge; and I think not only that it becomes the modesty of philosophy not to pronounce magisterially, where we want that evidence that can produce knowledge; but also, that it is of use to us to discern how far our knowledge does reach; for the state we are at present in, not being that of vision, we must in many things content ourselves with faith and probability: and in the present question, about the Immateriality of the Soul, if our faculties cannot arrive at demonstrative certainty, we need not think it strange. All the great ends of morality and religion are well enough secured, without philosophical proofs of the soul's immateriality; since it is evident, that he who made us at the beginning to subsist here, sensible intelligent beings, and for several years continued us in such a state, can and will restore us to the like state of sensibility in another world, and make us capable there to receive the retribution he has designed to men, according to their doings in this life. And therefore it is not of such mighty necessity to determine one way or the other, as some, over-zealous for or against the immateriality of the soul, have been forward to make the world believe. Who, either on the one side, indulging too much their thoughts immersed altogether in matter, can allow no existence to what is not material: or who, on the other side, finding not *cogitation* within the natural powers of matter, examined over and over again by the utmost intention of mind, have the confidence to conclude – That Omnipotency itself cannot give perception and thought to a substance which has the modification of solidity. He that considers how hardly sensation is, in our thoughts, reconcilable to extended matter; or existence to anything that has no extension at all, will confess that he is very far from certainly knowing what his soul is. It is a point which seems to me to be put out of the reach of our knowledge: and he who will give himself leave to consider freely, and look into the dark and intricate part of each hypothesis, will scarce find his reason able to determine him fixedly for or against the soul's materiality. Since, on which side soever he views it, either as an *unextended substance*, or as a *thinking extended matter*, the difficulty to conceive either will, whilst either alone is in his thoughts, still drive him to the contrary side. An unfair way which some men take with themselves: who, because of the inconceivableness of something they find in one, throw themselves violently into the contrary hypothesis, though altogether as unintelligible to an unbiassed understanding. This serves not only to show the weakness and the scantiness of our knowledge, but the insignificant triumph of such sort of arguments; which, drawn from our own views, may satisfy us that we can find no certainty on one side of the question: but do not at all thereby help us to truth by running into the opposite opinion; which, on examination, will be found clogged with equal difficulties. For what safety, what advantage to any one is it, for the avoiding the seeming absurdities, and to him unsurmountable rubs, he meets with in one opinion, to take refuge in the contrary, which is built on something altogether as inexplicable, and as far remote from his comprehension? It is past controversy, that we have in us *something* that thinks; our very doubts about what it is, confirm the certainty of its being, though we must content ourselves in the ignorance of what *kind* of being it is: and it is in vain to go about to be sceptical in this, as it is unreasonable in most other cases to be positive against the being of anything, because we cannot comprehend its nature. For I would fain know what substance exists, that has not something in it which manifestly baffles our understandings. Other spirits, who see and know the nature and inward constitution of things, how much must they exceed us in knowledge? To which, if we add larger comprehension, which enables them at one glance to see the connexion and agreement of very many ideas, and readily supplies to them the intermediate proofs, which we by single and slow steps, and long poring in the dark, hardly at last find out, and are often ready to forget one before we have hunted out another; we may guess at some part of the happiness of superior ranks of spirits, who have a quicker and more penetrating sight, as well as a larger field of knowledge.

But to return to the argument in hand: our knowledge, I say, is not only limited to the paucity and imperfections of the ideas we have, and which we employ it about, but even comes short of that too: but how far it reaches, let us now inquire. [...]

Of Our Knowledge of the Existence of a God

1. Though God has given us no innate ideas of himself; though he has stamped no original

characters on our minds, wherein we may read his being; yet having furnished us with those faculties our minds are endowed with, he hath not left himself without witness: since we have sense, perception, and reason, and cannot want a clear proof of him, as long as we carry *ourselves* about us. Nor can we justly complain of our ignorance in this great point; since he has so plentifully provided us with the means to discover and know him; so far as is necessary to the end of our being, and the great concernment of our happiness. But, though this be the most obvious truth that reason discovers, and though its evidence be (if I mistake not) equal to mathematical certainty: yet it requires thought and attention; and the mind must apply itself to a regular deduction of it from some part of our intuitive knowledge, or else we shall be as uncertain and ignorant of this as of other propositions, which are in themselves capable of clear demonstration. To show, therefore, that we are capable of *knowing*, i.e. *being certain* that there is a God, and *how we may come by* this certainty, I think we need go no further than *ourselves*, and that undoubted knowledge we have of our own existence.

2. I think it is beyond question, that man has a clear idea of his own being; he knows certainly he exists, and that he is something. He that can doubt whether he be anything or no, I speak not to; no more than I would argue with pure nothing, or endeavour to convince nonentity that it were something. If any one pretends to be so sceptical as to deny his own existence, (for really to doubt of it is manifestly impossible,) let him for me enjoy his beloved happiness of being nothing, until hunger or some other pain convince him of the contrary. This, then, I think I may take for a truth, which every one's certain knowledge assures him of, beyond the liberty of doubting, viz. that he is *something that actually exists*.

3. In the next place, man knows, by an intuitive certainty, that bare *nothing can no more produce any real being, than it can be equal to two right angles*. If a man knows not that nonentity, or the absence of all being, cannot be equal to two right angles, it is impossible he should know any demonstration in Euclid. If, therefore, we know there is some real being, and that nonentity cannot produce any real being, it is an evident demonstration, that *from eternity there has been something*; since what was not from eternity had a beginning; and what had a beginning must be produced by something else.

4. Next, it is evident, that what had its being and beginning from another, must also have all that which is in and belongs to its being from another too. All the powers it has must be owing to and received from the same source. This eternal source, then, of all being must also be the source and original of all power; and so *this eternal Being must be also the most powerful*.

5. Again, a man finds in *himself* perception and knowledge. We have then got one step further; and we are certain now that there is not only some being, but some knowing, intelligent being in the world. There was a time, then, when there was no knowing being, and when knowledge began to be; or else there has been also *a knowing being from eternity*. If it be said, there was a time when no being had any knowledge, when that eternal being was void of all understanding; I reply, that then it was impossible there should ever have been any knowledge: it being as impossible that things wholly void of knowledge, and operating blindly, and without any perception, should produce a knowing being, as it is impossible that a triangle should make itself three angles bigger than two right ones. For it is as repugnant to the idea of senseless matter, that it should put into itself sense, perception, and knowledge, as it is repugnant to the idea of a triangle, that it should put into itself greater angles than two right ones.

6. Thus, from the consideration of ourselves, and what we infallibly find in our own constitutions, our reason leads us to the knowledge of this certain and evident truth, – *That there is an eternal, most powerful, and most knowing Being*; which whether any one will please to call God, it matters not. The thing is evident; and from this idea duly considered, will easily be deduced all those other attributes, which we ought to ascribe to this eternal Being. If, nevertheless, any one should be found so senselessly arrogant, as to suppose man alone knowing and wise, but yet the product of mere ignorance and chance; and that all the rest of the universe acted only by that blind haphazard; I shall leave with him that very rational and emphatical rebuke of Tully (l. ii. De Leg.), to be considered at his leisure: "What can be more sillily arrogant and misbecoming, than for a man to think that he has a mind and understanding in him, but yet in all the universe beside there is no such thing? Or that those things, which with the utmost stretch of his reason he can scarce comprehend, should be moved and managed without any reason at all?" *Quid est enim verius, quam neminem esse oportere tam stulte arrogantem, ut in se mentem et rationem putet inesse, in cœlo mundoque non putet? Aut ea quæ vix*

summa ingenii ratione comprehendat, nulla ratione moveri putet?

From what has been said, it is plain to me we have a more certain knowledge of the existence of a God, than of anything our senses have not immediately discovered to us. Nay, I presume I may say, that we more certainly know that there is a God, than that there is anything else without us. When I say we *know*, I mean there is such a knowledge within our reach which we cannot miss, if we will but apply our minds to that, as we do to several other inquiries. [. . .]

18

Of the Conduct of the Understanding

Of Truth and Error

[...] 42. Right understanding consists in the discovery and adherence to truth, and that in the perception of the visible or probable agreement or disagreement of ideas, as they are affirmed and denied one of another. From whence it is evident, that the right use and conduct of the understanding, whose business is purely truth and nothing else, is, that the mind should be kept in a perfect indifferency, not inclining to either side, any farther than evidence settles it by knowledge, or the over-balance of probability gives it the turn of assent and belief; but yet it is very hard to meet with any discourse wherein one may not perceive the author not only maintain (for that is reasonable and fit) but inclined and biassed to one side of the question, with marks of a desire that that should be true. If it be asked me, how authors who have such a bias and lean to it may be discovered? I answer, by observing how in their writings or arguings they are often led by their inclinations to change the ideas of the question, either by changing the terms, or by adding and joining others to them, whereby the ideas under consideration are so varied as to be more serviceable to their purpose, and to be thereby brought to an easier and nearer agreement, or more visible and remoter disagreement one with another. This is plain and direct sophistry; but I am far from thinking that wherever it is found it is made use of

Of the Conduct of the Understanding (1706). From *The Works of John Locke*, vol. 3 (Germany: Scientia Verlag Aalen, 1963). Selection: sects 42–44, pp. 278–83.

with design to deceive and mislead the readers. It is visible that men's prejudices and inclinations by this way impose often upon themselves; and their affection for truth, under their prepossession in favour of one side, is the very thing that leads them from it. Inclination suggests and slides into their discourse favourable terms, which introduce favourable ideas; till at last, by this means, that is concluded clear and evident, thus dressed up, which, taken in its native state, by making use of none but the precise determined ideas, would find no admittance at all. The putting these glosses on what they affirm; these, as they are thought, handsome, easy, and graceful explications of what they are discoursing on, is so much the character of what is called and esteemed writing well, that it is very hard to think that authors will ever be persuaded to leave what serves so well to propagate their opinions, and procure themselves credit in the world, for a more jejune and dry way of writing, by keeping to the same terms precisely annexed to the same ideas; a sour and blunt stiffness, tolerable in mathematicians only, who force their way, and make truth prevail by irresistible demonstration.

But yet if authors cannot be prevailed with to quit the looser, though more insinuating ways of writing; if they will not think fit to keep close to truth and instruction by unvaried terms, and plain unsophisticated arguments; yet it concerns readers not to be imposed on by fallacies, and the prevailing ways of insinuation. To do this, the surest and most effectual remedy is to fix in the mind the clear and distinct ideas of the question stripped of words; and so likewise in the train of argumentation, to take up the author's ideas, neglecting his words, observing how they connect or separate those in the question. He that does this will be able to cast off all that is superfluous; he will see what is pertinent, what coherent, what is direct to, what slides by, the question. This will readily show him all the foreign ideas in the discourse, and where they were brought in; and though they perhaps dazzled the writer, yet he will perceive that they give no light nor strength to his reasonings.

This, though it be the shortest and easiest way of reading books with profit, and keeping one's self from being misled by great names or plausible discourses; yet it being hard and tedious to those who have not accustomed themselves to it, it is not to be expected that every one (amongst those few who really pursue truth) should this way guard his understanding from being imposed on by the wilful, or at least undesigned sophistry, which creeps into most of the books of argument. They, that write against their conviction, or that, next to them, are resolved to maintain the tenets of a party they are engaged in, cannot be supposed to reject any arms that may help to defend their cause, and therefore such should be read with the greatest caution. And they, who write for opinions they are sincerely persuaded of, and believe to be true, think they may so far allow themselves to indulge their laudable affection to truth, as to permit their esteem of it to give it the best colours, and set it off with the best expressions and dress they can, thereby to gain it the easiest entrance into the minds of their readers, and fix it deepest there.

One of those being the state of mind we may justly suppose most writers to be in, it is fit their readers, who apply to them for instruction, should not lay by that caution which becomes a sincere pursuit of truth, and should make them always watchful against whatever might conceal or misrepresent it. If they have not the skill of representing to themselves the author's sense by pure ideas separated from sounds, and thereby divested of the false lights and deceitful ornaments of speech; this yet they should do, they should keep the precise question steadily in their minds, carry it along with them through the whole discourse, and suffer not the least alteration in the terms, either by addition, subtraction, or substituting any other. This every one can do who has a mind to it; and he that has not a mind to it, it is plain, makes his understanding only the warehouse of other men's lumber; I mean false and unconcluding reasonings, rather than a repository of truth for his own use; which will prove substantial, and stand him in stead, when he has occasion for it. And whether such

an one deals fairly by his own mind, and conducts his own understanding right, I leave to his own understanding to judge.

43. The mind of man being very narrow, and so slow in making acquaintance with things, and taking in new truths, that no one man is capable, in a much longer life than ours, to know all truths; it becomes our prudence, in our search after knowledge, to employ our thoughts about fundamental and material questions, carefully avoiding those that are trifling, and not suffering ourselves to be diverted from our main even purpose, by those that are merely incidental. How much of many young men's time is thrown away in purely logical inquiries, I need not mention. This is no better than if a man, who was to be a painter, should spend all his time in examining the threads of the several cloths he is to paint upon, and counting the hairs of each pencil and brush he intends to use in the laying on of his colours. Nay, it is much worse than for a young painter to spend his apprenticeship in such useless niceties; for he, at the end of all his pains to no purpose, finds that it is not painting, nor any help to it, and so is really to no purpose: whereas men designed for scholars have often their heads so filled and warmed with disputes on logical questions, that they take those airy useless notions for real and substantial knowledge, and think their understanding so well furnished with science, that they need not look any farther into the nature of things, or descend to the mechanical drudgery of experiment and inquiry. This is so obvious a mismanagement of the understanding, and that in the professed way to knowledge, that it could not be passed by; to which might be joined abundance of questions, and the way of handling of them in the schools. What faults in particular of this kind every man is, or may be guilty of, would be infinite to enumerate; it suffices to have shown that superficial and slight discoveries and observations that contain nothing of moment in themselves, nor serve as clues to lead us into farther knowledge, should not be thought worth our searching after.

There are fundamental truths that lie at the bottom, the basis upon which a great many others rest, and in which they have their consistency. These are teeming truths, rich in store, with which they furnish the mind, and, like the lights of heaven, are not only beautiful and entertaining in themselves, but give light and evidence to other things, that without them could not be seen or known. Such is that admirable discovery of

Mr. Newton, that all bodies gravitate to one another, which may be counted as the basis of natural philosophy; which, of what use it is to the understanding of the great frame of our solar system, he has to the astonishment of the learned world shown; and how much farther it would guide us in other things, if rightly pursued, is not yet known. Our Saviour's great rule, that "we should love our neighbour as ourselves," is such a fundamental truth for the regulating human society, that, I think, by that alone, one might without difficulty determine all the cases and doubts in social morality. These and such as these are the truths we should endeavour to find out, and store our minds with. Which leads me to another thing in the conduct of the understanding that is no less necessary, viz.

44. To accustom ourselves, in any question proposed, to examine and find out upon what it bottoms. Most of the difficulties that come in our way, when well considered and traced, lead us to some proposition, which, known to be true, clears the doubt, and gives an easy solution of the question; whilst topical and superficial arguments, of which there is store to be found on both sides, filling the head with variety of thoughts, and the mouth with copious discourse, serve only to amuse the understanding, and entertain company without coming to the bottom of the question, the only place of rest and stability for an inquisitive mind, whose tendency is only to truth and knowledge.

For example, if it be demanded, whether the grand seignior can lawfully take what he will from any of his people? This question cannot be resolved without coming to a certainty, whether all men are naturally equal; for upon that it turns; and that truth well settled in the understanding, and carried in the mind through the various debates concerning the various rights of men in society, will go a great way in putting an end to them, and showing on which side the truth is. [...]

19

A Discourse of Miracles

To discourse of miracles without defining what one means by the word miracle, is to make a show, but in effect to talk of nothing.

A miracle then I take to be a sensible operation, which, being above the comprehension of the spectator, and in his opinion contrary to the established course of nature, is taken by him to be divine.

He that is present at the fact, is a spectator: he that believes the history of the fact, puts himself in the place of a spectator.

This definition, it is probable, will not escape these two exceptions.

1. That hereby what is a miracle is made very uncertain; for it depending on the opinion of the spectator, that will be a miracle to one which will not be so to another.

In answer to which, it is enough to say, that this objection is of no force, but in the mouth of one who can produce a definition of a miracle not liable to the same exception, which I think not easy to do; for it being agreed, that a miracle must be that which surpasses the force of nature in the established, steady laws of causes and effects, nothing can be taken to be a miracle but what is judged to exceed those laws. Now every one being able to judge of those laws only by his own acquaintance with nature, and notions of its force (which are different in different men), it is unavoidable that that should be a miracle to one, which is not so to another.

2. Another objection to this definition will be, that the notion of a miracle, thus enlarged, may

A Discourse of Miracles (1706). From *The Works of John Locke*, vol. 9 (Germany: Scientia Verlag Aalen, 1963). Selection: pp. 256–65.

come sometimes to take in operations that have nothing extraordinary or supernatural in them, and thereby invalidate the use of miracles for the attesting of divine revelation.

To which I answer, not at all, if the testimony which divine revelation receives from miracles be rightly considered.

To know that any revelation is from God, it is necessary to know that the messenger that delivers it is sent from God, and that cannot be known but by some credentials given him by God himself. Let us see then whether miracles, in my sense, be not such credentials, and will not infallibly direct us right in the search of divine revelation.

It is to be considered, that divine revelation receives testimony from no other miracles, but such as are wrought to witness his mission from God who delivers the revelation. All other miracles that are done in the world, how many or great soever, revelation is not concerned in. Cases wherein there has been, or can be need of miracles for the confirmation of revelation, are fewer than perhaps is imagined. The heathen world, amidst an infinite and uncertain jumble of deities, fables, and worships, had no room for a divine attestation of any one against the rest. Those owners of many gods were at liberty in their worship; and no one of their divinities pretending to be the one only true God, no one of them could be supposed in the pagan scheme to make use of miracles to establish his worship alone, or to abolish that of the other; much less was there any use of miracles to confirm any articles of faith, since no one of them had any such to propose as necessary to be believed by their votaries. And therefore I do not remember any miracles recorded in the Greek or Roman writers, as done to confirm any one's mission and doctrine. Conformable hereunto we find St. Paul, 1 Cor. i. 22, takes notice that the Jews (it is true) required miracles, but as for the Greeks they looked after something else; they knew no need or use there was of miracles to recommend any religion to them. And indeed it is an astonishing mark how far the god of this world had blinded men's minds, if we consider that the Gentile world received and stuck to a religion, which, not being derived from reason, had no sure foundation in revelation. They knew not its original, nor the authors of it, nor seemed concerned to know from whence it came, or by whose authority delivered; and so had no mention or use of miracles for its confirmation. For though there were here and there some pretences to revelation, yet there were not so much as pretences to miracles that attested it.

If we will direct our thoughts by what has been, we must conclude that miracles, as the credentials of a messenger delivering a divine religion, have no place but upon a supposition of one only true God; and that it is so in the nature of the thing, and cannot be otherwise, I think will be made appear in the sequel of this discourse. Of such who have come in the name of the one only true God, professing to bring a law from him, we have in history a clear account but of three, viz. Moses, Jesus, and Mahomet. For what the Persees say of their Zoroaster, or the Indians of their Brama (not to mention all the wild stories of the religions farther East) is so obscure, or so manifestly fabulous, that no account can be made of it. Now of the three before-mentioned, Mahomet having none to produce, pretends to no miracles for the vouching his mission; so that the only revelations that come attested by miracles, being those of Moses and Christ, and they confirming each other; the business of miracles, as it stands really in matter of fact, has no manner of difficulty in it; and I think the most scrupulous or sceptical cannot from miracles raise the least doubt against the divine revelation of the Gospel.

But since the speculative and learned will be putting of cases which never were, and it may be presumed never will be; since scholars and disputants will be raising of questions where there are none, and enter upon debates whereof there is no need; I crave leave to say, that he who comes with a message from God to be delivered to the world, cannot be refused belief if he vouches his mission by a miracle, because his credentials have a right to it. For every rational thinking man must conclude, as Nicodemus did, "we know that thou art a teacher come from God, for no man can do these signs which thou doest, except God be with him."

For example, Jesus of Nazareth professes himself sent from God: he with a word calms a tempest at sea. This one looks on as a miracle, and consequently cannot but receive his doctrine. Another thinks this might be the effect of chance, or skill in the weather, and no miracle, and so stands out; but afterwards seeing him walk on the sea, owns that for a miracle, and believes: which yet upon another has not that force, who suspects it may possibly be done by the assistance of a spirit. But yet the same person, seeing afterwards our Saviour cure an inveterate palsy by a word, admits that for a miracle, and becomes a convert. Another overlooking it in this instance, afterwards finds a miracle in his giving sight to one born blind, or in raising the dead, or his raising himself from the dead, and so receives his doctrine as a revelation coming from God. By all which it is plain, that where the miracle is admitted, the doctrine cannot be rejected; it comes with the assurance of a divine attestation to him that allows the miracle, and he cannot question its truth.

The next thing then is, what shall be a sufficient inducement to take any extraordinary operation to be a miracle, i.e. wrought by God himself for the attestation of a revelation from him?

And to this I answer, the carrying with it the marks of a greater power than appears in opposition to it. For,

1. First, this removes the main difficulty where it presses hardest, and clears the matter from doubt, when extraordinary and supernatural operations are brought to support opposite missions, about which methinks more dust has been raised by men of leisure than so plain a matter needed. For since God's power is paramount to all, and no opposition can be made against him with an equal force to his; and since his honour and goodness can never be supposed to suffer his messenger and his truth to be borne down by the appearance of a greater power on the side of an impostor, and in favour of a lie; wherever there is an opposition, and two pretending to be sent from heaven clash, the signs, which carry with them the evident marks of a greater power, will always be a certain and unquestionable evidence, that the truth and divine mission are on that side on which they appear. For though the discovery, how the lying wonders are or can be produced, be beyond the capacity of the ignorant, and often beyond the conception of the most knowing

spectator, who is therefore forced to allow them in his apprehension to be above the force of natural causes and effects; yet he cannot but know they are not seals set by God to his truth for the attesting of it, since they are opposed by miracles that carry the evident marks of a greater and superior power, and therefore they cannot at all shake the authority of one so supported. God can never be thought to suffer that a lie, set up in opposition to a truth coming from him, should be backed with a greater power than he will show for the confirmation and propagation of a doctrine which he has revealed, to the end it might be believed. The producing of serpents, blood, and frogs, by the Egyptian sorcerers and by Moses, could not to the spectators but appear equally miraculous: which of the pretenders then had their mission from God, and the truth on their side, could not have been determined, if the matter had rested there. But when Moses's serpent eat up theirs, when he produced lice, which they could not, the decision was easy. It was plain Jannes and Jambres acted by an inferior power, and their operations, how marvellous and extraordinary soever, could not in the least bring in question Moses's mission; that stood the firmer for this opposition, and remained the more unquestionable after this, than if no such signs had been brought against it.

So likewise the number, variety, and greatness of the miracles wrought for the confirmation of the doctrine delivered by Jesus Christ, carry with them such strong marks of an extraordinary divine power, that the truth of his mission will stand firm and unquestionable, till any one rising up in opposition to him shall do greater miracles than he and his apostles did. For any thing less will not be of weight to turn the scales in the opinion of any one, whether of an inferior or more exalted understanding. This is one of those palpable truths and trials, of which all mankind are judges; and there needs no assistance of learning, no deep thought, to come to a certainty in it. Such care has God taken that no pretended revelation should stand in competition with what is truly divine, that we need but open our eyes to see and be sure which came from him. The marks of his over-ruling power accompany it; and therefore to this day we find, that wherever the Gospel comes, it prevails to the beating down the strong holds of Satan, and the dislodging the prince of the power of darkness, driving him away with all his lying wonders; which is a standing miracle, carrying with it the testimony of superiority.

What is the uttermost power of natural agents or created beings, men of the greatest reach cannot discover; but that it is not equal to God's omnipotency, is obvious to every one's understanding; so that the superior power is an easy as well as sure guide to divine revelation, attested by miracles, where they are brought as credentials to an embassy from God.

And thus upon the same grounds of superiority of power, uncontested revelation will stand too.

For the explaining of which, it may be necessary to premise,

1. That no mission can be looked on to be divine, that delivers any thing derogating from the honour of the one, only, true, invisible God, or inconsistent with natural religion and the rules of morality: because God having discovered to men the unity and majesty of his eternal godhead, and the truths of natural religion and morality, by the light of reason, he cannot be supposed to back the contrary by revelation; for that would be to destroy the evidence and the use of reason, without which men cannot be able to distinguish divine revelation from diabolical imposture.

2. That it cannot be expected that God should send any one into the world on purpose to inform men of things indifferent, and of small moment, or that are knowable by the use of their natural faculties. This would be to lessen the dignity of his majesty in favour of our sloth, and in prejudice to our reason.

3. The only case, then, wherein a mission of any one from heaven can be reconciled to the high and awful thoughts men ought to have of the Deity, must be the revelation of some supernatural truths relating to the glory of God, and some great concern of men. Supernatural operations attesting such a revelation may with reason be taken to be miracles, as carrying the marks of a superior and over-ruling power, as long as no revelation accompanied with marks of a greater power appears against it. Such supernatural signs may justly stand good, and be received for divine, i.e. wrought by a power superior to all, till a mission attested by operations of a greater force shall disprove them: because it cannot be supposed God should suffer his prerogative to be so far usurped by any inferior being, as to permit any creature, depending on him, to set his seals, the marks of his divine authority, to a mission coming from him. For these supernatural signs being the only means God is conceived to have to satisfy men, as rational

creatures, of the certainty of any thing he would reveal, as coming from himself, can never consent that it should be wrested out of his hands, to serve the ends and establish the authority of an inferior agent that rivals him. His power being known to have no equal, always will, and always may be, safely depended on, to show its superiority in vindicating his authority, and maintaining every truth that he hath revealed. So that the marks of a superior power accompanying it, always have been, and always will be, a visible and sure guide to divine revelation; by which men may conduct themselves in their examining of revealed religions, and be satisfied which they ought to receive as coming from God; though they have by no means ability precisely to determine what is or is not above the force of any created being; or what operations can be performed by none but a divine power, and require the immediate hand of the Almighty. And therefore we see it is by that our Saviour measures the great unbelief of the Jews, John xv. 24, saying, "If I had not done among them the works which no other man did, they had not had sin; but now have they both seen and hated both me and my Father;" declaring, that they could not but see the power and presence of God in those many miracles he did, which were greater than ever any other man had done. When God sent Moses to the children of Israel with a message, that now, according to his promise, he would redeem them by his hand out of Egypt, and furnished him with signs and credentials of his mission; it is very remarkable what God himself says of those signs, Exod. iv. 8, "And it shall come to pass, if they will not believe thee, nor hearken to the voice of the first sign" (which was turning his rod into a serpent), that "they will believe the voice of the latter sign" (which was the making his hand leprous by putting it in his bosom). God farther adds, ver. 9, "And it shall come to pass, if they will not believe also these two signs, neither hearken unto thy voice, that thou shalt take of the water of the river, and pour upon the dry land: and the water which thou takest out of the river shall become blood upon the dry land." Which of those operations was or was not above the force of all created beings, will, I suppose, be hard for any man, too hard for a poor brick-maker, to determine; and therefore the credit and certain reception of the mission was annexed to neither of them, but the prevailing of their attestation was heightened by the increase of their number; two supernatural operations showing more power than

one, and three more than two. God allowed that it was natural, that the marks of greater power should have a greater impression on the minds and belief of the spectators. Accordingly the Jews, by this estimate, judged of the miracles of our Saviour, John vii. 31, where we have this account, "And many of the people believed on him, and said, When Christ cometh, will he do more miracles than these which this man hath done?" This, perhaps, as it is the plainest, so it is also the surest way to preserve the testimony of miracles in its due force to all sorts and degrees of people. For miracles being the basis on which divine mission is always established, and consequently that foundation on which the believers of any divine revelation must ultimately bottom their faith, this use of them would be lost, if not to all mankind, yet at least to the simple and illiterate (which is the far greatest part) if miracles be defined to be none but such divine operations as are in themselves beyond the power of all created beings, or at least operations contrary to the fixed and established laws of nature. For as to the latter of those, what are the fixed and established laws of nature, philosophers alone, if at least they, can pretend to determine. And if they are to be operations performable only by divine power, I doubt whether any man, learned or unlearned, can in most cases be able to say of any particular operation, that can fall under his senses, that it is certainly a miracle. Before he can come to that certainty, he must know that no created being has a power to perform it. We know good and bad angels have abilities and excellencies exceedingly beyond all our poor performances or narrow comprehensions. But to define what is the utmost extent of power that any of them has, is a bold undertaking of a man in the dark, that pronounces without seeing, and sets bounds in his narrow cell to things at an infinite distance from his model and comprehension.

Such definitions, therefore, of miracles, however specious in discourse and theory, fail us when we come to use, and an application of them in particular cases.

"These thoughts concerning miracles were occasioned by my reading Mr. Fleetwood's Essay on Miracles, and the letter writ to him on that subject. The one of them defining a miracle to be an extraordinary operation performable by God alone: and the other writing of miracles without any definition of a miracle at all."

20

The Second Treatise of Government

Chapter VIII: Of the Beginning of Political Societies

95. Men being, as has been said, by nature all free, equal, and independent, no one can be put out of this estate and subjected to the political power of another without his own consent. The only way whereby any one divests himself of his natural liberty and puts on the bonds of civil society is by agreeing with other men to join and unite into a community for their comfortable, safe, and peaceable living one amongst another, in a secure enjoyment of their properties and a greater security against any that are not of it. This any number of men may do, because it injures not the freedom of the rest; they are left as they were in the liberty of the state of nature. When any number of men have so consented to make one community or government, they are thereby presently incorporated and make one body politic wherein the majority have a right to act and conclude the rest.

96. For when any number of men have, by the consent of every individual, made a community, they have thereby made that community one body, with a power to act as one body, which is only by the will and determination of the majority; for that which acts any community being only the consent of the individuals of it, and it being necessary to that which is one body to move one way, it is necessary the body should move that way whither

Two Treatises of Government (1690). From *The Second Treatise of Government*, ed. Thomas P. Peardon (Indianapolis: Bobbs-Merrill Co., Inc., 1952). Selection: "Of the Beginning of Political Societies," pp. 54–70.

the greater force carries it, which is the consent of the majority; or else it is impossible it should act or continue one body, one community, which the consent of every individual that united into it agreed that it should; and so every one is bound by that consent to be concluded by the majority. And therefore we see that in assemblies impowered to act by positive laws, where no number is set by that positive law which impowers them, the act of the majority passes for the act of the whole and, of course, determines, as having by the law of nature and reason the power of the whole.

97. And thus every man, by consenting with others to make one body politic under one government, puts himself under an obligation to every one of that society to submit to the determination of the majority and to be concluded by it; or else this original compact, whereby he with others incorporates into one society, would signify nothing, and be no compact, if he be left free and under no other ties than he was in before in the state of nature. For what appearance would there be of any compact? What new engagement if he were no further tied by any decrees of the society than he himself thought fit and did actually consent to? This would be still as great a liberty as he himself had before his compact, or any one else in the state of nature has who may submit himself and consent to any acts of it if he thinks fit.

98. For if the consent of the majority shall not in reason be received as the act of the whole and conclude every individual, nothing but the consent of every individual can make anything to be the act of the whole; but such a consent is next to impossible ever to be had if we consider the infirmities of health and avocations of business which in a

number, though much less than that of a commonwealth, will necessarily keep many away from the public assembly. To which, if we add the variety of opinions and contrariety of interests which unavoidably happen in all collections of men, the coming into society upon such terms would be only like Cato's coming into the theatre only to go out again. Such a constitution as this would make the mighty leviathan of a shorter duration than the feeblest creatures, and not let it outlast the day it was born in; which cannot be supposed till we can think that rational creatures should desire and constitute societies only to be dissolved; for where the majority cannot conclude the rest, there they cannot act as one body, and consequently will be immediately dissolved again.

99. Whosoever, therefore, out of a state of nature unite into a community must be understood to give up all the power necessary to the ends for which they unite into society to the majority of the community, unless they expressly agreed in any number greater than the majority. And this is done by barely agreeing to unite into one political society, which is all the compact that is, or needs be, between the individuals that enter into or make up a commonwealth. And thus that which begins and actually constitutes any political society is nothing but the consent of any number of freemen capable of a majority to unite and incorporate into such a society. And this is that, and that only, which did or could give beginning to any lawful government in the world.

100. To this I find two objections made:

First, That there are no instances to be found in history of a company of men independent and equal one amongst another that met together and in this way began and set up a government.

Secondly, It is impossible of right that men should do so, because all men being born under government, they are to submit to that and are not at liberty to begin a new one.

101. To the first there is this to answer: that it is not at all to be wondered at that history gives us but a very little account of men that lived together in the state of nature. The inconveniences of that condition, and the love and want of society, no sooner brought any number of them together, but they presently united and incorporated if they designed to continue together. And if we may not suppose men ever to have been in the state of nature, because we hear not much of them in such a state, we may as well suppose the armies of Salmanasser or Xerxes were never children be-

cause we hear little of them till they were men and embodied in armies. Government is everywhere antecedent to records, and letters seldom come in amongst a people till a long continuation of civil society has, by other more necessary arts, provided for their safety, ease, and plenty; and then they begin to look after the history of their founders and search into their original, when they have outlived the memory of it; for it is with commonwealths as with particular persons – they are commonly ignorant of their own births and infancies; and if they know anything of their original, they are beholden for it to the accidental records that others have kept of it. And those that we have of the beginning of any politics in the world, excepting that of the Jews, where God himself immediately interposed, and which favors not at all paternal dominion, are all either plain instances of such a beginning as I have mentioned, or at least have manifest footsteps of it.

102. He must show a strange inclination to deny evident matter of fact when it agrees not with his hypothesis, who will not allow that the beginnings of Rome and Venice were by the uniting together of several men free and independent one of another, amongst whom there was no natural superiority or subjection. And if Josephus Acosta's word may be taken, he tells us that in many parts of America there was no government at all.

"There are great and apparent conjectures," says he, "that these men," speaking of those of Peru, "for a long time had neither kings nor commonwealths, but lived in troops, as they do this day in Florida, the Cheriquanas, those of Brazil, and many other nations which have no certain kings, but as occasion is offered, in peace or war, they choose their captains as they please."

If it be said that every man there was born subject to his father or the head of his family, that the subjection due from a child to a father took not away his freedom of uniting into what political society he thought fit has been already proved. But be that as it will, these men, it is evident, were actually free; and whatever superiority some politicians now would place in any of them, they themselves claimed it not, but by consent were all equal till by the same consent they set rulers over themselves. So that their politic societies all began from a voluntary union and the mutual agreement of men freely acting in the choice of their governors and forms of government.

103. And I hope those who went away from Sparta with Palantus, mentioned by Justin, *lib.* iii. c. 4, will be allowed to have been freemen, independent one of another, and to have set up a government over themselves by their own consent. Thus I have given several examples out of history of people free and in the state of nature that, being met together, incorporated and began a commonwealth. And if the want of such instances be an argument to prove that governments were not nor could not be so begun, I suppose the contenders for paternal empire were better let it alone than urge it against natural liberty; for if they can give so many instances out of history of governments begun upon paternal right, I think – though at best an argument from what has been to what should of right be has no great force – one might, without any great danger, yield them the cause. But if I might advise them in the case, they would do well not to search too much into the original of governments as they have begun *de facto*, lest they should find at the foundation of most of them something very little favorable to the design they promote and such a power as they contend for.

104. But to conclude, reason being plain on our side that men are naturally free, and the examples of history showing that the governments of the world that were begun in peace had their beginning laid on that foundation, and were made by the consent of the people, there can be little room for doubt either where the right is, or what has been the opinion or practice of mankind about the first erecting of governments.

105. I will not deny that, if we look back as far as history will direct us toward the original of commonwealths, we shall generally find them under the government and administration of one man. And I am also apt to believe that where a family was numerous enough to subsist by itself, and continued entire together without mixing with others, as it often happens where there is much land and few people, the government commonly began in the father; for the father, having by the law of nature the same power with every man else to punish as he thought fit any offenses against that law, might thereby punish his transgressing children even when they were men and out of their pupilage; and they were very likely to submit to his punishment and all join with him against the offender, in their turns, giving him thereby power to execute his sentence against any transgression, and so in effect make him the lawmaker and governor over all that remained in conjunction with his family. He was fittest to be trusted; paternal affection secured their property and interest under his care; and the custom of obeying him in their childhood made it easier to submit to him rather than to any other. If, therefore, they must have one to rule them, as government is hardly to be avoided amongst men that live together, who so likely to be the man as he that was their common father, unless negligence, cruelty, or any other defect of mind or body made him unfit for it? But when either the father died and left his next heir, for want of age, wisdom, courage, or any other qualities, less fit for rule, or where several families met and consented to continue together, there it is not to be doubted but they used their natural freedom to set up him whom they judged the ablest and most likely to rule well over them. Conformable hereunto we find the people of America, who – living out of the reach of the conquering swords and spreading domination of the two great empires of Peru and Mexico – enjoyed their own natural freedom, though, *caeteris paribus*, they commonly prefer the heir of their deceased king; yet, if they find him any way weak or incapable, they pass him by and set up the stoutest and bravest man for their ruler.

106. Thus, though looking back as far as records give us any account of peopling the world and the history of nations, we commonly find the government to be in one hand; yet it destroys not that which I affirm – viz., that the beginning of politic society depends upon the consent of the individuals to join into and make one society; who, when they are thus incorporated, might set up what form of government they thought fit. But this having given occasion to men to mistake and think that by nature government was monarchical and belonged to the father, it may not be amiss here to consider why people in the beginning generally pitched upon this form, which though perhaps the father's pre-eminence might in the first institution of some commonwealth give rise to, and place in the beginning the power in one hand; yet it is plain that the reason that continued the form of government in a single person was not any regard or respect to paternal authority, since all petty monarchies, that is, almost all monarchies, near their original, have been commonly, at least upon occasion, elective.

107. First, then, in the beginning of things, the father's government of the childhood of those sprung from him having accustomed them to the rule of one man and taught them that where it was

exercised with care and skill, with affection and love to those under it, it was sufficient to procure and preserve to men all the political happiness they sought for in society. It was no wonder that they should pitch upon and naturally run into that form of government which from their infancy they had been all accustomed to and which, by experience, they had found both easy and safe. To which, if we add that monarchy being simple and most obvious to men whom neither experience had instructed in forms of government, nor the ambition or insolence of empire had taught to beware of the encroachments of prerogative or the inconveniences of absolute power which monarchy in succession was apt to lay claim to and bring upon them, it was not at all strange that they should not much trouble themselves to think of methods of restraining any exorbitancies of those to whom they had given the authority over them, and of balancing the power of government by placing several parts of it in different hands. They had neither felt the oppression of tyrannical dominion, nor did the fashion of the age, nor their possessions, or way of living, which afforded little matter for covetousness or ambition, give them any reason to apprehend or provide against it; and therefore it is no wonder they put themselves into such a frame of government as was not only, as I said, most obvious and simple, but also best suited to their present state and condition, which stood more in need of defense against foreign invasions and injuries than of multiplicity of laws. The equality of a simple, poor way of living, confining their desires within the narrow bounds of each man's small property, made few controversies, and so no need of many laws to decide them or variety of officers to superintend the process or look after the execution of justice, where there were but few trespasses and offenders. Since, then, those who liked one another so well as to join into society cannot but be supposed to have some acquaintance and friendship together and some trust one in another, they could not but have greater apprehensions of others than of one another; and therefore their first care and thought cannot but be supposed to be how to secure themselves against foreign force. It was natural for them to put themselves under a frame of government which might best serve to that end, and choose the wisest and bravest man to conduct them in their wars and lead them out against their enemies, and in this chiefly be their ruler.

108. Thus we see that the kings of the Indians in America, which is still a pattern of the first ages in Asia and Europe, while the inhabitants were too few for the country, and want of people and money gave men no temptation to enlarge their possessions of land or contest for wider extent of ground, are little more than generals of their armies; and though they command absolutely in war, yet at home and in time of peace they exercise very little dominion and have but a very moderate sovereignty, the resolutions of peace and war being ordinarily either in the people or in a council, though the war itself, which admits not of plurality of governors, naturally devolves the command into the king's sole authority.

109. And thus, in Israel itself, the chief business of their judges and first kings seems to have been to be captains in war and leaders of their armies; which – besides what is signified by "going out and in before the people," which was to march forth to war, and home again at the heads of their forces – appears plainly in the story of Jephthah. The Ammonites making war upon Israel, the Gileadites in fear send to Jephthah, a bastard of their family whom they had cast off, and article with him, if he will assist them against the Ammonites, to make him their ruler; which they do in these words: "And the people made him head and captain over them" (Judges xi. 11), which was, as it seems, all one as to be judge. "And he judged Israel" (Judges xii. 7), that is, was their captain-general, six years. So when Jotham upbraids the Shechemites with the obligation they had to Gideon, who had been their judge and ruler, he tells them, "He fought for you, and adventured his life far, and delivered you out of the hands of Midian" (Judges ix. 17). Nothing is mentioned of him but what he did as a general; and indeed that is all is found in his history, or in any of the rest of the judges. And Abimelech particularly is called king, though at most he was but their general. And when, being weary of the ill conduct of Samuel's sons, the children of Israel desired a king, "like all the nations, to judge them, and to go out before them, and to fight their battles" (1 Sam. viii. 20), God granting their desire says to Samuel: "I will send thee a man, and thou shalt anoint him to be captain over my people Israel, that he may save my people out of the hands of the Philistines" (ix. 16), as if the only business of a king had been to lead out their armies and fight in their defense; and, accordingly, Samuel, at his inauguration, pouring a vial of oil upon him, declares to Saul that "the Lord had anointed him to be captain over his inheritance" (x. 1). And, therefore, those who,

after Saul's being solemnly chosen and saluted king by the tribes of Mispeh, were unwilling to have him their king, made no other objection but this: "How shall this man save us?" (vs. 27), as if they should have said, "This man is unfit to be our king, not having skill and conduct enough in war to be able to defend us." And when God resolved to transfer the government to David, it is in these words: "But now thy kingdom shall not continue. The Lord hath sought him a man after his own heart, and the Lord hath commanded him to be captain over his people" (xiii. 14), as if the whole kingly authority were nothing else but to be their general. And, therefore, the tribes who had stuck to Saul's family and opposed David's reign, when they came to Hebron with terms of submission to him, they tell him, amongst other arguments, they had to submit to him as their king; that he was in effect their king in Saul's time, and, therefore, they had no reason but to receive him as their king now. "Also," say they, "in time past, when Saul was king over us, thou wast he that leddest out and broughtest in Israel, and the Lord said unto thee, 'Thou shalt feed my people Israel and thou shalt be a captain over Israel.'"

110. Thus, whether a family by degrees grew up into a commonwealth and, the fatherly authority being continued on to the elder son, every one in his turn growing up under it tacitly submitted to it, and the easiness and equality of it not offending any one, every one acquiesced, till time seemed to have confirmed it and settled a right of succession by prescription; or whether several families, or the descendants of several families, whom chance, neighborhood, or business brought together, uniting into society, the need of a general whose conduct might defend them against their enemies in war, and the great confidence the innocence and sincerity of that poor but virtuous age – such as are almost all those which begin governments that ever come to last in the world – gave men of another, made the first beginners of commonwealths generally put the rule into one man's hand, without any other express limitation or restraint but what the nature of the thing and the end of government required. Whichever of those it was that at first put the rule into the hands of a single person, certain it is that nobody was intrusted with it but for the public good and safety, and to those ends, in the infancies of commonwealths, those who had it commonly used it. And unless they had done so, young societies could not have subsisted; without such nursing fathers, tender and careful of the public weal, all governments would have sunk under the weakness and infirmities of their infancy, and the prince and the people had soon perished together.

111. But though the golden age – before vain ambition and *amor sceleratus habendi*, evil concupiscence, had corrupted men's minds into a mistake of true power and honor – had more virtue and, consequently, better governors, as well as less vicious subjects; and there was then no stretching prerogative on the one side to oppress the people, nor, consequently, on the other, any dispute about privilege to lessen or restrain the power of the magistrate, and so no contest betwixt rulers and people about governors or government; yet, when ambition and luxury in future ages would retain and increase the power, without doing the business for which it was given, and, aided by flattery, taught princes to have distinct and separate interests from their people, men found it necessary to examine more carefully the original and rights of government, and to find out ways to restrain the exorbitancies and prevent the abuses of that power which, they having entrusted in another's hands only for their own good, they found was made use of to hurt them.

112. Thus we may see how probable it is that people that were naturally free and by their own consent either submitted to the government of their father, or united together out of different families to make a government, should generally put the rule into one man's hands and choose to be under the conduct of a single person, without so much as by express conditions limiting or regulating his power which they thought safe enough in his honesty and prudence, though they never dreamed of monarchy being *jure divino*, which we never heard of among mankind till it was revealed to us by the divinity of this last age, nor ever allowed paternal power to have a right of dominion or to be the foundation of all government. And thus much may suffice to show that, as far as we have any light from history, we have reason to conclude that all peaceful beginnings of government have been laid in the consent of the people. I say peaceful, because I shall have occasion in another place to speak of conquest, which some esteem a way of beginning of governments.

The other objection I find urged against the beginning of politics in the way I have mentioned is this:

113. That all men being born under government, some or other, it is impossible any of them

should ever be free and at liberty to unite together and begin a new one, or ever be able to erect a lawful government.

If this argument be good, I ask, how came so many lawful monarchies into the world? For if anybody, upon this supposition, can show me any one man in any age of the world free to begin a lawful monarchy, I will be bound to show him ten other free men at liberty at the same time to unite and begin a new government under a regal or any other form, it being demonstration that if any one, born under the dominion of another, may be so free as to have a right to command others in a new and distinct empire, every one that is born under the dominion of another may be so free, too, and may become a ruler or subject of a distinct separate government. And so, by this their own principle, either all men, however born, are free, or else there is but one lawful prince, one lawful government in the world. And then they have nothing to do but barely to show us which that is; which, when they have done, I doubt not but all mankind will easily agree to pay obedience to him.

114. Though it be a sufficient answer to their objection to show that it involves them in the same difficulties that it does those they use it against, yet I shall endeavor to discover the weakness of this argument a little further. "All men," say they, "are born under government, and therefore they cannot be at liberty to begin a new one. Everyone is born a subject to his father, or his prince, and is therefore under the perpetual tie of subjection and allegiance." It is plain mankind never owned nor considered any such natural subjection that they were born in, to one or to the other that tied them without their own consents, to a subjection to them and their heirs.

115. For there are no examples so frequent in history, both sacred and profane, as those of men withdrawing themselves and their obedience from the jurisdiction they were born under, and the family or community they were bred up in, and setting up new governments in other places; from whence sprang all that number of petty commonwealths in the beginning of ages, and which always multiplied as long as there was room enough, till the stronger or more fortunate swallowed the weaker, and those great ones, again breaking to pieces, dissolved into lesser dominions. All which are so many testimonies against paternal sovereignty, and plainly prove that it was not the natural right of the father descending to his heirs that made governments in the beginning, since it was

impossible, upon that ground, there should have been so many little kingdoms; all must have been but only one universal monarchy if men had not been at liberty to separate themselves from their families and the government, be it what it will, that was set up in it, and go and make distinct commonwealths and other governments as they thought fit.

116. This has been the practice of the world from its first beginning to this day; nor is it now any more hindrance to the freedom of mankind that they are born under constituted and ancient polities that have established laws and set forms of government, than if they were born in the woods, amongst the unconfined inhabitants that run loose in them; for those who would persuade us that "by being born under any government we are naturally subjects to it" and have no more any title or pretense to the freedom of the state of nature, have no other reason – bating that of paternal power, which we have already answered – to produce for it but only because our fathers or progenitors passed away their natural liberty, and thereby bound up themselves and their posterity to a perpetual subjection to the government which they themselves submitted to. It is true that, whatever engagement or promises any one has made for himself, he is under the obligation of them, but cannot by any compact whatsoever bind his children or posterity; for his son, when a man, being altogether as free as the father, any act of the father can no more give away the liberty of the son than it can of anybody else. He may indeed annex such conditions to the land he enjoyed as a subject of any commonwealth as may oblige his son to be of that community, if he will enjoy those possessions which were his father's, because that estate, being his father's property, he may dispose or settle it as he pleases.

117. And this has generally given the occasion to mistake in this matter; because commonwealths not permitting any part of their dominions to be dismembered, nor to be enjoyed by any but those of their community, the son cannot ordinarily enjoy the possessions of his father but under the same terms his father did, by becoming a member of the society; whereby he puts himself presently under the government he finds there established as much as any other subject of that commonwealth. And thus "the consent of freemen, born under government, which only makes them members of it," being given separately in their turns, as each comes to be of age, and not in a multitude

together, people take no notice of it and, thinking it not done at all, or not necessary, conclude they are naturally subjects as they are men.

118. But, it is plain, governments themselves understand it otherwise; they claim no power over the son because of that they had over the father; nor look on children as being their subjects, by their father's being so. If a subject of England have a child by an English woman in France, whose subject is he? Not the King of England's, for he must have leave to be admitted to the privileges of it; nor the King of France's, for how then has his father a liberty to bring him away and breed him as he pleases? And who ever was judged as a traitor or deserter, if he left or warred against a country, for being barely born in it of parents that were aliens there? It is plain, then, by the practice of governments themselves as well as by the law of right reason, that a child is born a subject of no country or government. He is under his father's tuition and authority till he comes to age of discretion; and then he is a freeman, at liberty what government he will put himself under, what body politic he will unite himself to; for if an Englishman's son, born in France, be at liberty, and may do so, it is evident there is no tie upon him by his father's being a subject of this kingdom, nor is he bound up by any compact of his ancestors. And why then has not his son, by the same reason, the same liberty though he be born anywhere else? Since the power that a father has naturally over his children is the same wherever they be born, and the ties of natural obligations are not bounded by the positive limits of kingdoms and commonwealths.

119. Every man being, as has been shown, naturally free, and nothing being able to put him into subjection to any earthly power but only his own consent, it is to be considered what shall be understood to be a sufficient declaration of a man's consent to make him subject to the laws of any government. There is a common distinction of an express and a tacit consent which will concern our present case. Nobody doubts but an express consent of any man entering into any society makes him a perfect member of that society, a subject of that government. The difficulty is, what ought to be looked upon as a tacit consent, and how far it binds – i.e., how far any one shall be looked upon to have consented and thereby submitted to any government, where he has made no expressions of it at all. And to this I say that every man that has any possessions or enjoyment of any part of the

dominions of any government does thereby give his tacit consent and is as far forth obliged to obedience to the laws of that government, during such enjoyment, as anyone under it; whether this his possession be of land to him and his heirs for ever, or a lodging only for a week, or whether it be barely traveling freely on the highway; and, in effect, it reaches as far as the very being of anyone within the territories of that government.

120. To understand this the better, it is fit to consider that every man, when he at first incorporates himself into any commonwealth, he, by his uniting himself thereunto, annexes also, and submits to the community, those possessions which he has or shall acquire that do not already belong to any other government; for it would be a direct contradiction for any one to enter into society with others for the securing and regulating of property, and yet to suppose his land, whose property is to be regulated by the laws of the society, should be exempt from the jurisdiction of that government to which he himself, the proprietor of the land, is a subject. By the same act, therefore, whereby any one unites his person, which was before free, to any commonwealth, by the same he unites his possessions which were before free to it also; and they become, both of them, person and possession, subject to the government and dominion of that commonwealth as long as it has a being. Whoever, therefore, from thenceforth by inheritance, purchase, permission, or otherwise, enjoys any part of the land so annexed to, and under the government of that commonwealth, must take it with the condition it is under – that is, of submitting to the government of the commonwealth under whose jurisdiction it is as far forth as any subject of it.

121. But since the government has a direct jurisdiction only over the land, and reaches the possessor of it – before he has actually incorporated himself in the society – only as he dwells upon and enjoys that, the obligation anyone is under by virtue of such enjoyment, to submit to the government, begins and ends with the enjoyment; so that whenever the owner, who has given nothing but such a tacit consent to the government, will, by donation, sale, or otherwise, quit the said possession, he is at liberty to go and incorporate himself into any other commonwealth, or to agree with others to begin a new one *in vacuis locis*, in any part of the world they can find free and unpossessed. Whereas he that has once, by actual agreement and any express declaration, given his

consent to be of any commonwealth is perpetually and indispensably obliged to be and remain unalterably a subject to it, and can never be again in the liberty of the state of nature, unless by any calamity the government he was under comes to be dissolved, or else, by some public act, cuts him off from being any longer a member of it.

122. But submitting to the laws of any country, living quietly and enjoying privileges and protection under them, makes not a man a member of that society; this is only a local protection and homage due to and from all those who, not being in a state of war, come within the territories belonging to any government, to all parts whereof the force of its laws extends. But this no more makes a man a member of that society, a perpetual subject of that commonwealth, than it would make a man a subject to another in whose family he found it convenient to abide for some time, though, while he continued in it, he were obliged to comply with the laws and submit to the government he found there. And thus we see that foreigners, by living all their lives under another government and enjoying the privileges and protection of it, though they are bound, even in conscience, to submit to its administration as far forth as any denizen, yet do not thereby come to be subjects or members of that commonwealth. Nothing can make any man so but his actually entering into it by positive engagement and express promise and compact. That is that which I think concerning the beginning of political societies and that consent which makes any one a member of any commonwealth.

PART VII

George Berkeley (1685–1753)

Introduction

Berkeley's most influential works were written early in his career. *An Essay Towards a New Theory of Vision*, written in 1709, focuses on several key questions about the nature of human perception. In our selection from this work, Berkeley discusses the relation between the objects of sight and touch, presenting his own distinctive solution to the Molyneux problem (see Locke, "Of Perception," in chapter 17 above). This is followed by an excerpt from *A Treatise Concerning the Principles of Human Knowledge* (1710) in which Berkeley introduces the celebrated "*esse* is *percipi*" thesis, the "master argument" against the metaphysical realism of Locke and his rationalist predecessors. The third selection, from Berkeley's essay *Concerning Motion* (*De Motu*), was written in 1720. Of special interest in this piece is the manner in which Berkeley distinguishes between metaphysical and scientific accounts of motion. Our final selection is drawn from a little-known essay by the title *Passive Obedience* (1712). In it Berkeley presents the main outline of his moral and political philosophy, arguing that the duty to obey the sovereign is "in strict truth a law of nature, universal reason, and morality."

21

An Essay Towards a New Theory of Vision

On the Relation Between Objects of Sight and Touch

[...] 121. We have shown the way wherein the mind, by mediation of visible ideas, perceives or apprehends the distance, magnitude, and situation of tangible objects. We come now to inquire more particularly concerning the difference between the ideas of sight and touch which are called by the same names, and see whether there be any idea common to both senses. From what we have at large set forth and demonstrated in the foregoing parts of this treatise, it is plain there is no one selfsame numerical extension, perceived both by sight and touch; but that the particular figures and extensions perceived by sight, however they may be called by the same names and reputed the same things with those perceived by touch, are nevertheless different, and have an existence distinct and separate from them. So that the question is not now concerning the same numerical ideas, but whether there be any one and the same sort or species of ideas equally perceivable to both senses? Or, in other words, whether extension, figure, and motion perceived by sight, are not specifically distinct from extension, figure, and motion perceived by touch?

122. But before I come more particularly to discuss this matter, I find it proper to consider extension in abstract. For of this there is much talk; and I am apt to think that when men speak of

An Essay Towards a New Theory of Vision (1709). From *Works on Vision*, ed. **Colin Murray Turbayne** (Indianapolis: Bobbs-Merrill Co., Inc., 1963). Selection: sects 121–48, pp. 77–92.

extension as being an idea common to two senses, it is with a secret supposition that we can single out extension from all other tangible and visible qualities, and form thereof an abstract idea, which idea they will have common both to sight and touch. We are therefore to understand by extension in abstract, an idea of extension – for instance, a line or surface entirely stripped of all other sensible qualities and circumstances that might determine it to any particular existence; it is neither black, nor white, nor red, nor has it any color at all, or any tangible quality whatsoever, and consequently it is of no finite determinate magnitude; for that which bounds or distinguishes one extension from another is some quality or circumstance wherein they disagree.

123. Now, I do not find that I can perceive, imagine, or anywise frame in my mind such an abstract idea as is here spoken of. A line or surface which is neither black, nor white, nor blue, nor yellow, etc., nor long, nor short, nor rough, nor smooth, nor square, nor round, etc., is perfectly incomprehensible. This I am sure of as to myself; how far the faculties of other men may reach they best can tell.

124. It is commonly said that the object of geometry is abstract extension. But geometry contemplates figures: now, figure is the termination of magnitude; but we have shown that extension in abstract has no finite determinate magnitude; whence it clearly follows that it can have no figure, and consequently is not the object of geometry. It is indeed a tenet, as well of the modern as of the ancient philosophers, that all general truths are concerning universal abstract ideas; without which, we are told, there could be no science, no

demonstration of any general proposition in geometry. But it were no hard matter, did I think it necessary to my present purpose, to show that propositions and demonstrations in geometry might be universal, though they who make them never think of abstract general ideas of triangles or circles.

125. After reiterated endeavors to apprehend the general idea of a triangle, I have found it altogether incomprehensible. And surely, if anyone were able to introduce that idea into my mind, it must be the author of the *Essay Concerning Human Understanding*: he, who has so far distinguished himself from the generality of writers by the clearness and significancy of what he says. Let us therefore see how this celebrated author describes the general or abstract idea of a triangle. "It must be," says he, "neither oblique nor rectangular, neither equilateral, equicrural, nor scalenum; but all and none of these at once. In effect it is somewhat imperfect that cannot exist; an idea, wherein some parts of several different and inconsistent ideas are put together." (*Essay on Human Understanding*, Bk. IV, chap. 7, sec. 9.) This is the idea which he thinks needful for the enlargement of knowledge, which is the subject of mathematical demonstration, and without which we could never come to know any general proposition concerning triangles. That author acknowledges it does "require some pains and skill to form this general idea of a triangle." (*Ibid.*) But, had he called to mind what he says in another place, to wit, "that ideas of mixed modes wherein any inconsistent ideas are put together cannot so much as exist in the mind, i.e., be conceived" (*vide* Bk. III, chap. 10, sec. 33, *ibid.*) – I say, had this occurred to his thoughts, it is not improbable he would have owned it above all the pains and skill he was master of, to form the above-mentioned idea of a triangle, which is made up of manifest staring contradictions. That a man who laid so great a stress on clear and determinate ideas should nevertheless talk at this rate seems very surprising. But the wonder will lessen if it be considered that the source whence this opinion flows is the prolific womb which has brought forth innumerable errors and difficulties, in all parts of philosophy, and in all the sciences. But this matter, taken in its full extent, were a subject too comprehensive to be insisted on in this place. And so much for extension in abstract.

126. Some, perhaps, may think pure space, vacuum, or trine dimension to be equally the object of sight and touch. But, though we have a very great propension to think the ideas of outness and space to be the immediate object of sight, yet, if I mistake not, in the foregoing parts of this essay that has been clearly demonstrated to be a mere delusion, arising from the quick and sudden suggestion of fancy, which so closely connects the idea of distance with that of sight that we are apt to think it is itself a proper and immediate object of that sense, till reason corrects the mistake.

127. It having been shown that there are no abstract ideas of figure, and that it is impossible for us, by any precision of thought, to frame an idea of extension separate from all other visible and tangible qualities which shall be common both to sight and touch, the question now remaining is whether the particular extensions, figures, and motions perceived by sight be of the same kind with the particular extensions, figures, and motions perceived by touch? In answer to which I shall venture to lay down the following proposition: *The extension, figures, and motions perceived by sight are specifically distinct from the ideas of touch, called by the same names; nor is there any such thing as one idea, or kind of idea, common to both senses.* This proposition may, without much difficulty, be collected from what has been said in several places of this essay. But, because it seems so remote from, and contrary to, the received notions and settled opinion of mankind, I shall attempt to demonstrate it more particularly and at large by the following arguments.

128. When upon perception of an idea I range it under this or that sort, it is because it is perceived after the same manner, or because it has a likeness or conformity with, or affects me in the same way as the ideas of the sort I rank it under. In short, it must not be entirely new, but have something in it old and already perceived by me. It must, I say, have so much, at least, in common with the ideas I have before known and named as to make me give it the same name with them. But, it has been, if I mistake not, clearly made out that a man born blind would not, at first reception of his sight, think the things he saw were of the same nature with the objects of touch, or had anything in common with them; but that they were a new set of ideas, perceived in a new manner, and entirely different from all he had ever perceived before. So that he would not call them by the same name, nor repute them to be of the same sort, with anything he had hitherto known.

129. *Secondly*, light and colors are allowed by all to constitute a sort of species entirely different

from the ideas of touch; nor will any man, I presume, say they can make themselves perceived by that sense. But there is no other immediate object of sight besides light and colors. It is therefore a direct consequence that there is no idea common to both senses.

130. It is a prevailing opinion, even amongst those who have thought and written most accurately concerning our ideas, and the ways whereby the enter into the understanding, that something more is perceived by sight than barely light and colors with their variations. Mr. Locke terms sight "the most comprehensive of all our senses, conveying to our minds the ideas of light and colors, which are peculiar only to that sense; and also the far different ideas of space, figure, and motion." (*Essay on Human Understanding*, Bk. II, chap. 9, sec. 9.) Space or distance, we have shown, is not otherwise the object of sight than of hearing (*vide* sec. 46). And as for figure and extension, I leave it to anyone that shall calmly attend to his own clear and distinct ideas to decide whether he has any idea intromitted immediately and properly by sight save only light and colors; or whether it be possible for him to frame in his mind a distinct abstract idea of visible extension, or figure, exclusive of all color; and, on the other hand, whether he can conceive color without visible extension? For my own part, I must confess, I am not able to attain so great a nicety of abstraction; in a strict sense, I see nothing but light and colors, with their several shades and variations. He who beside these also perceives by sight ideas far different and distinct from them, has that faculty in a degree more perfect and comprehensive than I can pretend to. It must be owned that, by the mediation of light and colors, other far different ideas are suggested to my mind: but so they are by hearing which, beside sounds which are peculiar to that sense, does, by their mediation, suggest not only space, figure, and motion, but also all other ideas whatsoever that can be signified by words.

131. *Thirdly*, it is, I think, an axiom universally received that quantities of the same kind may be added together and make one entire sum. Mathematicians add lines together; but they do not add a line to a solid, or conceive it as making one sum with a surface. These three kinds of quantity being thought incapable of any such mutual addition, and consequently of being compared together in the several ways of proportion, are by them esteemed entirely disparate and heterogeneous.

Now let anyone try in his thoughts to add a visible line or surface to a tangible line or surface so as to conceive them making one continued sum or whole. He that can do this may think them homogeneous; but he that cannot must, by the foregoing axiom, think them heterogeneous. A blue and a red line I can conceive added together into one sum and making one continued line; but, to make, in my thoughts, one continued line of a visible and tangible line added together is, I find, a task far more difficult, and even insurmountable; and I leave it to the reflection and experience of every particular person to determine for himself.

132. A further confirmation of our tenet may be drawn from the solution of Mr. Molyneux's problem, published by Mr. Locke in his *Essay*: which I shall set down as it there lies, together with Mr. Locke's opinion of it: "*Suppose a man born blind, and now adult, and taught by his touch to distinguish between a cube and a sphere of the same metal, and nighly of the same bigness, so as to tell when he felt one and the other, which is the cube, and which the sphere. Suppose then the cube and sphere placed on a table, and the blind man made to see:* quaere, *whether by his sight, before he touched them, he could now distinguish and tell which is the globe, which the cube?* To which the acute and judicious proposer answers: *Not. For, though he has obtained the experience of how a globe, how a cube affects his touch; yet he has not yet attained the experience that what affects his touch so or so must affect his sight so or so; or that a protuberant angle in the cube, that pressed his hand unequally, shall appear to his eye as it does in the cube.* I agree with this thinking gentleman, whom I am proud to call my friend, in his answer to this his problem; and am of opinion that the blind man, at first sight, would not be able with certainty to say which was the globe, which the cube, while he only saw them" (*Essay on Human Understanding*, Bk. II, chap. 9, sec. 8).

133. Now, if a square surface perceived by touch be the same sort with a square surface perceived by sight, it is certain the blind man here mentioned might know a square surface as soon as he saw it. It is no more but introducing into his mind, by a new inlet, an idea he has been already well acquainted with. Since therefore he is supposed to have known by his touch that a cube is a body terminated by square surfaces; and that a sphere is not terminated by square surfaces – upon the supposition that a visible and tangible square differ only *in numero*, it follows that he might know, by the unerring mark of the square

surfaces, which was the cube, and which not, while he only saw them. We must therefore allow either that visible extension and figures are specifically distinct from tangible extension and figures, or else that the solution of this problem given by those two thoughtful and ingenious men is wrong.

134. Much more might be laid together in proof of the proposition I have advanced. But, what has been said is, if I mistake not, sufficient to convince anyone that shall yield a reasonable attention. And, as for those that will not be at the pains of a little thought, no multiplication of words will ever suffice to make them understand the truth or rightly conceive my meaning.

135. I cannot let go the above-mentioned problem without some reflection on it. It has been made evident that a man blind from his birth would not, at first sight, denominate anything he saw by the names he had been used to appropriate to ideas of touch (*vide* sec. 106). "Cube," "sphere," "table," are words he has known applied to things perceivable by touch, but to things perfectly intangible he never knew them applied. Those words, in their wonted application, always marked out to his mind bodies or solid things which were perceived by the resistance they gave. But there is no solidity, no resistance or protrusion, perceived by sight. In short, the ideas of sight are all new perceptions to which there be no names annexed in his mind; he cannot therefore understand what is said to him concerning them. And to ask of the two bodies he saw placed on the table which was the sphere, which the cube, were to him a question downright bantering and unintelligible, nothing he sees being able to suggest to his thoughts the idea of body, distance, or, in general, of anything he had already known.

136. It is a mistake to think the same thing affects both sight and touch. If the same angle or square which is the object of touch be also the object of vision, what should hinder the blind man, at first sight, from knowing it? For, though the manner wherein it affects the sight be different from that wherein it affected his touch, yet, there being beside this manner or circumstance which is new and unknown the angle or figure which is old and known, he cannot choose but discern it.

137. Visible figure and extension having been demonstrated to be of a nature entirely different and heterogeneous from tangible figure and extension, it remains that we inquire concerning motion. Now, that visible motion is not of the same sort with tangible motion seems to need no further proof; it

being an evident corollary from what we have shown concerning the difference there is betwixt visible and tangible extension. But for a more full and express proof hereof, we need only observe that one who had not yet experienced vision would not at first sight know motion. Whence it clearly follows that motion perceivable by sight is of a sort distinct from motion perceivable by touch. The antecedent I prove thus: By touch he could not perceive any motion but what was up or down, to the right or left, nearer or farther from him; besides these, and their several varieties or complications, it is impossible he should have any idea of motion. He would not therefore think anything to be motion, or give the name "motion" to any idea which he could not range under some or other of those particular kinds thereof. But from sec. 95 it is plain that, by the mere act of vision, he could not know motion upward or downward, to the right or left, or in any other possible direction. From which I conclude, he would not know motion at all at first sight. As for the idea of motion in abstract, I shall not waste paper about it, but leave it to my reader to make the best he can of it. To me it is perfectly unintelligible.

138. The consideration of motion may furnish a new field for inquiry. But, since the manner wherein the mind apprehends by sight the motion of tangible objects, with the various degrees thereof, may be easily collected from what has been said concerning the manner wherein that sense does suggest their various distances, magnitudes, and situations, I shall not enlarge any further on this subject, but proceed to consider what may be alleged with greatest appearance of reason, against the proposition we have shown to be true: For, where there is so much prejudice to be encountered, a bare and naked demonstration of the truth will scarce suffice. We must also satisfy the scruples that men may raise in favor of their preconceived notions, show whence the mistake arises, how it came to spread, and carefully disclose and root out those false persuasions that an early prejudice might have implanted in the mind.

139. *First*, therefore, it will be demanded how visible extension and figures come to be called by the same name with tangible extension and figures, if they are not of the same kind with them? It must be something more than humor or accident that could occasion a custom so constant and universal as this, which has obtained in all ages and nations of the world, and amongst all ranks of men, the learned as well as the illiterate.

140. To which I answer, we can no more argue a visible and tangible square to be of the same species from their being called by the same name, than we can that a tangible square and the monosyllable consisting of six letters whereby it is marked are of the same species, because they are both called by the same name. It is customary to call written words and the things they signify by the same name; for, words not being regarded in their own nature, or otherwise than as they are marks of things, it had been superfluous and beside the design of language to have given them names distinct from those of the things marked by them. The same reason holds here also. Visible figures are the marks of tangible figures; and, from sec. 59, it is plain that in themselves they are little regarded, or upon any other score than for their connection with tangible figures, which by nature they are ordained to signify. And, because this language of nature does not vary in different ages or nations, hence it is that in all times and places visible figures are called by the same names as the respective tangible figures suggested by them; and not because they are alike, or of the same sort with them.

141. But, say you, surely a tangible square is liker to a visible square than to a visible circle: It has four angles, and as many sides; so also has the visible square; but the visible circle has no such thing, being bounded by one uniform curve, without right lines or angles, which makes it unfit to represent the tangible square, but very fit to represent the tangible circle. Whence it clearly follows that visible figures are patterns of, or of the same species with, the respective tangible figures represented by them; that they are like unto them, and of their own nature fitted to represent them, as being of the same sort; and that they are in no respect arbitrary signs, as words.

142. I answer, it must be acknowledged the visible square is fitter than the visible circle to represent the tangible square, but then it is not because it is liker, or more of a species with it, but because the visible square contains in it several distinct parts whereby to mark the several distinct corresponding parts of a tangible square, whereas the visible circle does not. The square perceived by touch has four distinct equal sides, so also has it four distinct equal angles. It is therefore necessary that the visible figure which shall be most proper to mark it contain four distinct equal parts, corresponding to the four sides of the tangible square; as likewise four other distinct and equal parts,

whereby to denote the four equal angles of the tangible square. And accordingly we see the visible figures contain in them distinct visible parts, answering to the distinct tangible parts of the figures signified or suggested by them.

143. But it will not hence follow that any visible figure is like unto or of the same species with its corresponding tangible figure – unless it be also shown that not only the number but also the kind of the parts be the same in both. To illustrate this, I observe that visible figures represent tangible figures much after the same manner that written words do sounds. Now, in this respect, words are not arbitrary; it not being indifferent what written word stands for any sound. But it is requisite that each word contain in it so many distinct characters as there are variations in the sound it stands for. Thus, the single letter "a" is proper to mark one simple uniform sound; and the word "adultery" is accommodated to represent the sound annexed to it – in the formation whereof, there being eight different collisions or modifications of the air by the organs of speech, each of which produces a difference of sound, it was fit the word representing it should consist of as many distinct characters, thereby to mark each particular difference or part of the whole sound. And yet nobody, I presume, will say the single letter "a," or the word "adultery," are alike unto or of the same species with the respective sounds by them represented. It is indeed arbitrary that, in general, letters of any language represent sounds at all; but, when that is once agreed, it is not arbitrary what combination of letters shall represent this or that particular sound. I leave this with the reader to pursue, and apply it in his own thoughts.

144. It must be confessed that we are not so apt to confound other signs with the things signified, or to think them of the same species, as we are visible and tangible ideas. But, a little consideration will show us how this may be, without our supposing them of a like nature. These signs are constant and universal; their connection with tangible ideas has been learned at our first entrance into the world; and ever since, almost every moment of our lives, it has been occurring to our thoughts, and fastening and striking deeper on our minds. When we observe that signs are variable, and of human institution; when we remember there was a time they were not connected in our minds with those things they now so readily suggest, but that their signification was learned by the slow steps of experience: this preserves us from

confounding them. But, when we find the same signs suggest the same things all over the world; when we know they are not of human institution, and cannot remember that we ever learned their signification, but think that at first sight they would have suggested to us the same things they do now – all this persuades us they are of the same species as the things respectively represented by them, and that it is by a natural resemblance they suggest them to our minds.

145. Add to this that whenever we make a nice survey of any object, successively directing the optic axis to each point thereof, there are certain lines and figures, described by the motion of the head or eye which, being in truth perceived by feeling, do nevertheless so mix themselves, as it were, with the ideas of sight that we can scarce think but they appertain to that sense. Again, the ideas of sight enter into the mind several at once, more distinct and unmingled than is usual in the other senses beside the touch. Sounds, for example, perceived at the same instant, are apt to coalesce, if I may so say, into one sound; but we can perceive, at the same time, great variety of visible objects, very separate and distinct from each other. Now, tangible extension being made up of several distinct coexistent parts, we may hence gather another reason that may dispose us to imagine a likeness or analogy between the immediate objects of sight and touch. But nothing, certainly, does more contribute to blend and confound them together than the strict and close connection they have with each other. We cannot open our eyes but the ideas of distance, bodies, and tangible figures are suggested by them. So swift, and sudden, and unperceived is the transition from visible to tangible ideas that we can scarce forbear thinking them equally the immediate object of vision.

146. The prejudice which is grounded on these, and whatever other causes may be assigned thereof, sticks so fast that it is impossible, without obstinate striving and labor of the mind, to get entirely clear of it. But then the reluctancy we find in rejecting any opinion can be no argument of its truth, to whoever considers what has been already shown with regard to the prejudices we entertain concerning the distance, magnitude, and situation of objects; prejudices so familiar to our minds, so confirmed and inveterate, as they will hardly give way to the clearest demonstration.

147. Upon the whole, I think we may fairly conclude that the proper objects of vision constitute a universal language of the Author of nature, whereby we are instructed how to regulate our actions in order to attain those things that are necessary to the preservation and well-being of our bodies, as also to avoid whatever may be hurtful and destructive of them. It is by their information that we are principally guided in all the transactions and concerns of life. And the manner wherein they signify and mark unto us the objects which are at a distance is the same with that of languages and signs of human appointment; which do not suggest the things signified by any likeness or identity of nature, but only by a habitual connection that experience has made us to observe between them.

148. Suppose one who had always continued blind be told by his guide that after he has advanced so many steps he shall come to the brink of a precipice, or be stopped by a wall; must not this to him seem very admirable and surprising? He cannot conceive how it is possible for mortals to frame such predictions as these, which to him seem as strange and unaccountable as prophecy does to others. Even they who are blessed with the visive faculty may (though familiarity make it less observed) find therein sufficient cause of admiration. The wonderful art and contrivance wherewith it is adjusted to those ends and purposes for which it was apparently designed; the vast extent, number, and variety of objects that are at once, with so much ease, and quickness, and pleasure, suggested by it – all these afford subject for much and pleasing speculation, and may, if anything, give us some glimmering analogous prenotion of things that are placed beyond the certain discovery and comprehension of our present state. [...]

22

A Treatise Concerning the Principles of Human Knowledge

Argument Against the Existence of Material Substance

[...] 17. If we inquire into what the most accurate philosophers declare themselves to mean by *material substance*, we shall find them acknowledge they have no other meaning annexed to those sounds but the idea of being in general together with the relative notion of its supporting accidents. The general idea of being appears to me the most abstract and incomprehensible of all other; and as for its supporting accidents, this, as we have just now observed, cannot be understood in the common sense of those words; it must, therefore, be taken in some other sense, but what that is they do not explain. So that when I consider the two parts or branches which make the signification of the words *material substance*, I am convinced there is no distinct meaning annexed to them. But why should we trouble ourselves any further in discussing this material *substratum* or support of figure and motion and other sensible qualities? Does it not suppose they have an existence without the mind? And is not this a direct repugnance and altogether inconceivable?

18. But, though it were possible that solid, figured, movable substances may exist without the mind, corresponding to the ideas we have of bodies, yet how is it possible for us to know this? Either we must know it by sense or by reason. As for our senses, by them we have the knowledge

only of our sensations, ideas, or those things that are immediately perceived by sense, call them what you will; but they do not inform us that things exist without the mind, or unperceived, like to those which are perceived. This the materialists themselves acknowledge. It remains therefore that if we have any knowledge at all of external things, it must be by reason, inferring their existence from what is immediately perceived by sense. But what reason can induce us to believe the existence of bodies without the mind, from what we perceive, since the very patrons of matter themselves do not pretend there is any necessary connection betwixt them and our ideas? I say it is granted on all hands (and what happens in dreams, frenzies, and the like, puts it beyond dispute) that it is possible we might be affected with all the ideas we have now, though no bodies existed without resembling them. Hence it is evident the supposition of external bodies is not necessary for the producing our ideas; since it is granted they are produced sometimes, and might possibly be produced always in the same order we see them in at present, without their concurrence.

19. But though we might possibly have all our sensations without them, yet perhaps it may be thought easier to conceive and explain the manner of their production by supposing external bodies in their likeness rather than otherwise; and so it might be at least probable there are such things as bodies that excite their ideas in our minds. But neither can this be said, for, though we give the materialists their external bodies, they by their own confession are never the nearer knowing how our ideas are produced, since they own themselves unable to comprehend in what manner body

A Treatise Concerning the Principles of Human Knowledge (1710), ed. Colin Murray Turbayne (Indianapolis: Bobbs-Merrill Co., Inc., 1957). Selection: sects 17–33, pp. 30–8.

can act upon spirit, or how it is possible it should imprint any idea in the mind. Hence it is evident the production of ideas or sensations in our minds can be no reason why we should suppose matter or corporeal substances, since that is acknowledged to remain equally inexplicable with or without this supposition. If therefore it were possible for bodies to exist without the mind, yet to hold they do so must needs be a very precarious opinion, since it is to suppose, without any reason at all, that God has created innumerable beings that are entirely useless and serve to no manner of purpose.

20. In short, if there were external bodies, it is impossible we should ever come to know it; and if there were not, we might have the very same reasons to think there were that we have now. Suppose – what no one can deny possible – an intelligence without the help of external bodies, to be affected with the same train of sensations or ideas that you are, imprinted in the same order and with like vividness in his mind. I ask whether that intelligence has not all the reason to believe the existence of corporeal substances, represented by his ideas and exciting them in his mind, that you can possibly have for believing the same thing? Of this there can be no question – which one consideration is enough to make any reasonable person suspect the strength of whatever arguments he may think himself to have for the existence of bodies without the mind.

21. Were it necessary to add any further proof against the existence of matter after what has been said, I could instance several of those errors and difficulties (not to mention impieties) which have sprung from that tenet. It has occasioned numberless controversies and disputes in philosophy, and not a few of far greater moment in religion. But I shall not enter into the detail of them in this place as well because I think arguments *a posteriori* are unnecessary for confirming what has been, if I mistake not, sufficiently demonstrated *a priori*, as because I shall hereafter find occasion to speak somewhat of them.

22. I am afraid I have given cause to think me needlessly prolix in handling this subject. For to what purpose is it to dilate on that which may be demonstrated with the utmost evidence in a line or two to anyone that is capable of the least reflection? It is but looking into your own thoughts, and so trying whether you can conceive it possible for a sound, or figure, or motion, or color to exist without the mind or unperceived. This easy trial may make you see that what you contend for is a downright contradiction. Insomuch that I am content to put the whole upon this issue: if you can but conceive it possible for one extended movable substance, or, in general, for any one idea, or anything like an idea, to exist otherwise than in a mind perceiving it, I shall readily give up the cause. And, as for all that compages of external bodies which you contend for, I shall grant you its existence, though you cannot either give me any reason why you believe it exists, or assign any use to it when it is supposed to exist. I say the bare possibility of your opinion's being true shall pass for an argument that it is so.

23. But, say you, surely there is nothing easier than to imagine trees, for instance, in a park, or books existing in a closet, and nobody by to perceive them. I answer you may so, there is no difficulty in it; but what is all this, I beseech you, more than framing in your mind certain ideas which you call books and trees, and at the same time omitting to frame the idea of anyone that may perceive them? But do not you yourself perceive or think of them all the while? This therefore is nothing to the purpose; it only shows you have the power of imagining or forming ideas in your mind; but it does not show that you can conceive it possible the objects of your thought may exist without the mind. To make out this, it is necessary that you conceive them existing unconceived or unthought of, which is a manifest repugnancy. When we do our utmost to conceive the existence of external bodies, we are all the while only contemplating our own ideas. But the mind, taking no notice of itself, is deluded to think it can and does conceive bodies existing unthought of or without the mind, though at the same time they are apprehended by or exist in itself. A little attention will discover to anyone the truth and evidence of what is here said, and make it unnecessary to insist on any other proofs against the existence of *material substance*.

24. It is very obvious, upon the least inquiry into our own thoughts, to know whether it be possible for us to understand what is meant by the *absolute existence of sensible objects in themselves, or without the mind*. To me it is evident those words mark out either a direct contradiction or else nothing at all. And to convince others of this, I know no readier or fairer way than to entreat they would calmly attend to their own thoughts; and if by this attention the emptiness or repugnance of those expressions does appear, surely nothing more is requisite for their conviction. It is on this, there-

fore, that I insist, to wit, that "the absolute existence of unthinking things" are words without a meaning, or which include a contradiction. This is what I repeat and inculcate, and earnestly recommend to the attentive thoughts of the reader.

25. All our ideas, sensations, or the things which we perceive, by whatsoever names they may be distinguished, are visibly inactive – there is nothing of power or agency included in them. So that one idea or object of thought cannot produce or make any alteration in another. To be satisfied of the truth of this, there is nothing else requisite but a bare observation of our ideas. For since they and every part of them exist only in the mind, it follows that there is nothing in them but what is perceived; but whoever shall attend to his ideas, whether of sense or reflection, will not perceive in them any power or activity; there is, therefore, no such thing contained in them. A little attention will discover to us that the very being of an idea implies passiveness and inertness in it, insomuch that it is impossible for an idea to do anything or, strictly speaking, to be the cause of anything; neither can it be the resemblance or pattern of any active being, as is evident from sect. 8. Whence it plainly follows that extension, figure, and motion cannot be the cause of our sensations. To say, therefore, that these are the effects of powers resulting from the configuration, number, motion, and size of corpuscles must certainly be false.

26. We perceive a continual succession of ideas, some are anew excited, others are changed or totally disappear. There is, therefore, some cause of these ideas, whereon they depend and which produces and changes them. That this cause cannot be any quality or idea or combination of ideas is clear from the preceding section. It must therefore be a substance; but it has been shown that there is no corporeal or material substance: it remains, therefore, that the cause of ideas is an incorporeal, active substance or spirit.

27. A spirit is one simple, undivided, active being – as it perceives ideas it is called the *understanding*, and as it produces or otherwise operates about them it is called the *will*. Hence there can be no *idea* formed of a soul or spirit; for all ideas whatever, being passive and inert (*vide* sect. 25), they cannot represent unto us, by way of image or likeness, that which acts. A little attention will make it plain to anyone that to have an idea which shall be like that active principle of motion and change of ideas is absolutely impossible. Such is the nature of *spirit*, or that which acts, that it

cannot be of itself perceived, but only by the effects which it produces. If any man shall doubt of the truth of what is here delivered, let him but reflect and try if he can frame the idea of any power or active being, and whether he has ideas of two principal powers marked by the names *will* and *understanding*, distinct from each other as well as from a third idea of substance or being in general, with a relative notion of its supporting or being the subject of the aforesaid powers – which is signified by the name *soul* or *spirit*. This is what some hold; but, so far as I can see, the words *will*, *soul*, *spirit* do not stand for different ideas or, in truth, for any idea at all, but for something which is very different from ideas, and which, being an agent, cannot be like unto, or represented by, any idea whatsoever. Though it must be owned at the same time that we have some notion of soul, spirit, and the operations of the mind, such as willing, loving, hating – in as much as we know or understand the meaning of those words.

28. I find I can excite ideas in my mind at pleasure, and vary and shift the scene as oft as I think fit. It is no more than willing, and straightway this or that idea arises in my fancy; and by the same power it is obliterated and makes way for another. This making and unmaking of ideas does very properly denominate the mind active. Thus much is certain and grounded on experience; but when we talk of unthinking agents or of exciting ideas exclusive of volition, we only amuse ourselves with words.

29. But, whatever power I may have over my own thoughts, I find the ideas actually perceived by sense have not a like dependence on my will. When in broad daylight I open my eyes, it is not in my power to choose whether I shall see or no, or to determine what particular objects shall present themselves to my view; and so likewise as to the hearing and other senses; the ideas imprinted on them are not creatures of my will. There is therefore some *other* will or spirit that produces them.

30. The ideas of sense are more strong, lively, and distinct than those of the imagination; they have likewise a steadiness, order, and coherence, and are not excited at random, as those which are the effects of human wills often are, but in a regular train or series, the admirable connection whereof sufficiently testifies the wisdom and benevolence of its Author. Now the set rules or established methods wherein the mind we depend on excites in us the ideas of sense are called the *laws of nature*; and these we learn by experience,

which teaches us that such and such ideas are attended with such and such other ideas in the ordinary course of things.

31. This gives us a sort of foresight which enables us to regulate our actions for the benefit of life. And without this we should be eternally at a loss; we could not know how to act anything that might procure us the least pleasure or remove the least pain of sense. That food nourishes, sleep refreshes, and fire warms us; that to sow in the seedtime is the way to reap in the harvest; and in general that to obtain such or such ends, such or such means are conducive – all this we know, not by discovering any necessary connection between our ideas, but only by the observation of the settled laws of nature, without which we should be all in uncertainty and confusion, and a grown man no more know how to manage himself in the affairs of life than an infant just born.

32. And yet this consistent, uniform working which so evidently displays the goodness and wisdom of that Governing Spirit whose Will constitutes the laws of nature, is so far from leading our thoughts to Him that it rather sends them awandering after second causes. For when we perceive certain ideas of sense constantly followed by other ideas, and we know this is not of our own doing, we forthwith attribute power and agency to the ideas themselves and make one the cause of another, than which nothing can be more absurd and unintelligible. Thus, for example, having observed that when we perceive by sight a certain round, luminous figure, we at the same time perceive by touch the idea or sensation called heat, we do from thence conclude the sun to be the cause of heat. And in like manner perceiving the motion and collision of bodies to be attended with sound, we are inclined to think the latter an effect of the former.

33. The ideas imprinted on the senses by the Author of Nature are called *real things*; and those excited in the imagination, being less regular, vivid, and constant, are more properly termed *ideas* or *images of things* which they copy and represent. But then our sensations, be they never so vivid and distinct, are nevertheless ideas, that is, they exist in the mind, or are perceived by it, as truly as the ideas of its own framing. The ideas of sense are allowed to have more reality in them, that is, to be more strong, orderly, and coherent than the creatures of the mind; but this is no argument that they exist without the mind. They are also less dependent on the spirit, or thinking substance which perceives them, in that they are excited by the will of another and more powerful spirit; yet still they are *ideas*; and certainly no idea, whether faint or strong, can exist otherwise than in a mind perceiving it. [...]

23

Concerning Motion

[...]

2. The consideration of motion has strangely distorted the minds of ancient philosophers, giving rise to varying opinions that are extraordinarily difficult, if not absurd. Since these opinions have virtually died out, there is no need to tarry over them. But even recent and sensible philosophers of the present age, when they treat of motion, use a fair number of terms that are extremely abstract and obscure, *e.g. solicitation of gravity*, *effort*, *dead forces*, *etc.*, which throw darkness over writings otherwise competent, and suggest views that are as repugnant to truth as to common sense. These it is necessary to discuss, and not for love of refutation, but for truth's sake.

3. *Solicitation*, and *striving* or *effort*, really refer only to beings that have life. When they are applied to other things, they must be taken metaphorically. But philosophers should avoid metaphors. That those words have no clear and distinct meaning when not referring to either animal sensibility or the motion of the body will be plain to anyone who considers the subject seriously.

4. While we are supporting heavy bodies we are aware of effort, fatigue and discomfort in ourselves. In falling bodies of some weight we perceive an accelerating motion towards the centre of the earth; and by means of the senses we perceive nothing else. Reason, however, tells us that there is some cause or principle of these phenomena; and this is commonly called *gravity*. Now since the cause of the falling of bodies is blind and unknown, gravity in that sense cannot properly be called a sensible quality. It must, then, be an occult quality. But it is scarcely (if at all) possible to conceive what an occult quality is, or how any mere quality can act or effect anything. It would be better, therefore, to leave the notion of occult quality out of account, and attend only to the sensible effects; in other words, to exclude from our thinking abstract terms (however useful these may be for discourse) and fix the mind on what is particular and concrete, that is, on the things themselves.

5. *Force* also is attributed to bodies. The term is used, however, as if it meant a quality that is known, yet is not motion, shape or any other sensible object, nor a feature of animal sensibility; which a little inspection will show to be nothing but an occult quality. Animal effort and bodily motion are commonly regarded as concomitants and measures of this occult quality.

6. Obviously, then, gravity or force cannot be laid down as the source or principle of motion, for can that principle be any more clearly known by calling it an occult quality? That which is itself occult explains nothing – not to mention that an unknown acting cause could be more rightly called a substance than a quality. Further, *force*, *gravity* and suchlike terms are more often and more suitably used with a concrete meaning, to stand for the body moved, difficulty in our resisting, etc. When they are used by philosophers to mean something altogether different from that – something that neither falls under the senses, nor can be understood by any power of the mind, nor can be fashioned in the imagination – sooner or later they beget error and confusion. [...]

Concerning Motion (*De Motu*, 1721). From *Berkeley: Philosophical Writings*, ed. T. E. Jessop (New York: Greenwood Press, 1969). Selection: pp. 203–16.

17. *Force, gravity, attraction* and suchlike terms are useful in reasonings and calculations about motion and moved bodies, but not for the understanding of the simple nature of motion itself, or for the designation of as many distinct qualities. As for *attraction*, it is evidently used by Newton to indicate not a real and physical quality but only a mathematical hypothesis; and Leibniz, while distinguishing elementary effort from impetus, admits that such entities are not actually found in Nature, but have to be constructed by abstraction. [...]

21. No light can be thrown on Nature by adducing anything that is neither accessible to the senses nor intelligible to reason. In every case, therefore, we have to see what evidence is offered by sense, by the course of experience, and by reason so far as it is dependent on these. Now all things fall into two classes, body and mind. Things that are extended, solid, mobile, shaped, and possess any other sensory qualities, we know by means of the senses; and things that are sentient, percipient and understanding, we know by a sort of internal awareness; and that these two groups of things are extremely different in kind is evident to us. I am writing of things that are known; things that are unknown it would be useless to discuss.

22. No known thing that we would call a *body* contains within itself anything that could be the origin or efficient cause of motion. For impenetrability, extension and shape do not include or mean any power of producing motion; on the contrary, not only they, but also all other bodily qualities whatsoever, gone through one by one, will be seen to be in fact passive, having in them nothing active, nothing that can in any way be understood as the fount and origin of motion. As for gravity, we have already shown that that term cannot stand for any known thing that is other than the sensible effect the cause of which is in question: for example, when we say that a body is heavy, we can mean nothing more than it is borne downwards, with no notion whatever concerning the cause of this sensible effect.

23. Of body we may declare quite confidently, then, as an established fact, that it is not the origin of motion; so that if anyone should maintain that the term *body* includes as a part of its meaning not only solid extension and its modifications but in addition some occult quality, potency, form or essence, it would be idle to dispute with him, there being no ideas to dispute with, and words being wasted when used with no definite meaning. The sane rule of philosophising seems rather to be that we should abstain as far as possible from all abstract and general notions – if, indeed, we can use the term *notion* for what has no meaning for us.

24. The whole content of the idea of body is open to us, and it is certain that what we find in it is not the origin of motion. Anyone who talks of an unknown something in matter, while having no idea of it, and calls that the origin of motion, is really saying nothing more than that the origin of motion is unknown. But it would be tedious to tarry over subtleties of that sort.

25. Besides bodily things there is the other class of thinking things. That these, on the contrary, do have in themselves the power of moving bodies we learn from our experience of ourselves, for the mind can at will rouse and stop the motion of our limbs, however puzzling the fact may be. This much is certain, that bodies are moved at the will of minds, so that mind can rightly be called the source of motion, though a particular and dependent source, since it itself depends on the primary and universal source. [...]

27. Body in fact persists in either of the two states it may be in, as much in motion as in rest. Such inertia can no more be called an action of body than the existence of body can be. Inertia is nothing but continuance in the same manner of existing, and this cannot properly be called an action. Similarly, when we suppose that the resistance which we experience in stopping a body in motion is an action of that body, we are deceived. Such felt resistance is in fact a passion in ourselves, is a proof not that the body acts but that we are acted upon; and anyhow it is plain that this experience of being acted upon would be the same whether the body were moved by itself or were impelled by something else. [...]

29. If extension, solidity and shape were taken away from the idea of body, what would remain would be nothing. But those qualities are indifferent in respect of motion, having in them nothing that can be called the source of motion. This is perfectly evident in the ideas we have of them. If the term *body* mean, then, what we do apprehend, we obviously cannot look for the principle of motion in it, for no part or attribute of it is an efficient cause productive of motion. Now to utter a word and mean nothing by it is unworthy of a philosopher.

30. Something thinking and active is a fact, and we experience it in ourselves as a source of motion. We call it soul, mind, or spirit. Also a fact is

something extended, inert, impenetrable and mobile, which is completely different from the former, constituting a distinct class. How great the difference is between thinking beings and extended beings was first noticed by Anaxagoras, a man of great sagacity, who asserted that mind has nothing in common with bodies, as we learn from Book I of Aristotle's *De Anima*. Among the moderns, Descartes is the one who has done most justice to that distinction. After him, other writers, by their use of obscure terms, have turned a clear point into an obstacle and a difficulty.

31. From what has been said it is plain that those who declare that active force, action, or the source of motion really is in bodies have adopted a view that has no foundation in any experience whatever, and prop up that view with obscure and general terms, and do not themselves understand what they are after. Those, on the other hand, who hold that mind is the source of motion are making a judgment that rests on their experience of themselves, and is supported by the most competent thinkers of every age. [...]

41. Mechanical principles and the universal laws of motion or of Nature, happily discovered in the last century, and treated of and applied with the help of geometry, have thrown remarkable light on natural philosophy. But metaphysical principles, and the real efficient causes of motion and of the existence of bodies and of bodily attributes, fall entirely outside the scope of mechanics and experimental inquiries and can throw no light on these, except so far as, being prior in the order of knowledge, they serve to prescribe the boundaries of Physics, and in that way remove difficulties and problems that are alien to this science.

42. Those who look to spirits for the origin of motion understand by the term *spirit* either something corporeal or something incorporeal. If corporeal, however tenuous it may be supposed to be, the difficulty referred to recurs; and if incorporeal, this view, however true it may be, takes us beyond the proper field of physics. Of course, if we were to extend natural philosophy beyond the limits of experiments and of mechanics, so as to include the study of incorporeal and unextended things, such a wider use of the term would bring under it the consideration of the soul [*anima*], mind or vital principle. But it will be more convenient to distinguish, in accordance with general usage, the branches of knowledge by assigning to each its own boundaries. The natural philosopher would then be confined to experiments, the laws of motion and mechanical principles, and the arguments that can be drawn from these; and whatever he may allege concerning other matters he would regard as falling within the field of some higher science. On the one hand, from the Laws of Nature now known some very elegant theories, and also some mechanical rules of practical value, have resulted. On the other hand, from the knowledge of the very Author of Nature far more important reflexions have sprung, but they belong to metaphysics, theology, and moral philosophy.

43. So far concerning the principles of motion: we must now discuss its nature. Since motion is clearly perceived by the senses, what has made it obscure is not so much its own nature as the opinions of learned philosophers. Motion never appears to sense without bodily mass, space and time. There are some thinkers, however, who try to apprehend motion as if it were a simple and abstract idea, distinct from everything else; but such an idea is too tenuous or subtle for the intellect to grasp – as anyone may see if he will make the attempt. From it spring great difficulties concerning the nature of motion, and definitions far more obscure than the very thing which they ought to illuminate. ...

44. Not content with that, they go further, distinguishing and dividing parts of motion from one another, and trying to form distinct ideas of them, as if they were really distinct beings. There are as well thinkers who distinguish motion and movement, regarding the former as the instantaneous element of the latter. They will have it besides that velocity, effort, force and impetus are so many things different in essence, of each of which we have before the intellect a peculiar and abstract idea distinct from all other ideas. But there is no point in dwelling on these matters, in view of what has been said above.

45. Many have defined motion in terms of transition, forgetting that transition is unintelligible apart from motion and has to be defined in terms of motion. This is one instance of the truth that definitions, while in some matters bringing light, in others bring darkness. As for the things perceived by the senses, they can scarcely be made clearer or better known by definition. In the vain hope of making them so, philosophers have made easy matters hard, and have entangled their minds in difficulties which for the most part they have themselves created. Because of this passion for defining and abstracting, many extremely subtle

questions, of no use whatever, about motion as about other matters, have perverted the intelligence of men, so much so that Aristotle, for example, has freely confessed in several places that he finds motion to be "something hard to know"; and some of the ancients have gone so far in their trifling as to deny outright the existence of motion.

46. It would be tedious to linger over petty points of that kind. It must suffice to have indicated the grounds on which they can be dissolved; to which we may add that what has been handed down in mathematics concerning the infinite division of space and time has brought, because of a natural affinity, paradoxes and thorny theories (all theories that treat of the infinite are thorny) into the inquiries concerning motion. . . .

47. Just as on the one hand there has been too much abstraction or division of things that are in reality inseparable, so on the other hand there has been a composition, or rather confusion, of things that are very diverse, with the result that the nature of motion has been made to seem intricate. It has become usual, for instance, to confuse motion with the efficient cause of motion, so that motion is thought of as having two aspects, one open to the senses and the other wrapped in gloomy night. Hence obscurity and confusion, and various paradoxes about motion, due to attributing to an effect what really belongs to the cause. [. . .]

52. . . . Motion cannot be understood without an understanding of place. This is defined by the moderns as the part of space that is occupied by body, and consequently it is divided, with respect to space, into relative and absolute − for they distinguish space too into absolute or real, and relative or apparent. They maintain that there is a space that is infinite in all directions, immobile, not perceivable by the senses, permeating and containing all bodies; and this they call absolute space. The space that is included in or marked out by bodies, and to that extent open to the senses, is called relative, apparent, or everyday space.

53. Let us imagine, then, all bodies to be utterly destroyed. What is left the moderns call absolute space, every relation that springs from the place and distances of bodies having been removed along with the bodies themselves. Further, that space is infinite, immobile, indivisible, imperceptible, without relation and without internal distinction. All its attributes, that is, are privative or negative; so that it seems to me to be just nothing − except that it gives rise to the difficulty that, since it

remains extended, extension is a positive quality. Now what sort of extension can it be that cannot be divided or measured, and whose parts cannot be either perceived by the senses or imagined? − for nothing can be formed in imagination that cannot by its nature be perceived by sense, since imagination is simply the power of representing sensible things actual or possible. Such extension also escapes pure intellect, since this faculty has to do only with spiritual and unextended things, such as minds and their states, passions, virtues and similar objects. If, then, we take away from absolute space nothing but the above terms, nothing will remain in sense, imagination, or intellect, so that those terms do mean no more than privation or negation, that is, just nothing.

54. It must be admitted that about this matter we have the strongest prejudices, to free ourselves from which requires the utmost effort of mind. Many, for example, are so far from regarding absolute space as nothing that they count it to be the only thing there is (other than God) that cannot be annihilated: they declare that by virtue of its own nature it exists necessarily, is eternal and uncreated, and to that extent shares in the attributes of the Divine. Since, however, it is entirely certain that everything to which we give a name is known because of some quality, relation, or other aspect (for it would be pointless to use words that stood for nothing known, for no notion, idea or concept), let us carefully examine whether it be possible to form any idea of that pure, real and absolute space which is supposed to persist when all bodies have been annihilated. On inspecting such an idea with some exactness, I find it to be the perfectly pure idea of nothing, if indeed, it may be called an idea at all. . . .

55. We tend to be deceived because when in imagination we have abolished all other bodies, each of us nevertheless assumes that his own body remains. On this assumption, we imagine the motion of our limbs to be completely free in every direction. But motion cannot be conceived without space. If we think the matter over carefully, it will become clear to us, first that what we are thinking of is relative space, marked out by reference to the parts of the body, and secondly, that our power to move our limbs is not being hindered by any obstacle. Besides these two aspects there is nothing. We falsely believe, however, that there is a third thing, namely, infinite space, really existing and allowing us the power to move our own body. For this power, however,

nothing is required but the absence of other bodies, which absence or privation, we are surely bound to admit, is not a positive thing at all. [...]

58. From what has been said it is evidently not right to define the real place of a body as that part of absolute space which the body occupies, and real or absolute motion as a change of real and absolute place; for all place is relative, just as all motion is. This will become clearer if we observe that no motion can be understood without some determination or direction, which cannot itself be understood unless, besides the body moved, we suppose our own body, or some other, to exist at the same time. For upwards, downwards, to the left, to the right, and all areas or regions, are what they are in virtue of some relation, and necessarily include or suppose a body other than the one that is moved. If, then, we suppose, say, a globe as being the only thing that exists, all other bodies being annihilated, we could not conceive any motion in it at all. [...]

63. No motion can be perceived or measured except by means of sensory objects. Since, then, absolute space never appears in any guise to the senses, it follows that it is utterly useless for distinguishing motions. Besides, some determination or direction is an essential feature of motion, and direction is essentially relative. Therefore absolute motion is inconceivable.

64. Further, since the motion of the same body will vary with variation in its relative place, and since, indeed, anything can be said to be moved in one respect and in another to be at rest, for the determination of true motion and true rest in a way that would remove ambiguity and serve the purpose of mechanical philosophers, who view the system of things more broadly, it would be enough to suppose, instead of an absolute space, relative space bounded by the heaven of the fixed stars, this being regarded as at rest. Motion and rest marked out within such a relative space can be conveniently used instead of absolute motion and rest, which latter cannot be distinguished in any empirical way from the former. Let forces be impressed as you please, let there be whatever impelling tendencies you please, and let me concede that motion is distinguished by means of actions applied to bodies, nevertheless it can never follow that there is an absolute space, and an absolute place, and that change of this is true motion. [...]

66. It is evident from the preceding considerations that for the understanding of the true nature of motion it is of the greatest importance (1) to distinguish between mathematical hypotheses and the actual natures of things; (2) to beware of abstractions; (3) to treat motion as something sensible, or at any rate imaginable, and to be content with relative measurements. If we observe these points, we shall both preserve intact the best theorems of the mechanical philosophy, which open up the secret places of nature and make the system of the world susceptible of mathematical treatment, and free the study of motion from a thousand minutiae, subtleties, and abstract ideas. Let so much suffice concerning the nature of motion.

67. We have now to discuss the question of the cause of the communication of motions....

68. Let it be laid down that a new motion is maintained in the struck body, either by the inherent force in virtue of which every body continues in its state of rest or of uniform motion in a straight line, or by the impressed force received at the time of percussion and remaining in the struck body – for in both these cases the effect apprehended is the same, the difference being one of words only. Similarly, when the striking body loses and the struck body acquires motion, it is idle to dispute whether the motion acquired is numerically the same as the motion lost, for such a dispute would lead us into metaphysical and entirely verbal minutiae about identity. It follows that, whether we say that motion is transmitted from the striking to the struck body, or that it is generated anew in the latter and is destroyed in the former, the fact or effect is the same. In either case all that is understood is that one body has lost motion and the other has acquired it.

69. That the Mind which moves and controls this bodily universe and is the true efficient cause of motion is, strictly speaking, the cause of the communication of motion, I would by no means deny. In physical philosophy, however, the causes and explanations of phenomena have to be derived from mechanical principles. A thing is physically explained, therefore, not by assigning its really operative and incorporeal cause, but by demonstrating the connexion of the thing with mechanical principles – as, for example, the principle that action and reaction are always opposite and equal, from which, as a primary principle and source, spring rules concerning the communication of motions, which to the great benefit of the sciences have already been discovered and demonstrated by our modern investigators. [...]

71. In physics, sensation and experience, which have to do with manifest effects only, have their place. In mechanics, the abstract notions of mathematics are admitted. In First Philosophy or metaphysics we are treating of incorporeal things, of the causes, truth and existence of things. The physicist considers the series or successions of sensible things, noting by what laws they are connected, and in what order, what preceding as if it were a cause, and what following as if it were an effect. From this point of view we say that one moved body is the cause of motion in another, or impresses motion upon it, and also that it draws or impels. In this use of *cause* we are to understand secondary corporeal causes, no account being taken of the real seat of the forces or active powers, or of the real cause in which these reside. Besides body, shape and motion, we may also call causes or mechanical principles the primary axioms of mechanics, regarded as if they were the causes of what follows from them.

72. The truly active causes can be drawn out of the darkness in which they are wrapped, and to some extent be known, only by means of meditation and reasoning. It is, however, the function of First Philosophy or metaphysics to treat of them. If to every science we allotted its own province and boundaries, and distinguished with precision the principles and objects that belong to it, we should be able to pursue our inquiries with both greater ease and greater clearness.

24

Passive Obedience

Romans, chap. xiii. ver. 2: "Whosoever resisteth the Power, resisteth the ordinance of God."

1. It is not my design to inquire into the particular nature of the government and constitution of these kingdoms; much less to pretend to determine concerning the merits of the different parties now reigning in the state. Those topics I profess to lie out of my sphere, and they will probably be thought by most men improper to be treated of in an audience almost wholly made up of young persons, set apart from the business and noise of the world, for their more convenient instruction in learning and piety. But surely it is in no respect unsuitable to the circumstances of this place to inculcate and explain every branch of the Law of Nature; or those virtues and duties which are equally binding in every kingdom or society of men under heaven. And of this kind I take to be that Christian Duty of not resisting the supreme Power, implied in my text – "Whosoever resisteth the Power, resisteth the ordinance of God."

In treating on which words I shall observe the following method: –

2. First, I shall endeavour to prove that there is an absolute unlimited non-resistance, or passive obedience, due to the supreme civil power, wherever placed in any nation.

Secondly, I shall inquire into the grounds and reasons of the contrary opinion.

Passive Obedience (1712). From *The Works of George Berkeley*, vol. 4, ed. Alexander Campbell Fraser (Oxford University Press, 1901). Selection: sects 1–21, pp. 102–14.

Thirdly, I shall consider the objections drawn from the pretended consequences of non-resistance to the supreme power.

In handling these points I intend not to build on the authority of Holy Scripture, but altogether on the Principles of Reason common to all mankind; and that, because there are some very rational and learned men, who, being verily persuaded an absolute passive subjection to any earthly power is repugnant to right reason, can never bring themselves to admit such an interpretation of Holy Scripture (however natural and obvious from the words) as shall make that a part of Christian religion which seems to them in itself manifestly absurd, and destructive of the original inherent rights of human nature.

3. I do not mean to treat of that submission which men are, either in duty or prudence, obliged to pay inferior or executive powers; neither shall I consider where or in what persons the supreme or legislative power is lodged in this or that government. Only thus much I shall take for granted: that there is in every civil community, somewhere or other, placed a Supreme Power of making laws, and enforcing the observation of them. The fulfilling of those laws, either by a punctual performance of what is enjoined in them, or, if that be inconsistent with reason or conscience, by a patient submission to whatever penalties the supreme power hath annexed to the neglect or transgression of them, is termed *loyalty*; as, on the other hand, the making use of force and open violence, either to withstand the execution of the laws, or ward off the penalties appointed by the supreme power, is properly named *rebellion*.

Now, to make it evident that every degree of rebellion is criminal in the subject, I shall, in the first place, endeavour to prove that Loyalty is a natural or moral duty; and Disloyalty, or Rebellion, in the most strict and proper sense, a vice or breach of the law of nature. And, secondly, I propose to shew that the prohibitions of vice, or negative precepts of the law of nature, as, "Thou shalt not commit adultery, Thou shalt not forswear thyself, Thou shalt not resist the supreme power," and the like, ought to be taken in a most absolute, necessary, and immutable sense: insomuch that the attainment of the greatest good, or deliverance from the greatest evil, that can befal any man or number of men in this life, may not justify the least violation of them.

First then, I am to shew that Loyalty is a moral duty, and Disloyalty or Rebellion, in the most strict and proper sense, a vice, or breach of the Law of Nature.

4. Though it be a point agreed amongst all wise men, that there are certain moral rules or laws of nature, which carry with them an eternal and indispensable obligation; yet, concerning the proper methods for discovering those laws, and distinguishing them from others dependent on the humour and discretion of men, there are various opinions. Some direct us to look for them in the Divine Ideas; others in the natural inscriptions on the mind: some derive them from the authority of learned men, and the universal agreement and consent of nations: lastly, others hold that they are only to be discovered by the deductions of reason. The three first methods must be acknowledged to labour under great difficulties; and the last has not, that I know, been anywhere distinctly explained, or treated of so fully as the importance of the subject doth deserve.

I hope therefore it will be pardoned, if, in a discourse of passive obedience, in order to lay the foundation of that duty the deeper, we make some inquiry into the origin, nature, and obligation of moral duties in general, and the criterions whereby they are to be known.

5. Self-love being a principle of all others the most universal, and the most deeply engraven in our hearts, it is natural for us to regard things as they are fitted to augment or impair our own happiness; and accordingly we denominate them *good* or *evil*. Our judgment is ever employed in distinguishing between these two; and it is the whole business of our lives to endeavour, by a proper application of our faculties, to procure the one and avoid the other. At our first coming into the world, we are entirely guided by the impressions of sense; sensible pleasure being the infallible characteristic of present good, as pain is of evil. But, by degrees, as we grow up in our acquaintance with the nature of things, experience informs us that present good is afterwards often attended with a greater evil; and, on the other side, that present evil is not less frequently the occasion of procuring to us a greater future good. Besides, as the nobler faculties of the human soul begin to display themselves, they discover to us goods far more excellent than those which affect the senses. Hence an alteration is wrought in our judgments; we no longer comply with the first solicitations of sense, but stay to consider the remote consequences of an action; what good may be hoped, or what evil feared from it, according to the wonted course of things. This obliges us frequently to overlook present momentary enjoyments, when they come in competition with greater and more lasting goods; though too far off, or of too refined a nature to affect our senses.

6. But, as the whole Earth and the entire duration of those perishing things contained in it is altogether inconsiderable, or, in the prophet's expressive style, "less than nothing" in respect of Eternity, who sees not that every reasonable man ought so to frame his actions as that they may most effectually contribute to promote his eternal interest? And, since it is a truth, evident by the light of nature, that there is a sovereign omniscient Spirit, who alone can make us for ever happy, or for ever miserable; it plainly follows that a conformity to His will, and not any prospect of temporal advantage, is the sole rule whereby every man who acts up to the principles of reason must govern and square his actions. The same conclusion doth likewise evidently result from the relation which God bears to His creatures. God alone is maker and preserver of all things. He is, therefore, with the most undoubted right, the great legislator of the world; and mankind are, by all the ties of duty, no less than interest, bound to obey His laws.

7. Hence we should above all things endeavour to trace out the Divine will, or the general design of Providence with regard to mankind, and the methods most directly tending to the accomplishment of that design. And this seems the genuine and proper way for discovering the laws of nature. For, laws being rules directive of our actions to the end intended by the legislator, in order to attain

the knowledge of God's laws, we ought first to inquire what that end is which He designs should be carried on by human actions. Now, as God is a being of infinite goodness, it is plain the end He proposes is good. But, God enjoying in Himself all possible perfection, it follows that it is not His own good, but that of His creatures. Again, the moral actions of men are entirely terminated within themselves, so as to have no influence on the other orders of intelligences or reasonable creatures; the end therefore to be procured by them can be no other than the good of men. But, as nothing in a natural state can entitle one man more than another to the favour of God, except only moral goodness; which, consisting in a conformity to the laws of God, doth presuppose the being of such laws, and law ever supposing an end, to which it guides our actions – it follows that, antecedent to the end proposed by God, no distinction can be conceived between men: that end therefore itself, or general design of Providence, is not determined or limited by any respect of persons. It is not therefore the private good of this or that man, nation, or age, but the general well-being of all men, of all nations, of all ages of the world, which God designs should be procured by the concurring actions of each individual.

Having thus discovered the great end to which all moral obligations are subordinate, it remains that we inquire what methods are necessary for the obtaining that end.

8. The well-being of mankind must necessarily be carried on in one of these two ways: – Either, first, without the injunction of any certain universal rules of morality; only by obliging every one, upon each particular occasion, to consult the public good, and always to do that which to him shall seem, in the present time and circumstances, most to conduce to it: or, secondly, by enjoining the observation of some determinate, established laws, which, if universally practised, have, from the nature of things, an essential fitness to procure the well-being of mankind; though, in their particular application, they are sometimes, through untoward accidents, and the perverse irregularity of human wills, the occasions of great sufferings and misfortunes, it may be, to very many good men.

Against the former of these methods there lie several strong objections. For brevity I shall mention only two: –

9. First, it will thence follow that the best men, for want of judgment, and the wisest, for want of knowing all the hidden circumstances and consequences of an action, may very often be at a loss how to behave themselves; which they would not be, in case they judged of each action by comparing it with some particular precept, rather than by examining the good or evil which in that single instance it tends to procure: it being far more easy to judge with certainty, whether such or such an action be a transgression of this or that precept, than whether it will be attended with more good or ill consequences. In short, to calculate the events of each particular action is impossible; and, though it were not, would yet take up too much time to be of use in the affairs of life.

Secondly, if that method be observed, it will follow that we can have no sure standard to which, comparing the actions of another, we may pronounce them good or bad, virtues or vices. For, since the measure and rule of every good man's actions is supposed to be nothing else but his own private disinterested opinion of what makes most for the public good at that juncture; and, since this opinion must unavoidably in different men, from their particular views and circumstances, be very different: it is impossible to know, whether any one instance of parricide or perjury, for example, be criminal. The man may have had his reasons for it; and that which in me would have been a heinous sin may be in him a duty. Every man's particular rule is buried in his own breast, invisible to all but himself, who therefore can only tell whether he observes it or no. And, since that rule is fitted to particular occasions, it must ever change as they do: hence it is not only various in different men, but in one and the same man at different times.

10. From all which it follows, there can be no harmony or agreement between the actions of good men: no apparent steadiness or consistency of one man with himself; no adhering to principles: the best actions may be condemned, and the most villainous meet with applause. In a word, there ensues the most horrible confusion of vice and virtue, sin and duty, that can possibly be imagined. It follows, therefore, that the great end to which God requires the concurrence of human actions must of necessity be carried on by the second method proposed, namely, the observation of certain, universal, determinate rules or moral precepts, which, in their own nature, have a necessary tendency to promote the well-being of the sum of mankind, taking in all nations and ages, from the beginning to the end of the world.

11. Hence, upon an equal comprehensive survey of the general nature, the passions, interests, and mutual respects of mankind; whatsoever practical proposition doth to right reason evidently appear to have a necessary connexion with the Universal well-being included in it, is to be looked upon as enjoined by the will of God. For, he that willeth the end doth will the necessary means conducive to that end; but it hath been shewn that God willeth the universal well-being of mankind should be promoted by the concurrence of each particular person; therefore, every such practical proposition necessarily tending thereto is to be esteemed a decree of God, and is consequently a law to man.

12. These propositions are called *laws of nature*, because they are universal, and do not derive their obligation from any civil sanction, but immediately from the Author of nature himself. They are said to be *stamped on the mind*, to be *engraven on the tables of the heart*, because they are well known to mankind, and suggested and inculcated by conscience. Lastly, they are termed *eternal rules of reason*, because they necessarily result from the nature of things, and may be demonstrated by the infallible deductions of reason.

13. And, notwithstanding that these rules are too often, either by the unhappy concurrence of events, or more especially by the wickedness of perverse men who will not conform to them, made accidental causes of misery to those good men who do, yet this doth not vacate their obligation: they are ever to be esteemed the fixed unalterable standards of moral good and evil; no private interest, no love of friends, no regard to the public good, should make us depart from them. Hence, when any doubt arises concerning the morality of an action, it is plain this cannot be determined by computing the public good which in that particular case it is attended with, but only by comparing it with the Eternal Law of Reason. He who squares his actions by this rule can never do amiss, though thereby he should bring himself to poverty, death, or disgrace: no, not though he should involve his family, his friends, his country, in all those evils which are accounted the greatest and most insupportable to human nature. Tenderness and benevolence of temper are often motives to the best and greatest actions; but we must not make them the sole rule of our actions: they are passions rooted in our nature, and, like all other passions, must be restrained and kept under, otherwise they may possibly betray us into as great

enormities as any other unbridled lust. Nay, they are more dangerous than other passions, insomuch as they are more plausible, and apt to dazzle and corrupt the mind with the appearance of goodness and generosity.

14. For the illustration of what has been said, it will not be amiss, if from the moral we turn our eyes on the natural world. *Homo ortus est* (says Balbus in Cicero [*De Natura Deorum*, Lib. II. § 37]) *ad mundum contemplandum, et imitandum*. And, surely, it is not possible for free intellectual agents to propose a nobler pattern for their imitation than Nature; which is nothing else but a series of free actions, produced by the best and wisest Agent. But, it is evident that those actions are not adapted to particular views, but all conformed to certain general rules, which, being collected from observation, are by philosophers termed laws of nature. And these indeed are excellently suited to promote the general well-being of the creation: but, what from casual combinations of events, and what from the voluntary motions of animals, it often falls out, that the natural good not only of private men but of entire cities and nations would be better promoted by a particular suspension, or contradiction, than an exact observation of those laws. Yet, for all that, nature still takes its course; nay, it is plain that plagues, famines, inundations, earthquakes, with an infinite variety of pains and sorrows – in a word, all kinds of calamities public and private, do arise from a uniform steady observation of those General Laws which are once established by the Author of Nature, and which He will not change or deviate from upon any of those accounts, how wise or benevolent soever it may be thought by foolish men to do so. As for the miracles recorded in Scripture, they were always wrought for confirmation of some doctrine or mission from God, and not for the sake of the particular natural goods, as health or life, which some men might have reaped from them. From all which it seems sufficiently plain that we cannot be at a loss which way to determine, in case we think God's own methods the properest to obtain His ends, and that it is our duty to copy after them, so far as the frailty of our nature will permit.

15. Thus far in general, of the nature and necessity of Moral Rules, and the criterion or mark whereby they may be known.

As for the particulars, from the foregoing discourse, the principal of them may without much difficulty be deduced. It hath been shewn that the Law of Nature is a system of such rules or precepts as that, if they be all of them, at all times, in all places, and by all men observed, they will necessarily promote the well-being of mankind, so far as it is attainable by human actions. Now, let any one who hath the use of reason take but an impartial survey of the general frame and circumstances of human nature, and it will appear plainly to him that the constant observation of truth, for instance, or of justice, and chastity hath a necessary connexion with their universal well-being; that, therefore, they are to be esteemed virtues or duties; and that "Thou shalt not forswear thyself," "Thou shalt not commit adultery," "Thou shalt not steal," are so many unalterable moral rules, which to violate in the least degree is vice or sin. I say, the agreement of these particular practical propositions with the definition or criterion premised doth so clearly result from the nature of things, that it were a needless digression, in this place, to enlarge upon it.

And, from the same principle, by the very same reasoning, it follows that Loyalty is a moral virtue, and "Thou shalt not resist the Supreme Power" a rule or law of nature, the least breach whereof hath the inherent stain of moral turpitude.

16. The miseries inseparable from a state of anarchy are easily imagined. So insufficient is the wit or strength of any single man, either to avert the evils, or procure the blessings of life, and so apt are the wills of different persons to contradict and thwart each other, that it is absolutely necessary several independent powers be combined together, under the direction (if I may so speak) of one and the same will – I mean the Law of the Society. Without this there is no politeness, no order, no peace, among men, but the world is one great heap of misery and confusion; the strong as well as the weak, the wise as well as the foolish, standing on all sides exposed to all those calamities which man can be liable to, in a state where he has no other security than the not being possessed of any thing which may raise envy or desire in another. A state by so much more ineligible than that of brutes as a reasonable creature hath a greater reflexion and foresight of miseries than they. From all which it plainly follows, that Loyalty, or submission to the supreme authority, hath, if universally practised in conjunction with all other virtues, a necessary connexion with the well-being of the whole sum of mankind; and, by consequence, if the criterion we have laid down be true, it is, strictly speaking, a moral duty, or branch of natural religion. And, therefore, the least degree of Rebellion is, with the utmost strictness and propriety, a sin: not only in Christians, but also in those who have the light of reason alone for their guide. Nay, upon a thorough and impartial view, this submission will, I think, appear one of the very first and fundamental laws of nature; inasmuch as it is civil government which ordains and marks out the various relations between men, and regulates property; thereby giving scope and laying a foundation for the exercise of all other duties. And, in truth, whoever considers the condition of man will scarce conceive it possible that the practice of any one moral virtue should obtain, in the naked, forlorn state of nature.

17. But, since it must be confessed that in all cases our actions come not within the direction of certain fixed moral rules, it may possibly be still questioned, whether obedience to the Supreme Power be not one of those exempted cases; and consequently to be regulated by the prudence and discretion of every single person rather than adjusted to the rule of absolute non-resistance. I shall therefore endeavour to make it yet more plain, that "Thou shalt not resist the Supreme Power" is an undoubted precept of morality; as will appear from the following considerations: –

First, then, submission to government is a point important enough to be established by a moral rule. Things of insignificant and trifling concern are, for that very reason, exempted from the rules of morality. But government, on which so much depend the peace, order, and well-being, of mankind, cannot surely be thought of too small importance to be secured and guarded by a moral rule. Government, I say, which is itself the principal source under heaven of those particular advantages for the procurement and conservation whereof several unquestionable moral rules were prescribed to men.

18. Secondly, obedience to government is a case universal enough to fall under the direction of a law of nature. Numberless rules there may be for regulating affairs of great concernment, at certain junctures, and to some particular persons or societies, which, notwithstanding, are not to be esteemed moral or natural laws, but may be either totally abrogated or dispensed with; because the private ends they were intended to promote respect only some particular persons, as engaged in relations not founded in the general nature of men; who, on various occasions, and in different postures of things, may prosecute their own designs by different measures, as in human prudence shall

seem convenient. But what relation is there more extensive and universal than that of *subject* and *law*? This is confined to no particular age or climate, but universally obtains, at all times, and in all places, wherever men live in a state exalted above that of brutes. It is, therefore, evident that the rule forbidding resistance to the Law or Supreme Power is not, upon pretence of any defect in point of universality, to be excluded from the number of the laws of nature.

19. Thirdly, there is another consideration which confirms the necessity of admitting this rule for a moral or natural law: namely, because the case it regards is of too nice and difficult a nature to be left to the judgment and determination of each private person. Some cases there are so plain and obvious to judge of that they may safely be trusted to the prudence of every reasonable man. But in all instances to determine, whether a civil law is fitted to promote the public interest; or whether submission or resistance will prove most advantageous in the consequence; or when it is that the general good of a nation may require an alteration of government, either in its form, or in the hands which administer it; – these are points too arduous and intricate, and which require too great a degree of parts, leisure, and liberal education, as well as disinterestedness and thorough knowledge in the particular state of a kingdom, for every subject to take upon him the determination of them. From which it follows that, upon this account also, Non-resistance, which in the main, nobody can deny to be a most profitable and wholesome duty, ought not to be limited by the judgment of private persons to particular occasions, but esteemed a most sacred law of nature.

20. The foregoing arguments do, I think, make it manifest, that the precept against Rebellion is on a level with other moral rules. Which will yet further appear from this fourth and last consideration. It cannot be denied that right reason doth require some common stated rule or measure, whereby subjects ought to shape their submission to the Supreme Power; since any clashing or disagreement in this point must unavoidably tend to weaken and dissolve the society. And it is unavoidable that there should be great clashing, where it is left to the breast of each individual to suit his fancy with a different measure of obedience. But this common stated measure must be either the general precept forbidding resistance, or else the public good of the whole nation; which last, though it is allowed to be in itself something certain and determinate, yet, forasmuch as men can regulate their conduct only by what appears to them, whether in truth it be what it appears or no; and, since the prospects men form to themselves of a country's public good are commonly as various as its landscapes, which meet the eye in several situations: it clearly follows, that to make the public good the rule of obedience is, in effect, not to establish any determinate, agreed, common measure of loyalty, but to leave every subject to the guidance of his own particular mutable fancy.

21. From all which arguments and considerations it is a most evident conclusion, that the law prohibiting Rebellion is in strict truth a law of nature, universal reason, and morality. [...]

PART VIII

David Hume (1711–76)

Introduction

Hume's debut as a philosophical author was not an auspicious one. His first major work, *A Treatise of Human Nature* (1739–40), in which Hume ambitiously proposed to introduce experimental method into the moral sciences, fell well short of his expectations. Though there were some who, like Reid and Kant, immediately recognized the importance of the work, it was not widely read. Hume successfully restated the main arguments of the *Treatise* in two shorter works. We have drawn our opening selections from these. The first, from *An Enquiry Concerning Human Understanding* (originally published in 1748 under the title *Philosophical Essays Concerning Human Understanding*),

is an elegant and concise statement of Hume's skepticism, and the implications of that view for inquiries into moral, scientific, and theological questions. In the second, from *An Enquiry Concerning the Principles of Morals* (1751), Hume presents a series of examples to show that morality is not a matter of reason, which judges of facts and relations, but a matter of taste and sentiment. Next we have the essay *Of the Original Contract* (1748). Here Hume presents an argument against the social contract and the principle of popular sovereignty. We conclude the chapter with a selection from Hume's essay *The Natural History of Religion*, which was published in 1757 in a volume entitled *Four Dissertations*. In this excerpt, Hume draws the implications of his skeptical philosophy for religious belief.

25

An Enquiry Concerning Human Understanding

Section XII: Of the Academical or Sceptical Philosophy

Part I

There is not a greater number of philosophical reasonings, displayed upon any subject, than those, which prove the existence of a Deity, and refute the fallacies of *Atheists*; and yet the most religious philosophers still dispute whether any man can be so blinded as to be a speculative atheist. How shall we reconcile these contradictions? The knights-errant, who wandered about to clear the world of dragons and giants, never entertained the least doubt with regard to the existence of these monsters.

The *Sceptic* is another enemy of religion, who naturally provokes the indignation of all divines and graver philosophers; though it is certain, that no man ever met with any such absurd creature, or conversed with a man, who had no opinion or principle concerning any subject, either of action or speculation. This begets a very natural question; What is meant by a sceptic? And how far it is possible to push these philosophical principles of doubt and uncertainty?

There is a species of scepticism, *antecedent* to all study and philosophy, which is much inculcated by DES CARTES and others, as a sovereign pre-

An Enquiry Concerning Human Understanding (1748). From *David Hume: Philosophical Works*, vol. 4, ed. Thomas Hill Green and Thomas Hodge Grose (Scientia Verlag Aalen, 1964). Selection: sect. 12, "Of the Academical or Sceptical Philosophy," Parts 1–3, pp. 122–35.

servative against error and precipitate judgment. It recommends an universal doubt, not only of all our former opinions and principles, but also of our very faculties; of whose veracity, say they, we must assure ourselves, by a chain of reasoning, deduced from some original principle, which cannot possibly be fallacious or deceitful. But neither is there any such original principle, which has a prerogative above others, that are self-evident and convincing: Or if there were, could we advance a step beyond it, but by the use of those very faculties, of which we are supposed to be already diffident. The CARTESIAN doubt, therefore, were it ever possible to be attended by any human creature (as it plainly is not) would be entirely incurable; and no reasoning could ever bring us to a state of assurance and conviction upon any subject.

It must, however, be confessed, that this species of scepticism, when more moderate, may be understood in a very reasonable sense, and is a necessary preparative to the study of philosophy, by preserving a proper impartiality in our judgments, and weaning our mind from all those prejudices, which we may have imbibed from education or rash opinion. To begin with clear and self-evident principles, to advance by timorous and sure steps, to review frequently our conclusions, and examine accurately all their consequences; though by these means we shall make both a slow and a short progress in our systems; are the only methods, by which we can ever hope to reach truth, and attain a proper stability and certainty in our determinations.

There is another species of scepticism, *consequent* to science and enquiry, when men are supposed to have discovered, either the absolute fallaciousness of their mental faculties, or their unfitness to reach any fixed determination in all those curious subjects of speculation, about which they are commonly employed. Even our very senses are brought into dispute, by a certain species of philosophers; and the maxims of common life are subjected to the same doubt as the most profound principles or conclusions of metaphysics and theology. As these paradoxical tenets (if they may be called tenets) are to be met with in some philosophers, and the refutation of them in several, they naturally excite our curiosity, and make us enquire into the arguments, on which they may be founded.

I need not insist upon the more trite topics, employed by the sceptics in all ages, against the evidence of *sense*; such as those which are derived from the imperfection and fallaciousness of our organs, on numberless occasions; the crooked appearance of an oar in water; the various aspects of objects, according to their different distances; the double images which arise from the pressing one eye; with many other appearances of a like nature. These sceptical topics, indeed, are only sufficient to prove, that the senses alone are not implicitly to be depended on; but that we must correct their evidence by reason, and by considerations, derived from the nature of the medium, the distance of the object, and the disposition of the organ, in order to render them, within their sphere, the proper *criteria* of truth and falsehood. There are other more profound arguments against the senses, which admit not of so easy a solution.

It seems evident, that men are carried, by a natural instinct or prepossession, to repose faith in their senses; and that, without any reasoning, or even almost before the use of reason, we always suppose an external universe, which depends not on our perception, but would exist, though we and every sensible creature were absent or annihilated. Even the animal creation are governed by a like opinion, and preserve this belief of external objects, in all their thoughts, designs, and actions.

It seems also evident, that, when men follow this blind and powerful instinct of nature, they always suppose the very images, presented by the senses, to be the external objects, and never entertain any suspicion, that the one are nothing but representations of the other. This very table, which we see white, and which we feel hard, is believed to exist, independent of our perception, and to be something external to our mind, which perceives it. Our presence bestows not being on it: Our absence does not annihilate it. It preserves its existence uniform and entire, independent of the situation of intelligent beings, who perceive or contemplate it.

But this universal and primary opinion of all men is soon destroyed by the slightest philosophy, which teaches us, that nothing can ever be present to the mind but an image or perception, and that the senses are only the inlets, through which these images are conveyed, without being able to produce any immediate intercourse between the mind and the object. The table, which we see, seems to diminish, as we remove farther from it: But the real table, which exists independent of us, suffers no alteration: It was, therefore, nothing but its image, which was present to the mind. These are the obvious dictates of reason; and no man, who reflects, ever doubted, that the existences, which we consider, when we say, *this house* and *that tree*, are nothing but perceptions in the mind, and fleeting copies or representations of other existences, which remain uniform and independent.

So far, then, are we necessitated by reasoning to contradict or depart from the primary instincts of nature, and to embrace a new system with regard to the evidence of our senses. But here philosophy finds herself extremely embarrassed, when she would justify this new system, and obviate the cavils and objections of the sceptics. She can no longer plead the infallible and irresistible instinct of nature: For that led us to a quite different system, which is acknowledged fallible and even erroneous. And to justify this pretended philosophical system, by a chain of clear and convincing argument, or even any appearance of argument, exceeds the power of all human capacity.

By what argument can it be proved, that the perceptions of the mind must be caused by external objects, entirely different from them, though resembling them (if that be possible) and could not arise either from the energy of the mind itself, or from the suggestion of some invisible and unknown spirit, or from some other cause still more unknown to us? It is acknowledged, that, in fact, many of these perceptions arise not from any thing external, as in dreams, madness, and other diseases. And nothing can be more inexplicable than the manner, in which body should so operate upon mind as ever to convey an image of itself to a substance, supposed of so different, and even contrary a nature.

It is a question of fact, whether the perceptions of the senses be produced by external objects, resembling them: How shall this question be determined? By experience surely; as all other questions of a like nature. But here experience is, and must be entirely silent. The mind has never any thing present to it but the perceptions, and cannot possibly reach any experience of their connexion with objects. The supposition of such a connexion is, therefore, without any foundation in reasoning.

To have recourse to the veracity of the supreme Being, in order to prove the veracity of our senses, is surely making a very unexpected circuit. If his veracity were at all concerned in this matter, our senses would be entirely infallible; because it is not possible that he can ever deceive. Not to mention, that, if the external world be once called in question, we shall be at a loss to find arguments, by which we may prove the existence of that Being or any of his attributes.

This is a topic, therefore, in which the profounder and more philosophical sceptics will always triumph, when they endeavour to introduce an universal doubt into all subjects of human knowledge and enquiry. Do you follow the instincts and propensities of nature, may they say, in assenting to the veracity of sense? But these lead you to believe, that the very perception or sensible image is the external object. Do you disclaim this principle, in order to embrace a more rational opinion, that the perceptions are only representations of something external? You here depart from your natural propensities and more obvious sentiments; and yet are not able to satisfy your reason, which can never find any convincing argument from experience to prove, that the perceptions are connected with any external objects.

There is another sceptical topic of a like nature, derived from the most profound philosophy; which might merit our attention, were it requisite to dive so deep, in order to discover arguments and reasonings, which can so little serve to any serious purpose. It is universally allowed by modern enquirers, that all the sensible qualities of objects, such as hard, soft, hot, cold, white, black, &c., are merely secondary, and exist not in the objects themselves, but are perceptions of the mind, without any external archetype or model, which they represent. If this be allowed, with regard to secondary qualities, it must also follow, with regard to the supposed primary qualities of extension and solidity; nor can the latter be any more entitled to that denomination than the former. The idea of extension is entirely acquired from the senses of

sight and feeling; and if all the qualities, perceived by the senses, be in the mind, not in the object, the same conclusion must reach the idea of extension, which is wholly dependent on the sensible ideas or the ideas of secondary qualities. Nothing can save us from this conclusion, but the asserting, that the ideas of those primary qualities are attained by *Abstraction*; an opinion, which, if we examine it accurately, we shall find to be unintelligible, and even absurd. An extension, that is neither tangible nor visible, cannot possibly be conceived: And a tangible or visible extension, which is neither hard nor soft, black nor white, is equally beyond the reach of human conception. Let any man try to conceive a triangle in general, which is neither *Isoceles* nor *Scalenum*, nor has any particular length or proportion of sides; and he will soon perceive the absurdity of all the scholastic notions with regard to abstraction and general ideas.[1]

Thus the first philosophical objection to the evidence of sense or to the opinion of external existence consists in this, that such an opinion, if rested on natural instinct, is contrary to reason, and if referred to reason, is contrary to natural instinct, and at the same time carries no rational evidence with it, to convince an impartial enquirer. The second objection goes farther, and represents this opinion as contrary to reason: at least, if it be a principle of reason, that all sensible qualities are in the mind, not in the object. Bereave matter of all its intelligible qualities, both primary and secondary, you in a manner annihilate it, and leave only a certain unknown, inexplicable *something*, as the cause of our perceptions; a notion so imperfect, that no sceptic will think it worth while to contend against it.

Part II

It may seem a very extravagant attempt of the sceptics to destroy *reason* by argument and ratiocination; yet is this the grand scope of all their enquiries and disputes. They endeavour to find objections, both to our abstract reasonings, and to those which regard matter of fact and existence.

The chief objection against all *abstract* reasonings is derived from the ideas of space and time; ideas, which, in common life and to a careless view, are very clear and intelligible, but when they pass through the scrutiny of the profound sciences (and they are the chief object of these sciences) afford principles, which seem full of absurdity and contradiction. No priestly *dogmas*, invented on purpose to tame and subdue the rebellious reason of mankind, ever shocked common sense more than the doctrine of the infinite divisibility of extension, with its consequences; as they are pompously displayed by all geometricians and metaphysicians, with a kind of triumph and exultation. A real quantity, infinitely less than any finite quantity, containing quantities infinitely less than itself, and so on *in infinitum*; this is an edifice so bold and prodigious, that it is too weighty for any pretended demonstration to support, because it shocks the clearest and most natural principles of human reason.[2] But what renders the matter more extraordinary, is, that these seemingly absurd opinions are supported by a chain of reasoning, the clearest and most natural; nor is it possible for us to allow the premises without admitting the consequences. Nothing can be more convincing and satisfactory than all the conclusions concerning the properties of circles and triangles; and yet, when these are once received, how can we deny, that the angle of contact between a circle and its tangent is infinitely less than any rectilineal angle, that as you may encrease the diameter of the circle *in infinitum*, this angle of contact becomes still less, even *in infinitum*, and that the angle of contact between other curves and their tangents may be infinitely less than those between any circle and its tangent, and so on, *in infinitum?* The demonstration of these principles seems as unexceptionable as that which proves the three angles of a triangle to be equal to two right ones, though the latter opinion be natural and easy, and the former big with contradiction and absurdity. Reason here seems to be thrown into a kind of amazement and suspence, which, without the suggestions of any sceptic, gives her a diffidence of herself, and of the ground on which she treads. She sees a full light, which illuminates certain places; but that light borders upon the most profound darkness. And between these she is so dazzled and confounded, that she scarcely can pronounce with certainty and assurance concerning any one object.

The absurdity of these bold determinations of the abstract sciences seems to become, if possible, still more palpable with regard to time than extension. An infinite number of real parts of time, passing in succession, and exhausted one after another, appears so evident a contradiction, that no man, one should think, whose judgment is not corrupted, instead of being improved, by the sciences, would ever be able to admit of it.

Yet still reason must remain restless, and unquiet, even with regard to that scepticism, to which she is driven by these seeming absurdities and contradictions. How any clear, distinct idea can contain circumstances, contradictory to itself, or to any other clear, distinct idea, is absolutely incomprehensible; and is, perhaps, as absurd as any proposition, which can be formed. So that nothing can be more sceptical, or more full of doubt and hesitation, than this scepticism itself, which arises from some of the paradoxical conclusions of geometry or the science of quantity.[3]

The sceptical objections to *moral* evidence, or to the reasonings concerning matter of fact, are either *popular* or *philosophical*. The popular objections are derived from the natural weakness of human understanding; the contradictory opinions, which have been entertained in different ages and nations; the variations of our judgment in sickness and health, youth and old age, prosperity and adversity; the perpetual contradiction of each particular man's opinions and sentiments; with many other topics of that kind. It is needless to insist farther on this head. These objections are but weak. For as, in common life, we reason every moment concerning fact and existence, and cannot possibly subsist, without continually employing this species of argument, any popular objections, derived from thence, must be insufficient to destroy that evidence. The great subverter of *Pyrrhonism* or the excessive principles of scepticism, is action, and employment, and the occupations of common life. These principles may flourish and triumph in the schools; where it is, indeed, difficult, if not impossible, to refute them. But as soon as they leave the shade, and by the presence of the real objects, which actuate our passions and sentiments, are put in opposition to the more powerful principles of our nature, they vanish like smoke, and leave the most determined sceptic in the same condition as other mortals.

The sceptic, therefore, had better keep within his proper sphere, and display those *philosophical* objections, which arise from more profound researches. Here he seems to have ample matter of triumph; while he justly insists, that all our evidence for any matter of fact, which lies beyond the testimony of sense or memory, is derived entirely from the relation of cause and effect; that we have no other idea of this relation than that of two objects, which have been frequently *conjoined* together; that we have no argument to convince us, that objects, which have, in our experience, been frequently conjoined, will likewise, in other instances, be conjoined in the same manner; and that nothing leads us to this inference but custom or a certain instinct of our nature; which it is indeed difficult to resist, but which, like other instincts, may be fallacious and deceitful. While the sceptic insists upon these topics, he shews his force, or rather, indeed, his own and our weakness; and seems, for the time at least, to destroy all assurance and conviction. These arguments might be displayed at greater length, if any durable good or benefit to society could ever be expected to result from them.

For here is the chief and most confounding objection to *excessive* scepticism, that no durable good can ever result from it; while it remains in its full force and vigour. We need only ask such a sceptic, *What his meaning is? And what he proposes by all these curious researches?* He is immediately at a loss, and knows not what to answer. A COPERNICAN or PTOLEMAIC, who supports each his different system of astronomy, may hope to produce a conviction, which will remain constant and durable, with his audience. A STOIC or EPICUREAN displays principles, which may not only be durable, but which have an effect on conduct and behaviour. But a PYRRHONIAN cannot expect, that his philosophy will have any constant influence on the mind: Or if it had, that its influence would be beneficial to society. On the contrary, he must acknowledge, if he will acknowledge any thing, that all human life must perish, were his principles universally and steadily to prevail. All discourse, all action would immediately cease; and men remain in a total lethargy, till the necessities of nature, unsatisfied, put an end to their miserable existence. It is true; so fatal an event is very little to be dreaded. Nature is always too strong for principle. And though a PYRRHONIAN may throw himself or others into a momentary amazement and confusion by his profound reasonings; the first and most trivial event in life will put to flight all his doubts and scruples, and leave him the same, in every point of action and speculation, with the philosophers of every other sect, or with those who never concerned themselves in any philosophical researches. When he awakes from his dream, he will be the first to join in the laugh against himself, and to confess, that all his objections are mere amusement, and can have no other tendency than to show the whimsical condition of mankind, who must act and reason and believe; though they are not able, by their most diligent enquiry, to satisfy themselves concerning the foundation of these operations, or to remove the objections, which may be raised against them.

Part III

There is, indeed, a more *mitigated* scepticism or *academical* philosophy, which may be both durable and useful, and which may, in part, be the result of this PYRRHONISM, or *excessive* scepticism, when its undistinguished doubts are, in some measure, corrected by common sense and reflection. The greater part of mankind are naturally apt to be affirmative and dogmatical in their opinions; and while they see objects only on one side, and have no idea of any counterpoising argument, they throw themselves precipitately into the principles, to which they are inclined; nor have they any indulgence for those who entertain opposite sentiments. To hesitate or balance perplexes their understanding, checks their passion, and suspends their action. They are, therefore, impatient till they escape from a state, which to them is so uneasy; and they think, that they can never remove themselves far enough from it, by the violence of their affirmations and obstinacy of their belief. But could such dogmatical reasoners become sensible of the strange infirmities of human understanding, even in its most perfect state, and when most accurate and cautious in its determinations; such a reflection would naturally inspire them with more modesty and reserve, and diminish their fond opinion of themselves, and their prejudice against antagonists. The illiterate may reflect on the disposition of the learned, who, amidst all the advantages of study and reflection, are commonly still diffident in their determinations: And if any of the learned be inclined, from their natural temper, to haughtiness and obstinacy, a small tincture of PYRRHONISM might abate their pride, by shewing them, that the few advantages, which they may have attained over their fellows, are but inconsiderable, if compared with the universal perplexity and confusion, which is inherent in human nature. In general, there is a degree of doubt, and caution, and modesty, which, in all kinds of scrutiny and decision, ought for ever to accompany a just reasoner.

Another species of *mitigated* scepticism, which may be of advantage to mankind, and which may be the natural result of the PYRRHONIAN doubt and scruples, is the limitation of our enquiries to such subjects as are best adapted to the narrow capacity of human understanding. The *imagination* of man is naturally sublime, delighted with whatever is remote and extraordinary, and running, without controul, into the most distant parts of space and time in order to avoid the objects, which custom has rendered too familiar to it. A correct *Judgment* observes a contrary method, and avoiding all distant and high enquiries, confines itself to common life, and to such subjects as fall under daily practice and experience; leaving the more sublime topics to the embellishment of poets and orators, or to the arts of priests and politicians. To bring us to so salutary a determination, nothing can be more serviceable, than to be once thoroughly convinced of the force of the PYRRHO-NIAN doubt, and of the impossibility, that any thing, but the strong power of natural instinct, could free us from it. Those who have a propensity to philosophy, will still continue their researches; because they reflect, that, besides the immediate pleasure, attending such an occupation, philosophical decisions are nothing but the reflections of common life, methodized and corrected. But they will never be tempted to go beyond common life, so long as they consider the imperfection of those faculties which they employ, their narrow reach, and their inaccurate operations. While we cannot give a satisfactory reason, why we believe, after a thousand experiments, that a stone will fall, or fire burn; can we ever satisfy ourselves concerning any determination, which we may form, with regard to the origin of worlds, and the situation of nature, from, and to eternity?

This narrow limitation, indeed, of our enquiries, is, in every respect, so reasonable, that it suffices to make the slightest examination into the natural powers of the human mind, and to compare them with their objects, in order to recommend it to us. We shall then find what are the proper subjects of science and enquiry.

It seems to me, that the only objects of the abstract sciences or of demonstration are quantity and number, and that all attempts to extend this more perfect species of knowledge beyond these bounds are mere sophistry and illusion. As the component parts of quantity and number are entirely similar, their relations become intricate and involved; and nothing can be more curious, as well as useful, than to trace, by a variety of mediums, their equality or inequality, through their different appearances. But as all other ideas are clearly distinct and different from each other, we can never advance farther, by our utmost scrutiny, than to observe this diversity, and, by an obvious reflection, pronounce one thing not to be another. Or if there be any difficulty in these decisions, it proceeds entirely from the undeterminate meaning of words, which is corrected by juster definitions. That *the square of the hypothenuse is equal to the squares of the other two sides*, cannot be known, let the terms be ever so exactly defined, without a train of reasoning and enquiry. But to convince us of this proposition, *that where there is no property, there can be no injustice*, it is only necessary to define the terms, and explain injustice to be a violation of property. This proposition is, indeed, nothing but a more imperfect definition. It is the same case with all those pretended syllogistical reasonings, which may be found in every other branch of learning, except the sciences of quantity and number; and these may safely, I think, be pronounced the only proper objects of knowledge and demonstration.

All other enquiries of men regard only matter of fact and existence; and these are evidently incapable of demonstration. Whatever *is* may *not be*. No negation of a fact can involve a contradiction. The non-existence of any being, without exception, is as clear and distinct an idea as its existence. The proposition, which affirms it not to be, however false, is no less conceivable and intelligible, than that which affirms it to be. The case is different with the sciences, properly so called. Every proposition, which is not true, is there confused and unintelligible. That the cube root of 64 is equal to the half of 10, is a false proposition, and can never be distinctly conceived. But that CÆSAR, or the angel GABRIEL, or any being never existed, may be a false proposition, but still is perfectly conceivable, and implies no contradiction.

The existence, therefore, of any being can only be proved by arguments from its cause or its effect; and these arguments are founded entirely on experience. If we reason *à priori*, any thing may appear able to produce any thing. The falling of a pebble may, for aught we know, extinguish the sun; or the wish of a man controul the planets in their orbits. It is only experience, which teaches us the nature and bounds of cause and effect, and enables us to infer the existence of one object from that of another.[4] Such is the foundation of moral reasoning, which forms the greater part of human knowledge, and is the source of all human action and behaviour.

Moral reasonings are either concerning particular or general facts. All deliberations in life regard the former; as also all disquisitions in history, chronology, geography, and astronomy.

The sciences, which treat of general facts, are politics, natural philosophy, physic, chymistry, &c. where the qualities, causes and effects of a whole species of objects are enquired into.

Divinity or Theology, as it proves the existence of a Deity, and the immortality of souls, is composed partly of reasonings concerning particular, partly concerning general facts. It has a foundation in *reason*, so far as it is supported by experience. But its best and most solid foundation is *faith* and divine revelation.

Morals and criticism are not so properly objects of the understanding as of taste and sentiment.

Beauty, whether moral or natural, is felt, more properly than perceived. Or if we reason concerning it, and endeavour to fix its standard, we regard a new fact, to wit, the general taste of mankind, or some such fact, which may be the object of reasoning and enquiry.

When we run over libraries, persuaded of these principles, what havoc must we make? If we take in our hand any volume; of divinity or school metaphysics, for instance; let us ask, *Does it contain any abstract reasoning concerning quantity or number?* No. *Does it contain any experimental reasoning concerning matter of fact and existence?* No. Commit it then to the flames: For it can contain nothing but sophistry and illusion.

Notes

1 This argument is drawn from Dr. BERKELEY; and indeed most of the writings of that very ingenious author form the best lessons of scepticism, which are to be found either among the ancient or modern philosophers, BAYLE not excepted. He professes, however, in his title-page (and undoubtedly with great truth) to have composed his book against the sceptics as well as against the atheists and free-thinkers. But that all his arguments, though otherwise intended, are, in reality, merely sceptical, appears from this, *that they admit of no answer and produce no conviction.* Their only effect is to cause that momentary amazement and irresolution and confusion, which is the result of scepticism.

2 Whatever disputes there may be about mathematical points, we must allow that there are physical points; that is, parts of extension, which cannot be divided or lessened, either by the eye or imagination. These images, then, which are present to the fancy or senses, are absolutely indivisible, and consequently must be allowed by mathematicians to be infinitely less than any real part of extension; and yet nothing appears more certain to reason, than that an infinite number of them composes an infinite extension. How much more an infinite number of those infinitely small parts of extension, which are still supposed infinitely divisible?

3 It seems to me not impossible to avoid these absurdities and contradictions, if it be admitted, that there is no such thing as abstract or general ideas, properly speaking; but that all general ideas are, in reality, particular ones, attached to a general term, which recalls, upon occasion, other particular ones, that resemble, in certain circumstances, the idea, present to the mind. Thus when the term Horse, is pronounced, we immediately figure to ourselves the idea of a black or a white animal, of a particular size or figure: But as that term is also usually applied to animals of other colours, figures and sizes, these ideas, though not actually present to the imagination, are easily recalled; and our reasoning and conclusion proceed in the same way, as if they were actually present. If this be admitted (as seems reasonable) it follows that all the ideas of quantity, upon which mathematicians reason, are nothing but particular, and such as are suggested by the senses and imagination, and consequently, cannot be infinitely divisible. It is sufficient to have dropped this hint at present, without prosecuting it any farther. It certainly concerns all lovers of science not to expose themselves to the ridicule and contempt of the ignorant by their conclusions; and this seems the readiest solution of these difficulties.

4 That impious maxim of the ancient philosophy, *Ex nihilo, nihil fit,* by which the creation of matter was excluded, ceases to be a maxim, according to this philosophy. Not only the will of the supreme Being may create matter; but, for aught we know *à priori,* the will of any other being might create it, or any other cause, that the most whimsical imagination can assign.

26

An Enquiry Concerning the Principles of Morals

Appendix I: Concerning Moral Sentiment

If the foregoing hypothesis be received, it will now be easy for us to determine the question first started, concerning the general principles of morals; and though we postponed the decision of that question, lest it should then involve us in intricate speculations, which are unfit for moral discourses, we may resume it at present, and examine how far either *reason* or *sentiment* enters into all decisions of praise or censure.

One principal foundation of moral praise being supposed to lie in the usefulness of any quality or action, it is evident that *reason* must enter for a considerable share in all decisions of this kind; since nothing but that faculty can instruct us in the tendency of qualities and actions, and point out their beneficial consequences to society and to their possessor. In many cases this is an affair liable to great controversy: doubts may arise; opposite interests may occur; and a preference must be given to one side, from very nice views, and a small overbalance of utility. This is particularly remarkable in questions with regard to justice; as is, indeed, natural to suppose, from that species of utility which attends this virtue. Were every single instance of justice, like that of benevolence, useful to society; this would be a more simple state of the case, and seldom liable to great controversy. But as single instances of justice are often pernicious in

An Enquiry Concerning the Principles of Morals (1751), ed. L. A. Selby-Bigge, rev. P. H. Nidditch (Oxford University Press, 1975). Selection: Appendix I, "Concerning Moral Sentiment," pp. 285–94.

their first and immediate tendency, and as the advantage to society results only from the observance of the general rule, and from the concurrence and combination of several persons in the same equitable conduct; the case here becomes more intricate and involved. The various circumstances of society; the various consequences of any practice; the various interests which may be proposed; these, on many occasions, are doubtful, and subject to great discussion and inquiry. The object of municipal laws is to fix all the questions with regard to justice: the debates of civilians; the reflections of politicians; the precedents of history and public records, are all directed to the same purpose. And a very accurate *reason* or *judgement* is often requisite, to give the true determination, amidst such intricate doubts arising from obscure or opposite utilities.

But though reason, when fully assisted and improved, be sufficient to instruct us in the pernicious or useful tendency of qualities and actions; it is not alone sufficient to produce any moral blame or approbation. Utility is only a tendency to a certain end; and were the end totally indifferent to us, we should feel the same indifference towards the means. It is requisite a *sentiment* should here display itself, in order to give a preference to the useful above the pernicious tendencies. This sentiment can be no other than a feeling for the happiness of mankind, and a resentment of their misery; since these are the different ends which virtue and vice have a tendency to promote. Here therefore *reason* instructs us in the several tendencies of actions, and *humanity* makes a distinction in favour of those which are useful and beneficial.

This partition between the faculties of understanding and sentiment, in all moral decisions, seems clear from the preceding hypothesis. But I shall suppose that hypothesis false: it will then be requisite to look out for some other theory that may be satisfactory; and I dare venture to affirm that none such will ever be found, so long as we suppose reason to be the sole source of morals. To prove this, it will be proper to weigh the five following considerations.

I. It is easy for a false hypothesis to maintain some appearance of truth, while it keeps wholly in generals, makes use of undefined terms, and employs comparisons, instead of instances. This is particularly remarkable in that philosophy, which ascribes the discernment of all moral distinctions to reason alone, without the concurrence of sentiment. It is impossible that, in any particular instance, this hypothesis can so much as be rendered intelligible, whatever specious figure it may make in general declamations and discourses. Examine the crime of *ingratitude*, for instance; which has place, wherever we observe good-will, expressed and known, together with good-offices performed, on the one side, and a return of ill-will or indifference, with ill-offices or neglect on the other: anatomize all these circumstances, and examine, by your reason alone, in what consists the demerit or blame. You never will come to any issue or conclusion.

Reason judges either of *matter of fact* or of *relations*. Enquire then, *first*, where is that matter of fact which we here call *crime*; point it out; determine the time of its existence; describe its essence or nature; explain the sense or faculty to which it discovers itself. It resides in the mind of the person who is ungrateful. He must, therefore, feel it, and be conscious of it. But nothing is there, except the passion of ill-will or absolute indifference. You cannot say that these, of themselves, always, and in all circumstances, are crimes. No, they are only crimes when directed towards persons who have before expressed and displayed good-will towards us. Consequently, we may infer, that the crime of ingratitude is not any particular individual *fact*; but arises from a complication of circumstances, which, being presented to the spectator, excites the *sentiment* of blame, by the particular structure and fabric of his mind.

This representation, you say, is false. Crime, indeed, consists not in a particular *fact*, of whose reality we are assured by *reason*; but it consists in certain *moral relations*, discovered by reason, in the same manner as we discover by reason the truths of geometry or algebra. But what are the relations, I ask, of which you here talk? In the case stated above, I see first good-will and good-offices in one person; then ill-will and ill-offices in the other. Between these, there is a relation of *contrariety*. Does the crime consist in that relation? But suppose a person bore me ill-will or did me ill-offices; and I, in return, were indifferent towards him, or did him good-offices. Here is the same relation of *contrariety*; and yet my conduct is often highly laudable. Twist and turn this matter as much as you will, you can never rest the morality on relation; but must have recourse to the decisions of sentiment.

When it is affirmed that two and three are equal to the half of ten, this relation of equality I understand perfectly. I conceive, that if ten be divided into two parts, of which one has as many units as the other; and if any of these parts be compared to two added to three, it will contain as many units as that compound number. But when you draw thence a comparison to moral relations, I own that I am altogether at a loss to understand you. A moral action, a crime, such as ingratitude, is a complicated object. Does the morality consist in the relation of its parts to each other? How? After what manner? Specify the relation: be more particular and explicit in your propositions, and you will easily see their falsehood.

No, say you, the morality consists in the relation of actions to the rule of right; and they are denominated good or ill, according as they agree or disagree with it. What then is this rule of right? In what does it consist? How is it determined? By reason, you say, which examines the moral relations of actions. So that moral relations are determined by the comparison of action to a rule. And that rule is determined by considering the moral relations of objects. Is not this fine reasoning?

All this is metaphysics, you cry. That is enough; there needs nothing more to give a strong presumption of falsehood. Yes, reply I, here are metaphysics surely; but they are all on your side, who advance an abstruse hypothesis, which can never be made intelligible, nor quadrate with any particular instance or illustration. The hypothesis which we embrace is plain. It maintains that morality is determined by sentiment. It defines virtue to be *whatever mental action or quality gives to a spectator the pleasing sentiment of approbation;* and vice the contrary. We then proceed to examine a plain matter of fact, to wit, what actions have this influence. We consider all the circumstances in which these actions agree, and thence endeavour to extract some general observations with regard to these sentiments. If you call this metaphysics, and find anything abstruse here, you need only conclude that your turn of mind is not suited to the moral sciences.

II. When a man, at any time, deliberates concerning his own conduct (as, whether he had better, in a particular emergence, assist a brother or a benefactor), he must consider these separate relations, with all the circumstances and situations of the persons, in order to determine the superior duty and obligation; and in order to determine the proportion of lines in any triangle, it is necessary to examine the nature of that figure, and the relations which its several parts bear to each other. But notwithstanding this appearing similarity in the two cases, there is, at bottom, an extreme difference between them. A speculative reasoner concerning triangles or circles considers the several known and given relations of the parts of these figures, and thence infers some unknown relation, which is dependent on the former. But in moral deliberations we must be acquainted beforehand with all the objects, and all their relations to each other; and from a comparison of the whole, fix our choice or approbation. No new fact to be ascertained; no new relation to be discovered. All the circumstances of the case are supposed to be laid before us, ere we can fix any sentence of blame or approbation. If any material circumstance be yet unknown or doubtful, we must first employ our inquiry or intellectual faculties to assure us of it; and must suspend for a time all moral decision or sentiment. While we are ignorant whether a man were aggressor or not, how can we determine whether the person who killed him be criminal or innocent? But after every circumstance, every relation is known, the understanding has no further room to operate, nor any object on which it could employ itself. The approbation or blame which then ensues, cannot be the work of the judgement, but of the heart; and is not a speculative proposition or affirmation, but an active feeling or sentiment. In the disquisitions of the understanding, from known circumstances and relations, we infer some new and unknown. In moral decisions, all the circumstances and relations must be previously known; and the mind, from the contemplation of the whole, feels some new impression of affection or disgust, esteem or contempt, approbation or blame.

Hence the great difference between a mistake of *fact* and one of *right*; and hence the reason why the one is commonly criminal and not the other. When Oedipus killed Laius, he was ignorant of the relation, and from circumstances, innocent and involuntary, formed erroneous opinions concerning the action which he committed. But when Nero killed Agrippina, all the relations between himself and the person, and all the circumstances of the fact, were previously known to him; but the motive of revenge, or fear, or interest, prevailed in his savage heart over the sentiments of duty and humanity. And when we express that detestation against him to which he himself, in a little time, became insensible, it is not that we see any relations, of which he was ignorant; but that, from the rectitude of our disposition, we feel sentiments against which he was hardened from flattery and a long perseverance in the most enormous crimes. In these sentiments then, not in a discovery of relations of any kind, do all moral determinations consist. Before we can pretend to form any decision of this kind, everything must be known and ascertained on the side of the object or action. Nothing remains but to feel, on our part, some sentiment of blame or approbation; whence we pronounce the action criminal or virtuous.

III. This doctrine will become still more evident, if we compare moral beauty with natural, to which in many particulars it bears so near a resemblance. It is on the proportion, relation, and position of parts, that all natural beauty depends; but it would be absurd thence to infer, that the perception of beauty, like that of truth in geometrical problems, consists wholly in the perception of relations, and was performed entirely by the understanding or intellectual faculties. In all the sciences, our mind from the known relations investigates the unknown. But in all decisions of taste or external beauty, all the relations are beforehand obvious to the eye; and we thence proceed to feel a sentiment of complacency or disgust, according to the nature of the object, and disposition of our organs.

Euclid has fully explained all the qualities of the circle; but has not in any proposition said a word of its beauty. The reason is evident. The beauty is not a quality of the circle. It lies not in any part of the line, whose parts are equally distant from a common centre. It is only the effect which that figure produces upon the mind, whose peculiar fabric or structure renders it susceptible of such sentiments. In vain would you look for it in the circle, or seek it, either by your senses or by mathematical reasonings, in all the properties of that figure.

Attend to Palladio and Perrault, while they explain all the parts and proportions of a pillar. They talk of the cornice, and frieze, and base, and entablature, and shaft and architrave; and give the description and position of each of these members. But should you ask the description and position of its beauty, they would readily reply, that the beauty is not in any of the parts or members of a pillar, but results from the whole, when that complicated figure is presented to an intelligent mind, susceptible to those finer sensations. Till such a spectator appear, there is nothing but a figure of such particular dimensions and proportions: from his sentiments alone arise its elegance and beauty.

Again; attend to Cicero, while he paints the crimes of a Verres or a Catiline. You must acknowledge that the moral turpitude results, in the same manner, from the contemplation of the whole, when presented to a being whose organs have such a particular structure and formation. The orator may paint rage, insolence, barbarity on the one side; meekness, suffering, sorrow, innocence on the other. But if you feel no indignation or compassion arise in you from this complication of circumstances, you would in vain ask him, in what consists the crime or villainy, which he so vehemently exclaims against? At what time, or on what subject it first began to exist? And what has a few months afterwards become of it, when every disposition and thought of all the actors is totally altered or annihilated? No satisfactory answer can be given to any of these questions, upon the abstract hypothesis of morals; and we must at last acknowledge, that the crime or immorality is no particular fact or relation, which can be the object of the understanding, but arises entirely from the sentiment of disapprobation, which, by the structure of human nature, we unavoidably feel on the apprehension of barbarity or treachery.

IV. Inanimate objects may bear to each other all the same relations which we observe in moral agents; though the former can never be the object of love or hatred, nor are consequently susceptible of merit or iniquity. A young tree, which over-tops and destroys its parent, stands in all the same relations with Nero, when he murdered Agrippina; and if morality consisted merely in relations, would no doubt be equally criminal.

V. It appears evident that the ultimate ends of human actions can never, in any case, be accounted for by *reason*, but recommend themselves entirely to the sentiments and affections of mankind, without any dependance on the intellectual faculties. Ask a man *why he uses exercise*; he will answer, *because he desires to keep his health*. If you then enquire, *why he desires health*, he will readily reply, *because sickness is painful*. If you push your enquiries farther, and desire a reason *why he hates pain*, it is impossible he can ever give any. This is an ultimate end, and is never referred to any other object.

Perhaps to your second question, *why he desires health*, he may also reply, that *it is necessary for the exercise of his calling*. If you ask, *why he is anxious on that head*, he will answer, *because he desires to get money*. If you demand *Why? It is the instrument of pleasure*, says he. And beyond this it is an absurdity to ask for a reason. It is impossible there can be a progress *in infinitum*; and that one thing can always be a reason why another is desired. Something must be desirable on its own account, and because of its immediate accord or agreement with human sentiment and affection.

Now as virtue is an end, and is desirable on its own account, without fee or reward, merely for the immediate satisfaction which it conveys; it is requisite that there should be some sentiment which it touches, some internal taste or feeling, or whatever you please to call it, which distinguishes moral good and evil, and which embraces the one and rejects the other.

Thus the distinct boundaries and offices of *reason* and of *taste* are easily ascertained. The former conveys the knowledge of truth and falsehood: the latter gives the sentiment of beauty and deformity, vice and virtue. The one discovers objects as they really stand in nature, without addition or diminution: the other has a productive faculty, and gilding or staining all natural objects with the colours, borrowed from internal sentiment, raises in a manner a new creation. Reason being cool and disengaged, is no motive to action, and directs only the impulse received from appetite or inclination, by showing us the means of attaining happiness or avoiding misery: Taste, as it gives pleasure or pain, and thereby constitutes happiness or misery, becomes a motive to action, and is the first spring or impulse to desire and volition. From circumstances and relations, known or supposed, the former leads us to the discovery of the concealed and unknown: after all circumstances and relations are laid before us, the latter makes us feel from the whole a new sentiment of blame or approbation. The standard of the one, being founded on the nature of things, is eternal and inflexible, even by the will of the Supreme Being: the standard of the other, arising from the internal frame and constitution of animals, is ultimately derived from that Supreme Will, which bestowed on each being its peculiar nature, and arranged the several classes and orders of existence.

27

Of the Original Contract

As no party, in the present age, can well support itself without a philosophical or speculative system of principles annexed to its political or practical one, we accordingly find that each of the factions into which this nation is divided has reared up a fabric of the former kind in order to protect and cover that scheme of actions which it pursues. The people being commonly very rude builders, especially in this speculative way, and more especially still when actuated by party zeal, it is natural to imagine that their workmanship must be a little unshapely, and discover evident marks of that violence and hurry in which it was raised. The one party, by tracing up government to the Deity, endeavor to render it so sacred and inviolate that it must be little less than sacrilege, however tyrannical it may become, to touch or invade it in the smallest article. The other party, by founding government altogether on the consent of the people, suppose that there is a kind of *original contract* by which the subjects have tacitly reserved the power of resisting their sovereign whenever they find themselves aggrieved by that authority with which they have, for certain purposes, voluntarily entrusted him. These are the speculative principles of the two parties, and these, too, are the practical consequences deduced from them.

I shall venture to affirm *that both these systems of speculative principles are just, though not in the sense intended by the parties*; and *that both the schemes of practical consequences are prudent, though not in the*

Of the Original Contract (1748). From *David Hume's Political Essays*, ed. Charles W. Hendel (Indianapolis: Bobbs-Merrill Co., Inc., 1953). Selection: pp. 43–61.

extremes to which each party, in opposition to the other, has commonly endeavored to carry them.

That the Deity is the ultimate author of all government will never be denied by any who admit a general providence and allow that all events in the universe are conducted by a uniform plan and directed to wise purposes. As it is impossible for the human race to subsist, at least in any comfortable or secure state, without the protection of government, this institution must certainly have been intended by that beneficent Being who means the good of all his creatures. And as it has universally, in fact, taken place in all countries and all ages, we may conclude, with still greater certainty, that it was intended by that omniscient Being who can never be deceived by any event or operation. But since he gave rise to it, not by any particular or miraculous interposition, but by his concealed and universal efficacy, a sovereign cannot, properly speaking, be called his vicegerent in any other sense than every power or force, being derived from him, may be said to act by his commission. Whatever actually happens is comprehended in the general plan or intention of Providence; nor has the greatest and most lawful prince any more reason, upon that account, to plead a peculiar sacredness or inviolable authority than an inferior magistrate, or even a usurper, or even a robber and a pirate. The same Divine Superintendent who, for wise purposes, invested a Titus or a Trajan with authority did also, for purposes no doubt equally wise though unknown, bestow power on a Borgia or an Angria. The same causes which gave rise to the sovereign power in every state established likewise every petty jurisdiction in it and every limited authority. A constable, therefore, no less than a king, acts by a divine commission and possesses an indefeasible right.

When we consider how nearly equal all men are in their bodily force, and even in their mental powers and faculties, till cultivated by education, we must necessarily allow that nothing but their own consent could at first associate them together and subject them to any authority. The people, if we trace government to its first origin in the woods and deserts, are the source of all power and jurisdiction, and voluntarily, for the sake of peace and order, abandoned their native liberty and received laws from their equal and companion. The conditions upon which they were willing to submit were either expressed or were so clear and obvious that it might well be esteemed superfluous to express them. If this, then, be meant by the *original contract*, it cannot be denied that all government is, at first, founded on a contract and that the most ancient rude combinations of mankind were formed chiefly by that principle. In vain are we asked in what records this charter of our liberties is registered. It was not written on parchment, nor yet on leaves or barks of trees. It preceded the use of writing and all the other civilized arts of life. But we trace it plainly in the nature of man and in the equality, or something approaching equality, which we find in all the individuals of that species. The force which now prevails, and which is founded on fleets and armies, is plainly political and derived from authority, the effect of established government. A man's natural force consists only in the vigor of his limbs and the firmness of his courage, which could never subject multitudes to the command of one. Nothing but their own consent and their sense of the advantages resulting from peace and order could have had that influence.

Yet even this consent was long very imperfect and could not be the basis of a regular administration. The chieftain, who had probably acquired his influence during the continuance of war, ruled more by persuasion than command; and till he could employ force to reduce the refractory and disobedient, the society could scarcely be said to have attained a state of civil government. No compact or agreement, it is evident, was expressly formed for general submission, an idea far beyond the comprehension of savages. Each exertion of authority in the chieftain must have been particular and called forth by the present exigencies of the case. The sensible utility resulting from his interposition made these exertions become daily more frequent; and their frequency gradually produced a habitual and, if you please to call it so, a voluntary and therefore precarious acquiescence in the people.

But philosophers who have embraced a party – if that be not a contradiction in terms – are not content with these concessions. They assert not only that government in its earliest infancy arose from consent, or rather the voluntary acquiescence of the people, but also that, even at present, when it has attained its full maturity, it rests on no other foundation. They affirm that all men are still born equal and owe allegiance to no prince or government unless bound by the obligation and sanction of a *promise*. And as no man, without some equivalent, would forego the advantages of his native liberty and subject himself to the will of another, this promise is always understood to be conditional and imposes on him no obligation, unless he meet with justice and protection from his sovereign. These advantages the sovereign promises him in return; and if he fail in the execution, he has broken on his part the articles of engagement, and has thereby freed his subject from all obligations to allegiance. Such, according to these philosophers, is the foundation of authority in every government, and such the right of resistance possessed by every subject.

But would these reasoners look abroad into the world, they would meet with nothing that in the least corresponds to their ideas or can warrant so refined and philosophical a system. On the contrary, we find everywhere princes who claim their subjects as their property and assert their independent right of sovereignty from conquest or succession. We find also everywhere subjects who acknowledge this right in their prince and suppose themselves born under obligations of obedience to a certain sovereign, as much as under the ties of reverence and duty to certain parents. These connections are always conceived to be equally independent of our consent, in Persia and China, in France and Spain, and even in Holland and England, wherever the doctrines above mentioned have not been carefully inculcated. Obedience or subjection becomes so familiar that most men never make any inquiry about its origin or cause, more than about the principle of gravity, resistance, or the most universal laws of nature. Or if curiosity ever move them, as soon as they learn that they themselves and their ancestors have, for several ages, or from time immemorial, been subject to such a form of government or such a family, they immediately acquiesce and acknowledge their obligation to allegiance. Were you to preach, in most parts of the world, that political connections are founded altogether on voluntary consent or a mutual promise, the magistrate would soon imprison you as seditious for loosening the ties of obedience, if your friends did not before shut you up as delirious for advancing such absurdities. It is strange that an act of the mind which every individual is supposed to have formed, and after he came to the use of reason too – otherwise it could have no authority – that this act, I say, should be so much unknown to all of them that over the face of the whole earth there scarcely remain any traces or memory of it.

But the contract on which government is founded is said to be the *original contract*, and consequently may be supposed too old to fall under the knowledge of the present generation. If the agreement by which savage men first associated and conjoined their force be here meant, this is acknowledged to be real; but being so ancient and being obliterated by a thousand changes of government and princes, it cannot now be supposed to retain any authority. If we would say anything to the purpose, we must assert that every particular government which is lawful and which imposes any duty of allegiance on the subject was at first founded on consent and a voluntary compact. But besides that this supposes the consent of the fathers to bind the children, even to the most remote generations – which republican writers will never allow – besides this, I say, it is not justified by history or experience in any age or country of the world.

Almost all the governments which exist at present, or of which there remains any record in story, have been founded originally either on usurpation or conquest or both, without any pretense of a fair consent or voluntary subjection of the people. When an artful and bold man is placed at the head of an army or faction, it is often easy for him, by employing sometimes violence, sometimes false pretenses, to establish his dominion over a people a hundred times more numerous than his partisans. He allows no such open communication that his enemies can know with certainty their number or force. He gives them no leisure to assemble together in a body to oppose him. Even all those who are the instruments of his usurpation may wish his fall, but their ignorance of each other's intention keeps them in awe and is the sole cause of his security. By such arts as these

many governments have been established, and this is all the *original contract* which they have to boast of.

The face of the earth is continually changing by the increase of small kingdoms into great empires, by the dissolution of great empires into smaller kingdoms, by the planting of colonies, by the migration of tribes. Is there anything discoverable in all these events but force and violence? Where is the mutual agreement or voluntary association so much talked of?

Even the smoothest way by which a nation may receive a foreign master, by marriage or a will, is not extremely honorable for the people, but supposes them to be disposed like a dowry or a legacy, according to the pleasure or interest of their rulers.

But where no force interposes and election takes place, what is this election so highly vaunted? It is either the combination of a few great men who decide for the whole and will allow of no opposition or it is the fury of a multitude that follow a seditious ringleader who is not known, perhaps, to a dozen among them and who owes his advancement merely to his own impudence or to the momentary caprice of his fellows.

Are these disorderly elections, which are rare too, of such mighty authority as to be the only lawful foundation of all government and allegiance?

In reality there is not a more terrible event than a total dissolution of government, which gives liberty to the multitude and makes the determination or choice of a new establishment depend upon a number which nearly approaches to that of the body of the people. For it never comes entirely to the whole body of them. Every wise man, then, wishes to see at the head of a powerful and obedient army a general who may speedily seize the prize and give to the people a master which they are so unfit to choose for themselves – so little correspondent is fact and reality to those philosophical notions.

Let not the establishment at the Revolution deceive us or make us so much in love with a philosophical origin to government as to imagine all others monstrous and irregular. Even that event was far from corresponding to these refined ideas. It was only the succession, and that only in the regal part of the government, which was then changed. And it was only the majority of seven hundred who determined that change for near ten millions. I doubt not, indeed, but the bulk of those ten millions acquiesced willingly in the determination. But was the matter left in the least to their choice? Was it not justly supposed to be from that moment decided and every man punished who refused to submit to the new sovereign? How otherwise could the matter have ever been brought to any issue or conclusion?

The republic of Athens was, I believe, the most extensive democracy that we read of in history. Yet if we make the requisite allowances for the women, the slaves, and the strangers, we shall find that that establishment was not at first made, nor any law ever voted, by a tenth part of those who were bound to pay obedience to it, not to mention the islands and foreign dominions which the Athenians claimed as theirs by right of conquest. And as it is well known that popular assemblies in that city were always full of license and disorder, notwithstanding the institutions and laws by which they were checked, how much more disorderly must they prove where they form not the established constitution, but meet tumultuously on the dissolution of the ancient government in order to give rise to a new one? How chimerical must it be to talk of a choice in such circumstances?

The Achaeans enjoyed the freest and most perfect democracy of all antiquity; yet they employed force to oblige some cities to enter into their league, as we learn from Polybius [Lib. ii. cap. 38].

Harry IV and Harry VII of England had really no title to the throne but a parliamentary election; yet they never would acknowledge it, lest they should thereby weaken their authority. Strange if the only real foundation of all authority be consent and promise.

It is in vain to say that all governments are or should be at first founded on popular consent as much as the necessity of human affairs will admit. This favors entirely my pretension. I maintain that human affairs will never admit of this consent, seldom of the appearance of it; but that conquest or usurpation – that is, in plain terms, force – by dissolving the ancient governments, is the origin of almost all the new ones which were ever established in the world. And that in the few cases where consent may seem to have taken place, it was commonly so irregular, so confined, or so much intermixed either with fraud or violence that it cannot have any great authority.

My intention here is not to exclude the consent of the people from being one just foundation of government. Where it has place, it is surely the best and most sacred of any. I only contend that it

has very seldom had place in any degree, and never almost in its full extent, and that, therefore, some other foundation of government must also be admitted.

Were all men possessed of so inflexible a regard to justice that of themselves they would totally abstain from the properties of others, they had forever remained in a state of absolute liberty, without subjection to any magistrate or political society. But this is a state of perfection of which human nature is justly deemed incapable. Again, were all men possessed of so perfect an understanding as always to know their own interests, no form of government had ever been submitted to but what was established on consent and was fully canvassed by every member of the society. But this state of perfection is likewise much superior to human nature. Reason, history, and experience show us that all political societies have had an origin much less accurate and regular; and were one to choose a period of time when the people's consent was the least regarded in public transactions, it would be precisely on the establishment of a new government. In a settled constitution their inclinations are often consulted, but during the fury of revolutions, conquests, and public convulsions, military force or political craft usually decides the controversy.

When a new government is established, by whatever means, the people are commonly dissatisfied with it and pay obedience more from fear and necessity than from any idea of allegiance or of moral obligation. The prince is watchful and jealous, and must carefully guard against every beginning or appearance of insurrection. Time, by degrees, removes all these difficulties and accustoms the nation to regard as their lawful or native princes that family which at first they considered as usurpers or foreign conquerors. In order to found this opinion, they have no recourse to any notion of voluntary consent or promise which, they know, never was in this case either expected or demanded. The original establishment was formed by violence and submitted to from necessity. The subsequent administration is also supported by power and acquiesced in by the people, not as a matter of choice but of obligation. They imagine not that their consent gives their prince a title. But they willingly consent because they think that, from long possession, he has acquired a title independent of their choice or inclination.

Should it be said that, by living under the dominion of a prince which one might leave, every individual has given a *tacit* consent to his authority and promised him obedience, it may be answered that such an implied consent can only have place where a man imagines that the matter depends on his choice. But where he thinks – as all mankind do who are born under established governments – that by his birth he owes allegiance to a certain prince or certain form of government, it would be absurd to infer a consent or choice which he expressly in this case renounces and disclaims.

Can we seriously say that a poor peasant or artisan has a free choice to leave his country when he knows no foreign language or manners and lives from day to day by the small wages which he acquires? We may as well assert that a man, by remaining in a vessel, freely consents to the dominion of the master, though he was carried on board while asleep and must leap into the ocean and perish the moment he leaves her.

What if the prince forbid his subjects to quit his dominions, as in Tiberius' time it was regarded as a crime in a Roman knight that he had attempted to fly to the Parthians in order to escape the tyranny of that emperor [Tacit. *Ann.* lib. vi. cap. 14]? Or as the ancient Muscovites prohibited all traveling under pain of death? And did a prince observe that many of his subjects were seized with the frenzy of migrating to foreign countries, he would doubtless, with great reason and justice, restrain them in order to prevent the depopulation of his own kingdom. Would he forfeit the allegiance of all his subjects by so wise and reasonable a law? Yet the freedom of their choice is surely, in that case, ravished from them.

A company of men who should leave their native country in order to people some uninhabited region might dream of recovering their native freedom, but they would soon find that their prince still laid claim to them and called them his subjects even in their new settlement. And in this he would but act conformably to the common ideas of mankind.

The truest *tacit* consent of this kind that is ever observed is when a foreigner settles in any country and is beforehand acquainted with the prince and government and laws to which he must submit; yet is his allegiance, though more voluntary, much less expected or depended on than that of a natural-born subject. On the contrary, his native prince still asserts a claim to him. And if he punish not the renegade when he seizes him in war with his new prince's commission, this clemency is not founded on the municipal law, which in all countries condemns the prisoner, but on the consent of princes, who have agreed to this indulgence in order to prevent reprisals.

Did one generation of men go off the stage at once and another succeed, as is the case with silkworms and butterflies, the new race, if they had sense enough to choose their government, which surely is never the case with men, might voluntarily and by general consent establish their own form of civil polity without any regard to the laws or precedents which prevailed among their ancestors. But as human society is in perpetual flux, one man every hour going out of the world, another coming into it, it is necessary in order to preserve stability in government that the new brood should conform themselves to the established constitution and nearly follow the path which their fathers, treading in the footsteps of theirs, had marked out to them. Some innovations must necessarily have place in every human institution; and it is happy where the enlightened genius of the age give these a direction to the side of reason, liberty, and justice. But violent innovations no individual is entitled to make. They are even dangerous to be attempted by the legislature. More ill than good is ever to be expected from them. And if history affords examples to the contrary, they are not to be drawn into precedent and are only to be regarded as proofs that the science of politics affords few rules which will not admit of some exception and which may not sometimes be controlled by fortune and accident. The violent innovations in the reign of Henry VIII proceeded from an imperious monarch seconded by the appearance of legislative authority; those in the reign of Charles I were derived from faction and fanaticism; and both of them have proved happy in the issue. But even the former were long the source of many disorders, and still more dangers; and if the measures of allegiance were to be taken from the latter, a total anarchy must have place in human society and a final period at once be put to every government.

Suppose that a usurper, after having banished his lawful prince and royal family, should establish his dominion for ten or a dozen years in any country and should preserve so exact a discipline in his troops and so regular a disposition in his garrisons that no insurrection had ever been raised or even murmur heard against his administration. Can it be asserted that the people, who in their hearts abhor his treason, have tacitly consented to his authority and promised him allegiance merely because, from necessity, they live under his dominion? Suppose again their native prince restored by means of an army which he levies in foreign countries. They receive him with joy and exultation, and show plainly with what reluctance they had submitted to any other yoke. I may now ask upon what foundation the prince's title stands? Not on popular consent surely; for though the people willingly acquiesce in his authority, they never imagine that their consent made him sovereign. They consent because they apprehend him to be already, by birth, their lawful sovereign. And as to tacit consent, which may now be inferred from their living under his dominion, this is no more than what they formerly gave to the tyrant and usurper.

When we assert that all lawful government arises from the consent of the people, we certainly do them a great deal more honor than they deserve or even expect and desire from us. After the Roman dominions became too unwieldy for the republic to govern them, the people over the whole known world were extremely grateful to Augustus for that authority which, by violence, he had established over them; and they showed an equal disposition to submit to the successor whom he left them by his last will and testament. It was afterward their misfortune that there never was, in one family, any long regular succession, but that their line of princes was continually broken either by private assassinations or public rebellions. The *praetorian* bands, on the failure of every family, set up one emperor, the legions in the East a second, those in Germany, perhaps, a third; and the sword alone could decide the controversy. The condition of the people in that mighty monarchy was to be lamented, not because the choice of the emperor was never left to them, for that was impracticable, but because they never fell under any succession of masters who might regularly follow each other. As to the violence and wars and bloodshed occasioned by every new settlement, these were not blamable because they were inevitable.

The house of Lancaster ruled in this island about sixty years; yet the partisans of the White Rose seemed daily to multiply in England. The present establishment has taken place during a still longer period. Have all views of right in another family been utterly extinguished, even though scarce any man now alive had arrived at the years of discretion when it was expelled, or could have consented to its dominion or have promised it

allegiance? – a sufficient indication, surely, of the general sentiment of mankind on this head. For we blame not the partisans of the abdicated family merely on account of the long time during which they have preserved their imaginary loyalty. We blame them for adhering to a family which we affirm has been justly expelled and which, from the moment the new settlement took place, had forfeited all title to authority.

But would we have a more regular, at least a more philosophical, refutation of this principle of an original contract or popular consent, perhaps the following observations may suffice.

All *moral* duties may be divided into two kinds. The *first* are those to which men are impelled by a natural instinct or immediate propensity which operates on them, independent of all ideas of obligation and of all views either to public or private utility. Of this nature are love of children, gratitude to benefactors, pity to the unfortunate. When we reflect on the advantage which results to society from such humane instincts, we pay them the just tribute of moral approbation and esteem. But the person actuated by them feels their power and influence antecedent to any such reflection.

The *second* kind of moral duties are such as are not supported by any original instinct of nature, but are performed entirely from a sense of obligation, when we consider the necessities of human society and the impossibility of supporting it if these duties were neglected. It is thus *justice*, or a regard to the property of others, *fidelity*, or the observance of promises, become obligatory and acquire an authority over mankind. For as it is evident that every man loves himself better than any other person, he is naturally impelled to extend his acquisitions as much as possible; and nothing can restrain him in this propensity but reflection and experience, by which he learns the pernicious effects of that license and the total dissolution of society which must ensue from it. His original inclination, therefore, or instinct, is here checked and restrained by a subsequent judgment or observation.

The case is precisely the same with the political or civil duty of *allegiance* as with the natural duties of justice and fidelity. Our primary instincts lead us either to indulge ourselves in unlimited freedom or to seek dominion over others; and it is reflection only which engages us to sacrifice such strong passions to the interests of peace and public order. A small degree of experience and observation suffices to teach us that society cannot possibly be maintained without the authority of magistrates, and that this authority must soon fall into contempt where exact obedience is not paid to it. The observation of these general and obvious interests is the source of all allegiance and of that moral obligation which we attribute to it.

What necessity, therefore, is there to found the duty of *allegiance*, or obedience to magistrates, on that of *fidelity*, or a regard to promises, and to suppose that it is the consent of each individual which subjects him to government, when it appears that both allegiance and fidelity stand precisely on the same foundation and are both submitted to by mankind on account of the apparent interests and necessities of human society? We are bound to obey our sovereign, it is said, because we have given a tacit promise to that purpose. But why are we bound to observe our promise? It must here be asserted that the commerce and intercourse of mankind, which are of such mighty advantage, can have no security where men pay no regard to their engagements. In like manner may it be said that men could not live at all in society, at least in a civilized society, without laws and magistrates and judges to prevent the encroachments of the strong upon the weak, of the violent upon the just and equitable. The obligation to allegiance being of like force and authority with the obligation to fidelity, we gain nothing by resolving the one into the other. The general interests or necessities of society are sufficient to establish both.

If the reason be asked of that obedience which we are bound to pay to government, I readily answer, "Because society could not otherwise subsist"; and this answer is clear and intelligible to all mankind. Your answer is, "Because we should keep our word." But besides that nobody, till trained in a philosophical system, can either comprehend or relish this answer; besides this, I say, you find yourself embarrassed when it is asked, *Why we are bound to keep our word?* Nor can you give any answer but what would immediately, without any circuit, have accounted for our obligation to allegiance.

But *to whom is allegiance due, and who is our lawful sovereign?* This question is often the most difficult of any and liable to infinite discussions. When people are so happy that they can answer, "Our present sovereign, who inherits, in a direct line, from ancestors that have governed us for many ages," this answer admits of no reply, even though historians in tracing up to the remotest antiquity the origin of that royal family may find, as commonly happens, that its first authority was derived from usurpation and violence. It is confessed that private justice, or the abstinence from the properties of others, is a most cardinal virtue. Yet reason tells us that there is no property in durable objects, such as land or houses, when carefully examined in passing from hand to hand, but must in some period have been founded on fraud and injustice. The necessities of human society, neither in private nor public life, will allow of such an accurate inquiry; and there is no virtue or moral duty but what may with facility be refined away, if we indulge a false philosophy in sifting and scrutinizing it, by every captious rule of logic, in every light or position in which it may be placed.

The questions with regard to private property have filled infinite volumes of law and philosophy if in both we add the commentators to the original text; and in the end we may safely pronounce that many of the rules there established are uncertain, ambiguous, and arbitrary. The like opinion may be formed with regard to the succession and rights of princes and forms of government. Several cases no doubt occur, especially in the infancy of any constitution, which admit of no determination from the laws of justice and equity; and our historian Rapin pretends that the controversy between Edward the Third and Philip de Valois was of this nature and could be decided only by an appeal to heaven, that is, by war and violence.

Who shall tell me whether Germanicus or Drusus ought to have succeeded to Tiberius, had he died while they were both alive without naming any of them for his successor? Ought the right of adoption to be received as equivalent to that of blood in a nation where it had the same effect in private families and had already, in two instances, taken place in the public? Ought Germanicus to be esteemed the elder son because he was born before Drusus, or the younger because he was adopted after the birth of his brother? Ought the right of the elder to be regarded in a nation where he had no advantage in the succession of private families? Ought the Roman Empire at that time to be deemed hereditary because of two examples; or ought it, even so early, to be regarded as belonging to the stronger or to the present possessor, as being founded on so recent a usurpation?

Commodus mounted the throne after a pretty long succession of excellent emperors who had acquired their title, not by birth or public election, but by the fictitious rite of adoption. The bloody debauche being murdered by a conspiracy suddenly formed between his wench and her gallant, who happened at that time to be praetorian praefect, these immediately deliberated about choosing a master to human kind, to speak in the style of those ages, and they cast their eyes on Pertinax. Before the tyrant's death was known, the praefect went secretly to that senator who, on the appearance of the soldiers, imagined that his execution had been ordered by Commodus. He was immediately saluted emperor by the officer and his attendants, cheerfully proclaimed by the populace, unwillingly submitted to by the guards, formally recognized by the senate, and passively received by the provinces and armies of the empire.

The discontent of the praetorian bands broke out in a sudden sedition, which occasioned the murder of that excellent prince; and the world being now without a master and without government, the guards thought proper to set the empire formally to sale. Julian, the purchaser, was proclaimed by the soldiers, recognized by the senate, and submitted to by the people; and must also have been submitted to by the provinces had not the envy of the legions begotten opposition and resistance. Pescennius Niger in Syria elected himself emperor, gained the tumultuary consent of his army, and was attended with the secret good will of the senate and people of Rome. Albinus in Britain found an equal right to set up his claim, but Severus, who governed Pannonia, prevailed in the end above both of them. That able politician and warrior, finding his own birth and dignity too much inferior to the imperial crown, professed at first an intention only of revenging the death of Pertinax. He marched as general into Italy, defeated Julian, and without our being able to fix any precise commencement even of the soldiers' consent he was from necessity acknowledged emperor by the senate and people, and fully established in his violent authority by subduing Niger and Albinus [Herodian, lib. ii].

"*Inter haec Gordianus Caesar,*" says Capitolinus, speaking of another period, "*sublatus a militibus. Imperator est appellatus, quia non erat alius in praesenti*" ["In the midst of these events Gordian Caesar was acclaimed by the army. He was declared 'imperator,' because there was no other 'imperator' at the moment"]. It is to be remarked that Gordian was a boy of fourteen years of age.

Frequent instances of a like nature occur in the history of the emperors, in that of Alexander's successors, and of many other countries. Nor can anything be more unhappy than a despotic government of this kind where the succession is disjointed and irregular and must be determined on every vacancy by force or election. In a free government the matter is often unavoidable, and is also much less dangerous. The interests of liberty may there frequently lead the people, in their own defense, to alter the succession of the crown. And the constitution, being compounded of parts, may still maintain a sufficient stability by resting on the aristocratical or democratical members, though the monarchical be altered from time to time in order to accommodate it to the former.

In an absolute government, when there is no legal prince who has a title to the throne, it may safely be determined to belong to the first occupant. Instances of this kind are but too frequent, especially in the eastern monarchies. When any race of princes expires, the will or destination of the last sovereign will be regarded as a title. Thus the edict of Louis XIV, who called the bastard princes to the succession in case of the failure of all the legitimate princes, would in such an event have some authority.[1] Thus the will of Charles the Second disposed of the whole Spanish monarchy. The cession of the ancient proprietor, especially when joined to conquest, is likewise deemed a good title. The general obligation which binds us to government is the interest and necessities of society; and this obligation is very strong. The determination of it to this or that particular prince or form of government is frequently more uncertain and dubious. Present possession has considerable authority in these cases, and greater than in private property because of the disorders which attend all revolutions and changes of government.

We shall only observe, before we conclude, that though an appeal to general opinion may justly, in the speculative sciences of metaphysics, natural philosophy, or astronomy, be deemed unfair and inconclusive, yet in all questions with regard to morals, as well as criticism, there is really no other standard by which any controversy can ever be decided. And nothing is a clearer proof that a theory of this kind is erroneous than to find that it leads to paradoxes repugnant to the common sentiments of mankind and to the practice and opinion of all nations and all ages. The doctrine which founds all lawful government on an *original contract*, or consent of the people, is plainly of this kind; nor has the most noted of its partisans, in prosecution of it, scrupled to affirm *that absolute monarchy is inconsistent with civil society and so can be no form of civil government at all,*[2] and *that the supreme power in a state cannot take from any man by taxes and impositions any part of his property without his own consent or that of his representatives.*[3] What authority any moral reasoning can have which leads into opinions so wide of the general practice of mankind in every place but this single kingdom, it is easy to determine.

The only passage I meet with in antiquity where the obligation of obedience to government is ascribed to a promise is in Plato's *Crito*, where Socrates refuses to escape from prison because he had tacitly promised to obey the laws. Thus he builds a *Tory* consequence of passive obedience on a *Whig* foundation of the original contract.

New discoveries are not to be expected in these matters. If scarce any man, till very lately, ever imagined that government was founded on compact, it is certain that it cannot in general have any such foundation. [. . .]

Notes

1 It is remarkable that, in the remonstrance of the Duke of Bourbon and the legitimate princes against this destination of Louis XIV, the doctrine of the *original contract* is insisted on, even in that absolute government. The French nation, say they, choosing Hugh Capet and his posterity to rule over them and their posterity, where the former line fails, there is a tacit right reserved to choose a new royal family; and this right is invaded by calling the bastard princes to the throne without the consent of the nation. But the Comte de Boulainvilliers, who wrote in defense of the bastard princes, ridicules this notion of an original contract, especially when applied to Hugh Capet, who mounted the throne, says he, by the same arts which have ever been employed by all conquerors and usurpers. He got his title, indeed, recognized by the states after he had put himself in possession. But is this a choice or contract? The Comte de Boulainvilliers, we may observe, was a noted republican; but being a man of learning and very conversant in history, he knew that the people were almost never consulted in these revolutions and new establishments, and that time alone bestowed right and authority on what was commonly at first founded on force and violence. See *Etat de la France*, Vol. III.

2 See Locke, *On Government*, Chap. VII, § 90.

3 Locke, *On Government*, Chap. XI, §§ 138, 139, 140.

28

The Natural History of Religion

XIV: Bad Influence of Popular Religions on Morality

Here I cannot forbear observing a fact, which may be worth the attention of such as make human nature the object of their enquiry. It is certain, that, in every religion, however sublime the verbal definition which it gives of its divinity, many of the votaries, perhaps the greatest number, will still seek the divine favour, not by virtue and good morals, which alone can be acceptable to a perfect being, but either by frivolous observances, by intemperate zeal, by rapturous extasies, or by the belief of mysterious and absurd opinions. The least part of the *Sadder*, as well as of the *Pentateuch*, consists in precepts of morality; and we may also be assured, that that part was always the least observed and regarded. When the old ROMANS were attacked with a pestilence, they never ascribed their sufferings to their vices, or dreamed of repentance and amendment. They never thought, that they were the general robbers of the world, whose ambition and avarice made desolate the earth, and reduced opulent nations to want and beggary. They only created a dictator, in order to drive a nail into a door; and by that means, they thought that they had sufficiently appeased their incensed deity.

The Natural History of Religion (1757). From *David Hume: Philosophical Works*, vol. 4, ed. Thomas Hill Green and Thomas Hodge Grose (Scientia Verlag Aalen, 1964). Selection: sects 14–15, "Bad Influence of Popular Religions on Morality/General Corollary," pp. 357–63.

In ÆGINA, one faction forming a conspiracy, barbarously and treacherously assassinated seven hundred of their fellow-citizens; and carried their fury so far, that, one miserable fugitive having fled to the temple, they cut off his hands, by which he clung to the gates, and carrying him out of holy ground, immediately murdered him. *By this impiety*, says HERODOTUS, (not by the other many cruel assassinations) *they offended the gods, and contracted an inexpiable guilt.*

Nay, if we should suppose, what never happens, that a popular religion were found, in which it was expressly declared, that nothing but morality could gain the divine favour; if an order of priests were instituted to inculcate this opinion, in daily sermons, and with all the arts of persuasion; yet so inveterate are the people's prejudices, that, for want of some other superstition, they would make the very attendance on these sermons the essentials of religion, rather than place them in virtue and good morals. The sublime prologue of ZALEUCUS'S laws inspired not the LOCRIANS, so far as we can learn, with any sounder notions of the measures of acceptance with the deity, than were familiar to the other GREEKS.

This observation, then, holds universally: But still one may be at some loss to account for it. It is not sufficient to observe, that the people, every where, degrade their deities into a similitude with themselves, and consider them merely as a species of human creatures, somewhat more potent and intelligent. This will not remove the difficulty. For there is no *man* so stupid, as that, judging by his natural reason, he would not esteem virtue and honesty the most valuable qualities, which any person could possess. Why not ascribe the same sentiment to his deity? Why not make all religion, or the chief part of it, to consist in these attainments?

Nor is it satisfactory to say, that the practice of morality is more difficult than that of superstition; and is therefore rejected. For, not to mention the excessive penances of the *Brachmans* and *Talapoins*; it is certain, that the *Rhamadan* of the TURKS, during which the poor wretches, for many days, often in the hottest months of the year, and in some of the hottest climates of the world, remain without eating or drinking from the rising to the setting sun; this *Rhamadan*, I say, must be more severe than the practice of any moral duty, even to the most vicious and depraved of mankind. The four lents of the MUSCOVITES, and the austerities of some *Roman Catholics*, appear more disagreeable than meekness and benevolence. In short, all virtue, when men are reconciled to it by ever so little practice, is agreeable: All superstition is for ever odious and burthensome.

Perhaps, the following account may be received as a true solution of the difficulty. The duties, which a man performs as a friend or parent, seem merely owing to his benefactor or children; nor can he be wanting to these duties, without breaking through all the ties of nature and morality. A strong inclination may prompt him to the performance: A sentiment of order and moral obligation joins its force to these natural ties: And the whole man, if truly virtuous, is drawn to his duty, without any effort or endeavour. Even with regard to the virtues, which are more austere, and more founded on reflection, such as public spirit, filial duty, temperance, or integrity; the moral obligation, in our apprehension, removes all pretension to religious merit; and the virtuous conduct is deemed no more than what we owe to society and to ourselves. In all this, a superstitious man finds nothing, which he has properly performed for the sake of his deity, or which can peculiarly recommend him to the divine favour and protection. He considers not, that the most genuine method of serving the divinity is by promoting the happiness of his creatures. He still looks out for some more immediate service of the supreme Being, in order to allay those terrors, with which he is haunted. And any practice, recommended to him, which either serves to no purpose in life, or offers the strongest violence to his natural inclinations; that practice he will the more readily embrace, on account of those very circumstances, which should make him absolutely reject it. It seems the more purely religious, because it proceeds from no mixture of any other motive or consideration. And if, for its sake, he sacrifices much of his ease and quiet, his claim of merit appears still to rise upon him, in proportion to the zeal and devotion which he discovers. In restoring a loan, or paying a debt, his divinity is nowise beholden to him; because these acts of justice are what he was bound to perform, and what many would have performed, were there no god in the universe. But if he fast a day, or give himself a sound whipping; this has a direct reference, in his opinion, to the service of God. No other motive could engage him to such austerities. By these distinguished marks of devotion, he has now acquired the divine favour; and may expect, in recompence, protection and safety in this world, and eternal happiness in the next.

Hence the greatest crimes have been found, in many instances, compatible with a superstitious piety and devotion: Hence, it is justly regarded as unsafe to draw any certain inference in favour of a man's morals, from the fervour or strictness of his religious exercises, even though he himself believe them sincere. Nay, it has been observed, that enormities of the blackest dye have been rather apt to produce superstitious terrors, and encrease the religious passion. BOMILCAR, having formed a conspiracy for assassinating at once the whole senate of CARTHAGE, and invading the liberties of his country, lost the opportunity, from a continual regard to omens and prophecies. *Those who undertake the most criminal and most dangerous enterprizes are commonly the most superstitious*; as an ancient historian remarks on this occasion. Their devotion and spiritual faith rise with their fears. CATILINE was not contented with the established deities and received rites of the national religion: His anxious terrors made him seek new inventions of this kind; which he never probably had dreamed of, had he remained a good citizen, and obedient to the laws of his country.

To which we may add, that, after the commission of crimes, there arise remorses and secret horrors, which give no rest to the mind, but make it have recourse to religious rites and ceremonies, as expiations of its offences. Whatever weakens or disorders the internal frame promotes the interests of superstition: And nothing is more destructive to them than a manly, steady virtue, which either preserves us from disastrous, melancholy accidents, or teaches us to bear them.

211

During such calm sunshine of the mind, these spectres of false divinity never make their appearance. On the other hand, while we abandon ourselves to the natural undisciplined suggestions of our timid and anxious hearts, every kind of barbarity is ascribed to the supreme Being, from the terrors with which we are agitated; and every kind of caprice, from the methods which we embrace in order to appease him. *Barbarity, caprice;* these qualities, however nominally disguised, we may universally observe, form the ruling character of the deity in popular religions. Even priests, instead of correcting these depraved ideas of mankind, have often been found ready to foster and encourage them. The more tremendous the divinity is represented, the more tame and submissive do men become to his ministers: And the more unaccountable the measures of acceptance required by him, the more necessary does it become to abandon our natural reason, and yield to their ghostly guidance and direction. Thus it may be allowed, that the artifices of men aggravate our natural infirmities and follies of this kind, but never originally beget them. Their root strikes deeper into the mind, and springs from the essential and universal properties of human nature.

XV: General Corollary

Though the stupidity of men, barbarous and uninstructed, be so great, that they may not see a sovereign author in the more obvious works of nature, to which they are so much familiarized; yet it scarcely seems possible, that any one of good understanding should reject that idea, when once it is suggested to him. A purpose, an intention, a design is evident in every thing; and when our comprehension is so far enlarged as to contemplate the first rise of this visible system, we must adopt, with the strongest conviction, the idea of some intelligent cause or author. The uniform maxims too, which prevail throughout the whole frame of the universe, naturally, if not necessarily, lead us to conceive this intelligence as single and undivided, where the prejudices of education oppose not so reasonable a theory. Even the contrarieties of nature, by discovering themselves every where, become proofs of some consistent plan, and establish one single purpose or intention, however inexplicable and incomprehensible.

Good and ill are universally intermingled and confounded; happiness and misery, wisdom and folly, virtue and vice. Nothing is pure and entirely of a piece. All advantages are attended with disadvantages. An universal compensation prevails in all conditions of being and existence. And it is not possible for us, by our most chimerical wishes, to form the idea of a station or situation altogether desirable. The draughts of life, according to the poet's fiction, are always mixed from the vessels on each hand of JUPITER: Or if any cup be presented altogether pure, it is drawn only, as the same poet tells us, from the left-handed vessel.

The more exquisite any good is, of which a small specimen is afforded us, the sharper is the evil, allied to it; and few exceptions are found to this uniform law of nature. The most sprightly wit borders on madness; the highest effusions of joy produce the deepest melancholy; the most ravishing pleasures are attended with the most cruel lassitude and disgust; the most flattering hopes make way for the severest disappointments. And, in general, no course of life has such safety (for happiness is not to be dreamed of) as the temperate and moderate, which maintains, as far as possible, a mediocrity, and a kind of insensibility, in every thing.

As the good, the great, the sublime, the ravishing are found eminently in the genuine principles of theism; it may be expected, from the analogy of nature, that the base, the absurd, the mean, the terrifying will be equally discovered in religious fictions and chimeras.

The universal propensity to believe in invisible, intelligent power, if not an original instinct, being at least a general attendant of human nature, may be considered as a kind of mark or stamp, which the divine workman has set upon his work; and nothing surely can more dignify mankind, than to be thus selected from all other parts of the creation, and to bear the image or impression of the universal Creator. But consult this image, as it appears in the popular religions of the world. How is the deity disfigured in our representations of him! What caprice, absurdity, and immorality are attributed to him! How much is he degraded even below the character, which we should naturally, in common life, ascribe to a man of sense and virtue!

What a noble privilege is it of human reason to attain the knowledge of the supreme Being; and, from the visible works of nature, be enabled to infer so sublime a principle as its supreme Creator? But turn the reverse of the medal. Survey most nations and most ages. Examine the religious principles, which have, in fact, prevailed in the world. You will scarcely be persuaded, that they are any thing but sick men's dreams: Or perhaps will regard them more as the playsome whimsies of monkies in human shape, than the serious, positive, dogmatical asseverations of a being, who dignifies himself with the name of rational.

Hear the verbal protestations of all men: Nothing so certain as their religious tenets. Examine their lives: You will scarcely think that they repose the smallest confidence in them.

The greatest and truest zeal gives us no security against hypocrisy: The most open impiety is attended with a secret dread and compunction.

No theological absurdities so glaring that they have not, sometimes, been embraced by men of the greatest and most cultivated understanding. No religious precepts so rigorous that they have not been adopted by the most voluptuous and most abandoned of men.

Ignorance is the mother of Devotion: A maxim that is proverbial, and confirmed by general experience. Look out for a people, entirely destitute of religion: If you find them at all, be assured, that they are but few degrees removed from brutes.

What so pure as some of the morals, included in some theological systems? What so corrupt as some of the practices, to which these systems give rise?

The comfortable views, exhibited by the belief of futurity, are ravishing and delightful. But how quickly vanish on the appearance of its terrors, which keep a more firm and durable possession of the human mind?

The whole is a riddle, an ænigma, an inexplicable mystery. Doubt, uncertainty, suspence of judgment appear the only result of our most accurate scrutiny, concerning this subject. But such is the frailty of human reason, and such the irresistible contagion of opinion, that even this deliberate doubt could scarcely be upheld; did we not enlarge our view, and opposing one species of superstition to another, set them a quarrelling; while we ourselves, during their fury and contention, happily make our escape into the calm, though obscure regions of philosophy.

PART IX

Thomas Reid (1710–96)

Introduction

Reid's philosophical outlook was decisively shaped by an early reading of Hume's *Treatise of Human Nature* – an experience which led him to reject any philosophy proceeding from a theory of ideas. The first two selections in this chapter are taken from Reid's *Essays on the Intellectual Powers of Man* (1785). In the first, Reid describes the direct realist account of perception that underpins his own common-sense philosophy. In the second, he presents a thoroughgoing critique of Hume's skepticism. Our third selection, "Of Morals," is from *Essays on the Active Powers of the Human Mind* (1788). Here again, Reid takes his critical point of departure in the work of Hume, arguing that judgments of right and wrong are not the product of mere feelings or passions but the expression of objective moral truths. Our final selection is from a collection of manuscripts which were edited and published by Paul Wood under the title *Thomas Reid on the Animate Creation: Papers Relating to the Life Sciences*. The excerpt, "Some Observations on the Modern System of Materialism," contains Reid's critique of the doctrine of materialism as it was advanced and defended by Joseph Priestley. Of special interest is the way Reid characterizes Locke as a materialist and criticizes him accordingly. There is no precise dating of this manuscript. But in his excellent scholarly introduction, Wood adduces strong evidence that it was written in the 1790s and may well have been Reid's last major philosophical work.

29

Essays on the Intellectual Powers of Man

V: Of Perception

In speaking of the impressions made on our organs in perception, we build upon facts borrowed from anatomy and physiology, for which we have the testimony of our senses. But being now to speak of perception itself, which is solely an act of the mind, we must appeal to another authority. The operations of our minds are known not by sense, but by consciousness, the authority of which is as certain and as irresistible as that of sense.

In order, however, to our having a distinct notion of any of the operations of our own minds, it is not enough that we be conscious of them, for all men have this consciousness: it is further necessary that we attend to them while they are exerted, and reflect upon them with care, while they are recent and fresh in our memory. It is necessary that, by employing ourselves frequently in this way, we get the habit of this attention and reflection; and therefore, for the proof of facts which I shall have occasion to mention upon this subject, I can only appeal to the reader's own thoughts, whether such facts are not agreeable to what he is conscious of in his own mind.

If, therefore, we attend to that act of our mind which we call the perception of an external object of sense, we shall find in it these three things. *First*, Some conception or notion of the object perceived.

Essays on the Intellectual Powers of Man (1785), ed. Baruch A. Brody (Cambridge, MA: MIT Press, 1969). Selections: Essay 2, ch. 5, "Of Perception," pp. 111–18; Essay 7, ch. 4, "Of Mr. Hume's Skepticism With Regard to Reason," pp. 738–52.

Secondly, A strong and irresistible conviction and belief of its present existence. And, *thirdly*, That this conviction and belief are immediate, and not the effect of reasoning.

1st, It is impossible to perceive an object without having some notion or conception of that which we perceive. We may indeed conceive an object which we do not perceive; but when we perceive the object, we must have some conception of it at the same time; and we have commonly a more clear and steady notion of the object while we perceive it, than we have from memory or imagination when it is not perceived. Yet, even in perception, the notion which our senses give of the object may be more or less clear, more or less distinct, in all possible degrees.

Thus we see more distinctly an object at a small than at a great distance. An object at a great distance is seen more distinctly in a clear than in a foggy day. An object seen indistinctly with the naked eye, on account of its smallness, may be seen distinctly with a microscope. The objects in this room will be seen by a person in the room less and less distinctly as the light of the day fails; they pass through all the various degrees of distinctness according to the degrees of the light, and at last, in total darkness, they are not seen at all. What has been said of the objects of sight is so easily applied to the objects of the other senses, that the application may be left to the reader.

In a matter so obvious to every person capable of reflection, it is necessary only further to observe, that the notion which we get of an object, merely by our external sense, ought not to be confounded with that more scientific notion which a man, come to the years of understanding, may have of the same object, by attending to its various attributes, or to its various parts, and their relation to each other, and to the whole. Thus the notion which a child has of a jack for roasting meat, will be acknowledged to be very different from that of a man who understands its construction, and perceives the relation of the parts to one another, and to the whole. The child sees the jack and every part of it as well as the man. The child, therefore, has all the notion of it which sight gives; whatever there is more in the notion which the man forms of it, must be derived from other powers of the mind, which may afterward be explained. This observation is made here only, that we may not confound the operations of different powers of the mind, which, by being always conjoined after we grow up to understanding, are apt to pass for one and the same.

2dly, In perception we not only have a notion more or less distinct of the object perceived, but also an irresistible conviction and belief of its existence. This is always the case when we are certain that we perceive it. There may be a perception so faint and indistinct, as to leave us in doubt whether we perceive the object or not. Thus, when a star begins to twinkle as the light of the sun withdraws, one may, for a short time, think he sees it, without being certain, until the perception acquires some strength and steadiness. When a ship just begins to appear in the utmost verge of the horizon, we may at first be dubious whether we perceive it or not: but when the perception is in any degree clear and steady, there remains no doubt of its reality; and when the reality of the perception is ascertained, the existence of the object perceived can no longer be doubted.

By the laws of all nations, in the most solemn judicial trials wherein men's fortunes and lives are at stake, the sentence passes according to the testimony of eye or ear witnesses of good credit. An upright judge will give a fair hearing to every objection that can be made to the integrity of a witness, and allow it to be possible that he may be corrupted; but no judge will ever suppose, that witnesses may be imposed upon by trusting to their eyes and ears: and if a skeptical counsel should plead against the testimony of the witnesses, that they had no other evidence for what they declared, but the testimony of their eyes and ears, and that we ought not to put so much faith in our senses, as to deprive men of life or fortune upon their testimony; surely no upright judge would admit a plea of this kind. I believe no

counsel, however skeptical, ever dared to offer such an argument; and if it was offered, it would be rejected with disdain.

Can any stronger proof be given, that it is the universal judgment of mankind that the evidence of sense is a kind of evidence which we may securely rest upon in the most momentous concerns of mankind; that it is a kind of evidence against which we ought not to admit any reasoning; and therefore, that to reason either for or against it, is an insult to common sense?

The whole conduct of mankind, in the daily occurrences of life, as well as the solemn procedure of judicatories in the trial of causes, civil and criminal, demonstrates this. I know only of two exceptions that may be offered against this being the universal belief of mankind.

The first exception is that of some lunatics, who have been persuaded of things that seem to contradict the clear testimony of their senses. It is said there have been lunatics and hypochondriacal persons, who seriously believed themselves to be made of glass; and, in consequence of this, lived in continual terror of having their brittle frame shivered into pieces.

All I have to say to this is, that our minds, in our present state, are, as well as our bodies, liable to strong disorders; and as we do not judge of the natural constitution of the body, from the disorders or diseases to which it is subject from accidents, so neither ought we to judge of the natural powers of the mind from its disorders, but from its sound state. It is natural to man, and common to the species, to have two hands, and two feet; yet I have seen a man, and a very ingenious one, who was born without either hands or feet. It is natural to man to have faculties superior to those of brutes; yet we see some individuals, whose faculties are not equal to those of many brutes; and the wisest man may, by various accidents, be reduced to this state. General rules that regard those whose intellects are sound, are not overthrown by instances of men whose intellects are hurt by any constitutional or accidental disorder.

The other exception that may be made to the principle we have laid down, is that of some philosophers who have maintained, that the testimony of sense is fallacious, and therefore ought never to be trusted. Perhaps it might be a sufficient answer to this to say, that there is nothing so absurd which some philosophers have not maintained. It is one thing to profess a doctrine of this kind, another seriously to believe it, and to be governed by it in the conduct of life. It is evident, that a man who did not believe his senses, could not keep out of harm's way an hour of his life; yet, in all the history of philosophy, we never read of any skeptic that ever stepped into fire or water because he did not believe his senses, or that showed, in the conduct of life, less trust in his senses than other men have. This gives us just ground to apprehend, that philosophy was never able to conquer that natural belief which men have in their senses; and that all their subtle reasonings against this belief were never able to persuade themselves.

It appears, therefore, that the clear and distinct testimony of our senses carries irresistible conviction along with it, to every man in his right judgment.

I observed, 3dly, That this conviction is not only irresistible, but it is immediate; that is, it is not by a train of reasoning and argumentation that we come to be convinced of the existence of what we perceive; we ask no argument for the existence of the object, but that we perceive it; perception commands our belief upon its own authority, and disdains to rest its authority upon any reasoning whatsoever.

The conviction of a truth may be irresistible, and yet not immediate. Thus, my conviction that the three angles of every plain triangle, are equal to two right angles, is irresistible, but it is not immediate: I am convinced of it by demonstrative reasoning. There are other truths in mathematics of which we have not only an irresistible, but an immediate conviction. Such are the axioms. Our belief of the axioms in mathematics is not grounded upon argument. Arguments are grounded upon them, but their evidence is discerned immediately by the human understanding.

It is, no doubt, one thing to have an immediate conviction of a self-evident axiom; it is another thing to have an immediate conviction of the existence of what we see: but the conviction is equally immediate and equally irresistible in both cases. No man thinks of seeking a reason to believe what he sees; and, before we are capable of reasoning, we put no less confidence in our senses than after. The rudest savage is as fully convinced of what he sees, and hears, and feels, as the most expert logician. The constitution of our understanding determines us to hold the truth of a mathematical axiom as a first principle, from which other truths may be deduced, but it is deduced from none; and the constitution of our power of perception determines us to hold the existence of what we distinctly perceive as a first principle, from which other truths may be deduced, but it is deduced from none. What has been said of the irresistible and immediate belief of the existence of objects distinctly perceived, I mean only to affirm with regard to persons so far advanced in understanding, as to distinguish objects of mere imagination from things which have a real existence. Every man knows that he may have a notion of Don Quixote, or of Garagantua, without any belief that such persons ever existed; and that of Julius Cesar and of Oliver Cromwell, he has not only a notion, but a belief that they did really exist. But whether children, from the time that they begin to use their senses, make a distinction between things which are only conceived or imagined, and things which really exist, may be doubted. Until we are able to make this distinction, we cannot properly be said to believe or to disbelieve the existence of any thing. The belief of the existence of any thing seems to suppose a notion of existence; a notion too abstract, perhaps, to enter into the mind of an infant. I speak of the power of perception in those that are adult, and of a sound mind, who believe that there are some things which do really exist; and that there are many things conceived by themselves, and by others, which have no existence. That such persons do invariably ascribe existence to everything which they distinctly perceive, without seeking reasons or arguments for doing so, is perfectly evident from the whole tenor of human life.

The account I have given of our perception of external objects, is intended as a faithful delineation of what every man, come to years of understanding, and capable of giving attention to what passes in his own mind, may feel in himself. In what manner the notion of external objects, and the immediate belief of their existence, is produced by means of our senses, I am not able to show, and I do not pretend to show. If the power of perceiving external objects in certain circumstances, be a part of the original constitution of the human mind, all attempts to account for it will be vain. No other account can be given of the constitution of things, but the will of Him that made them. As we can give no reason why matter is extended and inert, why the mind thinks, and is conscious of its thoughts, but the will of Him who made both; so I suspect we can give no other reason why, in certain circumstances, we perceive external objects, and in others do not.

The Supreme Being intended, that we should have such knowledge of the material objects that surround us, as is necessary in order to our supplying the wants of nature, and avoiding the dangers to which we are constantly exposed; and he has admirably fitted our powers of perception to this purpose. If the intelligence we have of external objects were to be got by reasoning only, the greatest part of men would be destitute of it; for the greatest part of men hardly ever learn to reason; and in infancy and childhood no man can reason. Therefore, as this intelligence of the objects that surround us, and from which we may receive so much benefit or harm, is equally necessary to children and to men, to the ignorant and to the learned, God in his wisdom conveys it to us in a way that puts all upon a level. The information of the senses is as perfect, and gives as full conviction to the most ignorant, as to the most learned.

IV: Of Mr. Hume's Skepticism With Regard to Reason

In the Treatise of Human Nature, book 1. part 4. sect. 1. the author undertakes to prove two points: 1st, that all that is called human knowledge, meaning demonstrative knowledge, is only probability; and 2dly, that this probability, when duly examined, vanishes by degrees, and leaves at last no evidence at all: so that in the issue, there is no ground to believe any one proposition rather than its contrary, and "all those are certainly fools who reason or believe any thing."

According to this account, reason, that boasted prerogative of man, and the light of his mind, is an *ignis fatuus*, which misleads the wandering traveller, and leaves him at last in absolute darkness.

How unhappy is the condition of man, born under a necessity of believing contradictions, and of trusting to a guide who confesses herself to be a false one!

It is some comfort, that this doctrine can never be seriously adopted by any man in his senses. And after this author had shown that "all the rules of logic require a total extinction of all belief and evidence," he himself, and all men that are not insane, must have believed many things, and yielded assent to the evidence which he had extinguished.

This indeed he is so candid as to acknowledge. "He finds himself absolutely and necessarily determined to live and talk and act like other people

in the common affairs of life. And since reason is incapable of dispelling these clouds, most fortunately it happens, that nature herself suffices to that purpose, and cures him of this philosophical melancholy and delirium." See sect. 7.

This was surely a very kind and friendly interposition of nature; for the effects of this philosophical delirium, if carried into life, must have been very melancholy.

But what pity is it, that nature, whatever is meant by that personage, so kind in curing this delirium, should be so cruel as to cause it. Doth the same fountain send forth sweet waters and bitter? Is it not more probable, that if the cure was the work of nature, the disease came from another hand, and was the work of the philosopher?

To pretend to prove by reasoning that there is no force in reason, does indeed look like a philosophical delirium. It is like a man's pretending to see clearly, that he himself and all other men are blind.

A common symptom of delirium is, to think that all other men are fools or mad. This appears to have been the case of our author, who concluded, "That all those are certainly fools who reason or believe any thing."

Whatever was the cause of this delirium, it must be granted, that if it was real and not feigned, it was not to be cured by reasoning: for what can be more absurd than to attempt to convince a man by reasoning who disowns the authority of reason. It was therefore very fortunate that nature found other means of curing it.

It may, however, not be improper to inquire, whether, as the author thinks, it was produced by a just application of the rules of logic, or, as others may be apt to think, by the misapplication and abuse of them.

First, Because we are fallible, the author infers that all knowledge degenerates into probability.

That man, and probably every created being, is fallible; and that a fallible being cannot have that perfect comprehension and assurance of truth which an infallible being has, I think ought to be granted. It becomes a fallible being to be modest, open to new light, and sensible, that by some false bias, or by rash judging, he may be misled. If this be called a degree of skepticism, I cannot help approving of it, being persuaded, that the man who makes the best use he can of the faculties which God has given him, without thinking them more perfect than they really are, may have all the belief that is necessary in the conduct of life, and all that is necessary to his acceptance with his Maker.

It is granted then, that human judgments ought always to be formed with an humble sense of our fallibility in judging.

This is all that can be inferred by the rules of logic from our being fallible. And if this be all that is meant by our knowledge degenerating into probability, I know no person of a different opinion.

But it may be observed, that the author here uses the word *probability* in a sense for which I know no authority but his own. Philosophers understand probability as opposed to demonstration; the vulgar as opposed to certainty; but this author understands it as opposed to infallibility, which no man claims.

One who believes himself to be fallible, may still hold it to be certain that two and two make four, and that two contradictory propositions cannot both be true. He may believe some things to be probable only, and other things to be demonstrable, without making any pretence to infallibility.

If we use words in their proper meaning, it is impossible that demonstration should degenerate into probability from the imperfection of our faculties. Our judgment cannot change the nature of the things about which we judge. What is really demonstration, will still be so, whatever judgment we form concerning it. It may likewise be observed, that when we mistake that for demonstration, which really is not, the consequence of this mistake is, not that demonstration degenerates into probability, but that what we took to be demonstration is no proof at all; for one false step in a demonstration destroys the whole, but cannot turn it into another kind of proof.

Upon the whole, then, this first conclusion of our author, that the fallibility of human judgment turns all knowledge into probability, if understood literally, is absurd; but if it be only a figure of speech, and means no more, but that, in all our judgments, we ought to be sensible of our fallibility, and ought to hold our opinions with that modesty that becomes fallible creatures, which I take to be what the author meant, this, I think, nobody denies, nor was it necessary to enter into a laborious proof of it.

One is never in greater danger of transgressing against the rules of logic, than in attempting to prove what needs no proof. Of this we have an instance in this very case: for the author begins his proof, that all human judgments are fallible, with affirming that some are infallible.

"In all demonstrative sciences," says he, "the rules are certain and infallible; but when we apply them, our fallible and uncertain faculties are very apt to depart from them, and fall into error."

He had forgot, surely, that the rules of demonstrative sciences are discovered by our fallible and uncertain faculties, and have no authority but that of human judgment. If they be infallible, some human judgments are infallible; and there are many in various branches of human knowledge which have as good a claim to infallibility as the rules of the demonstrative sciences.

We have reason here to find fault with our author for not being skeptical enough, as well as for a mistake in reasoning, when he claims infallibility to certain decisions of the human faculties, in order to prove that all their decisions are fallible.

The *second* point which he attempts to prove, is, that this probability, when duly examined, suffers a continual diminution, and at last a total extinction.

The obvious consequence of this is, that no fallible being can have good reason to believe any thing at all; but let us hear the proof.

"In every judgment, we ought to correct the first judgment derived from the nature of the object, by another judgment derived from the nature of the understanding. Besides the original uncertainty inherent in the subject, there arises another, derived from the weakness of the faculty which judges. Having adjusted these two uncertainties together, we are obliged, by our reason, to add a new uncertainty, derived from the possibility of error in the estimation we make of the truth and fidelity of our faculties. This is a doubt, of which, if we would closely pursue our reasoning, we cannot avoid giving a decision. But this decision, though it should be favourable to our preceding judgment, being founded only on probability, must weaken still further our first evidence. The third uncertainty must in like manner be criticised by a fourth, and so on without end.

"Now, as every one of these uncertainties takes away a part of the original evidence, it must at last be reduced to nothing. Let our first belief be ever so strong, it must infallibly perish, by passing through so many examinations, each of which carries off somewhat of its force and vigour. No finite object can subsist under a decrease repeated *in infinitum*.

"When I reflect on the natural fallibility of my judgment, I have less confidence in my opinions, than when I only consider the objects concerning which I reason. And when I proceed still further, to turn the scrutiny against every successive estimation I make of my faculties, all the rules of logic require a continual diminution, and at last a total extinction of belief and evidence."

This is the author's Achillean argument against the evidence of reason, from which he concludes, that a man who would govern his belief by reason, must believe nothing at all, and that belief is an act not of the cogitative, but of the sensitive part of our nature.

If there be any such thing as motion, said an ancient skeptic, the swift-footed Achilles could never overtake an old man in a journey. For, suppose the old man to set out a thousand paces before Achilles, and that while Achilles has travelled the thousand paces, the old man has gone five hundred; when Achilles has gone the five hundred, the old man has gone two hundred and fifty; and when Achilles has gone the two hundred and fifty, the old man is still one hundred and twenty-five before him. Repeat these estimations *in infinitum*, and you will still find the old man foremost; therefore Achilles can never overtake him; therefore there can be no such thing as motion.

The reasoning of the modern skeptic against reason is equally ingenious, and equally convincing. Indeed, they have a great similarity.

If we trace the journey of Achilles two thousand paces, we shall find the very point where the old man is overtaken: but this short journey, by dividing it into an infinite number of stages, with corresponding estimations, is made to appear infinite. In like manner, our author, subjecting every judgment to an infinite number of successive probable estimations, reduces the evidence to nothing.

To return then to the argument of the modern skeptic. I examine the proof of a theorem of Euclid. It appears to me to be strict demonstration. But I may have overlooked some fallacy; therefore I examine it again and again, but can find no flaw in it. I find all that have examined it agree with me. I have now that evidence of the truth of the proposition, which I and all men call demonstration, and that belief of it, which we call certainty.

Here my skeptical friend interposes, and assures me, that the rules of logic reduce this demonstration to no evidence at all. I am willing to hear what step in it he thinks fallacious, and why. He makes no objection to any part of the demonstration, but pleads my fallibility in judging. I have made the proper allowance for this already, by being open to conviction. But, says he, there are two uncertain-

ties, the first inherent in the subject, which I have already shown to have only probable evidence; the second arising from the weakness of the faculty that judges. I answer, It is the weakness of the faculty only that reduces this demonstration to what you call probability. You must not therefore make it a second uncertainty; for it is the same with the first. To take credit twice in an account for the same article is not agreeable to the rules of logic. Hitherto therefore there is but one uncertainty; to wit, my fallibility in judging.

But, says my friend, you are obliged by reason to add a new uncertainty, derived from the possibility of error in the estimation you make of the truth and fidelity of your faculties. I answer,

This estimation is ambiguously expressed; it may either mean an estimation of my liableness to err by the misapplication and abuse of my faculties; or it may mean an estimation of my liableness to err, by conceiving my faculties to be true and faithful while they may be false and fallacious in themselves, even when applied in the best manner. I shall consider this estimation in each of these senses.

If the first be the estimation meant, it is true that reason directs us, as fallible creatures, to carry along with us, in all our judgments, a sense of our fallibility. It is true also, that we are in greater danger of erring in some cases, and less in others; and that this danger of erring may, according to the circumstances of the case, admit of an estimation, which we ought likewise to carry along with us in every judgment we form.

When a demonstration is short and plain; when the point to be proved does not touch our interest or our passions; when the faculty of judging in such cases, has acquired strength by much exercise, there is less danger of erring; when the contrary circumstances take place, there is more.

In the present case, every circumstance is favourable to the judgment I have formed. There cannot be less danger of erring in any case, excepting perhaps when I judge of a self-evident axiom.

The skeptic further urges, that this decision, though favourable to my first judgment, being founded only on probability, must still weaken the evidence of that judgment.

Here I cannot help being of a quite contrary opinion, nor can I imagine how an ingenious author could impose upon himself so grossly, for surely he did not intend to impose upon his reader.

After repeated examination of a proposition of Euclid, I judge it to be strictly demonstrated; this is my first judgment. But as I am liable to err from various causes, I consider how far I may have been misled by any of these causes in this judgment. My decision upon this second point is favourable to my first judgment, and therefore, as I apprehend, must strengthen it. To say, that this decision, because it is only probable, must weaken the first evidence, seems to me contrary to all rules of logic, and to common sense.

The first judgment may be compared to the testimony of a credible witness; the second, after a scrutiny into the character of the witness, wipes off every objection that can be made to it, and therefore surely must confirm and not weaken his testimony.

But let us suppose, that, in another case, I examine my first judgment upon some point, and find, that it was attended with unfavourable circumstances. What, in reason, and according to the rules of logic, ought to be the effect of this discovery?

The effect surely will be, and ought to be, to make me less confident in my first judgment, until I examine the point anew in more favourable circumstances. If it be a matter of importance, I return to weigh the evidence of my first judgment. If it was precipitate before, it must now be deliberate in every point. If at first I was in passion, I must now be cool. If I had an interest in the decision, I must place the interest on the other side.

It is evident, that this review of the subject may confirm my first judgment, notwithstanding the suspicious circumstances that attended it. Though the judge was biassed or corrupted, it does not follow, that the sentence was unjust. The rectitude of the decision does not depend upon the character of the judge, but upon the nature of the case. From that only, it must be determined whether the decision be just. The circumstances that rendered it suspicious are mere presumptions, which have no force against direct evidence.

Thus, I have considered the effect of this estimation of our liableness to err in our first judgment, and have allowed to it all the effect that reason and the rules of logic permit. In the case I first supposed, and in every case where we can discover no cause of error, it affords a presumption in favour of the first judgment. In other cases, it may afford a presumption against it. But the rules of logic require, that we should not judge by presumptions, where we have direct evidence. The effect of an unfavourable presumption should

only be, to make us examine the evidence with the greater care.

The skeptic urges, in the last place, that this estimation must be subjected to another estimation, that to another, and so on *in infinitum*; and as every new estimation takes away from the evidence of the first judgment, it must at last be totally annihilated.

I answer, *first*, It has been shown above, that the first estimation, supposing it unfavourable, can only afford a presumption against the first judgment; the second, upon the same supposition, will be only the presumption of a presumption; and the third, the presumption that there is a presumption of a presumption. This infinite series of presumption resembles an infinite series of quantities decreasing in geometrical proportion, which amounts only to a finite sum. The infinite series of stages of Achilles's journey after the old man, amounts only to two thousand paces; nor can this infinite series of presumptions outweigh one solid argument in favour of the first judgment, supposing them all to be unfavourable to it.

2dly, I have shown, that the estimation of our first judgment may strengthen it; and the same thing may be said of all the subsequent estimations. It would, therefore, be as reasonable to conclude, that the first judgment will be brought to infallible certainty when this series of estimations is wholly in its favour, as that its evidence will be brought to nothing by such a series supposed to be wholly unfavourable to it. But, in reality, one serious and cool re-examination of the evidence by which our first judgment is supported, has, and in reason ought to have, more force to strengthen or weaken it, than an infinite series of such estimations as our author requires.

3dly, I know no reason nor rule in logic, that requires that such a series of estimations should follow every particular judgment.

A wise man who has practised reasoning knows that he is fallible, and carries this conviction along with him in every judgment he forms. He knows likewise, that he is more liable to err in some cases than in others. He has a scale in his mind, by which he estimates his liableness to err, and by this he regulates the degree of his assent in his first judgment upon any point.

The author's reasoning supposes, that a man, when he forms his first judgment, conceives himself to be infallible; that by a second and subsequent judgment, he discovers that he is not infallible; and that by a third judgment, subsequent to the second, he estimates his liableness to err in such a case as the present.

If the man proceed in this order, I grant, that his second judgment will, with good reason, bring down the first from supposed infallibility to fallibility; and that his third judgment will, in some degree, either strengthen or weaken the first, as it is corrected by the second.

But every man of understanding proceeds in a contrary order. When about to judge in any particular point, he knows already that he is not infallible. He knows what are the cases in which he is most or least liable to err. The conviction of these things is always present to his mind, and influences the degree of his assent in his first judgment, as far as to him appears reasonable.

If he should afterward find reason to suspect his first judgment, and desires to have all the satisfaction his faculties can give, reason will direct him not to form such a series of estimations upon estimations, as this author requires, but to examine the evidence of his first judgment carefully and cooly; and this review may very reasonably, according to its result, either strengthen or weaken, or totally overturn his first judgment.

This infinite series of estimations, therefore, is not the method that reason directs in order to form our judgment in any case. It is introduced without necessity, without any use but to puzzle the understanding, and to make us think, that to judge, even in the simplest and plainest cases, is a matter of insurmountable difficulty and endless labour; just as the ancient skeptic, to make a journey of two thousand paces appear endless, divided it into an infinite number of stages.

But we observed, that the estimation which our author requires may admit of another meaning, which indeed is more agreeable to the expression, but inconsistent with what he advanced before.

By the possibility of error in the estimation of the truth and fidelity of our faculties, may be meant, that we may err by esteeming our faculties true and faithful, while they may be false and fallacious, even when used according to the rules of reason and logic.

If this be meant, I answer, 1st, that the truth and fidelity of our faculty of judging is, and must be taken for granted in every judgment and in every estimation.

If the skeptic can seriously doubt of the truth and fidelity of his faculty of judging when properly used, and suspend his judgment upon that point till he finds proof, his skepticism admits of no cure

by reasoning, and he must even continue in it until he have new faculties given him, which shall have authority to sit in judgment upon the old. Nor is there any need of an endless succession of doubts upon this subject, for the first puts an end to all judgment and reasoning, and to the possibility of conviction by that means. The skeptic has here got possession of a strong hold which is impregnable to reasoning, and we must leave him in possession of it, till nature, by other means, makes him give it up.

2dly, I observe, that this ground of skepticism, from the supposed infidelity of our faculties, contradicts what the author before advanced in this very argument; to wit, that "the rules of the demonstrative sciences are certain and infallible, and that truth is the natural effect of reason, and that error arises from the irruption of other causes."

But perhaps he made these concessions unwarily. He is therefore at liberty to retract them, and to rest his skepticism upon this sole foundation, that no reasoning can prove the truth and fidelity of our faculties. Here he stands upon firm ground: for it is evident, that every argument offered to prove the truth and fidelity of our faculties, takes for granted the thing in question, and is therefore that kind of sophism which logicians call *petitio principi*.

All we would ask of this kind of skeptic is, that he would be uniform and consistent, and that his practice in life do not belie his profession of skepticism with regard to the fidelity of his faculties: for the want of faith, as well as faith itself, is best shown by works. If a skeptic avoid the fire as much as those who believe it dangerous to go into it, we can hardly avoid thinking his skepticism to be feigned, and not real.

Our author indeed was aware, that neither his skepticism, nor that of any other person, was able to endure this trial, and therefore enters a caveat against it. "Neither I," says he, "nor any other person, was ever sincerely and constantly of that opinion. Nature, by an absolute and uncontrollable necessity, has determined us to judge, as well as to breathe and feel. My intention, therefore," says he, "in displaying so carefully the arguments of that fantastic sect, is only to make the reader sensible of the truth of my hypothesis, that all our reasonings concerning causes and effects, are derived from nothing but custom, and that belief is more properly an act of the sensitive than of the cogitative part of our nature."

We have before considered the first part of this hypothesis, Whether our reasoning about causes be derived only from custom?

The other part of the author's hypothesis here mentioned is darkly expressed, though the expression seems to be studied, as it is put in italics. It cannot surely mean that belief is not an act of thinking. It is not, therefore, the power of thinking that he calls the cogitative part of our nature. Neither can it be the power of judging, for all belief implies judgment; and to believe a proposition means the same thing as to judge it to be true. It seems, therefore, to be the power of reasoning that he calls the cogitative part of our nature.

If this be the meaning, I agree to it in part. The belief of first principles is not an act of the reasoning power: for all reasoning must be grounded upon them. We judge them to be true, and believe them without reasoning. But why this power of judging of first principles should be called the sensitive part of our nature, I do not understand.

As our belief of first principles is an act of pure judgment without reasoning; so our belief of the conclusions drawn by reasoning from first principles, may, I think, be called an act of the reasoning faculty.

Upon the whole, I see only two conclusions that can be fairly drawn from this profound and intricate reasoning against reason. The first is, that we are fallible in all our judgments and in all our reasonings. The second, that the truth and fidelity of our faculties can never be proved by reasoning; and therefore our belief of it cannot be founded on reasoning. If the last be what the author calls his hypothesis, I subscribe to it, and think it not an hypothesis, but a manifest truth; though I conceive it to be very improperly expressed, by saying, that belief is more properly an act of the sensitive than of the cogitative part of our nature.

30

Essays on the Active Powers of the Human Mind

Essay V: Of Morals

Chap. I: Of the First Principles of Morals

Morals, like all other sciences, must have first principles, on which all moral reasoning is grounded.

In every branch of knowledge where disputes have been raised, it is useful to distinguish the first principles from the superstructure. They are the foundation on which the whole fabric of the science leans; and whatever is not supported by this foundation can have no stability.

In all rational belief, the thing believed is either itself a first principle, or it is by just reasoning deduced from first principles. When men differ about deductions of reasoning, the appeal must be made to the rules of reasoning, which have been very unanimously fixed from the days of Aristotle. But when they differ about a first principle, the appeal is made to another tribunal; to that of common sense.

How the genuine decisions of common sense may be distinguished from the counterfeit, has been considered in essay sixth, on the intellectual powers of man, chapter fourth, to which the reader is referred. What I would here observe is, that as first principles differ from deductions of reasoning in the nature of their evidence, and must be tried by a different standard when they are called in question, it is of importance to know to which of

Essays on the Active Powers of the Human Mind (1788), ed. Baruch A. Brody (Cambridge, MA: MIT Press, 1969). Selection: Essay 5, "Of Morals," ch. 1, pp. 360–70.

these two classes a truth which we would examine belongs. When they are not distinguished, men are apt to demand proof for every thing they think fit to deny: and when we attempt to prove by direct argument, what is really self-evident, the reasoning will always be inconclusive; for it will either take for granted the thing to be proved, or something not more evident; and so, instead of giving strength to the conclusion, will rather tempt those to doubt of it, who never did so before.

I propose, therefore, in this chapter, to point out some of the first principles of morals, without pretending to a complete enumeration.

The principles I am to mention, relate either to virtue in general, or to the different particular branches of virtue, or to the comparison of virtues where they seem to interfere.

1st, There are some things in human conduct, that merit approbation and praise, others that merit blame and punishment; and different degrees either of approbation or of blame, are due to different actions.

2dly, What is in no degree voluntary, can neither deserve moral approbation nor blame.

3dly, What is done from unavoidable necessity may be agreeable or disagreeable, useful or hurtful, but cannot be the object either of blame or of moral approbation.

4thly, Men may be highly culpable in omitting what they ought to have done, as well as in doing what they ought not.

5thly, We ought to use the best means we can to be well informed of our duty, by serious attention to moral instruction; by observing what we approve, and what we disapprove, in other men, whether our acquaintance, or those whose actions are recorded in history; by reflecting often, in a calm and dispassionate hour, on our own past conduct, that we may discern what was wrong, what was right, and what might have been better; by deliberating cooly and impartially upon our future conduct, as far as we can foresee the opportunities we may have of doing good, or the temptations to do wrong; and by having this principle deeply fixed in our minds, that as moral excellence is the true worth and glory of a man, so the knowledge of our duty is to every man, in every station of life, the most important of all knowledge.

6thly, It ought to be our most serious concern to do our duty as far as we know it, and to fortify our minds against every temptation to deviate from it; by maintaining a lively sense of the beauty of right conduct, and of its present and future reward, of the turpitude of vice, and of its bad consequences here and hereafter; by having always in our eye the noblest examples; by the habit of subjecting our passions to the government of reason; by firm purposes and resolutions with regard to our conduct; by avoiding occasions of temptation when we can; and by imploring the aid of him who made us, in every hour of temptation.

These principles concerning virtue and vice in general, must appear self-evident to every man who has a conscience, and who has taken pains to exercise this natural power of his mind. I proceed to others that are more particular.

1st, We ought to prefer a greater good, though more distant, to a less; and a less evil to a greater.

A regard to our own good, though we had no conscience, dictates this principle; and we cannot help disapproving the man that acts contrary to it, as deserving to loose the good which he wantonly threw away, and to suffer the evil which he knowingly brought upon his own head.

We observed before, that the ancient moralists, and many among the modern, have deduced the whole of morals from this principle, and that when we make a right estimate of goods and evils according to their degree, their dignity, their duration, and according as they are more or less in our power, it leads to the practice of every virtue: more directly, indeed, to the virtues of self-government, to prudence, to temperance, and to fortitude; and, though more indirectly even to justice, humanity, and all the social virtues, when their influence upon our happiness is well understood.

Though it be not the noblest principle of conduct, it has this peculiar advantage, that its force is felt by the most ignorant, and even by the most abandoned.

Let a man's moral judgment be ever so little improved by exercise, or ever so much corrupted by bad habits, he cannot be indifferent to his own happiness or misery. When he is become insensible to every nobler motive to right conduct, he cannot be insensible to this. And though to act from this motive solely, may be called *prudence* rather than *virtue*, yet this prudence deserves some regard upon its own account, and much more as it is the friend and ally of virtue, and the enemy of all vice; and as it gives a favourable testimony of virtue to those who are deaf to every other recommendation.

If a man can be induced to do his duty even from a regard to his own happiness, he will soon find reason to love virtue for her own sake, and to act from motives less mercenary.

I cannot therefore approve of those moralists, who would banish all persuasives to virtue taken from the consideration of private good. In the present state of human nature these are not useless to the best, and they are the only means left of reclaiming the abandoned.

2dly, As far as the intention of nature appears in the constitution of man, we ought to comply with that intention, and to act agreeably to it.

The Author of our being has given us not only the power of acting within a limited sphere, but various principles or springs of action, of different nature and dignity, to direct us in the exercise of our active power.

From the constitution of every species of the inferior animals, and especially from the active principles which nature has given them, we easily perceive the manner of life for which nature intended them; and they uniformly act the part to which they are led by their constitution, without any reflection upon it, or intention of obeying its dictates. Man only, of the inhabitants of this world, is made capable of observing his own constitution, what kind of life it is made for, and of acting according to that intention, or contrary to it. He only is capable of yielding an intentional obedience to the dictates of his nature, or of rebelling against them.

In treating of the principles of action in man, it has been shown, that as his natural instincts and bodily appetites, are well adapted to the preservation of his natural life, and to the continuance of the species; so his natural desires, affections, and passions, when uncorrupted by vicious habits, and under the government of the leading principles of reason and conscience, are excellently fitted for the rational and social life. Every vicious action shows an excess, or defect, or wrong direction of some natural spring of action, and therefore may, very justly, be said to be unnatural. Every virtuous action agrees with the uncorrupted principles of human nature.

The Stoics defined virtue to be a life according to nature. Some of them more accurately, a life according to the nature of man, in so far as it is superior to that of brutes. The life of a brute is according to the nature of the brute; but it is neither virtuous nor vicious. The life of a moral agent cannot be according to his nature, unless it be virtuous. That conscience, which is in every man's breast, is the law of God written in his heart, which he cannot disobey without acting unnaturally, and being self-condemned.

The intention of nature, in the various active principles of man, in the desires of power, of knowledge, and of esteem, in the affection to children, to near relations, and to the communities to which we belong, in gratitude, in compassion, and even in resentment and emulation, is very obvious, and has been pointed out in treating of those principles. Nor is it less evident, that reason and conscience are given us to regulate the inferior principles, so that they may conspire, in a regular and consistent plan of life, in pursuit of some worthy end.

3dly, No man is born for himself only. Every man, therefore, ought to consider himself as a member of the common society of mankind, and of those subordinate societies to which he belongs, such as family, friends, neighbourhood, country, and to do as much good as he can, and as little hurt to the societies of which he is a part.

This axiom leads directly to the practice of every social virtue, and indirectly to the virtues of self-government, by which only we can be qualified for discharging the duty we owe to society.

4thly, In every case, we ought to act that part toward another, which we would judge to be right in him to act toward us, if we were in his circumstances and he in ours; or, more generally, what we approve in others, that we ought to practise in like circumstances, and what we condemn in others we ought not to do.

If there be any such thing as right and wrong in the conduct of moral agents, it must be the same to all in the same circumstances.

We stand all in the same relation to Him who made us, and will call us to account for our conduct: for with him there is no respect of persons.

We stand in the same relation to one another as members of the great community of mankind. The duties consequent upon the different ranks, and offices, and relations of men, are the same to all in the same circumstances.

It is not want of judgment, but want of candour and impartiality, that hinders men from discerning what they owe to others. They are quicksighted enough in discerning what is due to themselves. When they are injured, or ill treated, they see it, and feel resentment. It is the want of candour that makes men use one measure for the duty they owe to others, and another measure for the duty that others owe to them in like circumstances. That men ought to judge with candour, as in all other cases, so especially in what concerns their moral conduct, is surely self-evident to every intelligent being. The man who takes offence when he is injured in his person, in his property, in his good name, pronounces judgment against himself if he act so toward his neighbour.

As the equity and obligation of this rule of conduct is self-evident to every man who has a conscience; so it is, of all the rules of morality, the most comprehensive, and truly deserves the encomium given it by the highest authority, that *it is the law and the prophets.*

It comprehends every rule of justice without exception. It comprehends all the relative duties, arising either from the more permanent relations of parent and child, of master and servant, of magistrate and subject, of husband and wife; or from the more transient relations of rich and poor, of buyer and seller, of debtor and creditor, of benefactor and beneficiary, of friend and enemy. It comprehends every duty of charity and humanity, and even of courtesy and good manners.

Nay, I think, that, without any force or straining, it extends even to the duties of self-government. For, as every man approves in others the virtues of prudence, temperance, self-command and fortitude, he must perceive, that what is right in others must be right in himself in like circumstances.

To sum up all, he who acts invariably by this rule will never deviate from the path of his duty, but from an error of judgment. And, as he feels the obligation that he and all men are under, to use the best means in his power to have his judgment well-informed in matters of duty, his errors will only be such as are invincible.

It may be observed, that this axiom supposes a faculty in man by which he can distinguish right conduct from wrong. It supposes also, that, by this faculty, we easily perceive the right and the wrong in other men that are indifferent to us; but are very apt to be blinded by the partiality of selfish passions when the case concerns ourselves. Every claim we have against others is apt to be magnified by self-love, when viewed directly. A change of persons removes this prejudice, and brings the claim to appear in its just magnitude.

5thly, To every man who believes the existence, the perfections, and the providence of God, the veneration and submission we owe to him is self-evident. Right sentiments of the Deity and of his works, not only make the duty we owe to him obvious to every intelligent being, but likewise add the authority of a divine law to every rule of right conduct.

There is another class of axioms in morals, by which, when there seems to be an opposition between the actions that different virtues lead to, we determine to which the preference is due.

Between the several virtues, as they are dispositions of mind, or determinations of will to act according to a certain general rule, there can be no opposition. They dwell together most amicably, and give mutual aid and ornament, without the possibility of hostility or opposition, and, taken altogether, make one uniform and consistent rule of conduct. But, between particular external actions, which different virtues would lead to, there may be an opposition. Thus, the same man may be in his heart, generous, grateful, and just. These dispositions strengthen, but never can weaken one another. Yet it may happen, that an external action which generosity or gratitude solicits, justice may forbid.

That in all such cases, unmerited generosity should yield to gratitude, and both to justice, is self-evident. Nor is it less so, that unmerited beneficence to those who are at ease should yield to compassion to the miserable, and external acts of piety to works of mercy, because God loves mercy more than sacrifice.

At the same time, we perceive, that those acts of virtue which ought to yield in the case of a competition, have most intrinsic worth when there is no competition. Thus, it is evident that there is more worth in pure and unmerited benevolence than in compassion, more in compassion than in gratitude, and more in gratitude than in justice.

I call these *first principles*, because they appear to me to have in themselves an intuitive evidence which I cannot resist. I find I can express them

in other words. I can illustrate them by examples and authorities, and perhaps can deduce one of them from another; but I am not able to deduce them from other principles that are more evident. And I find the best moral reasonings of authors I am acquainted with, ancient and modern, heathen and christian, to be grounded upon one or more of them.

The evidence of mathematical axioms is not discerned till men come to a certain degree of maturity of understanding. A boy must have formed the general conception of *quantity*, and of *more*, and *less*, and *equal*; of *sum*, and *difference*; and he must have been accustomed to judge of these relations in matters of common life, before he can perceive the evidence of the mathematical axiom, that equal quantities, added to equal quantities, make equal sums.

In like manner, our moral judgment, or conscience, grows to maturity from an imperceptible seed, planted by our Creator. When we are capable of contemplating the actions of other men, or of reflecting upon our own calmly and dispassionately, we begin to perceive in them the qualities of honest and dishonest, of honorable and base, of right and wrong, and to feel the sentiments of moral approbation and disapprobation.

These sentiments are at first feeble, easily warped by passions and prejudices, and apt to yield to authority. By use and time, the judgment, in morals as in other matters, gathers strength, and feels more vigour. We begin to distinguish the dictates of passion from those of cool reason, and to perceive, that it is not always safe to rely upon the judgment of others. By an impulse of nature, we venture to judge for ourselves, as we venture to walk by ourselves.

There is a strong analogy between the progress of the body from infancy to maturity, and the progress of all the powers of the mind. This progression in both is the work of nature, and in both may be greatly aided or hurt by proper education. It is natural to a man to be able to walk, or run, or leap; but if his limbs had been kept in fetters from his birth, he would have none of those powers. It is no less natural to a man trained in society, and accustomed to judge of his own actions, and those of other men, to perceive a right and a wrong, an honorable and a base, in human conduct; and to such a man, I think, the principles of morals I have above mentioned, will appear self-evident. Yet there may be individuals of the human species so little accustomed to think or judge of any thing, but of gratifying their animal appetites, as to have hardly any conception of right or wrong in conduct, or any moral judgment; as there certainly are some who have not the conceptions and the judgment necessary to understand the axioms of geometry.

From the principles above mentioned, the whole system of moral conduct follows so easily, and with so little aid of reasoning, that every man of common understanding, who wishes to know his duty, may know it. The path of duty is a plain path, which the upright in heart can rarely mistake. Such it must be, since every man is bound to walk in it. There are some intricate cases in morals which admit of disputation; but these seldom occur in practice; and, when they do, the learned disputant has no great advantage: for the unlearned man, who uses the best means in his power to know his duty, and acts according to his knowledge, is inculpable in the sight of God and man. He may err, but he is not guilty of immorality.

31

Some Observations on the Modern System of Materialism

Introduction

By the Modern System of Materialism I mean that which is advanced by the Reverend Dr. Priestley in his *Disquisitions relating to Matter and Spirit* published Anno 1777, and defended in his *Free Discussion of the Doctrines of Materialism and Philosophical Necessity*, and *Illustrations of the Disquisitions* published Anno 1778.

As I know no other Author who has explained and defended this System, I take the principles of it from him only.

The sum of them is, That Man is not, as is commonly believed, compounded of two Substances, to wit, an unthinking Substance which we call the body, and thinking Substance which we call the Mind, but is wholly Material; That Matter, however, is not that inert, solid and impenetrable Substance which it has commonly been supposed to be; That, in fact, it has no properties but those of extension and inherent powers of Attraction and Repulsion.

This account of the properties and powers of Matter I take to be new, and that which distinguishes Dr. Priestley's System from other Systems of Materialism, and it is to this part of his System that the following observations chiefly relate.

From *Thomas Reid on the Animate Creation*, ed. Paul Wood (University Park, PA: The Pennsylvania State University Press, 1995). Selection: "Some Observations on the Modern System of Materialism," pp. 173–82.

Chap. I: Of the Connection of this System with Other Philosophical Opinions

There are some Philosophical Opinions supported by very eminent modern Philosophers, which if they be true, subvert the very foundation of Materialism, which therefore we might expect would have been refuted and removed in order to build this System. Dr. Priestley, however, far from refuting those opinions, speaks more favourably of them than a consistent and zealous Materialist ought to do.

I. There are two contradictory opinions with regard to what we call a Substance as distinguished from the things we call Qualities.

The ancient Philosophers thought it selfevident that the things we call Qualities cannot possibly exist without a Substance in which they are inherent, to which they properly belong, and from which they necessarily result, as the properties of a mathematical figure result from its nature and definition. They conceived therefore that figure cannot, without absurdity, be supposed to exist but in something figured, nor motion but in something moved, nor Judgment and Memory but in something that judges and remembers.

This has been the opinion of the Vulgar in all ages, and is implied in the grammatical structure of all languages, and I cannot help assenting to it.

It is true indeed that we have no immediate perception of Substance either by sense or by consciousness, but we are led by our constitution to infer its existence from the qualities which we immediately perceive, and though the relation between a Substance and its qualities be in some respects obscure, it is easily distinguished from all other relations.

If this vulgar opinion concerning Substance be true, there is no impropriety in enquiring whether Soul and Body be two distinct Substances, or one and the same.

But the modern Philosophy, introduced by Des Cartes and improved by Locke, Berkeley, and Hume, is inimical to this notion of Substance, and leads us to conceive it as a vulgar prejudice.

Des Cartes the Father of this System seems to have had some apprehension of this, by his making extension to be, not a quality of Matter, but the very essence of it, and Thought, not to be an operation of Mind, but its essence. The different modes of thinking, such as judging, willing, remembering, his followers chose to call *Modifications of the Mind*, rather than *Operations of the Mind*, the first of these phrases implying that the Mind is nothing but Thought which may be variously modified, the last implying that the Mind is not Thought, but a Being or Substance which has the power of thinking.

Mr. Locke saw more clearly that his System did not admit any idea of Substance. He says expressly, "That we neither have nor can have any idea of Substance either by Sensation or reflection," and "that we signify nothing by that word but an uncertain supposition of, we know not what idea, which we take to be the *Substratum* or support of those ideas we do know." *Essay 1.4.18*. He observes, "That they who first ran into the notion of *Accidents*, as a sort of real beings, that needed something to inhere in, were forced to find out the word *Substance* to support them. That had the poor Indian Philosopher (who imagined that the earth also wanted something to bear it up) but thought of this word *Substance*, he needed not to have been at the trouble to find an Elephant to support it, and a Tortoise to support his Elephant: The word *Substance* would have done it effectually." *Essay 2.13.19*.

It is well known that Bishop Berkeley and Mr. Hume have employed their reason and wit against this poor word Substance, and treated a *Substratum* of qualities as a Chimera.

Now, this modern opinion concerning Substance seems to me inconsistent with the belief that the Soul is either a material or an immaterial Substance. Mr. Hume is perfectly consistent with himself when he makes Body to be only a certain collection of Qualities to which we give one name, and Mind to be a certain succession of Ideas and Impressions.

If I believe that Substance is a word without a meaning, or that it is an imaginary thing, invented to support Accidents, as the Indian invented his Elephant to support the Earth, how can I seriously believe that either Body or Soul is a Substance? Can it be a serious Question, worthy of a laboured discussion, whether Man be one Substance or compounded of two, if the existence of Substance be imaginary or uncertain?

It seems evident therefore that one who holds the System of Materialism to be true and important, ought not to be dubious with regard to the existence of Substance. Yet Dr. Priestley seems more dubious with regard to the last of these points, than accords with his zeal for the first.

He says, indeed, *Disquisitions page 125*, "It is true that a property, such as I conceive the power of thinking to be, cannot exist without its Substance." This is perfectly consistent with Materialism. For if neither properties nor powers can exist without a Substance to which they belong, it follows necessarily, that the body which has properties must be a Substance, and that the Mind which has powers must be a Substance, and it may reasonably be enquired whether they be one and the same Substance or not.

In many other places, however, this Author seems to be very dubious whether there be any such thing as Substance, and very positive that we have no proper idea of it.

Disquisitions page 104. "In fact we have no proper idea of any essence whatsoever." *Ibid*. "The term *Substance* or Essence therefore is, in fact, nothing more than a help to expression, as we may say, but not at all to conception."

If the term Substance express any conception of the mind, though even an obscure conception, it must be a help to conception; and if it be no help to conception, it can express no conception clear or obscure, and then I apprehend it can be no help to expression but an incumbrance upon it, as all unmeaning words are.

Disquisitions page 107. "The properties or powers being different, the Substance or Essence (if it be any convenience to us to use such terms at all) must be different also."

Here, I would be glad to know how, without the use of such terms, we should express the fundamental principle of Materialism, That Soul and Body are not two different Substances, but one and the same.

Free Discussion page 364. "Having again and again observed, what I believe will be universally admitted, that by the words *Being, Substance* or *Thing*, we only mean the unknown, and, perhaps, imaginary support of properties."

If this be so, will it not follow, that the whole dispute about Materialism, is a dispute about the unity or duplicity of an unknown, and, perhaps, an imaginary thing.

It seems therefore incumbent on those who support the doctrine of Materialism as a doctrine of real importance in Philosophy and in Religion, not only, not to adopt the scruples that have been raised by modern Philosophers about the existence of Substance, but to shew that they have no solid foundation, and that however imperfect or obscure our notion of Substance may be, we must admit their existence, and that qualities cannot subsist without them.

II. Another opinion subversive of Materialism is that which denies the existence of Matter.

If one believe, with Bishop Berkeley, that there is no such thing as a material world, that ideas and immaterial thinking Beings are the only existences in the Universe, it is impossible that he can believe at the same time that the human Soul is a piece of Matter. Bishop Berkeley thought it no small recommendation of his opinion, that, if it be true, Materialism is effectually refuted. And, indeed, the contradiction between these two opinions is selfevident. Every argument for Materialism supposes the existence of Matter, and, if matter do not exist, must be fallacious and inconclusive.

If the existence of Matter be an hypothesis only, brought to account for the production of ideas in our Minds, it will follow, that all that can be said for Materialism, is grounded upon an hypothesis; and this, to those who have a just taste in Philosophy, must appear to be a very slippery foundation.

It might therefore be expected of Materialists, that in order to lay a solid foundation for their system, they should shew that the subtile arguments of Bishop Berkeley against the existence, and even against the possibility of a material world, have no force.

Dr. Priestley expresses a more favourable opinion of Bishop Berkeley's system, than a confirmed Materialist ought to entertain.

Institutes of Natural and Revealed Religion, Pref page 12. "If this appears to any person a more natural and simple hypothesis to account for our Ideas, and therefore preferable to the supposition

of a real external world; by means of which and of a more general agency of the Deity, the same ideas may be presented to thousands and millions of Minds, I leave him to his imagination, from which no evil that I know will result."

Surely this evil will result, that he cannot be a Materialist.

Examination of Reid, Beattie and Oswald, Introd page 60. "The moment we have attained to the knowledge of Ideas, the external world is nothing more than an hypothesis, to account for those ideas, so probable indeed, that few persons seriously doubt of its real existence, and of its being the cause of our Ideas." *Ibid. page 155*, He calls it, "This same innocent theory of Berkeleys." And *page 312*, He says of Dr. Price, "This Philosopher had more good sense than to load his scheme with the belief of the real existence of the external world."

It happens that the scheme of Materialism is necessarily loaded with the belief of the real existence of the external world; and therefore it is incumbent upon the defenders of it to support that load.

It is true, Dr. Priestley thinks the existence of the external world a probable hypothesis, because it accounts for appearances. Supposing it to be so, the system of Materialism can have no more probability than that of an hypothesis that accounts for appearances. And those who have a just taste in Philosophy, pay no regard to such hypotheses.

Sir Isaac Newton has told us, that they have no place in Philosophy. "Hypotheses non fingo. Quiquid enim ex phaenom⟨e⟩nis non deducitur, hypothesis vocanda est, et hypotheses, seu Metaphysicae, seu physicae, seu qualitatum occultarum, seu Mechani⟨c⟩ae, in philosophia experimentali locum non habent." And his great Friend Roger Cotes, describing the experimental method of philosophizing, says, "Nihil autem principii loco assumunt quod nondum ex phaenomenis comprobatum fuerit. Hypotheses non comm⟨i⟩niscuntur, neque in Physicam recipiunt, nisi ut quaestiones de quarum veritate disputetur."

The probability of this hypothesis Dr. Priestley places in this. "That it exhibits particular appearances as arising from more general laws." This is a probability common to thousands of hypotheses which time has discovered to be false. But what is its claim to this probability?

Dr. Priestley has in two different works, and in the same words, shewn this at full length, first in the preface to the third volume of his *Institutes*, *pages 12 and 13*, and afterwards in his introductory observations to his *Examination of Reid, Beattie and Oswald, pages 58 and 59*. The words are, "Half the inhabitants of the globe, for instance, may be looking towards the heavens at the same time, and all their minds are impressed in the same manner: All see the moon, stars and planets precisely in the same situations; and even the observations of those who use Telescopes correspond with the utmost exactness. To explain this, Bishop Berkeley says, that the divine Being, attending particularly to each individual mind, impresses their *Sensoriums* in the same or in a corresponding manner, without the medium of any thing external to them. On the other hand, I, without pretending that his scheme is impossible, where divine power is concerned, think, however, that it is more natural to suppose, that there are really such bodies as the moon, stars and planets, placed at certain distances from us, and moving in certain directions, by means of which, without such an agency as he supposes, all our minds are necessarily impressed in this corresponding manner."

This is the probability on which the existence of an external world, and, of consequence, the truth of the system of Materialism is grounded by Dr. Priestley; and he acknowledges, that the hypothesis of there being no external world, is by no means so shocking to his understanding, as the supposition that we really perceive things that are external to us, and do not judge of all things that are without ourselves, by notices perceived within, how mistaken soever we may be in our judgments concerning them.

Were I to examine this probability on the principle which Berkeley assumes, and which to Dr. Priestley's understanding appears more evident than even the existence of an external world, I would say, that an inhabited globe, its numerous inhabitants, their observations and telescopes, as well as the Moon, stars and planets which they observe, are, according to this principle, nothing but Ideas in my Mind. The external existence of things corresponding or similar to these Ideas, is the very thing to be proved; and, in this argument, that external existence is taken for granted. So that though the consequence were not only probable but demonstrative, the argument is only what Logicians call a *Petitio principii*.

Besides this, we have no reason to think that an external world could possibly enter into the conception of a Being who never perceived any thing external. Our conceptions are limited by our perceptions. A man who never saw colours cannot conceive colours, nor can one who never heard sound conceive sound. We can in imagination mix and compound the materials got by perception in various ways, but to add other Materials to them is no more in our power than to create. According to Dr. Priestley, all that we really perceive is only sensations in our own Minds. No mixture or composition of Sensations can make up the conception of an external world. Sensations are fleeting and transient things, like the images in a Mirror; the external world has a real and permanent existence. Sensations cannot be but in a sentient mind, as their subject, the external world, has an existence given it independent of any subject, and is totally of a different kind from any sensation or composition of Sensations.

Let us suppose that man were such a Being as Dr. Priestley conceives him to be, that is, a being who really perceives nothing external to himself, and judges of all things only by notices perceived in his own mind; and let us suppose that in consequence of his reflection upon his inward notices, he puts this question to himself, What is the cause of his ideas and sensations, and of that regularity with which they are produced, with manifest marks of wisdom superior to his own, and of benevolent design? How would he judge in this case?

Would he attribute these effects to an unthinking cause such as a material world, granting that he could form a conception of such a cause? Surely, if he had understanding he would impute such effects to a Being of superior rank, who had power over him as a Potter has over his clay.

There is no reason therefore to think that, from any notices within himself, such a Being would be able to form any conception of an external world; or, if he could, that an inquiry into the cause of his Sensations and Ideas would lead him into the conception of such a world and the belief of its existence.

It appears therefore that in order to refute Berkeley's scheme, and consequently to lay a foundation for the system of Materialism, something more solid is wanted than the probability offered by Dr. Priestley.

III. I apprehend that to support the system of Materialism, the capital doctrines of Locke's system must be given up, and refuted.

To these doctrines Dr. Priestley has hitherto shewn a strong attachment; but if they leave no foundation for Materialism, the defenders of it must refute them.

In the preface to the third volume of his Institutes, page 21, He says, "I have no doubt, however, but the time will certainly come, when the general principles of Hartley, as well as of Locke, will be fully established, and when every contrary hypothesis will be forgotten."

In the Examination of Reid, Beattie and Oswald, after giving the outline of Locke's system, He adds, *pages 5 and 6,* "I think he has been hasty in concluding that there is some other source of our Ideas besides the external senses; but the rest of his system appears to me, and others, to be the cornerstone of all just and rational knowledge of ourselves. This solid foundation, however, has been attempted to be overturned by a set of pretended Philosophers, of whom the most conspicuous and assuming is Dr. Reid, Professor of Moral Philosophy in the University of Glasgow." And in a passage already quoted he acknowledges, "That the hypothesis of there being no external world, is by no means so shocking to his understanding as the supposition that we really perceive things that are external to us."

The reasons why I conceive Mr. Locke's system concerning Ideas to be subversive of Materialism are two. First, because it leaves us no idea of substance, and Secondly, because Berkeley's system is the necessary consequence of it.

Mr. Locke saw clearly, and has expressly said, that we neither have nor can have any idea of substance, either by sensation or by reflection. And indeed nothing is more evident. For, by our senses we perceive only the qualities of bodies, but not their substance; by consciousness we perceive only the operations of our minds, but not their substance; and there is not a third avenue according to Locke's system by which this idea can enter. Substance therefore is a word without an Idea, that is, without a meaning. And to say that Soul and Body are one Substance, or that they are two Substances, must be propositions that have no meaning.

I know there are many passages in Locke's Essay that imply our having an idea of Substance. When he came to consider our ideas in detail, it appeared that Substances occupy too large a share to be overlooked. Accordingly he divides them into three classes, to wit, the Ideas of Substances, of Modes, and of Relations, and treats of each particularly. One would think that, according to his principles, there can be no idea of Substances.

Whatever way we take to reconcile these things it is certain that no idea of Substance can be admitted, without overturning a fundamental article of Locke's system. The only account I can make of this apparent inconsistence is, that in candid minds, such as Mr. Locke's certainly was, selfevident truths, when, by some favourite hypothesis, they are shut out at one door, are apt to make good their entrance by another.

That Berkeley's system is the necessary consequence of Mr. Locke's appears to me very evident.

We are taught by Des Cartes, by Locke, and by all their followers, that all the evidence we can have of things external, must be drawn by reasoning from the Sensations and Ideas we are conscious of in ourselves, or, as it is very properly expressed by Dr. Priestley, that we really perceive nothing external, but judge of all things that are without ourselves by notices perceived within.

This principle, which I take to be the cornerstone of Locke's system, Berkeley assumes as an axiom; and draws his conclusion from it, by reasoning so clear and cogent, that they must stand or fall together. All attempts to disjoin them have been, and for ever will be vain. And therefore to establish the existence of Matter, and thereby lay a foundation for Materialism, this principle of Locke's System must be refuted.

PART X

Jean-Jacques Rousseau (1712–88)

Introduction

Though Rousseau's philosophical interests were confined mainly to social and political issues, his analysis of the condition of the individual in modern society was enormously influential for subsequent thinkers, and figured prominently in the ideology of the French Revolution. Our first selection is from the early *Discourse on the Arts and the Sciences* (1750) in which Rousseau argues that the progress of civilization has been accompanied by moral regress, and that the savage state was happier and more virtuous than life in a modern nation. This essay won an important prize and established Rousseau's reputation as a writer. The next is from *Discourse on the Origin of Inequality* (1754) and is a brilliant evocation of the rule of greed and hypocrisy in an advanced society: "Let us reflect what must be the state of things, when men are forced to caress and destroy one another at the same time; when they are born enemies by duty, and knaves by interest." Our third selection, from *Émile* (1762), is a summary discussion of the origin, nature, and forms of government. This excerpt presents an elegant synopsis of the main argument advanced in Rousseau's best-known work, *The Social Contract* (1762). We conclude our selections with the chapter "Civil Religion" from the latter work. Rousseau's discussion of the relation of religion to polity and his argument for religious toleration look back to Locke, Spinoza, and Hobbes, and forward to Kant and Hegel. His insights still throw light on our contemporary concerns about these matters.

32

Discourse on the Arts and the Sciences

[The Effect of the Arts and Sciences on Moral Development]

[...] We cannot reflect on the morality of mankind without contemplating with pleasure the picture of the simplicity which prevailed in the earliest times. This image may be justly compared to a beautiful coast, adorned only by the hands of nature; towards which our eyes are constantly turned, and which we see receding with regret. While men were innocent and virtuous and loved to have the gods for witnesses of their actions, they dwelt together in the same huts; but when they became vicious, they grew tired of such inconvenient on-lookers, and banished them to magnificent temples. Finally, they expelled their deities even from these, in order to dwell there themselves; or at least the temples of the gods were no longer more magnificent than the palaces of the citizens. This was the height of degeneracy; nor could vice ever be carried to greater lengths than when it was seen, supported, as it were, at the doors of the great, on columns of marble, and graven on Corinthian capitals.

As the conveniences of life increase, as the arts are brought to perfection, and luxury spreads, true courage flags, military virtues disappear; and all this is the effect of the sciences and of those arts which are exercised in the privacy of men's dwellings. When the Goths ravaged Greece, the libraries only escaped the flames owing to an opinion

Discourse on the Arts and the Sciences (1750). From *The Social Contract and Discourses*, tr. G. D. H. Cole, rev. J. H. Brumfitt and John C. Hall (London: J. M. Dent & Sons, Ltd., 1973). Selection: pp. 20–9.

that was set on foot among them, that it was best to leave the enemy with a possession so calculated to divert their attention from military exercises, and keep them engaged in indolent and sedentary occupations.

Charles the Eighth found himself master of Tuscany and the kingdom of Naples, almost without drawing sword; and all his court attributed this unexpected success to the fact that the princes and nobles of Italy applied themselves with greater earnestness to the cultivation of their understandings than to active and martial pursuits. In fact, says the sensible person who records these characteristics, experience plainly tells us, that in military matters and all that resemble them application to the sciences tends rather to make men effeminate and cowardly than resolute and vigorous.

The Romans confessed that military virtue was extinguished among them, in proportion as they became connoisseurs in the arts of the painter, the engraver, and the goldsmith, and began to cultivate the fine arts. Indeed, as if this famous country was to be for ever an example to other nations, the rise of the Medici and the revival of letters has once more destroyed, this time perhaps for ever, the martial reputation which Italy seemed a few centuries ago to have recovered.

The ancient republics of Greece, with that wisdom which was so conspicuous in most of their institutions, forbade their citizens to pursue all those inactive and sedentary occupations, which by enervating and corrupting the body diminish also the vigour of the mind. With what courage, in fact, can it be thought that hunger and thirst, fatigues, dangers, and death, can be faced by men whom the smallest want overwhelms and the slightest difficulty repels? With what resolution can soldiers support the excessive toils of war, when they are entirely unaccustomed to them? With what spirits can they make forced marches under officers who have not even the strength to travel on horseback? It is no answer to cite the reputed valour of all the modern warriors who are so scientifically trained. I hear much of their bravery in a day's battle; but I am told nothing of how they support excessive fatigue, how they stand the severity of the seasons and the inclemency of the weather. A little sunshine or snow, or the want of a few superfluities, is enough to cripple and destroy one of our finest armies in a few days. Intrepid warriors! permit me for once to tell you the truth, which you seldom hear. Of your bravery I am fully satisfied. I have no doubt that you would have triumphed with Hannibal at Cannae, and at Trasimene: that you would have passed the Rubicon with Caesar, and enabled him to enslave his country; but you never would have been able to cross the Alps with the former, or with the latter to subdue your own ancestors, the Gauls.

A war does not always depend on the events of battle: there is in generalship an art superior to that of gaining victories. A man may behave with great intrepidity under fire, and yet be a very bad officer. Even in the common soldier, a little more strength and vigour would perhaps be more useful than so much courage, which after all is no protection from death. And what does it matter to the State whether its troops perish by cold and fever, or by the sword of the enemy?

If the cultivation of the sciences is prejudicial to military qualities, it is still more so to moral qualities. Even from our infancy an absurd system of education serves to adorn our wit and corrupt our judgment. We see, on every side, huge institutions, where our youth are educated at great expense, and instructed in everything but their duty. Your children will be ignorant of their own language, when they can talk others which are not spoken anywhere. They will be able to compose verses which they can hardly understand; and, without being capable of distinguishing truth from error, they will possess the art of making them unrecognizable by specious arguments. But magnanimity, equity, temperance, humanity, and courage will be words of which they know not the meaning. The dear name of country will never strike on their ears; and if they ever hear speak of God,[1] it will be less to fear than to be frightened of Him. I would as soon, said a wise man, that my pupil

had spent his time in the tennis court as in this manner; for there his body at least would have got exercise.

I well know that children ought to be kept employed, and that idleness is for them the danger most to be feared. But what should they be taught? This is undoubtedly an important question. Let them be taught what they are to practise when they come to be men;[2] not what they ought to forget.

Our gardens are adorned with statues and our galleries with pictures. What would you imagine these masterpieces of art, thus exhibited to public admiration, represent? The great men who have defended their country, or the still greater men who have enriched it by their virtues? Far from it. They are the images of every perversion of heart and mind, carefully selected from ancient mythology, and presented to the early curiosity of our children, doubtless that they may have before their eyes the representations of vicious actions, even before they are able to read.

Whence arise all those abuses, unless it be from that fatal inequality introduced among men by the distinction of talents and the cheapening of virtue? This is the most evident effect of all our studies, and the most dangerous of all their consequences. The question is no longer whether a man is honest, but whether he is clever. We do not ask whether a book is useful, but whether it is well written. Rewards are lavished on wit and ingenuity, while virtue is left unhonoured. There are a thousand prizes for fine discourses, and none for good actions. I should be glad, however, to know whether the honour attaching to the best discourse that ever wins the prize in this Academy is comparable with the merit of having founded the prize.

A wise man does not go in chase of fortune; but he is by no means insensible to glory, and when he sees it so ill distributed, his virtue, which might have been animated by a little emulation, and turned to the advantage of society, droops and dies away in obscurity and indigence. Preferring the agreeable arts to the useful ones must, in the long run, inevitably result in this; and this truth has been but too much confirmed since the revival of the arts and sciences. We have physicists, geometricians, chemists, astronomers, poets, musicians, and painters in plenty; but we have no longer a citizen among us; or if there be found a few scattered over our abandoned countryside, they are left to perish there unnoticed and neglected. Such is the condition to which those who give us our daily bread, and our children milk, are reduced, and such are our feelings towards them.

I confess, however, that the evil is not so great as it might have become. The eternal providence, in placing salutary simples beside noxious plants, and making poisonous animals contain their own antidote, has taught the sovereigns of the earth, who are its ministers, to imitate its wisdom. It is by following this example that the truly great monarch, to whose glory every age will add new lustre, drew from the very bosom of the arts and sciences the very fountains of a thousand lapses from rectitude, those famous societies, which, while they are depositaries of the dangerous trust of human knowledge, are yet the sacred guardians of morals, by the attention they pay to their maintenance among themselves in all their purity, and by the demands which they make on every member whom they admit.

These wise institutions, confirmed by his august successor and imitated by all the kings of Europe, will serve at least to restrain men of letters, who, all aspiring to the honour of being admitted into these Academies, will keep watch over themselves, and endeavour to make themselves worthy of such honour by useful performances and irreproachable morals. Those Academies also, which, in proposing prizes for literary merit, make choice of such subjects are calculated to arouse the love of virtue in the hearts of citizens, prove that it prevails in themselves, and must give men the rare and real pleasure of finding learned societies devoting themselves to the enlightenment of mankind, not only by agreeable exercises of the intellect, but also by useful instructions.

An objection which may be made is, in fact, only an additional proof of my argument. So much precaution proves but too evidently the need for it. We never seek remedies for evils that do not exist. Why, indeed, must these bear all the marks of ordinary remedies, on account of their inefficacy? The numerous establishments in favour of the learned are only adapted to make men mistake the objects of the sciences, and turn men's attention to the cultivation of them. One would be inclined to think, from the precautions everywhere taken, that we are overstocked with husbandmen, and are afraid of a shortage of philosophers. I will not venture here to enter into a comparison between agriculture and philosophy, as they would not bear it. I shall only ask: What is philosophy? What is contained in the writings of the most celebrated philosophers? What are the lessons of these friends of wisdom? To hear them, should we not take them for so many mountebanks, exhibiting themselves in public, and crying out, *Here, Here, come to me, I am the only true doctor?* One of them teaches that there is no such thing as matter, but that everything exists only in representation. Another declares that there is no other substance than matter, and no other God than the world itself. A third tells you that there are no such things as virtue and vice, and that moral good and evil are chimeras; while a fourth informs you that men are only beasts of prey, and may conscientiously devour one another. Why, my great philosophers, do you not reserve these wise and profitable lessons for your friends and children? You would soon reap the benefit of them, nor should we be under any apprehension of our own becoming your disciples.

Such are the wonderful men, whom their contemporaries held in the highest esteem during their lives, and to whom immortality has been attributed since their decease. Such are the wise maxims we have received from them, and which are transmitted, from age to age, to our descendants. Paganism, though given over to all the extravagances of human reason, has left nothing to compare with the shameful monuments which have been prepared by the art of printing, during the reign of the gospel. The impious writings of Leucippus and Diagoras perished with their authors. The world, in their days, was ignorant of the art of immortalizing the errors and extravagances of the human mind. But thanks to the art of printing[3] and the use we make of it, the pernicious reflections of Hobbes and Spinoza will last for ever. Go, famous writings, of which the ignorance and rusticity of our forefathers would have been incapable. Go to our descendants, along with those still more pernicious works which reek of the corrupted manners of the present age! Let them together convey to posterity a faithful history of the progress and advantages of our arts and sciences. If they are read, they will leave not a doubt about the question we are now discussing, and unless mankind should then be still more foolish than we, they will lift up their hands to Heaven and exclaim in bitterness of heart: "Almighty God! Thou who holdest in Thy hand the minds of men, deliver us from the fatal arts and sciences of our forefathers; give us back ignorance, innocence, and poverty, which alone can make us happy and are precious in Thy sight."

But if the progress of the arts and sciences has added nothing to our real happiness; if it has corrupted our morals, and if that corruption has vitiated our taste, what are we to think of the herd of text-book authors, who have removed those impediments which nature purposely laid in the way to the Temple of the Muses, in order to guard its approach and try the powers of those who might be tempted to seek knowledge? What are we to think of those compilers who have indiscreetly broken open the door of the sciences, and introduced into their sanctuary a populace unworthy to approach it, when it was greatly to be wished that all who should be found incapable of making a considerable progress in the career of learning should have been repulsed at the entrance, and thereby cast upon those arts which are useful to society. A man who will be all his life a bad versifier, or a third-rate geometrician, might have made nevertheless an excellent clothier. Those whom nature intended for her disciples have not needed masters. Bacon, Descartes, and Newton, those teachers of mankind, had themselves no teachers. What guide indeed could have taken them so far as their sublime genius directed them? Ordinary masters would only have cramped their intelligence, by confining it within the narrow limits of their own capacity. It was from the obstacles they met with at first that they learned to exert themselves, and bestirred themselves to traverse the vast field which they covered. If it be proper to allow some men to apply themselves to the study of the arts and sciences, it is only those who feel themselves able to walk alone in their footsteps and to outstrip them. It belongs only to these few to raise monuments to the glory of the human understanding. But if we are desirous that nothing should be above their genius, nothing should be beyond their hopes. This is the only encouragement they require. The soul insensibly adapts itself to the objects on which it is employed, and thus it is that great occasions produce great men. The greatest orator in the world was Consul of Rome, and perhaps the greatest of philosophers Lord Chancellor of England. Can it be conceived that, if the former had only been a professor at some University, and the latter a pensioner of some Academy, their works would not have suffered from their situation? Let not princes disdain to admit into their councils those who are most capable of giving them good advice. Let them renounce the old prejudice, which was invented by the pride of the great, that the art of governing mankind is more difficult than that of instructing them; as if it were easier to induce men to do good voluntarily than to compel them to it by force. Let the learned of the first rank find an honourable refuge in their courts; let them there enjoy the only recompense worthy of them, that of promoting by their influence the happiness of the peoples they have enlightened by their wisdom. It is by this means only that we are likely to see what virtue, science, and authority can do, when animated by the noblest emulation, and working unanimously for the happiness of mankind.

But so long as power alone is on one side, and knowledge and understanding alone on the other, the learned will seldom make great objects their study, princes will still more rarely do great actions, and the peoples will continue to be, as they are, mean, corrupt, and miserable.

As for us, ordinary men, on whom Heaven has not been pleased to bestow such great talents; as we are not destined to reap such glory, let us remain in our obscurity. Let us not covet a reputation we should never attain, and which, in the present state of things, would never make up to us for the trouble it would have cost us, even if we were fully qualified to obtain it. Why should we build our happiness on the opinions of others, when we can find it in our own hearts? Let us leave to others the task of instructing mankind in their duty, and confine ourselves to the discharge of our own. We have no occasion for greater knowledge than this.

Virtue! sublime science of simple minds, are such industry and preparation needed if we are to know you? Are not your principles graven on every heart? Need we do more, to learn your laws, than examine ourselves and listen to the voice of conscience, when the passions are silent?

This is the true philosophy, with which we must learn to be content, without envying the fame of those celebrated men, whose names are immortal in the republic of letters. Let us, instead of envying them, endeavour to make, between them and us, that honourable distinction which was formerly seen to exist between two great peoples, that the one knew how to speak, and the other how to act, aright.

Notes

1 *Pensées philosophiques* (Diderot).

2 Such was the education of the Spartans according to one of the greatest of their kings. It is well worthy of notice, says Montaigne, that the excellent institutions of Lycurgus, which were in truth miraculously perfect, paid as much attention to the bringing up of youth as if this were their principal object, and yet, at the very seat of the Muses, they make so little mention of learning that it seems as if their generous-spirited youth disdained every other restraint, and required, instead of masters of the sciences, instructors in valour, prudence, and justice alone.

Let us hear next what the same writer says of the ancient Persians. Plato, says he, relates that the heir to the throne was thus brought up. At his birth he was committed, to not the care of women, but to eunuchs in the highest authority and near the person of the king, on account of their virtue. These undertook to render his body beautiful and healthy. At seven years of age they taught him to ride and go hunting. At fourteen he was placed in the hands of four, the wisest, the most just, the most temperate, and the bravest persons in the kingdom. The first instructed him in religion, the second taught him to adhere inviolably to truth, the third to conquer his passions, and the fourth to be afraid of nothing. All, I may add, taught him to be a good man; but not one taught him to be learned.

Astyages, in Xenophon, desires Cyrus to give him an account of his last lesson. It was this, answered Cyrus, one of the big boys of the school having a small coat, gave it to a little boy and took away from him his coat, which was larger. Our master having appointed me arbiter in the dispute, I ordered that matters should stand as they were, as each boy seemed to be better suited than before. The master, however, remonstrated with me, saying that I considered only convenience, whereas justice ought to have been the first concern, and justice teaches that no one should suffer forcible interference with what belongs to him. He added that he was punished for his wrong decision, just as boys are punished in our country schools when they forget the first aorist of τύπτω. My tutor must make me a fine harangue, *in genere demonstrativo*, before he will persuade me that his school is as good as this.

3 If we consider the frightful disorders which printing has already caused in Europe, and judge of the future by the progress of its evils from day to day, it is easy to foresee that sovereigns will hereafter take as much pains to banish this dreadful art from their dominions, as they ever took to encourage it. The Sultan Achmet, yielding to the importunities of certain pretenders to taste, consented to have a press erected at Constantinople; but it was hardly set to work before they were obliged to destroy it, and throw the plant into a well.

It is related that the Caliph Omar, being asked what should be done with the library at Alexandria, answered in these words: "If the books in the library contain anything contrary to the Alcoran, they are evil and ought to be burnt; if they contain only what the Alcoran teaches, they are superfluous." This reasoning has been cited by our men of letters as the height of absurdity; but if Gregory the Great had been in the place of Omar and the Gospel in the place of the Alcoran, the library would still have been burnt, and it would have been perhaps the finest action of his life.

33

A Discourse on the Origin of Inequality

Appendix

A famous author, reckoning up the good and evil of human life, and comparing the aggregates, finds that our pains greatly exceed our pleasures: so that, all things considered, human life is not at all a valuable gift. This conclusion does not surprise me; for the writer drew all his arguments from man in civilization. Had he gone back to the state of nature, his inquiries would clearly have had a different result, and man would have been seen to be subject to very few evils not of his own creation. It has indeed cost us not a little trouble to make ourselves as wretched as we are. When we consider, on the one hand, the immense labours of mankind, the many sciences brought to perfection, the arts invented, the powers employed, the deeps filled up, the mountains levelled, the rocks shattered, the rivers made navigable, the tracts of land cleared, the lakes emptied, the marshes drained, the enormous structures erected on land, and the teeming vessels that cover the sea; and, on the other hand, estimate with ever so little thought, the real advantages that have accrued from all these works to mankind, we cannot help being amazed at the vast disproportion there is between these things, and deploring the infatuation of man, which, to gratify his silly pride and vain self-admiration, induces him eagerly to pursue all

A Note to the *Discourse on the Origin of Inequality* (1754). From *The Social Contract and Discourses*, tr. G. D. H. Cole, rev. J. H. Brumfitt and John C. Hall (London: J. M. Dent & Sons, Ltd., 1973). Selection: Appendix: pp. 118–26.

the miseries he is capable of feeling, though beneficent nature had kindly placed them out of his way.

That men are actually wicked, a sad and continual experience of them proves beyond doubt: but, all the same I think I have shown that man is naturally good. What then can have depraved him to such an extent, except the changes that have happened in his constitution, the advances he has made, and the knowledge he has acquired? We may admire human society as much as we please; it will be none the less true that it necessarily leads men to hate each other in proportion as their interests clash, and to do one another apparent services, while they are really doing every imaginable mischief. What can be thought of a relation, in which the interest of every individual dictates rules directly opposite to those the public reason dictates to the community in general – in which every man finds his profit in the misfortunes of his neighbour? There is not perhaps any man in a comfortable position who has not greedy heirs, and perhaps even children, secretly wishing for his death; not a ship at sea, of which the loss would not be good news to some merchant or other; not a house, which some debtor of bad faith would not be glad to see reduced to ashes with all the papers it contains; not a nation which does not rejoice at the disasters that befall its neighbours. Thus it is that we find our advantage in the misfortunes of our fellow-creatures, and that the loss of one man almost always constitutes the prosperity of another. But it is still more pernicious that public calamities are the objects of the hopes and expectations of innumerable individuals. Some desire sickness, some mortality, some war, and some famine. I have seen men wicked enough to weep for sorrow at the prospect of a plentiful season; and the great and fatal fire of London, which cost so many unhappy persons their lives or their fortunes, made the fortunes of perhaps ten thousand others. I know that Montaigne censures Demades the Athenian for having caused to be punished a workman who, by selling his coffins very dear, was a great gainer by the deaths of his fellow-citizens; but, the reason alleged by Montaigne being that everybody ought to be punished, my point is clearly confirmed by it. Let us penetrate, therefore, the superficial appearances of benevolence, and survey what passes in the inmost recesses of the heart. Let us reflect what must be the state of things, when men are forced to caress and destroy one another at the same time; when they are born enemies by duty, and knaves by interest. It will perhaps be said that society is so formed that every man gains by serving the rest. That would be all very well, if he did not gain still more by injuring them. There is no legitimate profit so great, that it cannot be greatly exceeded by what may be made illegitimately; we always gain more by hurting our neighbours than by doing them good. Nothing is required but to know how to act with impunity; and to this end the powerful employ all their strength, and the weak all their cunning.

Savage man, when he has dined, is at peace with all nature, and the friend of all his fellow-creatures. If a dispute arises about a meal, he rarely comes to blows, without having first compared the difficulty of conquering his antagonist with the trouble of finding subsistence elsewhere: and, as pride does not come in, it all ends in a few blows; the victor eats, and the vanquished seeks provision somewhere else, and all is at peace. The case is quite different with man in the state of society, for whom first necessaries have to be provided, and then superfluities; delicacies follow next, then immense wealth, then subjects, and then slaves. He enjoys not a moment's relaxation; and what is yet stranger, the less natural and pressing his wants, the more headstrong are his passions, and, still worse, the more he has it in his power to gratify them; so that after a long course of prosperity, after having swallowed up treasures and ruined multitudes, the hero ends up by cutting every throat till he finds himself, at last, sole master of the world. Such is in miniature the moral picture, if not of human life, at least of the secret pretensions of the heart of civilized man.

Compare without partiality the state of the citizen with that of the savage, and trace out, if you can, how many inlets the former has opened to pain and death, besides those of his vices, his wants, and his misfortunes. If you reflect on the mental afflictions that prey on us, the violent passions that waste and exhaust us, the excessive labour with which the poor are burdened, the still more dangerous indolence to which the wealthy give themselves up, so that the poor perish of want, and the rich of surfeit; if you reflect but a moment on the heterogeneous mixtures and pernicious seasonings of foods; the corrupt state in which they are frequently eaten; on the adulteration of medicines, the wiles of those who sell them, the mistakes of those who administer them, and the poisonous vessels in which they are prepared; on the epidemics bred by foul air in consequence of great numbers of men being crowded together, or those which are caused by our delicate way of living, by our passing from our houses into the open air and back again, by the putting on or throwing off our clothes with too little care, and by all the precautions which sensuality has converted into necessary habits, and the neglect of which sometimes costs us our life or health; if you take into account the conflagrations and earthquakes, which, devouring or overwhelming whole cities, destroy the inhabitants by thousands; in a word, if you add together all the dangers with which these causes are always threatening us, you will see how dearly nature makes us pay for the contempt with which we have treated her lessons.

I shall not here repeat, what I have elsewhere said of the calamities of war; but wish that those, who have sufficient knowledge, were willing or bold enough to make public the details of the villainies committed in armies by the contractors for commissariat and hospitals: we should see plainly that their monstrous frauds, already none too well concealed, which cripple the finest armies in less than no time, occasion greater destruction among the soldiers than the swords of the enemy.

The number of people who perish annually at sea, by famine, the scurvy, pirates, fire, and shipwrecks, affords matter for another shocking calculation. We must also place to the credit of the establishment of property, and consequently to the institution of society, assassinations, poisonings, highway robberies, and even the punishments inflicted on the wretches guilty of these crimes; which, though expedient to prevent greater evils, yet by making the murder of one man cost the lives of two or more, double the loss to the human race.

What shameful methods are sometimes practised to prevent the birth of men, and cheat nature; either by brutal and depraved appetites which insult her most beautiful work – appetites unknown to savages or mere animals, which can spring only from the corrupt imagination of mankind in civilized countries; or by secret abortions, the fitting effects of debauchery and vitiated notions of honour; or by the exposure or murder of multitudes of infants, who fall victims to the poverty of their parents, or the cruel shame of their mothers; or, finally, by the mutilation of unhappy wretches, part of whose life, with their hope of posterity, is given up to vain singing, or, still worse, the brutal jealousy of other men: a mutilation which, in the last case, becomes a double outrage against nature from the treatment of those who suffer it, and from the use to which they are destined. But is it not a thousand times more common and more dangerous for paternal rights openly to offend against humanity? How many talents have not been thrown away, and inclinations forced, by the unwise constraint of fathers? How many men, who would have distinguished themselves in a fitting estate, have died dishonoured and wretched in another for which they had no taste! How many happy, but unequal, marriages have been broken or disturbed, and how many chaste wives have been dishonoured, by an order of things continually in contradiction with that of nature! How many good and virtuous husbands and wives are reciprocally punished for having been ill-assorted! How many young and unhappy victims of their parents' avarice plunge into vice, or pass their melancholy days in tears, groaning in the indissoluble bonds which their hearts repudiate and gold alone has formed! Fortunate sometimes are those whose courage and virtue remove them from life before inhuman violence makes them spend it in crime or in despair. Forgive me, fathers and mothers, who are ever to be pitied: I regret having to increase your pain; I only hope it may serve as an eternal and terrible example to anyone who dares, in the very name of nature, to violate the most sacred of natural rights.

If I have spoken only of those ill-starred unions which are the result of our system, is it to be thought that those over which love and sympathy preside are free from disadvantages? What if I should undertake to show humanity attacked in its very source, and even in the most sacred of all ties, in which fortune is consulted before nature, and, the disorders of society confounding all virtue and vice, continence becomes a criminal precaution, and a refusal to give life to a fellow-creature, an act of humanity? But, without drawing aside the veil which hides all these horrors, let us content ourselves with pointing out the evil which others will have to remedy.

To all this add the multiplicity of unhealthy trades, which shorten men's lives or destroy their bodies, such as working in the mines, and the preparing of metals and minerals, particularly lead, copper, mercury, cobalt, and arsenic: add those other dangerous trades which are daily fatal to many tilers, carpenters, masons, and miners; put all these together and we can see, in the establishment and perfection of societies, the reasons for that diminution of our species, which has been noticed by many philosophers.

Luxury, which cannot be avoided among men greedy for their own comfort and for the respect of others, soon completes the evil which society had begun and, under the pretence of giving bread to the poor whom it should never have made such, impoverishes all the rest, and sooner or later depopulates the State. Luxury is a remedy much worse than the disease it sets up to cure; or rather it is in itself the greatest of all evils, for every State, great or small: for, in order to maintain all the servants and vagabonds it creates, it brings oppression and ruin on the citizen and the labourer; it is like those scorching winds, which, covering the trees and plants with devouring insects, deprive useful animals of their subsistence and spread famine and death wherever they blow.

From society and the luxury to which it gives birth arise the liberal and mechanical arts, commerce, letters, and all those superfluities which make industry flourish, and enrich and ruin nations. The reason for such destruction is plain. It is easy to see, from the very nature of agriculture, that it must be the least lucrative of all the arts; for, its produce being the most universally necessary, the price must be proportionate to the abilities of the very poorest of mankind.

From the same principle may be deduced this rule, that the arts in general are more lucrative in proportion as they are less useful; and that, in the end, the most useful becomes the most neglected. From this we may learn what to think of the real advantages of industry and the actual effects of its progress.

Such are the sensible causes of all the miseries, into which opulence at length plunges the most celebrated nations. In proportion as arts and industry flourish, the despised husbandman, burdened with the taxes necessary for the support of luxury, and condemned to pass his days between labour and hunger, forsakes his native field, to seek in towns the bread he ought to carry thither. The more our capital cities strike the vulgar eye with admiration, the greater reason is there to lament the sight of the abandoned countryside, the large tracts of land that lie uncultivated, the roads crowded with unfortunate citizens turned beggars or highwaymen, and doomed to end their wretched lives either on a dunghill or on the gallows. Thus the State grows rich on the one hand, and feeble and depopulated on the other; the mightiest monarchies, after having taken immense pains to enrich and depopulate themselves, fall at last a prey to some poor nation, which has yielded to the fatal temptation of invading them, and then, growing opulent and weak in its turn, is itself invaded and ruined by some other.

Would someone be so kind as to explain to us what produced the hordes of barbarians who overran Europe, Asia and Africa for so many centuries? Was their prodigious increase due to their industry and arts, to the wisdom of their laws, or to the excellence of their political system? Let the learned tell us why, instead of multiplying to such a degree, these fierce and brutal men, without sense or science, without education, without restraint, did not destroy each other hourly in quarrelling over the productions of their fields and woods. Let them tell us how these wretches could have the presumption to oppose such clever people as we were, so well trained in military discipline, and possessed of such excellent laws and institutions: and why, since society has been brought to perfection in northern countries, and so much pains taken to instruct their inhabitants in their social duties and in the art of living happily and peaceably together, we see them no longer produce such numberless hosts as they used once to send forth to be the plague and terror of other nations. I fear someone may at last answer me by saying, that all these fine things, arts, sciences, and laws, were wisely invented by men, as a salutary plague, to prevent the too great multiplication of mankind, lest the world, which was given us for a habitation, should in time be too small for its inhabitants.

What, then, is to be done? Must we destroy society, abolish *mine* and *yours* and go back to living in the forests with the bears? This is the sort of conclusion my adversaries would come to and I would sooner forestall it than leave to them the shame of drawing it. O you, who have never heard the voice of heaven, who think man destined only to live this little life and die in peace; you, who can resign in the midst of populous cities your fatal acquisitions, your restless spirits, your corrupt hearts and endless desires; resume, since it depends entirely on yourselves, your ancient and primitive innocence: retire to the woods, there to lose the sight and remembrance of the crimes of your contemporaries; and be not apprehensive of degrading your species, by renouncing its advances in order to renounce its vices. As for men like me, whose passions have destroyed their original simplicity, who can no longer subsist on plants or acorns, or live without laws and magistrates; those who were honoured in their first father with supernatural instructions; those who discover, in the design of giving human actions at the start a morality which they must otherwise have been so long in acquiring, the reason for a precept in itself indifferent and inexplicable on every other system; those, in short, who are persuaded that the Divine Being has called all mankind to be partakers in the happiness and perfection of celestial intelligences, all these will endeavour to merit the eternal prize they are to expect from the practice of those virtues, which they make themselves follow in learning to know them. They will respect the sacred bonds of their respective communities; they will love their fellow-citizens, and serve them with all their might; they will scrupulously obey the laws, and all those who make or administer them; they will particularly honour those wise and good princes, who find means of preventing, curing, or even palliating all these evils and abuses, by which we are constantly threatened; they will animate the zeal of their deserving rulers, by showing them, without flattery or fear, the importance of their office and the severity of their duty. But they will not therefore have less contempt for a constitution that cannot support itself without the aid of so many splendid characters, much oftener wished for than found; and from which, notwithstanding all their pains and solicitude, there always arise more real calamities than even apparent advantages.

34

Émile

[On Government]

[. . .] The science of politics is and probably always will be unknown. Grotius, our leader in this branch of learning, is only a child, and what is worse an untruthful child. When I hear Grotius praised to the skies and Hobbes overwhelmed with abuse, I perceive how little sensible men have read or understood these authors. As a matter of fact, their principles are exactly alike, they only differ in their mode of expression. Their methods are also different: Hobbes relies on sophism; Grotius relies on the poets; they are agreed in everything else. In modern times the only man who could have created this vast and useless science was the illustrious Montesquieu. But he was not concerned with the principles of political law; he was content to deal with the positive laws of settled governments; and nothing could be more different than these two branches of study.

Yet he who would judge wisely in matters of actual government is forced to combine the two; he must know what ought to be in order to judge what is. The chief difficulty in the way of throwing light upon this important matter is to induce an individual to discuss and to answer these two questions. "How does it concern me; and what can I do?" Émile is in a position to answer both.

The next difficulty is due to the prejudices of childhood, the principles in which we were brought up; it is due above all to the partiality of authors, who are always talking about truth, though they care very little about it; it is only

Émile (1762), tr. Barbara Foxley (New York: Dutton, 1969). Selection: Bk 5, pp. 421–30.

their own interests that they care for, and of these they say nothing. Now the nation has neither professorships, nor pensions, nor membership of the academies to bestow. How then shall its rights be established by men of that type? The education I have given him has removed this difficulty also from Émile's path. He scarcely knows what is meant by government; his business is to find the best; he does not want to write books; if ever he did so, it would not be to pay court to those in authority, but to establish the rights of humanity.

There is a third difficulty, more specious than real; a difficulty which I neither desire to solve nor even to state; enough that I am not afraid of it; sure I am that in inquiries of this kind, great talents are less necessary than a genuine love of justice and a sincere reverence for truth. If matters of government can ever be fairly discussed, now or never is our chance.

Before beginning our observations we must lay down rules of procedure; we must find a scale with which to compare our measurements. Our principles of political law are our scale. Our actual measurements are the civil law of each country.

Our elementary notions are plain and simple, being taken directly from the nature of things. They will take the form of problems discussed between us, and they will not be formulated into principles, until we have found a satisfactory solution of our problems.

For example, we shall begin with the state of nature, we shall see whether men are born slaves or free, in a community or independent; is their association the result of free will or of force? Can the force which compels them to united action ever form a permanent law, by which this original force becomes binding, even when another has been imposed upon it, so that since the power of King Nimrod, who is said to have been the first conqueror, every other power which has overthrown the original power is unjust and usurping, so that there are no lawful kings but the descendants of Nimrod or their representatives; or if this original power has ceased, has the power which succeeded it any right over us, and does it destroy the binding force of the former power, so that we are not bound to obey except under compulsion, and we are free to rebel as soon as we are capable of resistance? Such a right is not very different from might; it is little more than a play upon words.

We shall inquire whether man might not say that all sickness comes from God, and that it is therefore a crime to send for the doctor.

Again, we shall inquire whether we are bound by our conscience to give our purse to a highwayman when we might conceal it from him, for the pistol in his hand is also a power.

Does this word power in this context mean something different from a power which is lawful and therefore subject to the laws to which it owes its being?

Suppose we reject this theory that might is right and admit the right of nature, or the authority of the father, as the foundation of society; we shall inquire into the extent of this authority; what is its foundation in nature? Has it any other grounds but that of its usefulness to the child, his weakness, and the natural love which his father feels towards him? When the child is no longer feeble, when he is grown-up in mind as well as in body, does not he become the sole judge of what is necessary for his preservation? Is he not therefore his own master, independent of all men, even of his father himself? For is it not still more certain that the son loves himself, than that the father loves the son?

The father being dead, should the children obey the eldest brother, or some other person who has not the natural affection of a father? Should there always be, from family to family, one single head to whom all the family owe obedience? If so, how has power ever come to be divided, and how is it that there is more than one head to govern the human race throughout the world?

Suppose the nations to have been formed each by its own choice; we shall then distinguish between right and fact; being thus subjected to their brothers, uncles, or other relations, not because they were obliged, but because they choose, we shall inquire whether this kind of society is not a sort of free and voluntary association?

Taking next the law of slavery, we shall inquire whether a man can make over to another his right to himself, without restriction, without reserve, without any kind of conditions; that is to say, can he renounce his person, his life, his reason, his very self, can he renounce all morality in his actions; in a word, can he cease to exist before his death, in spite of nature who places him directly in charge of his own preservation, in spite of reason and conscience which tell him what to do and what to leave undone?

If there is any reservation or restriction in the deed of slavery, we shall discuss whether this deed does not then become a true contract, in which both the contracting powers, having in this respect no common master,[1] remain their own judge as to the conditions of the contract, and therefore free to this extent, and able to break the contract so soon as it becomes hurtful.

If then a slave cannot convey himself altogether to his master, how can a nation convey itself altogether to its head? If a slave is to judge whether his master is fulfilling his contract, is not the nation to judge whether its head is fulfilling his contract?

Thus we are compelled to retrace our steps, and when we consider the meaning of this collective nation we shall inquire whether some contract, a tacit contract at the least, is not required to make a nation, a contract anterior to that which we are assuming.

Since the nation was a nation before it chose a king, what made it a nation, except the social contract? Therefore the social contract is the foundation of all civil society, and it is in the nature of this contract that we must seek the nature of the society formed by it.

We will inquire into the meaning of this contract; may it not be fairly well expressed in this formula? As an individual every one of us contributes his goods, his person, his life, to the common stock, under the supreme direction of the general will; while as a body we receive each member as an indivisible part of the whole.

Assuming this, in order to define the terms we require, we shall observe that, instead of the individual person of each contracting party, this deed of association produces a moral and collective body, consisting of as many members as there are votes in the Assembly. This public personality is usually called the *body politic*, which is called by its members the *State* when it is passive, and the *Sovereign* when it is active, and a *Power* when compared with its equals. With regard to the members themselves, collectively they are known as the *nation*, and individually as *citizens* as members of the *city* or partakers in the sovereign power, and *subjects* as obedient to the same authority.

We shall note that this contract of association includes a mutual pledge on the part of the public and the individual; and that each individual, entering, so to speak, into a contract with himself, finds himself in a twofold capacity, *i.e.*, as a member of the sovereign with regard to others, as member of the state with regard to the sovereign.

We shall also note that while no one is bound by any engagement to which he was not himself a party, the general deliberation which may be binding on all the subjects with regard to the sovereign, because of the two different relations under which each of them is envisaged, cannot be binding on the state with regard to itself. Hence we see that there is not, and cannot be, any other fundamental law, properly so called, except the social contract only. This does not mean that the body politic cannot, in certain respects, pledge itself to others; for in regard to the foreigner, it then becomes a simple creature, an individual.

Thus the two contracting parties, *i.e.*, each individual and the public, have no common superior to decide their differences; so we will inquire if each of them remains free to break the contract at will, that is to repudiate it on his side as soon as he considers it hurtful.

To clear up this difficulty, we shall observe that, according to the social pact, the sovereign power is only able to act through the common, general will; so its decrees can only have a general or common aim; hence it follows that a private individual cannot be directly injured by the sovereign, unless all are injured, which is impossible, for that would be to want to harm oneself. Thus the social contract has no need of any warrant but the general power, for it can only be broken by individuals, and they are not therefore freed from their engagement, but punished for having broken it.

To decide all such questions rightly, we must always bear in mind that the nature of the social pact is private and peculiar to itself, in that the nation only contracts with itself, *i.e.*, the people as a whole as sovereign, with the individuals as subjects; this condition is essential to the construction and working of the political machine, it alone makes pledges lawful, reasonable, and secure, without which it would be absurd, tyrannical, and liable to the grossest abuse.

Individuals having only submitted themselves to the sovereign, and the sovereign power being only the general will, we shall see that every man in obeying the sovereign only obeys himself, and how much freer are we under the social pact than in the state of nature.

Having compared natural and civil liberty with regard to persons, we will compare them as to property, the rights of ownership and the rights of sovereignty, the private and the common domain. If the sovereign power rests upon the right of ownership, there is no right more worthy of respect; it is inviolable and sacred for the sovereign power, so long as it remains a private individual right; as soon as it is viewed as common to all the citizens, it is subject to the common will, and this will may destroy it. Thus the sovereign has no right to touch the property of one or many; but he may lawfully take possession of the property of all, as was done in Sparta in the time of Lycurgus; while the abolition of debts by Solon was an unlawful deed.

Since nothing is binding on the subjects except the general will, let us inquire how this will is made manifest, by what signs we may recognise it with certainty, what is a law, and what are the true characters of the law? This is quite a fresh subject; we have still to define the term law.

As soon as the nation considers one or more of its members, the nation is divided. A relation is established between the whole and its part which makes of them two separate entities, of which the part is one, and the whole, minus that part, is the other. But the whole minus the part is not the whole; as long as this relation exists, there is no longer a whole, but two unequal parts.

On the other hand, if the whole nation makes a law for the whole nation, it is only considering itself; and if a relation is set up, it is between the whole community regarded from one point of view, and the whole community regarded from another point of view, without any division of that whole. Then the object of the statute is general, and the will which makes that statute is general too. Let us see if there is any other kind of decree which may bear the name of law.

If the sovereign can only speak through laws, and if the law can never have any but a general purpose, concerning all the members of the state, it follows that the sovereign never has the power to make any law with regard to particular cases; and yet it is necessary for the preservation of the state that particular cases should also be dealt with; let us see how this can be done.

The decrees of the sovereign can only be decrees of the general will, that is laws; there must also be determining decrees, decrees of power or government, for the execution of those laws; and these, on the other hand, can only have particular aims. Thus the decrees by which the sovereign decides that a chief shall be elected is a law; the decree by which that chief is elected, in pursuance of the law, is only a decree of government.

This is a third relation in which the assembled people may be considered, i.e., as magistrates or executors of the law which it has passed in its capacity as sovereign.[2]

We will now inquire whether it is possible for the nation to deprive itself of its right of sovereignty, to bestow it on one or more persons; for the decree of election not being a law, and the people in this decree not being themselves sovereign, we do not see how they can transfer a right which they do not possess.

The essence of sovereignty consisting in the general will, it is equally hard to see how we can be certain that an individual will shall always be in agreement with the general will. We should rather assume that it will often be opposed to it; for individual interest always tends to privileges, while the common interest always tends to equality, and if such an agreement were possible, no sovereign right could exist, unless the agreement were either necessary or indestructible.

We will inquire if, without violating the social pact, the heads of the nation, under whatever name they are chosen, can ever be more than the officers of the people, entrusted by them with the duty of carrying the law into execution. Are not these chiefs themselves accountable for their administration, and are not they themselves subject to the laws which it is their business to see carried out?

If the nation cannot alienate its supreme right, can it entrust it to others for a time? Cannot it give itself a master, cannot it find representatives? This is an important question and deserves discussion.

If the nation can have neither sovereign nor representatives we will inquire how it can pass its own laws; must there be many laws; must they be often altered; is it easy for a great nation to be its own lawgiver?

Was not the Roman people a great nation?

Is it a good thing that there should be great nations?

It follows from considerations already established that there is an intermediate body in the state between subjects and sovereign; and this intermediate body, consisting of one or more members, is entrusted with the public administration, the carrying out of the laws, and the maintenance of civil and political liberty.

The members of this body are called *magistrates* or *kings*, that is to say, rulers. This body, as a whole, considered in relation to its members, is called the *prince*, and considered in its actions it is called the *government*.

If we consider the action of the whole body upon itself, that is to say, the relation of the whole to the whole, of the sovereign to the state, we can compare this relation to that of the extremes in a proportion of which the government is the middle term. The magistrate receives from the sovereign the commands which he gives to the nation, and when it is reckoned up his product or his power is in the same degree as the product or power of the citizens who are subjects on one side of the proportion and sovereigns on the other. None of the three terms can be varied without at once destroying this proportion. If the sovereign tries to govern, and if the prince wants to make the laws, or if the subject refuses to obey them, disorder takes the place of order, and the state falls to pieces under despotism or anarchy.

Let us suppose that this state consists of ten thousand citizens. The sovereign can only be considered collectively and as a body, but each individual, as a subject, has his private and independent existence. Thus the sovereign is as ten thousand to one; that is to say, every member of the state has, as his own share, only one ten-thousandth part of the sovereign power, although he is subject to the whole. Let the nation be composed of one hundred thousand men, the position of the subjects is unchanged, and each continues to bear the whole weight of the laws, while his vote, reduced to the one hundred-thousandth part, has ten times less influence in the making of the laws. Thus the subject being always one, the sovereign is relatively greater as the number of the citizens is increased. Hence it follows that the larger the state the less liberty.

Now the greater the disproportion between private wishes and the general will, i.e., between manners and laws, the greater must be the power of repression. On the other side, the greatness of the state gives the depositaries of public authority greater temptations and additional means of abusing that authority, so that the more power is required by the government to control the people, the more power should there be in the sovereign to control the government.

From this twofold relation it follows that the continued proportion between the sovereign, the prince, and the people is not an arbitrary idea, but a consequence of the nature of the state. Moreover, it follows that one of the extremes, *i.e.*, the nation, being constant, every time the double ratio increases or decreases, the simple ratio increases or diminishes in its turn; which cannot be unless the middle term is as often changed. From this we may conclude that there is no single absolute form of government, but there must be as many different forms of government as there are states of different size.

If the greater the numbers of the nation the less the ratio between its manners and its laws, by a fairly clear analogy, we may also say, the more numerous the magistrates, the weaker the government.

To make this principle clearer we will distinguish three essentially different wills in the person of each magistrate; first, his own will as an individual, which looks to his own advantage only; secondly, the common will of the magistrates, which is concerned only with the advantage of the prince, a will which may be called corporate, and one which is general in relation to the government and particular in relation to the state of which the government forms part; thirdly, the will of the people, or the sovereign will, which is general, as much in relation to the state viewed as the whole as in relation to the government viewed as a part of the whole. In a perfect legislature the private individual will should be almost nothing; the corporate will belonging to the government should be quite subordinate, and therefore the general and sovereign will is the master of all the others. On the other hand, in the natural order, these different wills become more and more active in proportion as they become centralised; the general will is always weak, the corporate will takes the second place, the individual will is preferred to all; so that every one is himself first, then a magistrate, and then a citizen; a series just the opposite of that required by the social order.

Having laid down this principle, let us assume that the government is in the hands of one man. In this case the individual and the corporate will are absolutely one, and therefore this will has reached the greatest possible degree of intensity. Now the use of power depends on the degree of this intensity, and as the absolute power of the government is always that of the people, and therefore invariable, it follows that the rule of one man is the most active form of government.

If, on the other hand, we unite the government with the supreme power, and make the prince the sovereign and the citizens so many magistrates, then the corporate will is completely lost in the general will, and will have no more activity than the general will, and it will leave the individual will in full vigour. Thus the government, though its absolute force is constant, will have the minimum of activity.

These rules are incontestable in themselves, and other considerations only serve to confirm them. For example, we see the magistrates as a body far more active than the citizens as a body, so that the individual will always counts for more. For each magistrate usually has charge of some particular duty of government; while each citizen, in himself, has no particular duty of sovereignty. Moreover, the greater the state the greater its real power, although its power does not increase because of the increase in territory; but the state remaining unchanged, the magistrates are multiplied in vain, the government acquires no further real strength, because it is the depositary of that of the state, which I have assumed to be constant. Thus, this plurality of magistrates decreases the activity of the government without increasing its power.

Having found that the power of the government is relaxed in proportion as the number of magistrates is multiplied, and that the more numerous the people, the more the controlling power must be increased, we shall infer that the ratio between the magistrates and the government should be inverse to that between subjects and sovereign, that is to say, that the greater the state, the smaller the government, and that in like manner the number of chiefs should be diminished because of the increased numbers of the people.

In order to make this diversity of forms clearer, and to assign them their different names, we shall observe in the first place that the sovereign may entrust the care of the government to the whole nation or to the greater part of the nation, so that there are more citizen magistrates than private citizens. This form of government is called *Democracy*.

Or the sovereign may restrict the government in the hands of a lesser number, so that there are more plain citizens than magistrates; and this form of government is called *Aristocracy*.

Finally, the sovereign may concentrate the whole government in the hands of one man. This is the third and commonest form of government, and is called *Monarchy* or royal government.

We shall observe that all these forms, or the first and second at least, may be less or more, and that within tolerably wide limits. For the democracy may include the whole nation, or may be confined to one half of it. The aristocracy, in its turn, may shrink from the half of the nation to the smallest number. Even royalty may be shared, either between father and son, between two brothers, or in some other fashion. There were always two kings in Sparta, and in the Roman empire there were as many as eight emperors at once, and yet it cannot be said that the empire was divided. There is a point where each form of government blends with the next; and under the three specific forms there may be really as many forms of government as there are citizens in the state.

Nor is this all. In certain respects each of these governments is capable of subdivision into different parts, each administered in one of these three ways. From these forms in combination there may arise a multitude of mixed forms, since each may be multiplied by all the simple forms.

In all ages there have been great disputes as to which is the best form of government, and people have failed to consider that each is the best in some cases and the worst in others. For ourselves, if the number of magistrates[3] in the various states is to be in inverse ratio to the number of the citizens, we infer that generally a democratic government is adapted to small states, an aristocratic government to those of moderate size, and a monarchy to large states. [...]

Notes

1   If they had such a common master, he would be no other than the sovereign, and then the right of slavery resting on the right of sovereignty would not be its origin.

2   These problems and theorems are mostly taken from the *Treatise on the Social Contract*, itself a summary of a larger work, undertaken without due consideration of my own powers, and long since abandoned.

3   You will remember that I mean, in this context, the supreme magistrates or heads of the nation, the others being only their deputies in this or that respect.

35

The Social Contract

Civil Religion

At first men had no kings save the gods, and no government save theocracy. They reasoned like Caligula, and, at that period, reasoned aright. It takes a long time for feeling so to change that men can make up their minds to take their equals as masters, in the hope that they will profit by doing so.

From the mere fact that God was set over every political society, it followed that there were as many gods as peoples. Two peoples that were strangers the one to the other, and almost always enemies, could not long recognize the same master: two armies giving battle could not obey the same leader. National divisions thus led to polytheism, and this in turn gave rise to theological and civil intolerance, which, as we shall see hereafter, are by nature the same.

The fancy the Greeks had for rediscovering their gods among the barbarians arose from the way they had of regarding themselves as the natural Sovereigns of such peoples. But there is nothing so absurd as the erudition which in our days identifies and confuses gods of different nations. As if Moloch, Saturn, and Chronos could be the same god! As if the Phoenician Baal, the Greek Zeus, and the Latin Jupiter could be the same! As if there could still be anything common to imaginary beings with different names!

The Social Contract (1762). From *The Social Contract and Discourses*, tr. G. D. H. Cole, rev. J. H. Brumfitt and John C. Hall (London: J.M. Dent & Sons, Ltd., 1973). Selection: Bk 4, ch. 8, "Civil Religion," pp. 298–308.

If it is asked how in pagan times, where each State had its cult and its gods, there were no wars of religion, I answer that it was precisely because each State, having its own cult as well as its own government, made no distinction between its gods and its laws. Political war was also theological; the provinces of the gods were, so to speak, fixed by the boundaries of nations. The god of one people had no right over another. The gods of the pagans were not jealous gods; they shared among themselves the empire of the world: even Moses and the Hebrews sometimes lent themselves to this view by speaking of the God of Israel. It is true, they regarded as powerless the gods of the Canaanites, a proscribed people condemned to destruction, whose place they were to take; but remember how they spoke of the divisions of the neighbouring peoples they were forbidden to attack! "Is not the possession of what belongs to your god Chamos lawfully your due?" said Jephthah to the Ammonites. "We have the same title to the lands our conquering God has made his own."[1] Here, I think, there is a recognition that the rights of Chamos and those of the God of Israel are of the same nature.

But when the Jews, being subject to the kings of Babylon, and, subsequently, to those of Syria, still obstinately refused to recognize any god save their own, their refusal was regarded as rebellion against their conqueror, and drew down on them the persecutions we read of in their history, which are without parallel till the coming of Christianity.[2]

Every religion, therefore, being attached solely to the laws of the State which prescribed it, there was no way of converting a people except by enslaving it, and there could be no missionaries save conquerors. The obligation to change cults being the law to which the vanquished yielded, it was necessary to be victorious before suggesting such a change. So far from men fighting for the gods, the gods, as in Homer, fought for men; each asked his god for victory, and repaid him with new altars. The Romans, before taking a city, summoned its gods to quit it; and, in leaving the Tarentines their outraged gods, they regarded them as subject to their own and compelled to do them homage. They left the vanquished their gods as they left them their laws. A wreath to the Jupiter of the Capitol was often the only tribute they imposed.

Finally, when, along with their empire, the Romans had spread their cult and their gods, and had themselves often adopted those of the vanquished, by granting to both alike the rights of the city, the peoples of that vast empire insensibly found themselves with multitudes of gods and cults, everywhere almost the same; and thus paganism throughout the known world finally came to be one and the same religion.

It was in these circumstances that Jesus came to set up on earth a spiritual kingdom, which, by separating the theological from the political system, made the State no longer one, and brought about the internal divisions which have never ceased to trouble Christian peoples. As the new idea of a kingdom of the other world could never have occurred to pagans, they always looked on the Christians as really rebels, who, while feigning to submit, were only waiting for the chance to make themselves independent and their masters, and to usurp by guile the authority they pretended in their weakness to respect. This was the cause of the persecutions.

What the pagans had feared took place. Then everything changed its aspect: the humble Christians changed their language, and soon this so-called kingdom of the other world turned, under a visible leader, into the most violent of earthly despotisms.

However, as there have always been a prince and civil laws, this double power and conflict of jurisdiction have made all good polity impossible in Christian States; and men have never succeeded in finding out whether they were bound to obey the master or the priest.

Several peoples, however, even in Europe and its neighbourhood, have desired without success to preserve or restore the old system: but the spirit of Christianity has everywhere prevailed. The sacred cult has always remained or again become independent of the Sovereign, and there has been no necessary link between it and the body of the State. Mahomet held very sane views, and linked his political system well together; and, as long as the form of his government continued under the caliphs who succeeded him, that government was indeed one, and so far good. But the Arabs, having grown prosperous, lettered, civilized, slack, and cowardly, were conquered by barbarians: the division between the two powers began again; and, although it is less apparent among the Mahometans than among the Christians, it none the less exists, especially in the sect of Ali, and there are States, such as Persia, where it is continually making itself felt.

Among us, the Kings of England have made themselves heads of the Church, and the Czars have done the same: but this title has made them less its masters than its ministers; they have gained not so much the right to change it, as the power to maintain it: they are not its legislators, but only its princes. Wherever the clergy is a corporate body,[3] it is master and legislator in its own country. There are thus two powers, two Sovereigns, in England and in Russia, as well as elsewhere.

Of all Christian writers, the philosopher Hobbes alone has seen the evil and how to remedy it, and has dared to propose the reunion of the two heads of the eagle, and the restoration throughout of political unity, without which no State or government will ever be rightly constituted. But he must have seen that the masterful spirit of Christianity was incompatible with his system, and that the priestly interest would always be stronger than that of the State. It is not so much what is false and terrible in his political theory, as what is just and true, that has drawn hatred on it.[4]

I believe that if the study of history were developed from this point of view, it would be easy to refute the contrary opinions of Bayle and Warburton, one of whom holds that religion can be of no use to the body politic, while the other, on the contrary, maintains that Christianity is its strongest support. We should demonstrate to the former that no State has ever been founded without a religious basis, and to the latter, that the law of Christianity at bottom does more harm by weakening than good by strengthening the constitution of the State. To make myself understood, I have only to make a little more exact the too vague ideas of religion as relating to this subject.

Religion, considered in relation to society, which is either general or particular, may also be divided into two kinds: the religion of man, and that of the citizen. The first, which has neither temples, nor altars, nor rites, and is confined to the purely internal cult of the supreme God and the eternal obligations of morality, is the religion of the Gospel pure and simple, the true theism, what may be called natural divine right or law. The other, which is codified in a single country, gives it its gods, its own tutelary patrons; it has its dogmas, its rites and its external cult prescribed by law; outside the single nation that follows it, all the world is in its sight infidel, foreign, and barbarous; the duties and rights of man extend for it only as far as its own altars. Of this kind were all the religions of early peoples, which we may define as civil or positive divine right of law.

There is a third sort of religion of a more singular kind, which gives men two codes of legislation, two rulers, and two countries, renders them subject to contradictory duties, and makes it impossible for them to be faithful both to religion and to citizenship. Such are the religions of the Lamas and of the Japanese, and such is Roman Christianity, which may be called the religion of the priest. It leads to a sort of mixed and anti-social code which has no name.

In their political aspect, all these three kinds of religion have their defects. The third is so clearly bad, that it is waste of time to stop to prove it such. All that destroys social unity is worthless; all institutions that set man in contradiction to himself are worthless.

The second is good in that it unites the divine cult with love of the laws, and, making country the object of the citizens' adoration, teaches them the service done to the State is service done to its tutelary god. It is a form of theocracy, in which there can be no pontiff save the prince, and no priests save the magistrates. To die for one's country then becomes martyrdom; violation of its laws, impiety; and to subject one who is guilty to public execration is to condemn him to the anger of the gods: *Sacer estod.*

On the other hand, it is bad in that, being founded on lies and error, it deceives men, makes them credulous and superstitious, and drowns the true cult of the Divinity in empty ceremonial. It is bad, again, when it becomes tyrannous and exclusive, and makes a people bloodthirsty and intolerant, so that it breathes fire and slaughter, and regards as a sacred act the killing of every one who does not believe in its gods. The result is to place such a people in a natural state of war with all others, so that its security is deeply endangered.

There remains therefore the religion of man or Christianity – not the Christianity of today, but that of the Gospel, which is entirely different. By means of this holy, sublime, and real religion all men, being children of one God, recognize one another as brothers, and the society that unites them is not dissolved even at death.

But this religion, having no particular relation to the body politic, leaves the laws in possession of the force they have in themselves without making any addition to it; and thus one of the great bonds that unite society considered in severalty fails to operate. Nay, more, so far from binding the hearts of the citizens to the State, it has the effect of taking them away from all earthly things. I know of nothing more contrary to the social spirit.

We are told that a people of true Christians would form the most perfect society imaginable. I see in this supposition only one great difficulty: that a society of true Christians would not be a society of men.

I say further that such a society, with all its perfection, would be neither the strongest nor the most lasting: the very fact that it was perfect would rob it of its bond of union; the flaw that would destroy it would lie in its very perfection.

Every one would do his duty; the people would be law-abiding, the rulers just and temperate; the magistrates upright and incorruptible; the soldiers would scorn death; there would be neither vanity nor luxury. So far, so good; but let us hear more.

Christianity as a religion is entirely spiritual, occupied solely with heavenly things; the country of the Christian is not of this world. He does his duty, indeed, but does it with profound indifference to the good or ill success of his cares. Provided he has nothing to reproach himself with, it matters little to him whether things go well or ill here on earth. If the State is prosperous, he hardly dares to share in the public happiness, for fear he may grow proud of his country's glory; if the State is languishing, he blesses the hand of God that is hard upon His people.

For the State to be peaceable and for harmony to be maintained, all the citizens without exception would have to be good Christians; if by ill hap there should be a single self-seeker or hypocrite, a Catiline or a Cromwell, for instance, he would certainly get the better of his pious compatriots. Christian charity does not readily allow a man to think hardly of his neighbours. As soon as, by some trick, he has discovered the art of imposing on them and getting hold of a share in the public authority, you have a man established in dignity; it is the will of God that he be respected: very soon you have a power; it is God's will that it be obeyed: and if the power is abused by him who wields it, it is the scourge wherewith God punishes His children. There would be scruples about driving out the usurper: public tranquillity would have to be disturbed, violence would have to be employed, and blood spilt; all this accords ill with Christian meekness; and after all, in this vale of sorrows, what does it matter whether we are free men or serfs? The essential thing is to get to heaven, and resignation is only an additional means of doing so.

If war breaks out with another State, the citizens march readily out to battle; not one of them thinks of flight; they do their duty, but they have no passion for victory; they know better how to die than how to conquer. What does it matter whether they win or lose? Does not providence know better than they what is meet for them? Only think to what account a proud, impetuous, and passionate enemy could turn their stoicism! Set over against them those generous peoples who were devoured by ardent love of glory and of their country, imagine your Christian republic face to face with Sparta or Rome: the pious Christians will be beaten, crushed, and destroyed, before they know where they are, or will owe their safety only to the contempt their enemy will conceive for them. It was to my mind a fine oath that was taken by the soldiers of Fabius, who swore, not to conquer or die, but to come back victorious – and kept their oath. Christians would never have taken such an oath; they would have looked on it as tempting God.

But I am mistaken in speaking of a Christian republic; the terms are mutually exclusive. Christianity preaches only servitude and dependence. Its spirit is so favourable to tyranny that it always profits by such a regime. True Christians are made to be slaves, and they know it and do not much mind: this short life counts for too little in their eyes.

I shall be told that Christian troops are excellent. I deny it. Show me an instance. For my part, I know of no Christian troops. I shall be told of the Crusades. Without disputing the valour of the Crusaders, I answer that, so far from being Christians, they were the priests' soldiery, citizens of the Church. They fought for their spiritual country, which the Church had, somehow or other, made

temporal. Well understood, this goes back to paganism: as the Gospel sets up no national religion, a holy war is impossible among Christians.

Under the pagan emperors, the Christian soldiers were brave; every Christian writer affirms it, and I believe it: it was a case of honourable emulation of the pagan troops. As soon as the emperors were Christian, this emulation no longer existed, and, when the Cross had driven out the eagle, Roman valour wholly disappeared.

But, setting aside political considerations, let us come back to what is right, and settle our principles on this important point. The right which the social compact gives the Sovereign over the subjects does not, we have seen, exceed the limits of public expediency.[5] The subjects then owe the Sovereign an account of their opinions only to such an extent as they matter to the community. Now, it matters very much to the community that each citizen should have a religion. That will make him love his duty; but the dogmas of that religion concern the State and its members only so far as they have reference to morality and to the duties which he who professes them is bound to do to others. Each man may have, over and above, what opinions he pleases, without its being the Sovereign's business to take cognizance of them; for, as the Sovereign has no authority in the other world, whatever the lot of its subjects may be in the life to come, that is not its business, provided they are good citizens in this life.

There is therefore a purely civil profession of faith of which the Sovereign should fix the articles, not exactly as religious dogmas, but as social sentiments without which a man cannot be a good citizen or a faithful subject.[6] While it can compel no one to believe them, it can banish from the State whoever does not believe them – it can banish him, not for impiety, but as an anti-social being, incapable of truly loving the laws and justice, and of sacrificing, at need, his life to his duty. If any one, after publicly recognizing these dogmas, behaves as if he does not believe them, let him be punished by death: he has committed the worst of all crimes, that of lying before the law.

The dogmas of civil religion ought to be few, simple, and exactly worded, without explanation or commentary. The existence of a mighty, intelligent, and beneficent Divinity, possessed of foresight and providence, the life to come, the happiness of the just, the punishment of the wicked, the sanctity of the social contract and the laws: these are its positive dogmas. Its negative dogmas I confine to one, intolerance, which is a part of the cults we have rejected.

Those who distinguish civil from theological intolerance are, to my mind, mistaken. The two forms are inseparable. It is impossible to live at peace with those we regard as damned; to love them would be to hate God who punishes them: we positively must either reclaim or torment them. Wherever theological intolerance is admitted, it must inevitably have some civil effect;[7] and as soon as it has such an effect, the Sovereign is no longer Sovereign even in the temporal sphere: thenceforth priests are the real masters, and kings only their ministers.

Now that there is and can be no longer an exclusive national religion, tolerance should be given to all religions that tolerate others, so long as their dogmas contain nothing contrary to the duties of citizenship. But whoever dares to say: "Outside the Church is no salvation," ought to be driven from the State, unless the State is the Church, and the prince the pontiff. Such a dogma is good only in a theocratic government; in any other, it is fatal. The reason for which Henry IV is said to have embraced the Roman religion ought to make every honest man leave it, and still more any prince who knows how to reason.

Notes

1 "Nonne ea quae possidet Chamos deus tuus, tibi jure debentur?" (Judges xi. 24). Such is the text in the Vulgate. Father de Carrières translates: "Do you not regard yourselves as having a right to what your god possesses?" I do not know the force of the Hebrew text: but I perceive that, in the Vulgate, Jephthah positively recognizes the right of the god Chamos, and that the French translator weakened this admission by inserting an "according to you", which is not in the Latin.

2 It is quite clear that the Phocian war, which was called "the Sacred War", was not a war of religion. Its object was the punishment of acts of sacrilege, and not the conquest of unbelievers.

3 It should be noted that the clergy find their bond of union not so much in formal assemblies, as in the communion of Churches. Communion and excommunication are the social compact of the clergy, a compact which will always make them masters of peoples and kings. All priests who communicate together are fellow citizens, even if they come from opposite ends of the earth. This invention is a masterpiece of statesmanship: there is nothing like it among pagan priests; who have therefore never formed a clerical corporate body.

4 See, for instance, in a letter from Grotius to his brother (April 11, 1643), what that learned man found to praise and to blame in the *De Cive*. It is true that, with a bent for indulgence, he seems to pardon the writer the good for the sake of the bad; but all men are not so forgiving.

5 "In the republic", says the Marquis d'Argenson, "each man is perfectly free in what does not harm others." This is the invariable limitation, which it is impossible to define more exactly. I have not been able to deny myself the pleasure of occasionally quoting from this manuscript, though it is unknown to the public, in order to do honour to the memory of a good and illustrious man, who had kept even in the Ministry the heart of a good citizen, and views on the government of his country that were sane and right.

6 Caesar, pleading for Catiline, tried to establish the dogma that the soul is mortal: Cato and Cicero, in refutation, did not waste time in philosophizing. They were content to show that Caesar spoke like a bad citizen, and brought forward a doctrine that would have a bad effect on the State. This, in fact, and not a problem of theology, was what the Roman senate had to judge.

7 Marriage, for instance, being a civil contract, has civil effects without which society cannot even subsist. Suppose a body of clergy should claim the sole right of permitting this act, a right which every intolerant religion must of necessity claim, is it not clear that in establishing the authority of the Church in this respect, it will be destroying that of the prince, who will have thenceforth only as many subjects as the clergy choose to allow him? Being in a position to marry or not to marry people, according to their acceptance of such and such a doctrine, their admission or rejection of such and such a formula, their greater or less piety, the Church alone, by the exercise of prudence and firmness, will dispose of all inheritances, offices, and citizens, and even of the State itself, which could not subsist if it were composed entirely of bastards. But, I shall be told, there will be appeals on the ground of abuse, summonses, and decrees; the temporalities will be seized. How sad! The clergy, however little, I will not say courage, but sense it has, will take no notice and go its way; it will quietly allow appeals, summonses, decrees, and seizures, and, in the end, will remain the master. It is not, I think, a great sacrifice to give up a part, when one is sure of securing all.

PART XI

Immanuel Kant (1724–1804)

Introduction

The opening selection in this chapter is from a virtually unknown work entitled *What Real Progress Has Metaphysics Made in Germany since the Time of Leibniz and Wolff?* (1804). In our excerpt, commencing "The History of Transcendental Philosophy in Modern Times," Kant presents a retrospective summary of the central arguments in the *First Critique*, and the major considerations that led to them. This is followed by the introduction to *The Metaphysics of Morals* (1797). The introduction is especially useful for its precise definitions of key concepts such as *duty* and *person*, as well as its lucid explanation of the categorical imperative. Our next selection is drawn from Kant's lectures on logic. These lectures, which were compiled, edited, and published in 1800 by Gottlob Benjamin Jäsche, formed the basis for the second part of Kant's *First Critique*. In this excerpt, Kant presents a clear statement of the proper scope and method of philosophy. For

Kant's political thought we turn next to *On the Common Saying: "This May be True in Theory, but It Does not Apply in Practice"* (1793). In the second part of this essay, "On the Relationship of Theory to Practice in Political Right," Kant offers a critical response to Hobbes's *De Cive*. Whereas Hobbes claimed that the rights of persons exist only within a state, which confers and protects those rights, Kant argues that the very possibility of a legitimate state presupposes the existence of *a priori* principles such as freedom, equality, and independence. We conclude the chapter with an example of Kant's writing on moral theology. Although much of what is contained in the *Lectures on Philosophical Theology* (1830) was already presented in the *First Critique*, there is material here that is original and valuable for understanding Kant's thought. This is true of the present selection, "The Nature and Certainty of Moral Faith," in which Kant presents a unique version of the moral argument for the existence of God.

36

What Real Progress Has Metaphysics Made in Germany since the Time of Leibniz and Wolff?

The History of Transcendental Philosophy in Modern Times

The *first step* to be taken in this rational investigation is to make the general distinction between analytic and synthetic judgments. Had this distinction been clearly understood during Leibniz's or Wolff's time, we would have found every logic or metaphysics that has since appeared not only to have depended on it but also to have stressed its importance. For the first form of judgment is always a priori and accompanied by the consciousness of its necessity. The second can be empirical, and logic cannot permit specification of the conditions under which a synthetic judgment a priori will occur.

The *second step* consists solely in raising the question: How are synthetic judgments a priori possible? For that there are such is proven by numerous examples drawn from the general science of nature, but principally, from pure mathematics. *Hume* had already performed a service by bringing forth a case – the one concerning the law of causality – that constituted an embarrassment

What Real Progress Has Metaphysics Made in Germany since the Time of Leibniz and Wolff? ("Welches sind die wirklichen Fortschritte, die die Metaphysik seit Leibnizens und Wolffs Zeiten in Deutschland gemacht hat," 1804), tr. Ted Humphrey (New York: Abaris Books, Inc., 1983). Selection: pp. 63–93 [odd numbered pages].

for all metaphysicians. What would have happened if he or any one else had stated the problem in universal form! All metaphysics would have had to have been set to one side until it was solved.

The *third step* is the problem: How is it possible to gain a priori cognition from synthetic judgments? Cognition is a judgment from which arises a concept possessing objective reality, that is, one for which a corresponding object can be given in experience. However, all experience is constituted from (1) an intuition of an object, i.e., an immediate, singular presentation through which an object is given for knowledge, and (2) a concept, i.e., a mediate representation through a characteristic common to several objects, by means of which, therefore, the object is thought. By themselves neither of the kinds of representation constitutes cognition. For there to be a priori synthetic cognition, then, there must be a priori intuitions and a priori concepts, whose possibility must be discussed; after that, their objective reality must be demonstrated by showing that their use is necessary for the possibility of experience.

An intuition that is to be possible a priori can concern only the form under which an object is intuited. For to intuit something a priori means to represent it a priori, before perception – i.e., empirical consciousness – and to make a representation of this object independently of perception. The empirical element of perception – sensation or the impression (*impressio*) – is the matter of intuition, with respect to which intuition would not thus be an a priori representation. An intuition concerned only with form is called pure intuition. And if such be possible, it must be independent of experience.

However, it is not the form of the object as it is constituted in itself, but rather that of the subject – specifically, the kind of representations its senses are capable [of having] – that makes intuition a priori possible. For if this form were taken from objects themselves, we would have had previously to perceive those objects, and we could be conscious of their constitution only in this perception. But that would then be an empirical intuition a priori. We can be satisfied as to whether or not the latter can exist as soon as we take note of whether or not the judgment that attributes this form to objects is necessary; for if not, the judgment is merely empirical.

The form of objects, which is all that can be presented in an intuition a priori, is not based on the constitution of this object in itself but on the natural constitution of a subject capable of representing objects in intuition. And it is only this subjective [element] in the formal constitution of the senses – as the receptivity to sensation in intuiting objects – which a priori makes possible a priori intuition, i.e., intuition preceding all perception. This, and the possibility of a priori synthetic judgments, is easily conceived from the point of view of intuition.

One can know a priori, then, how and under what form the objects of the senses will be intuited, namely, in accordance with the subjective form of sensibility – that is, in accordance with the inherent capacity for receiving sensations that the subject brings with it – and in order to speak precisely, one must not, as a matter of fact, say that the form of objects is represented by us in pure intuition, but that what is represented is merely the formal and subjective condition of sensibility under which we a priori intuit given objects.

That is the special constitution of our (human) intuition insofar as the representation of objects is possible for us simply as sensuous beings. We can, to be sure, think of an immediate (*direkte*) manner of representing an object, one that does not depend on conditions of sensibility and, consequently, that intuits objects through the understanding. However, we do not have a defensible concept of such [a mode of intuiting], even though it is necessary to think of such an understanding in order not to attribute our form of intuition to all beings possessing capacities for knowledge. For it may be that some beings in this world are able to intuit the same objects under another form; it may also be that this form is the same in all beings in this world, and, indeed, necessarily so. But we have just as little insight into this necessity as into the possibility of a supreme understanding, which, free from all reliance on sensibility and the need to use concepts in knowing, knows objects perfectly by means of mere (intellectual) intuition.

Now the *Critique of Pure Reason* proves that the presentations of space and time are precisely such pure intuitions as we require – that they must be in order to provide an a priori basis for all our knowledge of things – and I can confidently refer to it, without being concerned about objections.

Regarding inner sense, I will now remark only that to many the double I in the consciousness of myself – namely, the I of inner sensuous intuition and the I of the thinking subject – seems to presuppose two subjects in a single person.

Now this is the theory: space and time are nothing but subjective forms of our sensible intuition and in no way proper determinations of objects themselves; but for precisely this reason, we can determine our intuitions a priori with a consciousness of the necessity of the judgments that determine them, as, e.g., in geometry. To determine means, however, to judge synthetically.

This theory can be called the doctrine of the ideality of space and time, since it presents them as being absolutely independent of things in themselves, a doctrine that is not merely an hypothesis to clarify the possibility of synthetic knowledge a priori, but one that is rather a demonstrated truth; for without intuition it is absolutely impossible to extend knowledge beyond [the content of] a given concept. And if this extension is to occur a priori, it must be based on a priori intuition, because unless one seeks such an a priori intuition in the formal constitution of the subject, rather than in that of the object, it is impossible. For on the former assumption, all objects of the senses will be represented as in conformity with intuition, and it must thus be possible to know them a priori and as necessarily conforming with the constitution of the subject, while on the latter assumption, a priori synthetic judgments would have to be empirical and contingent, which is self-contradictory.

This [doctrine of the] ideality of space and time is nonetheless at the same time a doctrine of their complete reality in respect to the objects of the senses (both outer and inner) as *appearances*, that is, as intuitions. This is true insofar as the form of appearances depends on the subjective constitution of the senses, whose knowledge, since it is based on a priori principles of pure intuition, provides for a secure and demonstrable science. Therefore, what is subjective, what concerns the properties of sensuous intuition in regard to its material content, namely sensation – for example, bodies in light as colors, in vibration as sounds, in salts as acids, and so on – remains merely subjective and yields no knowledge of objects, and, consequently, what is subjective cannot provide examples of representations in empirical intuition that are valid for everyone, for it contains no data for a priori cognition, as do space and time. In general, then, the subjective element [of sensible intuition] cannot be counted as knowledge of objects.

It has further to be noted that appearance, taken in the transcendental sense, where one says of things that they are appearances (*Phaenomena*), is a concept that means something entirely different from when I say, this thing appears to me in this or that way. Saying the latter merely indicates physical appearance, which can be regarded as [its] appearance (*Apparenz*) or semblance. In the language of experience, the objects of the senses are regarded as things in themselves, for I can only compare them with other objects of the senses thought of as things in themselves – e.g., heaven with all its stars, even though it is merely appearance; and if one says of the starry heaven that it gives the illusion of a vault, the term semblance [denotes] the subjective [element] in the representation of a thing, which can be a reason for falsely judging that it [the thing] is objective.

And so the proposition that all sensuous representations provide knowledge of objects only as appearances is altogether different from the proposition that such representations comprise only the semblance of objects, which the idealist would maintain.

But nothing is as strange or more astounding in the theory that all objects of the senses are mere appearances, than that I, as the object of inner sense, that is, considered as soul, am acquainted with myself only as appearance, not as that which I am as a thing in itself. Yet the representation of time, as mere a priori form of inner intuition underlying all knowledge of myself, permits of no other explanation of the possibility of recognizing that form to be the condition of self-consciousness.

The *subjective* [element] that constitutes the form of sensibility, which a priori underlies all intuition of objects, makes it possible for us to have a priori knowledge of objects as they *appear* to us. We want now to define this expression still more explicitly, since we explain this subjective (element of representation) as the manner of representing how those objects – outer or inner (i.e., ourselves) – affect our senses, and thus we can say that we know these objects only as appearances.

That I am conscious of myself is a thought that already contains a twofold self, the I as subject and the I as object. How it might be possible for the I that I think to be an object (of intuition) for me, one that enables me to distinguish me from myself, is absolutely impossible to explain, even though it is an indubitable fact; it indicates, however, a capacity so highly elevated above sensuous intuition that, as the basis for the possibility of understanding, it has the effect of separating us from all animals, to which we have no reason for ascribing the ability to say I to themselves, and results in an infinity of self-constituted representations and concepts. But a double personality is not meant by this double I. Only the I that I think and intuit is a person; the I that belongs to the object that is intuited by me is, similarly to other objects outside me, a thing.

Absolutely no further knowledge regarding the I in the first sense (the subject of apperception) – the logical I, considered as an a priori representation – is possible, neither with respect to what sort of being it is nor [with regard to] its natural constitution. It is as if the substance were what remains when all of its inhering accidents have been stripped away, but cannot in any way be further known [when stripped of its accidents], because its accidents are precisely that by means of which I can know its nature.

But the I in the second sense (as subject of perception), the psychological I, as empirical consciousness, is capable of [providing] all sorts of cognition, and in regard to it the form of inner sense, time, is the a priori ground underlying all perceptions and their connection, whose apprehension (*apprehensio*) is the way the subject is thereby affected, i.e., in conformity with the condition of time, whereas the sensible I is determined by the intellectual I in the former's reception of the latter into consciousness.

Every inner psychological observation we make serves as a proof and example that this is so; for such observation requires that one can affect inner sense by means of attention – even if doing so involves a certain degree of difficulty (for thoughts, as factual determinations of the capacity for representing, belong to the empirical representation of our state) – so as to gain knowledge of what in the first place inner sense discloses in the intuition of our own selves. This, of course, presents us to ourselves only in the way in which we appear, whereas the logical I, which is indeed the subject as it is in itself in pure consciousness, signifies pure spontaneity, not receptivity. Beyond this no knowledge of the nature of the logical I is possible.

Of A Priori Concepts

When the subjective form of sensibility is applied to objects as their form – and this must occur, given the theory that sensuous objects are appearances – its determination of objects entails a representation that is inseparable from those objects, namely, that of composedness. For we cannot represent a determinate space to ourselves except by drawing it, i.e., by joining one [portion of] space to another, and it is exactly the same for time.

Now the representation of a composedness as such is not a mere intuition, but instead requires the concept of a composition, insofar as it is applied to intuition in space and time. Thus, this concept (together with that of its contrary, simplicity) is not abstracted from intuitions, as one of the partial representations they contain. Rather, it is a fundamental concept, indeed an a priori one. Finally, it is the sole a priori fundamental concept originally in the understanding that is the basis for all concepts of the objects of the senses.

Thus, in understanding there will be as many a priori concepts, under which the objects given by the senses must be subsumed, as there are modes of conscious composition (*Synthesis*), that is, as there are modes of synthetic unity of apperception of the manifold given in intuition.

These concepts are the pure concepts of the understanding that pertain to all objects that may be met with by our senses. They were presented by Aristotle under the name of categories, although mixed with heterogeneous concepts, and by the Scholastics under the name of *predicaments*, with the very same errors. They probably could have been presented in a systematically ordered table if what logic teaches concerning the manifold in the form of judgments had previously been presented with the coherence of a system.

Understanding manifests its power solely in judgments, which are nothing but the unity of consciousness in the relation of concepts in general, regardless of whether this unity is analytic or synthetic. Now understanding's pure concepts of the objects given in intuition are the same logical functions, but only insofar as they represent the synthetic unity of apperception a priori with what is given in a manifold in an intuition in general. Thus, the table of categories could have been completely sketched out parallel to the [table of] logical [judgments]. But this did not happen until the appearance of the *Critique of Pure Reason*.

But it is well to note that these categories, or, as they are otherwise known, *predicaments*, do not presuppose any determinate mode of intuition (as, for instance, the sole one possible for us humans), like space and time, that is sensible. They are forms of thought for the concept of an object of intuition in general, no matter what kind it may be, even if it is non-sensible, of which we can specifically form no concept. For by means of pure understanding we must always constitute a concept of an object about which we want to judge something a priori, even if we later find that it is transcendent and that no objective reality can be provided it. In itself, the category does not depend on the forms of sensibility, space and time, but may have other forms of which we simply cannot think as its foundation, if these [forms] pertain only to what is subjective that a priori precedes all cognition and makes synthetic a priori judgments possible.

Additionally, the predicaments belong among the categories as original concepts of the understanding; thus, they are derivative and are either pure concepts of the understanding or sensibly conditioned a priori concepts. The former are represented by existence as quantity, that is, duration, or as alteration, that is, as existence with opposing determinations; the latter sort are exemplified by the concept of motion as change of location in space, which likewise can be completely enumerated and systematically presented in a table.

Transcendental philosophy – that is, the doctrine of all a priori knowledge in general, which the *Critique of Pure Reason* is, and whose elements have now been completely laid out – has as its purpose the foundation of a metaphysics, which, as the ultimate end of pure reason, in turn has as its objective the extension of reason beyond the boundaries of the sensible to the field of the super-sensible. This is a transition that – if it is not to be a dangerous leap, inasmuch as it does not involve a continuous development in the same order of principles – requires careful consideration that checks progress at the boundaries of both realms.

From this there follows the division of the stages of pure reason into the doctrine of scientific knowledge, progress – the doctrine of doubt, as stagnation – and the doctrine of wisdom, as a transition to the ultimate end of metaphysics. The first contains a theoretical-dogmatic doctrine, the second a skeptical discipline, and the third a practical-dogmatic doctrine.

The Extent of Pure Reason's Theoretical-Dogmatic Use

The content of this section is the proposition that the extent of pure reason's theoretical knowledge reaches only to objects of the senses.

This proposition, insofar as it is an exponible judgment, contains two propositions:

(1) As a capacity for a priori cognition of things, reason extends to objects of the senses.
(2) In its theoretical use, reason is certainly capable of concepts, but not of having theoretical cognition of what cannot be an object of the senses.

An explanation of how a priori cognition of the objects of the senses is possible belongs to the proof of the first proposition, for without an explanation we would not be genuinely certain whether the judgments concerning those objects would in fact be cognition; however, as regards the property [by virtue of which] they are a priori judgments, it announces itself through consciousness of their necessity.

For a representation to be cognition (here I always mean theoretical cognition), a concept must be combined in the same representation with an intuition of an object so that the former is represented as containing the latter. Now if a concept is taken as a sensible representation, that is, as empirical, it contains as a characteristic, i.e., as a partial representation, something already conceived in sensible intuition, and is distinguished from the intuition of the senses only by its logical form, namely, its general validity, e.g., the concept of a four footed animal in the representation of a horse.

However, if the concept is a category, a pure concept of the understanding, it is independent of all intuition; yet a concept must be given an intuition if it is to be employed in cognition. And if this cognition is to be a priori, it must be given a pure intuition, and, of course, this must conform to the synthetic unity of apperception of the manifold of intuition that is thought through the categories; that is, the power of representation must give an a priori schema to the pure concept of the understanding, without which it can have no object and cannot serve as cognition.

Now because all the cognition of which man is capable is sensible, and because the a priori intuition of either space or time – both of which represent objects only as objects of sense, not as things in general – our theoretical cognition in general is limited to objects of the senses, even though it may be cognition a priori. To be sure, cognition can proceed dogmatically within these boundaries by using laws, as the essence of objects of sense, that it prescribes for nature a priori. However, it can never extend itself theoretically beyond this boundary.

Cognition of the objects of the senses as such, that is, through those empirical representations which one is conscious of (through connected perceptions), is experience. Accordingly, our theoretical cognition never transcends the field of experience. Now since all theoretical cognition must agree with experience, and since this agreement is possible only in one or another way, that is, either experience is the foundation of our cognition, or cognition is the foundation of experience, then, if there is synthetic cognition a priori, there is no alternative but that it must contain the a priori conditions of the possibility of experience in general. But then it also contains the conditions of the possibility of objects of experience in general, for only through experience can objects of experience be cognizable objects for us. The a priori principles in accordance with which any experience is possible are the forms of objects – space, time, and the categories, which contain a priori the synthetic unity of consciousness, insofar as empirical representations can be subsumed under it.

The highest task of transcendental philosophy is thus [to determine]: how is experience possible?

The principle that all cognition begins only with experience concerns a *quaestio facti* that does not properly belong here, and the fact will be conceded without scruple. But whether it is to be derived from experience alone as its ultimate foundation is a *quaestio iuris*, an affirmative answer to which would introduce an empiricism of transcendental philosophy and a denial of its rationalism.

The first view is self-contradictory. For if all cognition is of empirical origin, then, without prejudice to reflection and its logical principle in conformity to the law of contradiction, which may be grounded a priori in the understanding and whose existence one can always concede, synthetic cognition, which comprises the essence of experience, is merely empirical and is possible only as cognition a posteriori. Transcendental philosophy itself is then a non-entity.

But nevertheless – since propositions that prescribe a priori rules for possible experience, as for example, *All change has a cause*, are strictly universal and necessary, yet for all that it cannot be disputed that they are synthetic – empiricism, which construes all the synthetic unity of our representations in knowledge as mere matters of custom, is totally indefensible. Transcendental philosophy is so firmly rooted in our reason that if one were to represent it as self-negating, another absolutely insoluble problem would arise. [That problem is] from whence comes the coherence and the regularity of sensible objects' existence together, [a coherence and regularity] that makes it possible for understanding to apprend them under universal law and to discover their unity in accordance with principles for which the principle of contradiction alone is not sufficient, since [if it were] rationalism would have inevitably to be invoked?

We find ourselves therefore compelled to seek an a priori principle of experience itself: So the question is, what can serve as one? All representations that constitute an experience can be ascribed to sensibility, excepting only one, namely, composedness as such.

Since composition cannot occur in the senses, but rather we must do it ourselves, it does not belong to sensibility's receptivity, but to understanding's spontaneity, as an a priori concept.

Subjectively considered, space and time are forms of intuition; but in order to make concepts of them as objects of pure intuition (without doing which we could not say anything about them) an a priori concept of composedness, consequently, of a composition (*Synthesis*) of the manifold is required. [Consequently, there must be] synthetic unity of apperception in the connection of this manifold; this unity of consciousness requires different functions to connect elements in the manifold in accordance with the differences in the intuitive representations of the objects in space and time. These are called categories and are a priori concepts of the understanding. To be sure, by themselves, they are not sufficient for *cognition* of an object in general. But still, they are the basis of the cognition of an object given in empirical intuition, which would then be experience. But the empirical element, i.e., that by means of which the existence of an object is represented as given, is called sensation (*sensatio, impressio*), which constitutes the matter of experience and, when connected with consciousness, is called perception. To produce experience as empirical cognition, the form of it – that is, the synthetic unity of apperception of it in the understanding, which is thus thought a priori – must still be added. For this, principles a priori in accord with mere concepts of the understanding are necessary, since we do not perceive space and time themselves directly and yet we must indicate the place of every object of perception in them through concepts. These concepts demonstrate their reality in sensible intuition, and in conjunction with intuition they make *experience* possible according to its form, which is given a priori. This experience is completely certain cognition a posteriori.

But an important doubt arises so far as the certainty of outer experience is concerned, not, to be sure, regarding whether our cognition of objects by means of such experience might perhaps be uncertain; rather, [the doubt is] whether the object that we posit as outside ourselves could not perhaps always be in us and that it would be quite impossible to recognize something as external with certainty. In leaving this question wholly undecided metaphysics would lose nothing of its progress, for, since the perceptions out of which, and the form of intuition in which, we constitute experience according to principles by means of categories may always be in us, whether or not they correspond to something outside us effects no change in the extension of cognition. For we can never have any commerce with objects, but must always stop with our perception, which is always in us.

From this follows the principle of the division of all metaphysics: knowledge of the supersensible, which is the concern of reason's speculative capacity, is not possible (*Noumenorum non datur scientia*).

This much has happened in recent times in transcendental philosophy and must have happened before reason could have taken one step in metaphysics proper, or even one step towards metaphysics. Indeed, it is the only thing that could have happened so long as for its part the Leibnizian-Wolffian philosophy still confidently proceeded on its way in Germany, believing that in addition to the old Aristotelian law of contradiction, it had given philosophy a new compass to guide it, namely, the principle of sufficient reason for the existence of things, as distinguished from their mere possibility according to concepts. The new guide also used the principle of the distinction between obscure, and clear but still confused representations and distinct ones for the distinction between intuition and conceptual knowledge. But with all of this, it [the Leibnizio-Wolffian Philosophy] unknowingly remained only in the field of logic – taking no steps into that of metaphysics, much less conquering any of it – proving that it had no clear knowledge of the distinction between synthetic and analytic judgments.

Now the proposition "Everything has its cause," which goes hand-in-hand with "Everything is an effect," can only belong to logic and permit the difference between judgments that are thought problematically and those supposed to have assertoric validity. It is merely analytic, because if it were to be valid for things, to wit, that all things must be regarded only as the effect of the existence of another, the sufficient reason that was so esteemed could be found nowhere. Refuge from this absurdity is then sought in the proposition that a thing (*ens a se*) does indeed always have a reason for its existence, but [that the] reason [may] be in itself, i.e., that the thing exists as an effect of itself. Here, assuming the absurdity is not apparent, the principle has nothing to do with things, but only judgments, and is only valid for those that are analytic. For example, the proposition, "Every body is divisible" surely has a reason and, indeed, in itself. That is, it can be regarded as a deduction of the predicate from the concept of the subject concept according to the law of contradiction, thus according to the principle of analytic judgments. Thus it is based only on an a priori principle of logic and does not take one step into the field of metaphysics, where the concern at hand is to extend a priori knowledge, [an enterprise] to which analytic judgments contribute nothing. Should the putative metaphysician introduce in addition the equally logical law of [sufficient]

reason to the law of contradiction, he would still not have completely enumerated the modality of judgments, because he would still have to add the law of excluded middle between two contradictory judgments. Then he would have established the logical principles of the possibility, truth or logical actuality, and the necessity of judgments as problematic, assertoric and apodictic judgments, so far as all of these stand under a single principle, that is, the principle of analytic judgments. The neglect of this proves that the metaphysician never got clear about logic, which concerns the completeness of the division.

But so far as the Leibnizian principle of the logical difference between indistinct and distinct representations is concerned, if it maintains that the former kind of representation that we called mere intuition is properly only the confused concept of its object and, consequently, intuition is distinguished from concepts of things only in virtue of the degree of consciousness, not specifically, so that, for example, if one were completely conscious of all the representations contained in the intuition of a body, that would [Leibnizians contend] provide a concept of it as an aggregate of monads. In opposition, the critical philosopher will maintain that a proposition such as "Bodies are constituted of monads" can derive – if we could only see sufficiently acutely (i.e., with complete consciousness of all partial representations) – only from experience and solely by means of an analysis of perception. However, since the existence of these monads together can be represented only in space, the metaphysician of the good old kind can grant the validity of space only as a merely empirical and confused representation of the juxtaposition of the [elements of the] manifold outside one another.

How, then, is he going to be in a position to maintain the proposition that space has three dimensions as an apodictic a priori proposition? He has not been able to show that this must be so from even the clearest consciousness of all partial representations of a body. Rather, at best perception teaches him that it is so. But if he assumes that the existence of three dimensional space is necessary and that it a priori underlies all representations of bodies, how will he explain this necessity, which he cannot reason away? For this form of representation, according to his own contention, is of mere empirical origin, which provides no necessity. If he desires to set aside this demand and assume [the existence of] space with those of its properties as may be constituted by that allegedly confused presentation – then geometry demonstrates to him, and consequently to reason, not by means of concepts, which float in the mind, but by means of the construction of concepts, that space and therefore that which fills it, bodies, can in no way be constituted of simple parts. Although, of course, if we want to make the possibility of the latter comprehensible to ourselves through mere concepts, we begin with particles and proceed from them to the composite, and the simples must then be the basis of this. In this way, we will be forced to confess that intuition (which is the type of representation that space is) and concept are wholly different species of presentation and that the former cannot be changed into the latter merely by analyzing the confusion in its presentation. Precisely the same holds for the representation of time!

How to Provide Objective Reality for Pure Concepts of Understanding and Reason

To represent a pure concept of the understanding as thinkable in an object of possible experience is to provide objective reality for it and to represent it in general. When this cannot be accomplished the concept is *empty*, that is, insufficient for cognition. When objective reality is directly attributed (*directe*) to a concept by an intuition corresponding to it, that is, when the concept is immediately represented, this action is schematism; however, if the concept cannot be represented immediately, but rather only through its consequences (*indirecte*), it can be called the symbolization of the concept. The former occurs with concepts of the sensible; the latter is an aid for concepts of the supersensible, which are thus not represented and cannot be given in any possible experience; and yet they necessarily belong to knowledge, even if it is possible only as practical knowledge.

The symbol of an idea (or a concept of reason) is an analogical representation of an object. That is, its relation to certain consequences is the same as the one that is attributed to the object in itself and its consequences, even though the objects themselves are of wholly different orders, as for example, when I represent to myself certain products of nature, perhaps the organized things, animals and plants, in relation to their cause, and a clock in relation to a man as its maker, because the relation of causality in general as a category is the same in the two cases. But the inner constitution of the subject of this relation remains unknown to me, and thus only the former can be represented, never the latter.

In this way, although I can have no properly theoretical cognition of the nonsensible, e.g., God, I can have knowledge by analogy and, to be sure, knowledge that it is necessary for reason to think. The categories are the basis of this knowledge, since they necessarily belong to the form of thought, whether it be directed toward the sensible or the supersensible, even though and just because by themselves they determine no object and do not constitute cognition.

The Illusion in Attempting to Provide Objective Reality for the Concepts of Understanding Independently of Sensibility

According to mere concepts of understanding, it is contradictory to think of two things external to one another that are completely identical with respect to all inner determinations (of quantity and quality). It is always just one and the same (numerically identical) thing thought twice.

This is Leibniz's principle of the identity of indiscernibles, to which he ascribed no small importance, but which, nonetheless, grossly offends reason. For one cannot conceive why a drop of water in one place should prevent an exactly identical drop of water from being in another. However, this attack immediately proves (1) that things in space cannot be represented by rational concepts as things in themselves – rather, in order to be known, they must be represented in sensible intuition as appearances – (2) that space is not a property or relation of things-in-themselves, as Leibniz assumes, and (3) that by themselves pure rational concepts do not yield cognition. [...]

37

The Metaphysics of Morals (Introduction)

IV: Rudimentary Concepts of the Metaphysics of Morals

(Philosophia practica universalis)

The concept of freedom is a pure concept of reason. In consequence it is transcendent for theoretical philosophy; that is, it is a concept for which no corresponding example can be given in any possible experience. Accordingly, it does not constitute an object of any theoretical knowledge that is possible for us; and it can by no means be valid as a constitutive principle of speculative reason, but can be valid only as a regulative and, indeed, merely negative principle of speculative reason. In the practical exercise of reason, however, the concept of freedom proves its reality through practical basic principles. As laws of a causality of pure reason, these principles determine the will independently of all empirical conditions (independently of anything sensible) and prove the existence in us of a pure Will in which moral concepts and laws have their origin.

On this concept of freedom, which is positive (from a practical point of view), are founded unconditional practical laws, which are called *moral*. For us, these moral laws are imperatives (commands or prohibitions), for the will is sensibly affected and therefore does not of itself conform to the pure Will, but often opposes it. Moreover,

The Metaphysics of Morals ("Metaphysik der Sitten," 1797). From *The Metaphysical Elements of Justice*, tr. John Ladd (Indianapolis: Bobbs-Merrill Co., Inc., 1965). Selection: Introduction, "Rudimentary Concepts of the Metaphysics of Morals," pp. 21–30.

they are categorical (unconditional) imperatives. In being unconditional, they are distinguished from technical imperatives (percepts of skill), which always give only conditional commands. According to these categorical imperatives, certain actions are allowed or not allowed, that is, are morally possible or impossible. However, some actions or their opposites are, according to these imperatives, morally necessary, that is, obligatory. Hence, for such actions there arises the concept of a duty, the obedience to or transgression of which is, to be sure, combined with a pleasure or displeasure of a special kind (that of a moral feeling). But we can take no account of this pleasure or displeasure in the practical laws of reason because these feelings do not relate to the ground of the practical laws, but only to the subjective effect on the mind that accompanies the determination of our will by these laws, and because such feelings can differ greatly in different persons without objectively – that is, in the judgment of reason – adding or taking away anything from the validity or influence of these laws.

The following concepts are common to both parts of the metaphysics of morals.

Obligation is the necessity of a free action under a categorical imperative of reason.

An imperative is a practical rule through which an action, in itself contingent, is made necessary. An imperative is distinguished from a practical law by the fact that, though the latter represents the necessity of an action, it does not consider whether this necessity already necessarily resides internally in the acting subject (as in the case of a holy being) or whether it is contingent (as in man). Where the former is the case, there is no imperative. Accordingly, an imperative is a rule the representation of which makes necessary a subjectively contingent action and thus represents the subject as one who must be constrained (necessitated) to conform to this rule.

The categorical (unconditional) imperative is one that does not command mediately, through the representation of an end that could be attained by an action, but immediately, through the mere representation of this action itself (its form), which the categorical imperative thinks as objectively necessary and makes necessary. Examples of this kind of imperative can be supplied by no other practical discipline than the one that prescribes obligation (moral philosophy). All other imperatives are technical and altogether conditional. The ground of the possibility of categorical imperatives lies in the fact that they refer to no determination of will (through which a purpose can be ascribed to it) other than its freedom.

An action is *allowed* (*licitum*) if it is not opposed to obligation, and this freedom that is not limited by any opposing imperative is called competence (*facultas moralis*). Hence it is obvious what is meant by unallowed (*illicitum*).

Duty is that action to which a person is bound. It is therefore the content [*Materie*] of obligation. And there can be one and the same duty (so far as the action is concerned), even though we could be obligated thereto in different ways.

The categorical imperative, inasmuch as it asserts an obligation with regard to certain actions, is a morally practical law. But, because obligation includes, not only practical necessity (of the sort that a law in general asserts), but also constraint, the imperative mentioned is a law either of command or of prohibition, according to whether the performance or the nonperformance is represented as a duty. An action that is neither commanded nor prohibited is merely allowed, because with respect to it there is no law that limits freedom (competence) and, therefore, also no duty. Such an action is called morally indifferent (*indifferens, adiaphoron, res merae facultatis*). We may ask whether there are any such actions and, if there are, whether in order to be free to do or forbear as one wants there must be a law of

permission (*lex permissiva*) in addition to the laws of command (*lex praeceptiva, lex mandati*) and of prohibition (*lex prohibitiva, lex vetiti*). If so, then competence would not always relate to an indifferent action (*adiaphoron*), for no special law would be required for an indifferent action when it is considered under moral laws.

An action is called a *deed* insofar as it stands under laws of obligation and, consequently, insofar as the subject is considered in this action [or obligation] under the aspect of the freedom of his will. Through such an act, the agent is regarded as the originator of the effect, and this effect together with the action itself can be imputed to him if he is previously acquainted with the law by virtue of which an obligation rests on him.

A *person* is the subject whose actions are susceptible to imputation. Accordingly, moral personality is nothing but the freedom of a rational being under moral laws (whereas psychological personality is merely the capacity to be conscious of the identity of one's self in the various conditions of one's existence). Hence it follows that a person is subject to no laws other than those that he (either alone or at least jointly with others) gives to himself.

A *thing* is something that is not susceptible to imputation. Every object of free will that itself lacks freedom is therefore called a thing (*res corporalis*).

A deed is *right* or *wrong* in general (*rectum aut minus rectum*) insofar as it is in accordance with or opposed to duty (*factum licitum aut illicitum*), no matter what the content or the origin of the duty may be. A deed opposed to duty is called a *transgression* (*reatus*).

An unintentional transgression that can be imputed is called mere neglect (*culpa*). An intentional transgression (that is, one accompanied by the consciousness that it is a transgression) is called a crime (*dolus*). That which is right according to external laws is called just (*justum*); what is not so is unjust (*injustum*).

A conflict of duties (*collisio officiorum s. obligationum*) would be that relationship between duties by virtue of which one would (wholly or partially) cancel the other. Because, however, duty and obligation are in general concepts that express the objective practical necessity of certain actions and because two mutually opposing rules cannot be necessary at the same time, then, if it is a duty to act according to one of them, it is not only not a duty but contrary to duty to act according to the other. It follows, therefore, that a conflict of duties and obligations is inconceivable (*obligationes non colliduntur*). It may, however, very well happen that two grounds of obligation (*rationes obligandi*), one or the other of which is inadequate to bind as a duty [*Verpflichtung*] (*rationes obligandi non obligantes*), are conjoined in a subject and in the rule that he prescribes to himself, and then one of the grounds is not a duty. When two such grounds are in conflict, practical philosophy does not say that the stronger obligation prevails (*fortior obligatio vincit*), but that the stronger ground binding to a duty [*Verpflichtungsgrund*] prevails (*fortior obligandi ratio vincit*).

In general, those binding laws for which an external legislation is possible are called *external laws* (*leges externae*). Among external laws, those to which an obligation can be recognized a priori by reason without external legislation are *natural laws*, whereas those that would neither obligate nor be laws without actual external legislation are called *positive laws*. Hence it is possible to conceive of an external legislation which contains only positive laws; but then it would have to be preceded by a natural law providing the ground of the authority of the legislator (that is, his authorization to obligate others through his mere will).

A basic principle that makes certain actions a duty is a practical law. The rule that the agent adopts on subjective grounds as his principle is called his *maxim*; hence, the maxims of agents may differ greatly with regard to the same laws.

The categorical imperative, which in general only asserts what obligation is, is this: act according to a maxim that can at the same time be valid as a universal law. You must therefore first of all consider your actions according to their basic subjective principle. But you can recognize whether this basic principle is also objectively valid only by this: that, when your reason puts this principle to the test of conceiving yourself as at the same time universally legislating by means of it, it qualifies for such a universal legislation.

In comparison to the great and manifold consequences that can be drawn from this law, its simplicity must at first seem surprising, as must also its authority to command without appearing to carry any incentive with it. But, in our astonishment at the capacity of our reason to determine will by the mere Idea of the qualification of a maxim for the universality of a practical law, we learn that it is just these practical (moral) laws that

first make known a property of will at which speculative reason could never have arrived either from a priori grounds or through experience, and the possibility of which speculative reason could by no means prove even if it did arrive at it, although such practical laws incontestably prove this property, namely, freedom. Consequently, it should surprise us less to find these laws indemonstrable and yet apodeictic, like mathematical postulates. At the same time, we will see a whole field of practical knowledge open before us, a field that is absolutely closed to reason in its theoretical use when it treats the same Idea of freedom or, indeed, any other of its Ideas of the supersensible.

The agreement of an action with the law of duty is its *legality* (*legalitas*); that of the maxim of the action with the law is its *morality* (*moralitas*). A *maxim* is the subjective principle of action that the subject adopts as a rule for himself (namely, how he wants to act). On the other hand, the basic principle of duty is that which reason absolutely and therefore objectively commands (how he should act).

The supreme basic principle of moral philosophy is therefore: act according to a maxim that can at the same time be valid as a universal law. Every maxim that does not so qualify is opposed to morality [*Moral*].

Laws proceed from the Will; maxims, from the will. In man, the will is free. The Will, which relates to nothing but the law, cannot be called either free or unfree, for it relates, not to actions, but immediately to legislation for the maxims of action (and is therefore practical reason itself). Consequently, it is absolutely necessary and is itself incapable of constraint. Only will can, therefore, be called free.

Freedom of will cannot be defined, however, as the capacity to choose [*Wahl*] to act for or against the law (*libertas indifferentiae*), as some people have tried to define it, even though as a phenomenon it provides frequent examples of this in experience. For freedom (as it first becomes known to us through the moral law) is known only as a negative property within us, the property of not being constrained to action by any sensible determining grounds. As a noumenon, however – that is, according to the capacity of man considered merely as an intelligence – freedom cannot by any means be theoretically described in its positive character as it constrains sensible will. But we can see clearly that, although experience tells us that man as a sensible being exhibits a capacity to choose [*zu wählen*], not only in accordance with the law, but also in opposition to it, yet his freedom as an intelligible being cannot be thus defined, for appearances can never enable us to comprehend a supersensible object (as is free will). Furthermore, we can see that freedom can never be posited on the fact that the rational subject is able to choose in opposition to his (legislative) reason, even though experience proves often enough that this does happen (and yet we cannot comprehend the possibility of this).

It is one thing to admit a proposition (of experience) and quite another to make it both the defining principle (of the concept of free will) and the universal mark distinguishing free will from *arbitrio bruto s. servo* ["brute or servile will"], since in the first case we do not claim that the mark necessarily belongs to the concept, which we are required to do in the latter case. Only the freedom relating to the internal legislation of reason is properly a capacity; the possibility of deviating from it is an incapacity. How, then, can the former be explained by the latter? Such an explanation is a bastard definition (*definitio hybrida*), for it adds to the practical concept the exercise of it as experience teaches it; it presents the concept in a false light.

A *law* (a morally practical one) is a proposition that contains a categorical imperative (a command). He who commands (*imperans*) through a law is the *lawgiver* (*legislator*). He is the originator (*auctor*) of the obligation imposed by the law, but is not always the originator of the law. If he is, then the law is positive (contingent) and arbitrary. The law that binds us a priori and unconditionally through our own reason can also be expressed as proceeding from the Will of a supreme lawgiver, that is, of one who has only rights and no duties (accordingly, from the divine Will). But this only signifies the Idea of a moral being whose Will is law for all, yet without conceiving of him as the originator of the law.

Imputation (*imputatio*) in its moral meaning is the judgment by which someone is regarded as the originator (*causa libera* ["free cause"]) of an action,

which is then called a "deed" (*factum*) and stands under laws. If this judgment also carries with it the juridical consequences of this deed, it is a judicial [*rechtskräftig*] imputation (*imputatio judiciaria s. valida*); otherwise it is only a criticizing imputation (*imputatio diiudicatoria*). That person (physical or moral) who is authorized to exercise judicial imputation is called the *judge* or the *court* (*judex s. forum*).

What anyone does in accordance with duty beyond what he can be compelled to do by the law is *meritorious* (*meritum*); what he does only in accordance with the law is *debt owed* (*debitum*); finally, what he does that is less than the law demands is *moral demerit* (*demeritum*). The juridical effect of demerit is punishment (*poena*); that of a meritorious deed is reward (*praemium*), provided that the reward promised in the law was the moving cause of the deed. Conduct that agrees with debt owed has no juridical effect. Charitable recompense (*remuneratio s. repensio benefica*) relates to the deed in no way that involves justice [*Rechtsverhältnis*].

The good or bad consequences of an action owed as well as the consequences of omitting a meritorious action cannot be imputed to the subject (*modus imputationis tollens*).

The good consequences of a meritorious action as well as the bad consequences of an illegitimate action can be imputed to the subject (*modus imputationis ponens*).

Subjectively considered, the degree of imputability (*imputabilitas*) of actions must be estimated by the magnitude of the obstacles that have to be overcome. The greater the natural obstacles (of sensibility) and the less the moral obstacle (of duty), the higher is the imputation of merit in a good deed, for example, if, at a considerable sacrifice, I rescue from dire necessity a man who is a complete stranger to me.

On the other hand, the less the natural obstacle and the greater the obstacle from grounds of duty, so much the more is transgression (as demerit) imputed. Therefore, the state of mind of the subject, namely, whether he committed the deed with emotion or in cool deliberation, makes a significant difference in imputation.

38

Logic

Concept of Philosophy in General

It is sometimes difficult to explain what is understood by a science. A science gains in precision by establishing its definite concept; and quite a few mistakes are thus avoided, which for various reasons slip in when one is not yet able to distinguish the science from those related to it.

Before we try to give a definition of philosophy, we must first investigate the character of the different cognitions themselves; and since philosophic cognitions belong to the cognitions of reason, we must explain what is to be understood by the latter.

Cognitions of reason are opposed to *historical* cognitions. The former are cognitions out of *principles* (*ex principiis*), the latter out of *data* (*ex datis*). A cognition, however, may have arisen out of reason and notwithstanding be historical; when a mere copyist, for example, learns the products of the reason of others, his cognition of such rational products is merely historical.

Cognitions may be distinguished

(1) according to their *objective* origin, i.e. according to the sources from which alone a cognition is possible. In this respect all cognitions are either *rational* or *empirical*;

(2) according to their *subjective* origin, i.e. according to the manner in which a cognition can be acquired by man. When seen from this latter viewpoint, cognitions are either *rational* or *historical*, whichever way they in themselves may have arisen. Something that *subjectively* is mere historical cognition, may therefore *objectively* be a cognition of reason.

It is harmful to know some rational cognitions merely historically; this does not matter with others. For example, the navigator knows the rules of navigation historically from his tables, and that is enough for him. But if a lawyer knows jurisprudence merely historically, he is completely ruined for being truly a judge, let alone a legislator.

From the aforementioned distinction between *objectively* and *subjectively* rational cognitions it becomes clear that, in a certain way, one can learn philosophy without being able to philosophize. He who truly wants to become a philosopher must practice the free use of his reason and not merely an imitative and, so to speak, mechanical use.

We have explained cognitions of reason as cognitions out of principles; and from this follows that they must be *a priori*. There are, however, two kinds of cognition which both are *a priori* and yet have many pronounced differences, namely, mathematics and philosophy.

One customarily maintains that mathematics and philosophy are distinguished from one another *by their subject*, in that the former deals with *quantity*, the latter with *quality*. This, however, is wrong. The difference between these sciences cannot rest on the subject, for philosophy is

Immanuel Kant's Logic: A Manual for Lectures ("Immanuel Kants Logik, ein Handbuch zu Vorlesungen," ed. Gottlob Benjamin Jäsche, 1800). From *Logic*, tr. Robert S. Hartman and Wolfgang Schwarz (Indianapolis: Bobbs-Merrill Co., Inc., 1974). Selection: Introduction, sect. 3, "Concept of Philosophy in General...," pp. 25–30.

directed toward everything, therefore also toward *quanta*, and mathematics in part also [toward everything], as far as everything has a quantity. Only *the different manner of rational cognition or of the use of reason* in mathematics and philosophy is decisive for the specific difference between these two sciences. Philosophy, namely, is the *cognition of reason out of mere concepts*; mathematics, on the contrary, is the *cognition of reason out of the construction of concepts*.

We *construct* concepts when we exhibit them in intuition *a priori* without experience or when we exhibit in intuition the object that corresponds to our concept. The mathematician can never avail himself of his reason according to mere concepts, the philosopher can never avail himself of it through construction of concepts. In mathematics one uses reason *in concreto*, but the [corresponding] intuition is not empirical; rather one here constructs something for himself, *a priori*, as object of intuition.

And herein, as we see, mathematics has an advantage over philosophy, in that the cognitions of the former are *intuitive*, those of the latter, on the contrary, only *discursive*. The reason, however, why in mathematics we ponder more the quantities lies in this, that quantities can be constructed *a priori* in intuition, whereas qualities cannot be exhibited in intuition.

Philosophy, thus, is the system of philosophic cognitions or of cognitions of reason out of concepts. This is the *scholastic* [or *school*] *concept* of this science. According to its *world concept* it is the science of the ultimate ends of human reason. This high concept gives philosophy its *dignity*, i.e. an absolute value. And actually it is philosophy alone that has an inner value and first gives value to all other cognitions.

In the end the question is always, What is philosophizing good for and what is its ultimate end? and this even when philosophy is considered as a science according to the *scholastic concept*.

In this scholastic meaning of the word, philosophy relates only to *skill*; in reference to the world concept, on the contrary, it relates to *usefulness*. In the former respect it is a *doctrine of skill*; in the latter a *doctrine of wisdom*, the *lawgiver* of reason, and to that extent the philosopher is not a *theoretician of reason, but lawgiver*.

The mere theoretician or, as *Socrates* calls him, the *philodoxus*, strives only after speculative knowledge, without caring how much his knowledge contributes to the ultimate end of human reason;

he gives rules for the use of reason to all kinds of ends. The practical philosopher, the teacher of wisdom through doctrine and example, is the philosopher in the true sense. For philosophy is the idea of a perfect wisdom that shows us the ultimate ends of human reason.

Two things belong to philosophy according to the scholastic concept:

First, a sufficient store of cognitions of reason; *second*, systematic coherence of these cognitions, or their conjunction in the idea of a whole.

Philosophy not only provides such strictly systematic coherence, but is the only science that has systematic coherence in the proper sense and gives systematic unity to all other sciences.

As concerns philosophy according to the world concept, however (*in sensu cosmico*), one may call it a *science of the highest maxim of the use of our reason*, if by maxim one understands the inner principle of choice among different ends.

For, in the latter meaning, philosophy is the science of relating all cognition and every use of reason to the ultimate end of human reason, to which, as the supreme end, all others are subordinated and in which they must be joined into unity.

The field of philosophy in this cosmopolitan meaning may be summed up in the following questions:

(1) *What can I know?* –
(2) *What ought I to do?*
(3) What may I hope?
(4) What is man?

The first question is answered by *metaphysics*, the second by *morality*, the third by *religion*, and the fourth by *anthropology*. At bottom all this could be reckoned to be anthropology, because the first three questions are related to the last.

The philosopher, therefore, must be able to determine

(1) the sources of human knowledge,
(2) the extent of the possible and advantageous use of all knowledge, and finally
(3) the limits of reason.

The last is the most urgent but also the most difficult task, of which the *philodoxus*, however, takes no notice.

Two things, primarily, make the philosopher. (1) Cultivation of talents and skill to use them for various ends. (2) Readiness in the use of all means to any ends one may choose. Both must be united, for without knowledge one never becomes a philosopher, but knowledge alone will never make the philosopher, unless there is added a purposeful joining of all cognitions and skills into unity, and an insight into their agreement with the highest ends of human reason.

No one at all can call himself a philosopher who cannot philosophize. Philosophizing, however, can be learned only through practice and the use of one's own reason.

How, indeed, should it be possible to learn philosophy? Every philosophical thinker builds his own work, so to speak, on the ruins of another; never, however, has a work come about that would have lasted in all its parts. Merely for that reason one cannot learn philosophy, because *it is not yet given*. Supposing, however, there *actually* were a philosophy: then no one who learned it could yet say of himself that he is a philosopher, for his knowledge of it would still be only *subjective-historical*.

In mathematics things are different. This science can in a certain way be learned, for here the proofs are so evident that everyone can become convinced of them; and because of its evidence it also can, as it were, be preserved as a *certain* and *permanent* doctrine.

He who wants to learn to philosophize must, on the contrary, regard all systems of philosophy only as the *history of the use of reason* and as objects for exercising his philosophical talent.

The true philosopher, as self-thinker, thus must make free, not slavishly imitating use of his reason. But not a *dialectical* use, i.e. one that aims only at giving cognitions a *semblance* of *truth* and *wisdom*. This is the business of the mere sophist, totally incompatible though with the dignity of the philosopher as one who knows and teaches wisdom.

For science has a true inner value only as an *organ of wisdom*. As such, however, it is indispensable, so that one may well maintain that wisdom without science is the shadowy outline of a perfection that we shall never reach.

He who hates science and so much the more loves wisdom is called a *misologist*. Misology usually springs from an emptiness of scientific attainments and a certain kind of vanity coupled with it. Sometimes, however, those also fall into the mistake of misology who at first pursued the sciences with much diligence and fortunate results but in the end found no satisfaction in all their knowledge.

Philosophy is the only science that can provide this inner satisfaction, for it closes, as it were, the scientific circle, and only through it do the sciences receive order and coherence.

For the sake of practice in self-thinking or philosophizing, we shall, therefore, have to look more to the *method* of our use of reason than to the propositions themselves that we have attained through it. [...]

39

On the Relationship of Theory to Practice in Political Right

(Against Hobbes)

Among all the contracts by which a large group of men unites to form a society (*pactum sociale*), the contract establishing a *civil constitution* (*pactum unionis civilis*) is of an exceptional nature. For while, so far as its execution is concerned, it has much in common with all others that are likewise directed towards a chosen end to be pursued by joint effort, it is essentially different from all others in the principle of its constitution (*constitutionis civilis*). In all social contracts, we find a union of many individuals for some common end which they all *share*. But a union as an end in itself which they all *ought to share* and which is thus an absolute and primary duty in all external relationships whatsoever among human beings (who cannot avoid mutually influencing one another), is only found in a society in so far as it constitutes a civil state, i.e. a commonwealth. And the end which is a duty in itself in such external relationships, and which is indeed the highest formal condition (*conditio sine qua non*) of all other external duties, is the *right* of men *under coercive public laws* by which each can be given what is due to him and secured against attack from any others. But the whole concept of an external right is derived entirely from the concept of *freedom* in the mutual

On the Common Saying: "This May be True in Theory, but It Does not Apply in Practice" ("Über den Gemeinspruch: 'Das mag in der Theorie richtig sein, taugt aber nicht für die Praxis,'" 1793). From *Kant's Political Writings*, ed. Hans Reiss, tr. H. B. Nisbet (Cambridge University Press, 1970). Selection: "On the Relationship of Theory to Practice in Political Right," pp. 73–9.

external relationships of human beings, and has nothing to do with the end which all men have by nature (i.e. the aim of achieving happiness) or with the recognised means of attaining this end. And thus the latter end must on no account interfere as a determinant with the laws governing external right. *Right* is the restriction of each individual's freedom so that it harmonises with the freedom of everyone else (in so far as this is possible within the terms of a general law). And *public right* is the distinctive quality of the *external laws* which make this constant harmony possible. Since every restriction of freedom through the arbitrary will of another party is termed *coercion*, it follows that a civil constitution is a relationship among *free* men who are subject to coercive laws, while they retain their freedom within the general union with their fellows. Such is the requirement of pure reason, which legislates *a priori*, regardless of all empirical ends (which can all be summed up under the general heading of happiness). Men have different views on the empirical end of happiness and what it consists of, so that as far as happiness is concerned, their will cannot be brought under any common principle nor thus under any external law harmonising with the freedom of everyone.

The civil state, regarded purely as a lawful state, is based on the following *a priori* principles:

(1) The *freedom* of every member of society as a *human being*.

(2) The *equality* of each with all the others as a *subject*.

(3) The *independence* of each member of a commonwealth as a *citizen*.

These principles are not so much laws given by an already established state, as laws by which a state can alone be established in accordance with pure rational principles of external human right. Thus:

1. Man's *freedom* as a human being, as a principle for the constitution of a commonwealth, can be expressed in the following formula. No-one can compel me to be happy in accordance with his conception of the welfare of others, for each may seek his happiness in whatever way he sees fit, so long as he does not infringe upon the freedom of others to pursue a similar end which can be reconciled with the freedom of everyone else within a workable general law – i.e. he must accord to others the same right as he enjoys himself. A government might be established on the principle of benevolence towards the people, like that of a father towards his children. Under such a *paternal government* (*imperium paternale*), the subjects, as immature children who cannot distinguish what is truly useful or harmful to themselves, would be obliged to behave purely passively and to rely upon the judgement of the head of state as to how they *ought* to be happy, and upon his kindness in willing their happiness at all. Such a government is the greatest conceivable *despotism*, i.e. a constitution which suspends the entire freedom of its subjects, who thenceforth have no rights whatsoever. The only conceivable government for men who are capable of possessing rights, even if the ruler is benevolent, is not a *paternal* but a *patriotic* government (*imperium non paternale, sed patrioticum*). A *patriotic* attitude is one where everyone in the state, not excepting its head, regards the commonwealth as a maternal womb, or the land as the paternal ground from which he himself sprang and which he must leave to his descendants as a treasured pledge. Each regards himself as authorised to protect the rights of the commonwealth by laws of the general will, but not to submit it to his personal use at his own absolute pleasure. This right of freedom belongs to each member of the commonwealth as a human being, in so far as each is a being capable of possessing rights.

2. Man's *equality* as a subject might be formulated as follows. Each member of the commonwealth has rights of coercion in relation to all the others, except in relation to the head of state.

For he alone is not a member of the commonwealth, but its creator or preserver, and he alone is authorised to coerce others without being subject to any coercive law himself. But all who are subject to laws are the subjects of a state, and are thus subject to the right of coercion along with all other members of the commonwealth; the only exception is a single person (in either the physical or the moral sense of the word), the head of state, through whom alone the rightful coercion of all others can be exercised. For if he too could be coerced, he would not be the head of state, and the hierarchy of subordination would ascend infinitely. But if there were two persons exempt from coercion, neither would be subject to coercive laws, and neither could do to the other anything contrary to right, which is impossible.

This uniform equality of human beings as subjects of a state is, however, perfectly consistent with the utmost inequality of the mass in the degree of its possessions, whether these take the form of physical or mental superiority over others, or of fortuitous external property and of particular rights (of which there may be many) with respect to others. Thus the welfare of the one depends very much on the will of the other (the poor depending on the rich), the one must obey the other (as the child its parents or the wife her husband), the one serves (the labourer) while the other pays, etc. Nevertheless, they are all equal as subjects *before the law*, which, as the pronouncement of the general will, can only be single in form, and which concerns the form of right and not the material or object in relation to which I possess rights. For no-one can coerce anyone else other than through the public law and its executor, the head of state, while everyone else can resist the others in the same way and to the same degree. No-one, however, can lose this authority to coerce others and to have rights towards them except through committing a crime. And no-one can voluntarily renounce his rights by a contract or legal transaction to the effect that he has no rights but only duties, for such a contract would deprive him of the right to make a contract, and would thus invalidate the one he had already made.

From this idea of the equality of men as subjects in a commonwealth, there emerges this further formula: every member of the commonwealth must be entitled to reach any degree of rank which a subject can earn through his talent, his industry and his good fortune. And his fellow-subjects may not stand in his way by *hereditary* prerogatives or privileges of rank and thereby hold him and his descendants back indefinitely.

All right consists solely in the restriction of the freedom of others, with the qualification that their freedom can co-exist with my freedom within the terms of a general law; and public right in a commonwealth is simply a state of affairs regulated by a real legislation which conforms to this principle and is backed up by power, and under which a whole people live as subjects in a lawful state (*status iuridicus*). This is what we call a civil state, and it is characterised by equality in the effects and counter-effects of freely willed actions which limit one another in accordance with the general law of freedom. Thus the *birthright* of each individual in such a state (i.e. before he has performed any acts which can be judged in relation to right) is absolutely *equal* as regards his authority to coerce others to use their freedom in a way which harmonises with his freedom. Since birth is not an act on the part of the one who is born, it cannot create any inequality in his legal position and cannot make him submit to any coercive laws except in so far as he is a subject, along with all the others, of the one supreme legislative power. Thus no member of the commonwealth can have a hereditary privilege as against his fellow-subjects; and no-one can hand down to his descendants the privileges attached to the rank he occupies in the commonwealth, nor act as if he were qualified as a ruler by birth and forcibly prevent others from reaching the higher levels of the hierarchy (which are *superior* and *inferior*, but never *imperans* and *subiectus*) through their own merit. He may hand down everything else, so long as it is material and not pertaining to his person, for it may be acquired and disposed of as property and may over a series of generations create considerable inequalities in wealth among the members of the commonwealth (the employee and the employer, the landowner and the agricultural servants, etc.). But he may not prevent his subordinates from raising themselves to his own level if they are able and entitled to do so by their talent, industry and good fortune. If this were not so, he would be allowed to practise coercion without himself being subject to coercive counter-measures from others, and would thus be more than their fellow-subject. No-one who lives within the lawful state of a commonwealth can forfeit this equality other than through some crime of his own, but never by contract or through

military force (*occupatio bellica*). For no legal transaction on his part or on that of anyone else can make him cease to be his own master. He cannot become like a domestic animal to be employed in any chosen capacity and retained therein without consent for any desired period, even with the reservation (which is at times sanctioned by religion, as among the Indians) that he may not be maimed or killed. He can be considered happy in any condition so long as he is aware that, if he does not reach the same level as others, the fault lies either with himself (i.e. lack of ability or serious endeavour) or with circumstances for which he cannot blame others, and not with the irresistible will of any outside party. For as far as right is concerned, his fellow-subjects have no advantage over him.[1]

3. The *independence* (*sibisufficientia*) of a member of the commonwealth as a *citizen*, i.e. as a co-legislator, may be defined as follows. In the question of actual legislation, all who are free and equal under existing public laws may be considered equal, but not as regards the right to make these laws. Those who are not entitled to this right are nonetheless obliged, as members of the commonwealth, to comply with these laws, and they thus likewise enjoy their protection (not as *citizens* but as co-beneficiaries of this protection). For all right depends on laws. But a public law which defines for everyone that which is permitted and prohibited by right, is the act of a public will, from which all right proceeds and which must not therefore itself be able to do an injustice to any one. And this requires no less than the will of the entire people (since all men decide for all men and each decides for himself). For only towards oneself can one never act unjustly. But on the other hand, the will of another person cannot decide anything for someone without injustice, so that the law made by this other person would require a further law to limit his legislation. Thus an individual will cannot legislate for a commonwealth. For this requires freedom, equality and *unity* of the will of *all* the members. And the prerequisite for unity, since it necessitates a general vote (if freedom and equality are both present), is independence. The basic law, which can come only from the general, united will of the people, is called the *original contract*.

Anyone who has the right to vote on this legislation is a *citizen* (*citoyen*, i.e. citizen of a state, not *bourgeois* or citizen of a town). The only qualification required by a citizen (apart, of course, from being an adult male) is that he must be his *own master* (*sui iuris*), and must have some *property* (which can include any skill, trade, fine art or science) to support himself. In cases where he must earn his living from others, he must earn it only by *selling* that which is his,[2] and not by allowing others to make use of him; for he must in the true sense of the word *serve* no-one but the commonwealth. In this respect, artisans and large or small landowners are all equal, and each is entitled to one vote only. As for landowners, we leave aside the question of how anyone can have rightfully acquired more land than he can cultivate with his own hands (for acquisition by military seizure is not primary acquisition), and how it came about that numerous people who might otherwise have acquired permanent property were thereby reduced to serving someone else in order to live at all. It would certainly conflict with the above principle of equality if a law were to grant them a privileged status so that their descendants would always remain feudal landowners, without their land being sold or divided by inheritance and thus made useful to more people; it would also be unjust if only those belonging to an arbitrarily selected class were allowed to acquire land, should the estates in fact be divided. The owner of a large estate keeps out as many smaller property owners (and their votes) as could otherwise occupy his territories. He does not vote on their behalf, and himself has only *one* vote. It should be left exclusively to the ability, industry and good fortune of each member of the commonwealth to enable each to acquire a part and all to acquire the whole, although this distinction cannot be observed within the general legislation itself. The number of those entitled to vote on matters of legislation must be calculated purely from the number of property owners, not from the size of their properties.

Those who possess this right to vote must agree *unanimously* to the law of public justice, or else a legal contention would arise between those who agree and those who disagree, and it would require yet another higher legal principle to resolve it. An entire people cannot, however, be expected to reach unanimity, but only to show a majority of votes (and not even of direct votes, but simply of the votes of those delegated in a large nation to represent the people). Thus the actual principle of being content with majority decisions must be accepted unanimously and embodied in a contract; and this itself must be the ultimate basis on which a civil constitution is established. [...]

Notes

1   If we try to find a definite meaning for the word *gracious*, as distinct from kind, beneficent, protective etc., we see that it can be attributed only to a person to whom no *coercive rights* apply. Thus only the head of the *state's government*, who enacts and distributes all benefits that are possible within the public laws (for the *sovereign* who provides them is, as it were, invisible, and is not an agent but the personified law itself), can be given the title of *gracious lord*, for he is the only individual to whom coercive rights do not apply. And even in an aristocratic government, as for example in Venice, the *senate* is the only "gracious lord". The nobles who belong to it, even including the *Doge* (for only the *plenary council* is the sovereign), are all subjects and equal to the others so far as the exercise of rights is concerned, for each subject has coercive rights towards every one of them. Princes (i.e. persons with a hereditary right to become rulers) are themselves called gracious lords only with future reference, an account of their claims to become rulers (i.e. by courtly etiquette, *par courtoisie*). But as owners of property, they are nonetheless fellow-subjects of the others, and even the humblest of their servants must possess a right of coercion against them through the head of state. Thus there can be no more than one gracious lord in a state. And as for gracious (more correctly *distinguished*) ladies, they can be considered entitled to this appellation by their *rank* and their *sex* (thus only as opposed to the *male* sex), and this only by virtue of a refinement of manners (known as gallantry) whereby the male sex imagines that it does itself greater honour by giving the fair sex precedence over itself.

2   He who does a piece of work (*opus*) can sell it to someone else, just as if it were his own property. But guaranteeing one's labour (*praestatio operae*) is not the same as selling a commodity. The domestic servant, the shop assistant, the labourer, or even the barber, are merely labourers (*operarii*), not *artists* (*artifices*, in the wider sense) or members of the state, and are thus unqualified to be citizens. And although the man to whom I give my firewood to chop and the tailor to whom I give material to make into clothes both appear to have a similar relationship towards me, the former differs from the latter in the same way as the barber from the wig-maker (to whom I may in fact have given the requisite hair) or the

labourer from the artist or tradesman, who does a piece of work which belongs to him until he is paid for it. For the latter, in pursuing his trade, exchanges his property with someone else (*opus*), while the for- mer allows someone else to make use of him. – But I do admit that it is somewhat difficult to define the qualifications which entitle anyone to claim the status of being his own master.

40

Lectures on Philosophical Theology

The Nature and Certainty of Moral Faith

Probability has a place only regarding the knowledge of things in the world. For anything of which I am to have probable knowledge must be homogeneous with (or a thing of the same kind as) some other thing of which my knowledge is certain. For instance, I know with probability that the moon is inhabited, because many similarities between it and the earth have been discovered (mountains, valleys, seas, and perhaps also an atmosphere). But this knowledge of the moon's habitability is probable only because I see with certainty that the earth is homogeneous with it in many ways, and from this I conclude that it would also be similar to it in this way. But when it is a question of a thing which does not belong to this world at all, then no homogeneity and hence no probability can apply to it. So I cannot say that it is probable that God exists. Such an expression would also be unsuited to the dignity of this knowledge. And it is improper too because no analogy between God and the world is thinkable. Hence in this case I must be content to have knowledge of something, or at least to be fully convinced of its existence.

Conviction is of two kinds, *dogmatic* and *practical*. The former has to be sought in mere concepts a priori, and has to be apodictic. But we have

Lectures on Philosophical Theology ("Vorlesungen über die philosophische Religionslehre," 1830), tr. Allen W. Wood and Gertrude M. Clark (Ithaca and London: Cornell University Press, 1978). Selection: sect. 2, "The Nature and Certainty of Moral Faith," pp. 121–31.

already seen that by the path of mere speculation we cannot convince ourselves with certainty of God's existence. At most the speculative interest of our reason compels us to assume such a being as a subjectively necessary hypothesis. But reason has no capacity sufficient to *demonstrate* it. Our need makes us wish for such a demonstration, but our reason cannot lay hold of it. It is true that I can argue from the existence of the world and from its accidental appearances to the existence of some supreme original being. Yet there still remains to us another kind of conviction, a *practical* one. It is a special field, which gives us far more satisfying prospects than dry speculation can ever yield. For if something presupposed on subjective grounds is only a hypothesis, a presupposition on objective grounds is a necessary *postulate*. These objective grounds are either theoretical (as in mathematics) or practical (as in morality). For moral imperatives, since they are grounded in the nature of our being as free and rational creatures, have as much evidence and certainty as mathematical propositions originating in the nature of things ever could have. Thus a necessary practical postulate is the same thing in regard to our practical interest as an axiom is in regard to our speculative interest. For the practical interest which we have in the existence of God as a wise ruler of the world is as great as it possibly can be, since if we cancel this fundamental principle, we renounce at the same time all prudence and honesty, and we have to act against our own reason and our conscience.

Such a moral theology not only provides us with a convincing certainty of God's being, but it also has the great advantage that it leads us to *religion*, since it joins the thought of God firmly to our morality, and in this way it even makes better men of us. Our moral faith is a practical postulate, in that anyone who denies it is brought *ad absurdum practicum*. An *absurdum logicum* is an absurdity in judgments; but there is an *absurdum practicum* when it is shown that anyone who denies this or that would have to be a scoundrel. And this is the case with moral faith. This moral belief is not one of my opinions concerning some hypothesis, that is, concerning some presupposition founded on contingent appearances. If one argues from the contingency of the world to a supreme author, then this is only a hypothesis, even if it is one which is necessary for us as an explanation, and hence something like a highly probable opinion. But such presuppositions, which flow from some absolutely necessary datum (as in morality and mathematics), are not mere opinions, but demand of us a firm belief. Hence our faith is not scientific knowledge, and thank heaven it is not! For God's wisdom is apparent in the very fact that we do not *know* that God exists, but should *believe* that God exists. For suppose we could attain to scientific knowledge of God's existence, through our experience or in some other way (even if the possibility of this knowledge cannot immediately be thought). And suppose further that we could really reach as much certainty through this knowledge as we do in intuition. Then in this case, all our morality would break down. In his every action, man would represent God to himself as a rewarder or avenger. This image would force itself involuntarily on his soul, and his hope for reward and fear of punishment would take the place of moral motives. Man would be virtuous out of sensuous impulses.

Baumgarten [*Metaphysica*; Halle, 1739] speaks of God's *sincerity*, but this expression is far beneath the dignity of the highest being. For negative perfections like sincerity (which consists only in God's not behaving hypocritically) could only be predicated of God insofar as it might occur to someone to *deny* them. But sincerity and truth are already contained in the concept of God in such a way that anyone who rejected these attributes would have to deny God himself as well. Such perfections, moreover, are already contained in God's holiness, since a holy being would certainly never lie. And why set up a special rubric and classification for each of the *corollaria*? If we really want to cite sincerity and truth as special attributes of God, it would be better to define

them in terms of the sincerity and truth which God demands of us. So there are still only three moral attributes of God, the three we have treated above: holiness, benevolence, and justice.

We can think of God's justice in two ways: either as justice within the order of nature, or justice by special decree. But as long as we have no instruction concerning the latter, or as long as we can make everything given in nature harmonize with God's holiness and benevolence, it is our duty to stop with a justice which gives us what our deeds are worth in the present course of things. This justice within the order of nature consists in the fact that God has already laid down in the course of things, and in his universal plan for the world, the way in which man's state will be proportioned to the degree of morality he has attained. Well-being is inseparably combined with good conduct, just as punishment is combined with moral corruption. Moral perfection in this life will be followed by moral growth in the next, just as moral deterioration in this life will bring a still greater decline. After death man will continue with his development and the predisposition of his abilities. Thus if in this world he strives to act in a morally good way and gradually attains to moral accomplishment, he may hope to continue his moral improvement in the world to come. On the other hand, if he has acted contrary to the eternal and necessary laws of morality, and has gradually made himself worse by frequent transgressions, then he must fear that his moral corruption will continue and increase. Or at least he has no reason to believe that a sudden reversal will occur in the next life. Instead, the experience of his state in the world and in the order of nature in general gives him clear proof that his moral deterioration (and with it the essentially necessary punishment) will last indefinitely or eternally, just like moral perfection and the well-being inseparable from it.

God's justice is usually divided into (1) *justitiam remunerativam* and (2) *justitiam punitivam*, since God punishes evil and rewards goodness. But the rewards which God bestows on us proceed not from his justice, but from his benevolence. For if they came to us from justice, then there could be no *praemia gratuita* [gifts of grace]. We would have to possess some right to demand them, and God would have to be bound to give them to us. Justice gives nothing gratuitously, it gives to each only the reward he merits. But even if we unceasingly observe all moral laws, we can never do more than our duty. Hence we can never expect rewards from

God's justice. Men may certainly merit things of one another and demand rewards based on their mutual justice. But we can give nothing to God, and so we can never have any right for rewards against him. It is written in a sublime and moving text: "He that hath pity on the poor lendeth to the Lord" [Proverbs 19:17]. Here the reward which is due us for the sake of the unfortunate is ascribed to God's benevolence, and God himself is regarded as our debtor. It is represented that when God bestows a promise on us, we are justified in demanding what he has promised us and expecting from his justice that it will be fulfilled. But promises of this kind, where someone pledges a wholly undeserved benefit to another, do not appear actually to bind the promisor to grant this benefit to the other. Or at least they do not give him the right to demand it. For they always remain good deeds, bestowed on us undeservedly, and they carry the mark not of justice but of benevolence. Hence in God there is no *justitiam remunerativam* toward us. Instead, all the rewards he shows us must be ascribed to his benevolence. His justice is concerned only with punishment. These punishments are either (1) *poenae correctivae* [punishments for correction], (2) *poenae exemplares* [punishments for an example], or (3) *poenae vindicativae* [vindictive punishments]. The first two are given *ne peccatur* [not on account of any wrongdoing]; the third, *quia peccatum est* [because there is wrongdoing]. But all *poenis correctivis* and *poenis exemplaribus* are always grounded on *poenae vindicativae*. For an innocent man may never be punished as an example for others unless he deserves the punishment himself. Hence all corrective punishments ordained for the guilty as a warning to others, must always accord with the rules of justice. Hence they must be avenging punishments. But the expression *poenae vindicativae*, like the expression *justitia ultrix* [avenging justice], is really too harsh. For we cannot think of vengeance in God, because vengeance always presupposes a feeling of pain impelling one to do something similar to the offender. So it is better to regard the punishments inflicted by divine justice on sins in general as an actus of *justitiae distributivae* [distributive justice], that is, as a justice limiting the apportionment of benevolence by the laws of holiness. Hence we see that there must be *poenae vindicativae*, because they alone constitute what is proper to justice; if they were rejected, this attribute could not be assumed in God at all. For *poenae correctivae* and *exemplares* are really acts of benevolence, because

they promote what is best either for the individual men improved by them or for the whole people for whom the punishment serves as a warning. How, then, is the essence of divine justice to be posited in them? His justice must limit benevolence so that it distributes good only according to the subject's worthiness. Hence justice will not ordain punishments for the criminal merely in order to teach what is best for him or for someone else. Rather, it does so in order to punish the offense by which he has violated the law and made himself unworthy of happiness. These retributive punishments will become obvious only when our whole existence is considered, and hence can be correctly determined and appraised only in it. It is from this that we get the majestic idea of a universal judgment of the world.

The *patience* of God consists in the fact that he executes his punishment of evil in the criminal only after he has given him the opportunity to improve himself. But after that, God's justice is unrelenting. For a judge who *pardons* is quite unthinkable. A judge must rather weigh all conduct strictly according to the laws of holiness and allow to each only that measure of happiness which is proportionate to his worthiness. It is enough to expect from God's benevolence that in this life it gives us the capacity to observe the laws of morality and to become worthy of happiness. God himself, the all-benevolent, can make us worthy of his good deeds. But unless we become worthy of this through our morality, God the just still cannot make us participants in happiness.

Impartiality belongs to those attributes which should not be special predicates of God. For no one could doubt that it belongs to him, because it is already contained in the concept of a holy God. God's impartiality consists in the fact that God has no favorites. For this would presuppose some predilection in him, and it is only a human imperfection (as, for example, when parents have a special love for a child which has not especially distinguished itself). But it cannot be thought of God that he would choose some individual subject over others as his favorite, with no regard to the subject's worthiness; for this would have to be an anthropomorphic representation. But if it should happen that one nation becomes enlightened sooner than another and is brought nearer to the destination of the human species, then this would belong rather to the wisest plan of a universal providence, which we are in no position to survey. It is far from a proof that God has a special interest in this nation and cares about this people with a particular favor. For in the kingdom of ends as in the kingdom of nature, God governs according to universal laws, which do not appear to be in conjunction with our shortsighted understanding. Man is certainly in the habit of taking any special bit of undeserved good fortune befalling him for a special testimony of the favor of divine providence. But this is the work of our self-preference, which would gladly persuade us that we are really worthy of the happiness we enjoy.

Equity is also a property which is beneath the majesty of the supreme being. For we can think of genuine equity only among human beings. Equity is an obligation arising from the right of another insofar as it is not combined with a license to compel someone else. Hence it is distinguished from strict right, where I can compel someone else to fulfill his obligation. For instance, if I have promised to give a servant a certain allowance, then I must pay it to him whatever happens. But now suppose there comes a time of scarcity, so that the servant cannot live on the agreed wages. In this case according to strict right I have no obligation to accord him more for his maintenance than I have promised him. He cannot compel me to do so, since he has no further obligation as a ground for his rights. But it is only equitable that I not let him go hungry, and that I add to his wages a proportion large enough that he can live on it. Before the bar of conscience it counts as a strict right that I owe to others what is due them merely from equity. And even if everyone were to think me just, because I fulfill everything to which I can be compelled and to which I have an external obligation, my conscience will still reproach me if I have offended the rules of equity. And God judges according to our conscience, which is his representative here on earth.

Absolute *immortality*, the impossibility of perishing, is ascribed to God. This attribute belongs by right only and solely to him, as a consequence of the absolute necessity of his existence. But the expression *immortality* is improper, because it is only a mere negation of an anthropomorphic representation. It is to be remarked in general that in theory the concept of God must be carefully purified and freed of all such human ideas; from a practical point of view, though, we may momentarily represent God using such predicates whenever by this means the thought of God affords more power and strength to our morality. But in the present case it is much better to use the expression *eternal* rather than *immortal*, since it is nobler and more appropriate to the dignity of God.

Since Baumgarten praises God as the *most happy being*, it will be necessary for us to investigate the true concept of happiness to see whether it fits God. Pleasure in one's state is called *welfare*. And insofar as this pleasure applies to the whole of our existence, it is called *happiness*. Happiness is consequently pleasure in our state as a whole. Pleasure in one's own person is called *self-contentment*. But freedom constitutes that which is most proper to us. Consequently, self-contentment is a pleasure in one's own freedom, or in the quality of one's will. If this self-contentment were to extend to the whole of our existence, it would be called *blessedness*. The distinction between self-contentment and happiness is just as necessary as it is important. For one can be fortunate, and in that sense, happy, without being blessed, even though the consciousness of one's own worth or self-contentment belongs to a perfect happiness. But self-contentment can certainly be found without good fortune, because at least in this life good conduct is not always combined with well-being. Self-contentment arises from morality, while happiness depends on physical conditions. No creature has the powers of nature in its control, so as to be able to make them agree with its self-contentment. Hence the highest degree of self-contentment (or in other words, blessedness) cannot be ascribed to any creature. But we can be more fortunate, and in that sense happier, if our whole state is such that we are able to be well-pleased with it. Yet in the present life happiness itself will hardly be our lot, and the stoics probably exaggerated things considerably when they believed that in this world virtue is always coupled with being well-pleased. The most infallible witness against this is experience.

For man, good fortune is not a possession, but a progression towards happiness. Yet full self-contentment, the comforting consciousness of integrity, is a good which can never be stolen from us, whatever the quality of our external state may be. And in fact all earthly happiness is far outweighed by the thought that as morally good men we have made ourselves worthy of an uninterrupted future happiness. Of course, this inner pleasure in our own person can never compensate for the loss of an externally happy state. But it can still uplift us even in the most troubled life when it is combined with its future prospects.

Now let us raise the question whether happiness may be ascribed to God. Since happiness relates only to one's external state, we must first ask whether God can be thought of as in a state. And then we first have to see what a state is. The ontological definition of a state is this: the coexistence of the changeable determinations of a thing along with the constant ones. In man, for instance, the constant determination is that he is human, and the changeable determinations are whether he is learned or ignorant, rich or poor. This coexistence of his changeable determinations (such as wealth or poverty) with the constant one (his humanity) constitutes his state. But in God everything is permanent. For how could changeable determinations be thought in him, existing along with what is constant in his essence? And how then can the eternal be thought of as in a state? But if no state can be predicated of God, then a state of happiness cannot be ascribed to him either. But supreme blessedness, the greatest possible self-contentment, belongs to him of itself; a blessedness, in fact, so understood that no creature can ever boast of anything even similar to it. For with creatures many external, sensible objects have an influence on their inner pleasure. But God is completely independent of all physical conditions. He is conscious of himself as the source of all blessedness. He is as it were the moral law itself personified. Hence he is also the only blessed one.

At the conclusion of moral theology it should be remarked that the three articles of moral faith, *God*, *freedom* of the human will, and a *moral world*, are the only articles in which it is permissible for us to transport ourselves in thought beyond all experience and out of the sensible world; only here may we assume and believe something from a practical point of view for which we otherwise have no adequate speculative grounds. But however necessary and dependable this procedure may be for the purposes of our morality, we are in no way justified in admitting ourselves further into this idea, and venturing to go with our speculation to a region with which only our practical interest is concerned. If we do so, then we are *fanatics*. For at this point the limits of our reason are clearly indicated, and whoever dares to transcend them will be punished by reason itself for his boldness with both pain and error. But if we remain within these boundaries, then our reward will be to become wise and good men.

PART XII

Jeremy Bentham (1748–1832)

Introduction

Modern philosophy anthologies draw almost exclusively from Bentham's *An Introduction to the Principles of Morals and Legislation* (1789). There is some justification for this: in addition to being one of the few texts Bentham personally saw into print, the *Introduction* offers a lucid statement of the principle of utility. To orient the reader, we have followed convention in including the first chapter of that work. But in order to give the reader a better sense of the breadth and interconnectedness of Bentham's writings, we have added selections from five other works. Three letters from a collection of papers entitled *The Panopticon, or the Inspection-House* (1791) contain Bentham's design and rationale for the construction of a modern prison. "Panopticon" derives from the most prominent feature of Bentham's plan: the prison was to be circular, with the warden located at the center. From this vantage, the warden would, in theory, be able to see all, while being seen by none. Despite years of planning and considerable personal investment, Bentham's prison was never built. The next two selections introduce the theory of fictions. Bentham believed that legal and moral terms such as *obligation*, *duty*, *power*, and *right* are mere fictions, empty sounds, which make sense only when understood in terms of real, perceptible entities such as pain and pleasure. The first excerpt, from Bentham's *A Fragment on Ontology*, explains the distinction between real and fictional entities, and how these are denominated in speech. This is followed by an excerpt from the *Essay on Logic* in which Bentham describes a technique for translating discourse about fictional entities into discourse about real entities. Next we have a selection from one of Bentham's earliest writings, *A Fragment on Government* (1776), in which he comments on the legal fiction of an "original contract." Finally, we turn to Bentham's unpublished and much neglected work on educational reform, *Chrestomathia*. In this excerpt, Bentham discusses the concept of motion.

41

An Introduction to the Principles of Morals and Legislation

Chapter I: Of the Principle of Utility

I. Nature has placed mankind under the governance of two sovereign masters, *pain* and *pleasure*. It is for them alone to point out what we ought to do, as well as to determine what we shall do. On the one hand the standard of right and wrong, on the other the chain of causes and effects, are fastened to their throne. They govern us in all we do, in all we say, in all we think: every effort we can make to throw off our subjection, will serve but to demonstrate and confirm it. In words a man may pretend to abjure their empire: but in reality he will remain subject to it all the while. The *principle of utility*[1] recognises this subjection, and assumes it for the foundation of that system, the object of which is to rear the fabric of felicity by the hands of reason and of law. Systems which attempt to question it, deal in sounds instead of sense, in caprice instead of reason, in darkness instead of light.

But enough of metaphor and declamation: it is not by such means that moral science is to be improved.

II. The principle of utility is the foundation of the present work: it will be proper therefore at the outset to give an explicit and determinate account of what is meant by it. By the principle[2] of utility is meant that principle which approves or disapproves of every action whatsoever, according to the tendency which it appears to have to augment or diminish the happiness of the party whose interest is in question: or, what is the same thing in other words, to promote or to oppose that happiness. I say of every action whatsoever; and therefore not only of every action of a private individual, but of every measure of government.

III. By utility is meant that property in any object, whereby it tends to produce benefit, advantage, pleasure, good, or happiness, (all this in the present case comes to the same thing) or (what comes again to the same thing) to prevent the happening of mischief, pain, evil, or unhappiness to the party whose interest is considered: if that party be the community in general, then the happiness of the community: if a particular individual, then the happiness of that individual.

IV. The interest of the community is one of the most general expressions that can occur in the phraseology of morals: no wonder that the meaning of it is often lost. When it has a meaning, it is this. The community is a fictitious *body*, composed of the individual persons who are considered as constituting as it were its *members*. The interest of the community then is, what? – the sum of the interests of the several members who compose it.

V. It is in vain to talk of the interest of the community, without understanding what is the interest of the individual.[3] A thing is said to promote the interest, or to be *for* the interest, of an individual, when it tends to add to the sum total of his pleasures: or, what comes to the same thing, to diminish the sum total of his pains.

VI. An action then may be said to be conformable to the principle of utility, or, for shortness sake, to utility, (meaning with respect to the community at large) when the tendency it has to

An Introduction to the Principles of Morals and Legislation (1789), ed. Laurence J. Lafleur (New York: Hafner Publishing Co., 1948). Selection: "Of the Principle of Utility," pp. 1–7.

augment the happiness of the community is greater than any it has to diminish it.

VII. A measure of government (which is but a particular kind of action, performed by a particular person or persons) may be said to be conformable to or dictated by the principle of utility, when in like manner the tendency which it has to augment the happiness of the community is greater than any which it has to diminish it.

VIII. When an action, or in particular a measure of government, is supposed by a man to be conformable to the principle of utility, it may be convenient, for the purposes of discourse, to imagine a kind of law or dictate, called a law or dictate of utility: and to speak of the action in question, as being conformable to such law or dictate.

IX. A man may be said to be a partizan of the principle of utility, when the approbation or disapprobation he annexes to any action, or to any measure, is determined by and proportioned to the tendency which he conceives it to have to augment or to diminish the happiness of the community: or in other words, to its conformity or unconformity to the laws or dictates of utility.

X. Of an action that is conformable to the principle of utility one may always say either that it is one that ought to be done, or at least that it is not one that ought not to be done. One may say also, that it is right it should be done; at least that it is not wrong it should be done: that it is a right action; at least that it is not a wrong action. When thus interpreted, the words *ought*, and *right* and *wrong*, and others of that stamp, have a meaning: when otherwise, they have none.

XI. Has the rectitude of this principle been ever formally contested? It should seem that it had, by those who have not known what they have been meaning. Is it susceptible of any direct proof? it should seem not: for that which is used to prove every thing else, cannot itself be proved: a chain of proofs must have their commencement somewhere. To give such proof is as impossible as it is needless.

XII. Not that there is or ever has been that human creature breathing, however stupid or perverse, who has not on many, perhaps on most occasions of his life, deferred to it. By the natural constitution of the human frame, on most occasions of their lives men in general embrace this principle, without thinking of it: if not for the ordering of their own actions, yet for the trying of their own actions, as well as of those of other men. There have been, at the same time, not many, perhaps, even of the most intelligent, who have been disposed to embrace it purely and without reserve. There are even few who have not taken some occasion or other to quarrel with it, either on account of their not understanding always how to apply it, or on account of some prejudice or other which they were afraid to examine into, or could not bear to part with. For such is the stuff that man is made of: in principle and in practice, in a right track and in a wrong one, the rarest of all human qualities is consistency.

XIII. When a man attempts to combat the principle of utility, it is with reasons drawn, without his being aware of it, from that very principle itself.[4] His arguments, if they prove any thing, prove not that the principle is *wrong*, but that, according to the applications he supposes to be made of it, it is *misapplied*. Is it possible for a man to move the earth? Yes; but he must first find out another earth to stand upon.

XIV. To disprove the propriety of it by arguments is impossible; but, from the causes that have been mentioned, or from some confused or partial view of it, a man may happen to be disposed not to relish it. Where this is the case, if he thinks the settling of his opinions on such a subject worth the trouble, let him take the following steps, and at length, perhaps, he may come to reconcile himself to it.

1. Let him settle with himself, whether he would wish to discard this principle altogether; if so, let him consider what it is that all his reasonings (in matters of politics especially) can amount to?

2. If he would, let him settle with himself, whether he would judge and act without any principle, or whether there is any other he would judge and act by?

3. If there be, let him examine and satisfy himself whether the principle he thinks he has found is really any separate intelligible principle; or whether it be not a mere principle in words, a kind of phrase, which at bottom expresses neither more nor less than the mere averment of his own unfounded sentiments; that is, what in another person he might be apt to call caprice?

4. If he is inclined to think that his own approbation or disapprobation, annexed to the idea of an act, without any regard to its consequences, is a sufficient foundation for him to judge and act upon, let him ask himself whether his sentiment is to be a standard of right and wrong, with respect

to every other man, or whether every man's sentiment has the same privilege of being a standard to itself?

5. In the first case, let him ask himself whether his principle is not despotical, and hostile to all the rest of the human race?

6. In the second case, whether it is not anarchial, and whether at this rate there are not as many different standards of right and wrong as there are men? and whether even to the same man, the same thing, which is right to-day, may not (without the least change in its nature) be wrong to-morrow? and whether the same thing is not right and wrong in the same place at the same time? and in either case, whether all argument is not at an end? and whether, when two men have said, "I like this," and "I don't like it," they can (upon such a principle) have any thing more to say?

7. If he should have said to himself, No: for that the sentiment which he proposes as a standard must be grounded on reflection, let him say on what particulars the reflection is to turn? if on particulars having relation to the utility of the act, then let him say whether this is not deserting his own principle, and borrowing assistance from that very one in opposition to which he sets it up: or if not on those particulars, on what other particulars?

8. If he should be for compounding the matter, and adopting his own principle in part, and the principle of utility in part, let him say how far he will adopt it?

9. When he has settled with himself where he will stop, then let him ask himself how he justifies to himself the adopting it so far? and why he will not adopt it any farther?

10. Admitting any other principle than the principle of utility to be a right principle, a principle that it is right for a man to pursue; admitting (what is not true) that the word *right* can have a meaning without reference to utility, let him say whether there is any such thing as a *motive* that a man can have to pursue the dictates of it: if there is, let him say what that motive is, and how it is to be distinguished from those which enforce the dictates of utility: if not, then lastly let him say what it is this other principle can be good for?

Notes

1   *Note by the Author, July 1822.* To this denomination has of late been added, or substituted, the *greatest happiness* or *greatest felicity* principle: this for shortness, instead of saying at length *that principle* which states the greatest happiness of all those whose interest is in question, as being the right and proper, and only right and proper and universally desirable, end of human action: of human action in every situation, and in particular in that of a functionary or set of functionaries exercising the powers of Government. The word *utility* does not so clearly point to the ideas of *pleasure* and *pain* as the words *happiness* and *felicity* do: nor does it lead us to the consideration of the *number*, of the interests affected; to the *number*, as being the circumstance, which contributes, in the largest proportion, to the formation of the standard here in question; the *standard of right and wrong*, by which alone the propriety of human conduct, in every situation, can with propriety be tried. This want of a sufficiently manifest connexion between the ideas of *happiness* and *pleasure* on the one hand, and the idea of *utility* on the other, I have every now and then found operating, and with but too much efficiency, as a bar to the acceptance, that might otherwise have been given, to this principle.

2   The word principle is derived from the Latin *principium*: which seems to be compounded of the two words *primus*, first, or chief, and *cipium*, a termination which seems to be derived from *capio*, to take, as in *mancipium, municipium*; to which are analogous, *auceps, forceps*, and others. It is a term of very vague and very extensive signification: it is applied to any thing which is conceived to serve as a foundation or beginning to any series of operations: in some cases, of physical operations; but of mental operations in the present case.

The principle here in question may be taken for an act of the mind; a sentiment; a sentiment of approbation; a sentiment which, when applied to an action, approves of its utility, as that quality of it by which the measure of approbation or disapprobation bestowed upon it ought to be governed.

3   Interest is one of those words, which not having any superior *genus*, cannot in the ordinary way be defined.

4   "The principle of utility, (I have heard it said) is a dangerous principle: it is dangerous on certain occasions to consult it." This is as much as to say, what? that it is not consonant to utility, to consult utility: in short, that it is *not* consulting it, to consult it.

Addition by the Author, July 1822.

Not long after the publication of the Fragment on Government, anno 1776, in which, in the character of an all-comprehensive and all-commanding principle, the principle of *utility* was brought to view, one person by whom observation to the above effect was made was *Alexander Wedderburn*, at that time Attorney or Solicitor General, afterwards successively Chief Justice of the Common Pleas, and Chancellor of England, under the successive titles of Lord Loughborough and Earl of Rosslyn. It was made – not indeed in my hearing, but in the hearing of a person by whom it was almost immediately communicated to me. So far from being self-contradictory, it was a shrewd and perfectly true one. By that distinguished functionary, the state of the Government was thoroughly understood: by the obscure individual, at that time not so much as supposed to be so: his disquisitions had not been as yet applied, with any thing like a comprehensive view, to the field of Constitutional Law, nor therefore to those features of the English Government, by which the greatest happiness of the ruling *one* with or without that of a favoured few, are now so plainly seen to be the only ends to which the course of it has at any time been directed. The *principle of utility* was an appellative, at that time employed – employed by me, as it had been by others, to designate that which, in a more perspicuous and instructive manner, may, as above, be designated by the name of the *greatest happiness principle*. "This principle (said Wedderburn) is a dangerous one." Saying so, he said that which, to a certain extent, is strictly true: a principle, which lays down, as the only *right* and justifiable end of Government, the greatest happiness of the greatest number – how can it be denied to be a dangerous one? dangerous it unquestionably is, to every government which has for its *actual* end or object, the greatest happiness of a certain *one*, with or without the addition of some comparatively small number of others, whom it is matter of pleasure or accommodation to him to admit, each of them, to a share in the concern, on the footing of so many junior partners. *Dangerous* it therefore really was, to the interest – the sinister interest – of all those functionaries, himself included, whose interest it was, to maximize delay, vexation, and expense, in judicial and other modes of procedure, for the sake of the profit, extractible out of the expense. In a Government which had for its end in view the greatest happiness of the greatest number, Alexander Wedderburn might have been Attorney General and then Chancellor: but he would not have been Attorney General with £15,000 a year, nor Chancellor, with a peerage with a veto upon all justice, with £25,000 a year, and with 500 sinecures at his disposal, under the name of Ecclesiastical Benefices, besides *et cæteras*.

42

The Panopticon,
or the Inspection-House

Letter II: Plan for a Penitentiary Inspection-House

Before you look at the plan, take in words the general idea of it.

The building is circular.

The apartments of the prisoners occupy the circumference. You may call them, if you please, the *cells*.

These *cells* are divided from one another, and the prisoners by that means secluded from all communication with each other, by *partitions* in the form of *radii* issuing from the circumference towards the centre, and extending as many feet as shall be thought necessary to form the largest dimension of the cell.

The apartment of the inspector occupies the centre; you may call it if you please the *inspector's lodge*.

It will be convenient in most, if not in all cases, to have a vacant space or *area* all round, between such centre and such circumference. You may call it if you please the *intermediate* or *annular* area.

About the width of a cell may be sufficient for a *passage* from the outside of the building to the lodge.

Each cell has in the outward circumference, a *window*, large enough, not only to light the cell,

The Panopticon, or the Inspection-House (1791). From *The Works of Jeremy Bentham*, vol. 4, ed. John Bowring (New York: Russell and Russell, Inc., 1962). Selections: Letter 2, "Plan for a Penitentiary Inspection-House," pp. 40–1; Letter 3, "Extent For a Single Building," pp. 42–3; Letter 5, "Essential Points of the Plan," pp. 44–5.

but, through the cell, to afford light enough to the correspondent part of the lodge.

The inner circumference of the cell is formed by an iron *grating*, so light as not to screen any part of the cell from the inspector's view.

Of this grating, a part sufficiently large opens, in form of a *door*, to admit the prisoner at his first entrance; and to give admission at any time to the inspector or any of his attendants.

To cut off from each prisoner the view of every other, the partitions are carried on a few feet beyond the grating into the intermediate area: such projecting parts I call the *protracted partitions*.

It is conceived, that the light, coming in in this manner through the cells, and so across the intermediate area, will be sufficient for the inspector's lodge. But, for this purpose, both the windows in the cells, and those corresponding to them in the lodge, should be as large as the strength of the building, and what shall be deemed a necessary attention to economy, will permit.

To the windows of the lodge there are *blinds*, as high up as the eyes of the prisoners in their cells can, by any means they can employ, be made to reach.

To prevent *thorough light*, whereby, notwithstanding the blinds, the prisoners would see from the cells whether or no any person was in the lodge, that apartment is divided into quarters, by *partitions* formed by two diameters to the circle, crossing each other at right angles. For these partitions the thinnest materials might serve; and they might be made removeable at pleasure; their height, sufficient to prevent the prisoners seeing over them from the cells. Doors to these partitions, if left open at any time, might produce the thorough light. To prevent this, divide each partition into two, at any part required, setting down the one-half at such distance from the other as shall be equal to the aperture of a door.

These windows of the inspector's lodge open into the intermediate area, in the form of *doors*, in as many places as shall be deemed necessary to admit of his communicating readily with any of the cells.

Small *lamps*, in the outside of each window of the lodge, backed by a reflector, to throw the light into the corresponding cells, would extend to the night the security of the day.

To save the troublesome exertion of voice that might otherwise be necessary, and to prevent one prisoner from knowing that the inspector was occupied by another prisoner at a distance, a small *tin tube* might reach from each cell to the inspector's lodge, passing across the area, and so in at the side of the correspondent window of the lodge. By means of this implement, the slightest whisper of the one might be heard by the other, especially if he had proper notice to apply his ear to the tube.

With regard to *instruction*, in cases where it cannot be duly given without the instructor's being close to the work, or without setting his hand to it by way of example before the learner's face, the instructor must indeed here as elsewhere, shift his station as often as there is occasion to visit different workmen; unless he calls the workmen to him, which in some of the instances to which this sort of building is applicable, such as that of imprisoned felons, could not so well be. But in all cases where directions, given verbally and at a distance, are sufficient, these tubes will be found of use. They will save, on the one hand, the exertion of voice it would require, on the part of the instructor, to communicate instruction to the workmen without quitting his central station in the lodge; and, on the other, the confusion which would ensue if different instructors or persons in the lodge were calling to the cells at the same time. And, in the case of hospitals, the quiet that may be insured by this little contrivance, trifling as it may seem at first sight, affords an additional advantage.

A *bell*, appropriated exclusively to the purposes of *alarm*, hangs in a *belfry* with which the building is crowned, communicating by a rope with the inspector's lodge.

The most economical, and perhaps the most convenient, way of *warming* the cells and area, would be by flues surrounding it, upon the principle of those in hot-houses. A total want of

every means of producing artificial heat might, in such weather as we sometimes have in England, be fatal to the lives of the prisoners; at any rate, it would often times be altogether incompatible with their working at any sedentary employment. The flues, however, and the fire-places belonging to them, instead of being on the outside, as in hot-houses, should be in the inside. By this means, there would be less waste of heat, and the current of air that would rush in on all sides through the cells, to supply the draught made by the fires, would answer so far the purpose of ventilation. But of this more under the head of Hospitals.[1]

Letter III: Extent for a Single Building

So far as to the characteristic parts of the principle of construction. You may now, perhaps, be curious to know to what extent a building upon this principle is capable of being carried, consistently with the various purposes to which it may come to be applied. Upon this subject, to speak with confidence belongs only to architects by profession. Indulge me, however, with a few words at a venture.

As to the *cells*, they will of course be more or less spacious, according to the employment which it is designed should be carried on in them.

As to the *whole building*, if it be too small, the circumference will not be large enough to afford a sufficient number of cells: if too large, the depth from the exterior windows will be too great; and there will not be light enough in the lodge.

As to this individual building of my brother's, the dimensions of it were determined by the consideration of the most convenient scantlings of the timbers, (that being in his situation the cheapest material,) and by other local considerations. It is to have two stories, and the diameter of the whole building is to be 100 feet out and out.

Merely to help conception, I will take this size for an example of such a building as he would propose for England.

Taking the diameter 100 feet, this admits of 48 *cells*, 6 feet wide each at the outside, walls included; with a *passage* through the building, of 8 or 9 feet.

I begin with supposing two stories of cells.

In the *under* story, thickness of the walls $2\frac{1}{2}$ feet.

From thence, clear *depth* of each cell from the window to the grating, 13 feet.

From thence to the ends of the *partition walls*, 3 feet more; which gives the length of the *protracted partitions*.

Breadth of the *intermediate area*, 14.

Total from the outside of the building to the *lodge*, $32\frac{1}{2}$ feet.

The double of this, 65 feet, leaves for the *diameter of the lodge*, 35 feet; including the thickness of its walls.

In the *upper* story, the *cells* will be but 9 feet deep; the difference between that and the 13 feet, which is their depth in the under story, being taken up by a *gallery* which surrounds the protracted partitions.

This gallery supplies, in the upper story, the place of an intermediate area on that floor; and by means of *steps*, which I shall come to presently, forms the communication between the upper story of cells to which it is attached, and the lower story of the cells, together with the intermediate area and the lodge.

The spot most remote from the place where the light comes in from, I mean the *centrical* spot of the building and of the lodge, will not be more than 50 feet distant from that place; a distance not greater, I imagine, than what is often times exemplified in churches; even in such as are not furnished in the manner of this building, with windows in every part of the exterior boundary. But the inspector's *windows* will not be more than about $32\frac{1}{2}$ feet from the open light.

It would be found convenient, I believe, on many accounts, and in most instances, to make *one story* of the *lodge* serve for *two stories* of the *cells*; especially in any situation where ground is valuable, the number of persons to be inspected large, the room necessary for each person not very considerable, and frugality and necessity more attended to than appearance.

For this purpose, the *floor* of the *ground story of the lodge* is elevated to within about $4\frac{1}{2}$ feet of the floor of the *first story* of the *cells*. By this means, the inspector's eye, when he stands up, will be on, or a little above, the level of the floor of the above mentioned upper story of the cells; and, at any rate, he will command both that and the ground story of the cells without difficulty, and without change of posture.

As to the *intermediate area*, the *floor* of it is upon a level, not with the *floor* of the *lodge*, but with that of the *lower story* of the cells. But at the *upper* story of the cells, its place, as I have already mentioned, is supplied by the above-mentioned *gallery*;

so that the altitude of this area from the floor to the ceiling is equal to that of both stories of the cells put together.

The floor of the lodge not being on a level with either story of the cells, but between both, it must at convenient intervals be provided with flights of *steps*, to go *down* to the ground story of the cells by the intermediate area, and *up* to the first floor of the cells by the gallery. The ascending flights, joined to the *descending*, enable the servants of the house to go to the upper story of the cells, without passing through the apartment of the inspector.

As to the *height* of the whole, and of the several parts, it is supposed that 18 feet might serve for *the two stories of cells*, to be inspected, as above, by *one story* of the *lodge*. This would hold 96 persons.

36 feet for four stories of *cells*, and two of the lodge: this would hold 192 persons.

54 feet for six stories of the cells, and three of the lodge: this would hold 288 persons.

And 54 feet, it is conceived, would not be an immoderate elevation.

The drawings which, I believe, will accompany this, suppose *four* for the number of stories of the cells.

You will see, under the head of hospitals, the reasons why I conceive that even a less height than 9 feet, deducting the thickness of a floor supported by arches, might be sufficient for the cells.

The *passage* might have, for its *height*, either the height of one story, or of two stories of the cells, according as the number of those cells was two or four. The part over the passage might, in either case, be added to the lodge, to which it would thereby give a communication, at each end, with the world without doors, and ensure a keeper against the danger of finding himself a prisoner among his prisoners.

Should it be thought, that, in this way, the lodge would not have light enough, for the convenience of a man of a station competent to the office, the deficiency might be supplied by a void space left in that part, all the way up. You may call it if you please the *central area*. Into this space windows may open where they are wanted, from the apartments of the lodge. It may be either left *open* at the top, or covered with a *sky-light*. But this expedient, though it might add, in some respects, to the convenience of the lodge, could not but add considerably to the quantity and expense of the building.

On the other hand, it would be assistant to ventilation. Here, too, would be a proper place for the *chapel*: the prisoners remaining in their cells, and the windows of the lodge, which is almost all window, being thrown open. The advantages derivable from it in point of light and ventilation depending upon its being kept vacant, it can never be wanted for any profane use. It may therefore, with the greater propriety, be allotted to divine service, and receive a regular consecration. The *pulpit* and *sounding-board* may be moveable. During the term of service, the sky-light, at all other times kept as open as possible, might be shut.

Letter V: Essential Points of the Plan

It may be of use, that among all the particulars you have seen, it should be clearly understood what circumstances are, and what are not, essential to the plan. The essence of it consists, then, in the *centrality* of the inspector's situation, combined with the well-known and most effectual contrivances for *seeing without being seen*. As to the *general form* of the building, the most commodious for most purposes seems to be the circular: but this is not an absolutely essential circumstance. Of all figures, however, this, you will observe, is the only one that affords a perfect view, and the same view, of an indefinite number of apartments of the same dimensions: that affords a spot from which, without any change of situation, a man may survey, in the same perfection, the whole number, and without so much as a change of posture, the half of the whole number, at the same time: that, within a boundary of a given extent, contains the greatest quantity of room: – that places the centre at the least distance from the light: – that gives the cells most width, at the part where, on account of the light, most light may, for the purposes of work, be wanted: – and that reduces to the greatest possible shortness the path taken by the inspector, in passing from each part of the field of inspection to every other.

You will please to observe, that though perhaps it is the most important point, that the persons to be inspected should always feel themselves as if under inspection, at least as standing a great chance of being so, yet it is not by any means the *only* one. If it were, the same advantage might be given to buildings of almost any form. What is also of importance is, that for the greatest proportion of time possible, each man should actually *be* under inspection. This is material in *all* cases, that the

inspector may have the satisfaction of knowing, that the discipline actually has the effect which it is designed to have: and it is more particularly material in such cases where the inspector, besides seeing that they conform to such standing rules as are prescribed, has more or less frequent occasion to give them such transient and incidental directions as will require to be given and enforced, at the commencement at least of every course of industry. And I think, it needs not much argument to prove, that the business of inspection, like every other, will be performed to a greater degree of perfection, the less trouble the performance of it requires.

Not only so, but the greater chance there is, of a given person's being at a given time actually under inspection, the more strong will be the persuasion – the more *intense*, if I may say so, the *feeling*, he has of his being so. How little turn soever the greater number of persons so circumstanced may be supposed to have for calculation, some rough sort of calculation can scarcely, under such circumstances, avoid forcing itself upon the rudest mind. Experiment, venturing first upon slight trangressions, and so on, in proportion to success, upon more and more considerable ones, will not fail to teach him the difference between a loose inspection and a strict one.

It is for these reasons, that I cannot help looking upon every form as less and less eligible, in proportion as it deviates from the *circular*.

A very material point is, that room be allotted to the lodge, sufficient to adapt it to the purpose of a complete and constant habitation for the principal inspector or head-keeper, and his family. The more numerous also the family, the better; since, by this means, there will in fact be as many inspectors, as the family consists of persons, though only one be paid for it. Neither the orders of the inspector himself, nor any interest which they may feel, or not feel, in the regular performance of his duty, would be requisite to find them motives adequate to the purpose. Secluded oftentimes, by their situation, from every other object, they will naturally, and in a manner unavoidably, give their eyes a direction conformable to that purpose, in every momentary interval of their ordinary occupations. It will supply in their instance the place of that great and constant fund of entertainment to the sedentary and vacant in towns – the looking out of the window. The scene, though a confined, would be a very various, and therefore, perhaps, not altogether an unamusing one.

Note

1   There is one subject, which, though not of the most dignified kind, nor of the most pleasant kind to expatiate upon, is of too great importance to health and safe custody to be passed over unconsidered: I mean the provision to be made for carrying off the result of necessary evacuations. A common necessary might be dangerous to security, and would be altogether incompatible with the plan of solitude. To have the filth carried off by the attendants, would be altogether as incompatible with cleanliness; since without such a degree of regularity as it would be difficult, if not ridiculous, to attempt to enforce in case of health, and altogether impossible in case of sickness, the air of each cell, and by that means the lodge itself would be liable to be kept in a state of constant contamination, in the intervals betwixt one visit and another. This being the case, I can see no other eligible means, than that of having in each cell a fixed provision made for this purpose in the construction of the building.

Betwixt every other two cells, at the end of the partition which divides them, a hollow shaft or tunnel is left in the brick-work of the exterior wall; which tunnel, if there be several stories to the building, is carried up through all of them.

Into this tunnel is inserted, under each cell, the bottom of an EARTHEN PIPE (like those applied in England to the tops of chimneys) glazed in the inside. The upper end, opening into the cell, is covered by a seat of cast-iron, bedded into the brick-work; with an aperture, which neither by its size nor shape shall be capable of admitting the body of a man. To gain the tunnel from the inside of the cell, the position of this pipe will of course be slanting. At the bottom of the tunnel, on the outside of the building, an arched opening, so low as scarcely to be discernible, admits of the filth being carried away. No one, who has been at all attentive to the history of prisons, but must have observed how often escapes have been effected or attempted through this channel.

A slight screen, which the prisoner might occasionally interpose, may perhaps not be thought superfluous. This, while it answers the purpose of decency, might be so adjusted as to prevent his concealing from the eye of the inspector any forbidden enterprise.

For each cell, the whole apparatus would not come to many shillings: a small consideration for a great degree of security. In this manner, without any relaxation of the discipline, the advantages of cleanliness, and its concomitant health, may be attained to as great a degree as in most private houses.

It would be regarded, perhaps, as a luxury too great for an establishment of this kind, were I to venture to propose the addition of a WATER-PIPE all around, with a cock to it in each cell. The clear expense would, however, not be quite so great as it might seem: since by this means a considerable quantity of attendance would be saved. To each prisoner, some allowance of water must necessarily be afforded, if it were only for drink, without regard to cleanliness. To forward that allowance by hand to two or three hundred prisoners in so many different apartments, might perhaps be as much as one man could do, if constantly employed. For the raising the water by pumps to necessary elevation, the labour of the prisoners would suffice.

As to the MATERIALS, brick, as every body knows, would be the cheapest in ***, and either brick or stone, in every other part of England. Thus much as to the shell. But in a building calculated for duration, as this would be, the expense of allowing the same materials to the FLOORS, and laying them upon ARCHES, would, I imagine, not be deemed an unsuitable one; especially when the advantage of a perfect security from fire is taken into the account.

43

A Fragment on Ontology

Introduction

The most general, that is, the most extensive propositions belonging to physics, to *somatology*, the only branch of physics that comes under the cognisance of sense, are considered as forming a separate branch of art and science, under the very uncharacteristic name of mathematics.

The most general and extensive propositions belonging to physics, in the largest sense of the word, including Somatology[1] and Psychology[2] taken together, have been considered as forming, in like manner, a separate discipline, to which the name of Ontology has been assigned.

The field of Ontology, or as it may otherwise be termed, the field of supremely abstract entities is a yet untrodden labyrinth, – a wilderness never hitherto explored.

In the endeavour to bring these entities to view, and place them under the reader's eye in such sort that to each of their names, ideas as clear, correct, and complete as possible, may by every reader who will take the trouble, be annexed and remain attached, the following is the course that will be pursued.

Those of which the conception is most simple, will all along precede those of which the conception is less simple; in other words, those words to the understanding of which, neither any other word, nor the import of any other word, will be necessary, will be brought to view in the first place, and before any of those which in their

A Fragment on Ontology. From *The Works of Jeremy Bentham*, vol. 8, ed. John Bowring (New York: Russell and Russell, Inc., 1962). Selection: pp. 195–9.

import bear a necessary and more or less explicit or implied reference to the ideas attached to this or that other word.

Chapter I: Classification of Entities

Section I: Division of entities

An entity is a denomination in the import of which every subject matter of discourse, for the designation of which the grammatical part of speech called a noun-substantive is employed, may be comprised.

Entities may be distinguished into *perceptible* and *inferential*.

An entity, whether perceptible or inferential, is either real or fictitious.

Section II: Of perceptible entities

A *perceptible* entity is every entity the existence of which is made known to human beings by the immediate testimony of their senses, without reasoning, *i.e.* without reflection. A perceptible real entity is, in one word, a body.[3]

The name *body* is the name of the genus generalissimum of that class of real entities. Under this genus generalissimum, a system of divisions which has for its limit the aggregate of all distinguishable individual bodies, may be pursued through as many stages as are found conducive to the purposes of discourse, at any such stage, and at any number of such stages, the mode of division may be bifurcate[4] and exhaustive, *i.e.* all-comprehensive.

The division according to which bodies are spoken of as subjects of one or other of the three physical kingdoms, viz. animal, vegetable, and mineral, is a *trifurcate* division. By substituting to this one stage of division, two stages, each of them bifurcate, the division may be rendered, or rather shown to be, exhaustive; as thus: –

A body is either endued with life, or not endued with life.

A body endued with life, is either endued with sensitive life, or with life not sensitive.

A body endued with sensitive life, is an animal; a body endued with a life not sensitive, is a vegetable; a body not endued with life, is a mineral.

Section III: Of inferential entities

An *inferential* entity, is an entity which, in these times at least, is not made known to human beings in general, by the testimony of sense, but of the existence of which the persuasion is produced by reflection – is inferred from a chain of reasoning.

An inferential entity is either, 1. Human; or, 2. Super-human.

1. A human inferential entity, is the soul considered as existing in a state of separation from the body.

Of a human soul, existing in a state of separation from the body, no man living will, it is believed, be found ready to aver himself to have had perception of any individual example; or, at any rate, no man who, upon due and apposite interrogation would be able to obtain credence.

Considered as existing and visiting any part of our earth in a state of separation from the body, a human soul would be a ghost: and, at this time of day, *custom* scarcely does, *fashion* certainly does not command us to believe in ghosts.

Of this description of beings, the reality not being, in any instance, attested by *perception*, cannot therefore be considered any otherwise than as a matter of *inference*.[5]

2. A superhuman entity is either supreme or subordinate.

The supreme, superhuman, inferential entity is God: sanctioned by revelation; sanctioned by the religion of Jesus as delivered by the apostle Paul, is the proposition that no man hath seen God at any time. If this proposition be correct, God not being consistently with the imperfection of the human senses capable of being referred to the class of perceptible real entities, cannot, in consequence of the imperfection under which human reason labours, cannot, any more than the soul of man considered as existing in a separate state, be referred by it to any other class than that of inferential real entities as above described.[6]

A subordinate superhuman entity is either *good* or *bad*. A good subordinate superhuman inferential entity is an angel; a bad subordinate superhuman inferential entity is a devil.

By the learner as well as by the teacher of logic, all these subjects of Ontology may, without much detriment, it is believed, to any other useful art, or any other useful science, be left in the places in which they are found.

Section IV: Of real entities

A real entity is an entity to which, on the occasion and for the purpose of discourse, existence is really meant to be ascribed.

Under the head of perceptible real entities may be placed, without difficulty, individual perceptions of all sorts:[7] the impressions produced in groups by the application of sensible objects to the organs of sense: the ideas brought to view by the recollection of those same objects; the new ideas produced under the influence of the imagination, by the decomposition and recomposition of those groups; – to none of these can the character, the denomination, of real entities be refused.

Faculties, powers of the mind, dispositions: all these are unreal; all these are but so many fictitious entities. When a view of them comes to be given, it will be seen how perfectly distinguishable, among psychical entities, are those which are recognised in the character of real, from those which are here referred to the class of fictitious entities.

To some it may seem matter of doubt whether, to a perception of any kind, the appellation of a real entity can, with propriety, be applied

Certain it is that it cannot, if either *solidity* or *permanence* be regarded as a quality belonging to the essence of reality.

But in neither of these instances can it, it is believed, any sufficient or just reason be assigned, why the field of reality should be regarded as confined within the limits which, on that supposition, would be applied to it.

Whatsoever title an object belonging to the class of bodies may be considered as possessing to the attribute of reality, i.e. of existence, every object belonging to the class of *perceptions* will be found to possess, in still higher degree, a title established by more immediate evidence: it is only by the evidence afforded by perceptions that the reality of a body of any kind can be established.

Of *Ideas*, our perception is still more direct and immediate than that which we have of corporeal substances: of their existence our persuasion is more necessary and irresistible than that which we have of the existence of corporeal substances.

Speaking of Entities, ideas might perhaps accordingly be spoken of as the *sole perceptible ones*, substances, those of the corporeal class, being, with reference, and in contradistinction to them, no other than *inferential* ones.

But if substances themselves be the subject of the division, and for the designation of the two branches of the division the words perceptible and inferential be employed, it is to corporeal substances that the characteristic and differential attribute, perceptible, cannot but be applied: the term inferential being thereupon employed for the designation of incorporeal ones.

The more correct and complete the consideration bestowed, the more clearly will it be perceived, that from the existence of perceptions, viz. of sensible ones, the inference whereby the existence of corporeal entities, viz. the bodies from which those perceptions are respectively derived, is much stronger, more necessary, and more irresistible, than the inference whereby the existence of incorporeal entities is inferred from the existence of perceptible entities, alias *corporeal* substances, alias bodies.

Suppose the non-existence of corporeal substances, of any hard corporeal substance that stands opposite to you, make this supposition, and as soon as you have made it, act upon it, pain, the perception of pain, will at once bear witness against you; and that by your punishment, your condign punishment. Suppose the non-existence of any inferential incorporeal substances, of any one of them, or of all of them, and the supposition made, act upon it accordingly, – be the supposition conformable or not conformable to the truth of the case, at any rate no such immediate counter-evidence, no such immediate punishment will follow.[8]

Section V: Of fictitious entities

A fictitious entity is an entity to which, though by the grammatical form of the discourse employed in speaking of it, existence be ascribed, yet in truth and reality existence is not meant to be ascribed.

Every noun-substantive which is not the name of a real entity, perceptible or inferential, is the name of a fictitious entity.

Every fictitious entity bears some relation to some real entity, and can no otherwise be understood than in so far as that relation is perceived, – a conception of that relation is obtained.

Reckoning from the real entity to which it bears relation, a fictitious entity may be styled a fictitious entity of the first remove, a fictitious entity of the second remove, and so on.

A fictitious entity of the first remove is a fictitious entity, a conception of which may be obtained by the consideration of the relation borne by it to a real entity, without need of considering the relation borne by it to any other fictitious entity.

A fictitious entity of the second remove is a fictitious entity, for obtaining a conception of which it is necessary to take into consideration some fictitious entity of the first remove.

Considered at any two contiguous points of time, every real entity is either in motion or at rest.

Now, when a real entity is said to be at rest, it is said to be so with reference to some other particular real entity or aggregate of real entities; for so far as any part of the system of the universe is perceived by us, we at all times perceive it not to be at rest. Such, at least, is the case not only with the bodies called planets, but with one or more of the bodies called fixed stars; and, by analogy, we infer this to be the case with all the rest.

This premised, considered with reference to any two contiguous points of time past, every perceptible real entity was, during that time, either in motion or not in motion; if not in motion, it was at rest.

Here, then, we have two correspondent and opposite fictitious entities of the first remove, viz. a motion and a rest.

A motion is a mode of speech commonly employed; a rest is a mode of speech not so commonly employed.

To be spoken of at all, every fictitious entity must be spoken of as if it were real. This, it will be seen, is the case with the above-mentioned pair of fictitious entities of the first remove.

A body is said to be in motion. This, taken in the literal sense, is as much as to say, here is a larger body, called a motion; *in* this larger body, the other body, namely, the really existing body, is contained.

So in regard to rest. To say this body is at rest is as much as to say, here is a body, and it will naturally be supposed a fixed body, and here is another body, meaning the real existing body, which is *at* that first-mentioned body, *i.e.* attached to it, as if the fictitious body were a stake, and the real body a beast tied to it.

An instance of a fictitious entity of the second remove is a quality. There are qualities that are qualities of real entities; there are qualities that are qualities of the above-mentioned fictitious entities of the first remove. For example, of motion, rectilinearity, curvilinearity, slowness, quickness, and so on.

Section VI: Uses of this distinction between names of real and names of fictitious entities

These uses are, 1. Attaching, in the only way in which they can be attached, clear ideas to the several all-comprehensive and leading terms in question. 2. Obviating and excluding the multitudinous errors and disputes of which the want of such clear ideas has been the source: disputes which, in many instances, have not terminated in words, but through words have produced antipathy, and through antipathy war with all its miseries.

Fictitious entity says some one, – of such a locution where can be the sense or use? By the word *entity* cannot but be represented something that has existence, – apply to the same subject the adjunct *fictitious*, the effect is to give instruction that it has not any existence. This, then, is a contradiction in terms, a species of locution from which, in proportion as it has any employment, confusion, and that alone, cannot but be the effect.

Entities are either real or fictitious, what can that mean? What but that of entities there are two species or sorts: viz. one which is itself, and another which is neither itself nor anything else? Instead of fictitious entity, or as synonymous with fictitious entity, why not here say, *nonentity*?

Answer. – Altogether inevitable will this seeming contradiction be found. The root of it is in the nature of language: that instrument without which, though of itself it be nothing, nothing can be said, and scarcely can anything be done.

Of the nature of that instrument, of the various forms under which it has been seen to present itself among different tribes of men, of the indis-

pensable parts (*i.e.* parts of speech) which may be seen to belong to it under every one of those forms, actual or possible, of the qualities desirable on the part of the collection of signs of which, under all these several forms, it is composed; – under all these several heads, sketches will be endeavoured to be given in another place.

All this while, antecedently to the stage at which these topics will present themselves, use is however making, as it could not but be made, of this same instrument. At that future stage, it will not only be the *instrument*, but the *subject* also of inquiry: at present and until then, employing it in the character of an instrument, we must be content to take it in hand, and make use of it, in the state in which we find it.

In like manner, the several operations, which by the help of language, and under the direction of logic, are performed by human minds upon language and thereby upon minds: such as distinction, division, definition, and the several other modes of exposition, including those of methodization, must be performed at and from the very outset of a work on logic, antecedently to the stage at which the task of examining into their nature and origination will be entered upon and come to be performed.

To language, then – to language alone – it is, that fictitious entities owe their existence – their impossible, yet indispensable, existence.[9]

In language the words which present themselves, and are employed in the character of *names*, are, some of them, names of real entities, – others, names of fictitious entities; and to one or other of these classes may all words which are employed in the character of *names* be referred.

What will, moreover, be seen, is, that the fiction – the mode of representation by which the fictitious entities thus created, in so far as fictitious entities can be created, are dressed up in the garb, and placed upon the level, of real ones, is a contrivance but for which language, or, at any rate, language in any form superior to that of the language of the brute creation, could not have existence.

And now, perhaps, may be seen the difference between a *fictitious entity* and a *non-entity*; or, to speak more strictly, the difference between the import of the two words – a difference such, that when, with propriety and use, the one is, the other cannot be employed.

In the house designated by such a number, (naming it) in such a street, in such a town, lives a being called the Devil, having a head, body, and limbs, like a man's – horns like a goat's – wings like a bat's, and a tail like a monkey's: – Suppose this assertion made, the observation naturally might be, that the Devil, as thus described, is a non-entity. The averment made of it is, that an object of that description really exists. Of that averment, if seriously made, the object or end in view cannot but be to produce in the minds to which communication is thus made, a serious persuasion of the existence of an object conformable to the description thus expressed.

Thus much concerning a non-entity. Very different is the notion here meant to be presented by the term fictitious entity.

By this term is here meant to be designated one of those sorts of objects, which in every language must, for the purpose of discourse, be spoken of as existing, – be spoken of in the like manner as those objects which really have existence, and to which existence is seriously meant to be ascribed, are spoken of; but without any such danger as that of producing any such persuasion as that of their possessing, each for itself, any separate, or strictly speaking, any real existence.

Take, for instances, the words motion, relation, faculty, power, and the like.

Real entities being the objects for the designation of which, in the first place, at the earliest stage of human intercourse, and in virtue of the most urgent necessity, words, in the character of names, were employed, – between the idea of a name and that of the reality of the object to which it was applied, an association being thus formed, from a connexion thus intimate, sprung a very natural propensity, viz. that of attributing reality to every object thus designated; – in a word, of ascribing reality to the objects designated by words, which, upon due examination, would be found to be nothing but so many names of so many fictitious entities.

To distinguish them from those fictitious entities, which, so long as language is in use among human beings, never can be spared, fabulous may be the name employed for the designation of the other class of *unreal* entities.

Of fictitious entities, whatsoever is predicated is not, consistently with strict truth, predicated (it then appears) of anything but their respective names.

But forasmuch as by reason of its length and compoundedness, the use of the compound denomination, *name of a fictitious entity*, would frequently be found attended with inconvenience; for the avoidance of this inconvenience, instead of this long denomination, the less long, though, unhappily, still compound denomination, fictitious entity, will commonly, after the above warning, be employed.

Of nothing that has place, or passes, in our minds can we give any account, any otherwise than by speaking of it as if it were a portion of space, with portions of matter, some of them at rest, others moving in it. Of nothing, therefore, that has place, or passes in our mind, can we speak, or so much as think, otherwise than in the way of *fiction*. To this word fiction we must not attach either those sentiments of pleasure, or those sentiments of displeasure, which, with so much propriety, attach themselves to it on the occasion in which it is most commonly in use. Very different in respect of purpose and necessity, very different is this logical species of fiction from the poetical and political; – very different the fiction of the Logician from the fictions of poets, priests, and lawyers.

For their object and effect, the fictions with which the Logician is conversant, without having been the author of them, have had neither more nor less than the carrying on of human converse; such communication and interchange of thought as is capable of having place between man and man. The fictions of the poet, whether in his character of historic fabulist or dramatic fabulist, putting or not putting the words of his discourse in metrical form, are pure of insincerity, and, neither for their object nor for their effect have anything but to amuse, unless it be in some cases to excite to action – to action in this or that particular direction for this or that particular purpose. By the priest and the lawyer, in whatsoever shape fiction has been employed, it has had for its object or effect, or both, to deceive, and, by deception, to govern, and, by governing, to promote the interest, real or supposed, of the party addressing, at the expense of the party addressed. In the mind of all, fiction, in the logical sense, has been the coin of necessity; – in that of poets of amusement – in that of the priest and the lawyer of mischievous immorality in the shape of mischievous ambition, – and too often both priest and lawyer have framed or made in part this instrument.

Notes

1 Somatology, the science that belongs to bodies.

2 Psychology, the science that belongs to mind.

3 The name *substance* has, by the logicians of former times, been used to comprise perceptible and inferential real entities: Souls, God, Angels, Devils, have been designated by them by the appellation *substance*.

4 The use of the exhaustive mode of division, as contra-distinguished from that which is not exhaustive, *i.e.* all-comprehensive, is to show, that your conception and comprehension of the subject, in so far as the particulars comprehended in it are in view, is complete.

5 Should there be any person in whose view the soul of man, considered in a state of separation from the body, should present itself as not capable of being, with propriety, aggregated to the class of real entities, to every such person, the class to which it belongs would naturally be that of fictitious entities; in which case it would probably be considered as being that whole, of which so many other psychical entities, none of which have ever been considered any otherwise than fictitious, such as the understanding, and the will, the perceptive faculty, the memory, and the imagination, are so many parts.

6 Should there be any person who, incapable of drawing those inferences by which the Creator and Preserver of all other entities, is referred to the class of real ones, should refuse to him a place in that class, the class to which such person would find himself, in a manner, compelled to refer that invisible and mysterious being would be, not as in the case of the human soul to that of fictitious entities, but that of non-entities.

7 Pathematic, *Apathematic*, to one or other of these denominations may all imaginable sorts of perceptions be referred. Pathematic, viz. such as either themselves consist of or are accompanied by pleasure or pain; *Apathematic*, such as have not any such accompaniment in any shape.

8 In the works of the authors who now (anno 1813) are in vogue, not a few are the notions of which the appearance will, at this time of day, be apt to excite a sensation of surprise in an unexperienced, and, one day perhaps, even in an experienced, mind.

Of this number are – 1. The denial of the existence of bodies. 2. The denial of the existence of general or abstract ideas.

Of these kindred paradoxes, – for such, in some sort, they will be found to be, – who were the first persons by whom they were respectively broached, is more than I recollect, if so it be that I ever knew; nor, supposing it attainable, would the trouble of the search be paid for by the value of the thing found.

Of those by whom the notion of the non-existence of matter, including the several bodies that present themselves to our senses, is maintained, Bishop Berkeley, if not the first in point of time, is, at any rate, the most illustrious partisan.

9 The division of entities into real and fictitious, is more properly the division of names into *names* of real and *names* of fictitious entities.

44

Essay on Logic

Section VII: Of Exposition by Paraphrasis, with its Subsidiary Operations, viz. Phraseoplerosis and Archetypation

Bisection 1: Explanation of these modes of exposition, and of the case in which they are necessary

Paraphrasis is that mode of exposition which is the only instructive mode, where the thing expressed being the name of a fictitious entity, has not any superior in the scale of logical subalternation.

Connected, and that necessarily, with paraphrasis, is an operation, for the designation of which the word Phraseoplerosis (*i.e.* the filling up of the phrase,) may be employed.

By the word paraphrasis may be designated that sort of exposition which may be afforded by transmuting into a proposition, having for its subject some real entity, a proposition which has not for its subject any other than a fictitious entity.

Nothing has no properties. A fictitious entity being, as this its name imports, being, by the very supposition, a mere nothing, cannot of itself have any properties: no proposition by which any property is ascribed to it can, therefore, be in itself, and of itself, a true one, nor, therefore, an instructive one. Whatsoever of truth is capable of belonging to it cannot belong to it in any other character than that of the representative – of the intended and supposed equivalent and adequate succedaneum,

of some proposition having for its subject some real entity.

Of any such fictitious entity, or fictitious entities, the real entity with which the import of their respective appellatives is connected, and on the import of which their import depends, may be termed the real source, efficient cause, or connecting principle.

In every proposition by which a property or affection of any kind is ascribed to an entity of any kind, real or fictitious, three parts or members are necessarily either expressly or virtually included, viz. 1. A *subject* being the name of the real or *fictitious entity* in question. – 2. A predicate by which is designated the property or affection attributed or ascribed to that subject; and 3. The *Copula*, or sign of the act of the mind, by which the attribution or ascription is performed.

By the sort of proposition here in question, viz., a proposition which has for its subject some fictitious entity, and for its predicate the name of an attribute attributed to that fictitious entity, some sort of image – the image of some real action or state of things, in every instance, is presented to the mind. This image may be termed the archetype, emblem, or archetypal image appertaining to the fictitious proposition, of which the name of the characteristic fictitious entity constitutes a part.

In so far as of this emblematic image indication is given, the act or operation by which such indication is given, may be termed Archetypation.

To a considerable extent Archetypation, *i.e.* the origin of the psychological, in some physical idea, is often, in a manner, lost; – its physical marks, being more or less obliterated by the frequency of

Essay on Logic. From *The Works of Jeremy Bentham*, vol. 8, ed. John Bowring (New York: Russell and Russell, Inc., 1962). Selection: sect. 7, pp. 246–8.

its use on psychological ground, while it is little, if at all, in use on the original physical ground.

Such psychological expressions, of which, as above, the physical origin is lost, are the most commodious for psychological use. Why? – Because in proportion as it is put out of sight, two psychological expressions, derived from two disparate and incongruous physical sources, are capable of being conjoined without bringing the incongruity to view.

When the expression applied to a psychological purpose is one of which the physical origin remains still prominent and conspicuous, it presents itself to view in the character of a figurative expression – for instance a *metaphor*. Carried for any considerable length through its connexions and dependencies, the metaphor becomes an allegory – a figure of speech, the unsuitableness of which, to serious and instructive discourse, is generally recognised. But the great inconvenience is, that it is seldom that for any considerable length of time, if any, the physical idea can be moulded and adapted to the psychological purpose.

In the case of a fictitious proposition which, for the exposition of it, requires a paraphrasis, having for its subject a real entity, (which paraphrasis, when exhibited, performs, in relation to the name of the fictitious subject, the same sort of office which, for the name of a real entity, is performed by a definition of the ordinary stamp, viz. a definition *per genus et differentiam*) – the name forms but a part of the fictitious proposition for the explanation of which, the sort of proposition having for its subject a real entity, is in the character of a paraphrastically-expository proposition required. To compose and constitute such a proposition as shall be ripe and qualified for the receiving for itself, and thereby for its subject, an exposition by *paraphrasis*, the addition of other matter is required, viz., besides the name of the subject, the name of the predicate, together with some sign performing the office of the copula; – the operation by which this completion of the phrase is performed, may be termed Phraseoplerosis.

Phraseoplerosis is thus another of the operations connected with, and subservient to, the main or principal operation, paraphrasis.

Bisection 2: Exemplification in the case of the fictitious entity obligation

For exposition and explanation of Paraphrasis, and of the other modes connected with it, and subsid-

iary to it, that which presents itself as the most instructive of all examples, which the nature of the case affords, is that which is afforded by the group of ethical fictitious entities, viz. *Obligations*, rights, and the other advantages dependent on obligation.

The fictitious entities which compose this group have all of them, for their real *source*, one and the same sort of real entity, viz. *sensation*, the word being taken in that sense in which it is significative not merely of perception, but of perception considered as productive of pain alone, of pleasure alone, or of both.

Pain (it is here to be observed) may have for its equivalent, loss of pleasure; pleasure, again, may have for its equivalent, exemption from pain.

An obligation (viz. the obligation of conducting himself in a certain manner,) is incumbent on a man, (*i.e.* is spoken of as incumbent on a man) in so far as, in the event of his failing to conduct himself in that manner, pain, or loss of pleasure, is considered as about to be experienced by him.[1]

In this example, –

1. The exponend, or say the word to be expounded, is *an obligation*.

2. It being the name not of a real, but only of a fictitious entity, and that fictitious entity not having any superior genus, it is considered as not susceptible of a definition in the ordinary shape, *per genus et differentiam*, but only of an exposition in the way of paraphrasis.

3. To fit it for receiving exposition in this shape, it is in the character of the subject of a proposition, by the help of the requisite compliments made up into a fictitious proposition. These compliments are, 1, the predicate, *incumbent on a man*; 2, the copula *is*; and of these, when thus added to the name of the subject, viz. *obligation*, the fictitious proposition which requires to be expounded by paraphrasis, viz. the proposition – *An obligation is incumbent on a man*, is composed.

4. Taking the name of the subject for the *basis*, by the addition of this predicate, *incumbent on a man*, and the copula *is*, the phrase is completed, the operation called *phraseoplerosis*, *i.e.* completion of the phrase is performed.

5. The source of the explanation thus given by paraphrasis, is the idea of eventual sensation, as expressed by the names of the different and opposite modes of sensation, viz., pain and pleasure, with their respective equivalents, and the designation of the event, on the happening of which such sensation is considered as being about to take place.

6. For the formation of the variety of fictitious propositions, of which the fictitious entity in question, viz. obligation, or an obligation, is in use to constitute the subject, the emblematical, or archetypal image, is that of a man lying down, with a heavy body pressing upon him, to wit, in such sort as either to prevent him from acting at all, or so ordering matters that if so it be that he does act, it cannot be in any other direction or manner than the direction or manner in question, – the direction or manner requisite.

The several distinguishable sources from any or all of which the pain and pleasure constitutive of the obligation in question, may be expected to be received, viz. the several sanctions, distinguished by the names of the physical sanction, the popular, or moral, sanction, the political (including the legal) sanction, and the religious sanction; – these particulars belong to another part of the field, and have received explanation in another place.[2]

To that other place it also belongs to bring to view the causes by which the attention and perception of mankind have, to so great an extent, been kept averted from the only true and intelligible source of obligation – from the only true and intelligible explanation of its nature, as thus indicated.

On the exposition thus given of the term obligation, may be built those other expositions, of which it will form the basis, viz., of rights, quasi rights or advantages analogous to rights, and their respective modifications, as well as of the several modifications of which the fictitious entity, *obligation*, is itself susceptible.

Notes

1 It is, however, only in so far as a man is aware of the probability, that in the event in question the unpleasant consequence in question will befal him, that the obligation can possess any probability of proving an effective one.

2 See *Principles of Morals and Legislation*, chapter iii. vol. i. p. 14.

45

A Fragment on Government

[Of the Original Contract]

XXXVI. As to the Original Contract, by turns embraced and ridiculed by our Author [Sir William Blackstone], a few pages, perhaps, may not be ill bestowed in endeavouring to come to a precise notion about its reality and use. The stress laid on it formerly, and still, perhaps, by some, is such as renders it an object not undeserving of attention. I was in hopes, however, till I observed the notice taken of it by our Author, that this chimera had been effectually demolished by Mr. HUME.[1] I think we hear not so much of it now as formerly. The indestructible prerogatives of mankind have no need to be supported upon the sandy foundation of a fiction.

XXXVII. With respect to this, and other fictions, there was once a time, perhaps, when they had their use. With instruments of this temper, I will not deny but that some political work may have been done, and that useful work, which, under the then circumstances of things, could hardly have been done with any other. But the season of *Fiction* is now over: insomuch, that what formerly might have been tolerated and countenanced under that name, would, if now attempted to be set on foot, be censured and stigmatized under the harsher appellations of *encroachment* or *imposture*. To attempt to introduce any *new* one, would be *now* a crime: for which reason there is much danger, without any use, in

A Fragment on Government (1776). From *The Works of Jeremy Bentham*, vol. 1, ed. John Bowring (New York: Russell and Russell, Inc., 1962). Selection: chs 36–41, pp. 268–270.

vaunting and propagating such as have been introduced already. In point of political discernment, the universal spread of learning has raised mankind in a manner to a level with each other, in comparison of what they have been in any former time: nor is any man now so far elevated above his fellows, as that he should be indulged in the dangerous licence of cheating them for their good.

XXXVIII. As to the fiction now before us, in the character of an *argumentum ad hominem*, coming when it did, and managed as it was, it succeeded to admiration.

That compacts, by whomsoever entered into, *ought* to be kept; – that men are *bound* by compacts, are propositions which men, without knowing or inquiring why, were disposed universally to accede to. The observance of promises they had been accustomed to see pretty constantly enforced. They had been accustomed to see Kings, as well as others, behave themselves as if bound by them. This proposition, then, "that men are bound by *compacts*;" and this other, "that, if one party performs not his part, the other is released from his," being propositions which no man disputed, were propositions which no man had any call to prove. In theory they were assumed for axioms: and in practice they were observed as rules.[2] If, on any occasion, it was thought proper to make a show of proving them, it was rather for form's sake than for any thing else; and that, rather in the way of momento or instruction to acquiescing auditors, than in the way of proof against opponents. On such an occasion, the common-place retinue of phrases was at hand: *Justice*, *Right Reason* required it; the *Law* of *Nature* commanded it, and so forth:

all which are but so many ways of intimating that a man is firmly persuaded of the truth of this or that moral proposition, though he either thinks he *need not*, or finds he *can't*, tell *why*. Men were too obviously and too generally interested in the observance of these rules, to entertain doubts concerning the force of any arguments they saw employed in their support. It is an old observation, how Interest smooths the road to Faith.

XXXIX. A compact, then, it was said, was made by the King and People: the terms of it were to this effect: – The People, on their part, promised to the King a *general obedience*: the King, on his part, promised to *govern* the People in such a *particular* manner always, as should be *subservient* to their happiness. I insist not on the words: I undertake only for the sense; as far as an imaginary engagement, so loosely and so variously worded by those who have imagined it, is capable of any decided signification. Assuming, then, as a general rule, that promises, when made, ought to be observed; and, as a point of fact, that a promise to this effect in particular had been made by the party in question, men were more ready to deem themselves qualified to judge when it was such a promise was *broken*, than to decide directly and avowedly on the delicate question, when it was that a King acted so far in *opposition* to the happiness of his People, that it were better no longer to obey him.

XL. It is manifest, on a very little consideration, that nothing was gained by this manœuvre after all: no difficulty removed by it. It was still necessary, and that as much as ever, that the question men studied to avoid should be determined, in order to determine the question they thought to substitute in its room. It was still necessary to determine, whether the King in question had, or had not, acted so far in *opposition* to the happiness of his people, that it were better no longer to obey him; in order to determine, whether the promise he was supposed to have made, had or had not been broken. For what was the supposed purport of this promise? It was no other than what has just been mentioned.

XLI. Let it be said, that part at least of this promise was to govern in *subservience to Law*: that hereby a more precise rule was laid down for his conduct, by means of this supposal of a promise,

than that other loose and general rule to govern in subservience to the *happiness of his people*: and that, by this means, it is the letter of the *Law* that forms the tenor of the rule.

Now true it is, that the governing in opposition to Law, is *one* way of governing in opposition to the happiness of the people: the natural effect of such a contempt of the Law being, if not actually to destroy, at least to threaten with destruction, all those rights and privileges that are founded on it: rights and privileges on the enjoyment of which that happiness depends. But still it is not this that can be safely taken for the entire purport of the promise here in question: and that for several reasons. *First*, Because the most mischievous, and under certain constitutions the most feasible, method of governing in opposition to the happiness of the people, is, by setting the Law itself in opposition to their happiness. *Second*, Because it is a case very conceivable, that a King may, to a great degree, impair the happiness of his people without violating the letter of any single Law. *Third*, Because extraordinary occasions may now and then occur, in which the happiness of the people may be better promoted by acting, for the moment, in *opposition* to the Law, than in *subservience* to it. *Fourth*, Because it is not any single violation of the Law, as such, that can properly be taken for a breach of his part of the contract, so as to be understood to have released the people from the obligation of performing theirs. For, to quit the fiction, and resume the language of plain truth, it is scarce ever any single violation of the Law that, by being *submitted to*, can produce so much mischief as shall surpass the probable mischief of *resisting* it. If every single instance whatever of such a violation were to be deemed an entire dissolution of the contract, a man who reflects at all would scarce find any where, I believe, under the sun, that Government which he could allow to subsist for twenty years together. It is plain, therefore, that to pass any sound decision upon the question which the inventors of this fiction substituted instead of the true one, the latter was still necessary to be decided. All they gained by their contrivance was, the convenience of deciding it obliquely, as it were, and by a side wind; that is, in a crude and hasty way, without any direct and steady examination. [. . .]

Notes

1   1. In the third volume of his TREATISE *on* HUMAN NATURE.

Our Author, one would think, had never so much as opened that celebrated book: of which the criminality in the eyes of some, and the merits in the eyes of others, have since been almost effaced by the splendour of more recent productions of the same pen. The magnanimity of our Author scorned, perhaps, or his circumspection feared, to derive instruction from an enemy: or, what is still more probable, he knew not that the subject had been so much as touched upon by that penetrating and acute metaphysician, whose works lie so much out of the beaten tract of Academic reading. But here, as it happens, there is no matter for such fears. Those men who are most alarmed at the dangers of a free inquiry; those who are most intimately convinced that the surest way to truth is by hearing nothing but on one side, will, I dare answer almost, find nothing of that which they deem poison in this third volume. I would not wish to send the reader to any other than this, which, if I recollect aright, stands clear of the objections that have of late been urged, with so much vehemence, against the work in general (by Dr. BEATTIE, in his *Essay on the Immutability of Truth*). As to the two first, the Author himself, I am inclined to think, is not ill-disposed, at present, to join with those who are of opinion, that they might, without any great loss to the science of Human Nature, be dispensed with. The like might be said, perhaps, of a considerable part, even of this. But after all retrenchments, there will still remain enough to have laid mankind under indelible obligations. That the foundations of all *virtue* are laid in *utility*, is there demonstrated, after a few exceptions made, with the strongest force of evidence: but I see not, any more than Helvetius saw, what need there was for the exceptions.

2. For my own part, I well remember, no sooner had I read that part of the work which touches on this subject, than I felt as if scales had fallen from my eyes. I then, for the first time, learned to call the cause of the People the cause of Virtue.

Perhaps a short sketch of the wanderings of a raw but well-intentioned mind, in its researches after moral truth, may, on this occasion, be not unuseful: for the history of one mind is the history of many. The writings of the honest, but prejudiced, Earl of Clarendon, to whose integrity nothing was wanting, and to whose wisdom little but the fortune of living something later; and the contagion of a monkish atmosphere: these, and other concurrent causes, had listed my infant affections on the side of despotism.

The Genius of the place I dwelt in, the authority of the State, the voice of the Church in her solemn offices: all these taught me to call Charles a Martyr, and his opponents rebels. I saw innovation, where indeed innovation, but a glorious innovation, was, in their efforts to withstand him. I saw falsehood, where indeed falsehood was, in their disavowals of innovation. I saw selfishness, and an obedience to the call of passion, in the efforts of the oppressed to rescue themselves from oppression. I saw strong countenance lent in the sacred writings to Monarchic government; and none to any other. I saw *passive obedience* deep stamped with the seal of the Christian Virtues of humility and self-denial.

Conversing with lawyers, I found them full of the virtues of their Original Contract, as a recipe of sovereign efficacy for reconciling the accidental necessity of resistance with the general duty of submission. This drug of theirs they administered to me to calm my scruples. But my unpractised stomach revolted against their opiate. I bid them open to me that page of history in which the solemnization of this important contract was recorded. They shrunk from this challenge; nor could they, when thus pressed, do otherwise than our Author has done, confess the whole to be a fiction. This, methought, looked ill. It seemed to me the acknowledgement of a bad cause, the bringing a fiction to support it. "To prove fiction, indeed," said I, "there is need of fiction; but it is the characteristic of truth to need no proof but truth. Have you then really any such privilege as that of coining facts? You are spending argument to no purpose. Indulge yourselves in the licence of supposing that to be true which is not, and as well may you suppose that proposition itself to be true, which you wish to prove, as that other whereby you hope to prove it." Thus continued I, unsatisfying and unsatisfied, till I learnt to see that *utility* was the test and measure of all virtue; of loyalty as much as any: and that the obligation to minister to general happiness was an obligation paramount to and inclusive of every other. Having thus got the instruction I stood in need of, I sat down to make my profit of it. I bid adieu to the original contract: and I left it to those to amuse themselves with this rattle, who could think they needed it.

2   A *compact* or *contract* (for the two words, on this occasion at least, are used in the same sense) may, I think, be defined a pair of promises, by two persons reciprocally given, the one promise in consideration of the other.

46

Chrestomathia

Appendix No. V: Sources of Motion

Analytical Sketch of the several *Sources of Motion*
with their correspondent *Primum Mobiles*.
Of *Motion in general – its generation and extinction.*

In the masses of matter with which man is conversant, and on which for his being, as well as his
well-being, he is at all times dependent, whatsoever change is effected – this change is either itself
some motion, or owes its origin to some motion of
which it is the result.

Motion is the motion of some *body* or *bodies*; of
some portion or portions of *matter*, of the aggregate mass of matter with which man is conversant.

Of this aggregate mass no particle can at any
time, or in any place, in any direction, enter or be
made to enter into a state of motion, without
having to encounter a perpetual and indefatigable
antagonist styled *Resistance*.

According to the commonly received distinction, this Resistance is susceptible of two different
modifications; viz. 1. *Counter Motion*, i.e. active;
and 2. *vis inertiæ*, or purely *passive* resisting force.
But, perhaps, upon a closer examination it might
be found, that that which presents itself in the
character of a purely passive resisting force, is no
other than an actively resisting force, produced by
the elasticity of the mass to which the moving
power is applied; that is, the repulsive power, the
countermotion, or tendency to countermotion, of

Chrestomathia. From *The Works of Jeremy Bentham*,
vol. 8, ed. John Bowring (New York: Russell and Russell, Inc., 1962). Selection: Appendix 5, pp. 128–32.

the particles of which the mass acted upon by the
moving force is composed.

To one or other of these powers, if between
them there can be any real difference, will be to
be referred that cause, to the designation of which,
when cessation of motion is considered as the
effect of it, the word *friction* is applied.

For the purpose of rendering, in the best
manner in which we are able, an account of the
motion of such bodies as are in motion, and of
the rest of such as are at rest, certain fictitious
entities are, by a sort of innocent falsehood, the
utterance of which is necessary to the purpose of
discourse, feigned to exist and operate in the character of causes, equally real with, and distinct
from, the perceptible and perceived effects, in
relation to which they are considered in the
character of causes.[1]

All bodies we are acquainted with, it is universally agreed, are compounds, as it were, of solid
matter and empty space. All bodies, viz. the ultimate particles of solid matter which enter into their
composition, are separated by intervals of space, in
which no matter at all, at any rate none that we
have any acquaintance with, is contained. To the
different distances at which, in different states of
its existence, the component particles of the same
body are placed, are owing, in some degree, the
different textures of which it is susceptible, and
which, under different circumstances, it exhibits
to our senses.

Take, for example, any mass of matter whatsoever: suppose an apple; the apple let it be from
which Newton derived the first hint of the attraction of gravitation; the ever memorable apple
which, as an object of worship to the latest poster-

ity, ought to have been preserved from corruption in a hermetically sealed glass-case; ought to have been transmitted as an object of worship to the latest inheritors of this our globe: – the particles of solid matter of which this apple is constituted are, each of them at a certain distance from each of the several others. How happens it that they are not more distant? What is the cause of such their propinquity? The necessary fiction above spoken of provides an answer and says, *the attraction of cohesion* is the cause by the operation of which they are thus kept together. How happens it that they are as distant as they are? What is the cause of such their distance? Here again steps in the same useful respondent, and answers, It is by mutual *repulsion* that they are thus kept asunder.

It is to distinguish it from the attraction of *gravity*, of which presently, that the attraction, termed the attraction of cohesion, has acquired that name. Of this species of attraction, repulsion, it has been seen, is the constant companion, and antagonist; each of the opposite and mutually balancing effects have equal need of a fictitious cause. Repulsion is the generic name applicable to other cases. *Attraction of cohesion* is a specific one. To match with this its antagonist, the particular species of repulsion here in question requires its specific name. Repulsion corresponding to the attraction of cohesion, let this be that specific name; or rather an appellation thus multitudinously worded, being too cumbersome for use, say, the *repulsion of cohesion*: and though taken by itself, and without explanation, the appellative would, upon the face of it, be self-contradictory, yet by this explanation, to which by its texture it would naturally point, it may perhaps be found not altogether unfit for use. Instead of this appellation, or for variety along with it, if for attraction of cohesion, the appellation internal attraction, or intestine attraction, be employed; for repulsion of cohesion, the term internal repulsion, or intestine repulsion, may be employed.

In the *Attraction of Gravity* may be seen one of the fictitious entities, to the operation of which, in the character of causes or sources, the birth of motion, howsoever modified, may, as far as we are acquainted with it, be referred. To the repulsion of cohesion – to this one simple cause, will, it is believed, be found referable, with equal propriety, the death of all these several motions; which, at the conclusion of the conflict maintained by the various species of attraction, endowed with their several unequal degrees of force, remains, consti-

tuting the only force by which matter is retained in that state of composition above-mentioned, which seems essential to its existence; and by which the whole multitude of its particles are prevented from being crowded together into one mass.

To account for the difference of bodies in point of distance, a sort of nominal entity is feigned, to represent the cause of it, and Motion is the name by which this imaginary cause is designated. Motion is thereupon considered (for such are the shifts that language is reduced to) as a sort of receptacle in which bodies are lodged; they are accordingly said to be *in* motion, as a man is said to be *in* a house.[2]

By laying out of consideration everything that concerns the particular nature of these bodies respectively; everything, in a word, concerning them, but the difference between the distance or interval between them at the one time, and the distance or interval between them at the other, we obtain the abstract idea, for the designation of which the word motion is employed. In speaking of it, we speak of it as if it were itself a substance: a hollow mass into which the body, the really and independently existing body, whatever it be, and how vast soever it be, is capable of being put, and which is capable of being communicated to that body, and so in regard to bodies in any number.

A philosopher, says the old Greek story, denying the existence of Motion, another to refute him, got up and walked. Good for a practical joke, not so for a serious refutation. Of the existence of the faculty of locomotion, the denier of the existence of motion, was not less perfectly aware before the experiment than after it. What he denied was, – not the universally exemplified, and universally known, and acknowledged matter of fact, that the same body is at one time in one place, at another time in another, and in that sense the existence of motion – but the existence of any real entity, corresponding to the appellation motion; any entity real and distinct from the body or bodies in which the motion is said to have place.

Thus early (as appears from this story) had a conception, however narrow and inadequate, been formed of the distinction between names of real entities and names of fictitious entities; a distinction by which much light has already been thrown, and by degrees much more will be thrown on the field of language; and through that medium, on the field of thought and action; and, in particular, on the nature of the relation between *cause* and *effect*. Cause, when the word is used in its proper signification, is perhaps in every instance the name of a fictitious entity; if you want the name of the correspondent real entity, substitute the word *author*, or the word *instrument*, to the word cause.

Rest is the absence, non-existence, or negation of this imaginary receptacle. When, after observation taken of the two bodies in question, at two different points of time, no such difference of distance is found, they are said to have been during that length of time each of them at rest. Rest is thus a sort of imaginary pillar, or anchor, to which, in the English language, they are considered or at least spoken of, as being fastened.[3]

Enclosed in that receptacle, or fastened to this pillar or anchor, – one or other is at every point of time the condition of every object to which the name of *body* has been attached.

The truth is, that absolutely and properly speaking, in as far as observation and inference have extended, motion is the state or condition in which, at every point, every body is, and so for ever is likely to continue. Rest is not the state of our own sun, about which the planet that we inhabit moves. If a state of rest were predicable of anything, it would be of the ideal point in the expanse of space, the *centre of gravity*, as it is called, about which, the sun on the one part, and the planets on the other, are observed or supposed to turn. The observations and inferences thus applied, in the first instance, to our sun, have been extended to those other bodies to which, to distinguish them from those companions to our earth called planets, we give the name of fixed stars; but which, determined as they have been by these observations and these inferences, it has seemed good to our astronomers not to tie to the above-mentioned pillar, but to put all together into the above-mentioned receptacle.

So it is then, that, for the purposes of discourse, as well as of thought and action, the pillar is not less necessary to us than the receptacle. For this purpose, rest requires to be distinguished into *absolute* and *relative*. Absolutely speaking, as above, no one body is at rest; but on this our little planet, the theatre of all our little doings and sufferings, bodies in abundance are to be found, which, as between any two given points of time, having been at the same distance from each other, have, during these two points of time, together with the whole interval, if any, that has been between them, been at rest. Upon the whole, then, absolute rest is not exemplified anywhere; but, on the surface of our planet, exemplifications of relative rest may be found everywhere. These things considered, henceforward as often as *rest* is spoken of as having place, relative rest, and that alone, will be intended.

The motions in which the various effects, as yet observed by us to be produced by the powers of nature, modified or not modified by human art and industry, have their essential causes, are derived from various sources. Of these motions, obvious, as when once brought to view, the task of giving a list may seem to be – obvious, and, by its conduciveness to the purpose of instruction, presenting an incontrovertible claim to the notice of the institutional writer, who, for the theatre of his labours, has chosen the field of Natural Philosophy, – the task of giving such a list, hath, it is believed, as yet, been undertaken by no one. No work in which that task has been executed, or endeavoured to be executed, is as yet anywhere to be found.

Consideration had of the utter absence of all information from more competent hands, to the author of these pages, how little soever accustomed to apply his industry to this department in the field of science, it occurred that an attempt to afford, in a manner however inadequate, a supply to this deficiency, might have its use, were it only by attracting to so interesting a subject, which presents so strong a claim to their notice, the attention of those from whose more adequate learning and ingenuity it may receive more correct and complete explanation.

Of these various sorts of motions, some are, as far as we have reason to believe, in their nature perpetual, unintermitting, or, if a common figure of speech may be allowed, immortal. Others, and by far the greater number, in their nature mortal and perishable.

Of these two so materially different heads, Which come under the former? Which under the latter? In any attempt to give answers to these questions, an answer to the question concerning the existence of what is called *perpetual motion*, is necessarily involved.

Of the following sketch the design is, in the first place, to perform the enumeration of the several distinguishable sources of motion, considered as it is wont to be produced, or capable of being produced by human art, in some determinate direction, for the purpose of accomplishing some determinate object or end in view. In the next place, by means of a systematical sketch, to bring to view the several points of relation between these several sources of motion, – the points in respect of which they agree with one another, and those on which they differ.

By this means a facility, it is hoped, will be given to the decision on the question, whether, in the preceding enumeration all such sources, actual and possible, are included; or whether any, and what are omitted.

Primum mobile is a term already in use; and by it, in each instance, is designated that mass of matter, which, when from the particular source in question, motion is considered as derived, is considered as being of all the bodies by which the motion is experienced, which, at the time in question, issues from that source, the first in which it has place. Accordingly, corresponding to every distinguishable source of motion, a *primum mobile* will be to be brought to view.

Of the two expressions, viz. sources of motion, and primum mobiles; the latter is the one, principally, if not exclusively, in use. To the other the preference has, notwithstanding, here been given, and that on several accounts.

1. It is only in as far as it points to the source whence it is derived, that the question, *what* or *which* is the *first mover?* (the body which, on the occasion in question, is of all the bodies in which the motion is observed to have place, the first in which it makes its appearance,) is an object of regard. In the class of objects designated by the generic word *motion*, men behold the cause of every effect, desirable or undesirable, which they perceive to take place. But various are the sources whence this important agent is seen to be derived. An object of anxious and continual research cannot but be, the determining, on every occasion, from which of all these sources, the article thus in universal demand, may be derived to most advantage.

Of this inquiry, source is the only direct and intrinsically important object: the primum mobile is so no otherwise than either in respect of its affording indication of the source, or, in respect of the need there is of commencing with this article, the plan of the operations instituted, for the deriving down to the ultimate object, whatsoever supply there may be occasion to draw from this source.

2. In many instances in which the source is sufficiently distinguishable to admit of a separate name, the primum mobile is altogether undiscernible; or, to speak more properly, a primum mobile is a thing that has no existence, – two bodies, or sets of bodies, move each of them towards the other, both beginning at the same instant of time; as is plainly the case, for example, in all those minute motions or dances of atoms, which belong to the experience of the chemical branch of science.

In a word, of the phrase, source of motion, the applicability will be seen to be universal; that of primum mobile, very confined; so much so that it is only in deference to usage, that any notice is here taken of it. [...]

Notes

1 The necessity to which we are subjected by the imperfection of the instrument for the purposes of discourse, the necessity of mixing falsehood with truth, on pain of being without ideas, as well as without conversation, on some of the most interesting of the subjects that lie within the pale of our cognizance, is productive but too abundantly of misconception and false reasoning; and this not only in the physical department of the field of thought, discourse, and action, but also in every other. On pain of having some of the most interesting subjects of thought, discourse, and action undiscoursed of, and even unthought of, we set to work the powers of our imaginations in the creation, as it were, of a multitude of imaginary beings, all spoken of as if they belonged to the class of bodies or substances; and on the occasion, and for the purpose of this creation, we attach to them a name or sign, called a part of speech: viz., a species of word, termed a noun substantive; the same species of word as that of which, in the character of a common name, we make use for the designation of real entities, appertaining strictly and properly to the class of substances. Beholding at a distance, in the dress of a man, sitting and playing upon an organ, an automaton figure, constructed for that purpose by the ingenuity of the mechanist, to take this creature of human art for a real man, is a sort of mistake which, at a certain distance, might happen for a time to be made by the most acute observer. In like manner, beholding a part of speech cast in the same mould with the name of a real entity, a really existing substance, no wonder if, on a variety of occasions, to the mental eye of a very acute observer, this fictitious entity thus accoutred, should present itself in the character of, and be regarded and treated as if it were a real one. How should it be otherwise, when on every occasion on which, and by every person by whom it is spoken of at all, it is spoken of as if it were

a real entity? and thus in a manner an universal attestation is given to the truth of a set of propositions, the falsity of which when once brought to view, cannot in any instance fail to be recognised.

2   The idea of *motion* is capable of being deduced from difference of position, without any difference of distance, as well as from difference of distance; but being much more complicated, the description of that case is, on that account, omitted.

3   Not so in every language, in the French, for example, (*en repos*) *rest*, is also a receptacle.

PART XIII

G. W. F. Hegel (1770–1831)

Introduction

The opening Hegel selection, "Who Thinks Abstractly?," may have been intended for publication in a newspaper. Written in 1806, it was not published during Hegel's lifetime. It is a witty sally in which common sense is convicted of abstractness while concreteness in thinking is shown to be the product of philosophical reflection. The second selection, which consists of the first twelve sections of the introduction to Hegel's *Logic* (first edition published in 1817), continues this theme in a more formal manner, characterizing the practice of philosophy and clarifying its relation to experience. The final excerpts are all from the *Phenomenology of Spirit* (1806) and include the introduction, which gives a good synopsis of the project, and the section on self-consciousness, "The Truth of Self-Certainty," that Alexander Kojève made so central to his interpretation of Hegel.

47

Who Thinks Abstractly?

Think? Abstractly? – *Sauve qui peut!* Let those who can save themselves! Even now I can hear a traitor, bought by the enemy, exclaim these words, denouncing this essay because it will plainly deal with metaphysics. For *metaphysics* is a word, no less than *abstract*, and almost *thinking* as well, from which everybody more or less runs away as from a man who has caught the plague.

But the intention here really is not so wicked, as if the meaning of thinking and of abstract were to be explained here. There is nothing the beautiful world finds as intolerable as explanations. I, too, find it terrible when somebody begins to explain, for when worst comes to worst I understand everything myself. Here the explanation of thinking and abstract would in any case be entirely superfluous; for it is only because the beautiful world knows what it means to be abstract that it runs away. Just as one does not desire what one does not know, one also cannot hate it. Nor is it my intent to try craftily to reconcile the beautiful world with thinking or with the abstract as if, under the semblance of small talk, thinking and the abstract were to be put over till in the end they had found their way into society incognito, without having aroused any disgust; even as if they were to be adopted imperceptibly by society, or, as the Swabians say, *hereingezäunselt*, before the author of this complication suddenly exposed this strange guest, namely the abstract, whom the whole party had long treated and recognized under a different title as if he were a good old acquaintance. Such scenes of recogni-

Who Thinks Abstractly? From *Hegel: Texts and Commentary*, tr. and ed. Walter Kaufmann (New York: Anchor Books, 1965). Selection: pp. 114–18.

tion which are meant to instruct the world against its will have the inexcusable fault that they simultaneously humiliate, and the wirepuller tries with his artifice to gain a little fame; but this humiliation and this vanity destroy the effect, for they push away again an instruction gained at such a price.

In any case, such a plan would be ruined from the start, for it would require that the crucial word of the riddle is not spoken at the outset. But this has already happened in the title. If this essay toyed with such craftiness, these words should not have been allowed to enter right in the beginning; but like the cabinet member in a comedy, they should have been required to walk around during the entire play in their overcoat, unbuttoning it only in the last scene, disclosing the flashing star of wisdom. The unbuttoning of the metaphysical overcoat would be less effective, to be sure, than the unbuttoning of the minister's: it would bring to light no more than a couple of words, and the best part of the joke ought to be that it is shown that society has long been in possession of the matter itself; so what they would gain in the end would be the mere name, while the minister's star signifies something real – a bag of money.

That everybody present should know what thinking is and what is abstract is presupposed in good society, and we certainly are in good society. The question is merely *who* thinks abstractly. The intent, as already mentioned, is not to reconcile society with these things, to expect it to deal with something difficult, to appeal to its conscience not frivolously to neglect such a matter that befits the rank and status of beings gifted with reason. Rather it is my intent to reconcile the beautiful world with itself, although it does not seem to have a bad conscience about this neglect; still, at least deep down, it has a certain respect for abstract thinking as something exalted, and it looks the other way not because it seems too lowly but because it appears too exalted, not because it seems too mean but rather too noble, or conversely because it seems an *Espèce*, something special; it seems something that does not lend one distinction in general society, like new clothes, but rather something that – like wretched clothes, or rich ones if they are decorated with precious stones in ancient mounts or embroidery that, be it ever so rich, has long become quasi-Chinese – excludes one from society or makes one ridiculous in it.

Who thinks abstractly? The uneducated, not the educated. Good society does not think abstractly because it is too easy, because it is too lowly (not referring to the external status) – not from an empty affectation of nobility that would place itself above that of which it is not capable, but on account of the inward inferiority of the matter.

The prejudice and respect for abstract thinking are so great that sensitive nostrils will begin to smell some satire or irony at this point; but since they read the morning paper they know that there is a prize to be had for satires and that I should therefore sooner earn it by competing for it than give up here without further ado.

I have only to adduce examples for my proposition: everybody will grant that they confirm it. A murderer is led to the place of execution. For the common populace he is nothing but a murderer. Ladies perhaps remark that he is a strong, handsome, interesting man. The populace finds this remark terrible: What? A murderer handsome? How can one think so wickedly and call a murderer handsome; no doubt, you yourselves are something not much better! This is the corruption of morals that is prevalent in the upper classes, a priest may add, knowing the bottom of things and human hearts.

One who knows men traces the development of the criminal's mind: he finds in his history, in his education, a bad family relationship between his father and mother, some tremendous harshness after this human being had done some minor wrong, so he became embittered against the social order – a first reaction to this that in effect expelled him and henceforth did not make it possible for him to preserve himself except through crime. – There may be people who will say when they hear such things: he wants to excuse this murderer! After all I remember how in my youth I heard a mayor lament that writers of books were going too far and sought to extirpate Christianity and righteousness altogether; somebody had written a defense of suicide; terrible, really too terrible! – Further questions revealed that *The Sufferings of Werther* [by Goethe, 1774] were meant.

This is abstract thinking: to see nothing in the murderer except the abstract fact that he is a murderer, and to annul all other human essence in him with this simple quality.

It is quite different in refined, sentimental circles – in Leipzig. There they strewed and bound flowers on the wheel and on the criminal who was tied to it. – But this again is the opposite abstraction. The Christians may indeed trifle with Rosicrucianism, or rather cross-rosism, and wreathe roses around the cross. The cross is the gallows and wheel that have long been hallowed. It has lost its one-sided significance of being the instrument of dishonorable punishment and, on the contrary, suggests the notion of the highest pain and the deepest rejection together with the most joyous rapture and divine honor. The wheel in Leipzig, on the other hand, wreathed with violets and poppies, is a reconciliation à la Kotzebue, a kind of slovenly sociability between sentimentality and badness.

In quite a different manner I once heard a common old woman who worked in a hospital kill the abstraction of the murderer and bring him to life for honor. The severed head had been placed on the scaffold, and the sun was shining. How beautifully, she said, the sun of God's grace shines on Binder's head! – You are not worthy of having the sun shine on you, one says to a rascal with whom one is angry. This woman saw that the murderer's head was struck by the sunshine and thus was still worthy of it. She raised it from the punishment of the scaffold into the sunny grace of God, and instead of accomplishing the reconciliation with violets and sentimental vanity, saw him accepted in grace in the higher sun.

Old woman, your eggs are rotten! the maid says to the market woman. What? she replies, my eggs rotten? You may be rotten! You say that about my eggs? You? Did not lice eat your father on the highways? Didn't your mother run away with the French, and didn't your grandmother die in a public hospital? Let her get a whole shirt instead of that flimsy scarf; we know well where she got that scarf and her hats: if it were not for those officers, many wouldn't be decked out like that these days, and if their ladyships paid more attention to their households, many would be in jail right now. Let her mend the holes in her stockings! – In brief, she does not leave one whole thread on her. She thinks abstractly and subsumes the other woman – scarf, hat, shirt, etc., as well as her fingers and other parts of her, and her father and whole family, too – solely under the crime that she has found the eggs rotten. Everything about her is colored through and through by these rotten eggs, while those officers of which the market woman spoke – if, as one may seriously doubt, there is anything to that – may have got to see very different things.

To move from the maid to a servant, no servant is worse off than one who works for a man of low class and low income; and he is better off the nobler his master is. The common man again thinks more abstractly, he gives himself noble airs vis-à-vis the servant and relates himself to the other man merely as to a servant; he clings to this one predicate. The servant is best off among the French. The nobleman is familiar with his servant, the Frenchman is his friend. When they are alone, the servant does the talking: see Diderot's *Jacques et son maître*; the master does nothing but take snuff and see what time it is and lets the servant take care of everything else. The nobleman knows that the servant is not merely a servant, but also knows the latest city news, the girls, and harbors good suggestions; he asks him about these matters, and the servant may say what he knows about these questions. With a French master, the servant may not only do this; he may also broach a subject, have his own opinions and insist on them; and when the master wants something, it is not done with an order but he has to argue and convince the servant of his opinion and add a good word to make sure that this opinion retains the upper hand.

In the army we encounter the same difference. Among the Austrians a soldier may be beaten, he is canaille; for whatever has the passive right to be beaten is canaille. Thus the common soldier is for the officer this *abstractum* of a beatable subject with whom a gentleman who has a uniform and *port d'epée* must trouble himself – and that could drive one to make a pact with the devil.

48

Logic

Introduction

§ 1

Philosophy misses an advantage enjoyed by the other sciences. It cannot like them rest the existence of its objects on the natural admissions of consciousness, nor can it assume that its method of cognition, either for starting or for continuing, is one already accepted. The objects of philosophy, it is true, are upon the whole the same as those of religion. In both the object is Truth, in that supreme sense in which God and God only is the Truth. Both in like manner go on to treat of the finite worlds of Nature and the human Mind, with their relation to each other and to their truth in God. Some *acquaintance* with its objects, therefore, philosophy may and even must presume, that and a certain interest in them to boot, were it for no other reason than this: that in point of time the mind makes general *images* of objects, long before it makes *notions* of them, and that it is only through these mental images, and by recourse to them, that the thinking mind rises to know and comprehend *thinkingly*.

But with the rise of this thinking study of things, it soon becomes evident that thought will be satisfied with nothing short of showing the *necessity* of its facts, of demonstrating the existence of its objects, as well as their nature and qualities. Our original acquaintance with them is thus discovered to be inadequate. We can assume nothing and assert nothing dogmatically; nor can we accept

The Logic of Hegel, tr. William Wallace (Oxford, 1873). Selection: Introduction, sects 1–12.

the assertions and assumptions of others. And yet we must make a beginning: and a beginning, as primary and underived, makes an assumption, or rather is an assumption. It seems as if it were impossible to make a beginning at all.

§ 2

This *thinking study of things* may serve, in a general way, as a description of philosophy. But the description is too wide. If it be correct to say, that thought makes the distinction between man and the lower animals, then everything human is human, for the sole and simple reason that it is due to the operation of thought. Philosophy, on the other hand, is a peculiar mode of thinking – a mode in which thinking becomes knowledge, and knowledge through notions. However great therefore may be the identity and essential unity of the two modes of thought, the philosophic mode gets to be different from the more general thought which acts in all that is human, in all that gives humanity its distinctive character. And this difference connects itself with the fact that the strictly human and thought-induced phenomena of consciousness do not originally appear in the form of a thought, but as a feeling, a perception, or mental image – all of which aspects must be distinguished from the form of thought proper.

According to an old preconceived idea, which has passed into a trivial proposition, it is thought which marks the man off from the animals. Yet trivial as this old belief may seem, it must, strangely enough, be recalled to mind in presence of certain preconceived ideas of the present day.

These ideas would put feeling and thought so far apart as to make them opposites, and would represent them as so antagonistic, that feeling, particularly religious feeling, is supposed to be contaminated, perverted, and even annihilated by thought. They also emphatically hold that religion and piety grow out of, and rest upon something else, and not on thought. But those who make this separation forget meanwhile that only man has the capacity for religion, and that animals no more have religion than they have law and morality.

Those who insist on this separation of religion from thinking usually have before their minds the sort of thought that may be styled *after-thought*. They mean "reflective" thinking, which has to deal with thoughts as thoughts, and brings them into consciousness. Slackness to perceive and keep in view this distinction which philosophy definitely draws in respect of thinking is the source of the crudest objections and reproaches against philosophy. Man – and that just because it is his nature to think – is the only being that possesses law, religion, and morality. In these spheres of human life, therefore, thinking, under the guise of feeling, faith, or generalized image, has not been inactive: its action and its productions are there present and therein contained. But it is one thing to have such feelings and generalized images that have been moulded and permeated by thought, and another thing to have thoughts about them. The thoughts, to which after-thought upon those modes of consciousness gives rise, are what is comprised under reflection, general reasoning, and the like, as well as under philosophy itself.

The neglect of this distinction between thought in general and the reflective thought of philosophy has also led to another and more frequent misunderstanding. Reflection of this kind has been often maintained to be the condition, or even the only way, of attaining a consciousness and certitude of the Eternal and True. The (now somewhat antiquated) metaphysical proofs of God's existence, for example, have been treated, as if a knowledge of them and a conviction of their truth were the only and essential means of producing a belief and conviction that there is a God. Such a doctrine would find its parallel, if we said that eating was impossible before we had acquired a knowledge of the chemical, botanical, and zoological characters of our food; and that we must delay digestion till we had finished the study of anatomy and physiology. Were it so, these sciences in their field, like philosophy in its, would gain greatly in point of utility; in fact, their utility would rise to the height of absolute and universal indispensableness. Or rather, instead of being indispensable, they would not exist at all.

§ 3

The *Content*, of whatever kind it be, with which our consciousness is taken up, is what constitutes the qualitative character of our feelings, perceptions, fancies, and ideas; of our aims and duties; and of our thoughts and notions. From this point of view, feeling, perception, etc., are the *forms* assumed by these contents. The contents remain one and the same, whether they are felt, seen, represented, or willed, and whether they are merely felt, or felt with an admixture of thoughts, or merely and simply thought. In any one of these forms, or in the admixture of several, the contents confront consciousness, or are its *object*. But when they are thus objects of consciousness, the modes of the several forms ally themselves with the contents; and each form of them appears in consequence to give rise to a special object. Thus what is the same at bottom may look like a different sort of fact.

The several modes of feeling, perception, desire, and will, so far as we are *aware* of them, are in general called ideas (mental representations): and it may be roughly said that philosophy puts thoughts, categories, or, in more precise language, adequate *notions*, in the place of the generalized images we ordinarily call ideas. Mental impressions such as these may be regarded as the metaphors of thoughts and notions. But to have these figurate conceptions does not imply that we appreciate their intellectual significance, the thoughts and rational notions to which they correspond. Conversely, it is one thing to have thoughts and intelligent notions, and another to know what impressions, perceptions, and feelings correspond to them.

This difference will to some extent explain what people call the unintelligibility of philosophy. Their difficulty lies partly in an incapacity – which in itself is nothing but want of habit – for abstract thinking; i.e. in an inability to get hold of pure thoughts and move about in them. In our ordinary state of mind, the thoughts are clothed upon and made one with the sensuous or spiritual material of the hour; and in reflection, meditation, and general reasoning, we introduce a blend of thoughts into feelings, percepts, and mental images. (Thus, in propositions where the subject-matter is due to the senses – e.g. "This leaf is green" – we have such categories introduced, as being and individuality.) But it is a very different thing to make the thoughts pure and simple our object.

But their complaint that philosophy is unintelligible is as much due to another reason; and that is an impatient wish to have before them as a mental picture that which is in the mind as a thought or notion. When people are asked to apprehend some notion, they often complain that they do not know what they have to think. But the fact is that in a notion there is nothing further to be thought than the notion itself. What the phrase reveals is a hankering after an image with which we are already familiar. The mind, denied the use of its familiar ideas, feels the ground where it once stood firm and at home taken away from beneath it, and, when transported into the region of pure thought, cannot tell where in the world it is.

One consequence of this weakness is that authors, preachers, and orators are found most intelligible, when they speak of things which their readers or hearers already know by rote – things which the latter are conversant with, and which require no explanation.

§ 4

The philosopher then has to reckon with popular modes of thought, and with the objects of religion. In dealing with the ordinary modes of mind, he will first of all, as we saw, have to prove and almost to awaken the need for his peculiar method of knowledge. In dealing with the objects of religion, and with truth as a whole, he will have to show that philosophy is capable of apprehending them from its own resources; and should a difference from religious conceptions come to light, he will have to justify the points in which it diverges.

§ 5

To give the reader a preliminary explanation of the distinction thus made, and to let him see at the same moment that the real import of our consciousness is retained, and even for the first time put in its proper light, when translated into the form of thought and the notion of reason, it may be

well to recall another of these old unreasoned beliefs. And that is the conviction that to get at the truth of any object or event, even of feelings, perceptions, opinions, and mental ideas, we must think it over. Now in any case to think things over is at least to transform feelings, ordinary ideas, etc. into thoughts.

Nature has given every one a faculty of thought. But thought is all that philosophy claims as the form proper to her business: and thus the inadequate view which ignores the distinction stated in § 3 leads to a new delusion, the reverse of the complaint previously mentioned about the unintelligibility of philosophy. In other words, this science must often submit to the slight of hearing even people who have never taken any trouble with it talking as if they thoroughly understood all about it. With no preparation beyond an ordinary education they do not hesitate, especially under the influence of religious sentiment, to philosophize and to criticize philosophy. Everybody allows that to know any other science you must have first studied it, and that you can only claim to express a judgement upon it in virtue of such knowledge. Everybody allows that to make a shoe you must have learned and practised the craft of the shoemaker, though every man has a model in his own foot, and possesses in his hands the natural endowments for the operations required. For philosophy alone, it seems to be imagined, such study, care, and application are not in the least requisite.

This comfortable view of what is required for a philosopher has recently received corroboration through the theory of immediate or intuitive knowledge.

§ 6

So much for the form of philosophical knowledge. It is no less desirable, on the other hand, that philosophy should understand that its content is no other than *actuality*, that core of truth which, originally produced and producing itself within the precincts of the mental life, has become the *world*, the inward and outward world, of consciousness. At first we become aware of these contents in what we call Experience. But even Experience, as it surveys the wide range of inward and outward existence, has sense enough to distinguish the mere appearance, which is transient and meaningless, from what in itself really deserves the name of actuality. As it is only in form that philosophy is distinguished from other modes of attaining an acquaintance with this same sum of being, it must necessarily be in harmony with actuality and experience. In fact, this harmony may be viewed as at least an extrinsic means of testing the truth of a philosophy. Similarly it may be held the highest and final aim of philosophic science to bring about, through the ascertainment of this harmony, a reconciliation of the self-conscious reason with the reason which *is* in the world – in other words, with actuality.

In the Preface to my *Philosophy of Law*, p. xix, are found the propositions:

What is reasonable is actual

and

What is actual is reasonable.

These simple statements have given rise to expressions of surprise and hostility, even in quarters where it would be reckoned an insult to presume absence of philosophy, and still more of religion. Religion at least need not be brought in evidence; its doctrines of the divine governments of the world affirm these propositions too decidedly. For their philosophic sense, we must presuppose intelligence enough to know, not only that God is actual, that He is the supreme actuality, that He alone is truly actual; but also, as regards the logical bearings of the question, that existence is in part mere appearance, and only in part actuality. In common life, any freak of fancy, any error, evil and everything of the nature of evil, as well as every degenerate and transitory existence whatever, gets in a casual way the name of actuality. But even our ordinary feelings are enough to forbid a casual (fortuitous) existence getting the emphatic name of an actual; for by fortuitous we mean an existence which has no greater value than that of something possible, which may as well not be as be. As for the term Actuality, these critics would have done well to consider the sense in which I employ it. In a detailed Logic I had treated among other things of actuality, and accurately distinguished it not only from the fortuitous, which, after all, has existence, but even from the cognate categories of existence and the other modifications of being.

The actuality of the rational stands opposed by the popular fancy that Ideas and ideals are nothing but chimeras, and philosophy a mere system of such phantasms. It is also opposed by the very different fancy that Ideas and ideals are something far too excellent to have actuality, or something too impotent to procure it for themselves. This divorce between idea and reality is especially dear to the analytic understanding which looks upon its own abstractions, dreams though they are, as something true and real, and prides itself on the imperative "ought", which it takes especial pleasure in prescribing even on the field of politics. As if the world had waited on it to learn how it ought to be, and was not! For, if it were as it ought to be, what would come of the precocious wisdom of that "ought"? When understanding turns this "ought" against trivial external and transitory objects, against social regulations or conditions, which very likely possess a great relative importance for a certain time and special circles, it may often be right. In such a case the intelligent observer may meet much that fails to satisfy the general requirements of right; for who is not acute enough to see a great deal in his own surroundings which is really far from being as it ought to be? But such acuteness is mistaken in the conceit that, when it examines these objects and pronounces what they ought to be, it is dealing with questions of philosophic science. The object of philosophy is the Idea: and the Idea is not so impotent as merely to have a right or an obligation to exist without actually existing. The object of philosophy is an actuality of which those objects, social regulations and conditions, are only the superficial outside.

§ 7

Thus reflection – thinking things over – in a general way involves the principle (which also means the beginning) of philosophy. And when the reflective spirit arose again in its independence in modern times, after the epoch of the Lutheran Reformation, it did not, as in its beginnings among the Greeks, stand merely aloof, in a world of its own, but at once turned its energies also upon the apparently illimitable material of the phenomenal world. In this way the name philosophy came to be applied to all those branches of knowledge, which are engaged in ascertaining the standard and Universal in the ocean of empirical individualities, as well as in ascertaining the Necessary element, or Laws, to be found in the apparent disorder of the endless masses of the fortuitous. It thus appears that modern philosophy derives its materials from our own personal observations and perceptions of the external and internal world, from nature as well as from the mind and heart of man, when both stand in the immediate presence of the observer.

This principle of Experience carries with it the unspeakably important condition that, in order to accept and believe any fact, we must be in contact with it; or, in more exact terms, that we must find the fact united and combined with the certainty of our own selves. We must be in touch with our subject-matter, whether it be by means of our external senses, or, else, by our profounder mind and our intimate self-consciousness. This principle is the same as that which has in the present day been termed faith, immediate knowledge, the revelation in the outward world, and, above all, in our own heart.

Those sciences, which thus got the name of philosophy, we call *empirical* sciences, for the reason that they take their departure from experience. Still the essential results which they aim at and provide are laws, general propositions, a theory – the thoughts of what is found existing. On this ground the Newtonian physics was called Natural Philosophy. Hugo Grotius, again, by putting together and comparing the behaviour of states towards each other as recorded in history, succeeded, with the help of the ordinary methods of general reasoning, in laying down certain general principles, and establishing a theory which may be termed the Philosophy of International Law. In England this is still the usual signification of the term philosophy. Newton continues to be celebrated as the greatest of philosophers: and the name goes down as far as the price-lists of instrument-makers. All instruments, such as the thermometer and barometer, which do not come under the special head of magnetic or electric apparatus, are styled philosophical instruments.[1] Surely thought, and not a mere combination of wood, iron, etc., ought to be called the instrument of philosophy! The recent science of Political Economy in particular, which in Germany is known as Rational Economy of the State, or intelligent national economy, has in England especially appropriated the name of philosophy.[2]

§ 8

In its own field this empirical knowledge may at first give satisfaction; but in two ways it is seen to come short. In the first place there is another circle of objects which it does not embrace. These are Freedom, Spirit, and God. They belong to a dif-

ferent sphere, not because it can be said that they have nothing to do with experience; for though they are certainly not experiences of the senses, it is quite an identical proposition to say that whatever is in consciousness is experienced. The real ground for assigning them to another field of cognition is that in their scope and *content* these objects evidently show themselves as infinite.

There is an old phrase often wrongly attributed to Aristotle, and supposed to express the general tenor of his philosophy. *Nihil est in intellectu quod non fuerit in sensu*: there is nothing in thought which has not been in sense and experience. If speculative philosophy refused to admit this maxim, it can only have done so from a misunderstanding. It will, however, on the converse side no less assert: *Nihil est in sensu quod non fuerit in intellectu*. And this may be taken in two senses. In the general sense it means that νοῦς or spirit (the more profound idea of νοῦς in modern thought) is the cause of the world. In its special meaning (see § 2) it asserts that the sentiment of right, morals, and religion is a sentiment (and in that way an experience) of such scope and such character that it can spring from and rest upon thought alone.

§ 9

But in the second place in point of *form* the subjective reason desires a further satisfaction than empirical knowledge gives; and this form is, in the widest sense of the term, Necessity (§ I). The method of empirical science exhibits two defects. The first is that the Universal or general principle contained in it, the genus, or kind, etc., is, on its own account, indeterminate and vague, and therefore not on its own account connected with the Particulars or the details. Either is external and accidental to the other; and it is the same with the particular facts which are brought into union: each is external and accidental to the others. The second defect is that the beginnings are in every case data and postulates, neither accounted for nor deduced. In both these points the form of necessity fails to get its due. Hence reflection, whenever it sets itself to remedy these defects, becomes speculative thinking, the thinking proper to philosophy. As a species of reflection, therefore, which, though it has a certain community of nature with the reflection already mentioned, is nevertheless different from it, philosophic thought thus possesses, in addition to the common forms, some forms of its own, of which the Notion may be taken as the type.

The relation of speculative science to the other sciences may be stated in the following terms. It does not in the least neglect the empirical facts contained in the several sciences, but recognizes and adopts them: it appreciates and applies towards its own structure the universal element in these sciences, their laws and classifications: but besides all this, into the categories of science it introduces, and gives currency to, other categories. The difference, looked at in this way, is only a change of categories. Speculative Logic contains all previous Logic and Metaphysics: it preserves the same forms of thought, the same laws and objects – while at the same time remodelling and expanding them with wider categories.

From *notion* in the speculative sense we should distinguish what is ordinarily called a notion. The phrase, that no notion can ever comprehend the Infinite, a phrase which has been repeated over and over again till it has grown axiomatic, is based upon this narrow estimate of what is meant by notions.

§ 10

This thought, which is proposed as the instrument of philosophic knowledge, itself calls for further explanation. We must understand in what way it possesses necessity or cogency: and when it claims to be equal to the task of apprehending the absolute objects (God, Spirit, Freedom), that claim must be substantiated. Such an explanation, however, is itself a lesson in philosophy, and properly falls within the scope of the science itself. A preliminary attempt to make matters plain would only be unphilosophical, and consist of a tissue of assumptions, assertions, and inferential pros and cons, i.e. of dogmatism without cogency, as against which there would be an equal right of counter-dogmatism.

A main line of argument in the Critical Philosophy bids us pause before proceeding to inquire into God or into the true being of things, and tells us first of all to examine the faculty of cognition and see whether it is equal to such an effort. We ought, says Kant, to become acquainted with the instrument, before we undertake the work for which it is to be employed; for if the instrument be insufficient, all our trouble will be spent in vain.

The plausibility of this suggestion has won for it general assent and admiration; the result of which has been to withdraw cognition from an interest in its objects and absorption in the study of them, and to direct it back upon itself; and so turn it to a question of form. Unless we wish to be deceived by words, it is easy to see what this amounts to. In the case of other instruments, we can try and criticize them in other ways than by setting about the special work for which they are destined. But the examination of knowledge can only be carried out by an act of knowledge. To examine this so-called instrument is the same thing as to know it. But to seek to know before we know is as absurd as the wise resolution of Scholasticus, not to venture into the water until he had learned to swim.

Reinhold saw the confusion with which this style of commencement is chargeable, and tried to get out of the difficulty by starting with a hypothetical and problematical stage of philosophizing. In this way he supposed that it would be possible, nobody can tell how, to get along, until we found ourselves, further on, arrived at the primary truth of truths. His method, when closely looked into, will be seen to be identical with a very common practice. It starts from a substratum of experiential fact, or from a provisional assumption which has been brought into a definition; and then proceeds to analyse this starting-point. We can detect in Reinhold's argument a perception of the truth, that the usual course which proceeds by assumptions and anticipations is no better than a hypothetical and problematical mode of procedure. But his perceiving this does not alter the character of this method; it only makes clear its imperfections.

§ 11

The special conditions which call for the existence of philosophy may be thus described. The mind or spirit, when it is sentient or perceptive, finds its object in something sensuous; when it imagines, in a picture or image; when it wills, in an aim or end. But in contrast to, or it may be only in distinction from, these forms of its existence and of its objects, the mind has also to gratify the cravings of its highest and most inward life. That innermost self is thought. Thus the mind renders thought its object. In the best meaning of the phrase, it comes to itself; for thought is its principle, and its very unadulterated self. But while thus occupied, thought entangles itself in contradictions, i.e. loses itself in the hard-and-fast non-identity of its thoughts, and so, instead of reaching itself, is caught and held in its counterpart. This result, to which honest but narrow thinking leads the mere understanding, is resisted by the loftier craving of which we have spoken. That craving expresses the perseverance of thought, which continues true to itself, even in this conscious loss of its native rest and independence, "that it may overcome" and work out in itself the solution of its own contradictions.

To see that thought in its very nature is dialectical, and that, as understanding, it must fall into contradiction – the negative of itself – will form one of the main lessons of logic. When thought grows hopeless of ever achieving, by its own means, the solution of the contradiction which it has by its own action brought upon itself, it turns back to those solutions of the question with which the mind had learned to pacify itself in some of its other modes and forms. Unfortunately, however, the retreat of thought has led it, as Plato noticed even in his time, to a very uncalled-for hatred of reason (misology); and it then takes up against its own endeavours that hostile attitude of which an example is seen in the doctrine that "immediate" knowledge, as it is called, is the exclusive form in which we become cognizant of truth.

§ 12

The rise of philosophy is due to these cravings of thought. Its point of departure is Experience; including under that name both our immediate consciousness and the inductions from it. Awakened, as it were, by this stimulus, thought is vitally characterized by raising itself above the natural state of mind, above the senses and inferences from the senses into its own unadulterated element, and by assuming, accordingly, at first a stand-aloof and negative attitude towards the point from which it started. Through this state of antagonism to the phenomena of sense its first satisfaction is found in itself, in the Idea of the universal essence of these phenomena: an Idea (the Absolute, or God) which may be more or less abstract. Meanwhile, on the other hand, the sciences, based on experience, exert upon the mind a stimulus to overcome the form in which their varied contents are presented, and to elevate these contents to the rank of necessary truth. For the facts of science

have the aspect of a vast conglomerate, one thing coming side by side with another, as if they were merely given and presented – as in short devoid of all essential or necessary connection. In consequence of this stimulus thought is dragged out of its unrealized universality and its fancied or merely possible satisfaction, and impelled onwards to a development from itself. On one hand this development only means that thought incorporates the contents of science, in all their speciality of detail as submitted. On the other it makes these contents imitate the action of the original creative thought, and present the aspect of a free evolution determined by the logic of the fact alone.

On the relation between "immediacy" and "mediation" in consciousness we shall speak later, expressly and with more detail. Here it may be sufficient to premise that, though the two "moments" or factors present themselves as distinct, still neither of them can be absent, nor can one exist apart from the other. Thus the knowledge of God, as of every supersensible reality, is in its true character an exaltation above sensations or perceptions: it consequently involves a negative attitude to the initial data of sense, and to that extent implies mediation. For to mediate is to take something as a beginning and to go onward to a second thing; so that the existence of this second thing depends on our having reached it from something else contradistinguished from it. In spite of this, the knowledge of God is no mere sequel, dependent on the empirical phase of consciousness: in fact, its independence is essentially secured through this negation and exaltation. No doubt, if we attach an unfair prominence to the fact of mediation, and represent it as implying a state of conditionedness, it may be said – not that the remark would mean much – that philosophy is the child of experience, and owes its rise to *a posteriori* fact. (As a matter of fact, thinking is always the negation of what we have immediately before us.) With as much truth however we may be said to owe eating to the means of nourishment, so long as we can have no eating without them. If we take this view, eating is certainly represented as ungrateful: it devours that to which it owes itself. Thinking, upon this view of its action, is equally ungrateful.

But there is also an *a priori* aspect of thought, whereby a mediation, not made by anything external but by a reflection into self, we have that immediacy which is universality, the self-complacency of thought which is so much at home with itself that it feels an innate indifference to descend to particulars, and in that way to the development of its own nature. It is thus also with religion, which whether it be rude or elaborate, whether it be invested with scientific precision of detail or confined to the simple faith of the heart, possesses, throughout, the same intensive nature of contentment and felicity. But if thought never gets further than the universality of the Ideas, as was perforce the case in the first philosophies (when the Eleatics never got beyond Being, or Heraclitus beyond Becoming), it is justly open to the charge of formalism. Even in a more advanced phase of philosophy, we may often find a doctrine which has mastered merely certain abstract propositions or formulae, such as, "In the absolute all is one", "Subject and object are identical" – and only repeating the same thing when it comes to particulars. Bearing in mind this first period of thought, the period of mere generality, we may safely say that experience is the real author of *growth* and *advance* in philosophy. For, firstly, the empirical sciences do not stop short at the mere observation of the individual features of a phenomenon. By the aid of thought, they are able to meet philosophy with materials prepared for it, in the shape of general uniformities, i.e. laws, and classifications of the phenomena. When this is done, the particular facts which they contain are ready to be received into philosophy. This, secondly, implies a certain compulsion on thought itself to proceed to these concrete specific truths. The reception into philosophy of these scientific materials, now that thought has removed their immediacy and made them cease to be mere data, forms at the same time a development of thought out of itself. Philosophy, then, owes its development to the empirical sciences. In return it gives their contents what is so vital to them, the freedom of thought – gives them, in short, an *a priori* character. These contents are now warranted necessary, and no longer depend on the evidence of facts merely, that they were so found and so experienced. The fact as experienced thus becomes an illustration and a copy of the original and completely self-supporting activity of thought.

Notes

1 The journal too, edited by Thomson, is called "Annals of Philosophy; or, Magazine of Chemistry, Mineralogy, Mechanics, Natural History, Agriculture, and Arts". We can easily guess from the title what sort of subjects are here to be understood under the term "philosophy". Among the advertisements of books just published, I lately found the following notice in an English newspaper: "The Art of Preserving the Hair, on Philosophical Principles, neatly printed in post 8vo, price seven shillings". By philosophical principles for the preservation of the hair are probably meant chemical or physiological principles.

2 In connection with the general principles of Political Economy, the term "philosophical" is frequently heard from the lips of English statesmen, even in their public speeches. In the House of Commons, on 2 Feb. 1825, Brougham, speaking on the address in reply to the speech from the throne, talked of "the statesman-like and philosophical principles of Free-trade – for philosophical they undoubtedly are – upon the acceptance of which his majesty this day congratulated the House". Nor is this language confined to members of the Opposition. At the ship-owners' yearly dinner in the same month, under the chairmanship of the Premier Lord Liverpool, supported by Canning the Secretary of State, and Sir C. Long the Paymaster-General of the Army, Canning in reply to the toast which had been proposed said: "A period has just begun, in which ministers have it in their power to apply to the administration of this country the sound maxims of a profound philosophy." Differences there may be between English and German philosophy: still, considering that elsewhere the name of philosophy is used only as a nickname and insult, or as something odious, it is a matter of rejoicing to see it still honoured in the mouth of the English Government.

49

Phenomenology of Spirit

Introduction

73. It is a natural assumption that in philosophy, before we start to deal with its proper subject-matter, viz. the actual cognition of what truly is, one must first of all come to an understanding about cognition, which is regarded either as the instrument to get hold of the Absolute, or as the medium through which one discovers it. A certain uneasiness seems justified, partly because there are different types of cognition, and one of them might be more appropriate than another for the attainment of this goal, so that we could make a bad choice of means; and partly because cognition is a faculty of a definite kind and scope, and thus, without a more precise definition of its nature and limits, we might grasp clouds of error instead of the heaven of truth. This feeling of uneasiness is surely bound to be transformed into the conviction that the whole project of securing for consciousness through cognition what exists in itself is absurd, and that there is a boundary between cognition and the Absolute that completely separates them. For, if cognition is the instrument for getting hold of absolute being, it is obvious that the use of an instrument on a thing certainly does not let it be what it is for itself, but rather sets out to reshape and alter it. If, on the other hand, cognition is not an instrument of our activity but a more or less passive medium through which the light of truth reaches us, then again we do not receive the truth as it is in itself, but only as it exists through

Phenomenology of Spirit (1806), tr. A. V. Miller (Oxford University Press, 1977). Selections: Introduction, pp. 46–57; "The Truth of Self-Certainty," pp. 104–19.

and in this medium. Either way we employ a means which immediately brings about the opposite of its own end; or rather, what is really absurd is that we should make use of a means at all.

It would seem, to be sure, that this evil could be remedied through an acquaintance with the way in which the *instrument* works; for this would enable us to eliminate from the representation of the Absolute which we have gained through it whatever is due to the instrument, and thus get the truth in its purity. But this "improvement" would in fact only bring us back to where we were before. If we remove from a reshaped thing what the instrument has done to it, then the thing – here the Absolute – becomes for us exactly what it was before this [accordingly] superfluous effort. On the other hand, if the Absolute is supposed merely to be brought nearer to us through this instrument, without anything in it being altered, like a bird caught by a lime-twig, it would surely laugh our little ruse to scorn, if it were not with us, in and for itself, all along, and of its own volition. For a ruse is just what cognition would be in such a case, since it would, with its manifold exertions, be giving itself the air of doing something quite different from creating a merely immediate and therefore effortless relationship. Or, if by testing cognition, which we conceive of as a *medium*, we get to know the law of its refraction, it is again useless to subtract this from the end result. For it is not the refraction of the ray, but the ray itself whereby truth reaches us, that is cognition; and if this were removed, all that would be indicated would be a pure direction or a blank space.

74. Meanwhile, if the fear of falling into error sets up a mistrust of Science, which in the absence

of such scruples gets on with the work itself, and actually cognizes something, it is hard to see why we should not turn round and mistrust this very mistrust. Should we not be concerned as to whether this fear of error is not just the error itself? Indeed, this fear takes something – a great deal in fact – for granted as truth, supporting its scruples and inferences on what is itself in need of prior scrutiny to see if it is true. To be specific, it takes for granted certain ideas about cognition as an *instrument* and as a *medium*, and assumes that there is a *difference between ourselves and this cognition*. Above all, it presupposes that the Absolute stands on one side and cognition on the other, independent and separated from it, and yet is something real; or in other words, it presupposes that cognition which, since it is excluded from the Absolute, is surely outside of the truth as well, is nevertheless true, an assumption whereby what calls itself fear of error reveals itself rather as fear of the truth.

75. This conclusion stems from the fact that the Absolute alone is true, or the truth alone is absolute. One may set this aside on the grounds that there is a type of cognition which, though it does not cognize the Absolute as Science aims to, is still true, and that cognition in general, though it be incapable of grasping the Absolute, is still capable of grasping other kinds of truth. But we gradually come to see that this kind of talk which goes back and forth only leads to a hazy distinction between an absolute truth and some other kind of truth, and that words like "absolute", "cognition", etc. presuppose a meaning which has yet to be ascertained.

76. Instead of troubling ourselves with such useless ideas and locutions about cognition as "an instrument for getting hold of the Absolute", or as "a medium through which we view the truth" (relationships which surely, in the end, are what all these ideas of a cognition cut off from the Absolute, and an Absolute separated from cognition, amount to); instead of putting up with excuses which create the incapacity of Science by assuming relationships of this kind in order to be exempt from the hard work of Science, while at the same time giving the impression of working seriously and zealously; instead of bothering to refute all these ideas, we could reject them out of hand as adventitious and arbitrary, and the words associated with them like "absolute", "cognition", "objective" and "subjective", and countless others whose meaning is assumed to be generally familiar,

could even be regarded as so much deception. For to give the impression that their meaning is generally well known, or that their Notion is comprehended, looks more like an attempt to avoid the main problem, which is precisely to provide this Notion. We could, with better justification, simply spare ourselves the trouble of paying any attention whatever to such ideas and locutions; for they are intended to ward off Science itself, and constitute merely an empty appearance of knowing, which vanishes immediately as soon as Science comes on the scene. But Science, just because it comes on the scene, is itself an appearance: in coming on the scene it is not yet Science in its developed and unfolded truth. In this connection it makes no difference whether we think of Science as the appearance because it comes on the scene alongside another mode of knowledge, or whether we call that other untrue knowledge its manifestation. In any case Science must liberate itself from this semblance, and it can do so only by turning against it. For, when confronted with a knowledge that is without truth, Science can neither merely reject it as an ordinary way of looking at things, while assuring us that its Science is a quite different sort of cognition for which that ordinary knowledge is of no account whatever; nor can it appeal to the vulgar view for the intimations it gives us of something better to come. By the former *assurance*, Science would be declaring its power to lie simply in its *being*; but the untrue knowledge likewise appeals to the fact that *it is*, and *assures* us that for it Science is of no account. *One* bare assurance is worth just as much as another. Still less can Science appeal to whatever intimations of something better it may detect in the cognition that is without truth, to the signs which point in the direction of Science. For one thing, it would only be appealing again to what merely *is*; and for another, it would only be appealing to itself, and to itself in the mode in which it exists in the cognition that is without truth. In other words, it would be appealing to an inferior form of its being, to the way it appears, rather than to what it is in and for itself. It is for this reason that an exposition of how knowledge makes its appearance will here be undertaken.

77. Now, because it has only phenomenal knowledge for its object, this exposition seems not to be Science, free and self-moving in its own peculiar shape; yet from this standpoint it can be regarded as the path of the natural consciousness which presses forward to true knowledge; or as the

way of the Soul which journeys through the series of its own configurations as though they were the stations appointed for it by its own nature, so that it may purify itself for the life of the Spirit, and achieve finally, through a completed experience of itself, the awareness of what it really is in itself.

78. Natural consciousness will show itself to be only the Notion of knowledge, or in other words, not to be real knowledge. But since it directly takes itself to be real knowledge, this path has a negative significance for it, and what is in fact the realization of the Notion, counts for it rather as the loss of its own self; for it does lose its truth on this path. The road can therefore be regarded as the pathway of *doubt*, or more precisely as the way of despair. For what happens on it is not what is ordinarily understood when the word "doubt" is used: shilly-shallying about this or that presumed truth, followed by a return to that truth again, after the doubt has been appropriately dispelled – so that at the end of the process the matter is taken to be what it was in the first place. On the contrary, this path is the conscious insight into the untruth of phenomenal knowledge, for which the supreme reality is what is in truth only the unrealized Notion. Therefore this thoroughgoing scepticism is also not the scepticism with which an earnest zeal for truth and Science fancies it has prepared and equipped itself in their service: the *resolve*, in Science, not to give oneself over to the thoughts of others, upon mere authority, but to examine everything for oneself and follow only one's own conviction, or better still, to produce everything oneself, and accept only one's own deed as what is true.

The series of configurations which consciousness goes through along this road is, in reality, the detailed history of the *education* of consciousness itself to the standpoint of Science. That zealous resolve represents this education simplistically as something directly over and done with in the making of the resolution; but the way of the Soul is the actual fulfilment of the resolution, in contrast to the untruth of that view. Now, following one's own conviction is, of course, more than giving oneself over to authority; but changing an opinion accepted on authority into an opinion held out of personal conviction, does not necessarily alter the content of the opinion, or replace error with truth. The only difference between being caught up in a system of opinions and prejudices based on personal conviction, and being caught up in one based on the authority of others, lies in the

added conceit that is innate in the former position. The scepticism that is directed against the whole range of phenomenal consciousness, on the other hand, renders the Spirit for the first time competent to examine what truth is. For it brings about a state of despair about all the so-called natural ideas, thoughts, and opinions, regardless of whether they are called one's own or someone else's, ideas with which the consciousness that sets about the examination [of truth] *straight away* is still filled and hampered, so that it is, in fact, incapable of carrying out what it wants to undertake.

79. The necessary progression and interconnection of the forms of the unreal consciousness will by itself bring to pass the *completion* of the series. To make this more intelligible, it may be remarked, in a preliminary and general way, that the exposition of the untrue consciousness in its untruth is not a merely *negative* procedure. The natural consciousness itself normally takes this one-sided view of it; and a knowledge which makes this one-sidedness its very essence is itself one of the patterns of incomplete consciousness which occurs on the road itself, and will manifest itself in due course. This is just the scepticism which only ever sees pure nothingness in its result and abstracts from the fact that this nothingness is specifically the nothingness of that *from which it results*. For it is only when it is taken as the result of that from which it emerges, that it is, in fact, the true result; in that case it is itself a *determinate* nothingness, one which has a *content*. The scepticism that ends up with the bare abstraction of nothingness or emptiness cannot get any further from there, but must wait to see whether something new comes along and what it is, in order to throw it too into the same empty abyss. But when, on the other hand, the result is conceived as it is in truth, namely, as a *determinate* negation, a new form has thereby immediately arisen, and in the negation the transition is made through which the progress through the complete series of forms comes about of itself.

80. But the *goal* is as necessarily fixed for knowledge as the serial progression; it is the point where knowledge no longer needs to go beyond itself, where knowledge finds itself, where Notion corresponds to object and object to Notion. Hence the progress towards this goal is also unhalting, and short of it no satisfaction is to be found at any of the stations on the way. Whatever is confined within the limits of a natural life cannot by its

own efforts go beyond its immediate existence; but it is driven beyond it by something else, and this uprooting entails its death. Consciousness, however, is explicitly the *Notion* of itself. Hence it is something that goes beyond limits, and since these limits are its own, it is something that goes beyond itself. With the positing of a single particular the beyond is also established for consciousness, even if it is only *alongside* the limited object as in the case of spatial intuition. Thus consciousness suffers this violence at its own hands: it spoils its own limited satisfaction. When consciousness feels this violence, its anxiety may well make it retreat from the truth, and strive to hold on to what it is in danger of losing. But it can find no peace. If it wishes to remain in a state of unthinking inertia, then thought troubles its thoughtlessness, and its own unrest disturbs its inertia. Or, if it entrenches itself in sentimentality, which assures us that it finds everything to be *good in its kind*, then this assurance likewise suffers violence at the hands of Reason, for, precisely in so far as something is merely a kind, Reason finds it *not* to be good. Or, again, its fear of the truth may lead consciousness to hide, from itself and others, behind the pretension that its burning zeal for truth makes it difficult or even impossible to find any other truth but the unique truth of vanity – that of being at any rate cleverer than any thoughts that one gets by oneself or from others. This conceit which understands how to belittle every truth, in order to turn back into itself and gloat over its own understanding, which knows how to dissolve every thought and always find the same barren Ego instead of any content – this is a satisfaction which we must leave to itself, for it flees from the universal, and seeks only to be for itself.

81. In addition to these preliminary general remarks about the manner and the necessity of the progression, it may be useful to say something about the *method of carrying out the inquiry*. If this exposition is viewed as a way of *relating Science* to *phenomenal* knowledge, and as an investigation and *examination of the reality of cognition*, it would seem that it cannot take place without some presupposition which can serve as its underlying *criterion*. For an examination consists in applying an accepted standard, and in determining whether something is right or wrong on the basis of the resulting agreement or disagreement of the thing examined; thus the standard as such (and Science likewise if it were the criterion) is accepted as the *essence* or as the *in-itself*. But here, where Science has just begun to come on the scene, neither Science nor anything else has yet justified itself as the essence or the in-itself; and without something of the sort it seems that no examination can take place.

82. This contradiction and its removal will become more definite if we call to mind the abstract determinations of truth and knowledge as they occur in consciousness. Consciousness simultaneously *distinguishes* itself from something, and at the same time *relates* itself to it, or, as it is said, this something exists *for* consciousness; and the determinate aspect of this *relating*, or of the *being* of something for a consciousness, is *knowing*. But we distinguish this being-for-another from *being-in-itself*; whatever is related to knowledge or knowing is also distinguished from it, and posited as existing outside of this relationship; this *being-in-itself* is called *truth*. Just what might be involved in these determinations is of no further concern to us here. Since our object is phenomenal knowledge, its determinations too will at first be taken directly as they present themselves; and they do present themselves very much as we have already apprehended them.

83. Now, if we inquire into the truth of knowledge, it seems that we are asking what knowledge is *in itself*. Yet in this inquiry knowledge is *our* object, something that exists *for us*; and the *in-itself* that would supposedly result from it would rather be the being of knowledge *for us*. What we asserted to be its essence would be not so much its truth but rather just our knowledge of it. The essence or criterion would lie within ourselves, and that which was to be compared with it and about which a decision would be reached through this comparison would not necessarily have to recognize the validity of such a standard.

84. But the dissociation, or this semblance of dissociation and presupposition, is overcome by the nature of the object we are investigating. Consciousness provides its own criterion from within itself, so that the investigation becomes a comparison of consciousness with itself; for the distinction made above falls within it. In consciousness one thing exists *for* another, i.e. consciousness regularly contains the determinateness of the moment of knowledge; at the same time, this other is to consciousness not merely *for it*, but is also outside of this relationship, or exists *in itself*: the moment of truth. Thus in what consciousness affirms from within itself as *being-in-itself* or the *True* we have the standard which consciousness itself sets up by

which to measure what it knows. If we designate *knowledge* as the Notion, but the essence or the *True* as what exists, or the *object*, then the examination consists in seeing whether the Notion corresponds to the object. But if we call the *essence* or in-itself of the *object* the *Notion*, and on the other hand understand by the *object* the Notion itself as *object*, viz. as it exists *for an other*, then the examination consists in seeing whether the object corresponds to its Notion. It is evident, of course, that the two procedures are the same. But the essential point to bear in mind throughout the whole investigation is that these two moments, "Notion" and "object", "being-for-another" and "being-in-itself", both fall *within* that knowledge which we are investigating. Consequently, we do not need to import criteria, or to make use of our own bright ideas and thoughts during the course of the inquiry; it is precisely when we leave these aside that we succeed in contemplating the matter in hand as it is *in and for itself*.

85. But not only is a contribution by us superfluous, since Notion and object, the criterion and what is to be tested, are present in consciousness itself, but we are also spared the trouble of comparing the two and really *testing* them, so that, since what consciousness examines is its own self, all that is left for us to do is simply to look on. For consciousness is, on the one hand, consciousness of the object, and on the other, consciousness of itself; consciousness of what for it is the True, and consciousness of its knowledge of the truth. Since both are *for* the same consciousness, this consciousness is itself their comparison; it is for this same consciousness to know whether its knowledge of the object corresponds to the object or not. The object, it is true, seems only to be for consciousness in the way that consciousness knows it; it seems that consciousness cannot, as it were, get behind the object as it exists for consciousness so as to examine what the object is *in itself*, and hence, too, cannot test its own knowledge by that standard. But the distinction between the in-itself and knowledge is already present in the very fact that consciousness knows an object at all. Something is *for it* the *in-itself*; and knowledge, or the being of the object for consciousness, is, *for it*, another moment. Upon this distinction, which is present as a fact, the examination rests. If the comparison shows that these two moments do not correspond to one another, it would seem that consciousness must alter its knowledge to make it conform to the object. But, in fact, in the

alteration of the knowledge, the object itself alters for it too, for the knowledge that was present was essentially a knowledge of the object: as the knowledge changes, so too does the object, for it essentially belonged to this knowledge. Hence it comes to pass for consciousness that what it previously took to be the *in-itself* is not an *in-itself*, or that it was only an in-itself *for consciousness*. Since consciousness thus finds that its knowledge does not correspond to its object, the object itself does not stand the test; in other words, the criterion for testing is altered when that for which it was to have been the criterion fails to pass the test; and the testing is not only a testing of what we know, but also a testing of the criterion of what knowing is.

86. *Inasmuch as the new true object issues from it*, this *dialectical* movement which consciousness exercises on itself and which affects both its knowledge and its object, is precisely what is called *experience* [*Erfahrung*]. In this connection there is a moment in the process just mentioned which must be brought out more clearly, for through it a new light will be thrown on the exposition which follows. Consciousness knows *something*; this object is the essence or the *in-itself*; but it is also for consciousness the in-itself. This is where the ambiguity of this truth enters. We see that consciousness now has two objects: one is the first *in-itself*, the second is the *being-for-consciousness of this in-itself*. The latter appears at first sight to be merely the reflection of consciousness into itself, i.e. what consciousness has in mind is not an object, but only its knowledge of that first object. But, as was shown previously, the first object, in being known, is altered for consciousness; it ceases to be the in-itself, and becomes something that is the *in-itself* only *for consciousness*. And this then is the True: the being-for-consciousness of this in-itself. Or, in other words, this is the *essence*, or the *object* of consciousness. This new object contains the nothingness of the first, it is what experience has made of it.

87. This exposition of the course of experience contains a moment in virtue of which it does not seem to agree with what is ordinarily understood by experience. This is the moment of transition from the first object and the knowledge of it, to the other object, which experience is said to be about. Our account implied that our knowledge of the first object, or the being-*for*-consciousness of the first in-itself, itself becomes the second object. It usually seems to be the case, on the contrary, that

our experience of the untruth of our first notion comes by way of a second object which we come upon by chance and externally, so that our part in all this is simply the pure *apprehension* of what is in and for itself. From the present viewpoint, however, the new object shows itself to have come about through a *reversal of consciousness itself*. This way of looking at the matter is something contributed by *us*, by means of which the succession of experiences through which consciousness passes is raised into a scientific progression – but it is not known to the consciousness that we are observing. But, as a matter of fact, we have here the same situation as the one discussed in regard to the relation between our exposition and scepticism, viz. that in every case the result of an untrue mode of knowledge must not be allowed to run away into an empty nothing, but must necessarily be grasped as the nothing *of that from which it results* – a result which contains what was true in the preceding knowledge. It shows up here like this: since what first appeared as the object sinks for consciousness to the level of its way of knowing it, and since the in-itself becomes a *being-for-consciousness* of the in-itself, the latter is now the new object. Herewith a new pattern of consciousness comes on the scene as well, for which the essence is something different from what it was at the preceding stage. It is this fact that guides the entire series of the patterns of consciousness in their necessary sequence. But it is just this necessity itself, or the *origination* of the new object, that presents itself to consciousness without its understanding how this happens, which proceeds for us, as it were, behind the back of consciousness. Thus in the movement of consciousness there occurs a moment of *being-in-itself* or *being-for-us* which is not present to the consciousness comprehended in the experience itself. The *content*, however, of what presents itself to us does exist *for it*; we comprehend only the formal aspect of that content, or its pure origination. *For it*, what has thus arisen exists only as an object; *for us*, it appears at the same time as movement and a process of becoming.

88. Because of this necessity, the way to Science is itself already *Science*, and hence, in virtue of its content, is the Science of the *experience of consciousness*.

89. The experience of itself which consciousness goes through can, in accordance with its Notion, comprehend nothing less than the entire system of consciousness, or the entire realm of the truth of Spirit. For this reason, the moments of this truth are exhibited in their own proper determinateness, viz. as being not abstract moments, but as they are for consciousness, or as consciousness itself stands forth in its relation to them. Thus the moments of the whole are *patterns of consciousness*. In pressing forward to its true existence, consciousness will arrive at a point at which it gets rid of its semblance of being burdened with something alien, with what is only for it, and some sort of "other", at a point where appearance becomes identical with essence, so that its exposition will coincide at just this point with the authentic Science of Spirit. And finally, when consciousness itself grasps this its own essence, it will signify the nature of absolute knowledge itself.

The Truth of Self-Certainty

166. In the previous modes of certainty what is true for consciousness is something other than itself. But the Notion of this truth vanishes in the experience of it. What the object immediately was *in itself* – mere being in sense-certainty, the concrete thing of perception, and for the Understanding, a Force – proves to be in truth, not this at all; instead, this *in-itself* turns out to be a mode in which the object is only for an other. The Notion of the object is superseded in the actual object, or the first, immediate presentation of the object is superseded in experience: certainty gives place to truth. But now there has arisen what did not emerge in these previous relationships, viz. a certainty which is identical with its truth; for the certainty is to itself its own object, and consciousness is to itself the truth. In this there is indeed an otherness; that is to say, consciousness makes a distinction, but one which at the same time is for consciousness *not* a distinction. If we give the name of *Notion* to the movement of knowing, and the name of *object* to knowing as a passive unity, or as the "I", then we see that not only for *us*, but for knowing itself, the object corresponds to the Notion. Or alternatively, if we call Notion what the object is *in itself*, but call the object what *it* is *qua* object or *for an other*, then it is clear that being-*in-itself* and being-*for-an-other* are one and the same. For the *in-itself* is consciousness; but equally it is that *for which* an other (the *in-itself*) is; and it is *for* consciousness that the in-itself of the object, and the being of the object for an other, are one and the same; the "I" is the *content* of the

connection and the connecting itself. Opposed to an other, the "I" is its own self, and at the same time it overarches this other which, for the "I", is equally only the "I" itself.

167. With self-consciousness, then, we have therefore entered the native realm of truth. We have now to see how the shape of self-consciousness first makes its appearance. If we consider this new shape of knowing, the knowing of itself, in relation to that which preceded, viz. the knowing of an other, then we see that though this other has indeed vanished, its moments have at the same time no less been preserved, and the loss consists in this, that here they are present as they are in themselves. The [mere] *being* of what is merely "meant", the *singleness* and the *universality* opposed to it of perception, as also the *empty inner being* of the Understanding, these are no longer essences, but are moments of self-consciousness, i.e. abstractions or distinctions which at the same time have no reality *for* consciousness itself, and are purely vanishing essences. Thus it seems that only the principal moment itself has been lost, viz. the *simple self-subsistent existence* for consciousness. But in point of fact self-consciousness is the reflection out of the being of the world of sense and perception, and is essentially the return from *otherness*. As self-consciousness, it is movement; but since what it distinguishes from itself is *only itself as* itself, the difference, as an otherness, is *immediately superseded* for it; the difference *is not*, and *it* [self-consciousness] is only the motionless tautology of: "I am I"; but since for it the difference does not have the form of *being*, it is *not* self-consciousness. Hence otherness is for it in the form of a *being*, or as a *distinct moment*; but there is also for consciousness the unity of itself with this difference as a *second distinct moment*. With that first moment, self-consciousness is in the form of *consciousness*, and the whole expanse of the sensuous world is preserved for it, but at the same time only as connected with the second moment, the unity of self-consciousness with itself; and hence the sensuous world is for it an enduring existence which, however, is only *appearance*, or a difference which, *in itself*, is no difference. This antithesis of its appearance and its truth has, however, for its essence only the truth, viz. the unity of self-consciousness with itself; this unity must become essential to self-consciousness, i.e. self-consciousness is *Desire* in general. Consciousness, as self-consciousness, henceforth has a double object: one is the immediate object, that of sense-certainty and perception, which however *for self-consciousness* has the character of a *negative*; and the second, viz. *itself*, which is the true *essence*, and is present in the first instance only as opposed to the first object. In this sphere, self-consciousness exhibits itself as the movement in which this antithesis is removed, and the identity of itself with itself becomes explicit for it.

168. But *for us*, or *in itself*, the object which for self-consciousness is the negative element has, on its side, returned into itself, just as on the other side consciousness has done. Through this reflection into itself the object has become Life. What self-consciousness distinguishes from itself as having *being*, also has in it, in so far as it is posited as being, not merely the character of sense-certainty and perception, but it is being that is reflected into itself, and the object of immediate desire is a *living thing*. For the *in-itself*, or the *universal* result of the relation of the Understanding to the inwardness of things, is the distinguishing of what is *not* to be distinguished, or the *unity* of what is distinguished. But this unity is, as we have seen, just as much its repulsion from itself; and this Notion sunders itself into the antithesis of self-consciousness and life: the former is the unity *for which* the infinite unity of the differences is; the latter, however, *is* only this unity itself, so that it is not at the same time *for itself*. To the extent, then, that consciousness is independent, so too is its object, but only *implicitly*. Self-consciousness which is simply *for itself* and directly characterizes its object as a negative element, or is primarily *desire*, will therefore, on the contrary, learn through experience that the object is independent.

169. The determination of Life as it has issued from the Notion, or the general result with which we enter this sphere, is sufficient to characterize it without having further to develop its nature. Its sphere is completely determined in the following moments. *Essence* is infinity as the *supersession* of all distinctions, the pure movement of axial rotation, its self-repose being an absolutely restless infinity; *independence* itself, in which the differences of the movement are resolved, the simple essence of Time which, in this equality with itself, has the stable shape of Space. The differences, however, are just as much present as *differences* in this simple universal medium; for this universal flux has its negative nature only in being the supersession of them; but it cannot supersede the different moments if they do not have an enduring existence [*Bestehen*]. It is this very flux, as a self-identical

independence which is itself an *enduring existence*, in which, therefore, they are present as distinct members and parts existing on their own account. *Being* no longer has the significance of *abstract* being, nor has their pure essentiality the significance of *abstract* universality; on the contrary, their being is precisely that simple fluid substance of pure movement within itself. The *difference*, however, *qua* difference, of these members with respect to one another consists in general in no other *determinateness* than that of the moments of infinity or of the pure movement itself.

170. The independent members are *for themselves*; but this *being-for-self* is really no less immediately their reflection into the unity than this unity is the splitting-up into independent shapes. The unity is divided within itself because it is an absolutely negative or infinite unity; and because it is what *subsists*, the difference, too, has independence only in *it*. This independence of the shape appears as something *determinate, for an other*, for the shape is divided within itself; and the supersession of this dividedness accordingly takes place through an other. But this supersession is just as much within the shape itself, for it is just that flux that is the substance of the independent shapes. This substance, however, is infinite, and hence the shape in its very subsistence is a dividedness within itself, or the supersession of its being-for-self.

171. If we distinguish more exactly the moments contained here, we see that we have, as the first moment, the subsistence of the independent shapes, or the suppression of what diremption is in itself, viz. that the shapes have no being in themselves, no enduring existence. The second moment, however is the subjection of that existence to the infinity of the difference. In the first moment there is the existent shape; as being *for itself*, or being in its determinateness infinite substance, it comes forward in antithesis to the *universal* substance, disowns this fluent continuity with it and asserts that it is not dissolved in this universal element, but on the contrary preserves itself by separating itself from this its inorganic nature, and by consuming it. Life in the universal fluid medium, a *passive* separating-out of the shapes becomes, just by so doing, a movement of those shapes or becomes Life as a *process*. The simple universal fluid medium is the *in-itself*, and the difference of the shapes is the *other*. But this fluid medium itself becomes the *other* through this difference; for now it is *for the difference* which

exists in and for itself, and consequently is the ceaseless movement by which this passive medium is consumed: Life as a *living thing*.

This *inversion*, however, is for that reason again an invertedness *in its own self*. What is consumed is the essence: the individuality which maintains itself at the expense of the universal, and which gives itself the feeling of its unity with itself, just by so doing supersedes its antithesis to the other by means of which it exists for itself. Its self-given unity with itself is just that *fluidity* of the differences or their *general dissolution*. But, conversely, the supersession of individual existence is equally the production of it. For since the *essence* of the individual shape – universal Life – and what exists for itself is in itself simple substance, when this substance places the *other* within itself it supersedes this its *simplicity* or its essence, i.e. it divides it, and this dividedness of the differenceless fluid medium is just what establishes individuality. Thus the simple substance of Life is the splitting-up of itself into shapes and at the same time the dissolution of these existent differences; and the dissolution of the splitting-up is just as much a splitting-up and a forming of members. With this, the two sides of the whole movement which before were distinguished, viz. the passive separatedness of the shapes in the general medium of independence, and the process of Life, collapse into one another. The latter is just as much an imparting of shape as a supersession of it; and the other, the imparting of shape, is just as much a supersession as an articulation of shape. The fluid element is itself only the *abstraction* of essence, or it is *actual* only as shape; and its articulation of itself is again a splitting-up of what is articulated into form or a dissolution of it. It is the whole round of this activity that constitutes Life: not what was expressed at the outset, the immediate continuity and compactness of its essence, nor the enduring form, the discrete moment existing for itself; nor the pure process of these; nor yet the simple taking-together of these moments. Life consists rather in being the self-developing whole which dissolves its development and in this movement simply preserves itself.

172. Since we started from the first immediate unity and returned through the moments of formation and of process to the unity of both these moments, and thus back again to the original simple substance, this *reflected* unity is different from the first. Contrasted with that *immediate* unity, or that unity expressed as a [mere] *being*,

this second is the *universal* unity which contains all these moments as superseded within itself. It is the simple genus which, in the movement of Life itself, does not *exist for itself qua* this *simple* determination; on the contrary, in this *result*, Life points to something other than itself, viz. to consciousness, for which Life exists as this unity, or as genus.

173. This other Life, however, for which the genus as such exists, and which is genus on its own account, viz. self-consciousness, exists in the first instance for self-consciousness only as this simple essence, and has itself as pure "I" for object. In the course of its experience which we are now to consider, this abstract object will enrich itself for the "I" and undergo the unfolding which we have seen in the sphere of Life.

174. The simple "I" is this genus or the simple universal, for which the differences are *not* differences only by its being the *negative essence* of the shaped independent moments; and self-consciousness is thus certain of itself only by superseding this other that presents itself to self-consciousness as an independent life; self-consciousness is Desire. Certain of the nothingness of this other, it explicitly affirms that this nothingness is *for it* the truth of the other; it destroys the independent object and thereby gives itself the certainty of itself as a *true* certainty, a certainty which has become explicit for self-consciousness itself *in an objective manner.*

175. In this satisfaction, however, experience makes it aware that the object has its own independence. Desire and the self-certainty obtained in its gratification, are conditioned by the object, for self-certainty comes from superseding this other: in order that this supersession can take place, there must be this other. Thus self-consciousness, by its negative relation to the object, is unable to supersede it; it is really because of that relation that it produces the object again, and the desire as well. It is in fact something other than self-consciousness that is the essence of Desire; and through this experience self-consciousness has itself realized this truth. But at the same time it is no less absolutely *for itself*, and it is so only by superseding the object; and it must experience its satisfaction, for it is the truth. On account of the independence of the object, therefore, it can achieve satisfaction only when the object itself effects the negation within itself; and it must carry out this negation of itself in itself, for it is *in itself* the negative, and must be *for* the other what it *is*. Since the object is

in its own self negation, and in being so is at the same time independent, it is consciousness. In the sphere of Life, which is the object of Desire, *negation* is present either *in an other*, viz. in Desire, or as a *determinateness* opposed to another indifferent form, or as the inorganic universal nature of Life. But this universal independent nature in which negation is present as absolute negation, is the genus as such, or the genus as *self-consciousness. Self-consciousness achieves its satisfaction only in another self-consciousness.*

176. The notion of self-consciousness is only completed in these three moments: (a) the pure undifferentiated "I" is its first immediate object. (b) But this immediacy is itself an absolute mediation, it *is* only as a supersession of the independent object, in other words, it is Desire. The satisfaction of Desire is, it is true, the reflection of self-consciousness into itself, or the certainty that has become truth. (c) But the truth of this certainty is really a double reflection, the duplication of self-consciousness. Consciousness has for its object one which, of its own self, posits its otherness or difference as a nothingness, and in so doing is independent. The differentiated, merely *living*, shape does indeed also supersede its independence in the process of Life, but it ceases with its distinctive difference to be what it is. The object of self-consciousness, however, is equally independent in this negativity of itself; and thus it is *for itself* a genus, a universal fluid element in the peculiarity of its own separate being; it is a living self-consciousness.

177. A self-consciousness exists *for a self-consciousness*. Only so is it in fact self-consciousness; for only in this way does the unity of itself in its otherness become explicit for it. The "I" which is the object of its Notion is in fact not "object"; the object of Desire, however, is only independent, for it is the universal indestructible substance, the fluid self-identical essence. A self-consciousness, in being an object, is just as much "I" as "object". With this, we already have before us the Notion of *Spirit*. What still lies ahead for consciousness is the experience of what Spirit is – this absolute substance which is the unity of the different independent self-consciousnesses which, in their opposition, enjoy perfect freedom and independence: "I" that is "We" and "We" that is "I". It is in self-consciousness, in the Notion of Spirit, that consciousness first finds its turning-point, where it leaves behind it the colourful show of the sensuous here-and-now and the nightlike void of the

supersensible beyond, and steps out into the spiritual daylight of the present.

Lordship and bondage

178. Self-consciousness exists in and for itself when, and by the fact that, it so exists for another; that is, it exists only in being acknowledged. The Notion of this its unity in its duplication embraces many and varied meanings. Its moments, then, must on the one hand be held strictly apart, and on the other hand must in this differentiation at the same time also be taken and known as not distinct, or in their opposite significance. The twofold significance of the distinct moments has in the nature of self-consciousness to be infinite, or directly the opposite of the determinateness in which it is posited. The detailed exposition of the Notion of this spiritual unity in its duplication will present us with the process of Recognition.

179. Self-consciousness is faced by another self-consciousness; it has come *out of itself*. This has a twofold significance: first, it has lost itself, for it finds itself as an *other* being; secondly, in doing so it has superseded the other, for it does not see the other as an essential being, but in the other sees its own self.

180. It must supersede this otherness of itself. This is the supersession of the first ambiguity, and is therefore itself a second ambiguity. First, it must proceed to supersede the *other* independent being in order thereby to become certain of *itself* as the essential being; secondly, in so doing it proceeds to supersede its *own* self, for this other is itself.

181. This ambiguous supersession of its ambiguous otherness is equally an ambiguous return *into itself*. For first, through the supersession, it receives back its own self, because, by superseding *its* otherness, it again becomes equal to itself; but secondly, the other self-consciousness equally gives it back again to itself, for it saw itself in the other, but supersedes this being of itself in the other and thus lets the other again go free.

182. Now, this movement of self-consciousness in relation to another self-consciousness has in this way been represented as the action of *one* self-consciousness, but this action of the one has itself the double significance of being both its own action and the action of the other as well. For the other is equally independent and self-contained, and there is nothing in it of which it is not itself the origin. The first does not have the object before it merely as it exists primarily for desire, but as something that has an independent existence of its own, which, therefore, it cannot utilize for its own purposes, if that object does not of its own accord do what the first does to it. Thus the movement is simply the double movement of the two self-consciousnesses. Each sees the *other* do the same as it does; each does itself what it demands of the other, and therefore also does what it does only in so far as the other does the same. Action by one side only would be useless because what is to happen can only be brought about by both.

183. Thus the action has a double significance not only because it is directed against itself as well as against the other, but also because it is indivisibly the action of one as well as of the other.

184. In this movement we see repeated the process which presented itself as the play of Forces, but repeated now in consciousness. What in that process was *for us*, is true here of the extremes themselves. The middle term is self-consciousness which splits into the extremes; and each extreme is this exchanging of its own determinateness and an absolute transition into the opposite. Although, as consciousness, it does indeed come *out of itself*, yet, though out of itself, it is at the same time kept back within itself, is *for itself*, and the self outside it, is for *it*. It is aware that it at once is, and is not, another consciousness, and equally that this other is *for itself* only when it supersedes itself as being for itself, and is for itself only in the being-for-self of the other. Each is for the other the middle term, through which each mediates itself with itself and unites with itself; and each is for itself, and for the other, an immediate being on its own account, which at the same time is such only through this mediation. They *recognize* themselves as *mutually recognizing* one another.

185. We have now to see how the process of this pure Notion of recognition, of the duplicating of self-consciousness in its oneness, appears to self-consciousness. At first, it will exhibit the side of the inequality of the two, or the splitting-up of the middle term into the extremes which, as extremes, are opposed to one another, one being only *recognized*, the other only *recognizing*.

186. Self-consciousness is, to begin with, simple being-for-self, self-equal through the exclusion from itself of everything else. For it, its essence and absolute object is "I"; and in this immediacy, or in this [mere] being, of its being-for-self, it is an *individual*. What is "other" for it is

an unessential, negatively characterized object. But the "other" is also a self-consciousness; one individual is confronted by another individual. Appearing thus immediately on the scene, they are for one another like ordinary objects, *independent* shapes, individuals submerged in the being [or immediacy] of *Life* – for the object in its immediacy is here determined as Life. They are, *for each other*, shapes of consciousness which have not yet accomplished the movement of absolute abstraction, of rooting-out all immediate being, and of being merely the purely negative being of self-identical consciousness; in other words, they have not as yet exposed themselves to each other in the form of pure being-for-self, or as self-consciousnesses. Each is indeed certain of its own self, but not of the other, and therefore its own self-certainty still has no truth. For it would have truth only if its own being-for-self had confronted it as an independent object, or, what is the same thing, if the object had presented itself as this pure self-certainty. But according to the Notion of recognition this is possible only when each is for the other what the other is for it, only when each in its own self through its own action, and again through the action of the other, achieves this pure abstraction of being-for-self.

187. The presentation of itself, however, as the pure abstraction of self-consciousness consists in showing itself as the pure negation of its objective mode, or in showing that it is not attached to any specific *existence*, not to the individuality common to existence as such, that it is not attached to life. This presentation is a twofold action: action on the part of the other, and action on its own part. In so far as it is the action of the *other*, each seeks the death of the other. But in doing so, the second kind of action, action on its own part, is also involved; for the former involves the staking of its own life. Thus the relation of the two self-conscious individuals is such that they prove themselves and each other through a life-and-death struggle. They must engage in this struggle, for they must raise their certainty of being *for themselves* to truth, both in the case of the other and in their own case. And it is only through staking one's life that freedom is won; only thus is it proved that for self-consciousness, its essential being is not [just] being, not the *immediate* form in which it appears, not its submergence in the expanse of life, but rather that there is nothing present in it which could not be regarded as a vanishing moment, that it is only pure *being-for-*

self. The individual who has not risked his life may well be recognized as a *person*, but he has not attained to the truth of this recognition as an independent self-consciousness. Similarly, just as each stakes his own life, so each must seek the other's death, for it values the other no more than itself; its essential being is present to it in the form of an "other", it is outside of itself and must rid itself of its self-externality. The other is an *immediate* consciousness entangled in a variety of relationships, and it must regard its otherness as a pure being-for-self or as an absolute negation.

188. This trial by death, however, does away with the truth which was supposed to issue from it, and so, too, with the certainty of self generally. For just as life is the *natural* setting of consciousness, independence without absolute negativity, so death is the *natural* negation of consciousness, negation without independence, which thus remains without the required significance of recognition. Death certainly shows that each staked his life and held it of no account, both in himself and in the other; but that is not for those who survived this struggle. They put an end to their consciousness in its alien setting of natural existence, that is to say, they put an end to themselves, and are done away with as *extremes* wanting to be *for themselves*, or to have an existence of their own. But with this there vanishes from their interplay the essential moment of splitting into extremes with opposite characteristics; and the middle term collapses into a lifeless unity which is split into lifeless, merely immediate, unopposed extremes; and the two do not reciprocally give and receive one another back from each other consciously, but leave each other free only indifferently, like things. Their act is an abstract negation, not the negation coming from consciousness, which supersedes in such a way as to preserve and maintain what is superseded, and consequently survives its own supersession.

189. In this experience, self-consciousness learns that life is as essential to it as pure self-consciousness. In immediate self-consciousness the simple "I" is absolute mediation, and has as its essential moment lasting independence. The dissolution of that simple unity is the result of the first experience; through this there is posited a pure self-consciousness, and a consciousness which is not purely for itself but for another, i.e. is a merely *immediate* consciousness, or consciousness in the form of *thinghood*. Both moments are

essential. Since to begin with they are unequal and opposed, and their reflection into a unity has not yet been achieved, they exist as two opposed shapes of consciousness; one is the independent consciousness whose essential nature is to be for itself, the other is the dependent consciousness whose essential nature is simply to live or to be for another. The former is lord, the other is bondsman.

190. The lord is the consciousness that exists *for itself*, but no longer merely the Notion of such a consciousness. Rather, it is a consciousness existing *for itself* which is mediated with itself through another consciousness, i.e. through a consciousness whose nature it is to be bound up with an existence that is independent, or thinghood in general. The lord puts himself into relation with both of these moments, to a *thing* as such, the object of desire, and to the consciousness for which thinghood is the essential characteristic. And since he is (a) *qua* the Notion of self-consciousness an immediate relation of *being-for-self*, but (b) is now at the same time mediation, or a being-for-self which is for itself only through another, he is related (a) immediately to both, and (b) mediately to each through the other. The lord relates himself mediately to the bondsman through a being [a thing] that is independent, for it is just this which holds the bondsman in bondage; it is his chain from which he could not break free in the struggle, thus proving himself to be dependent, to possess his independence in thinghood. But the lord is the power over this thing, for he proved in the struggle that it is something merely negative; since he is the power over this thing and this again is the power over the other [the bondsman], it follows that he holds the other in subjection. Equally, the lord relates himself mediately to the thing through the bondsman; the bondsman, *qua* self-consciousness in general, also relates himself negatively to the thing, and takes away its independence; but at the same time the thing is independent *vis-à-vis* the bondsman, whose negating of it, therefore, cannot go the length of being altogether done with it to the point of annihilation; in other words, he only *works* on it. For the lord, on the other hand, the *immediate* relation becomes through this mediation the sheer negation of the thing, or the enjoyment of it. What desire failed to achieve, he succeeds in doing, viz. to have done with the thing altogether, and to achieve satisfaction in the enjoyment of it. Desire failed to do this because of the thing's independence; but the lord,

who has interposed the bondsman between it and himself, takes to himself only the dependent aspect of the thing and has the pure enjoyment of it. The aspect of its independence he leaves to the bondsman, who works on it.

191. In both of these moments the lord achieves his recognition through another consciousness; for in them, that other consciousness is expressly something unessential, both by its working on the thing, and by its dependence on a specific existence. In neither case can it be lord over the being of the thing and achieve absolute negation of it. Here, therefore, is present this moment of recognition, viz. that the other consciousness sets aside its own being-for-self, and in so doing itself does what the first does to it. Similarly, the other moment too is present, that this action of the second is the first's own action; for what the bondsman does is really the action of the lord. The latter's essential nature is to exist only for himself; he is the sheer negative power for whom the thing is nothing. Thus he is the pure, essential action in this relationship, while the action of the bondsman is impure and unessential. But for recognition proper the moment is lacking, that what the lord does to the other he also does to himself, and what the bondsman does to himself he should also do to the other. The outcome is a recognition that is one-sided and unequal.

192. In this recognition the unessential consciousness is for the lord the object, which constitutes the *truth* of his certainty of himself. But it is clear that this object does not correspond to its Notion, but rather that the object in which the lord has achieved his lordship has in reality turned out to be something quite different from an independent consciousness. What now really confronts him is not an independent consciousness, but a dependent one. He is, therefore, not certain of *being-for-self* as the truth of himself. On the contrary, his truth is in reality the unessential consciousness and its unessential action.

193. The *truth* of the independent consciousness is accordingly the servile consciousness of the bondsman. This, it is true, appears at first *outside* of itself and not as the truth of self-consciousness. But just as lordship showed that its essential nature is the reverse of what it wants to be, so too servitude in its consummation will really turn into the opposite of what it immediately is; as a consciousness forced back into itself, it will withdraw into itself and be transformed into a truly independent consciousness.

194. We have seen what servitude is only in relation to lordship. But it is a self-consciousness, and we have now to consider what as such it is in and for itself. To begin with, servitude has the lord for its essential reality; hence the *truth* for it is the independent consciousness that is *for itself*. However, servitude is not yet aware that this truth is implicit in it. But it does in fact contain within itself this truth of pure negativity and being-for-self, for it has experienced this its own essential nature. For this consciousness has been fearful, not of this or that particular thing or just at odd moments, but its whole being has been seized with dread; for it has experienced the fear of death, the absolute Lord. In that experience it has been quite unmanned, has trembled in every fibre of its being, and everything solid and stable has been shaken to its foundations. But this pure universal movement, the absolute melting-away of everything stable, is the simple, essential nature of self-consciousness, absolute negativity, *pure being-for-self*, which consequently is *implicit* in this consciousness. This moment of pure being-for-self is also *explicit* for the bondsman, for in the lord it exists for him as his *object*. Furthermore, his consciousness is not this dissolution of everything stable merely in principle; in his service he *actually* brings this about. Through his service he rids himself of his attachment to natural existence in every single detail; and gets rid of it by working on it.

195. However, the feeling of absolute power both in general, and in the particular form of service, is only implicitly this dissolution, and although the fear of the lord is indeed the beginning of wisdom, consciousness is not therein aware that it is a being-for-self. Through work, however, the bondsman becomes conscious of what he truly is. In the moment which corresponds to desire in the lord's consciousness, it did seem that the aspect of unessential relation to the thing fell to the lot of the bondsman, since in that relation the thing retained its independence. Desire has reserved to itself the pure negating of the object and thereby its unalloyed feeling of self. But that is the reason why this satisfaction is itself only a fleeting one, for it lacks the side of objectivity and permanence. Work, on the other hand, is desire held in check, fleetingness staved off; in other words, work forms and shapes the thing. The negative relation to the object becomes its *form* and something *permanent*, because it is precisely for the worker that the object has independence.

This *negative* middle term or the formative *activity* is at the same time the individuality or pure being-for-self of consciousness which now, in the work outside of it, acquires an element of permanence. It is in this way, therefore, that consciousness, *qua* worker, comes to see in the independent being [of the object] its *own* independence.

196. But the formative activity has not only this positive significance that in it the pure being-for-self of the servile consciousness acquires an existence; it also has, in contrast with its first moment, the negative significance of *fear*. For, in fashioning the thing, the bondsman's own negativity, his being-for-self, becomes an object for him only through his setting at nought the existing *shape* confronting him. But this objective *negative* moment is none other than the alien being before which it has trembled. Now, however, he destroys this alien negative moment, posits *himself* as a negative in the permanent order of things, and thereby becomes *for himself*, someone existing on his own account. In the lord, the being-for-self is an "other" for the bondsman, or is only *for* him [i.e. is not his own]; in fear, the being-for-self is present in the bondsman himself; in fashioning the thing, he becomes aware that being-for-self belongs to *him*, that he himself exists essentially and actually in his own right. The shape does not become something other than himself through being made external to him; for it is precisely this shape that is his pure being-for-self, which in this externality is seen by him to be the truth. Through this rediscovery of himself by himself, the bondsman realizes that it is precisely in his work wherein he seemed to have only an alienated existence that he acquires a mind of his own. For this reflection, the two moments of fear and service as such, as also that of formative activity, are necessary, both being at the same time in a universal mode. Without the discipline of service and obedience, fear remains at the formal stage, and does not extend to the known real world of existence. Without the formative activity, fear remains inward and mute, and consciousness does not become explicitly *for itself*. If consciousness fashions the thing without that initial absolute fear, it is only an empty self-centred attitude; for its form or negativity is not negativity *per se*, and therefore its formative activity cannot give it a consciousness of itself as essential being. If it has not experienced absolute fear but only some lesser dread, the negative being has remained for it something external, its substance has not been infected by it through

and through. Since the entire contents of its natural consciousness have not been jeopardized, determinate being still *in principle* attaches to it; having a "mind of one's own" is self-will, a freedom which is still enmeshed in servitude. Just as little as the pure form can become essential being for it, just as little is that form, regarded as extended to the particular, a universal formative activity, an absolute Notion; rather it is a skill which is master over some things, but not over the universal power and the whole of objective being.

PART XIV

Søren Kierkegaard (1813–55)

Introduction

Until recently, scholars tended to focus mainly on Kierkegaard's pseudonymous writings from the period 1843–6. These include some of his best-known works, such as *Either/ Or, Fear and Trembling, Philosophical Fragments*, and the *Concluding Unscientific Postscript*. With the exception of our first selection, we have drawn from other, less familiar parts of Kierkegaard's work. As an example of the early pseudonymous series we have included a selection from *Fear and Trembling* (1843) in which Johannes de Silentio examines the potential conflict between ethics and religious faith in the story of Abraham and Isaac. This is followed by a selection from a volume of religious writings entitled *Upbuilding Discourses in Various Spirits*, which Kierkegaard published under his own name in 1847. The text is drawn from the first discourse, "On the Occasion of a Confession, Purity of Heart Is To Will One Thing," which focuses on one of the central themes in Kierkegaard's writing: what it means to be an authentic individual. Next we have two excerpts from *Prac-*

tice in Christianity (1850), a work which bears the name of Kierkegaard's Christian pseudonym, Anti-Climacus. These selections present a concise summary of the main ideas contained in the more familiar *Philosophical Fragments* (1844) and *Concluding Unscientific Postscript* (1846) by Johannes Climacus. Whereas Johannes regards the requirements of faith from a safe philosophical distance, Anti-Climacus is a committed Christian whose formulations have a mildly polemical tone. These writings preview the withering attack Kierkegaard would later launch against established Christianity. That attack began in 1854–5 in the columns of *The Fatherland*, a popular liberal newspaper of the day. This was followed by a series of polemical pamphlets entitled *The Instant*. In "Would It Be Best Now to 'Stop Ringing the Fire Alarm'?" (*The Fatherland*, 1855), Kierkegaard declares that "official Christianity is not the Christianity of the New Testament." In "What Says the Fire Chief?" (*The Instant* no. 6, 1855) and "When is 'the Instant'?" (*The Instant* no. 10, unpublished during Kierkegaard's lifetime), he calls our attention to the need for absolute decisiveness in spiritual matters.

50

Fear and Trembling

Problema I: Is There a Teleological Suspension of the Ethical?

The ethical as such is the universal, and as the universal it applies to everyone, which can be put from another point of view by saying that it applies at every moment. It rests immanently in itself, has nothing outside itself that is its *telos* [end, purpose] but is itself the *telos* for everything outside, and when that is taken up into it, it has no further to go. Seen as an immediate, no more than sensate and psychic, being, the single individual is the particular that has its *telos* in the universal, and the individual's ethical task is always to express himself in this, to abrogate his particularity so as to become the universal. As soon as the single individual wants to assert himself in his particularity, in direct opposition to the universal, he sins, and only by recognizing this can he again reconcile himself with the universal. Whenever, having entered the universal, the single individual feels an urge to assert his particularity, he is in a state of temptation, from which he can extricate himself only by surrendering his particularity to the universal in repentance. If that is the highest that can be said of man and his existence, then the ethical and a person's eternal blessedness, which is his *telos* in all eternity and at every moment, are identical; for in that case it would be a contradiction to say that one surrendered that *telos* (i.e., suspended it *teleologically*) since by suspending the *telos* one

Fear and Trembling (*Frygt og Bæven*, 1843), tr. Alastair Hannay (Penguin, 1985). Selection: "Is There a Teleological Suspension of the Ethical?," pp. 83–95.

would be forfeiting it, while what is said to be suspended in this sense is not forfeited but preserved in something higher, the latter being precisely its *telos*.

If that is the case, then Hegel is right in his "Good and Conscience" where he discusses man seen merely as the single individual and regards this way of seeing him as a "moral form of evil" to be annulled in the teleology of the ethical life, so that the individual who stays at this stage is either in sin or in a state of temptation. Where Hegel goes wrong, on the other hand, is in talking about faith, in not protesting loudly and clearly against the honour and glory enjoyed by Abraham as the father of faith when he should really be remitted to some lower court for trial and exposed as a murderer.

For faith is just this paradox, that the single individual is higher than the universal, though in such a way, be it noted, that the movement is repeated, that is, that, having been in the universal, the single individual now sets himself apart as the particular above the universal. If that is not faith, then Abraham is done for and faith has never existed in the world, just because it has always existed. For if the ethical life is the highest and nothing incommensurable is left over in man, except in the sense of what is evil, i.e. the single individual who is to be expressed in the universal, then one needs no other categories than those of the Greek philosophers, or whatever can be logically deduced from them. This is something Hegel, who has after all made some study of the Greeks, ought not to have kept quiet about.

One not infrequently hears people who prefer to lose themselves in clichés rather than studies say that light shines over the Christian world, while paganism is shrouded in darkness. This kind of talk has always struck me as strange, since any reasonably deep thinker, any reasonably serious artist will still seek rejuvenation in the eternal youth of the Greeks. The explanation may be that they know not what to say, only that they have to say something. There is nothing wrong with saying that paganism did not have faith, but if this is to mean anything one must be a little clearer what one means by faith, otherwise one falls back into those clichés. It is easy to explain the whole of existence, faith included, and he is not the worst reckoner in life who counts on being admired for having such an explanation; for it is as Boileau says: "*un sot trouve toujours un plus sot, qui l'admire*" ["a fool can always find a greater fool who admires him"].

Faith is just this paradox, that the single individual as the particular is higher than the universal, is justified before the latter, not as subordinate but superior, though in such a way, be it noted, that it is the single individual who, having been subordinate to the universal as the particular, now by means of the universal becomes that individual who, as the particular, stands in an absolute relation to the absolute. This position cannot be mediated, for all mediation occurs precisely by virtue of the universal; it is and remains in all eternity a paradox, inaccessible to thought. And yet faith *is* this paradox. Or else (these are implications which I would ask the reader always to bear in mind, though it would be too complicated for me to spell them out each time) – or else faith has never existed just because it has always existed. And Abraham is done for.

That the individual can easily take this paradox for a temptation is true enough. But one should not keep it quiet on that account. True enough, too, that many people may have a natural aversion to the paradox, but that is no reason for making faith into something else so that they too can have it; while those who do have faith should be prepared to offer some criterion for distinguishing the paradox from a temptation.

Now the story of Abraham contains just such a teleological suspension of the ethical. There has been no want of sharp intellects and sound scholars who have found analogies to it. Their wisdom amounts to the splendid principle that basically everything is the same. If one looks a little closer I doubt very much whether one will find in the whole world a single analogy, except a later one

that proves nothing, for the fact remains that Abraham represents faith, and that faith finds its proper expression in him whose life is not only the most paradoxical conceivable, but so paradoxical that it simply cannot be thought. He acts on the strength of the absurd; for it is precisely the absurd that as the single individual he is higher than the universal. This paradox cannot be mediated; for as soon as he tries Abraham will have to admit that he is in a state of temptation, and in that case he will never sacrifice Isaac, or if he has done so he must return repentantly to the universal. On the strength of the absurd he got Isaac back. Abraham is therefore at no instant the tragic hero, but something quite different, either a murderer or a man of faith. The middle-term that saves the tragic hero is something Abraham lacks. That is why I can understand a tragic hero, but not Abraham, even though in a certain lunatic sense I admire him more than all others.

Abraham's relation to Isaac, ethically speaking, is quite simply this, that the father should love the son more than himself. Yet within its own compass the ethical has several rankings; let us see whether this story contains any such higher expression of the ethical which might explain his behaviour ethically, justify him ethically for suspending the ethical duty to the son, yet without thereby exceeding the ethical's own teleology.

When an enterprise involving a whole nation is prevented, when such an enterprise is brought to a halt by heaven's disfavour, when divine wrath sends a dead calm which mocks every effort, when the soothsayer performs his sad task and proclaims that the deity demands a young girl as a sacrifice – then it is with heroism that the father has to make that sacrifice. Nobly will he hide his grief though he could wish he were "the lowly man who dares to weep" and not the king who must bear himself as befits a king. And however solitarily the pain enters his breast, for he has only three confidants among his people, soon the entire population will be privy to his pain, but also to his deed, to the fact that for the well-being of the whole he was willing to offer that girl, his daughter, this lovely young maiden. Oh, what bosom! What fair cheeks! What flaxen hair! And the daughter will touch him with her tears, and the father avert his face, but the hero will raise the knife. And when the news of this reaches the ancestral home all the beauteous maidens of Greece will blush with animation, and were the daughter a bride the betrothed would not be angered but proud to have been party to the father's deed, because the maiden belonged to him more tenderly than to the father.

When that bold judge, who saved Israel in the hour of need binds God and himself in one breath with the same promise, then it is with heroism that he is to transform the young girl's jubilation, the beloved daughter's joy, to sorrow, and all Israel will grieve with her maidenly youth; but every free-born man will understand Jephthah, every stout-hearted woman admire him, and every maiden in Israel will want to do as his daughter; for what good would it be for Jephthah to triumph by making his promise but fail to keep it? Would the victory not be taken once more from the people?

When a son forgets his duty, when the State entrusts the father with the sword of judgement, when the laws demand punishment at the father's hand, then it is with heroism that the father must forget that the guilty one is his son. Nobly will he hide his pain, but in the nation there will be not one, not even the son, who fails to admire the father, and every time the laws of Rome are interpreted it will be recalled that many interpreted them more learnedly but none more gloriously than Brutus.

On the other hand, if it had been while his fleet was being borne by wind under full sail to its destination that Agamemnon had sent that messenger who brought Iphigenia to the sacrifice; if unbound by any promise that would decide the fate of his people Jephthah had said to his daughter: "Sorrow now for two months henceforth over the short day of your youth, for I shall sacrifice you"; if Brutus had had a righteous son and still called upon the lictors to execute him – who would understand them? If to the question, why did you do it?, these three had replied: "It is a trial in which we are being tested", would one then have understood them better?

When at the decisive moment Agamemnon, Jephthah, and Brutus heroically overcome their pain, have heroically given up the loved one, and have only the outward deed to perform, then never a noble soul in the world will there be but sheds tears of sympathy for their pain, tears of admiration for their deed. But if at that decisive moment these three men had added to the heroism with which they bore their pain the little words "It won't happen", who then would understand them? If in explanation they added: "We believe it on the strength of the absurd", who then would

understand them better? For who would not readily understand that it was absurd? But who would understand that for that reason one could believe it?

The difference between the tragic hero and Abraham is obvious enough. The tragic hero stays within the ethical. He lets an expression of the ethical have its *telos* in a higher expression of the ethical; he reduces the ethical relation between father and son, or daughter and father, to a sentiment that has its dialectic in its relation to the idea of the ethical life. Here, then, there can be no question of a teleological suspension of the ethical itself.

With Abraham it is different. In his action he overstepped the ethical altogether, and had a higher *telos* outside it, in relation to which he suspended it. For how could one ever bring Abraham's action into relationship with the universal? How could any point of contact ever be discovered between what Abraham did and the universal other than that Abraham overstepped it? It is not to save a nation, not to uphold the idea of the State, that Abraham did it, not to appease angry gods. If there was any question of the deity's being angry, it could only have been Abraham he was angry with, and Abraham's whole action stands in no relation to the universal, it is a purely private undertaking. While, then, the tragic hero is great through his deed's being an expression of the ethical life, Abraham is great through an act of purely personal virtue. There is no higher expression of the ethical in Abraham's life than that the father shall love the son. The ethical in the sense of the ethical life is quite out of the question. In so far as the universal was there at all it was latent in Isaac, concealed as it were in his loins, and it would have to cry out with Isaac's mouth: "Don't do it, you are destroying everything."

Then why does Abraham do it? For God's sake, and what is exactly the same, for his own. He does it for the sake of God because God demands this proof of his faith; he does it for his own sake in order to be able to produce the proof. The unity here is quite properly expressed in the saying in which this relationship has always been described: it is a trial, a temptation. A temptation, but what does that mean? What we usually call a temptation is something that keeps a person from carrying out a duty, but here the temptation is the ethical itself which would keep him from doing God's will. But then what is the duty? For the duty is precisely the expression of God's will.

Here we see the need for a new category for understanding Abraham. Such a relationship to the divine is unknown to paganism. The tragic hero enters into no private relationship with God, but the ethical is the divine and therefore the paradox in the divine can be mediated in the universal.

Abraham cannot be mediated, which can also be put by saying he cannot speak. The moment I speak I express the universal, and when I do not no one can understand me. So the moment Abraham wants to express himself in the universal, he has to say that his situation is one of temptation, for he has no higher expression of the universal that overrides the universal he transgresses.

Thus while Abraham arouses my admiration, he also appals me. The person who denies himself and sacrifices himself for duty gives up the finite in order to grasp on to the infinite; he is secure enough. The tragic hero gives up what is certain for what is still more certain, and the eye of the beholder rests confidently upon him. But the person who gives up the universal to grasp something still higher that is not the universal, what does he do? Can this be anything but temptation? And if it were something else but the individual were mistaken, what salvation is there for him? He suffers all the pain of the tragic hero, he brings all his joy in the world to nothing, he abandons everything, and perhaps the same instant debars himself from that exalted joy so precious to him that he would buy it at any price. That person the beholder cannot at all understand, nor let his eye rest upon him with confidence. Perhaps what the believer intends just cannot be done, after all it is unthinkable. Or if it could be done and the individual had misunderstood the deity, what salvation would there be for him? The tragic hero, he needs tears and he claims them; yes, where was that envious eye so barren as not to weep with Agamemnon, but where was he whose soul was so confused as to presume to weep for Abraham? The tragic hero has done with his deed at a definite moment in time, but in the course of time he achieves something no less important, he seeks out the one whose soul is beset with sorrow, whose breast cannot draw air for its stifled sighs, whose thoughts, weighed down with tears, hang heavy upon him; he appears before him, he breaks the spell of grief, loosens the corset, coaxes forth the tear by making the sufferer forget his own suffering in his. Abraham one cannot weep over. One approaches him with a *horror religiosus* [holy terror] like that in which Israel approached Mount Sinai. What if the lonely man who climbs the mountain in Moriah, whose peak soars heaven-high over the plains of Aulis, is not a sleepwalker who treads surefootedly over the abyss, while someone standing at the foot of the mountain, seeing him there, trembles with anxiety and out of respect and fear dares not even shout to him – what if he should be distracted, what if he has made a mistake? – Thanks! And thanks again, to whoever holds out to one who has been assaulted and left naked by life's sorrows, holds out to him the leaf of the word with which to hide his misery. Thanks to you, great Shakespeare!, you who can say everything, everything, everything exactly as it is – and yet why was this torment one you never gave voice to? Was it perhaps that you kept it to yourself, like the beloved whose name one still cannot bear the world to mention? For a poet buys this power of words to utter all the grim secrets of others at the cost of a little secret he himself cannot utter, and a poet is not an apostle, he casts devils out only by the power of the devil.

But now when the ethical is thus teleologically suspended, how does the single individual in whom it is suspended exist? He exists as the particular in opposition to the universal. Does this mean he sins? For this is the form of sin looked at ideally, just as the fact that the child does not sin because it is not conscious of its own existence as such does not mean that, looked at ideally, its existence is not that of sin or that the ethical does not make its demands of the child at every moment. If this form cannot be said to repeat itself in a way other than that of sin, then judgement has been delivered upon Abraham. Then how did Abraham exist? He had faith. That is the paradox that keeps him at the extremity and which he cannot make clear to anyone else, for the paradox is that he puts himself as the single individual in an absolute relation to the absolute. Is he justified? His justification is, once again, the paradox; for if he is the paradox it is not by virtue of being anything universal, but of being the particular.

How does the single individual assure himself that he is justified? It is a simple enough matter to level the whole of existence down to the idea of the State or to a concept of society. If one does that one can no doubt also mediate; for in this way one does not come to the paradox at all, to the single individual's as such being higher than the universal, which I can also put pointedly in a proposition of Pythagoras's, that the odd numbers are more perfect than the even. Should one happen to catch word of an answer in the direction of the paradox in our time, it will no doubt go like this: "That's to be judged by the outcome." A hero who has become the scandal of his generation, aware that he is a paradox that cannot be understood, cries undaunted to his contemporaries: "The future will show I was right!" This cry is heard less frequently nowadays, for as our age to its detriment produces no heroes, so it has the advantage that it also produces few caricatures. Whenever nowadays we hear the words "That's to be judged by the outcome" we know immediately with whom we have the honour of conversing. Those who speak thus are a populous tribe which, to give them a common name, I shall call the "lecturers". They live in their thoughts, secure in life, they have a *permanent* position and *sure* prospects in a well-organized State; they are separated by centuries, even millennia, from the convulsions of existence; they have no fear that such things could happen again; what would the police and the newspapers say? Their lifework is to judge the great, to judge them according to the outcome. Such conduct in respect of greatness betrays a strange mixture of arrogance and pitifulness, arrogance because they feel called to pass judgement, pitifulness because they feel their lives unrelated in even the remotest manner to those of the great. Surely anyone with a speck of *erectior ingenii* [nobility of mind] cannot become so completely the cold and clammy mollusc as to lose sight altogether, in approaching the great, of the fact that ever since the Creation it has been accepted practice for the outcome to come last, and that if one is really to learn something from the great it is precisely the beginning one must attend to. If anyone on the verge of action should judge himself according to the outcome, he would never begin. Even though the result may gladden the whole world, that cannot help the hero; for he knows the result only when the whole thing is over, and that is not how he becomes a hero, but by virtue of the fact that he began.

But in any case the outcome in its dialectic (in so far as it is finitude's answer to the infinite question) is totally incompatible with the existence of the hero. Or are we to take it that Abraham was justified in relating himself as the single individual to the universal by the fact that he got Isaac by a *marvel*? Had Abraham actually sacrificed Isaac, would that have meant he was less justified?

But it is the outcome that arouses our curiosity, as with the conclusion of a book; one wants nothing of the fear, the distress, the paradox. One flirts with the outcome aesthetically; it comes as unexpectedly and yet as effortlessly as a prize in the lottery; and having heard the outcome one is improved. And yet no robber of temples hardlabouring in chains is so base a criminal as he who plunders the holy in this way, and not even Judas, who sold his master for thirty pieces of silver, is more contemptible than the person who would thus offer greatness for sale.

It goes against my nature to speak inhumanly of greatness, to let its grandeur fade into an indistinct outline at an immense distance, or represent it as great without the human element in it coming to the fore – whence it ceases to be the great; for it is not what happens to me that makes me great, but what I do, and there is surely no one who thinks that anyone became great by winning the big lottery prize. Even of a person born in humble circumstances I ask that he should not be so inhuman towards himself as to be unable to think of the king's castle except at a distance and by dreaming of its grandeur indistinctly, wanting to exalt it and simultaneously destroying its grandeur by exalting it in such a debasing way. I ask that he be human enough to approach and bear himself with confidence and dignity there too. He should not be so inhuman as shamelessly to want to violate every rule of respect by storming into the king's salon straight from the street – he loses more by doing that than the king; on the contrary he should find pleasure in observing every rule of decorum with a glad and confident enthusiasm, which is just what will make him frank and open-hearted. This is only an analogy, for the difference here is only a very imperfect expression of the spiritual distance. I ask everyone not to think so inhumanly of himself as to dare not set foot in those palaces where not just the memory of the chosen lives on but the chosen themselves. He should not push himself shamelessly forward and thrust upon them his kinship with them, he should feel happy every time he bows before them, but be frank and confident and always something more than a cleaning woman; for unless he wants to be more than that he will never come in there. And what will help him are exactly the fear and distress in which the great are tried, for otherwise, at least if there is a drop of red blood in him, they will merely arouse his righteous envy. And whatever can only be great at a distance, whatever people want to exalt with empty and hollow phrases, that they themselves reduce to nothing.

Was there ever in the world anyone as great as that blessed woman, the mother of God, the Virgin Mary? And yet how do people speak of her? To say she was favoured among women doesn't make her great, and if it were not for the odd fact that those who listen can think as inhumanly as those who speak, surely every young girl would ask, why am I not favoured too? And had I nothing more to say I should by no means dismiss such a question as stupid; for as regards favours, abstractly considered, everyone is equally entitled. What is left out is the distress, the fear, the paradox. My thought is as pure as the next man's and surely the thought of anyone able to think in this way will be pure; if not, something dreadful is in store; for a person who has once called these images to mind cannot be rid of them again, and if he sins against them, then in their quiet wrath, more terrifying than the clamour of ten voracious critics, they will wreak their awful vengeance on him. No doubt Mary bore the child miraculously, but it went with Mary "after the manner of women", and such a time is one of fear, distress, and paradox. No doubt the angel was a ministering spirit, but he was not an obliging one who went round to all the other young girls in Israel and said: "Do not despise Mary, something out of the ordinary is happening to her." The angel came only to Mary, and no one could understand her. Yet what woman was done greater indignity than Mary, and isn't it true here too that those whom God blesses he damns in the same breath? This is the spirit's understanding of Mary, and she is not at all – as it offends me to say, though even more so that people have mindlessly and irresponsibly thought of her thus – she is not at all the fine lady sitting in her finery and playing with a divine child. Yet for saying notwithstanding, "Behold the handmaid of the Lord", she is great, and it seems to me that it should not be difficult to explain why she became the mother of God. She needs no worldly admiration, as little as Abraham needs our tears, for she was no heroine and he no hero, but both of them became greater than that, not by any means by being relieved of the distress, the agony, and the paradox, but because of these.

Great indeed it is when the poet presents his tragic hero for popular admiration and dares to say: "Weep for him, for he deserves it"; for there is greatness in meriting the tears of those who deserve to shed them; great indeed for the poet to dare hold the crowd in check, dare discipline people into testing their own worthiness to weep for the hero, for the waste-water of snivellers is a degradation of the holy. But greater than all these is that the knight of faith dares to say even to the noble person who would weep for him: "Do not weep for me, but weep for yourself."

One is stirred, one harks back to those beautiful times, sweet tender longings lead one to the goal of one's desire, to see Christ walking about in the promised land. One forgets the fear, the distress, the paradox. Was it so easy a matter not to be mistaken? Was it not a fearful thought that this man who walked among the others was God? Was it not terrifying to sit down to eat with him? Was it so easy a matter to become an apostle? But the outcome, eighteen centuries, that helps; it helps that shabby deception wherein one deceives oneself and others. I do not feel brave enough to wish to be contemporary with such events, but for that reason I do not judge harshly of those who were mistaken, nor think meanly of those who saw the truth.

But now I return to Abraham. In the time before the outcome either Abraham was a murderer every minute or we stay with the paradox which is higher than all mediation.

So Abraham's story contains a teleological suspension of the ethical. He has, as the single individual, become higher than the universal. This is the paradox which cannot be mediated. How he got into it is just as inexplicable as how he stayed in it. If this is not how it is with Abraham, then he is not even a tragic hero but a murderer. To want to go on calling him the father of faith, to talk of this to those who are only concerned with words, is thoughtless. A tragic hero can become a human being by his own strength, but not the knight of faith. When a person sets out on the tragic hero's admittedly hard path there are many who could lend him advice; but he who walks the narrow path of faith no one can advise, no one understand. Faith is a marvel, and yet no human being is excluded from it; for that in which all human life is united is passion,[1] and faith is a passion.

Note

1 Lessing has somewhere made similar remarks from a purely aesthetic point of view. In the passage in question he actually wants to show that sorrow too can express itself with wit. To that end he quotes the words spoken on a particular occasion by the unfortunate English king, Edward II. As contrast he quotes from Diderot: a story of a farmer's wife and a remark of hers, and then continues: "That too was wit, and the wit of a peasant at that; but the situation made it inevitable. Consequently one mustn't try to find the excuse for the witty expression of pain and of sorrow in the fact that the person who uttered them was superior, well-educated, intelligent, and witty as well, *for the passions make all men again equal* . . . the explanation lies in the fact that in the same situation probably everyone would have said the same thing. The peasant woman's thought is one a queen might just as well have had, just as what the king said on that occasion could, and no doubt would, have been said by a peasant."

51

Purity of Heart Is To Will One Thing

Live as an "Individual"

The talk asks you, then, *whether you live in such a way that you are conscious of being an "individual."* The question is not of the inquisitive sort, as if one asked about that "individual" in some special sense, about the one whom admiration and envy unite in pointing out. No, it is the serious question, of what each man really is according to his eternal vocation, so that he himself shall be conscious that he is following it; and what is even more serious, to ask it as if he were considering his life before God. This consciousness is the fundamental condition for truthfully willing only one thing. For he who is not himself a unity is never really anything wholly and decisively; he only exists in an external sense – as long as he lives as a numeral within the crowd, a fraction within the earthly conglomeration. Alas, how indeed should such a one decide to busy himself with the thought: truthfully to will only one thing!

Indeed it is precisely this consciousness that must be asked for. Just as if the talk could not ask in generalities, but rather asks you as an individual. Or, better still, my listener, if you would ask yourself, whether you have this consciousness, whether you are actively contemplating the occasion of this talk. For in the outside world, the crowd is busy making a noise. The one makes a noise because he heads the crowd, the many because they are members of the crowd. But the all-

Purity of Heart Is To Will One Thing (1847), tr. Douglas V. Steere (New York: Harper & Row, Publishers, 1938). Selection: "Live as an 'Individual'," pp. 184–97.

knowing One, who in spite of anyone is able to observe it all, does not desire the crowd. He desires the individual; He will deal only with the individual, quite unconcerned as to whether the individual be of high or low station, whether he be distinguished or wretched.

Each man himself, as an individual, should render his account to God. No third person dares venture to intrude upon this accounting between God and the individual. Yet the talk, by putting its question, dares and ought to dare, to remind man, in a way never to be forgotten, that the most ruinous evasion of all is to be hidden in the crowd in an attempt to escape God's supervision of him as an individual, in an attempt to get away from hearing God's voice as an individual. Long ago, Adam attempted this same thing when his evil conscience led him to imagine that he could hide himself among the trees. It may even be easier and more convenient, and more cowardly to hide oneself among the crowd in the hope that God should not be able to recognize one from the other. But in eternity each shall render account as an individual. That is, eternity will demand of him that he shall have lived as an individual. Eternity will draw out before his consciousness, all that he has done as an individual, he who had forgotten himself in noisy self-conceit. In eternity, he shall be brought to account strictly as an individual, he who intended to be in the crowd where there should be no such strict reckoning. Each one shall render account to God as an individual. The King shall render account as an individual; and the most wretched beggar, as an individual. No one may pride himself at being more than an individual, and no one despondently think that he is not an individual, perhaps because here in earth's busyness he had not as much as a name, but was named after a number.

For, after all, what is eternity's accounting other than that the voice of conscience is forever installed with its eternal right to be the exclusive voice? What is it other than that throughout eternity an infinite stillness reigns wherein the conscience may talk with the individual about what he, as an individual, of what he has done of Good or of evil, and about the fact that during his life he did not wish to be an individual? What is it other than that within eternity there is infinite space so that each person, as an individual, is apart with his conscience? For in eternity there is no mob pressure, no crowd, no hiding place in the crowd, as little as there are riots or street fights! Here in the temporal order conscience is prepared to make each person into an individual. But here in the temporal order, in the unrest, in the noise, in the pressure of the mob, in the crowd, in the primeval forest of evasion, alas, it is true, the calamity still happens, that someone completely stifles the voice of his conscience – his conscience, for he can never rid himself of it. It continues to belong to him, or more accurately, he continues to belong to it. Yet we are not now talking about this calamity, for even among the better persons, it happens all too readily that the voice of conscience becomes merely one voice among many. Then it follows so easily that the isolated voice of conscience (as generally happens to a solitary one) becomes overruled – by the majority. But in eternity, conscience is the only voice that is heard. It must be heard by the individual, for the individual has become the eternal echo of this voice. It must be heard. There is no place to flee from it. For in the infinite there is no place, the individual is himself the place. It must be heard. In vain the individual looks about for the crowd. Alas, it is as if there were a world between him and the nearest individual, whose conscience is also speaking to him about what *he* as an individual has spoken, and done, and thought of good and of evil.

Do you now live so that you are conscious of yourself as an individual; that in each of your relations in which you come into touch with the outside world, you are conscious of yourself, and that at the same time you are related to yourself as an individual? Even in these relations which we men so beautifully style the most intimate of all, do you remember that you have a still more intimate relation, namely, that in which you as an individual are related to yourself before God? If you are bound to another human being by the holy bond of matrimony, do you consider in this intimate relation that still more intimate relation in which you as an individual are related to yourself before God? The talk does not ask you whether you now love your wife: it hopes so; nor whether she is the apple of your eye and the desire of your heart: it wishes you this. It does not ask what you have done to make your wife happy, about how you both have arranged your household life, about what good advice you have been able to get from others, or what harmful influence others have had upon you. It does not ask whether your marital life is more commendable than that of many others, or whether it perhaps might be looked upon by some as a worthy example. No, the talk asks about none of these things. It asks you neither in congratulation, nor inquisitively, nor watchfully, nor apologetically, nor comparatively. It asks you only about the ultimate thing: whether you yourself are conscious of that most intimate relation to yourself as an individual. You do not carry the responsibility for your wife, nor for other men, nor by any comparative standard with other men, but only as an individual, before God, where it is not asked whether your marriage was in accordance with others, with the common practice, or better than others, but where you as an individual will be asked only whether it was in accordance with your responsibility as an individual. For common practice changes, and all comparison goes lame, or is only half truth. But eternity's practice, which never goes out of fashion, is, that you are the individual, that you yourself in the intimate relation of marriage should have been conscious of this.

In truth, it is not divorce that eternity is aiming at, neither is it divorce, that eternity does away with the difference between man and woman. Your wife will have no occasion to grieve because you are pondering this, your most intimate relation to God. And should she be so foolish as to desire for herself only that which is earthly or even foolish enough to desire as well to draw you down to the earthly: yet a woman's folly shall certainly not be able to change the law of eternity. In eternity it will not be asked whether your wife seduced you (eternity will talk with her about that), but simply as an individual you will be asked whether you allowed yourself to be seduced. If your marriage is so blessed that you see a family growing up around you, may you be conscious that while you have an intimate relation to your children you have a still more intimate relation to yourself as an individual. You share the responsibility with your wife, and hence eternity will also ask her as an individual about her share of the responsibility. For in eternity there is not a single complication that is able to make the accounting difficult and evasion easy. Eternity does not ask concerning how far you brought up your children in the way that you saw others do it. It simply asks you, as an individual, how you brought up your children. It does not talk with you in the manner that you would talk with a friend in confidence. For alas, even this confidence can all too easily accustom you to evasions. For even the most trustworthy friend still speaks as a third person. And by much of such confidence, one easily gets used to speaking of himself as if he were a third person. But in eternity, you are the individual, and conscience when it talks with you is no third person, any more than you are a third person when you talk with conscience. For you and conscience are one. It knows all that you know, and it knows that you know it. With respect to your children's upbringing you can weigh various matters with your wife, or your friends. But how you act and the responsibility for it is finally wholly and solely yours as an individual. And if you fail to act, hiding from yourself and from others behind a screen of deliberation, you bring down the responsibility solely upon yourself as an individual.

Yes, in the temporal order where in all directions both this and that are asked about in the manifold complex complications of their reciprocal action, there one may rightly enough believe that it was a fantasy of the imagination, a chimera, that each one among these countless millions of people should be convinced accurately down to the least trifle of what his life consisted. But in eternity this is possible, because each becomes an individual. And this applies to every relation of your life.

If you do not live in some out-of-the-way place in the world, if you live in a populous city, and you direct your attention outwards, sympathetically engrossing yourself in the people and in what is going on, do you remember each time you throw yourself in this way into the world around you, that in this relation, you relate yourself to yourself as an individual with eternal responsibility? Or do you press yourself into the crowd, where the one excuses himself with the others, where at one moment there are, so to speak, many, and where in the next moment, each time that the talk

touches upon responsibility, there is no one? Do you judge like the crowd, in its capacity as a crowd? You are not obliged to have an opinion about what you do not understand. No, on the contrary, you are eternally excused from that. But you are eternally responsible as an individual to render an account for your opinion, and for your judgment. And in eternity, you will not be asked inquisitively and professionally, as though by a newspaper reporter, whether there were many that had the same – wrong opinion. You will be asked only whether you have held it, whether you have spoiled your soul by joining in this frivolous and thoughtless judging, because the others, because the many judged thoughtlessly. You will be asked only whether you may not have ruined the best within you by joining the crowd in its defiance, thinking that you were many and therefore you had the prerogative, because you were many, that is, because you were many who were wrong. In eternity it will be asked whether you may not have damaged a good thing, in order that you also might judge with them that did not know how to judge, but who possessed the crowd's strength, which in the temporal sense is significant but to which eternity is wholly indifferent.

You see, in the temporal order, a man counts and says: "One more or less, it makes no difference" – and he applies this even to himself! In the temporal order a man counts and says: "One over against a hundred, after all what can come of that?" So he grows cowardly in the face of – number. And numbers are usually false. Truth is content to be a unity. But a man wins something by this cowardly indulgence. He does not win a bed in a hospital. No, but he wins the amazing thing of becoming the strongest of all, because the crowd is always the strongest. Eternity, on the other hand, never counts. The individual is always only one and conscience in its meticulous way concerns itself with the individual. In eternity you will look in vain for the crowd. You will listen in vain to find whether you cannot hear where the noise and the gathering is, so that you may run to it. In eternity you, too, will be forsaken by the crowd. And this is terrifying. Yet in the temporal order to be forsaken by the crowd, provided that the Eternal comforts, may be something blessed, and the pain of it, a mere jest. What then in eternity will conscience demand of you by the consciousness that you are an individual? It will teach you that if you judge (for in very many cases it will restrain you from judging), you must bear the responsibility for your judgment. It will teach you that you should examine what you understand and what you do not understand as if you stood trembling in the presence of a departed one; it wishes to frighten you from resorting to the brilliant flights into wretchedness to which you are often subject. For many fools do not make a wise man, and the crowd is doubtful recommendation for a cause. Yes, the larger the crowd, the more probable that that which it praises is folly, and the more improbable that it is truth, and the most improbable of all that it is any eternal truth. For in eternity crowds simply do not exist. The truth is not such that it at once pleases the frivolous crowd – and at bottom it never does; to such a multitude the truth must appear as simply absurd. But the man who, conscious of himself as an individual, judges with eternal responsibility, he is slow to pass judgment upon the unusual. For it is possible that it is falsehood and deceit and illusion and vanity. But it is also possible that it is true. He remembers the word of the simple sage of ancient times: "This, that a man's eye cannot see by the light by which the majority see could be because he is used to darkness; but it could also be because he is used to a still clearer light, and when this is so, it is no laughing matter" [Socrates, in Plato's *Republic*, VII, 518A].

No, it is no laughing matter, but it is laughable, or it is pitiable, that the frivolous ones laugh at a man because he is wiser or better than they. For even laughter calls for a reasonable ground, and when this is absent, the laughter becomes the very thing that is laughable. But here in the temporal order, in the midst of earth's appalling prodigality with human beings, here number tempts. It tempts a man to count, to count himself in with the crowd. Here, by the use of round numbers, everything can be manipulated with ease. Yes, here in the temporal order it is possible that no individual can ever succeed, even if it were true that he sincerely willed the Good, in dispersing the crowd. But eternity can do it. Eternity seizes each one by the strong arm of conscience, holding him as an individual. Eternity sets him apart with his conscience. Woe unto him, if he is left to this judge alone! For in that case eternity will set him apart with his conscience in that place where there is pressure, to be sure, but not as in the temporal order where the pressure is the excuse, yes, the victory. No, eternity places him where to be under pressure is to be alone, stripped of every excuse; to be alone and to be lost. The royal psalm singer says

that: while the heathen clamor, God sits in his heaven and laughs at them [Psalms 2:4]. I dare not believe this. It would seem to be preferable to say that: while the crowd clamors and shouts and triumphs and celebrates; while one individual after another hastens to the place of tumult, where it is good to be if one is in search of oblivion and indulgence from that which is eternal; while at the same time the crowd shouts mockingly at God, "Yes, now see whether you can get hold of us"; yet since it is difficult in the rush of the crowd to distinguish the individual, difficult to see the single tree when one is looking at the wood, the sober countenance of eternity quietly waits. And if all the generations that have lived on earth rose up and gathered themselves in a single crowd in order to loose a storm against eternity, in order to coerce eternity by their colossal majority: eternity would scatter them as easily as the firmness of an immovable rock would scatter frothy scum; as easily as the wind when it rushes forward scatters chaff. Just as easily, but not in the same way. For the wind scatters the chaff, but then turns around and drifts it together again. Eternity scatters the crowd by giving each an infinite weight, by making him heavy – as an individual. For what in eternity is the highest blessing is also the deepest seriousness. What, there, is the most blessed comfort, is also the most appalling responsibility.

In eternity there are chambers enough so that each may be placed alone in one. For wherever conscience is present, and it is and shall be present in each person, there exists in eternity a lonely prison, or the blessed chamber of salvation. On that account this consciousness of being an individual is the primary consciousness in a man, which is his eternal consciousness. But that man is slow to pass judgment who bears in mind, that he is an individual, and that the final and highest responsibility for the judgment rests solely upon him. For even the most trusted friend in passing judgment as an impartial observer must necessarily leave out what is crucial. To be the party directly concerned, the one to whom conscience in this affair speaks the intimate "thou," is another matter, for conscience only speaks this intimate "thou" to your friend in regard to the manner in which he is to give counsel. Such a thoughtful one does not willingly pass judgment on many things, and just this helps him to will only one thing. He thinks it is not altogether an advantage to live in a populous city where because of the swiftness of the means of communication almost everyone can easily have a hasty and superficial judgment about everything possible. On the contrary, he looks upon this easiness as a temptation and a snare and he learns earnestness in order as an individual to be concerned about his eternal responsibility.

"Even a fool might be a wise man if he could keep silent," says the proverb. And this is so, not merely because then he would not betray his foolishness, but also because this self-control would help him to become conscious of himself as an individual, and would prevent him from adopting the crowd's opinion. Or if he had an opinion of his own, it would prevent him from hastening to get the crowd to adopt it. The one who is conscious of himself as an individual has his vision trained to look upon everything as inverted. His sense becomes familiar with eternity's true thought: that everything in this life appears in inverted form. The purely momentary, in the next moment, to say nothing of eternity, becomes nonsense and vanity: the fiery moment of lust (and what is so strong for the moment as lust!) is loathsome in memory; the fiery moment of anger, revenge, and passion whose gratification seems an irresistible impulse is horrible to remember. For the angry one, the vengeful one, the passionate one, thinks in the moment of passion that he revenges himself. But in the moment of remembrance, when the act of revenge comes back to him, he loathes himself, for he sees that precisely in that moment of revenge he lost himself. The purely momentary seems to be profitable. Yet in the next moment its deception becomes apparent and, eternally understood, calls for repentance. So it is with all things of the moment, and hence with the crowd's opinion or with membership in the crowd in so far as this opinion and this membership is a thing of the moment.

My listeners, do you at present live in such a way that you are yourself clearly and eternally conscious of being an individual? This was the question the address was to ask, or rather that you are to ask yourself, if you actively consider this occasion. The talk should not tell you only that which will disturb you, even though many are of the conviction that a man ought ever to live in such an aroused state of consciousness. Nor is it concerned how many or how few hold that conviction. The speaker will not attempt to win you to this conviction, even if he does as a rule hold it himself. He does not wish to force it upon you any more than you would desire to force it upon him if you were of this conviction. For the exalted earnestness of the Eternal wishes neither the commendation of the majority nor the commendation of eloquence. One thing alone the talk does not dare to promise you – nor does it wish to insult you. It does not dare to promise you earthly gain if you enter upon and in dedication persevere in this conviction. On the contrary, if persevered in, it will make your life more taxing, and frequently perhaps wearisome. If persevered in, it may make you the target of others' ridicule, not to mention even greater sacrifices that perseverance might choose to require of you. Of course, the ridicule does not distract you if you continue to persist in your conviction. Ridicule will even be a help to you, in the sense that it is a further proof to you that you are on the right path. For the judgment of the crowd has its significance. One should not remain proudly ignorant of it, no, one should be attentive to it. If after this he sees to it that he does the opposite from the judgment of the crowd, then he, for the most part, does the right thing. Or if at the outset a man does the opposite, and he is then so fortunate as to have the judgment of the crowd express itself to the contrary, then he can be fairly certain that he has laid hold of the right thing. Then he has not only himself inwardly weighed and tested the conviction properly, but he has also the advantage of having it tested a second time by the help of ridicule. Ridicule may wound his feelings but just by that wound it shows that he is on the right path – the path of honor and of victory, like a warrior's wound, when it is on the breast where both the wound and the badge of honor are to be borne.

You have surely noticed among schoolboys, that the one that is regarded by all as the boldest is the one who has no fear of his father, who dares to say to the others, "Do you think I am afraid of him?" On the other hand, if they sense that one of their number is actually and literally afraid of his father, they will readily ridicule him a little. Alas, in men's fear-ridden rushing together into a crowd (for why indeed does a man rush into a crowd except because he is afraid!) there, too, it is a mark of boldness not to be afraid, not even of God. And if someone notes that there is an individual outside the crowd who is really and truly afraid – not of the crowd, but of God, he is sure to be the target of some ridicule. The ridicule is usually glossed over somewhat and it is said: a man should *love* God.

Yes, to be sure, God knows that man's highest consolation is that God is love and that man is permitted to love Him. But let us not become too forward, and foolishly, yes, blasphemously, dismiss the tradition of our fathers, established by God Himself: that really and truly a man should fear God. This fear is known to the man who is himself conscious of being an individual, and thereby is conscious of his eternal responsibility before God. For he knows, that even if he could with the help of evasions and excuses, get on well in this life, and even if he could by this shady path have gained the whole world, yet there is still a place in the next world where there is no more evasion than there is shade in the scorching desert.

The talk will not go into this further. It will only ask you again and again, do you now live so that you are conscious of being an individual and thereby that you are conscious of your eternal responsibility before God? Do you live in such a way that this consciousness is able to secure the time and quiet and liberty of action to penetrate every relation of your life? This does not demand that you withdraw from life, from an honorable calling, from a happy domestic life. On the contrary, it is precisely that consciousness which will sustain and clarify and illuminate what you are to do in the relations of life. You should not withdraw and sit brooding over your eternal accounting. To do this is to deserve something further to account for. You will more and more readily find time to perform your duty and your task, while concern over your eternal responsibility will hinder you from being "busy" and busily having a hand in everything possible – an activity that can best be called: time-wasting.

52

Practice in Christianity

The Halt

"Come here to me, all you who labor and are burdened, I will give you rest."

Halt now! But before what is one to halt? Before that which at the same moment infinitely changes everything – so that instead of seeing what might be expected, a vast crowd of people who labor and are burdened who accepted the invitation, you eventually will actually see the opposite, a vast crowd of people who shudder and recoil until they storm ahead and trample down, so that, if from the outcome one were to infer what had been said, one might rather conclude that *"procul o procul este profani* [away, away, O unhallowed ones]" had been said instead of "Come here" – before that which is infinitely more important and infinitely more decisive: **the inviter.** Not as if he were not a human being, to do what he says, or God, to keep what he promises – no, in another sense.

I

That the inviter is and wants to be the specific historical person he was eighteen hundred years ago, and as that specific person, living under the conditions under which he lived at that time, he

Practice in Christianity (Indøvelse i Christendom, 1850), tr. Howard V. Hong and Edna H. Hong (Princeton University Press, 1991). Selections: "The Halt," pp. 23–32; "The Categories of *Offense,* That Is, of Essential Offense," pp. 123–44.

has spoken words of invitation. – He is not and does not want to be for anyone the person one has come to know something about incidentally from history (world history, history directly understood in contradistinction to sacred history) and nothing more than that, because we can learn nothing from history about him inasmuch as there is nothing at all that can be "known" about him. He does not want to be judged humanly by the results of his life, that is, he is and wants to be the sign of offense and the object of faith; to judge him according to the results of his life is blasphemy. As God, his life, that he lived and has lived, is infinitely more decisive than all the results of it in history.

(a): Who spoke those words of invitation?

The inviter. Who is the inviter? Jesus Christ. Which Jesus Christ, the Jesus Christ who sits in glory at the Father's right hand? No. From glory he has not spoken a word. So, then, it is Jesus Christ in his abasement, in the situation of abasement, who has spoken these words.

Is, then, Jesus Christ not the same? Yes, he is the same today and yesterday, the same as he was eighteen hundred years ago, the Jesus Christ who abased himself and took the form of a servant, the Jesus Christ who spoke these words of invitation. It is also he who said that he will come again in glory. In his coming again in glory he is again the same Jesus Christ, but this has not happened as yet.

Is he, then, not in glory now? Yes, of course, this the Christian *believes.* But it was in the condition of abasement that he spoke those words; he did not speak them from glory. Nothing can be known about his coming again in glory; that can only be believed in the strictest sense. But one cannot become a believer except by coming to him in his state of abasement, to him, the sign of offense and the object of faith. He does not exist [*existere*] in any other way, for only in this way has he existed. That he will come in glory is anticipated, but can be anticipated and believed only by the person who has adhered to him and adheres to him as he has existed.

So Jesus Christ is the same; but he lived eighteen hundred years ago in his abasement and is not changed until his coming again. He has not yet come again; therefore he still continues to be the abased one who, it is believed, will come again in glory. What he has said and taught, every word he has spoken, becomes *eo ipso* [precisely thereby] untrue if we make it appear as if it is Christ in glory who says it. No, *he* is silent; the *abased one* is speaking. The intervening period (between the abasement and the coming again in glory), which at this time is about eighteen hundred years and may still become many times eighteen hundred years, the intervening period, that is, what the intervening period wants to make him into, world history's or church history's secular information about Christ, about who Christ was, about who has spoken those words, is something irrelevant, neither here nor there, something that only misrepresents him and thereby makes his words of invitation untrue.

It is untrue if I make up words that someone has never said and say that he has said them. But it is also untrue and the words he has said become untrue, or it becomes untrue that he has said them, if I make him essentially different from what he was when he said them. Essentially different, for an untruth with regard to something or other incidental is not able to make it untrue that "he" has said it. – Thus if it pleases God to wander here on earth in as strict an incognito as only an Almighty can wear, impenetrable for all confidential knowing, if it pleases him (and why he does it, for what purpose, he himself certainly knows best, but whatever his reason and purpose, they testify that the incognito has something essential to signify) to teach people in the form of a lowly servant, judging from appearances just like any other human being, if it pleases him to teach people in this guise – and then when someone repeats verbatim what he said but makes it appear

that it was God who said these words, then it becomes untrue, for it is untrue that *he* said these words.

(b): Can one come to know something about Christ from history?[1]

No. Why not? Because one cannot *know* anything at all about *Christ*; he is the paradox, the object of faith, exists only for faith. But all historical communication is the communication of *knowledge*; consequently one can come to know nothing about Christ from history. For if one comes to know little or much or something about him, he is not the one he in truth is. Thus one comes to know something about him that is different from what he is. One comes to know nothing about him or one comes to know something incorrect about him – one is deceived. History makes Christ into someone else than he is in truth, and thus from history we come to know much about – Christ? No, not about Christ, for about him nothing can be known; he can only be believed.

(c): Can it be demonstrated from history that Christ was God?

Let me ask another question first: Can any more foolish contradiction be imagined than this, to want to **demonstrate** (for the present it is a matter of indifference whether we want to *demonstrate* it from history or from anything else in the world) that an individual human being is God? That an individual human being is God, that is, claims to be God, is indeed the offense κατ' ἐξοχήν [in an eminent sense]. But what is the offense, that which offends? That which conflicts with all (human) reason. And it is that which one wants to demonstrate! But to "demonstrate" is, after all, to make something into the rational-actual that it is. Can one, then, make that which conflicts with all reason into the rational-actual? Certainly not, unless one wants to contradict oneself. One can "demonstrate" only that it conflicts with reason. The demonstrations for the divinity of Christ that Scripture sets forth – his miracles, his resurrection from the dead, his ascension – are indeed only for faith, that is, they are not "demonstrations." Neither do they want to demonstrate that all this is in complete harmony with reason; on the contrary, they want to demonstrate that it conflicts with reason and consequently is the object of faith.

Back to the demonstration from history. "Is it not eighteen hundred years now since Christ lived, is not his name proclaimed and believed throughout the whole world, has not his teaching (Christianity) changed the shape of the world, victoriously penetrated all its relations, and therefore has not history adequately, or more than adequately, established who he was, that he was – God?" No, history has neither adequately nor more than adequately established that; never in all eternity can history establish that. But with regard to the first assertion, it is indeed certain enough that his name is proclaimed all over the world – whether it is believed, I shall not be able to decide; it is certain enough that Christianity has changed the shape of the world, victoriously penetrated all its relations, so victoriously that now all claim to be Christian.

But what does that demonstrate? At most it can demonstrate that Jesus Christ was a great man, perhaps the greatest of all. But that he was – God – no, stop; with the help of God that conclusion will surely miscarry.

If in wanting to proceed to this conclusion we begin with the assumption that Jesus Christ was a human being and then consider the eighteen hundred years of history (the results of his life), we can then conclude in steadily ascending superlatives: great, greater, greatest, exceedingly and amazingly the greatest man who has ever lived. – But if we begin with the assumption (of faith) that he was God, then we have *eo ipso* crossed out, canceled, the eighteen hundred years as making no difference either way, demonstrating neither *pro* nor *contra*, because the certitude of faith is infinitely higher. – And obviously we have to begin in one of these ways; if we begin in the latter way, everything is in order.

If we begin in the first way, we cannot, without somewhere or other being guilty of a μετάβασις εἰς ἄλλο γένος [shifting from one genus to another], suddenly by way of a conclusion obtain the new quality, God, so that as a consequence the result or results of a human being's life at some point suddenly demonstrate that this human being was God. If this could be done, then the following question could also be answered: What results must there be, how great the effects, how many centuries must pass in order to have it demonstrated from the results of a "human beings's" life (this, after all, is the as-

sumption) that he was God? If it perhaps is so that even in the year 300 Christ was not completely demonstrated to be God, there would be something to it; he was a little more than the exceedingly, amazingly greatest man who ever lived, but it would still take a few additional centuries. In that case, it presumably would follow in turn that the people who lived in the year 300 did not regard Christ as God, even less those who lived in the first century: whereas certainty that he was God increases with every century, so that in our century, the nineteenth, certainty is the greatest it has ever been, a certainty of which by comparison the first centuries had only a vague inkling. This question may be answered or ignored; it is basically a matter of indifference.

What, after all, does this mean? Would it be possible that by observing the ever-unfolding results of something one can by a simple deduction produce a quality different from that of the assumption? Is it not madness (if the person is not mad) that the first judgment, which is indeed that of the assumption from which one proceeds, can mistake which is which to such a degree that one goes wrong by a quality from the correct one? And if one begins with this error, how will one at any point be able to see from the results that a quite different, an infinitely different quality is involved? A footprint on a way is indeed a result of someone's having walked this way. It may happen that I make the mistake that it was, for example, a bird, but by closer scrutiny, following the prints further, ascertain that it must have been another animal. Fine, but here there is no infinite change of quality, either. But can I, by close scrutiny and by following prints of this sort, at some point reach the conclusion: ergo it is a spirit that has walked along this way, a spirit – which leaves no print? So it is also with concluding from the results of an – assumed – human existence that ergo it was God. Do God and man then resemble each other to such a degree, is there such scant difference between them, that I, if I am not mad, can start with the assumption that it was a human being; and on the other hand has not Christ himself claimed to be God? If God and man resemble each other to that degree, if they are to that degree kindred, consequently essentially within the same quality, then the conclusion "ergo it was God" is humbug; for if to be God is nothing else than that, then God does not exist [*er til*] at all. But if God does exist, and consequently is separated from what it is to be human by an infinite qualitative difference – if I, then, or anyone starts with the assumption that it was a human being, it can never in all eternity be shown that it was God. Even someone only moderately developed dialectically must easily perceive that the whole question of results is incommensurable with the decision whether it was God and that this decision confronts a person in an entirely different way: whether he will believe what he claimed to be, that he was God, or he will not believe.

Dialectically understood – that is, of course, if one takes the time to understand it – this is sufficient to block that conclusion from the results of Christ's life: ergo he was God. But faith as the authority makes an even more extreme charge against any attempt to approach Jesus Christ by means of what is known about him from history, which has preserved the results of Christ's life. Faith's claim is that this whole attempt is – *blasphemy*. Faith's claim is that the only demonstration that unbelief allowed to stand when it dispatched all the other demonstrations of the truth of Christianity, the demonstration that unbelief invented – yes, it is curiously complicated! – and invented in order to demonstrate the truth of Christianity! – excellent, unbelief invents demonstrations in order to defend Christianity – the demonstration that is then much paraded in Christendom, the demonstration of eighteen hundred years – faith's claim is that it is – *blasphemy*.

With regard to a *human being*, it is true that the results of his life are more important than his life. If, in order to find out who Christ was and to show this by means of a conclusion, we consider the results of his life, we then *eo ipso* make him into a human being, a human being who like other human beings must take his examination in history, which, incidentally, in this case is just as mediocre an examiner as an ordinary school teacher examining in Latin.

How strange! With the help of history and by looking at the results of his life, we want to arrive in conclusion at the "ergo": ergo he was God – and faith makes the very opposite claim, that the one who begins at all with this syllogism begins with a blasphemy. The blasphemy is not so much the hypothetical assumption that he was a human being. No, the blasphemy is what lies at the base of this whole enterprise, the idea without which one would not begin, the idea of whose correctness one is firmly and completely convinced, that it also applies to Christ, the idea that the result of his life is more important than his life, in other words,

that he is a human being. Hypothetically one says: Let us assume that Christ was a human being. But at the base of this hypothesis, which is still not blasphemy, lies the *assertum* [claim] that the view that the result of one's life is more important than one's life applies to Christ. If this is not assumed, then one admits to oneself that one's whole enterprise is meaningless, one admits it before beginning, and therefore why begin? But if one assumes it and begins, then the blasphemy is under way. The more engrossed one becomes in considering the results, but with the aim of drawing a conclusion as to whether he was God or not – the more blasphemous is one's conduct and is that at every moment as long as this consideration continues.

What a strange meeting: it is made to appear that if only a really thorough consideration of the results of Christ's life is made one will surely come to the "ergo" – and faith judges the very beginning of this attempt to be a mockery of God, and the continuation an increasing mockery of God.

"History," says faith, "has nothing at all to do with Jesus Christ; with regard to him we have only sacred history (which is qualitatively different from history in general), which relates the story of his life in the state of abasement, also that he claimed to be God. He is the paradox that history can never digest or convert into an ordinary syllogism. He is the same in his abasement as in his loftiness – but the eighteen hundred years, or if it came to be eighteen thousand years, has nothing at all to do with it. These brilliant results in world history, which almost convince even a professor of history that he was God, these brilliant results are certainly not his coming again in glory! But this is just about how one understands it; it shows again that Christ is made into a human being whose coming again in glory cannot be or become anything other than the result of his life in history – whereas Christ's coming again in glory is something entirely different from this, something that is to be believed. He abased himself and was wrapped in rags – he will come again in glory, but the brilliant results, especially on closer inspection, are too shabby a glory, in any case a totally incongruous glory that faith therefore never mentions when it speaks of his glory. He still exists only in his abasement, until he, something that is believed, comes again in glory. History may be an excellent branch of knowledge, but it must not become so conceited that it undertakes what the Father will do, to array Christ in glory, clothing him in the glittering trappings of results, as if this were the second coming. That in his abasement he was God, that he will come again in glory – this goes not a little beyond the understanding of history; this cannot be drawn from history, no matter how matchlessly one regards it, except through a matchless lack of dialectic."

How strange, and then history is the very thing that people have wanted to use to demonstrate that Christ was God.

(d): Is the result of Christ's life more important than his life?

No, by no means, just the opposite; if this were the case, then Christ was only a human being.

It is, namely, by no means extraordinary that a human being has lived; certainly millions and millions enough of them have lived. If that is to become extraordinary, then his life must have something extraordinary; that is, with regard to a human being's life, the extraordinariness consists only in something else. It is not extraordinary that he lived, but his life had this and this extraordinariness. This extraordinariness can be, among other things, what he has achieved, the results of his life.

But that God has lived here on earth as an individual human being is infinitely extraordinary. Even if it had had no results whatever, it makes no difference; it remains just as extraordinary, infinitely extraordinary, infinitely more extraordinary than all the results. Try here to situate the extraordinariness in something else, and one will readily perceive the foolishness; indeed, what extraordinariness would there be in the fact that God's life has had extraordinary results? To talk in this manner is nonsense.

No, that God has lived is the infinitely extraordinary, is the in-itself extraordinary. If it is assumed that Christ's life had had no results at all – if someone were then to say that his life was not extraordinary, this is a mockery of God. It is equally extraordinary, and if it were a matter of extraordinariness in something else, it would have to be: the extraordinariness that his life had had no results. If, however, someone says that Christ's life is extraordinary because of the results, then this is again mockery of God, because Christ's life is the in-itself extraordinary.

The emphasis does not fall upon the fact that a human being has lived, but the emphasis falls infinitely upon the fact that God has lived. Only God can attach that much importance to himself, so that the fact that he has lived is infinitely more important than all the results that are registered in history. [...]

The Categories of *Offense*, That Is, of Essential Offense

In the first period of Christendom, when even aberrations bore an unmistakable mark of one's nevertheless knowing what the issue was, the fallacy with respect to the God-man was either that in one way or another the term "God" was taken away (Ebionitism and the like) or the term "man" was taken away (Gnosticism). In the entire modern age, which so unmistakably bears the mark that it does not even know what the issue is, the confusion is something different and far more dangerous. By way of didacticism, the God-man has been made into that speculative unity of God and man *sub specie aeterni* [under the aspect of eternity] or made visible in that nowhere-to-be-found medium of pure being, rather than that the God-man is the unity of being God and an individual human being in a historically actual situation. Or Christ has been abolished altogether, thrown out and his teaching taken over, and finally he is almost regarded as one regards an anonymous writer: the teaching is the principal thing, is everything. This is why people delude themselves into thinking that all Christianity is nothing but *direct* communication, in its simplicity even more direct than the professor's profound dictations. In a loss of meaning, it is forgotten that here the teacher is more important than the teaching. Wherever it is the case that the teacher is an essential component, there is a reduplication; the reduplication lies in precisely this, that the teacher is integral; but wherever there is reduplication, the communication is not completely direct paragraph-communication or professor-communication. Reduplicated in the teacher through his existing in what he teaches, the communication is in manifold ways a self-differentiating art. And now when the teacher, who is inseparable from and more essential than the teaching, is a paradox, then all direct communication is impossible. But in our day everything is made abstract and everything personal is abolished: we take Christ's teaching – and abolish Christ. This is to abolish Christianity, for Christ is a person and is the teacher who is more important than the teaching. – Just as Christ's life, the fact that he has lived, is vastly more important than all the results of his life (as I have tried to show in another work), so also is Christ infinitely more important than his teaching. It is true only of a human being that his teaching is more important than he himself; to apply this to Christ is a blasphemy, inasmuch as it makes him into only a human being.

1: The God-man is a sign

What is meant by a *sign?* A sign is the denied immediacy or the second being that is different from the first being. This is not to say that the sign is not immediately something but that it is a sign, and it is not immediately that which it is as a sign or as a sign is not the immediate that it is. A navigation mark is a sign. Immediately it certainly is something, a post, a lamp, etc., but a sign it is not immediately; that it is a sign is something different from what it immediately is. – This underlies all the mystification by means of signs, for the sign is only for the one who knows that it is a sign and in the strictest sense only for the one who knows what it means; for everyone else the sign is that which it immediately is. – Even if it were not so, that there is someone who has made this or that into a sign and there is no agreement with anyone that this is supposed to be a sign, if I see something striking and call it a sign, this involves a term based on reflection. The striking thing is the immediate, but my regarding it as a sign (which is a reflection, something I in a certain sense take from myself) indeed expresses that I think that it is supposed to mean something. But that it is supposed to *mean* something is its being something different from what it immediately is. Consequently, I do not deny its immediacy in regarding it as a sign, although I do not know definitely either that it is a sign or what it is supposed to mean.

A *sign of contradiction* is a sign that intrinsically contains a contradiction in itself. There is no contradiction in its being immediately this or that and also a sign, for there must certainly be an immediate entity for it to be a sign; a literal nothing is not a sign either. A sign of contradiction, however, is a sign that contains a contradiction in its composition. To justify the name of "sign," there must be something by which it draws attention to itself or to the contradiction. But the contradictory parts must not annul each other in such a way that the sign comes to mean nothing or in such a way that it becomes the opposite of a sign, an unconditional concealment. – A communication that is the unity of jest and earnestness is thus a sign of contradiction. It is no direct communication; it is impossible for the recipient to say *directly* which is which, simply because the one communicating does not *directly* communicate either jest or earnestness. Therefore the earnestness in this communication lies in another place, or somewhere else, lies in making the recipient self-active – from the purely dialectical point of view, the highest earnestness with regard to communication. But such a communication must secure for itself a something by which it draws attention to itself, by which it occasions and invites a heeding of the communication; and on the other hand the combination of jest and earnestness must not be lunacy either, because then there is no communication; whereas, if jest or earnestness completely dominates, it is direct communication.

A sign is not what it is in its immediacy, because in its immediacy no sign *is*, inasmuch as "sign" is a term based on reflection. A sign of contradiction is that which draws attention to itself and, once attention is directed to it, shows itself to contain a contradiction.

In Scripture the God-man is called a sign of contradiction – but what contradiction, if any, could there be at all in the speculative unity of God and man? No, there is no contradiction in that, but the contradiction – and it is as great as possible, is the qualitative contradiction – is between being God and being an individual human being. In addition to being what one is immediately, to be a sign is to be a something else also. To be a sign of contradiction is to be a something else that stands in contrast to what one immediately is. So it is with the God-man. Immediately, he is an individual human being, just like others, a lowly, unimpressive human being, but now comes the contradiction – that *he* is God.

But lest this contradiction become a contradiction that exists for no one or does not exist for anyone – somewhat like a mystification that is so extraordinarily successful that its effect is nil – there must be something that draws attention to it. The miracle essentially serves this purpose, and a single direct statement about being God. Yet neither the miracle nor the single direct statement is absolutely direct communication; for in that case the contradiction is *eo ipso* canceled. As far as the miracle, which is the object of *faith*, is concerned, this is certainly easy to see; as for the second, that the single direct statement is nevertheless not direct communication, this will be shown later.

The God-man is the sign of contradiction, and why? Because, replies Scripture, because he was to disclose the thoughts of hearts. Does all the modern thought about the speculative unity of God and man, all this that regards Christianity only as a teaching, does this have the remotest resemblance to the essentially Christian? No, in the modern approach everything is made as direct as putting one's foot in a sock – and the Christian approach is the sign of contradiction that discloses the thoughts of hearts. The God-man is an individual human being – not a fantastic unity that has never existed except *sub specie aeterni* [under the aspect of eternity], and he is anything but an assistant professor who teaches directly to parroters or dictates paragraphs for shorthand writers – he does exactly the very opposite, he discloses the thoughts of hearts. Ah, it is so cozy to be listeners and transcribers when everything is so completely direct. Gentlemen listeners and transcribers must watch out – it is the thoughts of *their* hearts that are to be disclosed.

And only the sign of contradiction can do this: it draws attention to itself and then it presents a contradiction. There is a something that makes it impossible not to look – and look, as one is looking one sees as in a mirror, one comes to see oneself, or he who is the sign of contradiction looks straight into one's heart while one is staring into the contradiction. A contradiction placed squarely in front of a person – if one can get him to look at it – is a mirror; as he is forming a judgment, what dwells within him must be disclosed. It is a riddle, but as he is guessing the riddle, what dwells within him is disclosed by the way he guesses. The contradiction confronts him with a choice, and as he is choosing, together with what he chooses, he himself is disclosed.

Note. We see that direct communication is an impossibility for the God-man, for inasmuch as he is the sign of contradiction he cannot communicate himself directly; to be a sign is already a term based on reflection, to say nothing of being the sign of contradiction. One also perceives that the modern confusion has managed to make all Christianity into direct communication only by leaving out the communicator, the God-man. As soon as the communicator is not thoughtlessly taken away or the communication is taken and the communicator left out, as soon as the communicator is taken

into account and the communicator is the God-man, a sign, a sign of contradiction, then direct communication is impossible, as it was in the situation of contemporaneity. But nowadays we have managed to have it done in another way. It is eighteen hundred years since Christ lived; then he is forgotten – only his teaching lasts – yes, that is, Christianity has been abolished.

2: The form of a servant is unrecognizability (the incognito)

What is unrecognizability? Unrecognizability is not to be in the character of what one essentially is – for example, when a policeman is in plain clothes.

And thus it is unrecognizability, the absolute unrecognizability, when one is God, then to be an individual human being. To be the individual human being or an individual human being (in a certain sense it is a matter of indifference whether he is a high-ranking or a low-ranking person) is the greatest possible distance, the infinitely qualitative distance, from being God, and therefore it is the most profound incognito.

But the modern age has abolished Christ, has either thrown him out completely and taken his teaching or has made him fantastical and has fantastically imputed to him direct communication. Not so in the situation of contemporaneity; remember, too, that Christ willed to be incognito expressly because he wanted to be the sign of contradiction. But these eighteen hundred years, what supposedly has been learned from them, and on the other hand, the total ignorance and inexperience of most people with regard to what it means to want to be incognito, an ignorance and inexperience due to the rampant didacticizing, whereas what it means to exist is completely forgotten – this has confused the conception of the God-man.

The majority of people living in Christendom today no doubt live in the illusion that if they had been contemporary with Christ they would have recognized him immediately despite his unrecognizability. They utterly fail to see how they betray that they do not know themselves; it totally escapes them that this conviction they have, whereby they presumably think to glorify Christ, is blasphemy, contained in the nonsensical-undialectical climax of clerical roaring: *to such a degree* was Christ God that one could immediately and directly perceive it, instead of: he was true God, and therefore *to such a degree* God that he was unrecognizable – thus it was not flesh and blood but the opposite of flesh and blood that inspired Peter to recognize him.

Essentially, Christ is remodeled. He is made into a man who himself was aware of being the extraordinary – but whom his contemporaries failed to notice. This may still be true. But the fabricating does not stop there; we fabricate that Christ really would have liked to be *directly* recognizable as the extraordinary he was, but that the blind infatuation of his contemporaries iniquitously refused to understand him. In other words, we betray that we utterly fail to understand what it means to be an incognito. It was Christ's free resolve from eternity to want to be incognito. Thus to think that we honor him by saying or thinking: If I had lived contemporary with him, I certainly would have recognized him directly – we insult him, and since it is Christ we are insulting, this means that we are blasphemous.

But the majority of people do not exist [*existere*] at all in the more profound sense. They have never made themselves existentially familiar with – that is, they have never ventured in action – the idea of wanting to be incognito. Let us take a simple human situation. When I want to be incognito (omitting here the reason and whether I have a right to be that), is it then a compliment if someone comes up to me and says: I knew you right away; it is the very opposite, it is a satire on me. But perhaps the satire was justified and my incognito poor. But now let us imagine a person who managed to maintain an incognito: he *wants* to be incognito; he presumably wants to be recognized but not *directly*. That he is not recognized directly for what he is cannot be something that simply happens to him, for it is indeed his own free decision. But here is the real secret, most people have no intimation of this superiority over oneself, and this superiority over oneself of wanting to be incognito in such a way that one seems much lowlier than one is – of this they have no intimation whatsoever. Or if an intimation did dawn upon them, they would no doubt think: What lunacy, suppose the incognito succeeded so well that one was actually taken to be what one pretended to be! Most people come scarcely any further than that, if they come that far. They discover here a self-contradiction, which in the service of the good is genuine self-denial: the good man does his very best to maintain his incognito, and his

incognito is that he is something far lowlier than he is. Thus someone chooses an incognito that shows him far lowlier than he is; he perhaps thinks of the Socratic principle: In order truly to will the good, one must avoid even the appearance of doing it. The incognito is his free decision. Using all his inventiveness and intrepidity, he exerts himself to the utmost of his powers to maintain the incognito. Either he succeeds or he fails. If he succeeds – well, then he has, humanly speaking, done himself harm: he has made all people think the least of him. What self-denial! On the other hand, what an enormous exertion, for at every moment he has had it in his power to show his true character. What self-denial, for what is self-denial without freedom. What supreme self-denial if the incognito is so successful that, even if he were to speak directly, no one would believe him.

But that such a superiority exists or could exist, of this people have no conception at all. How far removed one is from it would be learned if one were to attempt to obtain a direct communication from such a superior person, or if he himself were to begin any such thing and gave it – one would learn it when he assumed the incognito again. So let us imagine, for example, a noble, sympathetic person who as a precaution or for any other reason whatsoever found an incognito to be necessary. For that he chooses, for example, to appear to be an egotist. Now he discloses himself to someone, shows him his true character, and the other person believes it, is gripped by it. So they understand each other. The other person is perhaps also of the opinion that he understands the incognito – he does not perceive that it was indeed removed, that he understood it with the aid of *direct* communication, that is, with the help of the person who *was* incognito but was not incognito as long as he communicated the understanding to him. Let us now imagine that for some reason or other the superior person has the notion or finds it necessary to reassume the incognito between the two who, as they say, understood each other – what then? Then it will be settled whether the other person is as great a dialectician as the first, or whether the other has faith in the possibility of this kind of self-denial. In other words, it will be settled whether the other person is capable of penetrating an incognito, or of steadfastly maintaining the understanding in the face of it, or of understanding it by himself. The moment the superior person assumes the incognito, he naturally does everything to maintain it and does not help the other person at all; on the contrary, he devises the strategy best calculated to deceive him – that is, to maintain his incognito. Now if he is essentially the superior one, he succeeds. The other person at first resists a little by way of direct communication, "This is a deception; you are not that way." But the incognito is maintained; no direct communication follows, and the other person once again believes that this person is an egotist and perhaps says, "For a moment I believed in him, but now even I see that he is an egotist." The point is that he cannot really hold to the idea that the unrecognizable person does not prefer to be recognized as the good man he is; the point is that he can understand an incognito only as long as the unrecognizable person shows him by direct communication that it is an incognito, that it is so and how – that is, as long as there is no incognito, or at least as long as the unrecognizable person is not in the character of being unrecognizable, gathering all his mental powers to maintain the unrecognizability and leaving the other person to himself. As long as the first person helps him with direct communication about the unrecognizability, he can understand it and – the self-denial, for then there really is none. But when there is, he cannot understand him. In other words, the other person really does not believe in the possibility that there could be self-denial such as that. – Whether a person has the right to mystify in this way, whether a person is capable of doing it, whether, if he could, his defense that he was maieutically developing the other person was adequate, or, from another point of view, whether it is not specifically his duty, assuming that it is self-denial and not pride – this I do not decide. Please regard this as merely an imaginary construction in thought that nevertheless does provide illumination regarding "unrecognizability."

And now the God-man! He is God but chooses to become this individual human being. This, as said before, is the most profound incognito or the most impenetrable unrecognizability that is possible, because the contradiction between being God and being an individual human being is the greatest possible, the infinitely qualitative contradiction. But it is his will, his free decision, and therefore it is an omnipotently maintained incognito. Indeed, by allowing himself to be born he has in a certain sense bound himself once and for all; his unrecognizability is so omnipotently maintained that in a way he himself is in the power of his own incognito, in which lies the literal *actuality* of his purely human suffering, that this is not merely appearance but in a certain sense is the assumed incognito's upper hand over him. Only in this way is there in the profoundest sense earnestness concerning his becoming true man; this is also why he suffers through the utmost suffering of feeling himself abandoned by God. He is not, therefore, at any moment beyond suffering but is actually in suffering, and this purely human experience befalls him, that the actuality proves to be even more terrible than the possibility, that he who freely assumed unrecognizability yet actually suffers as if he were trapped or had trapped himself in unrecognizability. It is a strange kind of dialectic: that he, omnipotent, binds himself and does it so omnipotently that he actually feels bound, suffers under the consequence of his loving and free decision to become an individual human being – to that degree there was earnestness in his becoming an actual human being. But so it had to be if he was to be the sign of contradiction that discloses the thoughts of the heart. – The imperfection in any human being's unrecognizability is the very arbitrariness with which he can annihilate it at any moment; the more he is able to prevent this and make it less possible, the more perfectly in earnest is the unrecognizability. But the God-man's unrecognizability is an omnipotently maintained incognito, and the divine earnestness is precisely this – that it was maintained to such an extent that he himself suffered purely humanly under the unrecognizability.

Note. It is easily seen that direct communication is an impossibility when one is so kind as to take the communicator into account and is not so absentminded about Christianity as to forget Christ. In relation to unrecognizability or for someone in unrecognizability, direct communication is an impossibility, because the direct communication does indeed directly state what one essentially is – but unrecognizability means not to be in the character of what one essentially is. Thus there is a contradiction that nevertheless makes direct communication indirect, that is, makes direct communication impossible. If there is to be a direct communication that remains a direct communication, one must step out of the incognito; otherwise that which in the first is direct communication (the direct statement) still does not become direct communication through the second (the incognito of the communicator).

3: The impossibility of direct communication

The opposite of direct communication is indirect communication. The latter can be produced in two ways.

Indirect communication can be an art of communication in redoubling the communication; the art consists in making oneself, the communicator, into a nobody, purely objective, and then continually placing the qualitative opposites in a unity. This is what some pseudonymous writers are accustomed to calling the double-reflection of the communication. For example, it is indirect communication to place jest and earnestness together in such a way that the composite is a dialectical knot – and then to be a nobody oneself. If anyone wants to have anything to do with this kind of communication, he will have to untie the knot himself. Or, to bring attack and defense into a unity in such a way that no one can directly say whether one is attacking or defending, so that the most zealous supporter of the cause and its most vicious foe can both seem to see in one an ally – and then to be nobody oneself, an absentee, an objective something, a nonperson. If, for example, at a given time faith seems to have vanished from the world, something one must advertise for in the Lost-and-Found columns, it perhaps can be beneficial in dialectically luring forth faith – yet I do not decide whether it can be beneficial. But here is an example of indirect communication or communication in double-reflection. One presents faith in the eminent sense and represents it in such a way that the most orthodox sees it as a defense of the faith and the atheist sees it as an attack, while the communicator is a zero, a nonperson, an objective something – yet he perhaps is an ingenious secret agent who with the aid of this communication finds out which is which, who is the believer, who the atheist; because this is disclosed when they form a judgment about what is presented, which is neither attack nor defense.

But indirect communication can also appear in another way, through the relation between the communication and the communicator. The communicator is present here, whereas in the first instance he was left out, yet, please note, by way of a negative reflection. But our age actually knows no other kind of communication than that mediocre method of didacticizing. What it means to exist has been completely forgotten. Any communication concerning existing requires a communicator; in other words, the communicator is the reduplication of the communication; to exist in what one understands is to reduplicate.

But this communication still cannot be called indirect communication just because there is a communicator who himself exists in what he communicates. If, however, the communicator himself is dialectically defined and his own being is based on reflection, then all direct communication is impossible.

So it is with the God-man. He is a sign, the sign of contradiction; he is unrecognizable – therefore any direct communication is impossible. In other words, if the communication by a communicator is to be direct, then not only the communication must be direct, but the communicator himself must be directly defined. If not, then even the most direct statement by such a communicator still does not – because of the communicator, because of what the communicator is – become direct communication.

If someone says directly: I am God; the Father and I are one, this is direct communication. But if the person who says it, the communicator, is this individual human being, an individual human being just like others, then this communication is not quite entirely direct, because it is not entirely direct that an individual human being should be God – whereas what he says is entirely direct. Because of the communicator the communication contains a contradiction, it becomes indirect communication; it confronts you with a choice: whether you will believe him or not.

One could very well weep when one reflects on the state of Christianity in Christendom with regard to what is used in sermon presentation again and again and with the greatest self-importance, as if one were saying something really striking and convincing. They say that Christ himself has directly said that he was God, the only begotten Son of the Father. They reject with horror any concealment as unworthy of Christ, as vanity and conceit in connection with so earnest a matter, the most earnest of all matters, the salvation of mankind. They maintain that Christ has given us a direct answer to a direct question. Alas, such pastors do not know at all whereof they speak; it is as if it were hidden from their eyes that they are abolishing Christianity. He who was an offense to the Jews, foolishness to the Greeks, the mystery by whom everything was revealed, but in the mystery – him they humanly make over into a kind of earnest public figure, almost as earnest as the pastor. If one will only take the trouble to say to such a person with a direct and cozy joviality, "Tell me now in all earnestness," then without any fear and trembling before the Deity, without the death throes that are the birth pangs of faith, without the shudder that is the beginning of worship, without the horror of the possibility of offense, one immediately and directly comes to know what cannot be known directly.

Yes, indeed, Christ himself did very directly say that he was the Father's only begotten Son, that is, the *sign of contradiction* – has *very directly* said it. What does that mean? See, here we are again. If he is the sign of contradiction, then he cannot give a direct communication – that is, the statement can be entirely direct, but the fact that he is involved, that he, the sign of contradiction, says it, makes it indirect communication. Yes, indeed, Christ did say: Believe in me, and it is an entirely direct statement. But if the one who says it is the sign of contradiction, what then? Then this direct statement in his mouth specifically expresses that to believe is not something so entirely direct or that even his call to believe is indirect communication.

And now with regard to *earnestness*, such pastors on the whole understand earnestness just about as well as they understand Christianity. The earnestness is precisely this – that Christ cannot give a direct communication, that the single direct statement, like the miracle, can serve only to make aware in order that the person who has been made aware, facing the offense of the contradiction, can choose whether he will believe or not.

But the essentially Christian is confused in every way. Christ is made into the speculative unity of God and man, or Christ is thrown out altogether and his teaching is taken, or Christ is really made into an idol. Spirit is the denial of direct immediacy. If Christ is true God, then he also must be unrecognizable, attired in unrecognizability, which is the denial of all straightforwardness. Direct recognizability is specifically characteristic of the idol. But this is what people make Christ into, and this is supposed to be earnestness. They take the direct statement and fantastically form a character corresponding to it (preferably sentimental, with the gentle look, the friendly eye, or whatever else such a foolish pastor can hit upon), and then it is *directly* altogether certain that Christ is God.

What abominable, sentimental frivolity! No, one does not manage to become a Christian at such a cheap price! He is the sign of contradiction, and by the direct statement he attaches himself to you only so that you must face the offense of the contradiction, and the thoughts of your heart are disclosed as you choose whether you will believe or not.

4: In Christ the secret of sufferings is the impossibility of direct communication

Christ's sufferings, how he was mocked, scourged, and crucified, have been much and often discussed, especially in earlier times. But in all this, an entirely different kind of suffering seems to be forgotten, the suffering of inwardness, suffering of soul, or what might be called the secret of the sufferings that were inseparable from his life in unrecognizability from the time he appeared until the very last.

It is always painful to have to conceal an inwardness and have to seem to be other than one is – so it is in a merely human situation. It is the most grievous human suffering, and the person who suffers in this way, alas, in one day he often has greater suffering than from all physical tortures combined. I do not presume to decide whether there actually are such collisions or whether a person when he experiences such a collision does not also sin every moment he remains in it – I am speaking only of the suffering. The collision is this, out of love for another person to have to conceal an inwardness and seem to be other than one is. The pains are purely psychical and are as compounded as possible. But it is not good for a pain to be compounded; with each new compounding it acquires one sting more. First there is the painfulness of one's own suffering, for if it is blissful to belong to another person in the mutual understanding of love, of friendship, then it is painful to have to keep this inwardness to oneself. In the next place, there is the suffering on behalf of the other person. That which is love's solicitude, a love that would do everything, sacrifice its life for the other, here finds its expression in something that has a likeness to the most extreme kind of cruelty – alas, and yet it is love. Finally, the painfulness is the suffering of responsibility. Thus it is out of love to annihilate, immediately and directly, one's own love, yet preserving it, out of love to be cruel to the beloved, out of love to take upon oneself this enormous responsibility.

But now the God-man! The true God *cannot* become directly recognizable, but direct recognizability is what the purely human, what the human beings to whom he came, would plead and implore him for as an indescribable alleviation. And out of love he becomes man! He is love, and yet at every moment he exists he must crucify, so to speak, all human compassion and solicitude – for he can become only the object of faith. But everything called purely human compassion is related to direct recognizability. Yet if he does not become the object of *faith*, he is not true God; and if he is not true God, then he does not save people either. Therefore, by the step he takes out of love he at the same time plunges that person, mankind, into the most horrible decision. Indeed, it is as if one heard a cry from human compassion: Oh, why are you doing this! And yet he does it out of love; he does it to save people. But out there in the horror of this decision he must keep them at a distance if, saved in faith, they are to belong to him at all – and he is love. Out of love he wants to do everything for people; he stakes his life for them, he suffers ignominious death for them – and for them he suffers this life – in divine love and compassion and mercy (compared with which all human compassion counts as nothing) to have to be, humanly speaking, so severe. His whole life is a suffering of inwardness. And then the last part of his life begins with the nocturnal betrayal, then he suffers physical pain and mistreatment; then he endures the suffering of being betrayed by a friend, of standing alone, ridiculed, mocked, spat upon, wearing a crown of thorns and dressed in purple, alone with his, humanly speaking, lost cause – see, what a man, alone among his infuriated enemies – what a dreadful setting, deserted by all his friends – what frightful loneliness! Yet a human being can also suffer in this way, suffer the same mistreatment, suffer even the desertion of his best friend, but then no more. If this is surmounted, then for a human being the cup of suffering is emptied. Here, however, the cup of suffering is filled again, the most bitter of all – he suffers so that this, his suffering, can become and does become an offense to the few believers. It is true that he suffers only once, but unlike a human being he does not escape with the first time of suffering – he suffers through the most grievous suffering the second time, in his concern and grief that his suffering is an occasion for offense.

No human being can comprehend this suffering; to want to comprehend it is presumption.

As far as I who am attempting to describe this am concerned, I perhaps owe a little explanation here.

I may at times betray such an acquaintance with concealed inwardness, the suffering of real self-denial, that someone could perhaps have the notion that I, even though an ordinary human being, nevertheless am such a person, one of those rare noble human beings. Far from it. In a strange manner, and not exactly on account of my virtues but rather on account of my sins, I have purely formally become aware of the secrets of existence and the secretiveness of existence in a way in which these and this presumably do not exist for many people. I do not pride myself on this, for it is not on account of my virtues. But I make an honest effort to use this knowledge to illuminate what is humanly true and what is humanly the true good. And this I use in turn to prompt, if possible, an awareness of the holy – about which I always add that no human being can comprehend this and that in regard to this the beginning and ending is worship. Even if one comprehended, fully comprehended, the purely human, this understanding is still a misunderstanding in regard to the God-man. – What responsibility I bear, no one understands as I do. Let no one take the trouble to terrify me on this account, for to him who can terrify me in a totally different way I relate myself in fear and trembling. But then, too, not very many understand as I do that Christianity has been abolished in Christendom.

5: The possibility of offense is to deny direct communication

The possibility of offense, as we have tried to show, is present at every moment, confirming at every moment the chasmic abyss between the single individual and the God-man over which faith and faith alone reaches. Thus it is not, to repeat again and again, an accidental relation, so that some perceive the possibility of offense and others not; no, the possibility of offense is the stumbling block for all, whether they choose to believe or they are offended.

Therefore the communication begins with a repulsion. But to begin with a repulsion is to deny direct communication. This is easy to perceive; it presents itself almost physically for perception. Anything that presents itself directly cannot be said to repulse first of all, but anything that presents itself in such a way that it first of all repulses cannot be said to present itself directly. On the other hand, it cannot be said to repulse only, because it presents itself, but in such a way that it first repulses.

But take away the possibility of offense, as has been done in Christendom, and all Christianity becomes direct communication, and then Christianity is abolished, has become something easy, a superficial something that neither wounds nor heals deeply enough; it has become the false invention of purely human compassion that forgets the infinite qualitative difference between God and man.

6: To deny direct communication is to require faith

The possibility of offense, the relation in which it begins, is in the most profound sense the expression for "making aware" or expresses that the greatest possible attention is required on the part of a human being (indeed, on a scale that is anything but the purely human, for it is on a divine scale) with respect to the decision to become a believer. Direct communication perhaps also seeks as well as it can to make the recipient aware: it pleads and implores him, it lays the importance of the cause right on his heart; it admonishes, threatens, etc. – this is all direct communication again, and therefore there is neither sufficient earnestness with regard to the supreme decision nor is sufficient awareness gained.

No, the way to begin is to deny direct communication – that is earnestness. The possibility of offense is frightful, and yet, just like the Law in relation to the Gospel, it is rigorousness that is part of the earnestness. There is no direct communication and no direct reception: there is a choice. It does not take place, as in direct communication, with coaxing and threatening and admonishing – and then, then, quite imperceptibly, little by little comes the transition, the transition to accepting it more or less, to keeping oneself convinced of it, to being of the opinion etc. No, a very specific kind of reception is required – that of faith. And faith itself is a dialectical qualification. Faith is a choice, certainly not direct reception – and the recipient is the one who is disclosed, whether he will believe or be offended.

But the whole of modern philosophy has done everything to delude us into thinking that faith is an immediate qualification, that it is the immediate – which in turn is linked up with having abolished the possibility of offense, having made Christianity

into a teaching, having abolished the God-man and the situation of contemporaneity. What modern philosophy understands by faith is really what is called having an opinion or what in everyday language some people call "to believe." Christianity is made into a teaching; this teaching is then proclaimed to a person, and he believes that it is as this teaching says. Then the next stage is to "comprehend" this teaching, and this philosophy does. All of this would be entirely proper if Christianity were a teaching, but since it is not, all this is totally wrong. Faith in a significant sense is related to the God-man. But the God-man, the sign of contradiction, denies direct communication – and calls for faith.

That to deny direct communication is to require faith can be simply pointed out in purely human situations if it is kept in mind that faith in its most eminent sense is related to the God-man. Let us examine this and to that end take the relationship between two lovers. I first assume this situation: in the most ardent terms, the lover assures the beloved of his love, and his entire bearing corresponds to this assurance, almost sheer adoration. He now asks the beloved, "Do you *believe* that I love you?" The beloved answers, "Yes, I *do believe* it." This is how we do indeed talk. But let us now suppose that the lover has the idea of wanting to test the beloved to see whether she does believe him. What does he do? He cuts off all direct communication, changes himself into a duplexity; as a possibility it looks deceptive, as if he possibly could be just as much a deceiver as the faithful lover. This is making oneself into a riddle, but what is a riddle? A riddle is a question, and what does the question ask about? It asks whether she loves him. – Now, I do not decide whether he has the right to do this; I merely follow the thought-categories, and in any case it must be kept in mind that a maieutic teacher to a certain extent does the same thing, poses the dialectical duplexity, but with the directly opposite intention, just to turn the other person away from him, to turn him inward in order to make him free, not in order to draw him to himself. – The difference in the lover's conduct is easy to see. In the first instance he asks directly: Do you believe me? In the second instance he makes himself into a question: whether she believes him. He perhaps bitterly comes to regret that he allowed himself to do such a thing – I have nothing to do with that; I merely follow the thought-categories. From a dialectical point of view, it is positively certain that the latter method is a far more basic way in which to require faith. The purpose of the latter method is to make the beloved disclose herself in a choice; that is, out of this duplexity she must choose which character she believes is the true one. If she chooses the good character, it is disclosed that she believes him. It is disclosed, since he does not help her at all; on the contrary, by means of the duplexity he has placed her entirely alone without any assistance whatsoever. He is a duplexity, and now the question is what she judges about him, but he understands it differently, for he sees that it is not he who is being judged but it is she who is disclosed in how she judges. Whether he is allowed to do this, I do not decide – I merely pursue the thought-categories. His method, which as long as it lasts may cause him indescribable suffering in unrest and concern, is simultaneously an almost chilling, inhuman indifference, and yet again the most intense passion. But he requires faith. Dialectically he is right, that to believe when one receives direct communication is altogether too direct.

Christianity has never understood by faith anything like this. The God-man must require faith and in order to require faith must deny direct communication. In a certain sense he cannot do otherwise, and he does not want it otherwise. As the God-man he is qualitatively different from any man, and therefore he must deny direct communication; he must *require* faith and require that he become the *object of faith*.

In the relation between individuals, one person must and shall be content with the other's assurance that he believes him; no one has the right to make himself into an object of faith for the other person. If one person is to use dialectical redoubling [*Fordoblelse*] in relation to another, he must in exactly the opposite way use it maieutically in order to avoid becoming an object of faith or an approximation thereof for another. The dialectical duplexity [*Dobbelthed*] is provisional; the next stage unconditionally brings falseness if, instead of using the dialectical duplexity for parrying, a person allows himself the presumption of becoming an object of faith for another person. But even with respect to the maieutic I do not decide to what extent, Christianly speaking, it is to be approved.

But only the God-man cannot do otherwise and, as qualitatively different from man, must insist upon being the object of faith. If he does not become this, he becomes an idol – and therefore he must deny direct communication because he must require faith.

7: The object of faith is the God-man precisely because the God-man is the possibility of offense

So inseparable is the possibility of offense from faith that if the God-man were not the possibility of offense he could not be the object of faith, either. Thus the possibility of offense is taken up into faith, is assimilated by faith, is the negative mark of the God-man. For if there were no possibility of offense, there would be direct recognizability, and then the God-man would be an idol; then direct recognizability is paganism.

One sees how little the gratitude of Christianity has been earned through the abolition of the possibility of offense, how it has been made into a pleasant, a sentimental paganism.

For this is the law: the person who abolishes faith abolishes the possibility of offense, such as when speculation substitutes comprehending for having faith; and the person who abolishes the possibility of offense abolishes faith, such as when the sentimental sermon presentation falsely attributes direct recognizability to Christ. But whether faith is abolished or whether the possibility of offense is abolished, something else is also abolished: the God-man. And if the God-man is abolished, Christianity is abolished.

And in truth, the eighteen hundred years have not contributed a jot to demonstrating the truth of Christianity; on the contrary, with steadily increasing power they have contributed to abolishing Christianity. It is not at all the case, either, as one might logically assume when the demonstration [*Bevis*] of the eighteen hundred years is applauded, that now in the nineteenth century one is convinced [*overbeviist*] of the truth of Christianity in a way totally different from the way the people were in the first and second generations – it is indeed rather the case (and this really sounds somewhat satirical on the worshipers and adorers of that demonstration) that in proportion as the demonstration increased in power – fewer and fewer were convinced. But this is what happens when once and for all the crucial point in something is missed: frightful confusions can result that increase from generation to generation. Now, since it has been *demonstrated*, and on an enormous scale, that Christianity is the truth, now there is no one, almost no one, who is willing to make any sacrifice for its sake. When one – shall I say when one "only" believed its truth – then one sacrificed life and blood. What a frightful delusion! If only, as that pagan who burned the libraries, one could push aside those eighteen hundred years – if one cannot do that, then Christianity is indeed abolished. If only it could be made evident to all those orators who demonstrate the truth of Christianity by the eighteen hundred years and win people, if only it could be made evident to them, frightful as it is, that they are betraying, denying, abolishing Christianity – if that cannot be done, then Christianity is abolished.

Note

1 Here and throughout the book, "history" is to be understood as profane history, world history, history directly understood in contradistinction to sacred history.

53

The *Fatherland*

Would It Be Best Now to "Stop Ringing the Fire Alarm"?

April 7, 1855.

This proposal has been made to me. However, I cannot in this respect humor anybody (supposing it is I who am ringing the bell); it would be inexcusable to leave off tolling as long as the fire is burning. But strictly speaking it is not I who am ringing the bell, it is I who am starting the fire in order to smoke out illusions and knavish tricks; it is a police raid, and a Christian police raid, for, according to the New Testament, Christianity is incendiarism, Christ Himself says, "I am come to set fire on the earth," and it is already burning, yea, and it is doubtless becoming a consuming conflagration, best likened to a forest fire, for it is "Christendom" that is set on fire. And it is the prolixities which have to go, the prodigiously prolix illusion fostered by the (well-meant or knavish) introduction of scientific learning into the Christian field, the prodigiously prolix conceit about millions of Christians, Christian kingdoms and lands, a whole world of Christians. This doubtless suits the convenience of princes of the Church, for the sake both of pecuniary advantage and of material power, and for the sake of what is the most exquisite and delicate refinement, that of scoffing at God and the New Testament, and being credited with zeal and fervor for spreading the doctrine. It is the prolixities which have to go, and that precisely by

The Fatherland (Fædrelandet, 1855). From Attack Upon "Christendom," tr. Walter Lowrie (Princeton University Press, 1968). Selection: "Would It Be Best Now to 'Stop Ringing the Fire Alarm'?," pp. 41–2.

means of the burning question (if the fire is not quenched), the burning question of the instant: that official Christianity is not the Christianity of the New Testament.

No, official Christianity is not the Christianity of the New Testament. Anybody can see that merely by casting a fleeting but impartial glance at the Gospels, and then looking at what we call "Christianity." The reason why this is not seen is that by all sorts of tricks of optical illusion the great mass of men are prevented from seeing impartially, and the reason for that is that there have been introduced by the State 1000 officials who have such difficulty about seeing impartially because the question of Christianity is stated for them at the same time in pecuniary terms, and naturally they do not want to have their eyes opened to what has hitherto been regarded as the surest way to bread, the surest of all, though it is a questionable way of livelihood, perhaps in a Christian sense even a "prohibited way"; the reason is that hundreds of men are introduced who instead of following Christ are snugly and comfortably settled, with family and steady promotion, under the guise that their activity is the Christianity of the New Testament, and who live off the fact that others have had to suffer for the truth (which precisely is Christianity), so that the relationship is completely inverted, and Christianity, which came into the world as the truth men die for, has now become the truth upon which they live, with family and steady promotion – "Rejoice then in life while thy springtime lasts."[1]

Otherwise everybody must be able to see that official Christianity is not the Christianity of the New Testament, does not resemble it any more than the square resembles the circle, no more than enjoyment resembles suffering, or loving oneself resembles hating oneself, or desiring the world resembles renouncing the world, being at home in the world resembles being a stranger and a pilgrim in the world, or going to business, to a dance, or a wooing, resembles following Christ – not a bit more; the Christian battalions which "Christendom" places in the field no more resemble what the New Testament understands by Christians than did the recruits which Falstaff enlisted resemble able-bodied, well-trained soldiers eager for battle; they cannot be more truly said to strive in the direction of what the New Testament understands by a Christian than a man who is walking with even pace out through West Gate can be said to be striving out through West Gate; and what we call a teacher in Christianity (a priest) no more resembles what the New Testament understands by a teacher in Christianity, no more resembles it than a chest of drawers resembles a dancer, has no more relation to what the New Testament understands by a teacher's task than a chest of drawers has to dancing – with this I say nothing disparaging of the priest from a civil or human point of view, any more than I deny that a chest of drawers may be an exceedingly useful and serviceable piece of furniture; I only say that it has no relation to dancing.

Note

1 [From a popular German drinking song, "Freut Euch des Lebens" (Usteri): Ed.]

54

The *Instant*

What Says the Fire Chief?

That when in any way one has what is called a cause, something he earnestly wishes to promote – and then there are others who propose to themselves the task of counteracting it, hindering it, harming it, that he then must take measures against these enemies of his, this everyone is aware of. But not everyone is aware that there is such a thing as honest good-intention which is far more dangerous and as if especially calculated with a view to preventing the cause from becoming truly serious.

When a man suddenly falls ill, well-meaning persons hasten at once to lend aid, one proposes one thing, and one another, if all of them had leave to advise at once, the patient's death would be certain; the well-meant advice of the individual may in itself be dangerous, in any case their bustling, flurried presence is injurious for the fact that it impedes the physician.

So also in the case of a fire. Hardly is the cry of "Fire!" heard before a crowd of people rush to the spot, nice, cordial, sympathetic, helpful people, one has a pitcher, another a basin, the third a squirt, etc., all of them nice, cordial, sympathetic, helpful people, so eager to help put out the fire.

But what says the Fire Chief? The Fire Chief, he says – yes, generally the Fire Chief is a very pleasant and polite man; but at a fire he is what one

The Instant (Øjeblikket, 1855). From *Attack Upon "Christendom,"* tr. Walter Lowrie (Princeton University Press, 1968). Selections: no. 6, "What Says the Fire Chief?," pp. 193–6; no. 10, "When is 'the Instant'?," pp. 280–1.

calls coarse-mouthed – he says, or rather he bawls, "Oh, go to hell with all your pitchers and squirts." And then, when these well-meaning people are perhaps offended and require at least to be treated with respect, what then says the Fire Chief? Yes, generally the Fire Chief is a very pleasant and polite man, who knows how to show everyone the respect that is due him; but at a fire he is rather different – he says, "Where the deuce is the police force?" And when some policemen arrive he says to them, "Rid me of these damn people with their pitchers and squirts; and if they won't yield to fair words, smear them a few over the back, so that we may be free of them and get down to work."

So then at a fire the whole way of looking at things is not the same as in everyday life. Good-natured, honest, well-meaning, by which in everyday life one attains the reputation of being a good fellow, is at a fire honored with coarse words and a few over the back.

And this is quite natural. For a fire is a serious thing, and whenever things are really serious, this honest good-intention by no means suffices. No, seriousness applies an entirely different law: either/or. Either thou art the man who in this instance can seriously do something, and seriously has something to do/or, if such be not thy case, then for thee the serious thing to do is precisely to get out. If by thyself thou wilt not understand this, then let the Fire Chief thrash it into thee by means of the police, from which thou mayest derive particular benefit, and which perhaps may after all contribute to making thee a bit serious, in correspondence with the serious thing which is a fire.

But as it is at a fire, so also it is in matters of the mind. Wherever there is a cause to be promoted, an undertaking to be carried out, an idea to be introduced – one can always be sure that when he who really is the man for it, the right man, who in a higher sense has and must have command, he who has seriousness and can give to the cause the seriousness it truly has – one can always be sure that when he comes (if I may so put it) to the spot, he will find there before him a genial company of twaddlers who under the name of seriousness lie around and bungle things by wanting to serve the cause, promote the undertaking, introduce the idea; a company of twaddlers who of course regard the fact that the person in question will not make common cause with them (precisely indicating his seriousness) as a certain proof that he lacks seriousness. I say, when the right man comes he will find things thus. I can also give this turn to it: the fact that he is the right man is really decided by the way he understands himself in relation to this company of twaddlers. If he has a notion that it is they who are to help, and that he must strengthen himself by union with them, he *eo ipso* is not the right man. The right man sees at once, like the Fire Chief, that this company of twaddlers must get out, that their presence and effect is the most dangerous assistance the fire could have. But in matters of the mind it is not as at a fire, where the Fire Chief merely has to say to the police, "Rid me of these men."

So it is in all matters of the mind, and so it is also in the religious field. History has so often been compared with what the chemists call a process. The metaphor may be quite suggestive, if only it is understood aright. They speak of a filtering process: water is filtered, and in the process it deposits impure ingredients. It is precisely in an opposite sense that history is a process. The idea is introduced – and with that it enters into the process of history. But unfortunately this does not (as one ludicrously assumes) result in the purification of the idea, which never is purer than in its primary form. No, it results, with steadily increasing momentum, in garbling the idea, in making it hackneyed, trite, in wearing it out, in introducing the impure ingredients which originally were not present (the very opposite of filtering), until at last, by the enthusiastic cooperation and mutual approbation of a series of successive generations the point is reached where the idea is entirely extinguished and the opposite of the idea has become what they now call the idea, and this they maintain has been accomplished by the historical process in which the idea has been purified and refined.

When at last the right man comes, he to whom in the highest sense the task belongs, who perhaps was early selected and slowly educated for this task, which is to let in light upon the affair, to set fire to this wilderness which is the asylum of all twaddle, all illusions, all knavish tricks – when he comes he will already find there before him a company of twaddlers who with cheerful cordiality have a sort of a notion that things are wrong, or are prepared to chatter about things being dreadfully wrong, and to be self-important for chattering about it. In case he, the right man, for a single instant sees amiss and thinks that it is this company that is to be a help, he is *eo ipso* not the right man. In case he makes a mistake and has anything to do with them, divine governance will instantly let go of him as unfit. But the right man sees with half an eye, as does the Fire Chief, that this company which well-meaningly would help to put out a fire with pitchers and squirts, that this same company which in the present instance, where it is not a question of extinguishing a fire but precisely of lighting a fire, would lend aid with a sulphur match without the sulphur, or with a damp paper-lighter, must get out, that he must not have the least thing to do with this company, that he must be as coarse-mouthed with them as possible, he who perhaps is usually anything but that. But everything depends upon getting rid of that company; for the effect of it is, in the form of hearty sympathy, to eradicate the real seriousness from the cause. Naturally the company will then rave against him, against this frightful pride, etc. But to him this must make no difference. Wherever there truly must be seriousness the law is this: either/or; either I am the one who seriously has to deal with the matter, is thereto called and is absolutely willing to venture decisively/or, if such is not my case, then seriousness is, not to engage in it at all. Nothing is more detestable and more vile, both betraying and bringing about a deeper demoralization, than this: to want to have somehow a little part in that which must be *aut/aut; aut Caesar/aut nihil* [either Caesar/or nothing], to want to have somehow a little part, and then with good-hearted moderation to prate about it, and so by this prattle to pretend mendaciously that one is better than those who have nothing to do with the whole concern – pretend to be better, and make the thing more difficult for him who properly has the task to do.

When is "the Instant"?

The Instant is when *the* man is there, the right man, the man of the Instant.

This is a secret which eternally will remain hidden from all worldly shrewdness, from everything which is only to a certain degree.

Worldly shrewdness stares and stares at events, at circumstances, it reckons and reckons, thinking that it might be able to distill the Instant out of the circumstances, and so become itself a power by the aid of the Instant, this breaking through of the eternal, hoping that itself might be rejuvenated, as it so greatly needs to be, by means of the new.

But in vain. Shrewdness does not succeed and never will to all eternity succeed by means of this surrogate – any more than all the arts of cosmetics succeed in producing natural beauty.

No, only when *the* man is there, and when he ventures as one must venture (which is precisely what worldly shrewdness and mediocrity want to avoid), then is the Instant – and the circumstances then obey the man of the Instant. In case nothing is brought into play but worldly shrewdness and mediocrity, the Instant never comes. Things may go on for hundreds of thousands and millions of years constantly the same – it looks perhaps as if it might now soon come; but so long as there is only worldly shrewdness and mediocrity, etc., the Instant comes not, no more than does an unfruitful man beget children.

But when the right man comes, yea, then the Instant is there. For the Instant is precisely that which does not lie in the circumstances, it is the new thing, the woof of eternity – but that same second it masters the circumstances to such a degree that (adroitly calculated to fool worldly shrewdness and mediocrity) it looks as if the Instant proceeded from the circumstances.

There is nothing worldly shrewdness so broods over and so hankers after as the Instant. What would it not give to be able to calculate rightly! Yet no one is more surely excluded from ever grasping the Instant than worldly shrewdness. For the Instant is heaven's gift to – a pagan would say, to the fortunate and the enterprising, but a Christian says, to the believer. Yea, this thing which by worldly shrewdness is so deeply despised, or at the most dressed up with borrowed phrases of Sunday solemnity, this thing of *believing*, that and that only is related as possibility to the Instant. Worldly shrewdness is eternally excluded, despised and abhorred, as things are in heaven, more than all vices and crimes, because in its nature it of all things most belongs to this wretched world, and most of all is remote from having anything to do with heaven and the eternal.

PART XV

Arthur Schopenhauer (1788–1860)

Introduction

Schopenhauer's main philosophical influences were Plato and Kant. To them he added an enthusiasm for the Upanishads and other ancient Indian wisdom literature. He was, by the end of his life, a popular cultural figure whose work clearly resonated with the needs and feelings of his time. Though Schopenhauer's effect on professional philosophy was neither immediate nor direct, he influenced important writers and artists whose work in turn shaped the context of later philosophizing. Wagner, Nietzsche, Freud, Thomas Mann, and Wittgenstein are among the many who learned from him. All our selections are taken from Schopenhauer's masterpiece, *The World as Will and Representation*. This was originally published in 1818 as a one-volume work. In 1844 a second edition appeared which added a second volume, consisting of a series of essays glossing and expanding on the material in the first. In the first selection, the only one from volume 1, Schopenhauer develops his view of the nature and value of philosophy. The brief final selection returns to this theme. The three intermediate selections describe in turn (1) Schopenhauer's version of idealism, (2) his wholly modern conception of conscious thought's dependence on the brain and nervous system, and (3) the metaphysical significance of death.

55

The World as Will and Representation

[On Philosophy]

[...] *Philosophy* has the peculiarity of presupposing absolutely nothing as known; everything to it is equally strange and a problem; not only the relations of phenomena, but also those phenomena themselves, and indeed the principle of sufficient reason itself, to which the other sciences are content to refer everything. In philosophy, however, nothing would be gained by such a reference, for one link of the series is just as foreign and strange to it as another. Moreover, that kind of connexion is itself just as much a problem for philosophy as what is joined together by that connexion, and this again is as much a problem after the combination thus explained as before it. For, as we have said, just what the sciences presuppose and lay down as the basis and limit of their explanation is precisely the real problem of philosophy, which consequently begins where the sciences leave off. Proofs cannot be its foundation, for these deduce unknown principles from others that are known; but to it everything is equally unknown and strange. There can be no principle in consequence of which the world with all its phenomena would first of all exist; therefore it is not possible, as Spinoza wished, to deduce a philosophy that demonstrates

The World as Will and Representation (1818; 2nd edn. 1844), tr. E. F. J. Payne, 2 vols (New York: Dover Publications, 1958). Selections: vol. 1, pp. 81–91 (excerpts); vol. 2, "On the Fundamental View of Idealism," pp. 3–18; "On the Primacy of the Will in Self-Consciousness," pp. 201–44 (excerpts); "On Death and Its Relation to the Indestructibility of Our Inner Nature," pp. 463–509 (excerpts); pp. 611–12.

ex firmis principiis. Philosophy is also the most universal rational knowledge (*Wissen*), whose main principles, therefore, cannot be deductions from another principle still more universal. The principle of contradiction establishes merely the agreement of concepts, and does not itself give concepts. The principle of sufficient reason explains connexions and combinations of phenomena, not the phenomena themselves. Therefore, philosophy cannot start from these to look for a *causa efficiens* or a *causa finalis* of the whole world. The present philosophy, at any rate, by no means attempts to say *whence* or *for what purpose* the world exists, but merely *what* the world is. But here the *Why* is subordinated to the *What*, for it already belongs to the world, as it springs merely from the form of its phenomenon, the principle of sufficient reason, and only to this extent has it meaning and validity. Indeed, it might be said that everyone knows without further help what the world is, for he himself is the subject of knowing of which the world is representation, and so far this would be true. But this knowledge is a knowledge of perception, is in the concrete. The task of philosophy is to reproduce this in the abstract, to raise to a permanent rational knowledge successive, variable perceptions, and generally all that the wide concept of *feeling* embraces and describes merely negatively as not abstract, distinct, rational knowledge. Accordingly, it must be a statement in the abstract of the nature of the whole world, of the whole as well as of all the parts. However, in order not to be lost in an endless multitude of particular judgements, it must make use of abstraction, and think everything individual in the universal, and its differences also in the universal.

It will therefore partly separate, partly unite, in order to present to rational knowledge the whole manifold of the world in general, according to its nature, condensed and summarized into a few abstract concepts. Yet through these concepts, in which it fixes the nature of the world, the whole individual as well as the universal must be known, and hence the knowledge of both must be closely bound up. Therefore, aptitude for philosophy consists precisely in what Plato put it in, namely in knowing the one in the many and the many in the one. Accordingly, philosophy will be a sum of very universal judgements, whose ground of knowledge is immediately the world itself in its entirety, without excluding anything, and hence everything to be found in human consciousness. It will be *a complete recapitulation, so to speak, a reflection of the world in abstract concepts*, and this is possible only by uniting the essentially identical into one concept, and by relegating the different and dissimilar to another. Bacon already set philosophy this task, when he said: *ea demum vera est philosophia, quae mundi ipsius voces fidelissime reddit, et veluti dictante mundo conscripta est, et nihil aliud est, quam ejusdem SIMULACRUM ET REFLECTIO, neque addit quidquam de proprio, sed tantum iterat et resonat* ("That philosophy only is the true one which reproduces most faithfully the statements of nature, and is written down, as it were, from nature's dictation, so that it is nothing but a *copy and a reflection* of nature, and adds nothing of its own, but is merely a repetition and echo" [Tr.]) (*De Augmentis Scientiarum*, 1. 2, c. 13). However, we take this in a more extended sense than Bacon could conceive at that time.

The agreement which all aspects and parts of the world have with one another, just because they belong to one whole, must also be found again in this abstract copy of the world. Accordingly, in this sum-total of judgements one could to a certain extent be derived from another, and indeed always reciprocally. Yet in addition to this they must first exist, and therefore be previously laid down as immediately established through knowledge of the world in the concrete, the more so as all direct proofs are more certain than those that are indirect. Their harmony with one another, by virtue of which they flow together even into the unity of one thought, and which springs from the harmony and unity of the world of perception itself, their common ground of knowledge, will therefore not be used as the first thing for establishing them, but will be added only as confirmation of their truth.

This problem itself can become perfectly clear only by its solution.

§ 16

After fully considering reason as a special faculty of knowledge peculiar to man alone, and the achievements and phenomena brought about by it and peculiar to human nature, it now remains for me to speak of reason in so far as it guides man's actions, and in this respect can be called *practical*. [...] At the beginning of our consideration of reason we remarked in general terms how the action and behaviour of man differ from those of the animal, and that this difference is to be regarded as solely the result of the presence of abstract concepts in consciousness. The influence of these on our whole existence is so decisive and significant that it places us to a certain extent in the same relation to the animals as that between animals that see and those without eyes (certain larvae, worms, and zoophytes). Animals without eyes know only by touch what is immediately present to them in space, what comes in contact with them. Animals that see, on the other hand, know a wide sphere of what is near and distant. In the same way, the absence of reason restricts the animals to representations of perception immediately present to them in time, in other words to real objects. We, on the other hand, by virtue of knowledge in the abstract, comprehend not only the narrow and actual present, but also the whole past and future together with the wide realm of possibility. We survey life freely in all directions, far beyond what is present and actual. Thus what the eye is in space and for sensuous knowledge, reason is, to a certain extent, in time and for inner knowledge. But just as the visibility of objects has value and meaning only by its informing us of their tangibility, so the whole value of abstract knowledge is always to be found in its reference to knowledge of perception. [...]

The universal survey of life as a whole, an advantage which man has over the animal through his faculty of reason, is also comparable to a geometrical, colourless, abstract, reduced plan of his way of life. He is therefore related to the animal as the navigator, who by means of chart, compass, and quadrant knows accurately at any moment his course and position on the sea, is related to the uneducated crew who see only the waves and skies. It is therefore worth noting, and indeed wonderful to see, how man, besides his life in the concrete, always lives a second life in the abstract. In the former he is abandoned to all the storms of reality and to the influence of the present; he must struggle, suffer, and die like the animal. But his life in the abstract, as it stands before his rational consciousness, is the calm reflection of his life in the concrete, and of the world in which he lives; it is precisely that reduced chart or plan previously mentioned. Here in the sphere of calm deliberation, what previously possessed him completely and moved him intensely appears to him cold, colourless, and, for the moment, foreign and strange; he is a mere spectator and observer. In respect of this withdrawal into reflection, he is like an actor who has played his part in one scene, and takes his place in the audience until he must appear again. In the audience he quietly looks on at whatever may happen, even though it be the preparation of his own death (in the play); but then he again goes on the stage, and acts and suffers as he must. From this double life proceeds that composure in man, so very different from the thoughtlessness of the animal. According to previous reflection, to a mind made up, or to a recognized necessity, a man with such composure suffers or carries out in cold blood what is of the greatest, and often most terrible, importance to him, such as suicide, execution, duels, hazardous enterprises of every kind fraught with danger to life, and generally things against which his whole animal nature rebels. We then see to what extent reason is master of the animal nature, and we exclaim to the strong: σιδήρειον νύ τοι ἦτορ! (*ferreum certe tibi cor!* "Truly hast thou a heart of iron!" [Tr.]) [*Iliad*, xxiv, 521.] Here it can really be said that the faculty of reason manifests itself *practically*, and thus *practical reason* shows itself, wherever action is guided by reason, where motives are abstract concepts, wherever the determining factors are not individual representations of perception, or the impression of the moment which guides the animal. But I have explained at length in the Appendix, and illustrated by examples, that this is entirely different from, and independent of, the ethical worth of conduct; that rational action and virtuous action are two quite different things; that reason is just as well found with great wickedness as with great kindness, and by its assistance gives great effectiveness to the one as to the other; that it is equally ready and of service for carrying out methodically and consistently the noble resolution as well as the bad, the wise maxim as well as the

imprudent. All this inevitably follows from the nature of reason, which is feminine, receptive, retentive, and not self-creative. [...]

The most perfect development of *practical reason* in the true and genuine sense of the word, the highest point to which man can attain by the mere use of his faculty of reason, and in which his difference from the animal shows itself most clearly, is the ideal represented in the *Stoic sage*. For the Stoic ethics is originally and essentially not a doctrine of virtue, but merely a guide to the rational life, whose end and aim is happiness through peace of mind. Virtuous conduct appears in it, so to speak, only by accident, as means, not as end. Therefore the Stoic ethics is by its whole nature and point of view fundamentally different from the ethical systems that insist directly on virtue, such as the doctrines of the *Vedas*, of Plato, of Christianity, and of Kant. The aim of Stoic ethics is happiness: τέλος τὸ εὐδαιμονεῖν (*virtutes omnes finem habere beatitudinem*) it says in the description of the Stoa by Stobaeus (*Eclogae*, 1. II, c. 7, p. 114, and also p. 138). Yet the Stoic ethics teaches that happiness is to be found with certainty only in inward calm and in peace of mind (ἀταραξία), and this again can be reached only through virtue. The expression that virtue is the highest good means just this. [...]

Taken as a whole, Stoic ethics is in fact a very valuable and estimable attempt to use reason, man's great prerogative, for an important and salutary purpose, namely to raise him by a precept above the sufferings and pains to which all life is exposed:

"*Qua ratione queas traducere leniter aevum:*
Ne te semper inops agitet vexetque cupido,
Ne pavor et rerum mediocriter utilium spes."
("That thou mayest be able to spend thy life smoothly, Let not ever-pressing desire torment and vex thee, Or fear or hope for things of little worth." [Tr.])

(Horace, *Epist.* I, xviii, 97.)

and in this way to make him partake in the highest degree of the dignity belonging to him as a rational being as distinct from the animal. We can certainly speak of a dignity in this sense, but not in any other. It is a consequence of my view of Stoic ethics that it had to be mentioned here with the description of what the faculty of *reason* is, and what it can achieve. But, however much this end is to a certain extent attainable through the application of reason and through a merely rational ethic, and although experience shows that the happiest are indeed those purely rational characters commonly called practical philosophers – and rightly so, because just as the real, i.e., theoretical, philosopher translates life into the concept, so they translate the concept into life – nevertheless we are still very far from being able to arrive at something perfect in this way, from being actually removed from all the burdens and sorrows of life, and led to the blissful state by the correct use of our reason. On the contrary, we find a complete contradiction in our wishing to live without suffering, a contradiction that is therefore implied by the frequently used phrase "blessed life." This will certainly be clear to the person who has fully grasped my discussion that follows. This contradiction is revealed in this ethic of pure reason itself by the fact that the Stoic is compelled to insert a recommendation of suicide in his guide to the blissful life (for this is what his ethics always remains). This is like the costly phial of poison to be found among the magnificent ornaments and apparel of oriental despots, and is for the case where the sufferings of the body, incapable of being philosophized away by any principles and syllogisms, are paramount and incurable. Thus its sole purpose, namely blessedness, is frustrated, and nothing remains as a means of escape from pain except death. But then death must be taken with unconcern, just as is any other medicine. Here a marked contrast is evident between the Stoic ethics and all those other ethical systems mentioned above. These ethical systems make virtue directly and in itself the aim and object, even with the most grievous sufferings, and will not allow a man to end his life in order to escape from suffering. But not one of them knew how to express the true reason for rejecting suicide, but they laboriously collected fictitious arguments of every kind. This true reason will appear in the fourth book in connexion with our discussion. But the above-mentioned contrast reveals and confirms just that essential difference to be found in the fundamental principle between the Stoa, really only a special form of eudaemonism, and the doctrines just mentioned, although both often agree in their results, and are apparently related. But the above-mentioned inner contradiction, with which the Stoic ethics is affected even in its fundamental idea, further shows itself in the fact that its ideal, the Stoic sage as represented by this ethical system, could never obtain life or inner poetical truth, but

remains a wooden, stiff lay-figure with whom one can do nothing. He himself does not know where to go with his wisdom, and his perfect peace, contentment, and blessedness directly contradict the nature of mankind, and do not enable us to arrive at any perceptive representation thereof. Compared with him, how entirely different appear the overcomers of the world and voluntary penitents, who are revealed to us, and are actually produced, by the wisdom of India; how different even the Saviour of Christianity, that excellent form full of the depth of life, of the greatest poetical truth and highest significance, who stands before us with perfect virtue, holiness, and sublimity, yet in a state of supreme suffering.

On the Fundamental View of Idealism

In endless space countless luminous spheres, round each of which some dozen smaller illuminated ones revolve, hot at the core and covered over with a hard cold crust; on this crust a mouldy film has produced living and knowing beings: this is empirical truth, the real, the world. Yet for a being who thinks, it is a precarious position to stand on one of those numberless spheres freely floating in boundless space, without knowing whence or whither, and to be only one of innumerable similar beings that throng, press, and toil, restlessly and rapidly arising and passing away in beginningless and endless time. Here there is nothing permanent but matter alone, and the recurrence of the same varied organic forms by means of certain ways and channels that inevitably exist as they do. All that empirical science can teach is only the more precise nature and rule of these events. But at last the philosophy of modern times, especially through Berkeley and Kant, has called to mind that all this in the first instance is only *phenomenon of the brain*, and is encumbered by so many great and different *subjective* conditions that its supposed absolute reality vanishes, and leaves room for an entirely different world-order that lies at the root of that phenomenon, in other words, is related to it as is the thing-in-itself to the mere appearance.

"The world is my representation" is, like the axioms of Euclid, a proposition which everyone must recognize as true as soon as he understands it, although it is not a proposition that everyone understands as soon as he hears it. To have brought this proposition to consciousness and to have connected it with the problem of the relation of the ideal to the real, in other words, of the world in the head to the world outside the head, constitutes, together with the problem of moral freedom, the distinctive characteristic of the philosophy of the moderns. For only after men had tried their hand for thousands of years at merely *objective* philosophizing did they discover that, among the many things that make the world so puzzling and precarious, the first and foremost is that, however immeasurable and massive it may be, its existence hangs nevertheless on a single thread; and this thread is the actual consciousness in which it exists. This condition, with which the existence of the world is irrevocably encumbered, marks it with the stamp of *ideality*, in spite of all *empirical* reality, and consequently with the stamp of the mere *phenomenon*. Thus the world must be recognized, from one aspect at least, as akin to a dream, indeed as capable of being put in the same class with a dream. For the same brain-function that conjures up during sleep a perfectly objective, perceptible, and indeed palpable world must have just as large a share in the presentation of the objective world of wakefulness. Though different as regards their matter, the two worlds are nevertheless obviously moulded from one form. This form is the intellect, the brain-function. Descartes was probably the first to attain the degree of reflection demanded by that fundamental truth; consequently, he made that truth the starting-point of his philosophy, although provisionally only in the form of sceptical doubt. By his taking *cogito ergo sum* ("I think, therefore I am" [Tr.]) as the only thing certain, and provisionally regarding the existence of the world as problematical, the essential and only correct starting-point, and at the same time the true point of support, of all philosophy was really found. This point, indeed, is essentially and of necessity *the subjective, our own consciousness*. For this alone is and remains that which is immediate; everything else, be it what it may, is first mediated and conditioned by consciousness, and therefore dependent on it. It is thus rightly considered that the philosophy of the moderns starts from Descartes as its father. Not long afterwards, Berkeley went farther along this path, and arrived at *idealism* proper; in other words, at the knowledge that what is extended in space, and hence the objective, material world in general, exists as such simply and solely in our *representation*, and that it is false and indeed absurd to attribute to it, *as such*, an existence outside all representation and independent of the knowing subject, and so to assume a matter positively and absolutely existing in itself. But this very correct and deep insight really constitutes the whole of Berkeley's philosophy; in it he had exhausted himself.

Accordingly, true philosophy must at all costs be *idealistic*; indeed, it must be so merely to be honest. For nothing is more certain than that no one ever came out of himself in order to identify himself immediately with things different from him; but everything of which he has certain, sure, and hence immediate knowledge, lies within his consciousness. Beyond this consciousness, therefore, there can be no *immediate* certainty; but the first principles of a science must have such a certainty. It is quite appropriate to the empirical standpoint of all the other sciences to assume the objective world as positively and actually existing; it is not appropriate to the standpoint of philosophy, which has to go back to what is primary and original. *Consciousness* alone is immediately given, hence the basis of philosophy is limited to the facts of consciousness; in other words, philosophy is essentially *idealistic*. Realism, which commends itself to the crude understanding by appearing to be founded on fact, starts precisely from an arbitrary assumption, and is in consequence an empty castle in the air, since it skips or denies the first fact of all, namely that all that we know lies within consciousness. For that the *objective existence* of things is conditioned by a representer of them, and that consequently the objective world exists only *as representation*, is no hypothesis, still less a peremptory pronouncement, or even a paradox put forward for the sake of debate or argument. On the contrary, it is the surest and simplest truth, and a knowledge of it is rendered more difficult only by the fact that it is indeed too simple, and that not everyone has sufficient power of reflection to go back to the first elements of his consciousness of things. There can never be an existence that is objective absolutely and in itself; such an existence, indeed, is positively inconceivable. For the objective, as such, always and essentially has its existence in the consciousness of a subject; it is therefore the representation of this subject, and consequently is conditioned by the subject, and moreover by the subject's forms of representation, which belong to the subject and not to the object.

That the *objective world would exist* even if there existed no knowing being at all, naturally seems at the first onset to be sure and certain, because it can be thought in the abstract, without the contradiction that it carries within itself coming to light. But if we try to *realize* this abstract thought, in other words, to reduce it to representations of perception, from which alone (like everything abstract) it can have content and truth; and if accordingly we attempt to *imagine an objective world without a knowing subject*, then we become aware that what we are imagining at that moment is in truth the opposite of what we intended, namely nothing but just the process in the intellect of a knowing being who perceives an objective world, that is to say, precisely that which we had sought to exclude. For this perceptible and real world is obviously a phenomenon of the brain; and so in the assumption that the world as such might exist independently of all brains there lies a contradiction.

The principal objection to the inevitable and essential *ideality of every object*, the objection which arises distinctly or indistinctly in everyone, is certainly as follows: Even my own person is object for another, and is therefore that other's representation, and yet I know certainly that I should exist even without that other representing me in his mind. But all other objects also stand in the same relation to his intellect as *I* stand; consequently, they too would exist without his representing them in his mind. The answer to this is as follows: That other being, whose object I am now considering my person to be, is not absolutely *the subject*, but is in the first instance a knowing individual. Therefore, if he too did *not* exist, in fact, even if there existed in general no other knowing being except myself, this would still by no means be the elimination of the *subject* in whose representation alone all objects exist. For I myself am in fact that *subject*, just as is every knowing being. Consequently, in the case here assumed, my person would certainly still exist, but again as representation, namely in my own knowledge. For even by myself it is always known only indirectly, never directly, since all existence as representation is an indirect existence. Thus as *object*, in other words as extended, filling space, and acting, I know my body only in the perception of my brain. This perception is brought about through the senses, and on their data the perceiving understanding carries out its function of passing from the effect to the cause. In this way, by the eye seeing the body, or the hands touching it, the understanding constructs the spatial figure that presents itself in space as my body. In no way, however, are there given to me directly, in some general feeling of the body or in inner self-consciousness, any extension, shape, and activity that would coincide with my inner being itself, and that inner being accordingly requires no other being in whose knowledge it would manifest itself, in order so to exist. On the contrary, that general feeling, just like self-consciousness, exists directly only in relation to the *will*, namely as comfortable or uncomfortable, and as active in the acts of will, which exhibit themselves for external perception as actions of the body. It follows from this that the existence of my person or of my body *as an extended and acting thing* always presupposes a *knowing being* different from it, since it is essentially an existence in the apprehension, in the representation, and hence an existence *for another being*. In fact, it is a phenomenon of the brain, no matter whether the brain in which it exhibits itself belongs to my own person or to another's. In the first case, one's own person is then split up into the knowing and the known, into object and subject, and here, as everywhere, these two face each other inseparable and irreconcilable. Therefore, if my own person, in order to exist as such, always requires a knower, this will apply at any rate just as much to all other objects; and to vindicate for these an existence independent of knowledge and of the subject of knowledge was the aim of the above objection.

However, it is evident that the existence conditioned through a knowing being is simply and solely existence *in space*, and hence that of a thing extended and acting. This alone is always a known thing, and consequently an existence *for another being*. At the same time, everything that exists in this way may still have *an existence for itself*, for which it requires no subject. This existence by itself, however, cannot be extension and activity (together space-occupation), but is necessarily another kind of being, namely that of a *thing-in-itself*, which, purely as such, can never be *object*. This, therefore, is the answer to the principal objection stated above, and accordingly this objection does not overthrow the fundamental truth that the objectively present and existing world can exist only in the representation, and so only for a subject.

It is also to be noted here that even Kant, at any rate so long as he remained consistent, cannot have thought of any *objects* among his things-in-themselves. For this follows already from the fact that he proved space as well as time to be a mere form of our intuition or perception, which in consequence does not belong to the things-in-themselves. What is not in space or in time cannot be *object*; therefore the being or existence of *things-in-themselves* can no longer be *objective*, but only of quite a different kind, namely a metaphysical being or existence. Consequently, there is already to be found in that Kantian principle also the proposition that the *objective* world exists only as *representation*.

In spite of all that may be said, nothing is so persistently and constantly misunderstood as *idealism*, since it is interpreted as meaning that the *empirical* reality of the external world is denied. On this rests the constant return of the appeal to common sense, which appears in many different turns and guises, for example, as "*fundamental conviction*" in the Scottish school, or as Jacobi's *faith or belief* in the reality of the external world. The external world by no means gives itself, as Jacobi explains, merely on credit; nor is it accepted by us on faith and trust. It gives itself as what it is, and performs directly what it promises. It must be remembered that Jacobi set up such a credit system of the world, and was lucky enough to impose it on a few professors of philosophy, who for thirty years went on philosophizing about it extensively and at their ease; and that it was this same Jacobi who once denounced Lessing as a Spinozist, and later Schelling as an atheist, and received from the latter the well-known and well-merited reprimand. In accordance with such zeal, by reducing the external world to a matter of faith, he wanted merely to open a little door for faith in general, and to prepare the credit for that which was afterwards actually to be offered on credit; just as if, to introduce paper money, we tried to appeal to the fact that the value of the ringing coin depended merely on the stamp the State put on it. In his philosopheme on the reality of the external world assumed on faith, Jacobi is precisely the "transcendental realist playing the part of the empirical idealist," whom Kant censured in the *Critique of Pure Reason*, first edition, p. 369.

True idealism, on the other hand, is not the empirical, but the transcendental. It leaves the *empirical* reality of the world untouched, but adheres to the fact that all *object*, and hence the empirically real in general, is conditioned by the *subject* in a twofold manner. In the first place it is conditioned *materially*, or as *object* in general, since an objective existence is conceivable only in face of a subject and as the representation of this subject. In the second place, it is conditioned *formally*, since the *mode and manner* of the object's existence, in other words, of its being represented (space, time, causality), proceed from the subject, and are predisposed in the subject. Therefore immediately connected with simple or *Berkeleian* idealism, which concerns the *object in general*, is *Kantian* idealism, which concerns the specially given *mode and manner* of objective existence. This proves that the whole of the material world with its bodies in space, extended and, by means of time, having causal relations with one another, and everything attached to this – all this is not something existing *independently* of our mind, but something that has its fundamental presuppositions in our brain-functions, *by means of* which and *in* which alone is *such* an objective order of things possible. For time, space, and causality, on which all those real and objective events rest, are themselves nothing more than functions of the brain; so that, therefore, this unchangeable *order* of things, affording the criterion and the clue to their empirical *reality*, itself comes first from the brain, and has its credentials from that alone. Kant has discussed this thoroughly and in detail; though he does not mention the brain, but says "the faculty of knowledge." He has even attempted to prove that that objective order in time, space, causality, matter, and so on, on which all the events of the real world ultimately rest, cannot even be *conceived*, when closely considered, as a self-existing order, i.e., an order of things-in-themselves, or as something absolutely objective and positively existing; for if we attempt to think it out to the end, it leads to contradictions. To demonstrate this was the purpose of the antinomies; in the appendix to my work, however, I have demonstrated the failure of the attempt. On the other hand, the Kantian teaching, even without the antinomies, leads to the insight that things and their whole mode and manner of existence are inseparably associated with our consciousness of them. Therefore he who has clearly grasped this soon reaches the conviction that the assumption that things exist as such, even outside and independently of our consciousness, is really absurd. Thus are we so deeply immersed in time, space, causality, and in the whole regular course of experience resting on these; we (and in fact even the animals) are so completely at home, and know how to find our way in experience from the very beginning. This would not be possible if our intellect were one thing and things another; but it can be explained only from the fact that the two constitute a whole; that the intellect itself creates that order, and exists only for things, but that things also exist only for it.

But even apart from the deep insight and discernment revealed only by the Kantian philosophy, the inadmissible character of the assumption of absolute *realism*, clung to so obstinately, can indeed be directly demonstrated, or at any rate felt, by the mere elucidation of its meaning through considerations such as the following. According to realism, the world is supposed to exist, as we know it, independently of this knowledge. Now let us once remove from it all knowing beings, and thus leave behind only inorganic and vegetable nature. Rock, tree, and brook are there, and the blue sky; sun, moon, and stars illuminate this world, as before, only of course to no purpose, since there exists no eye to see such things. But then let us subsequently put into the world a knowing being. That world then presents itself *once more* in his brain, and repeats itself inside that brain exactly as it was previously outside it. Thus to the *first* world a *second* has been added, which, although completely separated from the first, resembles it to a nicety. Now the *subjective* world of this perception is constituted in *subjective*, known space exactly as the *objective* world is in *objective*, infinite space. But the subjective world still has an advantage over the objective, namely the knowledge that that external space is infinite; in fact, it can state beforehand most minutely and accurately the full conformity to law of all the relations in that space which are possible and not yet actual, and it does not need to examine them first. It can state just as much about the course of time, as also about the relation of cause and effect which governs the changes in outer space. I think that, on closer consideration, all this proves absurd enough, and thus leads to the conviction that that absolutely *objective* world outside the head, independent of it and *prior* to all knowledge, which we at first imagined we had conceived, was really no other than the second world already known *subjectively*, the world of the representation, and that it is this alone which we are actually capable of conceiving. Accordingly the assumption is automatically forced on us that the world, as we know it, exists only for our knowledge, and consequently in the *representation* alone, and not once again outside that representation. In keeping with this assumption, then, the thing-in-itself, in other words, that which exists independently of our knowledge and of all knowledge, is to be regarded as something quite different from the *representation* and all its attributes, and hence from objectivity in general. What this is, will afterwards be the theme of our second book.

On the other hand, the controversy about the reality of the external world, considered in § 5 of our first volume, rests on the assumption, just criticized, of an objective and a subjective world both in *space*, and on the impossibility, arising in the case of this presupposition, of a transition, a bridge, between the two. On this controversy I have to make the following remarks.

Subjective and objective do not form a continuum. That of which we are immediately conscious is bounded by the skin, or rather by the extreme ends of the nerves proceeding from the cerebral system. Beyond this lies a world of which we have no other knowledge than that gained through pictures in our mind. Now the question is whether and to what extent a world existing independently of us corresponds to these pictures. The relation between the two could be brought about only by means of the law of causality, for this law alone leads from something given to something quite different from it. This law itself, however, has first of all to substantiate its validity. Now it must be either of *objective* or of *subjective* origin; but in either case it lies on one bank or the other, and therefore cannot serve as a bridge. If, as Locke and Hume assumed, it is *a posteriori*, and hence drawn from experience, it is of *objective* origin; it then itself belongs to the external world in question, and therefore cannot vouch for the reality of that world. For then, according to Locke's method, the law of causality would be demonstrated from experience, and the reality of experience from the law of causality. If, on the other hand, it is given *a priori*, as Kant more correctly taught, then it is of *subjective* origin; and so it is clear that with it we always remain in the *subjective*. For the only thing actually given *empirically* in the case of perception is the occurrence of a sensation in the organ of sense. The assumption that this sensation, even only in general, must have a *cause* rests on a law that is rooted in the form of our knowledge, in other words, in the functions of our brain. The origin of this law is therefore just as subjective as is that sensation itself. The *cause* of the given sensation, assumed as a result of this law, immediately manifests itself in perception as *object*, having space and time as the form of its appearance. But again, even *these* forms themselves are of entirely subjective origin, for they are the mode and manner of our faculty of perception. That transition from the sensation to its cause, which, as I have repeatedly shown, lies at the foundation of all sense-perception, is certainly sufficient for indicating to us the empirical presence in space and time of an empirical object, and is therefore fully satisfactory for practical life. But it is by no means sufficient for giving us information about the existence and real inner nature of the phenomena that arise for us in such a way, or rather of their intelligible substratum. Therefore, the fact that, on the occasion of certain sensations occurring in my organs of sense, there arises in my head a *perception* of things extended in space, permanent in time, and causally operative, by no means justifies me in assuming that such things also exist in themselves, in other words, that they exist with such properties absolutely belonging to them, independently of my head and outside it. This is the correct conclusion of the *Kantian* philosophy. It is connected with an earlier result of Locke which is just as correct, and very much easier to understand. Thus, although, as is allowed by Locke's teaching, external things are positively assumed to be the causes of the sensations, there cannot be any *resemblance* at all between the *sensation*, in which the *effect* consists, and the objective *nature* or *quality* of the *cause* that gives rise to this sensation. For the sensation, as organic function, is above all determined by the very artificial and complicated nature of our sense-organs; thus it is merely stimulated by the external cause, but is then perfected entirely in accordance with its own laws, and hence is wholly subjective. Locke's philosophy was the criticism of the functions of sense; but Kant has furnished the criticism of the functions of the brain. But to all this we still have to add the result of Berkeley, which has been revised by me, namely that every *object*, whatever its origin, is, *as object*, already conditioned by the subject, and thus is essentially only the subject's *representation*. The aim of realism is just the object without subject; but it is impossible even to conceive such an object clearly.

From the whole of this discussion it follows with certainty and distinctness that it is absolutely impossible to arrive at a comprehension of the *inner nature* of things on the path of mere *knowledge* and *representation*, since this knowledge always comes to things *from without*, and must therefore remain eternally *outside* them. This purpose could be attained only by our finding *ourselves* in the inside of things, so that this inside would be known to us directly. My second book considers to what extent this is actually the case. However, so long as we stop, as in this first book we do, at objective comprehension, and hence at *knowledge*, the world is and remains for us a mere *representation*, since no path is here possible which leads beyond this.

But in addition to this, adherence to the *idealistic* point of view is a necessary counterpoise to the *materialistic*. Thus the controversy over the real and the ideal can also be regarded as one concerning the existence of *matter*. For it is ultimately the reality or ideality of matter which is the point in question. Is matter as such present merely in our representation, or is it also independent thereof? In the latter case, it would be the thing-in-itself; and he who assumes a matter existing in itself must also consistently be a materialist, in other words, must make matter the principle of explanation of all things. On the other hand, he who denies it to be a thing-in-itself is *eo ipso* an idealist. Among the moderns only Locke has asserted positively and straightforwardly the reality of matter; therefore his teaching, through the instrumentality of Condillac, led to the sensualism and materialism of the French. Berkeley alone has denied matter positively and without modifications. Therefore the complete antithesis is that of idealism and materialism, represented in its extremes by Berkeley and the French materialists (Holbach). Fichte is not to be mentioned here; he deserves no place among real philosophers, those elect of mankind who with deep earnestness seek not their own affairs, but the *truth*. They must therefore not be confused with those who under this pretext have only their personal advancement in view. Fichte is the father of *sham philosophy*, of the *underhand* method that by ambiguity in the use of words, incomprehensible talk, and sophisms, tries to deceive, to impress by an air of importance, and thus to befool those eager to learn. After this method had been applied by Schelling, it reached its height, as is well known, in Hegel, with whom it ripened into real charlatanism. But whoever in all seriousness even mentions that Fichte along with Kant shows that he has no notion of what Kant is. On the other hand, materialism also has its justification. It is just as true that the knower is a product of matter as that matter is a mere representation of the knower; but it is also just as one-sided. For materialism is the philosophy of the subject who forgets to take account of himself. Therefore, against the assertion that I am a mere modification of matter, it must also be asserted that all matter exists merely in my representation, and this assertion is no less right. An as yet obscure knowledge of these relations appears to have evoked the Platonic saying ὕλη ἀληθινὸν ψεῦδος (*materia mendacium verax* "Matter is a lie, and yet true" [Tr.]).

Realism, as I have said, necessarily leads to *materialism*. For while empirical perception gives us things-in-themselves, as they exist independently of our knowledge, experience also gives us the *order* of things-in-themselves, in other words, the true and only world-order. But this way leads to the assumption that there is only *one* thing-in-itself, namely matter, of which everything else is a modification; for the course of nature is the absolute and only world-order. To avoid these consequences, *spiritualism* was set up along with *realism*, so long as the latter was in undisputed authority; thus the assumption was made of a second substance, outside and along with matter, namely an *immaterial substance*. This dualism and *spiritualism*, devoid equally of experience, proofs, and comprehensibility, was denied by Spinoza, and shown to be false by Kant, who ventured to do this because at the same time he established *idealism* in its rights. For with *realism*, *materialism*, as the counterpoise to which *spiritualism* had been devised, falls to the ground of its own accord, since matter and the course of nature then become mere *phenomenon*, conditioned by the intellect; for the phenomenon has its existence only in the *representation* of the intellect. Accordingly, *spiritualism* is the specious and false safeguard against *materialism*; but the real and true safeguard is *idealism*. By making the objective world dependent *on us*, idealism gives the necessary counterpoise to the dependence *on* the objective world in which *we* are placed by the course of nature. The world, from which I part at death, is, on the other hand, only my representation. The centre of gravity of existence falls back into the *subject*. What is proved is not, as in spiritualism, the knower's independence of matter, but the dependence of all matter on the knower. Of course, this is not so easy to understand and so convenient to handle as is spiritualism with its two substances; but χαλεπὰ τὰ καλά ("What is noble is difficult" [Tr.]).

In opposition to the *subjective* starting-point, namely "the world is my representation," there certainly is at the moment with equal justification the *objective* starting-point, namely "the world is matter," or "matter alone positively exists" (as it alone is not liable to becoming and to passing away), or "all that exists is matter." This is the starting-point of Democritus, Leucippus, and Epicurus. More closely considered, however, starting from the *subject* retains a real advantage; it has the advantage of one perfectly justified step, for consciousness alone is what is *immediate*. We skip this, however, when we go straight to matter and make that our starting-point. On the other hand, it would be possible to construct the world from matter and its properties, if these were correctly, completely, and exhaustively known (and many of them we still lack). For everything that has come into existence has become actual through *causes*, that were able to operate and come together only in consequence of the *fundamental forces of matter*. But these must be capable of complete demonstration at least *objectively*, even if we shall never get to know them *subjectively*. But such an explanation and construction of the world would always have as its foundation not only the assumption of an existence-in-itself of matter (whereas in truth such existence is conditioned by the subject), but it would also have to let all the *original properties* in this matter remain in force, and yet be absolutely inexplicable, that is, be *qualitates occultae*. (See § § 26, 27 of the first volume.) For matter is only the bearer of these forces, just as the law of causality is only the regulator of their phenomena. Consequently, such an explanation of the world would still be only relative and conditioned, really the work of a *physical science* that at every step longed for a *metaphysic*. On the other hand, even the subjective starting-point and axiom, "the world is my representation," has something inadequate about it, firstly inasmuch as it is one-sided, for the world is much more besides this (namely thing-in-itself, will); in fact, being representation is to a certain extent accidental to it; secondly also inasmuch as it expresses merely the object's being conditioned by the subject without at the same time stating that the subject as such is also conditioned by the object. For the proposition that "the subject would nevertheless be a knowing being, even if it had no object, in other words, no representation at all" is just as false as is the proposition of the crude understanding to the effect that "the world, the object, would still exist, even if there were no subject." A consciousness without object is no consciousness at all. A thinking subject has *concepts* for its object; a sensuously perceiving subject has objects with the qualities corresponding to its organization. Now if we deprive the *subject* of all the particular determinations and forms of its knowing, all the properties in the *object* also disappear, and nothing but *matter without form and quality* is left. This matter can occur in experience as little as can the subject without the forms of its knowledge, yet it remains opposed to the bare subject as such, as its reflex, which can only disappear simultaneously with it. Although materialism imagines that it postulates nothing more than this matter – atoms for instance – yet it unconsciously adds not only the subject, but also space, time, and causality, which depend on special determinations of the subject.

The world as representation, the objective world, has thus, so to speak, two poles, namely the knowing subject plain and simple without the forms of its knowing, and crude matter without form and quality. Both are absolutely unknowable; the subject, because it is that which knows; matter, because without form and quality it cannot be perceived. Yet both are the fundamental conditions of all empirical perception. Thus the knowing subject, merely as such, which is likewise a presupposition of all experience, stands in opposition, as its clear counterpart, to crude, formless, quite dead (i.e., will-less) matter. This matter is not given in any experience, but is presupposed in every experience. This subject is not in time, for time is only the more direct form of all its representing. Matter, standing in opposition to the subject, is accordingly eternal, imperishable, endures through all time; but properly speaking it is not extended, since extension gives form, and hence it is not spatial. Everything else is involved in a constant arising and passing away, whereas these two constitute the static poles of the world as representation. We can therefore regard the permanence of matter as the reflex of the timelessness of the pure subject, that is simply taken to be the condition of every object. Both belong to the phenomenon, not to the thing-in-itself; but they are the framework of the phenomenon. Both are discovered only through abstraction; they are not given immediately, pure and by themselves.

The fundamental mistake of all systems is the failure to recognize this truth, namely that *the intellect and matter are correlatives*, in other words, the one exists only for the other; both stand and fall together; the one is only the other's reflex. They are in fact really one and the same thing, considered from two opposite points of view; and this one thing – here I am anticipating – is the phenomenon of the will or of the thing-in-itself. Consequently, both are secondary, and therefore the origin of the world is not to be looked for in either of them. But in consequence of their failure to recognize this, all systems (with the possible exception of Spinoza's) have sought the origin of

all things in one of those two. Thus some of them suppose an intellect, νοῦς, as positively the first thing and the δημιουργός; and accordingly they allow a *representation* in this of things and of the world to precede their real existence; consequently they distinguish the real world from the world as representation, which is false. Therefore, *matter* now appears as that by which the two are distinguished, namely as a thing-in-itself. Hence arises the difficulty of producing this matter, the ὕλη, so that, when added to the mere representation of the world, it may impart reality thereto. That original intellect must either find it already in existence; matter is then an absolutely first thing just as much as that intellect is, and we then get two absolutely first things, the δημιουργός and the ὕλη. Or the intellect produces matter out of nothing, an assumption that our understanding combats, for this understanding is capable of grasping only changes in matter, not an arising or passing away of that matter. At bottom, this rests on the very fact that matter is the essential correlative of the understanding. The systems opposed to these, which make the other of the two correlatives, namely matter, the absolutely first thing, suppose a matter that exists without being represented by a subject; and, as is sufficiently clear from all that has been said above, this is a direct contradiction, for in the existence of matter we always think only of its being represented by a subject. But then there arises for them the difficulty of bringing to this matter, which alone is their absolutely first thing, the intellect that is ultimately to know it from experience. In § 7 of the first volume I have spoken of this weak side of materialism. With me, on the other hand, matter and intellect are inseparable correlatives, existing for each other, and therefore only relatively. Matter is the representation of the intellect; the intellect is that in the representation of which alone matter exists. Both together constitute the *world as representation*, which is precisely Kant's *phenomenon*, and consequently something secondary. What is primary is that which appears, namely the *thing-in-itself*, which we shall afterwards learn to recognize as the *will*. In itself this is neither the representer nor the represented, but is quite different from its mode of appearance.

As an impressive conclusion to this important and difficult discussion, I will now personify those two abstractions, and introduce them into a dialogue, after the manner of *Probodha Chandro Daya*. We may also compare it with a similar dialogue between matter and form in Raymond Lull's *Duo-decim Principia Philosophiae*, c. 1 and 2.

The Subject

I am, and besides me there is nothing. For the world is my representation.

Matter

Presumptuous folly! *I* am, and besides me there is nothing. For the world is my fleeting form. You are a mere result of a part of this form, and quite accidental.

The Subject

What silly conceit! Neither you nor your form would exist without me; you are conditioned through me. Whoever thinks me away, and then believes he can still think of you, is involved in a gross delusion; for your existence outside my representation is a direct contradiction, a wooden-iron. *You are*, simply means you are represented by me. My representation is the locality of your existence; I am therefore its first condition.

Matter

Fortunately the boldness of your assertion will soon be refuted in a real way, and not by mere words. A few more moments, and you – actually are no more; with all your boasting and bragging, you have sunk into nothing, floated past like a shadow, and suffered the fate of every one of my fleeting forms. But I, I remain intact and undiminished from millennium to millennium, throughout endless time, and behold unmoved the play of my changing forms.

The Subject

This endless time, to live through which is your boast, is, like the endless space you fill, present merely in my representation; in fact, it is the mere form of my representation which I carry already prepared within me, and in which you manifest yourself. It receives you, and in this way do you first of all exist. But the annihilation with which you threaten me does not touch me, otherwise you also would be annihilated. On the contrary, it concerns merely the individual which for a short time is my bearer, and which, like everything else, is my representation.

Matter

Even if I grant you this, and go so far as to regard your existence, which is inseparably linked to that of these fleeting individuals, as something existing by itself, it nevertheless remains dependent on mine. For you are subject only in so far as you have an object; and that object is I. I am its kernel and content, that which is permanent in it, that which holds it together, without which it would be as incoherent and as wavering and unsubstantial as the dreams and fancies of your individuals, that have borrowed even their fictitious content from me.

The Subject

You do well to refrain from disputing my existence on account of its being linked to individuals; for just as inseparably as I am tied to these, so are you tied to form, your sister, and you have never yet appeared without her. No eye has yet seen either you or me naked and isolated; for we are both only abstractions. At bottom it is *one* entity that perceives itself and is perceived by itself, but its being-in-itself cannot consist either in perceiving or in being perceived, as these are divided between us.

Both

So we are inseparably connected as necessary parts of one whole, which includes us both and exists through us both. Only a misunderstanding can set up the two of us as enemies in opposition to each other, and lead to the false conclusion that the one contests the existence of the other, with which its own existence stands and falls.

This whole, including both, is the world as representation, or the phenomenon. After this is taken away, there remains only the purely metaphysical, the thing-in-itself, which in the second book we shall recognize as the will.

On the Primacy of the Will in Self-Consciousness

The will, as the thing-in-itself, constitutes the inner, true, and indestructible nature of man; yet in itself it is without consciousness. For consciousness is conditioned by the intellect, and the intellect is a mere accident of our being, for it is a function of the brain. The brain, together with the nerves and spinal cord attached to it, is a mere fruit, a product, in fact a parasite, of the rest of the organism, in so far as it is not directly geared to the organism's inner working, but serves the purpose of self-preservation by regulating its relations with the external world. On the other hand, the organism itself is the visibility, the objectivity, of the individual will, its image, as this image presents itself in that very brain (which in the first book we learned to recognize as the condition of the objective world in general). Therefore, this image is brought about by the brain's forms of knowledge, namely space, time, and causality; consequently it presents itself as something extended, successively acting, and material, in other words, operative or effective. The parts of the body are both directly felt and perceived by means of the senses only in the brain. In consequence of this, it can be said that the intellect is the secondary phenomenon, the organism the primary, that is, the immediate phenomenal appearance of the will; the will is metaphysical, the intellect physical; the intellect, like its objects, is mere phenomenon, the will alone is thing-in-itself. Then, in a more and more *figurative* sense, and so by way of comparison, it can be said that the will is the substance of man, the intellect the accident; the will is the matter, the intellect the form; the will is heat, the intellect light.

We will now first of all verify, and at the same time elucidate, this thesis by the following facts appertaining to the inner life of man. Perhaps, on this occasion, more will be gained for knowledge of the inner man than is to be found in many systematic psychologies.

1. Not only the consciousness of other things, i.e., the apprehension of the external world, but also *self-consciousness*, as already mentioned, contains a knower and a known, otherwise it would not be a *consciousness*. For *consciousness* consists in knowing, but knowing requires a knower and a known. Therefore self-consciousness could not exist if there were not in it a known opposed to the knower and different therefrom. Thus, just as there can be no object without a subject, so there can be no subject without an object, in other words, no knower without something different from this that is known. Therefore, a consciousness that was through and through pure intelligence would be impossible. The intelligence is like the sun that does not illuminate space unless an object exists by which its rays are reflected. The knower himself, precisely as such, cannot be known, otherwise he would be the *known* of another knower. But as the *known* in self-consciousness we find exclusively the *will*. For not only willing and deciding in the narrowest sense, but also all

striving, wishing, shunning, hoping, fearing, loving, hating, in short all that directly constitutes our own weal and woe, desire and disinclination, is obviously only affection of the will, is a stirring, a modification, of willing and not-willing, is just that which, when it operates outwards, exhibits itself as an act of will proper. But in all knowledge the known, not the knower, is the first and essential thing, inasmuch as the former is the πρωτότυπος, the latter the ἔκτυπος ("prototype"; "copy," "ectype" [Tr.]). Therefore in self-consciousness the known, consequently the will, must be the first and original thing; the knower, on the other hand, must be only the secondary thing, that which has been added, the mirror. They are related somewhat as the self-luminous is to the reflecting body; or as the vibrating strings are to the sounding-board, where the resulting note would then be consciousness. We can also consider the plant as such a symbol of consciousness. As we know, it has two poles, root and corona; the former reaching down into darkness, moisture and cold, and the latter up into brightness, dryness and warmth; then as the point of indifference of the two poles where they part from each other close to the ground, the collum or root-stock (*rhizoma, le collet*). The root is what is essential, original, perennial, whose death entails the death of the corona; it is therefore primary. The corona, on the other hand, is the ostensible, that which has sprouted forth, that which passes away without the root dying; it is therefore the secondary. The root represents the will, the corona the intellect, and the point of indifference of the two, namely the collum, would be the *I*, which, as their common extreme point, belongs to both. This I is the *pro tempore* identical subject of knowing and willing, whose identity I call in my very first essay (*On the Principle of Sufficient Reason*) and in my first philosophical astonishment, the miracle κατ᾽ ἐξοχήν ("*par excellence*" [Tr.]). It is the point of departure and of contact of the whole phenomenon, in other words, of the objectification of the will; it is true that it conditions the phenomenon, but the phenomenon also conditions it. The comparison here given can be carried even as far as the individual character and nature of men. Thus, just as usually a large corona springs only from a large root, so the greatest mental abilities are found only with a vehement and passionate will. A genius of phlegmatic character and feeble passions would be like succulent plants that have very small roots in spite of an imposing corona consisting of thick leaves;

yet he will not be found. Vehemence of the will and passionate ardour of the character are a condition of enhanced intelligence, and this is shown physiologically through the brain's activity being conditioned by the movement communicated to it with every pulsation through the great arteries running up to the *basis cerebri*. Therefore an energetic pulse, and even, according to Bichat, a short neck are necessary for great activity of the brain. But the opposite of the above is of course found; that is, vehement desires, passionate, violent character, with weak intellect, in other words, with a small brain of inferior conformation in a thick skull. This is a phenomenon as common as it is repulsive; it might perhaps be compared to the beetroot.

2. But in order not merely to describe consciousness figuratively, but to know it thoroughly, we have first to find out what exists in every consciousness in the same manner, and what therefore will be, as the common and constant element, that which is essential. We shall then consider what distinguishes one consciousness from another, and this accordingly will be the accidental and secondary element.

Consciousness is known to us positively only as a property of animal nature; consequently we may not, indeed we cannot, think of it otherwise than as *animal consciousness*, so that this expression is in fact tautological. Therefore what is always to be found in *every* animal consciousness, even the most imperfect and feeblest, in fact what is always its foundation, is the immediate awareness of a *longing*, and of its alternate satisfaction and non-satisfaction in very different degrees. To a certain extent we know this *a priori*. For amazingly varied as the innumerable species of animals may be, and strange as some new form of them, never previously seen, may appear to us, we nevertheless assume beforehand with certainty its innermost nature as something well known, and indeed wholly familiar to us. Thus we know that the animal *wills*, indeed even *what* it wills, namely existence, well-being, life, and propagation. Since we here presuppose with perfect certainty an identity with ourselves, we have no hesitation in attributing to it unchanged all the affections of will known to us in ourselves; and we speak positively and plainly of its desire, aversion, fear, anger, hatred, love, joy, sorrow, longing, and so on. On the other hand, as soon as we come to speak of phenomena of mere knowledge, we run into uncertainty. We do not venture to say that the animal

conceives, thinks, judges, or knows; we attribute to it with certainty only representations in general, since without these its *will* could not be stirred or agitated in the ways previously mentioned. But as regards the animals' definite way of knowing, and its precise limits in a given species, we have only indefinite concepts, and make conjectures. Therefore understanding between us and them is often difficult, and is brought about ingeniously only in consequence of experience and practice. Here, then, are to be found distinctions of consciousness. On the other hand, longing, craving, willing, or aversion, shunning, and not-willing, are peculiar to every consciousness; man has them in common with the polyp. Accordingly, this is the essential and the basis of every consciousness. The difference of its manifestations in the various species of animal beings depends on the different extension of their spheres of knowledge in which the motives of those manifestations are to be found. Directly from our own nature we understand all the actions and attitudes of animals that express stirrings and agitations of the will; and so to this extent we sympathize with them in many different ways. On the other hand, the gulf between us and them arises simply and solely from a difference of intellect. The gulf between a very intelligent animal and a man of very limited capacity is possibly not much greater than that between a blockhead and a genius. Therefore here also, the resemblance between them in another aspect, springing from the likeness of their inclinations and emotions and again assimilating both, sometimes stands out surprisingly, and excites astonishment. This consideration makes it clear that in all animal beings the *will* is the primary and substantial thing; the *intellect*, on the other hand, is something secondary and additional, in fact a mere tool in the service of the will, which is more or less complete and complicated according to the requirements of this service. Just as a species of animals appears equipped with hoofs, claws, hands, wings, horns, or teeth according to the aims of its will, so is it furnished with a more or less developed brain, whose function is the intelligence requisite for its continued existence. Thus the more complicated the organization becomes in the ascending series of animals, the more manifold do its needs become, and the more varied and specially determined the objects capable of satisfying them, consequently the more tortuous and lengthy the paths for arriving at these, which must now all be known and found. Therefore, to the same extent, the animal's representations must also be more versatile, accurate, definite, and connected, and its attention more eager, more continuous, and more easily roused; consequently its intellect must be more developed and complete. Accordingly we see the organ of intelligence, the cerebral system, together with the organs of sense, keep pace with an increase of needs and wants, and with the complication of the organism. We see the increase of the *representing* part of consciousness (as opposed to the *willing* part) bodily manifesting itself in the ever-increasing proportion of the brain in general to the rest of the nervous system, and of the cerebrum to the cerebellum. For (according to Flourens) the former is the workshop of representations, while the latter is the guide and regulator of movements. But the last step taken by nature in this respect is disproportionately great. For in man not only does the power of representation in *perception*, which hitherto has existed alone, reach the highest degree of perfection, but the *abstract* representation, thinking, i.e., *reason (Vernunft)* is added, and with it reflection. Through this important enhancement of the intellect, and hence of the secondary part of consciousness, it obtains a preponderance over the primary part in so far as it becomes from now on the predominantly active part. Thus, whereas in the case of the animal the immediate awareness of its satisfied or unsatisfied desire constitutes by far the principal part of its consciousness, and indeed the more so the lower the animal stands, so that the lowest animals are distinguished from plants only by the addition of a dull representation, with man the opposite is the case. Intense as his desires may be, more intense even than those of any animal and rising to the level of passions, his consciousness nevertheless remains continuously and predominantly concerned and engrossed with representations and ideas. Undoubtedly this is mainly what has given rise to that fundamental error of all philosophers, by virtue of which they make thinking the essential and primary element of the so-called soul, in other words, of man's inner or spiritual life, always putting it first, but regard willing as a mere product of thinking, and as something secondary, additional, and subsequent. But if willing resulted merely from knowing, how could the animals, even the lowest of them, manifest a will that is often so indomitable and vehement, in spite of such extremely limited knowledge? Accordingly, since that fundamental error of the philosophers makes, so to speak, the accident into the substance, it leads them on to

wrong paths from which there is no longer a way out. Therefore that relative predominance of the *knowing* consciousness over the *desiring*, and consequently of the secondary part over the primary, which appears in man, can in certain abnormally favoured individuals go so far that, in moments of supreme enhancement, the secondary or knowing part of consciousness is entirely detached from the willing part, and passes by itself into free activity, in other words, into an activity not stimulated by the will, and therefore no longer serving it. Thus the knowing part of consciousness becomes purely objective and the clear mirror of the world, and from this the conceptions of *genius* arise, which are the subject of our third book.

3. If we descend through the series of grades of animals, we see the intellect becoming weaker and weaker and more and more imperfect; but we certainly do not observe a corresponding degradation of the will. On the contrary, the will everywhere retains its identical nature, and shows itself as a great attachment to life, care for the individual and for the species, egoism and lack of consideration for all others, together with the emotions springing therefrom. Even in the smallest insect the will is present complete and entire; it wills what it wills as decidedly and completely as does man. The difference lies merely in *what* it wills, that is to say, in the motives; but these are the business of the intellect. As that which is secondary and tied to bodily organs, the intellect naturally has innumerable degrees of perfection, and in general is essentially limited and imperfect. The *will*, on the other hand, as that which is original and the thing-in-itself, can never be imperfect, but every act of will is wholly what it can be. By virtue of the simplicity belonging to the will as the thing-in-itself, as the metaphysical in the phenomenon, its *essential nature* admits of no degrees, but is always entirely itself. Only its *stimulation or excitement* has degrees, from the feeblest inclination up to passion, and also its excitability, and thus its vehemence, from the phlegmatic to the choleric temperament. On the other hand, the *intellect* has not merely degrees of *excitement*, from sleepiness up to the mood and inspiration, but also degrees of its *real nature*, of the completeness thereof; accordingly, this rises gradually from the lowest animal which perceives only obscurely up to man, and in man again from the blockhead to the genius. The *will* alone is everywhere entirely itself, for its function is of the greatest simplicity, for this consists in willing and in not-willing, which operates with the

greatest ease and without effort, and requires no practice. On the other hand, knowing has many different functions, and never takes place entirely without effort, which it requires for fixing the attention and making the object clear, and at a higher degree, also for thinking and deliberation; it is therefore capable of great improvement through practice and training. If the intellect holds out to the will something simple and perceptible, the will at once expresses its approval or disapproval. This is the case even when the intellect has laboriously pondered and ruminated, in order finally to produce from numerous data by means of difficult combinations the result that seems most in agreement with the interests of the will. Meanwhile, the will has been idly resting; after the result is reached, it enters, as the sultan does on the divan, merely to express again its monotonous approval or disapproval. It is true that this can turn out different in degree, but in essence it remains always the same.

This fundamentally different nature of the will and the intellect, the simplicity and originality essential in the former in contrast to the complicated and secondary character of the latter, become even clearer to us when we observe their strange interplay within us, and see in a particular case how the images and ideas arising in the intellect set the will in motion, and how entirely separated and different are the roles of the two. Now it is true that we can already observe this in the case of actual events that vividly excite the will, whereas primarily and in themselves they are merely objects of the intellect. But, to some extent, it is not so obvious here that this reality as such primarily exists only in the intellect; and again, the change generally does not occur as rapidly as is necessary, if the thing is to be easily seen at a glance, and thus really comprehensible. On the other hand, both these are the case if it is mere ideas and fantasies that we allow to act on the will. If, for example, we are alone, and think over our personal affairs, and then vividly picture to ourselves, say, the menace of an actually present danger, and the possibility of an unfortunate outcome, anxiety at once compresses the heart, and the blood ceases to flow. But if the intellect then passes to the possibility of the opposite outcome, and allows the imagination to picture the happiness long hoped-for as thereby attained, all the pulses at once quicken with joy, and the heart feels as light as a feather, until the intellect wakes up from its dream. But then let some occasion lead

the memory to an insult or injury suffered long ago, and anger and resentment at once storm through the breast that a moment before was at peace. Then let the image of a long-lost love arise, called up by accident, with which is connected a whole romance with its magic scenes, and this anger will at once give place to profound longing and sadness. Finally, if there occur to us some former humiliating incident, we shrivel up, would like to be swallowed up, blush with shame, and often try to divert and distract ourselves forcibly from it by some loud exclamation, scaring away evil spirits as it were. We see that the intellect strikes up the tune, and the will must dance to it; in fact, the intellect causes it to play the part of a child whom its nurse at her pleasure puts into the most different moods by chatter and tales alternating between pleasant and melancholy things. This is due to the fact that the will in itself is without knowledge, but the understanding associated with it is without will. Therefore the will behaves like a body that is moved, the understanding like the causes that set it in motion, for it is the medium of motives. Yet with all this, the primacy of the will becomes clear again when this will, that becomes, as we have shown, the sport of the intellect as soon as it allows the intellect to control it, once makes its supremacy felt in the last resort. This it does by prohibiting the intellect from having certain representations, by absolutely preventing certain trains of thought from arising, because it knows, or in other words experiences from the self-same intellect, that they would arouse in it any one of the emotions previously described. It then curbs and restrains the intellect, and forces it to turn to other things. However difficult this often is, it is bound to succeed the moment the will is in earnest about it; for the resistance then comes not from the intellect, which always remains indifferent, but from the will itself; and the will has an inclination in one respect for a representation it abhors in another. Thus the representation is in itself interesting to the will, just because it excites it. At the same time, however, abstract knowledge tells the will that this representation will cause it a shock of painful and unworthy emotion to no purpose. The will then decides in accordance with this last knowledge, and forces the intellect to obey. This is called "being master of oneself"; here obviously the master is the will, the servant the intellect, for in the last instance the will is always in command, and therefore constitutes the real core, the being-in-itself, of man. In this respect Ἡγεμονικόν ("the principal faculty" (a Stoic term) [Tr.]) would be a fitting title for the *will*; yet again this title seems to apply to the *intellect*, in so far as that is the guide and leader, like the footman who walks in front of the stranger. In truth, however, the most striking figure for the relation of the two is that of the strong blind man carrying the sighted lame man on his shoulders.

The relation of the will to the intellect here described can further be recognized in the fact that the intellect is originally quite foreign to the decisions of the will. It furnishes the will with motives; but only subsequently, and thus wholly *a posteriori*, does it learn how these have acted, just as a man making a chemical experiment applies the reagents, and then waits for the result. In fact, the intellect remains so much excluded from the real resolutions and secret decisions of its own will that sometimes it can only get to know them, like those of a stranger, by spying out and taking unawares; and it must surprise the will in the act of expressing itself, in order merely to discover its real intentions. For example, I have devised a plan, but I still have some scruple regarding it; on the other hand, the feasibility of the plan, as regards its possibility, is completely uncertain, since it depends on external circumstances that are still undecided. Therefore at all events it is unnecessary for the present to come to a decision about it, and so for the time being I let the matter rest. Now I often do not know how firmly I am already attached in secret to this plan, and how much I desire that it be carried into effect, in spite of the scruple; in other words, my intellect does not know this. But only let a favourable report reach me as to its feasibility, and at once there arises within me a jubilant, irresistible gladness, diffused over my whole being and taking permanent possession of it, to my own astonishment. For only now does my intellect learn how firmly my will had already laid hold of the plan, and how entirely it was in agreement therewith, whereas the intellect had still regarded it as entirely problematical and hardly a match for that scruple. Or in another case, I have entered very eagerly into a mutual obligation that I believe to be very much in accordance with my wishes. As the matter progresses, the disadvantages and hardships make themselves felt, and I begin to suspect that I even repent of what I pursued so eagerly. However, I rid myself of this suspicion by assuring myself that, even if I were not bound, I should continue on the same course. But then the obligation is unexpectedly broken and

dissolved by the other party, and I observe with astonishment that this happens to my great joy and relief. We often do not know what we desire or fear. For years we can have a desire without admitting it to ourselves or even letting it come to clear consciousness, because the intellect is not to know anything about it, since the good opinion we have of ourselves would inevitably suffer thereby. But if the wish is fulfilled, we get to know from our joy, not without a feeling of shame, that this is what we desired; for example, the death of a near relation whose heir we are. Sometimes we do not know what we really fear, because we lack the courage to bring it to clear consciousness. In fact, we are often entirely mistaken as to the real motive from which we do or omit to do something, till finally some accident discloses the secret to us, and we know that our real motive was not what we thought of it as being, but some other that we were unwilling to admit to ourselves, because it was by no means in keeping with our good opinion of ourselves. For example, as we imagine we omit to do something for purely moral reasons; yet we learn subsequently that we were deterred merely by fear, since we do it as soon as all danger is removed. In individual cases this may go so far that a man does not even guess the real motive of his action, in fact does not regard himself as capable of being influenced by such a motive; yet it is the real motive of his action. Incidentally, we have in all this a confirmation and illustration of the rule of La Rochefoucauld: *"L'amour-propre est plus habile que le plus habile homme du monde"* ("Self-esteem is cleverer than the cleverest man of the world" [Tr.]), in fact even a commentary on the Delphic γνῶθι σαυτόν ("Know yourself" [Tr.]) and its difficulty. Now if, on the other hand, as all philosophers imagine, the intellect constituted our true inner nature, and the decisions of the will were a mere result of knowledge, then precisely *that* motive alone, from which we *imagined* we acted, would necessarily be decisive for our moral worth, on the analogy that the intention, not the result, is decisive in this respect. But then the distinction between imagined and actual motive would really be impossible. Therefore, all cases described here, and moreover the analogous cases which anyone who is attentive can observe in himself, enable us to see how the intellect is such a stranger to the will that occasionally it is even mystified thereby. For it is true that it furnishes the will with motives; but it does not penetrate into the secret workshop of the will's decisions. It is, of course, a confidant of the will, yet a confidant that does not get to know everything. A confirmation of this is also afforded by the fact that occasionally the intellect does not really trust the will; and at some time or other almost everyone will have an opportunity of observing this in himself. Thus, if we have formed some great and bold resolution – which, however, as such is only a promise given by the will to the intellect – there often remains within us a slight, unconfessed doubt whether we are quite in earnest about it, whether, in carrying it out, we shall not waver or flinch, but shall have firmness and determination enough to carry it through. It therefore requires the deed to convince us of the sincerity of the resolve.

All these facts are evidence of the complete difference between the will and the intellect, and demonstrate the former's primacy and the latter's subordinate position.

4. The *intellect* grows tired; the *will* is untiring. After continuous work with the head, we feel fatigue of the brain, just as we feel fatigue of the arm after continuous bodily work. All *knowing* is associated with effort and exertion; *willing*, on the contrary, is our very nature, whose manifestations occur without any weariness and entirely of their own accord. Therefore, if our *will* is strongly excited, as in all emotions such as anger, fear, desire, grief, and so on, and we are then called upon to *know*, perhaps with the intention of correcting the motives of those emotions, then the violence we must do to ourselves for this purpose is evidence of the transition from the original, natural activity proper to us to the activity that is derived, indirect, and forced. For the will alone is αὐτόματος and therefore ἀκάματος καὶ ἀγήρατος ἤματα πάντα (*lassitudinis et senii expers in sempiternum* "self-moving"; "untiring and not growing old for ever" [Tr.]). It alone is active, unbidden and of its own accord, and hence often too early and too much; and it knows no weariness. Infants, who show scarcely the first feeble trace of intelligence, are already full of self-will; through uncontrollable, aimless storming and screaming, they show the pressure of will with which they are full to overflowing, whereas their willing as yet has no object, in other words, they will without knowing what they will. [...]

This consideration, therefore, also shows us the will as something original and thus metaphysical, but the intellect as something secondary and physical. For as such the intellect, like everything physical, is subject to *vis inertiae* ("force of inertia" [Tr.]), and is therefore active only when it is put in motion by something else, by the will; and this will rules it, guides it, incites it to further effort, in short imparts to it the activity that is not originally inherent in it. Therefore it willingly rests as soon as it is allowed to do so, and often declares itself to be *indolent* and disinclined to activity. Through continued effort it becomes tired to the point of complete dullness; it is exhausted just as the voltaic pile is through repeated shocks. Therefore all continuous mental work requires pauses and rest, otherwise stupidity and incapacity are the result. Of course these are at first only temporary; but if this rest is constantly denied to the intellect, it becomes excessively and perpetually strained. The consequence is that it becomes permanently dull, and in old age this dullness can pass into complete incapacity, childishness, imbecility, and madness. It is not to be ascribed to old age in and by itself, but to long-continued tyrannical overstraining of the intellect or the brain, when these disorders appear in the last years of life. From this can be explained the fact that Swift became mad, Kant childish, Sir Walter Scott, and also Wordsworth, Southey, and many of less eminence, dull and incapable. Goethe to the end remained clear, and mentally vigorous and active, because he, who was always a man of the world and a courtier, never pursued his mental occupations with self-compulsion. The same holds good of Wieland and the ninety-one-year-old Knebel, as well as Voltaire. But all this proves how very secondary and physical the intellect is, what a mere tool it is. For this reason it needs, for almost a third of its life, the entire suspension of its activity in sleep, in resting the brain. The intellect is the mere function of the brain, which therefore precedes it just as the stomach precedes digestion, or as bodies precede their impact, and together with which it flags and becomes exhausted in old age. The *will*, on the contrary, as thing-in-itself, is never indolent, is absolutely untiring. Its activity is its essence; it never ceases to will, and when, during deep sleep, it is forsaken by the intellect, and is therefore unable to act outwardly from motives, it is active as vital force, looks after the inner economy of the organism with the less interruption, and, as *vis naturae medicatrix* ("the healing power of nature" [Tr.]), again sets in order the irregularities that had found their way into it. For it is not, like the intellect, a function of the body, but *the body is its function*; therefore *ordine rerum* it is prior to that body, as it is the metaphysical substratum of that body, the in-itself of that body's phenomenal appearance. For the duration of life it communicates its indefatigability to the *heart*, that *primum mobile* of the organism, which has therefore become its symbol and synonym. Moreover it does not disappear in old age, but still goes on willing what it has willed. It becomes, in fact, firmer and more inflexible than it was in youth, more irreconcilable, implacable, self-willed, and intractable, because the intellect has become less responsive and susceptible. Therefore we can perhaps get the better of a person in old age only by taking advantage of the weakness of his intellect.

The usual *weakness* and *imperfection* of the intellect, as shown in the want of judgement, narrow-mindedness, perversity, and folly of the great majority, would also be quite inexplicable if the intellect were not something secondary, adventitious, and merely instrumental, but the immediate and original essence of the so-called soul, or in general of the inner man, as was formerly assumed by all philosophers. For how could the original inner nature err and fail so frequently in its immediate and characteristic function? That which is *actually* original in human consciousness, namely *willing*, goes on all the time with perfect success; every being wills incessantly, vigorously, and decidedly. To regard the immoral element in the will as an imperfection of it would be a fundamentally false point of view; on the contrary, morality has a source that really lies beyond nature; hence it is in contradiction with the utterances of nature. For this reason, morality is directly opposed to the natural will, which in itself is absolutely egoistic; in fact, to pursue the path of morality leads to the abolition of the will. On this point I refer to our fourth book and to my essay *On the Basis of Morality*.

5. That the *will* is what is real and essential in man, whereas the *intellect* is only the secondary, the conditioned, and the produced, becomes clear from the fact that the intellect can fulfil its function quite properly and correctly only so long as the will is silent and pauses. On the other hand, the function of the intellect is disturbed by every observable excitement of the will, and its result is falsified by the will's interference; but the converse, namely that the intellect is in a similar manner a hindrance to the will, does not hold. Thus the moon cannot produce any effect when the sun is in the heavens; yet the moon in the heavens does not prevent the sun from shining.

A great *fright* often deprives us of our senses to such an extent that we become petrified, or do the most preposterous things; for example, when a fire has broken out, we run right into the flames. *Anger* makes us no longer know what we do, still less what we say. *Rashness*, for this reason called blind, makes us incapable of carefully considering the arguments of others, or even of picking out and putting in order our own. *Joy* makes us inconsiderate, thoughtless, and foolhardy; *desire* acts in almost the same way. *Fear* prevents us from seeing and seizing the resources that still exist, and are often close at hand. Therefore *equanimity*, *composure*, and *presence of mind* are the most essential qualifications for overcoming sudden dangers, and also for contending with enemies and opponents. Composure consists in the silence of the will, so that the intellect can act; presence of mind consists in the undisturbed activity of the intellect under the pressure of events that act on the will. Therefore composure is the condition of presence of mind, and the two are closely related; they are rare, and exist always only in a limited degree. But they are of inestimable advantage, because they allow of the use of the intellect just at those times when we are most in need of it; and in this way they confer decided superiority. He who does not possess them knows what he ought to have done or said only after the opportunity has passed. It is very appropriately said of him who is violently moved, in other words whose will is so strongly excited as to destroy the purity of the intellect's function, that he is *disarmed*; for the correct knowledge of circumstances and relations is our defence and weapon in the conflict with events and people. In this sense, Balthasar Gracián says: *Es la pasión enemiga declarada de la cordura* (Passion is the declared enemy of prudence). Now if the intellect were not something completely different from the will, but, as has hitherto been supposed, knowing and willing were radically one, and were equally original functions of an absolutely simple substance, then with the rousing and heightening of the will, in which emotion consists, the intellect also would of necessity be heightened. But, as we have seen, it is rather hindered and depressed by this; and for this reason, the ancients called emotion *animi perturbatio*. The intellect is really like the mirror-surface of water, the water itself being like the will; the agitation of the water therefore destroys at once the purity of that mirror and the distinctness of its images. The *organism* is the will itself, embodied will, in other words, *will* objectively perceived in the brain. For this reason many of its functions, such as respiration, blood circulation, bile secretion, and muscular force, are enhanced and accelerated by the pleasant, and generally robust, emotions. The *intellect*, on the other hand, is the mere function of the *brain*, which is nourished and sustained by the organism only parasitically. Therefore every perturbation of the *will*, and with it of the *organism*, must disturb or paralyse the function of the brain, a function existing by itself, and knowing no other needs than simply those of rest and nourishment.

But this disturbing influence of the will's activity on the intellect can be shown not only in the perturbations produced by the emotions, but also in many other more gradual, and therefore more lasting, falsifications of thought through our inclinations and tendencies. *Hope* makes us regard what we desire, and *fear* what we are afraid of, as being probable and near, and both magnify their object. Plato (according to Aelian, *Variae Historiae*, 13, 28) has very finely called *hope* the dream of him who is awake. Its nature lies in the fact that the will, when its servant, the *intellect*, is unable to produce the thing desired, compels this servant at any rate to picture this thing to it, and generally to undertake the role of comforter, to pacify its lord and master, as a nurse does a child, with fairy-tales, and to deck these out so that they obtain an appearance of verisimilitude. Here the intellect is bound to do violence to its own nature, which is aimed at truth, since it is compelled, contrary to its own laws, to regard as true things that are neither true nor probable, and often scarcely possible, merely in order to pacify, soothe, and send to sleep for a while the restless and unmanageable *will*. We clearly see here who is master and who is servant. Indeed, many may have made the observation that, if a matter of importance to them admits of several courses of development, and they have brought all these into one disjunctive judgement that in their opinion is complete, the outcome is nevertheless quite different and wholly unexpected by them. But possibly they will not have noticed that this result was then almost always the one most unfavourable to them. This can be explained from the fact that, while their *intellect* imagined that it surveyed the possibilities completely, the worst of all remained quite invisible to it, because the *will*, so to speak, kept this covered with its hand; in other words, the will so mastered the intellect that it was quite incapable of glancing at the worst case of all, although, this case

was the most probable, since it actually came to pass. However, in decidedly melancholy dispositions, or those which have grown wiser through like experience, the process is indeed reversed, since apprehension and misgiving in them play the part formerly played by hope. The first appearance of a danger puts them into a state of groundless anxiety. If the intellect begins to investigate matters, it is rejected as incompetent, in fact as a deceptive sophist, because the heart is to be believed. The heart's timidity and nervousness are now actually allowed to pass as arguments for the reality and magnitude of the danger. So then the intellect is not at all allowed to look for counter-arguments that it would soon recognize if left to itself, but is forced to picture to them at once the most unfortunate issue, even when it itself can conceive this as scarcely possible:

Such as we know is false, yet dread in sooth,
Because the worst is ever nearest truth.
(Byron, *Lara*, i, 28)

Love and *hatred* entirely falsify our judgement; in our enemies we see nothing but shortcomings, in our favourites nothing but merits and good points, and even their defects seem amiable to us. Our *advantage*, of whatever kind it may be, exercises a similar secret power over our judgement; what is in agreement with it at once seems to us fair, just, and reasonable; what runs counter to it is presented to us in all seriousness as unjust and outrageous, or inexpedient and absurd. Hence so many prejudices of social position, rank, profession, nationality, sect, and religion. A hypothesis, conceived and formed, makes us lynx-eyed for everything that confirms it, and blind to everything that contradicts it. What is opposed to our party, our plan, our wish, or our hope often cannot possibly be grasped and comprehended by us, whereas it is clear to the eyes of everyone else; on the other hand, what is favourable to these leaps to our eyes from afar. What opposes the heart is not admitted by the head. All through life we cling to many errors, and take care never to examine their ground, merely from a fear, of which we ourselves are unconscious, of possibly making the discovery that we have so long and so often believed and maintained what is false. Thus is our intellect daily befooled and corrupted by the deceptions of inclination and liking. This has been finely expressed by Bacon in the following words: *Intellectus LUMINIS SICCI non est; sed recipit infusionem a voluntate et affectibus: id quod generat ad quod vult scientias: quod enim mavult homo, id potius credit. Innumeris modis, iisque interdum imperceptibilibus, affectus intellectum imbuit et inficit* ("The intellect is no *light that would burn dry* (*without oil*), but receives its supply from the will and from the passions; and this produces knowledge according as we desire to have it. For man prefers most of all to believe what he would like to. Passion influences and infects the intellect in innumerable ways that are sometimes imperceptible" [Tr.]) (*Novum Organum*, I, 49). Obviously, it is also this that opposes all new fundamental views in the sciences and all refutations of sanctioned errors; for no one will readily see the correctness of that which convicts him of incredible want of thought. From this alone can be explained the fact that the truths of Goethe's colour theory, so clear and simple, are still denied by the physicists; and thus even he had to learn from experience how much more difficult is the position of one who promises people instruction rather than entertainment. It is therefore much more fortunate to have been born a poet than a philosopher. On the other hand, the more obstinately an error has been held, the more mortifying does the convincing proof subsequently become. With a system that is overthrown, as with a beaten army, the most prudent is he who runs away from it first. [. . .]

The disturbing influence of the will on the intellect, as all these phenomena prove, and, on the other hand, the intellect's frailty and feebleness, by virtue of which it is incapable of operating correctly whenever the will is in any way set in motion, give us yet another proof that the will is the radical part of our real nature, and acts with original force, whereas the intellect, as something adventitious and in many ways conditioned, can act only in a secondary and conditional manner.

There is no immediate disturbance of the will by knowledge, corresponding to the disturbance and clouding of knowledge by the will which has been discussed; in fact, we cannot really form any conception of such a thing. No one will try to explain it by saying that falsely interpreted motives lead the will astray, for this is a fault of the intellect in its own function. This fault is committed purely within the province of the intellect, and its influence on the will is wholly indirect. It would be more plausible to attribute *irresolution* to this, as in its case, through the conflict of the motives presented by the intellect to the will, the latter is brought to a standstill, and is therefore impeded.

But on closer consideration it becomes very clear that the cause of this hindrance is to be sought not in the activity of the *intellect* as such, but simply and solely in the *external objects* brought about by this activity. The objects stand for once precisely in such a relation to the will, which is here interested, that they pull it in different directions with nearly equal force. This real cause acts merely *through* the intellect as the medium of motives, although, of course, only on the assumption that the intellect is keen enough to comprehend the objects and their manifold relations exactly. Indecision as a trait of character is conditioned just as much by qualities of the will as by those of the intellect. It is, of course, not peculiar to extremely limited minds, because their feeble understanding does not enable them to discover so many different qualities and relations in things. Moreover, their understanding is so little fitted for the effort of reflecting on and pondering over those things, and so over the probable consequences of each step, that they prefer to decide at once in accordance with the first impression or some simple rule of conduct. The converse of this occurs in the case of people of considerable understanding. Therefore, whenever these have in addition a tender care for their own well-being, in other words, a very sensitive egoism that certainly does not want to come off too badly and wants to be always safe and secure, this produces at every step a certain uneasiness, and hence indecision. Therefore this quality points in every way to a want not of understanding, but of courage. Yet very eminent minds survey the relations and their probable developments with such rapidity and certainty that, if only they are supported by some courage, they thus acquire that quick peremptoriness and resoluteness which fits them to play an important role in world affairs, provided that times and circumstances afford the opportunity for so doing.

The only decided, direct hindrance and disturbance that the will can suffer from the intellect as such, may indeed be quite exceptional. This is the consequence of an abnormally predominant development of the intellect, and hence of that high endowment described as genius. Such a gift is indeed a decided hindrance to the energy of the character, and consequently to the power of action. Therefore it is not the really great minds that make historical characters, since such characters, capable of bridling and governing the mass of mankind, struggle with world-affairs. On the contrary, men of much less mental capacity are suitable for this, when they have great firmness, resolution, and inflexibility of will, such as cannot exist at all with very high intelligence. Accordingly, with such high intelligence a case actually occurs where the intellect directly impedes the will.

6. In contrast to the obstacles and hindrances mentioned, which the intellect suffers from the will, I wish now to show by a few examples how, conversely, the functions of the intellect are sometimes aided and enhanced by the incentive and spur of the will, so that here also we may recognize the primary nature of the one and the secondary nature of the other, and that it may become clear that the intellect stands to the will in the relation of a tool.

A powerfully acting motive, such as a yearning desire or pressing need, sometimes raises the intellect to a degree of which we had never previously believed it capable. Difficult circumstances, imposing on us the necessity of certain achievements, develop entirely new talents in us, the germs of which had remained hidden from us, and for which we did not credit ourselves with any capacity. The understanding of the stupidest person becomes keen when it is a question of objects that closely concern his willing. He now observes, notices, and distinguishes with great subtlety and refinement even the smallest circumstances that have reference to his desires or fears. This has much to do with that cunning of half-witted persons which is often observed with surprise. For this reason, Isaiah rightly says: *vexatio dat intellectum* ("Vexation bestows intellect," Isa. 28:19, Vulg. [Tr.]), which is therefore also used as a proverb: akin to it is the German proverb "*Die Not ist die Mutter der Künste*" (Necessity is the mother of the arts); the fine arts, however, must form an exception, since the kernel of every one of their works, namely the conception, must result from a perfectly will-less, and only thus a purely objective, perception, if they are to be genuine. Even the understanding of animals is considerably enhanced through necessity, so that in difficult cases they achieve things at which we are astonished. For example, almost all of them reckon that it is safer not to run away when they believe they are not seen; thus the hare lies still in the furrow of the field and lets the hunter pass close to it; if insects cannot escape, they pretend to be dead, and so on. We become more closely acquainted with this influence from the special story of the wolf's self-training under the spur of the great difficulty of its position in civilized Europe, to be found in the second letter of Leroy's excellent book *Lettres sur l'intelligence et la perfectibilité des animaux*. Immediately afterwards, in the third letter, there follows the high school of the fox; in an equally difficult position, he has far less physical strength, but in his case greater understanding compensates for this. Yet this understanding reaches the high degree of cunning, which distinguishes him especially in old age, only through constant struggle with want on the one hand and danger on the other, and thus under the spur of the will. In all these enhancements of the intellect, the will plays the part of the rider urging his horse with the spur beyond the natural measure of its strength.

In just the same way, *memory* is enhanced by pressure of the will. Even when otherwise weak, it preserves completely what is of value to the ruling passion. The lover forgets no opportunity favourable to him, the man of ambition no circumstance that suits his plans, the miser never forgets the loss he has suffered, the proud man never forgets an injury to his honour, the vain person remembers every word of praise and even the smallest distinction that falls to his lot. This also extends to the animals; the horse stops at the inn where it was once fed a long time ago; dogs have an excellent memory for all occasions, times, and places that have afforded them dainty morsels, and foxes for the various hiding-places in which they have stored their plunder. [...]

7. If, as is generally assumed, the will proceeded from knowledge as its result or product, then where there is much will there would necessarily be much knowledge, insight, and understanding. This, however, is by no means the case; on the contrary, we find in many men a strong, i.e., decided, resolute, persistent, inflexible, obstinate, and vehement will associated with a very feeble and incompetent understanding. Thus whoever has dealings with them is reduced to despair, since their will remains inaccessible to all arguments and representations, and is not to be got at, so that it is, so to speak, hidden in a sack out of which it *wills* blindly. Animals have less understanding by far in spite of a will that is often violent and stubborn. Finally, plants have mere will without any knowledge at all.

If willing sprang merely from knowledge, our *anger* would inevitably be exactly proportionate to its cause or occasion in each case, or at any rate to our understanding thereof, since it too would be nothing more than the result of the present knowledge. But it very rarely turns out like this; on the contrary, anger usually goes far beyond the occasion. Our fury and rage, the *furor brevis*, often with trifling occasions and without error in regard to them, are like the storming of an evil demon, which, having been shut up, only waited for the opportunity to dare to break loose, and now rejoices at having found it. This could not be the case if the ground of our true nature were a *knower*, and willing were a mere result of *knowledge*; for how could anything come into the result which did not lie in the elements thereof? The conclusion cannot contain more than is contained in the premises. Thus here also the will shows itself as an essence which is entirely different from knowledge, and makes use of knowledge merely for communication with the outside world. But then it follows the laws of its own nature without taking from knowledge anything more than the occasion.

The intellect, as the will's mere tool, is as different from it as is the hammer from the smith. So long as the intellect alone is active in a conversation, that conversation remains *cold*; it is almost as though the man himself were not there. Moreover, he cannot then really compromise himself, but can at most make himself ridiculous. Only when the will comes into play is the man really present; he now becomes *warm*, in fact matters often become *hot*. It is always the *will* to which we ascribe the warmth of life; on the other hand, we speak of the *cold* understanding, or to investigate a thing *coolly*, in other words, to think without the influence of the will. If we attempt to reverse the relation, and consider the will as the tool of the intellect, it is as if we were to make the smith the tool of the hammer.

Nothing is more tiresome and annoying than when we argue with a person with reasons and explanations, and take all the trouble to convince him, under the impression that we have to deal only with his *understanding*, and then finally discover that he *will* not understand; that we therefore had to deal with his *will*, which pays no heed to the truth, but brings into action wilful misunderstandings, chicaneries, and sophisms, entrenching itself behind its understanding and its supposed want of insight. Then he is of course not to be got at in this way, for *arguments and proofs applied against the will* are like the blows of a concave mirror's phantom against a solid body. Hence the oft-repeated saying: *Stat pro ratione voluntas* ("My will [to do something] is my reason [for doing it]" [Tr.]). Proofs enough of what has

been said are furnished by ordinary, everyday life; but unfortunately they are also to be found on the path of the sciences. Acknowledgement of the most important truths, of the rarest achievements, will be expected in vain from those who have an interest in not allowing them to be accepted. Such an interest springs either from the fact that such truths contradict what they themselves teach every day, or from their not daring to make use of it and afterwards teach it; or, even if all this is not the case, they do not acknowledge such truths, because the watchword of mediocrities will always be: *Si quelqu'un excelle parmi nous, qu'il aille exceller ailleurs* ("If anyone makes his mark among us, let him go and do so elsewhere" [Tr.]), as Helvetius has delightfully rendered the saying of the Ephesians in Cicero (*Tusc.* v, c. 36); or as a saying of the Abyssinian Fit Arari has it: "Among quartzes the diamond is outlawed." Therefore whoever expects from this always numerous band a just appreciation of his achievements will find himself very much deceived; and perhaps for a while he will not be able to understand their behaviour at all, until at last he finds out that, whereas he appealed to *knowledge*, he had to do with the *will*. Thus he finds himself entirely in the position above described; in fact, he is really like the man who brings his case before a court all of whose members are bribed. In individual cases, however, he will obtain the most conclusive proof that he was opposed by their *will* and not by their *insight*, when one or the other of them makes up his mind to plagiarize. He will then see with astonishment what shrewd judges they are, what an accurate judgement they have of the merit of others, and how well they are able to discover the best, like sparrows that never miss the ripest cherries.

The opposite of the will's victorious resistance to knowledge which I here describe, is seen when, in expounding our arguments and proofs, we have on our side the will of the persons addressed. All are then equally convinced, all arguments are striking, and the matter is at once as clear as daylight. Popular speakers know this. In the one case as in the other, the will shows itself as that which has original force, against which the intellect can do nothing. [...]

9. The universally used and generally very well understood expressions *heart* and *head* have sprung from a correct feeling of the fundamental distinction in question. They are therefore significant and to the point, and are found again and again in all languages. *Nec cor nec caput habet*

("He has neither heart nor head" [Tr.]), says Seneca of the Emperor Claudius (*Ludus de morte Claudii Caesaris*, c. 8). The *heart*, that *primum mobile* of animal life, has quite rightly been chosen as the symbol, indeed the synonym, of the *will*, the primary kernel of our phenomenon; and it denotes this in contrast with the *intellect* which is exactly identical with the *head*. All that which is the business of the *will* in the widest sense, such as desire, passion, joy, pain, kindness, goodness, wickedness, and also that which is usually understood by the term *"Gemüt"* (disposition, feeling), and what Homer expresses by φίλον ἦτορ ("the beloved heart" [*Iliad*, V, 250. Tr.]), is attributed to the *heart*. Accordingly, we say: He has a bad heart; his heart is in this business; it comes from his heart; it cut him to the heart; it breaks his heart; his heart bleeds; the heart leaps for joy; who can read a man's heart? it is heart-rending, heart-crushing, heart-breaking, heart-inspiring, heart-stirring; he is good-hearted, hard-hearted; heartless, stout-hearted, faint-hearted, and so on. Quite especially, however, love affairs are called affairs of the heart, *affaires du cœur* ("affairs of the heart" [Tr.]); because the sexual impulse is the focus of the will, and the selection with reference thereto constitutes the principal concern of natural, human willing, the ground of which I shall discuss at length in a chapter supplementary to the fourth book. In *Don Juan* (canto 11, v. 34) Byron is satirical about love being to women an affair of the head instead of an affair of the heart. On the other hand, the *head* denotes everything that is the business of *knowledge*. Hence a man of brains, a good head, a clever head, a fine head, a bad head, to lose one's head, to keep one's head, and so on. Heart and head indicate the whole person. But the head is always the secondary, the derived; for it is not the centre of the body, but its highest efflorescence. When a hero dies, his heart is embalmed, not his brain. On the other hand, we like to preserve the skulls of poets, artists, and philosophers. Thus Raphael's skull was preserved in the Accademia di S. Luca in Rome, though recently it was shown to be not genuine; in 1820 Descartes' skull was sold by auction in Stockholm.

A certain feeling of the true relation between will, intellect, and life is also expressed in the Latin language. The intellect is *mens*, νοῦς; the will, on the other hand, is *animus*, which comes from *anima*, and this from ἄνεμος. *Anima* is life itself, the breath, ψυχή; but *animus* is the life-giving principle and at the same time the will, the subject of inclinations, likings, purposes, passions, and emotions; hence also *est mihi animus, fert animus*, for "I feel inclined to," "I should like to," as well as *animi causa*, and so on; it is the Greek θυμός, the German *Gemüt*, and thus heart, not head. *Animi perturbatio* is emotion; *mentis perturbatio* would signify madness or craziness. The predicate *immortalis* is attributed to *animus*, not to *mens*. All this is the rule based on the great majority of passages, although, with concepts so closely related, it is bound to happen that the words are sometimes confused. By ψυχή the Greeks appear primarily and originally to have understood the vital force, the life-giving principle. In this way there at once arose the divination that it must be something metaphysical, consequently something that would not be touched by death. This is proved, among other things, by the investigations of the relation between νοῦς and ψυχή preserved by Stobaeus (*Eclogues*, Bk. I, c. 51, §§ 7, 8).

10. On what does the *identity of the person* depend? Not on the matter of the body; this becomes different after a few years. Not on the form of the body, which changes as a whole and in all its parts, except in the expression of the glance, by which we still recognize a man even after many years. This proves that, in spite of all the changes produced in him by time, there yet remains in him something wholly untouched by it. It is just this by which we recognize him once more, even after the longest intervals of time, and again find the former person unimpaired. It is the same with ourselves, for, however old we become, we yet feel within ourselves that we are absolutely the same as we were when we were young, indeed when we were still children. This thing which is unaltered and always remains absolutely the same, which does not grow old with us, is just the kernel of our inner nature, and that does not lie in time. It is assumed that the identity of the person rests on that of consciousness. If, however, we understand by this merely the continuous recollection of the course of life, then it is not enough. We know, it is true, something more of the course of our life than of a novel we have formerly read, yet only very little indeed. The principal events, the interesting scenes, have been impressed on us; for the rest, a thousand events are forgotten for one that has been retained. The older we become, the more does everything pass us by without leaving a trace. Great age, illness, injury to the brain, madness, can deprive a man entirely of memory, but the identity of his person has not in this way been

lost. That rests on the identical *will* and on its unalterable character; it is also just this that makes the expression of the glance unalterable. In the *heart* is the man to be found, not in the head. It is true that, in consequence of our relation to the external world, we are accustomed to regard the subject of knowing, the knowing I, as our real self which becomes tired in the evening, vanishes in sleep, and in the morning shines more brightly with renewed strength. This, however, is the mere function of the brain, and is not our real self. Our true self, the kernel of our inner nature, is that which is to be found behind this, and which really knows nothing but willing and not-willing, being contented and not contented, with all the modifications of the thing called feelings, emotions, and passions. This it is which produces that other thing, which does not sleep with it when it sleeps, which also remains unimpaired when that other thing becomes extinct in death. On the other hand, everything related to *knowledge* is exposed to oblivion; even actions of moral significance sometimes cannot be completely recalled by us years after, and we no longer know exactly and in detail how we behaved in a critical case. The *character itself*, however, to which the deeds merely testify, we cannot forget; it is still exactly the same now as then. The will itself, alone and by itself, endures; for it alone is unchangeable, indestructible, does not grow old, is not physical but metaphysical, does not belong to the phenomenal appearance, but to the thing itself that appears. How the identity of consciousness, so far as it goes, depends on the will, I have already shown in chapter 15; therefore I need not dwell on it here.

11. Incidentally, Aristotle says in the book on the comparison of the desirable: "To live well is better than to live" (βέλτιον τοῦ ζῆν τὸ εὖ ζῆν, *Topica*, iii, 2). From this it might be inferred, by twofold contraposition, that not to live is better than to live badly. This is evident to the intellect; yet the great majority live very badly rather than not at all. Therefore this attachment to life cannot have its ground in its own *object*, for life, as was shown in the fourth book, is really a constant suffering, or at any rate, as will be shown later in chapter 28, a business that does not cover the cost; hence that attachment can be founded only in its own *subject*. But it is not founded in the *intellect*, it is not result of reflection, and generally is not a matter of choice; on the contrary, this willing of life is something that is taken for granted; it is a *prius* of the *intellect* itself. We ourselves are the will-to-live; hence we must live, well or badly. Only from the fact that this attachment or clinging to a life so little worthy of it is entirely *a priori* and not *a posteriori*, can we explain the excessive fear of death inherent in every living thing. La Rochefoucauld expressed this fear with rare frankness and naivety in his last reflection; on it ultimately rests the effectiveness of all tragedies and heroic deeds. Such effectiveness would be lost if we assessed life only according to its objective worth. On this inexpressible *horror mortis* rests also the favourite principle of all ordinary minds that whoever takes his own life must be insane; yet no less is the astonishment, mingled with a certain admiration, which this action always provokes even in thinking minds, since such action is so much opposed to the nature of every living thing that in a certain sense we are forced to admire the man who is able to perform it. Indeed, we even find a certain consolation in the fact that, in the worst cases, this way out is actually open to us, and we might doubt it if it were not confirmed by experience. For suicide comes from a resolve of the intellect, but our willing of life is a *prius* of the intellect. Therefore this consideration, that will be discussed in detail in chapter 28, also confirms the primacy of the *will* in self-consciousness.

12. On the other hand, nothing more clearly demonstrates the *intellect's* secondary, dependent, and conditioned nature than its periodical intermission. In deep sleep all knowing and forming of representations entirely ceases; but the kernel of our true being, its metaphysical part, necessarily presupposed by the organic functions as their *primum mobile*, never dares to pause, if life is not to cease; moreover, as something metaphysical, and consequently incorporeal, it needs no rest. Therefore the philosophers who set up a *soul*, i.e., an originally and essentially *knowing* being, as this metaphysical kernel, saw themselves forced to the assertion that this soul is quite untiring in its representing and knowing, and consequently continues these even in the deepest sleep; only after waking up we are left with no recollection of this. However, the falsity of this assertion was easy to see, as soon as that *soul* had been set aside in consequence of Kant's teaching. For sleep and waking show the unprejudiced mind in the clearest manner that knowing is a secondary function, and is conditioned by the organism, just as is any other function. The *heart* alone is untiring, because its beating and the circulation of the blood are not conditioned directly by the nerves, but are just the

original expression of the will. All other physiological functions, governed merely by the ganglionic nerves that have only a very indirect and remote connexion with the brain, also continue in sleep, although the secretions take place more slowly. Even the beating of the heart, on account of its dependence on respiration which is conditioned by the cerebral system (*medulla oblongata*), becomes a little slower with this. The stomach is perhaps most active in sleep; this is to be ascribed to its special consensus with the brain that is now resting from its labours, such consensus causing mutual disturbances. The *brain* alone, and with it knowledge, pause completely in deep sleep; for it is merely the ministry of foreign affairs, just as the ganglionic system is the ministry of home affairs. The brain with its function of knowing is nothing more than a *guard* mounted by the will for its aims and ends that lie outside. Up in the watch-tower of the head this guard looks round through the windows of the senses, and watches the point from which mischief threatens and advantage is to be observed, and the will decides in accordance with its report. This *guard*, like everyone engaged on active service, is in a state of close attention and exertion, and therefore is glad when it is again relieved after discharging its duties of watching, just as every sentry likes to be withdrawn from his post. This withdrawal is falling asleep, which for that reason is so sweet and agreeable, and to which we are so ready to yield. On the other hand, being roused from sleep is unwelcome, because it suddenly recalls the *guard* to its post. Here we feel generally the reappearance of the hard and difficult diastole after the beneficent systole, the separation once more of the intellect from the will. On the other hand, a so-called *soul* that was originally and radically a *knowing* being would of necessity on waking up feel like a fish put back into water. In sleep, where only the vegetative life is carried on, the will alone operates according to its original and essential nature, undisturbed from outside, with no deduction from its force through activity of the brain and the exertion of knowing. Knowledge is the heaviest organic function, but is for the organism merely a means, not an end; therefore in sleep the whole force of the will is directed to the maintenance, and where necessary to the repair, of the organism. For this reason, all healing, all salutary and wholesome crises, take place in sleep, since the *vis naturae medicatrix* ("the healing power of nature" [Tr.]) has free play only when it is relieved of the burden of the function of knowledge. Therefore the embryo, that still has to form the body, sleeps continuously, and so for the greatest part of its time does the newborn child. In this sense Burdach (*Physiologie*, vol. III, p. 484) quite rightly declares sleep to be the *original state*.

With regard to the brain itself, I account in more detail for the necessity of sleep through a hypothesis that appears to have been advanced first in Neumann's book *Von den Krankheiten des Menschen*, 1834, vol. IV, § 216. This is that the nutrition of the brain, and hence the renewal of its substance from the blood, cannot take place while we are awake, since the highly eminent, organic function of knowing and thinking would be disturbed and abolished by the function of nutrition, low and material as it is. By this is explained the fact that sleep is not a purely negative state, a mere pausing of the brain's activity, but exhibits at the same time a positive character. This is seen from the fact that between sleep and waking there is no mere difference of degree, but a fixed boundary which, as soon as sleep intervenes, declares itself through dream-apparitions that are completely heterogeneous from our immediately preceding thoughts. A further proof of this is that, when we have dreams that frighten us, we try in vain to cry out, or to ward off attacks, or to shake off sleep, so that it is as if the connecting link between the brain and the motor nerves, or between the cerebrum and the cerebellum (as the regulator of movements), were abolished; for the brain remains in its isolation, and sleep holds us firmly as with brazen claws. Finally, the positive character of sleep is seen in the fact that a certain degree of strength is required for sleeping; therefore too much fatigue as well as natural weakness prevent us from seizing it, *capere somnum*. This can be explained from the fact that the *process of nutrition* must be introduced if sleep is to ensue; the brain must, so to speak, begin to take nourishment. Moreover, the increased flow of blood into the brain during sleep can be explained by the process of nutrition, as also the instinctively assumed position of the arms, which are laid together above the head because it promotes this process. This is also why children require a great deal of sleep, as long as the brain is still growing; whereas in old age, when a certain atrophy of the brain, as of all parts, occurs, sleep becomes scanty; and finally why excessive sleep produces a certain dullness of consciousness, in consequence of a temporary hypertrophy of the brain, which, in the case of habitual excess of sleep, can become permanent and produce imbecility: ἀνίη καὶ πολὺς ὕπνος (noxae est etiam multus somnus "Even copious sleep is a burden and a misery" [Tr.]). [Odyssey, 15, 394.] The need for sleep is accordingly directly proportional to the intensity of the brain-life, and thus to clearness of consciousness. Those animals whose brain-life is feeble and dull, reptiles and fishes for instance, sleep little and lightly. Here I remind the reader that the winter-sleep is a sleep almost in name only, since it is not an inactivity of the brain alone, but of the whole organism, and so a kind of suspended animation. Animals of considerable intelligence sleep soundly and long. Even human beings require more sleep the more developed, as regards quantity and quality, and the more active their brain is. Montaigne relates of himself that he had always been a heavy sleeper; that he had spent a large part of his life in sleeping; and that at an advanced age he still slept from eight to nine hours at a stretch (Bk. iii, ch. 13). It is also reported of Descartes that he slept a great deal (Baillet, Vie de Descartes (1693), p. 288). Kant allowed himself seven hours for sleep, but it became so difficult for him to manage with this that he ordered his servant to force him, against his will and without listening to his remonstrances, to get up at a fixed time (Jachmann, Immanuel Kant, p. 162). For the more completely awake a man is, in other words the clearer and more wide-awake his consciousness, the greater is his necessity for sleep, and thus the more soundly and longer he sleeps. Accordingly, much thinking or strenuous head-work will increase the need for sleep. That sustained muscular exertion also makes us sleepy can be explained from the fact that in such exertion the brain, by means of the medulla oblongata, the spinal marrow, and the motor nerves, continuously imparts to the muscles the stimulus affecting their irritability, and in this way its strength is exhausted. Accordingly the fatigue we feel in our arms and legs has its real seat in the brain, just as the pain felt in these parts is really experienced in the brain; for the brain is connected with the motor nerves just as it is with the nerves of sense. The muscles not actuated by the brain, e.g., those of the heart, therefore do not become tired. From the same reason we can explain why we cannot think acutely either during or after great muscular exertion. That we have far less mental energy in summer than in winter is partly explained by the fact that in summer we sleep less; for the more soundly we have slept, the more

completely wakeful, the more wide awake are we afterwards. But this must not lead us astray into lengthening our sleep unduly, since it then loses in intension, in other words, in depth and in soundness, what it gains in extension, and thus it becomes a mere waste of time. Goethe means this when he says (in the second part of Faust) of morning slumber: "Sleep's a shell, to break and spurn!" In general, therefore, the phenomenon of sleep most admirably confirms that consciousness, apprehension, perception, knowing, and thinking are not something original in us, but a conditioned, secondary state. It is a luxury of nature, and indeed her highest, which she is therefore the less able to continue without interruption, the higher the pitch to which it has been brought. It is the product, the efflorescence, of the cerebral nerve-system, which is itself nourished like a parasite by the rest of the organism. This is also connected with what is shown in our third book, that knowing is the purer and more perfect the more it has freed and severed itself from willing, whereby the purely objective, the aesthetic apprehension appears. In just the same way, an extract is so much the purer, the more it has been separated from that from which it has been extracted, and the more it has been refined and clarified of all sediment. The contrast is shown by the will, whose most immediate manifestation is the whole organic life, and primarily the untiring heart. [...]

On Death and Its Relation to the Indestructibility of Our Inner Nature

Death is the real inspiring genius or Musagetes of philosophy, and for this reason Socrates defined philosophy as θανάτου μελέτη ("preparation for death" [Tr.]). Indeed, without death there would hardly have been any philosophizing. It will therefore be quite in order for a special consideration of this subject to have its place here at the beginning of the last, most serious, and most important of our books.

The animal lives without any real knowledge of death; therefore the individual animal immediately enjoys the absolute imperishableness and immortality of the species, since it is conscious of itself only as endless. With man the terrifying certainty of death necessarily appeared along with the faculty of reason. But just as everywhere in nature a remedy, or at any rate a compensation, is given for every evil, so the same reflection that introduced the knowledge of death also assists us in obtaining *metaphysical* points of view. Such views console us concerning death, and the animal is neither in need of nor capable of them. All religions and philosophical systems are directed principally to this end, and are thus primarily the antidote to the certainty of death which reflecting reason produces from its own resources. The degree in which they attain this end is, however, very different, and *one* religion or philosophy will certainly enable man, far more than the others will, to look death calmly in the face. Brahmanism and Buddhism, which teach man to regard himself as Brahman, as the original being himself, to whom all arising and passing away are essentially foreign, will achieve much more in this respect than will those religions that represent man as being made out of nothing and as actually beginning at his birth the existence he has received from another. In keeping with this we find in India a confidence and a contempt for death of which we in Europe have no conception. It is indeed a ticklish business to force on man through early impression weak and untenable notions in this important respect, and thus to render him for ever incapable of adopting more correct and stable views. For example, to teach him that he came but recently from nothing, that consequently he has been nothing throughout an eternity, and yet for the future is to be imperishable and immortal, is just like teaching him that, although he is through and through the work of another, he shall nevertheless be responsible to all eternity for his commissions and omissions. Thus if with a mature mind and with the appearance of reflection the untenable nature of such doctrines forces itself on him, he has nothing better to put in their place; in fact, he is no longer capable of understanding anything better, and in this way is deprived of the consolation that nature had provided for him as compensation for the certainty of death. In consequence of such a development, we now (1844) see in England the Socialists among the demoralized and corrupted factory workers, and in Germany the young Hegelians among the demoralized and corrupted students, sink to the absolutely physical viewpoint. This leads to the result: *edite, bibite, post mortem nulla voluptas* ("Eat and drink, after death there is no more rejoicing" [Tr.]), and to this extent can be described as bestiality.

According, however, to all that has been taught about death, it cannot be denied that, at any rate in Europe, the opinion of men, often in fact even of the same individual, very frequently vacillates afresh between the conception of death as absolute annihilation and the assumption that we are, so to speak with skin and hair, immortal. Both are equally false, but we have not so much to find a correct mean as rather to gain the higher standpoint from which such views disappear of themselves.

With these considerations, I wish to start first of all from the entirely empirical viewpoint. Here we have primarily before us the undeniable fact that, according to natural consciousness, man not only fears death for his own person more than anything else, but also weeps violently over the death of his friends and relations. It is evident, indeed, that he does this not egoistically over his own loss, but out of sympathy for the great misfortune that has befallen them. He therefore censures as hardhearted and unfeeling those who in such a case do not weep and show no grief. Parallel with this is the fact that, in its highest degrees, the thirst for revenge seeks the death of the adversary as the greatest evil that can be inflicted on him. Opinions change according to time and place, but the voice of nature remains always and everywhere the same, and is therefore to be heeded before everything else. Now here it seems clearly to assert that death is a great evil. In the language of nature, *death* signifies annihilation; and that death is a serious matter could already be inferred from the fact that, as everyone knows, life is no joke. Indeed we must not deserve anything better than these two.

The fear of death is, in fact, independent of all knowledge, for the animal has it, although it does not know death. Everything that is born already brings this fear into the world. Such fear of death, however, is *a priori* only the reverse side of the will-to-live, which indeed we all are. Therefore in every animal the fear of its own destruction, like the care for its maintenance, is inborn. Thus it is this fear of death, and not the mere avoidance of pain, that shows itself in the anxious care and caution with which the animal seeks to protect itself, and still more its brood, from everyone who might become dangerous. Why does the animal flee, tremble, and try to conceal itself? Because it is simply the will-to-live, but as such it is forfeit to death and would like to gain time. By nature man is just the same. The greatest of evils, the worst thing that can threaten anywhere, is death; the greatest anxiety is the anxiety of death. Nothing excites us so irresistibly to the most lively interest as does danger to the lives of others; nothing is more dreadful than an execution. Now the boundless attachment to life which appears here cannot have sprung from knowledge and reflection. To these, on the contrary, it appears foolish, for the objective value of life is very uncertain, and it remains at least doubtful whether existence is to be preferred to non-existence; in fact, if experience and reflection have their say, non-existence must certainly win. If we knocked on the graves and asked the dead whether they would like to rise again, they would shake their heads. In Plato's *Apology* this is also the opinion of Socrates, and even the cheerful and amiable Voltaire cannot help saying: *On aime la vie; mais le néant ne laisse pas d'avoir du bon*: and again: *Je ne sais pas ce que c'est que la vie éternelle, mais celle-ci est une mauvaise plaisanterie* ("We like life, but all the same nothingness also has its good points.... I do not know what eternal life is, but this present life is a bad joke" [Tr.]). Moreover, in any case life must end soon, so that the few years which possibly we have still to exist vanish entirely before the endless time when we shall be no more. Accordingly, to reflection it appears even ludicrous for us to be so very anxious about this span of time, to tremble so much when our own life or another's is endangered, and to write tragedies whose terrible aspect has as its main theme merely the fear of death. Consequently, this powerful attachment to life is irrational and blind; it can be explained only from the fact that our whole being-in-itself is the will-to-live, to which life therefore must appear as the highest good, however embittered, short, and uncertain it may be; and that that will is originally and in itself without knowledge and blind. Knowledge, on the contrary, far from being the origin of that attachment to life, even opposes it, since it discloses life's worthlessness, and in this way combats the fear of death. When it is victorious, and man accordingly faces death courageously and calmly, this is honoured as great and noble. Therefore we then extol the triumph of knowledge over the blind will-to-live which is nevertheless the kernel of our own inner being. In the same way we despise him in whom knowledge is defeated in that conflict, who therefore clings unconditionally to life, struggles to the utmost against approaching death, and receives it with despair; yet in him is expressed only the original inner being of our own self and of nature. Incidentally, it may here be asked how the boundless love of life and the endeavour to maintain it in every way as long as possible could be regarded as base and contemptible, and likewise considered by the followers of every religion as unworthy thereof, if life were the gift of the good gods to be acknowledged with thanks. How then could it appear great and noble to treat it with contempt? Meanwhile, these considerations confirm for us: (1) that the will-to-live is the innermost essence of man; (2) that in itself the will is without knowledge and blind; (3) that knowledge is an adventitious principle, originally foreign to the will; (4) that knowledge conflicts with the will, and our judgement applauds the triumph of knowledge over the will.

If what makes death seem so terrible to us were the thought of *non-existence*, we should necessarily think with equal horror of the time when as yet we did not exist. For it is irrefutably certain that non-existence after death cannot be different from non-existence before birth, and is therefore no more deplorable than that is. An entire infinity ran its course when we did *not yet* exist, but this in no way disturbs us. On the other hand, we find it hard, and even unendurable, that after the momentary intermezzo of an ephemeral existence, a second infinity should follow in which we shall exist *no longer*. Now could this thirst for existence possibly have arisen through our having tasted it and found it so very delightful? As was briefly set forth above, certainly not; the experience gained would far rather have been capable of causing an infinite longing for the lost paradise of non-existence. To the hope of immortality of the soul there is always added that of a "better world"; an indication that the present world is not worth much. Notwithstanding all this, the question of our state after death has certainly been discussed verbally and in books ten thousand times more often than that of our state before birth. Theoretically, however, the one is a problem just as near at hand and just as legitimate as the other; moreover, he who answered the one would likewise be fully enlightened about the other. We have fine declamations about how shocking it would be to think that the mind of man, which embraces the world and has so many excellent ideas, should sink with him into the grave; but we hear nothing about this mind having allowed a whole infinity of time to elapse before it arose with these its qualities, and how for just as long a time the world had to manage without it. Yet to knowledge uncorrupted by the will no question presents itself more naturally than this, namely: An infinite time has run its course before my birth; what was I throughout all that time? Metaphysically, the answer might perhaps be: "I was always I; that is, all who throughout that time said I, were just I." But let us turn away from this to our present entirely empirical point of view, and assume that I did not exist at all. But I can then console myself for the infinite time after my death when I shall not exist, with the infinite time when I did not as yet exist, as a quite customary and really very comfortable state. For the infinity *a parte post* without me cannot be any more fearful than the infinity *a parte ante* ("after life"; "before life" [Tr.]) without me, since the two are not distinguished by anything except by the intervention of an ephemeral life-dream. All proofs of continued existence after death may also be applied just as well *in partem ante*, where they then demonstrate existence before life, in assuming which the Hindus and Buddhists therefore show themselves to be very consistent. Only Kant's ideality of time solves all these riddles; but we are not discussing this at the moment. But this much follows from what has been said, namely that to mourn for the time when we shall no longer exist is just as absurd as it would be to mourn for the time when we did not as yet exist; for it is all the same whether the time our existence does not fill is related to that which it does fill as future or as past.

But quite apart even from these considerations of time, it is in and by itself absurd to regard non-existence as an evil; for every evil, like every good, presupposes existence, indeed even consciousness. But this ceases with life, as well as in sleep and in a fainting fit; therefore the absence of consciousness is well known and familiar to us as a state containing no evil at all; in any case, its occurrence is a matter of a moment. Epicurus considered death from this point of view, and therefore said quite rightly: ὁ θάνατος μηδὲν πρὸς ἡμᾶς (Death does not concern us), with the explanation that when we are, death is not, and when death is, we are not (Diogenes Laërtius, x, 27). To have lost what cannot be missed is obviously no evil; therefore we ought to be just as little disturbed by the fact that we shall not exist as by the fact that we did not exist. Accordingly, from the standpoint of knowledge, there appears to be absolutely no ground for fearing death; but consciousness consists in knowing, and thus for consciousness death is no evil. Moreover, it is not really this *knowing* part of our *ego* that fears death, but *fuga mortis* comes simply and solely from the blind *will*, with which every living thing is filled. But, as already mentioned, this *fuga mortis* is essential to it, just because it is the will-to-live, whose whole inner nature consists in a craving for life and existence. Knowledge is not originally inherent in it, but appears only in consequence of the will's objectification in animal individuals. Now if by means of knowledge the will beholds death as the end of the phenomenon with which it has identified itself, and to which it therefore sees itself limited, its whole nature struggles against this with all its might. We shall investigate later on whether it really has anything to fear from death, and shall then remember the real source of the fear of death which is indicated here with a proper distinction between the willing and knowing part of our true nature.

According to this, what makes death so terrible for us is not so much the end of life – for this cannot seem to anyone specially worthy of regret – as the destruction of the organism, really because this organism is the will itself manifested as body. But actually, we feel this destruction only in the evils of illness or of old age; on the other hand, for the *subject*, death itself consists merely in the moment when consciousness vanishes, since the activity of the brain ceases. The extension of the stoppage to all the other parts of the organism which follows this is really already an event after death. Therefore, in a subjective respect, death concerns only consciousness. Now from going to sleep everyone can, to some extent, judge what the vanishing of consciousness may be; and whoever has had a real fainting fit knows it even better. The transition here is not so gradual, nor is it brought about by dreams; but first of all, while we are still fully conscious, the power of sight disappears, and then immediately supervenes the deepest unconsciousness. As far as the accompanying sensation goes, it is anything but unpleasant; and undoubtedly just as sleep is the brother of death, so is the fainting fit its twin-brother. Violent death also cannot be painful, for, as a rule, even severe wounds are not felt at all till some time afterwards, and are often noticed only from their external symptoms. If they are rapidly fatal, consciousness will vanish before this discovery; if they result in death later, it is the same as with other illnesses. All who have lost consciousness in water, through charcoal fumes, or through hanging, also state, as is well known, that it happened without pain. And finally, even death through natural causes proper, death through old age, euthanasia, is a gradual vanishing and passing out of existence in an imperceptible manner. In old age, passions and desires, together with the susceptibility to their objects, are gradually extinguished; the emotions no longer find any excitement, for the power to make representations or mental pictures becomes weaker and weaker, and its images feebler. The impressions no longer stick to us, but pass away without a trace; the days roll by faster and faster; events lose their significance; everything grows pale. The old man, stricken in years, totters about or rests in a corner, now only a shadow, a ghost, of his former self. What still remains there for death to destroy? One day a slumber is his last, and his dreams are ———. They are the dreams that Hamlet asks about in the famous monologue. I believe that we dream them just now.

I have still to observe that, although the maintenance of the life-process has a metaphysical basis, it does not take place without resistance, and hence without effort. It is this to which the organism yields every evening, for which reason it then suspends the brain-function, and diminishes certain secretions, respiration, pulse, and the development of heat. From this it may be concluded that the entire cessation of the life-process must be a wonderful relief for its driving force. Perhaps this is partly responsible for the expression of sweet contentment on the faces of most of the dead. In general, the moment of dying may be similar to that of waking from a heavy nightmare.

So far, the result for us is that death cannot really be an evil, however much it is feared, but that it often appears even as a good thing, as something desired, as a friend. All who have encountered insuperable obstacles to their existence or to their efforts, who suffer from incurable disease or from inconsolable grief, have the return into the womb of nature as the last resource that is often open to them as a matter of course. Like everything else, they emerged from this womb for a short time, enticed by the hope of more favourable conditions of existence than those that have fallen to their lot, and from this the same path always remains open to them. That return is the *cessio bonorum* ("surrender of property" [Tr.]) of the living. Yet even here it is entered into only after a physical or moral conflict, so hard does everyone struggle against returning to the place from which he came forth so readily and willingly to an existence that has so many sorrows and so few joys to offer. To Yama, the god of death, the Hindus give two faces, one very fearful and terrible, one very cheerful and benevolent. This is

already explained in part from the observations we have just made.

From the empirical standpoint, at which we are still placed, the following consideration is one which presents itself automatically, and therefore merits being defined accurately by elucidation, and thus kept within its limits. The sight of a corpse shows me that sensibility, irritability, blood circulation, reproduction, and so on in it have ceased. From this I conclude with certainty that that which previously actuated them, which was nevertheless something always unknown to me, now actuates them no longer, and so has departed from them. But if I now wished to add that this must have been just what I have known only as consciousness, and consequently as intelligence (soul), this would be a conclusion not merely unjustified, but obviously false. For consciousness has always shown itself to me not as the cause, but as a product and result of organic life, since it rose and sank in consequence thereof at the different periods of life, in health and sickness, in sleep, in a faint, in awaking, and so on. Thus it always appeared as the effect, never as a cause, of organic life, always showed itself as something arising and passing away and again arising, so long as the conditions for this still exist, but not apart from them. Indeed, I may also have seen that the complete derangement of consciousness, madness, far from dragging down with it and depressing the other forces, or even endangering life, greatly enhances these, especially irritability or muscular force, and lengthens rather than shortens life, if there are no other competing causes. Then I knew individuality as a quality or attribute of everything organic, and when this was a self-conscious organism, of consciousness also. But there exists no occasion for concluding now that individuality is inherent in that vanished principle which imparts life and is wholly unknown to me; the less so, as everywhere in nature I see each particular phenomenon to be the work of a universal force active in thousands of similar phenomena. But on the other hand there is just as little occasion for concluding that, because organized life has here ceased, the force that actuated it hitherto has also become nothing; just as little as there is to infer from the stopping of the spinning-wheel the death of the spinner. If, by finding its centre of gravity again, a pendulum finally comes to rest, and thus its individual apparent life has ceased, no one will suppose that gravitation is annihilated, but everyone sees that now as always it is active in innumerable phenomena. Of course, it might be objected to this comparison that even in the pendulum gravitation has not ceased to be active, but has merely given up manifesting its activity visibly. He who insists on this may think, instead, of an electrical body in which, after its discharge, electricity has really ceased to be active. I wished only to show by this that we directly attribute an eternity and ubiquity even to the lowest forces of nature; and the transitoriness of their fleeting phenomena does not for a moment confuse us with regard thereto. So much the less, therefore, should it occur to us to regard the cessation of life as the annihilation of the living principle, and thus death as the entire destruction of man. Because the strong arm that three thousand years ago bent the bow of Ulysses no longer exists, no reflective and well-regulated understanding will look upon the force that acted so energetically in it as entirely annihilated. Therefore, on further reflection, it will not be assumed that the force that bends the bow today, first began to exist with that arm. Much nearer to us is the idea that the force that formerly actuated a life now vanished is the same force that is active in the life now flourishing; indeed this thought is almost inevitable. However, we certainly know that, as was explained in the second book, only that is perishable which is involved in the causal chain; but merely the states and forms are so involved. Untouched, however, by the change of these, which is produced by causes, there remain matter on the one hand, and the natural forces on the other; for both are the presupposition of all those changes. But the principle that gives us life must first be conceived at any rate as a force of nature, until a profounder investigation may perhaps let us know what it is in itself. Thus, taken already as a force of nature, vital force remains entirely untouched by the change of forms and states, which the bond of cause and effect introduces and carries off again, and which alone are subject to arising and passing away, just as these processes lie before us in experience. To this extent, therefore, the imperishableness of our true inner nature could already be certainly demonstrated. But this, of course, will not satisfy the claims usually made on proofs of our continued existence after death, nor will it afford the consolation expected from such proofs. Yet it is always something, and whoever fears death as his absolute annihilation cannot afford to disdain the perfect certainty that the innermost principle of his life remains untouched by it. In fact, we might ad-

vance the paradox that that second thing which, like the forces of nature, remains untouched by the continuous change of states under the guidance of causality, i.e., matter, also assures us through its absolute permanence of an indestructibility; and by virtue of this, he who might be incapable of grasping any other could yet be confident of a certain imperishability. But it will be asked: "How is the permanence of mere dust, of crude matter, to be regarded as a continuance of our true inner nature?" Oh! do you know this dust then? Do you know what it is and what it can do? Learn to know it before you despise it. This matter, now lying there as dust and ashes, will soon form into crystals when dissolved in water; it will shine as metal; it will then emit electric sparks. By means of its galvanic tension it will manifest a force which, decomposing the strongest and firmest combinations, reduces earths to metals. It will, indeed of its own accord, form itself into plant and animal; and from its mysterious womb it will develop that life, about the loss of which you in your narrowness of mind are so nervous and anxious. Is it, then, so absolutely and entirely nothing to continue to exist as such matter? Indeed, I seriously assert that even this permanence of matter affords evidence of the indestructibility of our true inner being, although only as in an image and simile, or rather only as in a shadowy outline. To see this, we need only recall the discussion on matter given in chapter 24, the conclusion of which was that mere formless matter – this basis of the world of experience, never perceived by itself alone, but assumed as always permanent – is the immediate reflection, the visibility in general, of the thing-in-itself, that is, of the will. Therefore, what absolutely pertains to the will in itself holds good of matter under the conditions of experience, and it reproduces the true eternity of the will under the image of temporal imperishability. Because, as we have already said, nature does not lie, no view which has sprung from a purely objective comprehension of her, and has been logically thought out, can be absolutely and entirely false; in the worst case it is only very one-sided and imperfect. But such a view is unquestionably consistent materialism, for instance that of Epicurus, just as is the absolute idealism opposed to it, like that of Berkeley, and generally every fundamental view of philosophy which has come from a correct *aperçu* and has been honestly worked out. Only they are all extremely one-sided interpretations, and therefore, in spite of their contrasts, are *simultaneously* true, each from a definite point of view. But as soon as we rise above this point, they appear to be true only relatively and conditionally. The highest standpoint alone, from which we survey them all and recognize them in their merely relative truth, and also beyond this in their falseness, can be that of absolute truth, in so far as such a truth is in general attainable. Accordingly, as was shown above, we see even in the really very crude, and therefore very old, fundamental view of materialism the indestructibility of our true inner being-in-itself still represented as by a mere shadow of it, namely through the imperishability of matter; just as in the already higher naturalism of an absolute physics we see it represented by the ubiquity and eternity of natural forces, among which vital force is at least to be reckoned. Hence even these crude fundamental views contain the assertion that the living being does not suffer any absolute annihilation through death, but continues to exist in and with the whole of nature.

The considerations which have brought us to this point, and with which the further discussions are connected, started from the remarkable fear of death which affects all living beings. But now we wish to alter the point of view, and to consider how, in contrast to individual beings, the *whole* of nature behaves with regard to death; yet here we still remain always on the ground and soil of the empirical.

We know, of course, of no higher gamble than that for life and death. We watch with the utmost attention, interest, and fear every decision concerning them; for in our view all in all is at stake. On the other hand, *nature*, which never lies, but is always frank and sincere, speaks quite differently on this theme, as Krishna does in the *Bhagavadgita*. Her statement is that the life or death of the individual is of absolutely no consequence. She expresses this by abandoning the life of every animal, and even of man, to the most insignificant accidents without coming to the rescue. Consider the insect on your path; a slight unconscious turning of your foot is decisive as to its life or death. Look at the wood-snail that has no means of flight, of defence, of practising deception, of concealment, a ready prey to all. Look at the fish carelessly playing in the still open net; at the frog prevented by its laziness from the flight that could save it; at the bird unaware of the falcon soaring above it; at the sheep eyed and examined from the thicket by the wolf. Endowed with little caution, all these go about guilelessly among the dangers which at every moment threaten their existence. Now, since nature abandons without reserve her organisms constructed with such inexpressible skill, not only to the predatory instinct of the stronger, but also to the blindest chance, the whim of every fool, and the mischievousness of every child, she expresses that the annihilation of these individuals is a matter of indifference to her, does her no harm, is of no significance at all, and that in these cases the effect is of no more consequence than is the cause. Nature states this very clearly, and she never lies; only she does not comment on her utterances, but rather expresses them in the laconic style of the oracle. Now if the universal mother carelessly sends forth her children without protection to a thousand threatening dangers, this can be only because she knows that, when they fall, they fall back into her womb, where they are safe and secure; therefore their fall is only a jest. With man she does not act otherwise than she does with the animals; hence her declaration extends also to him; the life or death of the individual is a matter of indifference to her. Consequently, they should be, in a certain sense, a matter of indifference to us; for in fact, we ourselves are nature. If only we saw deeply enough, we should certainly agree with nature, and regard life or death as indifferently as does she. Meanwhile, by means of reflection, we must attribute nature's careless and indifferent attitude concerning the life of individuals to the fact that the destruction of such a phenomenon does not in the least disturb its true and real inner being.

As we have just been considering, not only are life and death dependent on the most trifling accidents, but the existence of organic beings generally is also ephemeral; animal and plant arise today and tomorrow pass away; birth and death follow in quick succession, whereas to inorganic things, standing so very much lower, an incomparably longer duration is assured, but an infinitely long one only to absolutely formless matter, to which we attribute this even *a priori*. Now if we ponder over all this, I think the merely empirical, but objective and unprejudiced, comprehension of such an order of things must be followed as a matter of course by the thought that this order is only a superficial phenomenon, that such a constant arising and passing away cannot in any way touch the root of things, but can be only relative, indeed only apparent. The true inner being of everything, which, moreover, evades our glance everywhere and is thoroughly mysterious, is not affected by that arising and passing away, but rather continues to exist undisturbed thereby. Of course, we can neither perceive nor comprehend the way in which this happens, and must therefore think of it only generally as a kind of *tour de passe-passe* ("conjuring trick" [Tr.]) that took place here. For whereas the most imperfect thing, the lowest, the inorganic, continues to exist unassailed, it is precisely the most perfect beings, namely living things with their infinitely complicated and inconceivably ingenious organizations, which were supposed always to arise afresh from the very bottom, and after a short span of time to become absolutely nothing, in order to make room once more for new ones like them coming into existence out of nothing. This is something so obviously absurd that it can never be the true order of things, but rather a mere veil concealing such an order, or more correctly a phenomenon conditioned by the constitution of our intellect. In fact, the entire existence and non-existence of these individual beings, in reference to which life and death are opposites, can be only relative. Hence the language of nature, in which it is given to us as something absolute, cannot be the true and ultimate expression of the quality and constitution of things and of the order of the world, but really only a *patois du pays* ("provincial dialect" [Tr.]), in other words, something merely relatively true, something self-styled, to be understood *cum grano salis*, or properly speaking, something conditioned by our intellect. I say that an immediate, intuitive conviction of the kind I have here tried to describe in words will force itself on everyone, of course only on everyone whose mind is not of the utterly common species. Such common minds are capable of knowing absolutely only the particular thing, simply and solely as such, and are strictly limited to knowledge of individuals, after the manner of the animal intellect. On the other hand, whoever, through an ability of an only somewhat higher power, even just begins to see in individual beings their universal, their Ideas, will also to a certain extent participate in that conviction, a conviction indeed that is immediate and therefore certain. Indeed, it is also only small, narrow minds that quite seriously fear death as their annihilation; those who are specially favoured with decided capacity are entirely remote from such terrors. Plato rightly founded the whole of philosophy on knowledge of the doctrine of Ideas, in other words, on the perception of the universal in the particular. But the conviction here described and arising directly out of the apprehension of nature must have been extremely lively in those sublime authors of the *Upanishads* of the *Vedas*, who can scarcely be conceived as mere human beings. For this conviction speaks to us so forcibly from an immense number of their utterances that we must ascribe this immediate illumination of their mind to the fact that, standing nearer to the origin of our race as regards time, these sages apprehended the inner essence of things more clearly and profoundly than the already enfeebled race, οἷοι νῦν βροτοί εἰσιν ("as mortals now are" [Tr.]), is capable of doing. But, of course, their comprehension was also assisted by the natural world of India, which is endowed with life in quite a different degree from that in which our northern world is. Thorough reflection, however, as carried through by Kant's great mind, also leads to just the same result by a different path; for it teaches us that our intellect, in which that rapidly changing phenomenal world exhibits itself, does not comprehend the true, ultimate essence of things, but merely its appearance or phenomenon; and indeed, as I add, because originally such an intellect is destined only to present motives to our will, in other words, to be serviceable to it in the pursuit of its paltry aims.

But let us continue still farther our objective and unprejudiced consideration of nature. If I kill an animal, be it a dog, a bird, a frog, or even only an insect, it is really inconceivable that this being, or rather the primary and original force by virtue of which such a marvellous phenomenon displayed itself only a moment before in its full energy and love of life, could through my wicked or thoughtless act have become nothing. Again, on the other hand, the millions of animals of every kind which come into existence at every moment in endless variety, full of force and drive, can never have been absolutely nothing before the act of their generation, and can never have arrived from nothing to an absolute beginning. If in this way I see one of these creatures withdraw from my sight without my ever knowing where it goes to, and another appear without my ever knowing where it comes from; moreover, if both still have the same form, the same inner nature, the same character, but not the same matter, which they nevertheless continue to throw off and renew during their existence; then of course the assumption that what vanishes and what appears in its place are one and the same thing, which has experienced only a slight change, a renewal of the form of its existence, and consequently that death is for the species what sleep is for the individual – this assumption, I say, is so close at hand, that it is impossible for it not to occur to us, unless our minds, perverted in early youth by the impression of false fundamental views, hurry it out of the way, even from afar, with superstitious fear. But the opposite assumption that an animal's birth is an arising out of nothing, and accordingly that its death is an absolute annihilation, and this with the further addition that man has also come into existence out of nothing, yet has an individual and endless future existence, and that indeed with consciousness, whereas the dog, the ape, and the elephant are annihilated by death – is really something against which the sound mind must revolt, and must declare to be absurd. If, as is often enough repeated, the comparison of a system's result with the utterances of common sense is supposed to be a touchstone of its truth, I wish that the adherents of that fundamental view, handed down by Descartes to the pre-Kantian eclectics, and indeed still prevalent even now among the great majority of cultured people in Europe, would once apply this touchstone here.

The genuine symbol of nature is universally and everywhere the circle, because it is the schema or form of recurrence; in fact, this is the most general form in nature. She carries it through in everything from the course of the constellations down to the death and birth of organic beings. In this way alone, in the restless stream of time and its content, a continued existence, i.e., a nature, becomes possible.

In autumn we observe the tiny world of insects, and see how one prepares its bed, in order to sleep the long, benumbing winter-sleep; another spins a cocoon, in order to hibernate as a chrysalis, and to awake in spring rejuvenated and perfected; finally, how most of them, intending to rest in the arms of death, carefully arrange a suitable place for depositing their eggs, in order one day to come forth from these renewed. This is nature's great doctrine of immortality, which tries to make it clear to us that there is no radical difference between sleep and death, but that the one endangers existence just as little as the other. The care with which the insect prepares a cell, or hole, or nest, deposits therein its egg, together with food for the larva that will emerge from it in the following spring, and then calmly dies, is just like the care with which a person in the evening lays out his clothes and his breakfast ready for the following morning, and then calmly goes to bed; and at

bottom it could not take place at all, unless the insect that dies in autumn were in itself and according to its true essence just as identical with the insect hatched in spring as the person who lies down to sleep is with the one who gets up.

After these considerations, we now return to ourselves and our species; we then cast our glance forward far into the future, and try to picture to ourselves future generations with the millions of their individuals in the strange form of their customs and aspirations. But then we interpose with the question: Whence will all these come? Where are they now? Where is the abundant womb of that nothing which is pregnant with worlds, and which still conceals them, the coming generations? Would not the smiling and true answer to this be: Where else could they be but there where alone the real always was and will be, namely in the present and its content? – hence with you, the deluded questioner, who in this mistaking of his own true nature is like the leaf on the tree. Fading in the autumn and about to fall, this leaf grieves over its own extinction, and will not be consoled by looking forward to the fresh green which will clothe the tree in spring, but says as a lament: "I am not these! These are quite different leaves!" Oh, foolish leaf! Whither do you want to go? And whence are the others supposed to come? Where is the nothing, the abyss of which you fear? Know your own inner being, precisely that which is so filled with the thirst for existence; recognize it once more in the inner, mysterious, sprouting force of the tree. This force is always *one* and the same in all the generations of leaves, and it remains untouched by arising and passing away. And now

οἵη περ φύλλων γενεή, τοίη δὲ καὶ ἀνδρῶν
(*Qualis foliorum generatio, talis et hominum.*)
("As the leaves on the tree, so are the generations of human beings." [*Iliad*, VI, 146. Tr.])

Whether the fly now buzzing round me goes to sleep in the evening and buzzes again the following morning, or whether it dies in the evening and in spring another fly buzzes which has emerged from its egg, this in itself is the same thing. But then the knowledge that presents these as two fundamentally different things is not unconditioned, but relative, a knowledge of the phenomenon, not of the thing-in-itself. In the morning the fly exists again; it also exists again in the spring. For the fly what distinguishes the winter from the night? In

Burdach's *Physiologie*, Vol. I, § 275, we read: "Up till ten o'clock in the morning no *Cercaria ephemera* (one of the infusoria) is yet to be seen (in the infusion), and at twelve the whole water swarms with them. In the evening they die, and the next morning new ones come into existence again. It was thus observed for six days in succession by Nitzsch."

Thus everything lingers only for a moment, and hurries on to death. The plant and the insect die at the end of the summer, the animal and man after a few years; death reaps unweariedly. But despite all this, in fact as if this were not the case at all, everything is always there and in its place, just as if everything were imperishable. The plant always flourishes and blooms, the insect hums, animal and man are there in evergreen youth, and every summer we again have before us the cherries that have already been a thousand times enjoyed. Nations also exist as immortal individuals, though sometimes they change their names. Even their actions, what they do and suffer, are always the same, though history always pretends to relate something different; for it is like the kaleidoscope, that shows us a new configuration at every turn, whereas really we always have the same thing before our eyes. Therefore, what forces itself on us more irresistibly than the thought that that arising and passing away do not concern the real essence of things, but that this remains untouched by them, hence is imperishable, consequently that each and every thing that *wills* to exist actually does exist continuously and without end? Accordingly, at every given point of time all species of animals, from the gnat to the elephant, exist together complete. They have already renewed themselves many thousands of times, and withal have remained the same. They know nothing of others like them who have lived before them, or who will live after them; it is the species that always lives, and the individuals cheerfully exist in the consciousness of the imperishability of the species and their identity with it. The will-to-live manifests itself in an endless present, because this is the form of the life of the species, which therefore does not grow old, but remains always young. Death is for the species what sleep is for the individual, or winking for the eye; when the Indian gods appear in human form, they are recognized by their not winking. Just as at nightfall the world vanishes, yet does not for a moment cease to exist, so man and animal apparently pass away through death, yet their true inner being continues to exist

just as undisturbed. Let us now picture to ourselves that alternation of birth and death in infinitely rapid vibrations, and we have before us the persistent and enduring objectification of the will, the permanent Ideas of beings, standing firm like the rainbow on the waterfall. This is temporal immortality. In consequence of this, in spite of thousands of years of death and decay, there is still nothing lost, no atom of matter, still less anything of the inner being exhibiting itself as nature. Accordingly we can at any moment cheerfully exclaim: "In spite of time, death, and decay, we are still all together!"

Perhaps an exception would have to be made of the man who should once have said from the bottom of his heart with regard to this game: "I no longer like it." But this is not yet the place to speak of that.

Attention, however, must indeed be drawn to the fact that the pangs of birth and the bitterness of death are the two constant conditions under which the will-to-live maintains itself in its objectification, in other words, our being-in-itself, untouched by the course of time and by the disappearance of generations, exists in an everlasting present, and enjoys the fruit of the affirmation of the will-to-live. This is analogous to our being able to remain awake during the day only on condition that we sleep every night; indeed, this is the commentary furnished by nature for an understanding of that difficult passage. For the suspension of the animal functions is sleep; that of the organic functions is death.

The substratum or filling out, the πλήρωμα or material of the *present*, is really the same through all time. The impossibility of directly recognizing this identity is just *time*, a form and limitation of our intellect. The fact that by virtue of it, for example, the future event does not as yet exist, rests on a delusion of which we become aware when the event has come to pass. The essential form of our intellect produces such a delusion, and this is explained and justified from the fact that the intellect has come forth from the hands of nature by no means for the purpose of comprehending the inner being of things, but merely for the purpose of comprehending motives, and hence to serve an individual and temporal phenomenon of will.[1] [. . .]

There is no greater contrast than that between the ceaseless, irresistible flight of time carrying its whole content away with it, and the rigid immobility of what is actually existing, which is at all times one and the same; and if, from this point of view, we fix our really objective glance on the immediate events of life, the *Nunc stans* becomes clear and visible to us in the centre of the wheel of time. To the eye of a being who lived an incomparably longer life and took in at a single glance the human race in its whole duration, the constant alternation of birth and death would present itself merely as a continuous vibration. Accordingly, it would not occur to it at all to see in it a constantly new coming out of nothing and passing into nothing, but, just as to our glance the rapidly turning spark appears as a continuous circle, the rapidly vibrating spring as a permanent triangle, the vibrating cord as a spindle, so to its glance the species would appear as that which is and remains, birth and death as vibrations.

We shall have false notions about the indestructibility of our true nature through death, so long as we do not make up our minds to study it first of all in the animals, and claim for ourselves alone a class apart from them under the boastful name of immortality. But it is this presumption alone and the narrowness of view from which it proceeds, on account of which most people struggle so obstinately against recognizing the obvious truth that, essentially and in the main, we are the same as the animals; in fact that such people recoil at every hint of our relationship with these. Yet it is this denial of the truth which, more than anything else, bars to them the way to real knowledge of the indestructibility of our true nature. For if we seek anything on a wrong path, we have in so doing forsaken the right; and on the wrong path we shall never attain to anything in the end but belated disillusionment. Therefore, pursue truth straight away, not according to preconceived freaks and fancies, but guided by the hand of nature! First of all learn to recognize, when looking at every young animal, the never-ageing existence of the species, which, as a reflection of its own eternal youth, bestows on every new individual a temporal youth, and lets it step forth as new, as fresh, as if the world were of today. Ask yourself honestly whether the swallow of this year's spring is an entirely different one from the swallow of the first spring, and whether actually between the two the miracle of creation out of nothing has been renewed a million times, in order to work just as often into the hands of absolute annihilation. I know quite well that anyone would regard me as mad if I seriously assured him that the cat, playing just now in the yard, is still the same one that did the same jumps and tricks there three

hundred years ago; but I also know that it is much more absurd to believe that the cat of today is through and through and fundamentally an entirely different one from that cat of three hundred years ago. We need only become sincerely and seriously engrossed in the contemplation of one of these higher vertebrates, in order to become distinctly conscious that this unfathomable inner being, taken as a whole as it exists, cannot possibly become nothing, and yet, on the other hand, we know its transitoriness. This rests on the fact that in this animal the eternity of its Idea (species) is distinctly marked in the finiteness of the individual. For in a certain sense it is of course true that in the individual we always have before us a different being, namely in the sense resting on the principle of sufficient reason, under which are also included time and space; these constitute the *principium individuationis*. But in another it is not true, namely in the sense in which reality belongs only to the permanent forms of things, to the Ideas, and which was so clearly evident to Plato that it became his fundamental thought, the centre of his philosophy; the comprehension of it became his criterion for the ability to philosophize generally.

Just as the spraying drops of the roaring waterfall change with lightning rapidity, while the rainbow, of which they are the supporter, remains immovably at rest, quite untouched by that restless change, so every Idea, i.e., every *species* of living beings remains entirely untouched by the constant change of its individuals. But it is the *Idea* or the species in which the will-to-live is really rooted and manifests itself; therefore the will is really concerned only in the continuance of the species. For example, the lions that are born and that die are like the drops of the waterfall; but *leonitas*, the Idea or form or shape of the lion, is like the unshaken and unmoved rainbow on the waterfall. Plato therefore attributed real and true being only to the *Ideas*, i.e., to the species; but to the individuals he attributed only a restless arising and passing away. From the deepest consciousness of his imperishable nature there also spring the confidence and serenity with which every animal and even every human individual move along lightheartedly amid a host of chances and hazards that may annihilate them at any moment, and moreover move straight on to death. Out of his eyes, however, there glances the peace of the species, which is unaffected and untouched by that destruction and extinction. Not even to man could this peace and calm be vouchsafed by uncertain and changing dogmas. As I have said, however, the sight of every animal teaches us that death is no obstacle to the kernel of life, the will in its manifestation. Yet what an unfathomable mystery lies in every animal! Look at the nearest one; look at your dog, and see how cheerfully and calmly he stands there! Many thousands of dogs have had to die before it was this dog's turn to live; but the death and extinction of those thousands have not affected the *Idea* of the dog. This Idea has not in the least been disturbed by all that dying. Therefore the dog stands there as fresh and endowed with original force as if this day were his first and none could be his last, and out of his eyes there shines the indestructible principle in him, the archaeus. Now what has died throughout those thousands of years? Not the dog; he stands there before us intact and unscratched; merely his shadow, his image or copy in our manner of knowing, which is bound to time. Yet how can we ever believe that that passes away which exists for ever and ever, and fills all time? The matter is, of course, explainable empirically, namely according as death destroyed the individuals, generation brought forth new ones. This empirical explanation, however, is only an apparent explanation; it puts one riddle in place of the other. Although a metaphysical understanding of the matter is not to be had so cheaply, it is nevertheless the only true and satisfactory one.

In his subjective method, Kant brought to light the great though negative truth that time cannot belong to the thing-in-itself, because it lies preformed in our apprehension. Now death is the temporal end of the temporal phenomenon; but as soon as we take away time, there is no longer any end at all, and the word has lost all meaning. But here, on the objective path, I am now trying to show the positive aspect of the matter, namely that the thing-in-itself remains untouched by time and by that which is possible only through time, that is, by arising and passing away, and that the phenomena in time could not have even that restless, fleeting existence that stands next to nothingness, unless there were in them a kernel of eternity. It is true that *eternity* is a concept having no perception as its basis; for this reason, it is also of merely negative content, and thus implies a timeless existence. *Time*, however, is a mere image of eternity, ὁ χρόνος εἰκὼν τοῦ αἰῶνος ("Time is a copy or image of eternity" [Tr.]), as Plotinus has it; and in just the same way, our temporal existence is the mere image of our true inner being. This must lie in eternity, just because time is only the form of

our knowing; but by virtue of this form alone we know our own existence and that of all things as transitory, finite, and subject to annihilation.

In the second book I have explained that the adequate objectivity of the will as thing-in-itself is the (Platonic) *Idea* at each of its grades. Similarly in the third book I have shown that the Ideas of beings have as their correlative the pure subject of knowing, consequently that the knowledge of them appears only by way of exception and temporarily under specially favourable conditions. For individual knowledge, on the other hand, and hence in time, the *Idea* exhibits itself under the form of the *species*, and this is the Idea drawn apart by entering into time. The *species* is therefore the most immediate objectification of the thing-in-itself, i.e., of the will-to-live. Accordingly, the innermost being of every animal and of man also lies in the *species*; thus the will-to-live, which is so powerfully active, has its root in the species, not really in the individual. On the other hand, immediate consciousness is to be found only in the individual; therefore it imagines itself to be different from the species, and thus fears death. The will-to-live manifests itself in reference to the individual as hunger and fear of death; in reference to the species, as sexual impulse and passionate care for the offspring. In agreement with this, we find nature, as being free from that delusion of the individual, just as careful for the maintenance of the species as she is indifferent to the destruction of the individuals; for her the latter are always only means, the former the end. Therefore, a glaring contrast appears between her niggardliness in the equipment of individuals and her lavishness when the species is at stake. From *one* individual often a hundred thousand seeds or more are obtained annually, for example, from trees, fish, crabs, termites, and many others. In the case of her niggardliness, on the other hand, only barely enough in the way of strength and organs is given to each to enable it with ceaseless exertion to maintain a bare living. If, therefore, an animal is crippled or weakened, it must, as a rule, die of starvation. And where an occasional economy was possible, through the circumstance that a part could be dispensed with in an emergency, it has been withheld, even out of order. Hence, for example, many caterpillars are without eyes; the poor animals grope about in the dark from leaf to leaf, and in the absence of antennae they do this by moving three quarters of their body to and fro in the air, till they come across an object. In this way they often miss their food that is to be found close at hand. But this happens in consequence of the *lex parsimoniae naturae*, to the expression of which, *natura nihil facit supervacaneum*, can still be added *et nihil largitur* ("Nature does nothing in vain and creates nothing superfluous; . . . and she gives away nothing" [Tr.]). The same tendency of nature shows itself also in the fact that the fitter an individual is for propagation by virtue of his age, the more powerfully does the *vis naturae medicatrix* ("the healing power of nature" [Tr.]) manifest itself in him. His wounds, therefore, heal easily, and he easily recovers from illnesses. This diminishes with the power of procreation, and sinks low after this power is extinguished; for in the eyes of nature the individual has now become worthless.

Now if we cast a glance at the scale of beings together with the gradation of consciousness that accompanies them, from the polyp to man, we see this wonderful pyramid kept in ceaseless oscillation certainly by the constant death of the individuals, yet enduring in the species throughout the endlessness of time by means of the bond of generation. Now, whereas, as was explained above, the *objective*, the species, manifests itself as indestructible, the *subjective*, consisting merely in the self-consciousness of these beings, seems to be of the shortest duration, and to be incessantly destroyed, in order just as often to come forth again out of nothing in an incomprehensible way. But a man must really be very short-sighted to allow himself to be deceived by this appearance, and not to understand that, although the form of temporal permanence belongs only to the objective, the subjective – i.e., the *will*, living and appearing in everything, and with it the subject of *knowing* in which this exhibits itself – must be no less indestructible. For the permanence of the objective, or the external, can indeed be only the phenomenal appearance of the indestructibility of the subjective, or the internal, since the former cannot possess anything that it had not received in fee from the latter; it cannot be essentially and originally something objective, a phenomenon, and then secondarily and accidentally something subjective, a thing-in-itself, something conscious of itself. For obviously, the former as phenomenon or appearance presupposes something that appears, just as being-for-another presupposes being-for-self, and object presupposes subject; but not conversely, since everywhere the root of things must lie in that which they are by themselves, hence in the subjective, not in the objective, not in that which they are only for others, not in the consciousness

of another. Accordingly we found in the first book that the correct starting-point for philosophy is essentially and necessarily the subjective, i.e., the idealistic, just as the opposite starting-point, proceeding from the objective, leads to materialism. Fundamentally, however, we are far more at one with the world than we usually think; its inner nature is our will, and its phenomenal appearance our representation. The difference between the continuance of the external world after his death and his own continuance after death would vanish for anyone who could bring this unity or identity of being to distinct consciousness; the two would present themselves to him as one and the same thing; in fact, he would laugh at the delusion that could separate them. For an understanding of the indestructibility of our true nature coincides with that of the identity of macrocosm and microcosm. Meanwhile we can elucidate what has here been said by a peculiar experiment that is to be carried out by means of the imagination, and might be called metaphysical. Let a person attempt to present vividly to his mind the time, not in any case very distant, when he will be dead. He then thinks himself away, and allows the world to go on existing; but soon, to his own astonishment, he will discover that nevertheless he still exists. For he imagined he made a mental representation of the world without himself; but the I or ego is in consciousness that which is immediate, by which the world is first brought about, and for which alone the world exists. This centre of all existence, this kernel of all reality, is to be abolished, and yet the world is to be allowed to go on existing; it is an idea that may, of course, be conceived in the abstract, but not realized. The endeavour to achieve this, the attempt to think the secondary without the primary, the conditioned without the condition, the supported without the supporter, fails every time, much in the same way as the attempt fails to conceive an equilateral right-angled triangle, or an arising and passing away of matter, and similar impossibilities. Instead of what was intended, the feeling here forces itself on us that the world is no less in us than we are in it, and that the source of all reality lies within ourselves. The result is really that the time when I shall not be will come objectively; but subjectively it can never come. Indeed, it might therefore be asked how far anyone in his heart actually believes in a thing that he cannot really conceive at all; or whether, since the deep consciousness of the indestructibility of our real inner nature is associated with that merely intellectual experiment that has, however, already been carried out more or less distinctly by everyone, whether, I say, our own death is not perhaps for us at bottom the most incredible thing in the world. [...]

He who conceives his existence as merely accidental, must certainly be afraid of losing it through death. On the other hand he who sees, even only in a general way, that his existence rests on some original necessity, will not believe that this necessity, which has produced so wonderful a thing, is limited to such a brief span of time, but that it is active at all times. But whoever reflects that up till now, when he exists, an infinite time, and thus an infinity of changes, has run its course, but yet notwithstanding this he exists, will recognize his existence as a necessary one. Therefore the entire possibility of all states and conditions has exhausted itself already without being able to eliminate his existence. *If ever he could not be, he would already not be now.* For the infinity of the time that has already elapsed, with the exhausted possibility of its events in it, guarantees that what *exists necessarily exists.* Consequently, everyone has to conceive himself as a necessary being, in other words, as a being whose existence would follow from its true and exhaustive definition, if only we had this. Actually in this train of thought is to be found the only immanent proof of the imperishableness of our real inner nature, that is to say, the only proof that keeps within the sphere of empirical data. Existence must be inherent in this inner nature, since it shows itself to be independent of all states or conditions that can possibly be brought about through the causal chain; for these states have already done what they could, and yet our existence has remained just as unshaken thereby, as the ray of light is by the hurricane that it cuts through. If from its own resources time could bring us to a happy state, we should already have been there long ago; for an infinite time lies behind us. But likewise, if time could lead us to destruction, we should already long ago have ceased to exist. It follows from the fact that we now exist, if the matter is well considered, that we are bound to exist at all times. For we ourselves are the inner nature that time has taken up into itself, in order to fill up its void; therefore this inner nature fills the *whole* of time, present, past, and future, in the same way; and it is just as impossible for us to fall out of existence as it is for us to fall out of space. If we carefully consider this, it is inconceivable that what once exists in all the force of reality

could ever become nothing, and then not exist throughout an infinite time. From this have arisen the Christian doctrine of the restoration of all things, the Hindu doctrine of the constantly renewed creation of the world by Brahma, together with similar dogmas of the Greek philosophers. The great mystery of our existence and non-existence, to explain which these and all kindred dogmas were devised, ultimately rests on the fact that the same thing that objectively constitutes an infinite course of time is subjectively a point, an indivisible, ever-present present-moment; but who comprehends it? It has been most clearly expounded by Kant in his immortal doctrine of the ideality of time and of the sole reality of the thing-in-itself. For it follows from this that what is really essential in things, in man, in the world, lies permanently and enduringly in the *Nunc stans*, firm and immovable; and that the change of phenomena and of events is a mere consequence of our apprehension of it by means of our perception-form of time. Accordingly, instead of saying to men: "Ye have arisen through birth, but are immortal," one should say: "Ye are not nothing," and teach them to understand this in the sense of the saying attributed to Hermes Trismegistus: Τὸ γὰρ ὂν ἀεὶ ἔσται. (*Quod enim est, erit semper* "For that which is must always be" [Tr.]; Stobaeus, *Eclogues*, I, 43, 6.) Yet if this does not succeed, but the anxious heart breaks out into its old lament: "I see all beings arise out of nothing through birth, and again after a brief term return to nothing; even my existence, now in the present, will soon lie in the remote past, and I shall be nothing!" then the right answer is: "Do you not exist? Do you not possess the precious present, to which you children of time all aspire so eagerly, actually at this moment? And do you understand how you have attained to it? Do you know the paths which have led you to it, that you could see them barred to you by death? An existence of yourself after the destruction of your body is not possibly conceivable to you; but can it be more inconceivable to you than are your present existence and the way you have attained to it? Why should you doubt that the secret paths that stood open to you up to this present, will not also stand open to you to every future present?"

Therefore, if considerations of this kind are certainly calculated to awaken the conviction that there is something in us that death cannot destroy, this nevertheless happens only by our being raised to a point of view from which birth is not the beginning of our existence. It follows from this, however, that what is proved to be indestructible through death is not really the individual. Moreover, having arisen through generation and carrying within himself the qualities of the father and mother, this individual exhibits himself as a mere difference of the species, and as such can be only finite. Accordingly, just as the individual has no recollection of his existence before his birth, so can he have no recollection of his existence after death. Everyone, however, places his I or ego in *consciousness*; therefore this seems to him to be tied to individuality. Moreover, with individuality there disappears all that which is peculiar to him, as to this, and which distinguishes him from others. Therefore his continued existence without individuality becomes for him indistinguishable from the continuance of all other beings, and he sees his I or ego become submerged. Now he who thus links his existence to the identity of *consciousness*, and therefore desires for this an endless existence after death, should bear in mind that in any case he can attain to this only at the price of just as endless a past before birth. For as he has no recollection of an existence before birth, and so his consciousness begins with birth, he must look upon his birth as an arising of his existence out of nothing. But then he purchases the endless time of his existence after death for just as long a time before birth; in this way the account is balanced without any profit to him. On the other hand, if the existence left untouched by death is different from that of individual consciousness, then it must be independent of birth just as it is of death. Accordingly, with reference to it, it must be equally true to say "I shall always be" and "I have always been," which then gives us two infinities for one. However, the greatest equivocation really lies in the word "I," as will be seen at once by anyone who calls to mind the contents of our second book and the separation there carried out of the willing part of our true inner nature from the knowing part. According as I understand this word, I can say: "Death is my entire end"; or else: "This my personal phenomenal appearance is just as infinitely small a part of my true inner nature as I am of the world." But the I or ego is the dark point in consciousness, just as on the retina the precise point of entry of the optic nerve is blind, the brain itself is wholly insensible, the body of the sun is dark, and the eye sees everything except itself. Our faculty of knowledge is directed entirely *outwards* in accordance with the fact that it is the product of a brain-function that has arisen for the purpose of mere self-maintenance, and hence for the search for nourishment and the seizing of prey. Therefore everyone knows of himself only as of this individual, just as it exhibits itself in external perception. If, on the other hand, he could bring to consciousness what he is besides and beyond this, he would willingly give up his individuality, smile at the tenacity of his attachment thereto, and say: "What does the loss of this individuality matter to me? for I carry within myself the possibility of innumerable individualities." He would see that, although there is not in store for him a continued existence of his individuality, it is nevertheless just as good as if he had such an existence, since he carries within himself a complete compensation for it. Besides this, however, it might also be taken into consideration that the individuality of most people is so wretched and worthless that they actually lose nothing in it, and that what in them may still have some value is the universal human element; but to this we can promise imperishableness. In fact, even the rigid unalterability and essential limitation of every individuality as such would, in the case of its endless duration, inevitably and necessarily produce ultimately such great weariness by its monotony, that we should prefer to become nothing, merely in order to be relieved of it. To desire immortality for the individual is really the same as wanting to perpetuate an error for ever; for at bottom every individuality is really only a special error, a false step, something that it would be better should not be, in fact something from which it is the real purpose of life to bring us back. This also finds confirmation in the fact that most, indeed really all, people are so constituted that they could not be happy, no matter in what world they might be placed. Insofar as such a world would exclude want and hardship, they would become a prey to boredom, and insofar as this was prevented, they would fall into misery, vexation, and suffering. Thus, for a blissful condition of man, it would not be by any means sufficient for him to be transferred to a "better world"; on the contrary, it would also be necessary for a fundamental change to occur in man himself, and hence for him to be no longer what he is, but rather to become what he is not. For this, however, he must first of all cease to be what he is; as a preliminary, this requirement is fulfilled by death, and the moral necessity of this can from this point of view already be seen. To be transferred to another world and to change one's entire nature are at bottom one and the same thing. On this also ultimately rests that dependence of the objective on the subjective which is explained by the idealism of our first book; accordingly, here is to be found the point of contact between transcendental philosophy and ethics. If we bear this in mind, we shall find that the awakening from the dream of life is possible only through the disappearance along with it of its whole fundamental fabric as well; but this is its organ itself, the intellect together with its forms. With this the dream would go on spinning itself for ever, so firmly is it incorporated with that organ. That which really dreamt the dream is, however, still different from it, and alone remains over. On the other hand, the fear that with death everything might be over and finished may be compared to the case of a person who in a dream should think that there were mere dreams without a dreamer. But would it even be desirable for an individual consciousness to be kindled again, after it had once been ended by death, in order that it might continue for ever? For the most part, often in fact entirely, its content is nothing but a stream of paltry, earthly, poor ideas, and endless worries and anxieties; let these then be finally silenced! Therefore with true instinct the ancients put on their tombstones: *Securitati perpetuae*; or *Bonae quieti* ("To eternal security; ... to good repose" [Tr.]). But if even here, as has happened so often, we wanted continued existence of the individual consciousness, in order to connect with it a reward or punishment in the next world, then at bottom the aim would be merely the compatibility of virtue with egoism. But these two will never embrace; they are fundamentally opposed. On the other hand, the immediate conviction, which the sight of noble actions calls forth, is well founded, that the spirit of love enjoining one man to spare his enemies, and another, even at the risk of his life, to befriend a person never previously seen, can never pass away and become nothing.

The most complete answer to the question of the individual's continued existence after death is to be found in Kant's great doctrine of the *ideality of time*. Just here does this doctrine show itself to be specially fruitful and rich in important results, since it replaces dogmas, which lead to the absurd on the one path as on the other, by a wholly theoretical but well proved insight, and thus at once settles the most exciting of all metaphysical questions. To begin, to end, and to continue are concepts that derive their significance simply and solely from time; consequently they are valid only on the presupposition of time. But time has no absolute existence; it is not the mode and manner of the being-in-itself of things, but merely the form of our *knowledge* of the existence and inner being of ourselves and of all things; and for this reason such knowledge is very imperfect, and is limited to mere phenomena. Thus in reference to this knowledge alone do the concepts of ceasing and continuing find application, not in reference to that which manifests itself in them, namely the being-in-itself of things; applied to this, such concepts therefore no longer have any true meaning. For this is also seen in the fact that an answer to the question arising from those time-concepts becomes impossible, and every assertion of such an answer, whether on the one side or the other, is open to convincing objections. We might indeed assert that our being-in-itself continues after death, because it would be wrong to say that it was destroyed; but we might just as well assert that it is destroyed, because it would be wrong to say that it continues; at bottom, the one is just as true as the other. Accordingly, something like an antinomy could certainly be set up here, but it would rest on mere negations. In it one would deprive the subject of the judgement of two contradictorily opposite predicates, but only because the whole category of these predicates would not be applicable to that subject. But if one deprives it of those two predicates, not together but separately, it appears as if the contradictory opposite of the predicate, denied in each case, were thus proved of the subject of the judgement. This, however, is due to the fact that incommensurable quantities are here compared, inasmuch as the problem removes us to a scene that abolishes time, but yet asks about time-determinations. Consequently, it is equally false to attribute these to the subject and to deny them, which is equivalent to saying that the problem is transcendent. In this sense death remains a mystery.

On the other hand, adhering to that very distinction between phenomenon and thing-in-itself, we can make the assertion that man as phenomenon is certainly perishable, yet his true inner being is not affected by this. Hence this true inner being is indestructible, although, on account of the elimination of the time-concepts which is connected with this, we cannot attribute continuance to it. Accordingly, we should be led here to the concept of an indestructibility that was nevertheless not a continuance. Now this concept is one which, obtained on the path of abstraction, may possibly be thought in the abstract; yet it cannot be supported by any perception; consequently, it cannot really become distinct. On the other hand, we must here keep in mind that we have not, like Kant, absolutely given up the ability to know the thing-in-itself; on the contrary, we know that it is to be looked for in the will. It is true that we have never asserted an absolute and exhaustive knowledge of the thing-in-itself; indeed, we have seen quite well that it is impossible to know anything according to what it may be absolutely in and by itself. For as soon as I *know*, I have a representation, a mental picture; but just because this representation is mine, it cannot be identical with what is known; on the contrary, it reproduces in an entirely different form that which is known by making it a being-for-others out of a being-for-self; hence it is still always to be regarded as the *phenomenal appearance* of this. However, therefore, a *knowing* consciousness may be constituted, there can always be for it only phenomena. This is not entirely obviated even by the fact that my own inner being is that which is known; for, in so far as it falls within my *knowing* consciousness, it is already a reflex of my inner being, something different from this inner being itself, and so already in a certain degree phenomenon. Thus, in so far as I am that which knows, I have even in my own inner being really only a phenomenon; on the other hand, in so far as I am directly this inner being itself, I am not that which knows. For it is sufficiently proved in the second book that knowledge is only a secondary property of our inner being, and is brought about through the animal nature of this. Strictly speaking, therefore, we know even our own will always only as phenomenon, and not according to what it may be absolutely in and by itself. But in that second book, as well as in my work *On the Will in Nature*, it is fully discussed and demonstrated that if, in order to penetrate into the essence of things, we leave what is given only indirectly and from outside, and stick to the only phenomenon into whose inner nature an immediate insight is accessible to us from within, we quite definitely find in this the will as the ultimate thing and the kernel of reality. In the will, therefore, we recognize the thing-in-itself in so far as it no longer has space, but time for its form; consequently, we really know it only in its most immediate manifestation, and thus with the reservation that this knowledge of it is still not exhaustive and entirely adequate. In this sense, therefore, we here retain the concept of the will as that of the thing-in-itself.

The concept of ceasing to be is certainly applicable to man as phenomenon in time, and empirical knowledge plainly presents death as the end of this temporal existence. The end of the person is just as real as was its beginning, and in just that sense in which we did not exist before birth, shall we no longer exist after death. But no more can be abolished through death than was produced through birth; and so that cannot be abolished by which birth first of all became possible. In this sense *natus et denatus* ("born and unborn" [Tr.]) is a fine expression. Now the whole of empirical knowledge affords us mere phenomena; thus only phenomena are affected by the temporal processes of arising and passing away, not that which appears, namely the being-in-itself. For this inner being the contrast, conditioned by the brain, between arising and passing away, does not exist at all; on the contrary, it has lost meaning and significance. This inner being, therefore, remains unaffected by the temporal end of a temporal phenomenon, and always retains that existence to which the concepts of beginning, end, and continuance are not applicable. But in so far as we can follow up this inner being, it is in every phenomenal being its will; so too in man. Consciousness, on the other hand, consists in knowledge; but this, as has been sufficiently demonstrated, belongs, as activity of the brain, and consequently as function of the organism, to the mere phenomenon, and therefore ends therewith. The will alone, of which the work or rather the copy was the body, is what is indestructible. The sharp distinction between will and knowledge, together with the former's primacy, a distinction that constitutes the fundamental characteristic of my philosophy, is therefore the only key to the contradiction that shows itself in many different ways, and always arises afresh in every consciousness, even the crudest. This contradiction is that death is our end, and yet we must be eternal and indestructible; hence it is the *sentimus, experimurque nos aeternos esse* of Spinoza ("We feel and experience that we are eternal" [Tr.]). All philosophers have made the mistake of placing that which is metaphysical, indestructible, and eternal in man in the *intellect*. It lies exclusively in the *will*, which is entirely different from the intellect, and alone is original. As was most thoroughly explained in the second book, the intellect is a secondary phenomenon, and is conditioned by the brain, and therefore begins and ends with this. The will alone is that which conditions, the kernel of the whole phenomenon; consequently, it is free from the forms of the phenomenon, one of which is time, and hence it is also indestructible. Accordingly, with death consciousness is certainly lost, but not what produced and maintained consciousness; life is extinguished, but with it not the principle of life which manifested itself in it. Therefore a sure and certain feeling says to everyone that there is in him something positively imperishable and indestructible. Even the freshness and vividness of recollections from earliest times, from early childhood, are evidence that something in us does not pass away with time, does not grow old, but endures unchanged. However, we were not able to see clearly what this imperishable element is. It is not consciousness any more than it is the body, on which consciousness obviously depends. On the contrary, it is that on which the body together with consciousness depends. It is, however, just that which, by entering into consciousness, exhibits itself as *will*. Of course, we cannot go beyond this most immediate phenomenal appearance of it, because we cannot go beyond consciousness. Therefore the question what that something may be in so far as it does *not* enter into consciousness, in other words, what it is absolutely in itself, remains unanswerable.

In the phenomenon, and by means of its forms time and space, as *principium individuationis*, it is thus evident that the human individual perishes, whereas the human race remains and continues to live. But in the being-in-itself of things which is free from these forms, the whole difference between the individual and the race is also abolished, and the two are immediately one. The entire will-to-live is in the individual, as it is in the race, and thus the continuance of the species is merely the image of the individual's indestructibility.

Now, since the infinitely important understanding of the indestructibility of our true nature by death rests entirely on the difference between phenomenon and thing-in-itself, I wish to put this very difference in the clearest light by elucidating it in the opposite of death, hence in the origin of animal beings, i.e., in *generation*. For this process, that is just as mysterious as death, places most directly before our eyes the fundamental contrast between phenomenon and the being-in-itself of things, i.e., between the world as representation and the world as will, and also shows us the entire heterogeneity of the laws of these two. The act of procreation thus presents itself to us in a twofold manner: firstly for self-consciousness, whose sole object is, as I have often shown, the will with all its affections; and secondly for the consciousness of other things, i.e., of the world of the representation, or the empirical reality of things. Now from the side of the will, and thus inwardly, subjectively, for self-consciousness, that act manifests itself as the most immediate and complete satisfaction of the will, i.e., as sensual pleasure. On the other hand, from the side of the representation, and thus outwardly, objectively, for the consciousness of other things, this act is just the woof of the most ingenious of all fabrics, the foundation of the inexpressibly complicated animal organism which then needs only development in order to become visible to our astonished eyes. This organism, whose infinite complication and perfection are known only to the student of anatomy, is not to be conceived and thought of, from the side of the representation, as other than a system, devised with the most carefully planned combination and carried out with the most consummate skill and precision, the most arduous work of the profoundest deliberation. Now from the side of the will, we know through self-consciousness that the production of the organism is the result of an act the very opposite of all reflection and deliberation, of an impetuous, blind craving, an exceedingly voluptuous sensation. This contrast is exactly akin to the infinite contrast, shown above, between the absolute facility with which nature produces her works, together with the correspondingly boundless carelessness with which she abandons such works to destruction – and the incalculably ingenious and well-thought-out construction of these very works. To judge from these, it must have been infinitely difficult to make them, and therefore to provide for their maintenance with every conceivable care, whereas we have the very opposite before our eyes. Now if, by this naturally very unusual consideration, we have brought together in the sharpest manner the two heterogeneous sides of the world, and so to speak grasped them with one hand, we must now hold them firmly, in order to convince ourselves of the entire invalidity of the laws of the phenomenon, or of the world as representation, for that of the will, or of things-in-themselves. It will then become clearer to us that whereas, on the side of the representation, i.e., in the phenomenal world, there is exhibited to us first an arising out of nothing, then a complete annihilation of what has arisen, from that other side, or in itself, there lies before us an essence or entity, and when the concepts of arising and passing away are applied to it, they have absolutely no meaning. For by going back to the root, where, by means of self-consciousness, the phenomenon and the being-in-itself meet, we have just palpably apprehended, as it were, that the two are absolutely incommensurable. The whole mode of being of the one, together with all the fundamental laws of this being, signifies nothing, and less than nothing, in the other. I believe that this last consideration will be rightly understood only by a few, and that it will be unpleasant and even offensive to all who do not understand it. However, I shall never on this account omit anything that can serve to illustrate my fundamental idea.

At the beginning of this chapter I explained that the great attachment to life, or rather the fear of death, by no means springs from *knowledge*, for in that case it would be the result of the known value of life, but that that fear of death has its root directly in the *will*; it proceeds from the will's original and essential nature, in which that will is entirely without knowledge, and is therefore the blind will-to-live. Just as we are allured into life by the wholly illusory inclination for sensual pleasure, so are we firmly retained in life by the fear of death, certainly just as illusory. Both spring directly from the will that is in itself without knowledge. On the other hand, if man were a merely *knowing* being, death would necessarily be not only a matter of indifference, but even welcome to him. Now the consideration we have reached here teaches us that what is affected by death is merely the *knowing* consciousness; that the *will*, on the other hand, in so far as it is the thing-in-itself that lies at the root of every individual phenomenon, is free from everything that depends on determinations of time, and so is imperishable. Its striving for existence and manifestation, from which the world results, is always satisfied, for it is accompanied by this world just as the body is by the shadow, since the world is merely the visibility of the true inner nature of the will. Nevertheless, the will in us fears death, and this is because knowledge presents to this will its true nature merely in the individual phenomenon. From this there arises for the will the illusion that it perishes with this phenomenon, just as when the mirror is smashed my image in it seems to be destroyed at the same time. Therefore this fills the will with horror, because it is contrary to its original nature, which is a blind craving for existence. It follows from this that that in us which alone is capable of fearing death, and also alone fears it, namely the *will*, is not affected by it; and that, on the other

hand, what is affected by it and actually perishes is that which, by its nature, is not capable of any fear, and generally of any desire or emotion, and is therefore indifferent to existence and non-existence. I refer to the mere subject of knowledge, the intellect, the existence of which consists in its relation to the world of the representation, in other words the objective world; it is the correlative of this objective world, with whose existence its own existence is at bottom identical. Thus, although the individual consciousness does not survive death, that survives it which alone struggles against it, the will. From this is also explained the contradiction that, from the standpoint of knowledge, philosophers have at all times with cogent arguments shown death to be no evil; yet the fear of death remains impervious to them all, simply because it is rooted not in knowledge, but in the will alone. Just because the will alone, not the intellect, is the indestructible element, it follows that all religions and philosophies promise a reward in eternity only to the virtues of the will or heart, not to those of the intellect or head.

The following may also serve to illustrate this consideration. The will, which constitutes our being-in-itself, is of a simple nature; it merely wills and does not know. The subject of knowing, on the other hand, is a secondary phenomenon, arising out of the objectification of the will; it is the point of unity of the nervous system's sensibility, the focus, as it were, in which the rays of activity of all parts of the brain converge. Therefore with this brain the subject of knowing is bound to perish. In self-consciousness, as that which alone knows, the subject of knowing stands facing the will as a spectator, and although it has sprung from the will, it knows that will as something different from itself, something foreign to it, and thus only empirically, in time, piecemeal, in the successive agitations and acts of the will; only *a posteriori* and often very indirectly does it come to know the will's decisions. This is why our own inner being is a riddle to us, in other words, to our intellect, and why the individual regards himself as newly arisen and as perishable, although his inner being-in-itself is something timeless, and therefore eternal. Now just as the *will* does not *know*, so, conversely, the intellect, or the subject of knowledge, is simply and solely *knowing*, without ever willing. This can be proved even physically from the fact that, as already mentioned in the second book, the various emotions, according to Bichat, directly affect all parts of the organism and disturb their functions, with the exception of the brain as that which can be affected by them at most indirectly, in other words, in consequence of those very disturbances (*De la vie et de la mort*, art. 6, § 2). Yet it follows from this that the subject of knowing, by itself and as such, cannot take any part or interest in anything, but that the existence or non-existence of everything, in fact even of itself, is a matter of indifference to it. Now why should this indifferent being be immortal? It ends with the temporal phenomenon of the will, i.e., with the individual, just as it originated therewith. It is the lantern that after it has served its purpose is extinguished. The intellect, like the world of perception which exists in it alone, is mere phenomenon; but the finiteness of both does not affect that of which they are the phenomenal appearance. The intellect is the function of the cerebral nervous system; but this, like the rest of the body, is the objectivity of the *will*. The intellect, therefore, depends on the somatic life of the organism; but this organism itself depends on the will. Thus, in a certain sense, the organic body can be regarded as the link between the will and the intellect; although, properly speaking, the body is only the will itself spatially exhibiting itself in the perception of the intellect. Death and birth are the constant renewal and revival of the will's consciousness. In itself this will is endless and beginningless; it alone is, so to speak, the substance of existence (every such renewal, however, brings a new possibility of the denial of the will-to-live). Consciousness is the life of the subject of knowing, or of the brain, and death is its end. Therefore consciousness is finite, is always new, beginning each time at the beginning. The *will* alone is permanent; but permanence also concerns it alone, for it is the will-to-live. Nothing is of any consequence to the knowing subject by itself; yet the will and the knowing subject are united in the I or ego. In every animal being the will has achieved an intellect, and this is the light by which the will here pursues its ends. Incidentally, the fear of death may also be due partly to the fact that the individual will is so reluctant to separate itself from the intellect that has fallen to its lot through the course of nature, from its guide and guard, without which it knows that it is helpless and blind.

Finally, this explanation agrees also with that daily moral experience, teaching us that the will alone is real, while its objects, on the other hand, as conditioned by knowledge, are only phenomena, mere froth and vapour, like the wine provided by Mephistopheles in Auerbach's cellar; thus after every pleasure of the senses we say; "And yet it seemed as I were drinking wine" [Goethe, *Faust*].

The terrors of death rest for the most part on the false illusion that then the I or ego vanishes, and the world remains. But rather is the opposite true, namely that the world vanishes; on the other hand, the innermost kernel of the ego endures, the bearer and producer of that subject in whose representation alone the world had its existence. With the brain the intellect perishes, and with the intellect the objective world, this intellect's mere representation. The fact that in other brains a similar world lives and moves, now as before, is a matter of indifference with reference to the intellect that is perishing. If, therefore, reality proper did not lie in the *will*, and if the *moral* existence were not that which extended beyond death, then, as the intellect and with it its world are extinguished, the true essence of things generally would be nothing more than an endless succession of short and troubled dreams without connexion among themselves; for the permanence of nature-without-knowledge consists merely in the time-representation of nature that knows. Therefore a world-spirit, dreaming without aim or purpose dreams that are often heavy and troubled, would then be all in all.

When an individual experiences the dread of death, we really have the strange, and even ludicrous, spectacle of the lord of the worlds, who fills everything with his true nature, and through whom alone everything that is has its existence, in despair and afraid of perishing, of sinking into the abyss of eternal nothingness; whereas, in truth, everything is full of him, and there is no place where he would not be, no being in whom he would not live, for existence does not support him, but he existence. Yet it is he who despairs in the individual who suffers the dread of death, since he is exposed to the illusion, produced by the *principium individuationis*, that his existence is limited to the being that is now dying. This illusion is part of the heavy dream into which he, as will-to-live, has fallen. However, we might say to the dying individual: "You are ceasing to be something which you would have done better never to become."

As long as no denial of that will has taken place, that of us which is left over by death is the seed and kernel of quite another existence, in which a new individual finds himself again so fresh and original, that he broods over himself in astonishment. Hence the enthusiastic, visionary, and dreamy disposition of noble youths at the time when this fresh consciousness has just been fully developed. What sleep is for the individual, death is for the will as thing-in-itself. It could not bear to continue throughout endless time the same actions and sufferings without true gain, if memory and individuality were left to it. It throws them off; this is Lethe; and through this sleep of death it reappears as a new being, refreshed and equipped with another intellect; "A new day beckons to a newer shore!" [Goethe, *Faust*] [...]

Death is the great reprimand that the will-to-live, and more particularly the egoism essential thereto, receive through the course of nature; and it can be conceived as a punishment for our existence.[2] Death is the painful untying of the knot that generation with sensual pleasure had tied; it is the violent destruction, bursting in from outside, of the fundamental error of our true nature, the great disillusionment. At bottom, we are something that ought not to be; therefore we cease to be. Egoism really consists in man's restricting all reality to his own person, in that he imagines he lives in this alone, and not in others. Death teaches him something better, since it abolishes this person, so that man's true nature, that is his will, will henceforth live only in other individuals. His intellect, however, which itself belonged only to the phenomenon, i.e., to the world as representation, and was merely the form of the external world, also continues to exist in the condition of being representation, in other words, in the *objective* being, *as such*, of things, hence also only in the existence of what was hitherto the external world. Therefore, from this time forward, his whole ego lives only in what he had hitherto regarded as non-ego; for the difference between external and internal ceases. Here we recall that the better person is the one who makes the least difference between himself and others, and does not regard them as absolutely non-ego; whereas to the bad person this difference is great, in fact absolute. I have discussed this at length in the essay *On the Basis of Morality*. The conclusion from the above remarks is that the degree in which death can be regarded as man's annihilation is in proportion to this difference. But if we start from the fact that the difference between outside me and inside me, as a spatial difference, is founded only in the phenomenon, not in the thing-in-itself, and so is not an absolutely real difference, then in the losing of our own individuality we shall see only the loss of a phenomenon, and thus only an apparent loss. However much reality that difference has in empirical consciousness, yet from the metaphysical standpoint the sentences "I perish, but the world endures," and "The world perishes, but I endure," are not really different at bottom.

But beyond all this, death is the great opportunity no longer to be I; to him, of course, who embraces it. During life, man's will is without freedom; on the basis of his unalterable character, his conduct takes place with necessity in the chain of motives. Now everyone carries in his memory very many things which he has done, about which he is not satisfied with himself. If he were to go on living, he would go on acting in the same way by virtue of the unalterability of his character. Accordingly, he must cease to be what he is, in order to be able to arise out of the germ of his true nature as a new and different being. Death, therefore, loosens those bonds; the will again becomes free, for freedom lies in the *esse*, not in the *operari*. *Finditur nodus cordis, dissolvuntur omnes dubitationes, ejusque opera evanescunt* ("[Whoever beholds the highest and profoundest], has his heart's knot cut, all his doubts are resolved, and his works come to nought" [Tr.]), is a very famous saying of the *Veda* often repeated by all Vedantists. Dying is the moment of that liberation from the one-sidedness of an individuality which does not constitute the innermost kernel of our true being, but is rather to be thought of as a kind of aberration thereof. The true original freedom again enters at this moment which in the sense stated can be regarded as a *restitutio in integrum* ("restoration to the former state" [Tr.]). The peace and composure on the countenance of most dead people seem to have their origin in this. As a rule, the death of every good person is peaceful and gentle; but to die willingly, to die gladly, to die cheerfully, is the prerogative of the resigned, of him who gives up and denies the will-to-live. For he alone wishes to die *actually* and not merely *apparently*, and consequently needs and desires no continuance of his person. He willingly gives up the existence that we know; what comes to him instead of it is in our eyes *nothing*, because our existence in reference to that one is *nothing*. The Buddhist faith calls that existence *Nirvana*, that is to say, extinction.

[On Philosophy]

[...] Philosophy has its value and virtue in its rejection of all assumptions that cannot be substantiated, and in its acceptance as its data only of that which can be proved with certainty in the external world given by perception, in the forms constituting our intellect for the apprehension of the world, and in the consciousness of one's own self common to all. For this reason it must remain cosmology, and cannot become theology. Its theme must restrict itself to the world; to express from every aspect *what* this world *is*, what it *may be* in its innermost nature, is all that it can honestly achieve. Now it is in keeping with this that, when my teaching reaches its highest point, it assumes a *negative* character, and so ends with a negation. Thus it can speak here only of what is denied or given up; but what is gained in place of this, what is laid hold of, it is forced (at the conclusion of the fourth book) to describe as nothing; and it can add only the consolation that it may be merely a relative, not an absolute, nothing. For, if something is no one of all the things that we know, then certainly it is for us in general nothing. Yet it still does not follow from this that it is nothing absolutely, namely that it must be nothing from every possible point of view and in every possible sense, but only that we are restricted to a wholly negative knowledge of it; and this may very well lie in the limitation of our point of view. [. . .]

Notes

1   There is only *one present*, and this always exists: for it is the sole form of actual existence. We must arrive at the insight that the *past* is not *in itself* different from the present, but is so only in our apprehension. This has *time* as its form, by virtue of which alone the present shows itself as different from the past. To make this insight easier, let us imagine all the events and scenes of human life, good and bad, fortunate and unfortunate, delightful and dreadful, which are presented to us successively in the course of time and variety of places, in the most motley multifariousness and succession, as existing *all at once and simultaneously* and for ever, in the *Nunc stans*, whereas only apparently now this now that exists; then we shall understand what the objectification of the will-to-live really means. Our pleasure in genre pictures is also due mainly to their fixing the fleeting scenes of life. The dogma of metempsychosis resulted from the feeling of the truth just expressed.

2   Death says: You are the product of an act that ought not to have taken place; therefore, to wipe it out, you must die.

PART XVI

John Stuart Mill (1806–73)

Introduction

Mill's thought, like Bentham's, was shaped by his commitment to the principle of utility. Our first selection is an early speech on the subject of perfectibility which Mill delivered to the London Debating Society in 1828. In it he identifies education and public opinion as the chief causes of moral improvement in society. However, Mill also recognized that whether or not a society succeeds in cultivating the moral development of its members depends on many factors, not the least of which is its political organization. In his later writings, especially in *Considerations on Representative Government* (1861), he argued for the superiority of representative democracy on the grounds that it offers the greatest opportunities for individual development. His enthusiasm for democracy was qualified, however, by his concern that the uninstructed masses are not competent to rule themselves. This concern is directly addressed in the second selection, entitled *On Democracy* (1835). The next two selections are from some of Mill's more familiar writings. The first, from *A System of Logic* (1843), inquires into the assumptions underlying inductive reasoning. This is followed by the third chapter of *Utilitarianism* (1863) in which Mill presents a justification of the utilitarian moral theory. The concluding selection is from a late essay entitled *The Utility of Religion* (1874). Here Mill argues that religion manifests itself in an individual's "deep feeling for the general good" and sense of common purpose, and that these are more fully realized in the "Religion of Humanity" than in any supernatural religion.

56

Speech on Perfectibility

Mr. President, if I had much anxiety to save my credit as a wise and practical person, I should not venture to stand forth in defence of the progressiveness of the human mind. I know that among all that class of persons who consider themselves to be *par excellence*, the wise and the practical, it is esteemed a proof of consummate judgment, to despair of doing good. I know that it is thought essential to a man who has any knowledge of the world, to have an extremely bad opinion of it: and that whenever there are two ways of explaining any fact, wise and practical people always take that way which attributes most folly, or most immorality, to the mass of mankind. Sir, it is not for me to dispute the palm of practicality with these sage and cautious persons. Howsoever it may be with all other aberrations of the human intellect, there is one description of errors from which it would be uncandid to deny that they are wholly free, viz. all those which arise from immoderate benevolence, or ill regulated philanthropy. It behoves those who have discarded errors so pleasing, so encouraging, so ennobling to every virtuous mind, to be very certain that they have discarded them in favour of truth. Those who have stripped themselves so philosophically of every prejudice which acts as a stimulus to our duty, should be very sure that they have left no other prejudices of a more discreditable description behind. They may be assured that the errors of benevolence are by no means those from which human prosperity has most to appre-

Speech on Perfectibility (delivered May 2, 1828). From *The Collected Works of John Stuart Mill*, vol. 26, ed. John M. Robson (University of Toronto Press, 1988). Selection: pp. 428–33.

hend, and however desirable it may be for the good of mankind that the love of virtue should never rise above temperate, we must be careful not to go on cooling it till it sinks to the freezing point. Sir, I do not feel my virtue to be of so warm and impetuous a character as to need any cooling, neither have I that confidence in my own judgment which would induce me to set up my opinion of truth in opposition to hopes and feelings which at least serve as a counteracting force against hopes and feelings far less pure, and I cannot but think far more pernicious. If we must err, at least let our errors not be on the side of selfishness; it is not that part, that element of the human constitution, which needs strengthening; there is not the slightest danger that it should ever be weaker than the good of human society requires.

But is it indeed an error to suppose mankind capable of great improvement? And is it really a mark of wisdom, to deride all grand schemes of human amelioration as visionary? I can assure honourable gentlemen that so far from being a proof of any wisdom it is what any fool can do as well as themselves, and I believe it is the fools principally, who have attached to that mode of proceeding the reputation of wisdom. For as I have observed that if there is a man in public or private life who is so impenetrably dull that reason and argument never make the slightest impression upon him, the dull people immediately set him down as a man of excellent judgment and strong sense, as if because men of talent and genius are sometimes deficient in judgment, it followed that it was only necessary to be without one spark of talent or genius in order to be a man of consummate judgment, because people are sometimes deceived by rash hopes in the same manner. I think I have observed that not the man who hopes when others despair, but the man who despairs when others hope, is admired by a large class of persons as a sage, and wisdom is supposed to consist not in seeing further than other people, but in not seeing so far. I mean no disrespect to some highly estimable persons, who are of a different opinion from myself on this question, but I am persuaded that a vast majority of those who laugh at the hopes of those who think that man can be raised to any higher rank as a moral and intellectual being, do so from a principle very different from wisdom or knowledge of the world. I believe that the great majority of those who speak of perfectibility as a dream do so because they feel that it is one which would afford them no pleasure if it were realised. I believe that they hold the progressiveness of the human mind to be chimerical, because they are conscious that they themselves are doing nothing to forward it and are anxious to believe that great work impossible, in which if it were possible they know it would be their duty to assist. I believe that there is something else which powerfully helps many persons to the same conclusion, a consciousness that they do not wish to get rid of their own imperfections, and a consequent unwillingness to believe it practicable that others should throw off theirs. I believe that if persons ignorant of the world sometimes miscalculate from expecting to find mankind wiser and better than they are, those persons who most affect to know the world are incessantly miscalculating the opposite way, and confidently reckoning upon a greater degree of knavery and folly among mankind than really exists. These last indeed differ from the others in not being so ready to correct their error, since the same utter incapacity of taking any generous and enlarged views which caused their mistake, prevents them from discovering it, and makes them impute those effects of the better part of man's nature which they did not calculate upon, only to a different species of selfishness. I will even say, that so far from its being a mark of wisdom to despair of human improvement there is no more certain indication of narrow views and a limited understanding, and that the wisest men of all political and religious opinions, from Condorcet to Mr. Coleridge, have been something nearly approaching to perfectibilians. Nay further, that the anti perfectibility doctrine, far from having the sanction of experience, is brought forward in opposition to one of the clearest cases of experience which human affairs present, and that by all just rules of induction we ought to conclude that an extremely high degree of moral and intellectual excellence may be made to prevail among mankind at large, since causes exist which have confessedly been found adequate to produce it in many particular instances.

In the little which I intend to say, I shall attempt little more than to expand and develope this last remark. There are others in this Society far more competent than myself to discuss in detail the past progress of the human mind, and the stages through which it is likely to pass in the road to further improvement. I leave it to them to point out how the difficulties are to be struggled with – it is enough for me if I can establish, on the ground of solid experience, that these difficulties may be overcome.

I shall confine myself in the first instance to the question of moral improvement. I shall not ask you, Sir, to expect among mankind any degree of moral excellence that is without parallel. My standard shall be one which we all know, which we all believe in, with which we are all familiar in our own experience. I suppose it will not be denied that there are and have been persons who have possessed a very high degree of virtue. Now here I take my stand: there have been such persons. I do not care how many; nor who they were. If I were to name any person, any historical character, to whom I think the designation applicable, without doubt that person might be cavilled at, and something raked up to throw a doubt upon his virtue, for it is difficult to adduce evidence on such a point that shall leave no possibility of cavil; but will those persons who say that this man or that man was not virtuous go farther and say that nobody was ever virtuous? I should think not. All they can say is that in the most virtuous there has been some frailty, some fault or weakness which has rendered even the best of them less than perfect. Certainly all this may be safely admitted. I shall not affirm that men in general can be made better than the best men whom the human race has hitherto produced.

Well then, here is a fact: there have been virtuous men: Now, what made them virtuous? I call upon the gentlemen on the other side to answer this question, for if it should turn out that those who are virtuous are so from causes which though they now act only upon a few, can be made to act upon all mankind, or the greater part, it is within the power of human exertion to make all or most men as virtuous as those are. I therefore challenge honourable gentlemen to say to what they attribute the superior moral excellence of some persons. If they do not answer, I will. It is to the original influence of good moral education, in their early years, and the insensible influence of the world, of society, of public opinion, upon their habits and associations in after life. Here then is specific experience. It is distinctly proved that these two forces, education and public opinion, when they are both of them brought fairly into play, and made to act in harmony with one another, are capable of producing high moral excellence. And yet the greater part of the arguments which have been advanced against us this evening are intended to prove that moral education and public opinion are *not* capable of producing these effects.

Why then have these causes not produced the same effects upon all, which they have upon some? Why but because they have not acted upon all. No pains have been taken with the moral education of mankind in general. The great business of moral education, to form virtuous habits of mind, is I may say entirely neglected: the child is indeed punished for certain immoral acts, but as for going to the root of the evil, and correcting the dispositions in which these acts originate, the thing is never thought of, or if it is thought of, nothing can be more ridiculously inefficacious than the means which are taken to effect it. And all this from sheer ignorance: for it is not that people do not set a sufficient value upon those habits of mind which lead to good habits of conduct; it is that they really do not know how such habits are generated, what they depend upon, and what mode of education favours or counteracts them. While that education which is called education is in this deplorable state, that insensible education which is not called education is still worse, for almost every where the great objects of ambition, those which ought to be the rewards of high intellectual and moral excellence, are the rewards either of wealth, as in this country, or of private favour, as in most others; and it is an established fact in the nature of man that whatever are the means by which the great recompenses of ambition are to be obtained, the person who possesses these means, and can therefore pretend to those recompenses, is the person who exercises influence over the public mind; he is the person whose favour is courted, whose actions are imitated, whose opinions are adopted, and the contagion of whose feelings is caught by the mass of mankind.

It is a very poor and ill divided public opinion, which can be formed out of an aggregate so ill composed. And yet that public opinion which is the result of so bad a moral education, is sufficient whenever it is combined with a better moral education to produce all the virtue which we see realized in some individuals of mankind as they now are.

It will of course be said that although good moral education and the operation of public opinion produce so much excellence in some persons, it does not follow that they can in all. I maintain on the contrary, that there is much less difficulty in producing it in all than there has been to produce it in some. Whatever of moral excellence now exists, has been produced in spite of a thousand obstacles: in spite of systems of education which if the names were altered and they were reported to us as existing in some far distant country would be considered incredible from the absolute fatuity, the utter abnegation of intellect which they exhibit; in spite of laws which in a hundred ways inflict evil upon one man for the benefit of another, and generate a spirit of domination and oppression on one side, of cringing and servility, mixed with bitter and vindictive resentment on the other; in spite of systems of judicial procedure which seem devised on purpose to give right and wrong an equal chance, and in which every possible encouragement is held out to the vice of insincerity – in spite of political institutions which in this at least, the most civilized country in the world, render wealth the only acquisition which is desired, poverty almost the only evil that is dreaded. All these evils might be remedied by the hand of God. If notwithstanding all these things the best moral education which the present circumstances of mankind admit of has produced, in those to whom it is given, so much excellence, what may not be expected if we remove these obstacles, and when they are taken away, give even as good a moral education to the greater portion of mankind – why not to all mankind: for moral excellence does not suppose a high order of intellectual cultivation, since it is often found in greatest perfection in the rudest minds.

With respect to such doctrines as have been advanced this evening on the other side, some of them I must confess have surprised me. We have been told that it is impossible to diminish the amount of vice, because vice arises from the passions, and it is impossible to vanquish the passions. Now, Sir, I demur to this, first, that it is taking a very narrow view of the principles of morals and the nature of the human mind to suppose that it is necessary for any good purpose to vanquish the passions. There is not one of the passions which by a well regulated education may not be converted into an auxiliary of the moral principle: there is not one of the passions which may not be as fully and much more permanently gratified, by a course of virtuous conduct than by vice. And if this be the case surely it would be the worst of policy even looking to moral excellence without regarding happiness in the least, to eradicate the passions, because it is they which furnish the active principle, the moving force; the passions are the spring, the moral principle only the regulator of human life.

But further, this very assertion that the passions cannot be vanquished may be taken as a specimen of the shallow philosophy of these gentlemen and their very superficial experience of mankind. They who profess to know human nature so well, seem to be very little aware what it is capable of. Have we not seen that men have lain for their whole lives upon beds of spikes; that they have stood all their lives upon the tops of pillars; that they have remained all their lives without stirring for one moment from a certain posture because they have willed it? Have they not swung by hooks drawn through their backs, and suffered themselves to be crushed by chariot wheels, and laid themselves voluntarily on funeral piles to be burned? Have not these things been done not by heroes and philosophers, but thousands and millions of common men, commonly educated? And then let gentlemen come and give us arguments which, if they prove any thing, prove the impossibility of all this. We could do none of these things: why? because we have never been accustomed to fix our imaginations on these things long enough for our first horror of them to wear off: but what caused these surprising achievements? It must have been either religion, conscience, or public opinion; gentlemen may choose, it shall be any one of the three: we have heard the force of each of the three separately explained away, and very plausible arguments adduced to prove that no one of them is strong enough to produce these effects. And yet the effects are produced. And let me ask these gentlemen the reason why? I will give up any two of the forces to them, if they grant me the third. If they ask, my own opinion is that all helped, but that the proximate motive had most

influence, that derived from public opinion: and some honourable gentlemen who have sometimes wondered at hearing public opinion spoken of in this Society as the immense force that it is, may perhaps now see from these instances why it is so spoken of.

But if such is the force of public opinion, what is wanting to produce that high state of general morality which we aspire to? Simply that public opinion should be well directed in respect of morality: that such a system of education should exist, as will give to the mass of mankind, not learning, but commonsense – practical judgment in ordinary affairs, and shall enable them to see that a thing is wrong when it is wrong, as shall make them despise humbug and see through casuistry and imposture, not to accept subterfuges and excuses for neglecting a duty, and not think the same thing laudable under a fine name and blamable under a vulgar one, for instance, not to think, like some persons in this room, that giving a man money, or money's worth, for voting against his conviction, is criminal when called bribery, but laudable when called legitimate influence of property: to judge of men by the manner in which they act, not by the manner in which they talk; not to estimate a man's moral excellence by the quantity of grimace which he exhibits in his own person, or by the quantity of hypocrisy which he exacts from his family and dependants; not to give men any credit for making great sacrifices at other people's expense, or for being philanthropic at a distance and prudent at home; not to think that charity consists in making laws to take away bread from the poor, and subscribing a few pounds annually to some institution for giving it to them; and in short not to see a great many other nice distinctions which the refined and cultivated people of the present day are able to see, and very ready to act upon. And there is another thing that is requisite – to take men out of the sphere of the opinion of their separate and private coteries, and make them amenable to the general tribunal of the public at large – to leave no class possessed of power sufficient to protect one another in defying public opinion, and to manufacture a separate code of morality for their private guidance; and so to organize the political institutions of a country that no one could possess any power save what might be given to him by the favourable sentiments, not of any separate class with a separate interest, but of the people.

57

On Democracy

From the principle of the necessity of identifying the interest of the government with that of the people, most of the practical maxims of a representative government are corollaries. All popular institutions are means towards rendering the identity of interest more complete. We say *more* complete, because (and this it is important to remark) perfectly complete it can never be. An approximation is all that is, in the nature of things, possible. By pushing to its utmost extent the accountability of governments to the people, you indeed take away from thcm thc power of prosecuting their own interests at the expense of the people by force, but you leave to them the whole range and compass of fraud. An attorney is accountable to his client, and removable at his client's pleasure; but we should scarcely say that his interest is identical with that of his client. When the accountability is perfect, the interest of rulers approximates more and more to identity with that of the people, in proportion as the people are more enlightened. The identity would be perfect, only if the people were so wise, that it should no longer be practicable to employ deceit as an instrument of government; a point of advancement only one stage below that at which they could do without government altogether; at least, without force, and penal sanctions, not (of course) without guidance and organized co-operation.

Identification of interest between the rulers and the ruled, being therefore, in a literal sense, impossible to be realized, ought not to be spoken of as

On Democracy (1835). From *J. S. Mill: A Selection of His Works*, ed. J. M. Robson (New York: Odyssey Press, 1966). Selection: pp. 453–8.

a condition which a government must absolutely fulfil; but as an end to be incessantly aimed at, and approximated to as nearly as circumstances render possible, and as is compatible with the regard due to other ends. For this identity of interest, even if it were wholly attainable, not being the sole requisite of good government, expediency may require that we should sacrifice some portion of it, or (to speak more precisely) content ourselves with a somewhat less approximation to it than might possibly be attainable, for the sake of some other end.

The only end, liable occasionally to conflict with that which we have been insisting on, and at all comparable to it in importance – the only other condition essential to good government – is this: That it be government by a select body, not by the public collectively: That political questions be not decided by an appeal, either direct or indirect, to the judgment or will of an uninstructed mass, whether of gentlemen or of clowns; but by the deliberately formed opinions of a comparatively few, specially educated for the task. This is an element of good government which has existed, in a greater or less degree, in some aristocracies, though unhappily not in our own; and has been the cause of whatever reputation for prudent and skilful administration those governments have enjoyed....

[The fortunate circumstances which lead to good aristocratic government], however, are seldom to be reckoned upon. But though the principle of government by persons specially brought up to it will not suffice to produce good government, good government cannot be had without it; and the grand difficulty in politics will for a long time be, how best to conciliate the two great elements on which good government depends; to combine the greatest amount of the advantage derived from the independent judgment of a specially instructed few, with the greatest degree of the security for rectitude of purpose derived from rendering those few responsible to the many.

What is necessary, however, to make the two ends perfectly reconcilable, is a smaller matter than might at first sight be supposed. It is not necessary that the many should themselves be perfectly wise; it is sufficient if they be duly sensible of the value of superior wisdom. It is sufficient if they be aware, that the majority of political questions turn upon considerations of which they, and all persons not trained for the purpose, must necessarily be very imperfect judges; and that their judgment must in general be exercised rather upon the characters and talents of the persons whom they appoint to decide these questions for them, than upon the questions themselves. They would then select as their representatives those whom the general voice of the instructed pointed out as the *most* instructed; and would retain them, so long as no symptom was manifested in their conduct, of being under the influence of interests or of feelings at variance with the public welfare. This implies no greater wisdom in the people than the very ordinary wisdom, of knowing what things they are and are not sufficient judges of. If the bulk of any nation possess a fair share of this wisdom, the argument for universal suffrage, so far as respects that people, is irresistible; for the experience of ages, and especially of all great national emergencies, bears out the assertion, that whenever the multitude are really alive to the necessity of superior intellect, they rarely fail to distinguish those who possess it.

The idea of a rational democracy is, not that the people themselves govern, but that they have security for good government. This security they cannot have by any other means than by retaining in their own hands the ultimate control. If they renounce this, they give themselves up to tyranny. A governing class not accountable to the people are sure, in the main, to sacrifice the people to the pursuit of separate interests and inclinations of their own. Even their feelings of morality, even their ideas of excellence, have reference, not to the good of the people, but to their own good: their very virtues are class virtues – their noblest acts of patriotism and self-devotion are but the sacrifice of their private interests to the interests of their class.

... In no government will the interests of the people be the object, except where the people are able to dismiss their rulers as soon as the devotion of those rulers to the interests of the people becomes questionable. But this is the only fit use to be made of popular power. Provided good intentions can be secured, the best government (need it be said?) must be the government of the wisest, and these must always be a few. The people ought to be the masters, but they are masters who must employ servants more skilful than themselves: like a ministry when they employ a military commander, or the military commander when he employs an army surgeon. When the minister ceases to confide in the commander, he dismisses him and appoints another; but he does not, if he is wise, send him instructions when and where to fight. He holds him responsible only for intentions and for results. The people must do the same. This does not render the control of the people nugatory. The control of a government over the commander of an army is not nugatory. A man's control over his physician is not nugatory, though he does not direct his physician what medicine to administer.

But in government, as in everything else, the danger is, lest those who can do whatever they will, may will to do more than is for their ultimate interest. The interest of the people is, to choose for their rulers the most instructed and the ablest persons who can be found; and having done so, to allow them to exercise their knowledge and ability for the good of the people, under the check of the freest discussion and the most unreserved censure, but with the least possible direct interference of their constituents – as long as it *is* the good of the people, and not some private end, that they are aiming at. A democracy thus administered would unite all the good qualities ever possessed by any government. Not only would its ends be good, but its means would be as well chosen as the wisdom of the age would allow; and the omnipotence of the majority would be exercised through the agency and according to the judgment of an enlightened minority, accountable to the majority in the last resort.

But it is not possible that the constitution of the democracy itself should provide adequate security for its being understood and administered in this spirit. This rests with the good sense of the people themselves. If the people can remove their rulers for one thing, they can for another. That ultimate control, without which they cannot have security for good government, may, if they please, be made the means of themselves interfering in the government, and making their legislators mere delegates for carrying into execution the preconceived judgment of the majority. If the people do this, they mistake their interest; and such a government, though better than most aristocracies, is not the kind of democracy which wise men desire.

Some persons, and persons too whose desire for enlightened government cannot be questioned, do not take so serious a view of this perversion of the true idea of an enlightened democracy. They say, it is well that the many should evoke all political questions to their own tribunal, and decide them according to their own judgment, because then philosophers will be compelled to enlighten the multitude, and render them capable of appreciating their more profound views. No one can attach greater value than we do to this consequence of popular government, so far as we believe it capable of being realized; and the argument would be irresistible, if, in order to instruct the people, all that is requisite were to will it; if it were only the *discovery* of political truths which required study and wisdom, and the evidences of them when discovered could be made apparent at once to any person of common sense, as well educated as every individual in the community might and ought to be. But the fact is not so. Many of the truths of politics (in political economy, for instance) are the result of a concatenation of propositions, the very first steps of which no one who has not gone through a course of study is prepared to concede; there are others, to have a complete perception of which requires much meditation, and experience of human nature. How will philosophers bring these home to the perceptions of the multitude? Can they enable common sense to judge of science, or inexperience of experience? Everyone who has even crossed the threshold of political philosophy knows, that on many of its questions the false view is greatly the most plausible; and a large portion of its truths are, and must always remain, to all but those who have specially studied them, paradoxes; as contrary, in appearance, to common sense, as the proposition that the earth moves round the sun. The multitude will never believe those truths, until tendered to them from an authority in which they have as unlimited confidence as they have in the unanimous voice of astronomers on a question of astronomy. That they should have no such confidence at present is no discredit to them; for where are the persons who are entitled to it? But we are well satisfied that it will be given, as soon as knowledge shall have made sufficient progress among the instructed classes themselves, to produce something like a general agreement in their opinions on the leading points of moral and political doctrine. Even now, on those points on which the instructed classes are agreed, the uninstructed have generally adopted their opinions.

58

A System of Logic

Of the Ground of Induction

1. Axiom of the uniformity of the course of nature

Induction properly so called, as distinguished from those mental operations, sometimes, though improperly, designated by the name, which I have attempted in the preceding chapter to characterize, may, then, be summarily defined as generalization from experience. It consists in inferring from some individual instances in which a phenomenon is observed to occur that it occurs in all instances of a certain class, namely, in all which *resemble* the former in what are regarded as the material circumstances.

In what way the material circumstances are to be distinguished from those which are immaterial, or why some of the circumstances are material and others not so, we are not yet ready to point out. We must first observe that there is a principle implied in the very statement of what induction is; an assumption with regard to the course of nature and the order of the universe, namely, that there are such things in nature as parallel cases; that what happens once will, under a sufficient degree of similarity of circumstances, happen again, and not only again, but as often as the same circumstances recur. This, I say, is an assumption involved in every case of induction. And, if we consult the actual course of nature, we find that the assumption is warranted. The universe, so far

A System of Logic (1843). From *J. S. Mill's Philosophy of Scientific Method*, ed. Ernest Nagel (New York: Hafner Publishing Co., 1950). Selection: ch. 3, "Of the Ground of Induction," pp. 181–6.

as known to us, is so constituted that whatever is true in any one case is true in all cases of a certain description; the only difficulty is to find what description.

This universal fact, which is our warrant for all inferences from experience, has been described by different philosophers in different forms of language: that the course of nature is uniform; that the universe is governed by general laws; and the like....

Whatever be the most proper mode of expressing it, the proposition that the course of nature is uniform is the fundamental principle or general axiom of induction. It would yet be a great error to offer this large generalization as any explanation of the inductive process. On the contrary, I hold it to be itself an instance of induction, and induction by no means of the most obvious kind. Far from being the first induction we make, it is one of the last or, at all events, one of those which are latest in attaining strict philosophical accuracy. As a general maxim, indeed, it has scarcely entered into the minds of any but philosophers; nor even by them, as we shall have many opportunities of remarking, have its extent and limits been always very justly conceived. The truth is that this great generalization is itself founded on prior generalizations. The obscurer laws of nature were discovered by means of it, but the more obvious ones must have been understood and assented to as general truths before it was ever heard of. We should never have thought of affirming that all phenomena take place according to general laws if we had not first arrived, in the case of a great multitude of phenomena, at some knowledge of the laws themselves, which could be done no otherwise than by induction. In what sense, then, can a principle which is so far from being our earliest induction be regarded as our warrant for all the others? In the only sense in which (as we have already seen) the general propositions which we place at the head of our reasonings when we throw them into syllogisms ever really contribute to their validity. As Archbishop Whately remarks, every induction is a syllogism with the major premise suppressed; or (as I prefer expressing it) every induction may be thrown into the form of a syllogism by supplying a major premise. If this be actually done, the principle which we are now considering, that of the uniformity of the course of nature, will appear as the ultimate major premise of all inductions and will, therefore, stand to all inductions in the relation in which, as has been shown at so much length, the major proposition of a syllogism always stands to the conclusion, not contributing at all to prove it, but being a necessary condition of its being proved; since no conclusion is proved for which there cannot be found a true major premise.

The statement that the uniformity of the course of nature is the ultimate major premise in all cases of induction may be thought to require some explanation. The immediate major premise in every inductive argument it certainly is not. Of that, Archbishop Whately's must be held to be the correct account. The induction, "John, Peter, etc., are mortal, therefore all mankind are mortal," may, as he justly says, be thrown into a syllogism by prefixing as a major premise (what is at any rate a necessary condition of the validity of the argument), namely, that what is true of John, Peter, etc., is true of all mankind. But how came we by this major premise? It is not self-evident; nay, in all cases of unwarranted generalization, it is not true. How, then, is it arrived at? Necessarily either by induction or ratiocination; and if by induction, the process, like all other inductive arguments, may be thrown into the form of a syllogism. This previous syllogism it is, therefore, necessary to construct. There is, in the long run, only one possible construction. The real proof that what is true of John, Peter, etc., is true of all mankind can only be that a different supposition would be inconsistent with the uniformity which we know to exist in the course of nature. Whether there would be this inconsistency or not may be a matter of long and delicate inquiry, but unless there would, we have no sufficient ground for the major [premise] of the inductive syllogism. It hence appears that, if we throw the whole course of any inductive argument into a series of syllogisms, we shall arrive by more or fewer steps at an ultimate syllogism which will have for its major premise the principle or axiom of the uniformity of the course of nature.[1] . . .

2. The question of inductive logic stated

In order to [reach] a better understanding of the problem which the logician must solve if he would establish a scientific theory of induction, let us compare a few cases of incorrect inductions with others which are acknowledged to be legitimate. Some, we know, which were believed for centuries to be correct were nevertheless incorrect. That all swans are white cannot have been a good induction, since the conclusion has turned out erroneous. The experience, however, on which the conclusion rested was genuine. From the earliest records, the testimony of the inhabitants of the known world was unanimous on the point. The uniform experience, therefore, of the inhabitants of the known world, agreeing in a common result, without one known instance of deviation from that result, is not always sufficient to establish a general conclusion.

But let us now turn to an instance apparently not very dissimilar to this. Mankind were wrong, it seems, in concluding that all swans were white; are we also wrong when we conclude that all men's heads grow above their shoulders and never below, in spite of the conflicting testimony of the naturalist Pliny? As there were black swans, though civilized people had existed for three thousand years on the earth without meeting with them, may there not also be "men whose heads do grow beneath their shoulders," notwithstanding a rather less perfect unanimity of negative testimony from observers? Most persons would answer, No; it was more credible that a bird should vary in its color than that men should vary in the relative position of their principal organs. And there is no doubt that in so saying they would be right; but to say why they are right would be impossible without entering more deeply than is usually done into the true theory of induction.

Again, there are cases in which we reckon with the most unfailing confidence upon uniformity, and other cases in which we do not count upon it at all. In some we feel complete assurance that the future will resemble the past, the unknown be precisely similar to the known. In others, however invariable may be the result obtained from the instances which have been observed, we draw from them no more than a very feeble presumption that the like result will hold in all other cases. That a straight line is the shortest distance between two points we do not doubt to be true even in the region of the fixed stars.[2] When a chemist announces the existence and properties of a newly-discovered substance, if we confide in his accuracy, we feel assured that the conclusions he has arrived at will hold universally, though the induction be founded but on a single instance. We do not withhold our assent, waiting for a repetition of the experiment; or if we do, it is from a doubt whether the one experiment was properly made, not whether if properly made it would be conclusive. Here, then, is a general law of nature inferred without hesitation from a single instance, a universal proposition from a singular one. Now mark another case, and contrast it with this. Not all the instances which have been observed since the beginning of the world in support of the general proposition that all crows are black would be deemed a sufficient presumption of the truth of the proposition to outweigh the testimony of one unexceptionable witness who should affirm that, in some region of the earth not fully explored, he had caught and examined a crow and had found it to be gray.

Why is a single instance, in some cases, sufficient for a complete induction, while, in others, myriads of concurring instances, without a single exception known or presumed, go such a very little way toward establishing a universal proposition? Whoever can answer this question knows more of the philosophy of logic than the wisest of the ancients and has solved the problem of induction.

Notes

1 But though it is a condition of the validity of every induction that there be uniformity in the course of nature, it is not a necessary condition that the uniformity should pervade all nature. It is enough that it pervades the particular class of phenomena to which the induction relates. An induction concerning the motions of the planets or the properties of the magnet would not be vitiated though we were to suppose that wind and weather are the sport of chance, provided it be assumed that astronomical and magnetic phenomena are under the dominion of general laws. Otherwise the early experience of mankind would have rested on a very weak foundation, for in the infancy of science it could not be known that *all* phenomena are regular in their course.

Neither would it be correct to say that every induction by which we infer any truth implies the general fact of uniformity *as foreknown*, even in reference to the kind of phenomena concerned. It implies *either* that this general fact is already known, *or* that we may now know it; as the conclusion, the Duke of Wellington is mortal, drawn from the instances A, B, and C, implies either that we have already concluded all men to be mortal, or that we are now entitled to do so from the same evidence. A vast amount of confusion and paralogism respecting the grounds of induction would be dispelled by keeping in view these simple considerations.

2 In strictness, wherever the present constitution of space exists, which we have ample reason to believe that it does in the region of the fixed stars.

59

Utilitarianism

Of the Ultimate Sanction of the Principle of Utility

The question is often asked, and properly so, in regard to any supposed moral standard, What is its sanction? what are the motives to obey it? or, more specifically, what is the source of its obligation? whence does it derive its binding force? It is a necessary part of moral philosophy to provide the answer to this question; which, though frequently assuming the shape of an objection to the utilitarian morality, as if it had some special applicability to that above others, really arises in regard to all standards. It arises, in fact, whenever a person is called on to *adopt* a standard, or refer morality to any basis on which he has not been accustomed to rest it. For the customary morality, that which education and opinion have consecrated, is the only one which presents itself to the mind with the feeling of being *in itself* obligatory: and, when a person is asked to believe that this morality *derives* its obligation from some general principle round which custom has not thrown the same halo, the assertion is to him a paradox; the supposed corollaries seem to have a more binding force than the original theorem; the superstructure seems to stand better without than with what is represented as its foundation. He says to himself, "I feel that I am bound not to rob or murder, betray or deceive; but why am I bound to promote the general hap-

Utilitarianism (1863). From *Dissertations and Discussions*, vol. 3 (New York: Henry Holt and Co., 1882). Selection: ch. 3, "Of the Ultimate Sanction of the Principle of Utility," pp. 336–47.

piness? If my own happiness lies in something else, why may I not give that the preference?"

If the view adopted by the utilitarian philosophy of the nature of the moral sense be correct, this difficulty will always present itself, until the influences which form moral character have taken the same hold of the principle which they have taken of some of the consequences; until, by the improvement of education, the feeling of unity with our fellow-creatures shall be (what it cannot be denied that Christ intended it to be) as deeply rooted in our character, and, to our own consciousness, as completely a part of our nature, as the horror of crime is in an ordinarily well brought up young person. In the mean time, however, the difficulty has no peculiar application to the doctrine of utility, but is inherent in every attempt to analyze morality, and reduce it to principles; which, unless the principle is already in men's minds invested with as much sacredness as any of its applications, always seems to divest them of a part of their sanctity.

The principle of utility either has, or there is no reason why it might not have, all the sanctions which belong to any other system of morals. Those sanctions are either external or internal. Of the external sanctions it is not necessary to speak at any length. They are, the hope of favor and the fear of displeasure from our fellow-creatures, or from the Ruler of the universe, along with whatever we may have of sympathy or affection for them; or of love and awe of him, inclining us to do his will independently of selfish consequences. There is evidently no reason why all these motives for observance should not attach themselves to the utilitarian morality as completely and as powerfully as to any other. Indeed, those of them which refer to our fellow-creatures are sure to do so, in proportion to the amount of general intelligence: for, whether there be any other ground of moral obligation than the general happiness or not, men do desire happiness; and, however imperfect may be their own practice, they desire and commend all conduct in others towards themselves by which they think their happiness is promoted. With regard to the religious motive, if men believe, as most profess to do, in the goodness of God, those who think that conduciveness to the general happiness is the essence, or even only the criterion, of good, must necessarily believe that it is also that which God approves. The whole force, therefore, of external reward and punishment, whether physical or moral, and whether proceeding from God or from our fellow-men, together with all that the capacities of human nature admit of disinterested devotion to either, become available to enforce the utilitarian morality, in proportion as that morality is recognized; and the more powerfully, the more the appliances of education and general cultivation are bent to the purpose.

So far as to external sanctions. The internal sanction of duty, whatever our standard of duty may be, is one and the same, – a feeling in our own mind; a pain, more or less intense, attendant on violation of duty, which, in properly cultivated moral natures, rises in the more serious cases into shrinking from it as an impossibility. This feeling, when disinterested, and connecting itself with the pure idea of duty, and not with some particular form of it, or with any of the merely accessory circumstances, is the essence of Conscience: though in that complex phenomenon, as it actually exists, the simple fact is, in general, all incrusted over with collateral associations, derived from sympathy, from love, and still more from fear; from all the forms of religious feeling; from the recollections of childhood, and of all our past life; from self-esteem, desire of the esteem of others, and occasionally even self-abasement. This extreme complication is, I apprehend, the origin of the sort of mystical character, which, by a tendency of the human mind of which there are many other examples, is apt to be attributed to the idea of moral obligation, and which leads people to believe that the idea cannot possibly attach itself to any other objects than those which, by a supposed mysterious law, are found in our present experience to excite it. Its binding force, however, consists in the existence of a mass of feeling which

must be broken through in order to do what violates our standard of right; and which, if we do nevertheless violate that standard, will probably have to be encountered afterwards in the form of remorse. Whatever theory we have of the nature of origin of conscience, this is what essentially constitutes it.

The ultimate sanction, therefore, of all morality (external motives apart) being a subjective feeling in our own minds, I see nothing embarrassing, to those whose standard is utility, in the question, What is the sanction of that particular standard? We may answer, The same as of all other moral standards, – the conscientious feelings of mankind. Undoubtedly this sanction has no binding efficacy on those who do not possess the feelings it appeals to; but neither will these persons be more obedient to any other moral principle than to the utilitarian one. On them, morality of any kind has no hold but through the external sanctions. Meanwhile the feelings exist, – a fact in human nature, the reality of which, and the great power with which they are capable of acting on those in whom they have been duly cultivated, are proved by experience. No reason has ever been shown why they may not be cultivated to as great intensity in connection with the utilitarian as with any other rule of morals.

There is, I am aware, a disposition to believe that a person who sees in moral obligation a transcendental fact, an objective reality belonging to the province of "things in themselves," is likely to be more obedient to it than one who believes it to be entirely subjective, having its seat in human consciousness only. But, whatever a person's opinion may be on this point of ontology, the force he is really urged by is his own subjective feeling, and is exactly measured by its strength. No one's belief that Duty is an objective reality is stronger than the belief that God is so; yet the belief in God, apart from the expectation of actual reward and punishment, only operates on conduct through, and in proportion to, the subjective religious feeling. The sanction, so far as it is disinterested, is always in the mind itself: and the notion, therefore, of the transcendental moralists must be, that this sanction will not exist *in* the mind, unless it is believed to have its root out of the mind; and that if a person is able to say to himself, "This which is restraining me, and which is called my conscience, is only a feeling in my own mind," he may possibly draw the conclusion, that, when the feeling ceases, the obligation ceases; and that, if he find the feeling inconvenient, he may disregard it, and endeavor to get rid of it. But is this danger confined to the utilitarian morality? Does the belief that moral obligation has its seat outside the mind make the feeling of it too strong to be got rid of? The fact is so far otherwise, that all moralists admit and lament the ease with which, in the generality of minds, conscience can be silenced or stifled. The question, Need I obey my conscience? is quite as often put to themselves by persons who never heard of the principle of utility as by its adherents. Those whose conscientious feelings are so weak as to allow of their asking this question, if they answer it affirmatively, will not do so because they believe in the transcendental theory, but because of the external sanctions.

It is not necessary, for the present purpose, to decide whether the feeling of duty is innate or implanted. Assuming it to be innate, it is an open question to what objects it naturally attaches itself; for the philosophic supporters of that theory are now agreed that the intuitive perception is of principles of morality, and not of the details. If there be any thing innate in the matter, I see no reason why the feeling which is innate should not be that of regard to the pleasures and pains of others. If there is any principle of morals which is intuitively obligatory, I should say it must be that. If so, the intuitive ethics would coincide with the utilitarian, and there would be no further quarrel between them. Even as it is, the intuitive moralists, though they believe that there are other intuitive moral obligations, do already believe this to be one; for they unanimously hold that a large *portion* of morality turns upon the consideration due to the interests of our fellow-creatures. Therefore, if the belief in the transcendental origin of moral obligation gives any additional efficacy to the internal sanction, it appears to me that the utilitarian principle has already the benefit of it.

On the other hand, if, as is my own belief, the moral feelings are not innate, but acquired, they are not for that reason the less natural. It is natural to man to speak, to reason, to build cities, to cultivate the ground, though these are acquired faculties. The moral feelings are not indeed a part of our nature, in the sense of being in any perceptible degree present in all of us; but this, unhappily, is a fact admitted by those who believe the most strenuously in their transcendental origin. Like the other acquired capacities above referred to, the moral faculty, if not a part of our nature, is a natural outgrowth from it; capable like them, in a certain small degree, of springing up spontaneously, and susceptible of being brought by cultivation to a high degree of development. Unhappily, it is also susceptible, by a sufficient use of the external sanctions and of the force of early impressions, of being cultivated in almost any direction; so that there is hardly any thing so absurd or so mischievous that it may not, by means of these influences, be made to act on the human mind with all the authority of conscience. To doubt that the same potency might be given by the same means to the principle of utility, even if it had no foundation in human nature, would be flying in the face of all experience.

But moral associations which are wholly of artificial creation, when intellectual culture goes on, yield by degrees to the dissolving force of analysis: and if the feeling of duty, when associated with utility, would appear equally arbitrary; if there were no leading department of our nature, no powerful class of sentiments, with which that association would harmonize, which would make us feel it congenial, and incline us not only to foster it in others (for which we have abundant interested motives), but also to cherish it in ourselves; if there were not, in short, a natural basis of sentiment for utilitarian morality, – it might well happen that this association also, even after it had been implanted by education, might be analyzed away.

But there *is* this basis of powerful natural sentiment; and this it is, which, when once the general happiness is recognized as the ethical standard, will constitute the strength of the utilitarian morality. This firm foundation is that of the social feelings of mankind; the desire to be in unity with our fellow-creatures, which is already a powerful principle in human nature, and happily one of those which tend to become stronger, even without express inculcation from the influences of advancing civilization. The social state is at once so natural, so necessary, and so habitual to man, that except in some unusual circumstances, or by an effort of voluntary abstraction, he never conceives himself otherwise than as a member of a body; and this association is riveted more and more as mankind are further removed from the state of savage independence. Any condition, therefore, which is essential to a state of society, becomes more and more an inseparable part of every person's conception of the state of things which he is born into, and which is the destiny of a human being. Now, society between human beings, except in the relation of master and slave, is manifestly impossible on any other footing than that the interests of all are to be consulted. Society between equals can only exist on the understanding that the interests of all are to be regarded equally. And since, in all states of civilization, every person except an absolute monarch has equals, every one is obliged to live on these terms with somebody; and, in every age, some advance is made towards a state in which it will be impossible to live permanently on other terms with anybody. In this way, people grow up unable to conceive as possible to them a state of total disregard of other people's interests. They are under a necessity of conceiving themselves as at least abstaining from all the grosser injuries, and (if only for their own protection) living in a state of constant protest against them. They are also familiar with the fact of co-operating with others, and proposing to themselves a collective, not an individual, interest as the aim (at least for the time being) of their actions. So long as they are co-operating, their ends are identified with those of others: there is at least a temporary feeling that the interests of others are their own interests. Not only does all strengthening of social ties, and all healthy growth of society, give to each individual a stronger personal interest in practically consulting the welfare of others: it also leads him to identify his *feelings* more and more with their good, or at least with an ever greater degree of practical consideration for it. He comes, as though instinctively, to be conscious of himself as a being who *of course* pays regard to others. The good of others becomes to him a thing naturally and necessarily to be attended to, like any of the physical conditions of our existence. Now, whatever amount of this feeling a person has, he is urged by the strongest motives, both of interest and of sympathy, to demonstrate it, and, to the utmost of his power, encourage it in others; and, even if he has none of it himself, he is as greatly interested as any one else that others should have it. Consequently, the smallest germs of the feeling are laid hold of and nourished by the contagion of sympathy and the influences of education, and a complete web of corroborative association is woven round it by the powerful agency of the external sanctions. This mode of conceiving ourselves and human life, as civilization goes on, is felt to be more and more natural. Every step in political improvement renders it more so, by removing the sources of opposition of interest, and levelling those inequalities of legal privilege between individuals or classes, owing to which there are large portions of mankind whose happiness it is still practicable to

disregard. In an improving state of the human mind, the influences are constantly on the increase which tend to generate in each individual a feeling of unity with all the rest, which, if perfect, would make him never think of or desire any beneficial condition for himself, in the benefits of which they are not included. If we now suppose this feeling of unity to be taught as a religion, and the whole force of education, of institutions, and of opinion, directed, as it once was in the case of religion, to make every person grow up from infancy surrounded on all sides both by the profession and the practice of it, I think that no one who can realize this conception will feel any misgiving about the sufficiency of the ultimate sanction for the Happiness morality. To any ethical student who finds the realization difficult, I recommend, as a means of facilitating it, the second of M. Comte's two principal works, the "Traité de Politique Positive." I entertain the strongest objections to the system of politics and morals set forth in that treatise: but I think it has superabundantly shown the possibility of giving to the service of humanity, even without the aid of belief in a Providence, both the psychological power and the social efficacy of a religion; making it take hold of human life, and color all thought, feeling, and action, in a manner of which the greatest ascendency ever exercised by any religion may be but a type and foretaste, and of which the danger is, not that it should be insufficient, but that it should be so excessive as to interfere unduly with human freedom and individuality.

Neither is it necessary to the feeling which constitutes the binding force of the utilitarian morality on those who recognize it, to wait for those social influences which would make its obligation felt by mankind at large. In the comparatively early state of human advancement in which we now live, a person cannot indeed feel that entireness of sympathy with all others which would make any real discordance in the general direction of their conduct in life impossible; but already a person in whom the social feeling is at all developed cannot bring himself to think of the rest of his fellow-creatures as struggling rivals with him for the means of happiness, whom he must desire to see defeated in their object in order that he may succeed in his. The deeply rooted conception which every individual even now has of himself as a social being tends to make him feel it one of his natural wants, that there should be harmony between his feelings and aims and those of his fellow-creatures.

If differences of opinion and of mental culture make it impossible for him to share many of their actual feelings, – perhaps make him denounce and defy those feelings, – he still needs to be conscious that his real aim and theirs do not conflict; that he is not opposing himself to what they really wish for, – namely, their own good, – but is, on the contrary, promoting it. This feeling in most individuals is much inferior in strength to their selfish feelings, and is often wanting altogether. But, to those who have it, it possesses all the characters of a natural feeling. It does not present itself to their minds as a superstition of education, or a law despotically imposed by the power of society, but as an attribute which it would not be well for them to be without. This conviction is the ultimate sanction of the greatest-happiness morality. This it is which makes any mind of well-developed feelings work with, and not against, the outward motives to care for others, afforded by what I have called the external sanctions; and when those sanctions are wanting, or act in an opposite direction, constitutes in itself a powerful internal binding force, in proportion to the sensitiveness and thoughtfulness of the character: since few but those whose mind is a moral blank could bear to lay out their course of life on the plan of paying no regard to others, except so far as their own private interest compels.

60

The Utility of Religion

[The Religion of Humanity]

[...] Religion and poetry address themselves, at least in one of their aspects, to the same part of the human constitution: they both supply the same want, that of ideal conceptions grander and more beautiful than we see realized in the prose of human life. Religion, as distinguished from poetry, is the product of the craving to know whether these imaginative conceptions have realities answering to them in some other world than ours. The mind, in this state, eagerly catches at any rumours respecting other worlds, especially when delivered by persons whom it deems wiser than itself. To the poetry of the supernatural, comes to be thus added a positive belief and expectation, which unpoetical minds can share with the poetical. Belief in a God or Gods, and in a life after death, becomes the canvas which every mind, according to its capacity, covers with such ideal pictures as it can either invent or copy. In that other life each hopes to find the good which he has failed to find on earth, or the better which is suggested to him by the good which on earth he has partially seen and known. More especially, this belief supplies the finer minds with material for conceptions of beings more awful than they *can* have known on earth, and more excellent than they probably *have* known. So long as human life is insufficient to satisfy human aspirations, so long there will be a craving for higher things, which

"The Utility of Religion" (1874). From *Three Essays on Religion: Nature, the Utility of Religion and Theism* by John Stuart Mill (London: Longmans, Green, Reader and Dyer, 1874).

finds its most obvious satisfaction in religion. So long as earthly life is full of sufferings, so long there will be need of consolations, which the hope of heaven affords to the selfish, the love of God to the tender and grateful.

The value, therefore, of religion to the individual, both in the past and present, as a source of personal satisfaction and of elevated feelings, is not to be disputed. But it has still to be considered, whether in order to obtain this good, it is necessary to travel beyond the boundaries of the world which we inhabit; or whether the idealization of our earthly life, the cultivation of a high conception of what *it* may be made, is not capable of supplying a poetry, and, in the best sense of the word, a religion, equally fitted to exalt the feelings, and (with the same aid from education) still better calculated to ennoble the conduct, than any belief respecting the unseen powers.

At the bare suggestion of such a possibility, many will exclaim, that the short duration, the smallness and insignificance of life, if there is no prolongation of it beyond what we see, makes it impossible that great and elevated feelings can connect themselves with anything laid out on so small a scale: that such a conception of life can match with nothing higher than Epicurean feelings, and the Epicurean doctrine "Let us eat and drink, for to-morrow we die."

Unquestionably, within certain limits, the maxim of the Epicureans is sound, and applicable to much higher things than eating and drinking. To make the most of the present for all good purposes, those of enjoyment among the rest; to keep under control those mental dispositions which lead to undue sacrifice of present good for a future which may never arrive; to cultivate the habit of deriving pleasure from things within our reach, rather than from the too eager pursuit of objects at a distance; to think all time wasted which is not spent either in personal pleasure or in doing things useful to oneself or others; these are wise maxims, and the "carpe diem" doctrine, carried thus far, is a rational and legitimate corollary from the shortness of life. But that because life is short we should care for nothing beyond it, is not a legitimate conclusion; and the supposition, that human beings in general are not capable of feeling deep and even the deepest interest in things which they will never live to see, is a view of human nature as false as it is abject. Let it be remembered that if individual life is short, the life of the human species is not short; its indefinite duration is practically equivalent to endlessness; and being combined with indefinite capability of improvement, it offers to the imagination and sympathies a large enough object to satisfy any reasonable demand for grandeur of aspiration. If such an object appears small to a mind accustomed to dream of infinite and eternal beatitudes, it will expand into far other dimensions when those baseless fancies shall have receded into the past.

Nor let it be thought that only the more eminent of our species, in mind and heart, are capable of identifying their feelings with the entire life of the human race. This noble capability implies indeed a certain cultivation, but not superior to that which might be, and certainly will be if human improvement continues, the lot of all. Objects far smaller than this, and equally confined within the limits of the earth (though not within those of a single human life), have been found sufficient to inspire large masses and long successions of mankind with an enthusiasm capable of ruling the conduct, and colouring the whole life. Rome was to the entire Roman people, for many generations as much a religion as Jehovah was to the Jews; nay, much more, for they never fell off from their worship as the Jews did from theirs. And the Romans, otherwise a selfish people, with no very remarkable faculties of any kind except the purely practical, derived nevertheless from this one idea a certain greatness of soul, which manifests itself in all their history where that idea is concerned and nowhere else, and has earned for them the large share of admiration, in other respects not at all deserved, which has been felt for them by most noble-minded persons from that time to this.

When we consider how ardent a sentiment, in favourable circumstances of education, the love of country has become, we cannot judge it impossible that the love of that larger country, the world, may be nursed into similar strength, both as a source of elevated emotion and as a principle of duty. He who needs any other lesson on this subject than the whole course of ancient history affords, let him read Cicero *de Officiis*. It cannot be said that the standard of morals laid down in that celebrated treatise is a high standard. To our notions it is on many points unduly lax, and admits capitulations of conscience. But on the subject of duty to our country there is no compromise. That any man, with the smallest pretensions to virtue, could hesitate to sacrifice life, reputation, family, everything valuable to him, to the love of country is a supposition which this eminent interpreter of Greek and Roman morality cannot entertain for a moment. If, then, persons could be trained, as we see they were, not only to believe in theory that the good of their country was an object to which all others ought to yield, but to feel this practically as the grand duty of life, so also may they be made to feel the same absolute obligation towards the universal good. A morality grounded on large and wise views of the good of the whole, neither sacrificing the individual to the aggregate nor the aggregate to the individual, but giving to duty on the one hand and to freedom and spontaneity on the other their proper province, would derive its power in the superior natures from sympathy and benevolence and the passion for ideal excellence: in the inferior, from the same feelings cultivated up to the measure of their capacity, with the superadded force of shame. This exalted morality would not depend for its ascendancy on any hope of reward; but the reward which might be looked for, and the thought of which would be a consolation in suffering, and a support in moments of weakness, would not be a problematical future existence, but the approbation, in this, of those whom we respect, and ideally of all those, dead or living, whom we admire or venerate. For, the thought that our dead parents or friends would have approved our conduct is a scarcely less powerful motive than the knowledge that our living ones do approve it: and the idea that Socrates, or Howard or Washington, or Antoninus, or Christ, would have sympathized with us, or that we are attempting to do our part in the spirit in which they did theirs, has operated on the very best minds, as a strong incentive to act up to their highest feelings and convictions.

To call these sentiments by the name morality, exclusively of any other title, is claiming too little for them. They are a real religion; of which, as of other religions, outward good works (the utmost meaning usually suggested by the word morality) are only a part, and are indeed rather the fruits of the religion than the religion itself. The essence of religion is the strong and earnest direction of the emotions and desires towards an ideal object, recognized as of the highest excellence, and as rightfully paramount over all selfish objects of desire. This condition is fulfilled by the Religion of Humanity in as eminent a degree, and in as high a sense, as by the supernatural religions even in their best manifestations, and far more so than in any of their others.

Much more might be added on this topic; but enough has been said to convince any one, who can distinguish between the intrinsic capacities of human nature and the forms in which those capacities happen to have been historically developed, that the sense of unity with mankind, and a deep feeling for the general good, may be cultivated into a sentiment and a principle capable of fulfilling every important function of religion and itself justly entitled to the name. I will now further maintain, that it is not only capable of fulfilling these functions, but would fulfil them better than any form whatever of supernaturalism. It is not only entitled to be called a religion: it is a better religion than any of those which are ordinarily called by that title.

For, in the first place, it is disinterested. It carries the thoughts and feelings of self, and fixes them on an unselfish object, loved and pursued as an end for its own sake. The religions which deal in promises and threats regarding a future life, do exactly the contrary: they fasten down the thoughts to the person's own posthumous interests; they tempt him to regard the performance of his duties to others mainly as a means to his own personal salvation; and are one of the most serious obstacles to the great purpose of moral culture, the strengthening of the unselfish and weakening of the selfish element in our nature; since they hold out to the imagination selfish good and evil of such tremendous magnitude, that it is difficult for any one who fully believes in their reality, to have feeling or interest to spare for any other distant and ideal object. It is true, many of the most unselfish of mankind have been believers in supernaturalism, because their minds have not dwelt on the threats and promises of their religion, but chiefly on the idea of a Being to whom they looked up with a confiding love, and in whose hands they willingly left all that related especially to themselves. But in its effect on common minds, what now goes by the name of religion operates mainly through the feelings of self-interest. Even the Christ of the gospels holds out the direct promise of reward from heaven as a primary inducement to the noble and beautiful beneficence towards our fellow-creatures which he so impressively inculcates. This is a radical inferiority of the best supernatural religions, compared with the Religion of Humanity; since the greatest thing which moral influences can do for the amelioration of human nature, is to cultivate the unselfish feelings in the only mode in which any active principle in human nature can be effectually cultivated, namely by habitual exercise: but the habit of expecting to be rewarded in another life for our conduct in this, makes even virtue itself no longer an exercise of the unselfish feelings.

Secondly, it is an immense abatement from the worth of the old religions as means of elevating and improving human character, that it is nearly, if not quite impossible for them to produce their best moral effects, unless we suppose a certain torpidity, if not positive twist in the intellectual faculties. For it is impossible that any one who habitually thinks, and who is unable to blunt his inquiring intellect by sophistry, should be able without misgiving to go on ascribing absolute perfection to the author and ruler of so clumsily made and capriciously governed a creation as this planet and the life of its inhabitants. The adoration of such a being cannot be with the whole heart, unless the heart is first considerably sophisticated. The worship must either be greatly overclouded by doubt, and occasionally quite darkened by it, or the moral sentiments must sink to the low level of the ordinances of Nature: the worshipper must learn to think blind partiality, atrocious cruelty, and reckless injustice, not blemishes in an object of worship, since all these abound to excess in the commonest phenomena of Nature. It is true, the God who is worshipped is not, generally speaking, the God of Nature only, but also the God of some revelation; and the character of the revelation will greatly modify and, it may be, improve the moral influences of the religion. This is emphatically true of Christianity; since the Author of the Sermon on the Mount is assuredly a far more benignant Being than the Author of Nature. But unfortunately, the believer in the christian revelation is obliged to believe that the same being is the author of both. This, unless he resolutely averts his mind from the subject, or practises the act of quieting his conscience by sophistry, involves him in moral perplexities without end; since the ways of his Deity in Nature are on many occasions totally at variance with the precepts, as he believes, of the same Deity in the Gospel. He who comes out with least moral damage from this embarrassment, is probably the one who never attempts to reconcile the two standards with one another, but confesses to himself that the purposes of Providence are mysterious, that its ways are not our ways, that its justice and goodness are not the justice and goodness which we can conceive and which it befits us to practise. When, however, this is the feeling of the believer, the worship of the Deity ceases to be the adoration of abstract moral perfection. It becomes the bowing down to a gigantic image of something not fit for us to imitate. It is the worship of power only.

I say nothing of the moral difficulties and perversions involved in revelation itself; though even in the Christianity of the Gospels, at least in its ordinary interpretation, there are some of so flagrant a character as almost to outweigh all the beauty and benignity and moral greatness which so eminently distinguish the sayings and character of Christ. The recognition, for example, of the object of highest worship, in a being who could make a Hell; and who could create countless generations of human beings with the certain foreknowledge that he was creating them for this fate. Is there any moral enormity which might not be justified by imitation of such a Deity? And is it possible to adore such a one without a frightful distortion of the standard of right and wrong? Any other of the outrages to the most ordinary justice and humanity involved in the common christian conception of the moral character of God, sinks into insignificance beside this dreadful idealization of wickedness. Most of them too, are happily not so unequivocally deducible from the very words of Christ as to be indisputably a part of christian doctrine. It may be doubted, for instance, whether Christianity is really responsible for atonement and redemption, original sin and vicarious punishment: and the same may be said respecting the doctrine which makes belief in the divine mission of Christ a necessary condition of salvation. It is nowhere represented that Christ himself made this statement, except in the huddled-up account of the Resurrection contained in the concluding verses of St. Mark, which some critics (I believe the best), consider to be an interpolation. Again, the proposition that "the powers that be are ordained of God" and the whole series of corollaries deduced from it in the Epistles, belong to St. Paul, and must stand or fall with Paulism, not with Christianity. But there is one moral contradiction inseparable from every form of Christianity, which no ingenuity can resolve, and no sophistry explain away. It is, that so precious a gift, bestowed on a few, should have been withheld from the many: that countless millions of human beings should have been allowed to live and die, to sin and suffer, without the one thing needful, the divine remedy for sin and suffering, which it would have cost the Divine Giver as little to have vouchsafed to all, as to have bestowed by special grace upon a favoured minority. Add to this, that the divine message, assuming it to be such, has been authenticated by credentials so insufficient, that they fail to convince a large proportion of the strongest and most cultivated minds, and the tendency to disbelieve them appears to grow with the growth of scientific knowledge and critical discrimination. He who can believe these to be the intentional shortcomings of a perfectly good Being, must impose silence on every prompting of the sense of goodness and justice as received among men.

It is, no doubt, possible (and there are many instances of it) to worship with the intensest devotion either Deity, that of Nature or of the Gospel, without any perversion of the moral sentiments: but this must be by fixing the attention exclusively on what is beautiful and beneficent in the precepts and spirit of the Gospel and in the dispensations of Nature, and putting all that is the reverse as entirely aside as if it did not exist. Accordingly, this simple and innocent faith can only, as I have said, co-exist with a torpid and inactive state of the speculative faculties. For a person of exercised intellect, there is no way of attaining anything equivalent to it, save by sophistication and perversion, either of the understanding or of the conscience. It may almost always be said both of sects and of individuals, who derive their morality from religion, that the better logicians they are, the worse moralists.

One only form of belief in the supernatural – one only theory respecting the origin and government of the universe – stands wholly clear both of intellectual contradiction and of moral obliquity. It is that which, resigning irrevocably the idea of an omnipotent creator, regards Nature and Life not as the expression throughout of the moral character and purpose of the Deity, but as the product of a struggle between contriving goodness and an intractable material, as was believed by Plato, or a Principle of Evil, as was the doctrine of the Manicheans. A creed like this, which I have known to be devoutly held by at least one cultivated and conscientious person of our own day, allows it to be believed that all the mass of evil which exists was undesigned by, and exists not by the appointment of, but in spite of the Being whom we are called upon to worship. A virtuous human being assumes in this theory the exalted character of a fellow-labourer with the Highest, a fellow-combatant in the great strife; contributing his little, which by the aggregation of many like himself becomes much, towards that progressive ascendancy, and ultimately complete triumph of good over evil, which history points to, and which this doctrine teaches us to regard as planned by the Being to whom we owe all the benevolent contrivance we behold in Nature. Against the moral tendency of this creed no possible objection can lie: It can produce on whoever can succeed in believing it, no other than an ennobling effect. The evidence for it, indeed, if evidence it can be called, is too shadowy and unsubstantial, and the promises it holds out too distant and uncertain, to admit of its being a permanent substitute for the religion of humanity; but the two may be held in conjunction: and he to whom ideal good, and the progress of the world towards it, are already a religion, even though that other creed may seem to him a belief not grounded on evidence, is at liberty to indulge the pleasing and encouraging thought, that its truth is possible. Apart from all dogmatic belief, there is for those who need it, an ample domain in the region of the imagination which may be planted with possibilities, with hypotheses which cannot be known to be false; and when there is anything in the appearances of nature to favour them, as in this case there is (for whatever force we attach to the analogies of Nature with the effects of human contrivance, there is no disputing the remark of Paley, that what is good in nature exhibits those analogies much oftener than what is evil), the contemplation of these possibilities is a legitimate indulgence, capable of bearing its part, with other influences, in feeding and animating the tendency of the feelings and impulses towards good.

One advantage, such as it is, the supernatural religions must always possess over the Religion of Humanity; the prospect they hold out to the individual of a life after death. For, though the scepticism of the understanding does not necessarily exclude the Theism of the imagination and feelings, and this, again, gives opportunity for a hope that the power which has done so much for us may be able and willing to do this also, such vague possibility must ever stop far short of a conviction. It remains then to estimate the value of this element – the prospect of a world to come – as a constituent of earthly happiness. I cannot but think that as the condition of mankind becomes improved, as they grow happier in their lives, and more capable of deriving happiness from unselfish sources, they will care less and less for this flattering expectation. It is not, naturally or generally, the happy who are the most anxious either for a prolongation of the present life, or for a life hereafter: it is those who never have been happy. They who have had their happiness can bear to part with existence: but it is hard to die without ever having lived. When mankind cease to need a future existence as a consolation for the sufferings of the present, it will have lost its chief value to them, for themselves. I am now speaking of the unselfish. Those who are so wrapped up in self that they are unable to identify their feelings with anything which will survive them, or to feel their life prolonged in their younger contemporaries and in all who help to carry on the progressive movement of human affairs, require the notion of another selfish life beyond the grave, to enable them to keep up any interest in existence, since the present life, as its termination approaches, dwindles into something too insignificant to be worth caring about. But if the Religion of Humanity were as sedulously cultivated as the supernatural religions are (and there is no difficulty in conceiving that it might be much more so), all who had received the customary amount of moral cultivation would up to the hour of death live ideally in the life of those who are to follow them: and though doubtless they would often willingly survive as individuals for a much longer period than the present duration of life, it appears to me probable that after a length of time different in different persons, they would have had enough of existence, and would gladly lie down and take their eternal rest. Meanwhile and without looking so far forward, we may remark, that those who believe the immortality of the soul, generally quit life with fully as much, if not more, reluctance, as those who have no such expectation. The mere cessation of existence is no evil to any one: the idea is only formidable through the illusion of imagination which makes one conceive oneself as if one were alive and feeling oneself dead. What is odious in death is not death itself, but the act of dying, and its lugubrious accompaniments: all of which must be equally undergone by the believer in immortality. Nor can I perceive that the sceptic loses by his scepticism any real and valuable consolation except one; the hope of reunion with those dear to him who have ended their earthly life before him. That loss, indeed, is neither to be denied nor extenuated. In many cases it is beyond the reach of comparison or estimate; and will always suffice to keep alive, in the more sensitive natures, the imaginative hope of a futurity which, if there is nothing to prove, there is as little in our knowledge and experience to contradict.

History, so far as we know it, bears out the opinion, that mankind can perfectly well do without the belief in a heaven. The Greeks had anything but a tempting idea of a future state. Their Elysian fields held out very little attraction to their feelings and imagination. Achilles in the Odyssey expressed a very natural, and no doubt a very common sentiment, when he said that he would rather be on earth the serf of a needy master, than reign over the whole kingdom of the dead. And the pensive character so striking in the address of the dying emperor Hadrian to his soul, gives evidence that the popular conception had not undergone much variation during that long interval. Yet we neither find that the Greeks enjoyed life less, nor feared death more, than other people. The Buddhist religion counts probably at this day a greater number of votaries than either the Christian or the Mahomedan. The Buddhist creed recognises many modes of punishment in a future life, or rather lives, by the transmigration of the soul into new bodies of men or animals. But the blessing from Heaven which it proposes as a reward, to be earned by perseverance in the highest order of virtuous life, is annihilation; the cessation, at least, of all conscious or separate existence. It is impossible to mistake in this religion, the work of legislators and moralists endeavouring to supply supernatural motives for the conduct which they were anxious to encourage; and they could find nothing more transcendant to hold out as the capital prize to be won by the mightiest efforts of labour and self-denial, than what we are so often told is the terrible idea of annihilation. Surely this is a proof that the idea is not really or naturally terrible; that not philosophers only, but the common order of mankind, can easily reconcile themselves to it, and even consider it as a good; and that it is no unnatural part of the idea of a happy life, that life itself be laid down, after the best that it can give has been fully enjoyed through a long lapse of time; when all its pleasures, even those of benevolence, are familiar, and nothing untasted and unknown is left to stimulate curiosity and keep up the desire of prolonged existence. It seems to me not only possible but probable, that in a higher, and, above all, a happier condition of human life, not annihilation but immortality may be the burdensome idea; and that human nature, though pleased with the present, and by no means impatient to quit it, would find comfort and not sadness in the thought that it is not chained through eternity to a conscious existence which it cannot be assured that it will always wish to preserve.

PART XVII

Karl Marx (1818–83)

Introduction

The selections from Marx begin with an excerpt from a youthful work which Marx left unfinished and which has come to be known in English as the *Economic and Philosophical Manuscripts* (1844). This work, the first systematic presentation of Marx's ideas, is important for its treatment of the concept of alienation. The text of our selection is from the Third Manuscript. This is followed by an excerpt from the *Communist Manifesto* (1847) which contains some of the most compelling language Marx ever wrote. In prophetic tones he describes history as the history of class conflict and lays out the internal contradictions he sees at the heart of capitalism. The final selection is from *Capital: A Critique of Political Economy*, Volume One (1867). Here Marx describes a distortion of human beings by capital which he calls "commodity fetishism." These selections acquaint one with the most important, and most vital, Marxian concepts.

61

Economic and Philosophical Manuscripts

Third Manuscript

(Private property and labor)

(I) *ad* page XXXVI. The *subjective essence* of private property, *private* property as activity for itself, as *subject*, as *person*, is labor. It is evident, therefore, that only the political economy which recognized labor as its principle (Adam Smith) and which no longer regarded private property as merely a *condition* external to man, can be considered as both a product of the real *dynamism* and *development* of private property, a product of modern *industry*, and a force which has accelerated and extolled the dynamism and development of industry and has made it a power in the domain of *consciousness*.

Thus, in the view of this enlightened political economy which has discovered the *subjective essence* of wealth within the framework of private property, the partisans of the monetary system, and of the mercantilist system, who consider private property as a *purely objective* being for man, are *fetishists* and *Catholics*. Engels is right, therefore, in calling Adam Smith the *Luther of political economy*. Just as Luther recognized religion and *faith* as the essence of the real *world*, and for that reason took up a position against Catholic paganism; just as he annulled *external* religiosity while making religiosity the *inner* essence of man; just as he negated the distinction between priest and

Economic and Philosophical Manuscripts (1844). From *Marx's Concept of Man*, ed. Erich Fromm, with translation by T. B. Bottomore (New York: Continuum Publishing Company, 1995). Selection: Third Manuscript, pp. 119–52 (excerpts).

layman because he transferred the priest into the heart of the layman; so wealth external to man and independent of him (and thus only to be acquired and conserved from outside) is annulled. That is to say, its *external* and *mindless* objectivity is annulled by the fact that private property is incorporated in man himself, and man himself is recognized as its essence. But as a result, man himself is brought into the sphere of private property, just as, with Luther, he is brought into the sphere of religion. Under the guise of recognizing man, political economy, whose principle is labor, carries to its logical conclusion the denial of man. Man himself is no longer in a condition of external tension with the external substance of private property; he has himself become the tension-ridden being of private property. What was previously a phenomenon of *being external to oneself*, a real external manifestation of man, has now become the act of objectification, of alienation. This political economy seems, therefore, at first, to recognize man with his independence, his personal activity, etc. It incorporates private property in the very essence of man, and it is no longer, therefore, conditioned by the local or national *characteristics of private property* regarded as *existing* outside itself. It manifests a cosmopolitan, universal activity which is destructive of every limit and every bond, and substitutes itself as the *only policy*, the *only* universality, the *only* limit and the *only* bond. But in its further development it is obliged to discard this hypocrisy and to show itself in all its cynicism. It does this, without any regard for the apparent contradictions to which its doctrine leads, by showing in a more *one-sided* fashion, and thus with greater *logic* and *clarity*, that *labor* is the sole *essence of wealth*, and by demonstrating that this doctrine, in contrast with the original conception, has consequences which are *inimical to man*. Finally, it gives the death blow to *ground rent*, that last individual and natural form of private property and source of wealth existing independently of the movement of labor which was the expression of feudal property, but has become entirely its economic expression and is no longer able to put up any resistance to political economy. (The Ricardo School.) Not only does the *cynicism* of political economy increase from Smith, through Say, to Ricardo, Mill, etc. inasmuch as for the latter the consequences of *industry* appeared more and more developed and contradictory; from a positive point of view they become more alienated, and more consciously alienated, from man, in comparison with their predecessors. This is *only* because their science develops with greater logic and truth. Since they make private property in its active form the subject, and since at the same time they make man as a non-being into a being, the contradiction in reality corresponds entirely with the contradictory essence which they have accepted as a principle. The divided (II) *reality* of *industry* is far from refuting, but instead confirms, its *self-divided* principle. Its principle is in fact the principle of this division.

The physiocratic doctrine of Quesnay forms the transition from the mercantilist system to Adam Smith. *Physiocracy* is in a direct sense the *economic* decomposition of feudal property, but for this reason it is equally directly the *economic transformation*, the re-establishment, of this same feudal property, with the difference that its language is no longer feudal but economic. All wealth is reduced to *land* and *cultivation* (agriculture). Land is not yet *capital* but is still a *particular* mode of existence of capital, whose value is claimed to reside in, and derive from, its natural particularity; but land is nonetheless a natural and universal *element*, whereas the mercantilist system regarded only precious metals as wealth. The *object* of wealth, its matter, has therefore been given the greatest universality within *natural limits* – inasmuch as it is also, as *nature*, directly objective wealth. And it is only by labor, by agriculture, that land exists for man. Consequently, the subjective essence of wealth is already transferred to labor. But at the same time agriculture is the *only productive labor*. Labor is therefore not yet taken in its universality and its abstract form; it is still bound to a particular *element of nature as its matter*,

and is only recognized in a particular *mode of existence determined by nature*. Labor is still only a *determinate, particular* alienation of man, and its product is also conceived as a determinate part of wealth due more to nature than to labor itself. Land is still regarded here as something which exists naturally and independently of man, and not yet as capital; i.e., as a factor of labor. On the contrary, labor appears to be a factor of *nature*. But since the fetishism of the old external wealth, existing only as an object, has been reduced to a very simple natural element, and since its essence has been partially, and in a certain way, recognized in its subjective existence, the necessary advance has been made in recognizing the *universal nature* of wealth and in raising labor in its absolute form, i.e., in abstraction, to the *principle*. It is demonstrated against the physiocrats that from the economic point of view (i.e., from the only valid point of view) agriculture does not differ from any other industry; and that it is not, therefore, a specific kind of labor, bound to a particular element, or a particular manifestation of labor, but *labor in general* which is the *essence* of wealth.

Physiocracy denies *specific*, external, purely objective wealth, in declaring that labor is its essence. For the physiocrats, however, labor is in the first place only the *subjective essence* of landed property. (They begin from that kind of property which appears historically as the predominant recognized type.) They merely turn landed property into alienated man. They annul its feudal character by declaring that *industry* (agriculture) is its *essence*; but they reject the industrial world and accept the feudal system by declaring that *agriculture* is the *only* industry.

It is evident that when the *subjective essence* – industry in opposition to landed property, industry forming itself as industry – is grasped, this essence includes within itself the opposition. For just as industry incorporates the superseded landed property, its subjective essence incorporates the subjective essence of the latter.

Landed property is the first form of private property, and industry first appears historically in simple opposition to it, as a particular form of private property (or rather, as the liberated slave of landed property); this sequence is repeated in the scientific study of the *subjective* essence of private property, and labor appears at first only as *agricultural labor* but later establishes itself as *labor in general*.

(III) All wealth has become *industrial* wealth, the *wealth* of labor, and *industry* is realized labor; just as the *factory system* is the realized essence of *industry* (i.e., of labor), and as *industrial capital* is the realized objective form of private property. Thus we see that it is only at this stage that private property can consolidate its rule over man and become, in its most general form, a world-historical power.

(Private property and communism)

ad page XXXIX. But the antithesis between *propertylessness* and *property* is still an indeterminate antithesis, which is not conceived in its *active reference* to its intrinsic relations, not yet conceived as a contradiction, so long as it is not understood as an antithesis between *labor* and *capital*. Even without the advanced development of private property, e.g., in ancient Rome, in Turkey, etc. this antithesis may be expressed in a primitive form. In this form it does not yet *appear* as established by private property itself. But labor, the subjective essence of private property as the exclusion of property, and capital, objective labor as the exclusion of labor, constitute *private property* as the developed relation of the contradiction and thus a dynamic relation which drives towards its resolution.

ad ibidem The supersession of self-estrangement follows the same course as self-estrangement. *Private property* is first considered only from its objective aspect, but with labor conceived as its essence. Its mode of existence is therefore *capital* which it is necessary to abolish "as such" (Proudhon). Or else the *specific form* of labor (labor which is brought to a common level, sub-divided, and thus unfree) is regarded as the source of the *noxiousness* of private property and of its existence alienated from man. Fourier, in accord with the Physiocrats, regards *agricultural labor* as being at least the exemplary kind of labor. Saint-Simon asserts on the contrary that *industrial labor* as such is the essence of labor, and consequently he desires the *exclusive* rule of the industrialists and an amelioration of the condition of the workers. Finally, *communism* is the *positive* expression of the abolition of private property, and in the first place of universal private property. In taking this relation in its *universal aspect* communism is (1) in its first form, only the generalization and fulfilment of the relation. As such it appears in a double form; the domination of material property looms so large that it aims to destroy everything which is incapable of being possessed by everyone as private property. It wishes to eliminate talent, etc. by *force*. Immediate physical possession seems to it the unique goal of life and existence. The role of *worker* is not abolished, but is extended to all men. The relation of private property remains the relation of the community to the world of things. Finally, this tendency to oppose general private property to private property is expressed in an animal form; *marriage* (which is incontestably a form of *exclusive private property*) is contrasted with the community of women, in which women become communal and common property. One may say that this idea of the *community of women* is the *open secret* of this entirely crude and unreflective communism. Just as women are to pass from marriage to universal prostitution, so the whole world of wealth (i.e., the objective being of man) is to pass from the relation of exclusive marriage with the private owner to the relation of universal prostitution with the community. This communism, which negates the *personality* of man in every sphere, is only the logical expression of private property, which is this negation. Universal *envy* setting itself up as a power is only a camouflaged form of cupidity which re-establishes itself and satisfies itself in a different way. The thoughts of every individual private property are *at least* directed against any *wealthier* private property, in the form of envy and the desire to reduce everything to a common level; so that this envy and leveling in fact constitute the essence of competition. Crude communism is only the culmination of such envy and leveling-down on the basis of a *preconceived* minimum. How little this abolition of private property represents a genuine appropriation is shown by the abstract negation of the whole world of culture and civilization, and the regression to the *unnatural* (IV) simplicity of the poor and wantless individual who has not only not surpassed private property but has not yet even attained to it.

The community is only a community of *work* and of *equality of wages* paid out by the communal capital, by the *community* as universal capitalist. The two sides of the relation are raised to a *supposed* universality; *labor* as a condition in which everyone is placed, and *capital* as the acknowledged universality and power of the community.

In the relationship with *woman*, as the prey and the handmaid of communal lust, is expressed the infinite degradation in which man exists for himself; for the secret of this relationship finds its *unequivocal*, incontestable, *open* and revealed expression in the relation of man to woman and in the way in which the *direct* and *natural* species relationship is conceived. The immediate, natural and necessary relation of human being to human being is also the *relation* of *man* to *woman*. In this *natural* species relationship man's relation to nature is directly his relation to man, and his relation to man is directly his relation to nature, to his own *natural* function. Thus, in this relation is *sensuously revealed*, reduced to an observable *fact*, the extent to which human nature has become nature for man and to which nature has become human nature for him. From this relationship man's whole level of development can be assessed. It follows from the character of this relationship how far *man* has become, and has understood himself as, a *species-being*, a *human being*. The relation of man to woman is the *most natural* relation of human being to human being. It indicates, therefore, how far man's *natural* behavior has become *human*, and how far his *human* essence has become a *natural* essence for him, how far his *human nature* has become *nature for him*. It also shows how far man's *needs* have become *human* needs, and consequently how far the other person, as a person, has become one of his needs, and to what extent he is in his individual existence at the same time a social being. The first positive annulment of private property, crude communism, is therefore only a *phenomenal form* of the infamy of private property representing itself as positive community.

(2) Communism (a) still political in nature, democratic or despotic; (b) with the abolition of the state, yet still incomplete and influenced by private property, that is, by the alienation of man. In both forms communism is already aware of being the reintegration of man, his return to himself, the supersession of man's self-alienation. But since it has not yet grasped the positive nature of private property, or the *human* nature of needs, it is still captured and contaminated by private property. It has well understood the concept, but not the essence.

(3) *Communism* is the *positive* abolition of *private property*, of *human self-alienation*, and thus the real *appropriation* of *human* nature through and for man. It is, therefore, the return of man himself as a *social*, i.e., really human, being, a complete and conscious return which assimilates all the wealth of previous development. Communism as a fully-developed naturalism is humanism and as a fully-developed humanism is naturalism. It is the *definitive* resolution of the antagonism between man and nature, and between man and man. It is the true solution of the conflict between existence and essence, between objectification and self-affirmation, between freedom and necessity, between individual and species. It is the solution of the riddle of history and knows itself to be this solution.

(V) Thus the whole historical development, both the *real* genesis of communism (the birth of its empirical existence) and its thinking consciousness, is its comprehended and conscious process of becoming; whereas the other, still undeveloped communism seeks in certain historical forms opposed to private property, a *historical* justification founded upon what already exists, and to this end tears out of their context isolated elements of this development (Cabet and Villegardelle are preeminent among those who ride this hobby horse) and asserts them as proofs of its historical pedigree. In doing so, it makes clear that by far the greater part of this development contradicts its own assertions, and that if it has ever existed its past existence refutes its pretension to *essential being*.

It is easy to understand the necessity which leads the whole revolutionary movement to find its empirical, as well as its theoretical, basis in the development of *private property*, and more precisely of the economic system.

This material, directly *perceptible* private property is the material and sensuous expression of *alienated human* life. Its movement – production and consumption – is the *sensuous* manifestation of the movement of all previous production, i.e., the realization or reality of man. Religion, the family, the state, law, morality, science, art, etc. are only *particular* forms of production and come under its general law. The positive supersession of *private property* as the appropriation of *human* life, is therefore the *positive* supersession of all alienation, and the return of man from religion, the family, the state, etc. to his *human*, i.e., *social* life. Religious alienation as such occurs only in the sphere of *consciousness*, in the inner life of man, but economic alienation is that of *real life* and its supersession therefore affects both aspects. Of course, the development in different nations has a different beginning according to whether the actual and *established* life of the people is more in the realm of mind or more in the external world, is a real or ideal life. Communism begins where atheism begins (Owen), but atheism is at the outset still far from being *communism*; indeed it is still for the most part an abstraction. Thus the philanthropy of atheism is at first only an abstract *philosophical* philanthropy, whereas that of communism is at once *real* and oriented towards *action*.

We have seen how, on the assumption that private property has been positively superseded, man produces man, himself and then other men; how the object which is the direct activity of his personality is at the same time his existence for other men and their existence for him. Similarly, the material of labor and man himself as a subject are the starting point as well as the result of this movement (and because there must be this starting point private property is a historical necessity). Therefore, the *social* character is the universal character of the whole movement; *as* society itself produces *man* as *man*, so it is *produced* by him. Activity and mind are social in their content as well as in their *origin*; they are *social* activity and *social* mind. The *human* significance of nature only exists for *social* man, because only in this case is nature a *bond* with other *men*, the basis of his existence for others and of their existence for him. Only then is nature the *basis* of his own *human* experience and a vital element of human reality. The *natural* existence of man has here become his *human* existence and nature itself has become human for him. Thus *society* is the accomplished union of man with nature, the veritable resurrection of nature, the realized naturalism of man and the realized humanism of nature.

(VI) Social activity and social mind by no means exist *only* in the form of activity or mind which is directly communal. Nevertheless, communal activity and mind, i.e., activity and mind which express and confirm themselves directly in a *real association* with other men, occur everywhere where this *direct* expression of sociability arises from the content of the activity or corresponds to the nature of mind.

Even when I carry out *scientific* work, etc., an activity which I can seldom conduct in direct association with other men, I perform a *social*, because *human*, act. It is not only the material of my activity – such as the language itself which the thinker uses – which is given to me as a social product. *My own existence* is a social activity. For this reason, what I myself produce I produce for society, and with the consciousness of acting as a social being.

My universal consciousness is only the *theoretical* form of that whose *living* form is the *real* community, the social entity, although at the present day this *universal* consciousness is an abstraction from real life and is opposed to it as an enemy. That is why the *activity* of my universal consciousness as such is my *theoretical* existence as a social being.

It is above all necessary to avoid postulating "society" once again as an abstraction confronting the individual. The individual *is* the *social being*. The manifestation of his life – even when it does not appear directly in the form of a communal manifestation, accomplished in association with other men – is therefore a manifestation and affirmation of *social life*. Individual human life and species-life are not *different things*, even though the mode of existence of individual life is necessarily either a more *specific* or a more *general* mode of species-life, or that of species-life a more *specific* or more *general* mode of individual life.

In his *species-consciousness* man confirms his real *social life*, and reproduces his real existence in thought; while conversely, species-life confirms itself in species-consciousness and exists for itself in its universality as a thinking being. Though man is a unique individual – and it is just his particularity which makes him an individual, a really *individual* communal being – he is equally the *whole*, the ideal whole, the subjective existence of society as thought and experienced. He exists in reality as the representation and the real mind of social existence, and as the sum of human manifestation of life.

Thought and being are indeed *distinct* but they also form a unity. *Death* seems to be a harsh victory of the species over the individual and to contradict their unity; but the particular individual is only a *determinate species-being* and as such he is mortal.

(4) Just as *private property* is only the sensuous expression of the fact that man is at the same time an *objective* fact for himself and becomes an alien and non-human object for himself; just as his manifestation of life is also his alienation of life and his self-realization a loss of reality, the emergence of an *alien* reality; so the positive supersession of private property, i.e., the *sensuous* appropriation of the human essence and of human life, of objective man and of human *creations*, by and for man, should not be taken only in the sense of *immediate*, exclusive *enjoyment*, or only in the sense of *possession* or *having*. Man appropriates his manifold being in an all-inclusive way, and thus as a whole man. All his *human* relations to the world – seeing, hearing, smelling, tasting, touching,

thinking, observing, feeling, desiring, acting, loving – in short all the organs of his individuality, like the organs which are directly communal in form (VII) are, in their objective action (their *action in relation to the object*) the appropriation of this object, the appropriation of human reality. The way in which they react to the object is the confirmation of *human reality*. It is human effectiveness and human *suffering*, for suffering humanly considered is an enjoyment of the self for man.

Private property has made us so stupid and partial that an object is only *ours* when we have it, when it exists for us as capital or when it is directly eaten, drunk, worn, inhabited, etc., in short, *utilized* in some way; although private property itself only conceives these various forms of possession as *means of life*, and the life for which they serve as means is the *life* of *private property* – labor and creation of capital.

Thus *all* the physical and intellectual senses have been replaced by the simple alienation of *all* these senses; the sense of *having*. The human being had to be reduced to this absolute poverty in order to be able to give birth to all his inner wealth. (On the category of *having* see Hess in *Einundzwanzig Bogen*.)

The supersession of private property is therefore the complete *emancipation* of all the human qualities and senses. It is this emancipation because these qualities and senses have become *human*, from the subjective as well as the objective point of view. The eye has become a *human* eye when its *object* has become a *human*, social object, created by man and destined for him. The senses have therefore become directly theoreticians in practice. They relate themselves to the thing for the sake of the thing, but the thing itself is an *objective human* relation to itself and to man, and vice versa. Need and enjoyment have thus lost their *egoistic* character, and nature has lost its mere *utility* by the fact that its utilization has become *human* utilization.

Similarly, the senses and minds of other men have become my *own* appropriation. Thus besides these direct organs, *social* organs are constituted, in the form of society; for example, activity in direct association with others has become an organ for the manifestation of life and a mode of appropriation of *human* life.

It is evident that the human eye appreciates things in a different way from the crude, non-human eye, the human *ear* differently from the crude ear. As we have seen, it is only when the object becomes a *human* object, or objective *humanity*, that man does not become lost in it. This is only possible when the object becomes a *social* object, and when he himself becomes a social being and society becomes a being for him in this object.

On the one hand, it is only when objective reality everywhere becomes for man in society the reality of human faculties, human reality, and thus the reality of his own faculties, that all *objects* become for him the *objectification of himself*. The objects then confirm and realize his individuality, they are *his own* objects, i.e., man himself becomes the object. *The manner in which* these objects become his own depends upon the *nature of the object* and the nature of the corresponding faculty; for it is precisely the *determinate character* of this relation which constitutes the specific *real* mode of affirmation. The object is not the same for the *eye* as for the *ear*, for the ear as for the eye. The *distinctive character* of each faculty is precisely its *characteristic* essence and thus also the characteristic mode of its objectification, of its *objectively real*, living *being*. It is therefore not only in thought, (VIII) but through *all* the senses that man is affirmed in the objective world.

Let us next consider the subjective aspect. Man's musical sense is only awakened by music. The most beautiful music has no meaning for the non-musical ear, is not an object for it, because my object can only be the confirmation of one of my own faculties. It can only be so for me in so far as my faculty exists for itself as a subjective capacity, because the meaning of an object for me extends only as far as the sense extends (only makes sense for an appropriate sense). For this reason, the *senses* of social man are *different* from those of non-social man. It is only through the objectively deployed wealth of the human being that the wealth of subjective *human* sensibility (a musical ear, an eye which is sensitive to the beauty of form, in short, senses which are capable of human satisfaction and which confirm themselves as human faculties) is cultivated or created. For it is not only the five senses, but also the so-called spiritual senses, the practical senses (desiring, loving, etc.), in brief, human sensibility and the human character of the senses, which can only come into being through the existence of *its* object, through humanized nature. The cultivation of the five senses is the work of all previous history. Sense which is subservient to crude needs has only a restricted meaning. For a starving man the human form of food does not exist, but only its abstract character as food. It could just as well exist in the most crude form, and it is impossible to say in what way this feeding-activity would differ from that of animals. The needy man, burdened with cares, has no appreciation of the most beautiful spectacle. The dealer in minerals sees only their commercial value, not their beauty or their particular characteristics; he has no mineralogical sense. Thus, the objectification of the human essence, both theoretically and practically, is necessary in order to *humanize* man's *senses*, and also to create the *human senses* corresponding to all the wealth of human and natural being.

Just as society at its beginnings finds, through the development of *private property* with its wealth and poverty (both intellectual and material), the materials necessary for this *cultural development, so* the fully constituted society produces man in all the plenitude of his being, the wealthy man endowed with all the senses, as an enduring reality. It is only in a social context that subjectivism and objectivism, spiritualism and materialism, activity and passivity, cease to be antinomies and thus cease to exist as such antinomies. The resolution of the *theoretical* contradictions is possible *only* through *practical* means, only through the practical energy of man. Their resolution is not by any means, therefore, only a problem of knowledge, but is a *real* problem of life which philosophy was unable to solve precisely because it saw there a purely theoretical problem.

It can be seen that the history of *industry* and industry as it *objectively* exists is an *open* book of the *human faculties*, and a human *psychology* which can be sensuously apprehended. This history has not so far been conceived in relation to human *nature*, but only from a superficial utilitarian point of view, since in the condition of alienation it was only possible to conceive real human faculties and *human* species-action in the form of general human existence, as religion, or as history in its abstract, general aspect as politics, art and literature, etc. *Everyday material industry* (which can be conceived as part of that general development; or equally, the general development can be conceived as a *specific* part of industry since all human activity up to the present has been labor, i.e., industry, self-alienated activity) shows us, in the form of *sensuous useful objects*, in an alienated form, the *essential human faculties* transformed into objects. No psychology for which this book, i.e., the most sensibly present and accessible part of history,

remains closed, can become a *real* science with a genuine content. What is to be thought of a science which stays aloof from this enormous field of human labor and which does not feel its own inadequacy even though this great wealth of human activity means nothing to it except perhaps what can be expressed in the single phrase – "need", "common need"?

The *natural sciences* have developed a tremendous activity and have assembled an ever-growing mass of data. But philosophy has remained alien to these sciences just as they have remained alien to philosophy. Their momentary *rapprochement* was only a *fantastic* illusion. There was a desire for union but the power to effect it was lacking. Historiography itself only takes natural science into account incidentally, regarding it as a factor making for enlightenment, for practical utility and for particular great discoveries. But natural science has penetrated all the more *practically* into human life through industry. It has transformed human life and prepared the emancipation of humanity even though its immediate effect was to accentuate the dehumanization of man. *Industry* is the actual historical relationship of nature, and thus of natural science, to man. If industry is conceived as the *exoteric* manifestation of the essential human *faculties*, the *human* essence of nature and the *natural* essence of man can also be understood. Natural science will then abandon its abstract materialist, or rather idealist, orientation, and will become the basis of a *human* science, just as it has already become – though in an alienated form – the basis of actual human life. One basis for life and another for science is *a priori* a falsehood. Nature, as it develops in human history, in the act of genesis of human society, is the *actual* nature of man; thus nature, as it develops through industry, though in an *alienated* form, is truly *anthropological* nature.

Sense experience (see Feuerbach) must be the basis of all science. Science is only *genuine* science when it proceeds from sense experience, in the two forms of *sense perception* and *sensuous* need; i.e., only when it proceeds from nature. The whole of history is a preparation for "man" to become an object of *sense perception*, and for the development of human needs (the needs of man as such). History itself is a *real* part of *natural history*, of the development of nature into man. Natural science will one day incorporate the science of man, just as the science of man will incorporate natural science; there will be a *single* science.

Man is the direct object of natural science, because directly *perceptible nature* is for man directly human sense experience (an identical expression) as the *other person* who is directly presented to him in a sensuous way. His own sense experience only exists as human sense experience for himself through the *other person*. But *nature* is the direct object of the *science of man*. The first object for man – man himself – is nature, sense experience; and the particular sensuous human faculties, which can only find objective realization in *natural* objects, can only attain self-knowledge in the science of natural being. The element of thought itself, the element of the living manifestation of thought, *language*, is sensuous in nature. The *social* reality of nature and *human* natural science or the *natural science of man*, are identical expressions.

It will be seen from this how, in place of the *wealth* and *poverty* of political economy, we have the *wealthy* man and the plenitude of *human* need. The wealthy man is at the same time one who *needs* a complex of human manifestations of life, and whose own self-realization exists as an inner necessity, a *need*. Not only the *wealth* but also the *poverty* of man acquires, in a socialist perspective, a *human* and thus a social meaning. Poverty is the passive bond which leads man to experience a need for the greatest wealth, the *other* person. The sway of the objective entity within me, the sensuous outbreak of my life-activity, is the passion which here becomes the *activity* of my being.

(5) A being does not regard himself as independent unless he is his own master, and he is only his own master when he owes his existence to himself. A man who lives by the favor of another considers himself a dependent being. But I live completely by another person's favor when I owe to him not only the continuance of my life but also *its creation*; when he is its *source*. My life has necessarily such a cause outside itself if it is not my own creation. The idea of *creation* is thus one which it is difficult to eliminate from popular consciousness. This consciousness is *unable to conceive* that nature and man exist on their own account, because such an existence contradicts all the tangible facts of practical life.

The idea of the creation of the *earth* has received a severe blow from the science of geogeny, i.e., from the science which portrays the formation and development of the earth as a process of spontaneous generation. *Generatio aequivoca* (spontaneous generation) is the only practical refutation of the theory of creation.

But it is easy indeed to say to the particular individual what Aristotle said: You are engendered by your father and mother, and consequently it is the coitus of two human beings, a human species-act, which has produced the human being. You see therefore that even in a physical sense man owes his existence to man. Consequently, it is not enough to keep in view only one of the two aspects, the *infinite* progression, and to ask further: who engendered my father and my grandfather? You must also keep in mind the *circular movement* which is perceptible in that progression, according to which man, in the act of generation reproduces himself; thus *man* always remains the subject. But you will reply: I grant you this circular movement, but you must in turn concede the progression, which leads even further to the point where I ask: who created the first man and nature as a whole? I can only reply: your question is itself a product of abstraction. Ask yourself how you arrive at that question. Ask yourself whether your question does not arise from a point of view to which I cannot reply because it is a perverted one. Ask yourself whether that progression exists as such for rational thought. If you ask a question about the creation of nature and man you abstract from nature and man. You suppose them *non-existent* and you want me to demonstrate that they *exist*. I reply: give up your abstraction and at the same time you abandon your question. Or else, if you want to maintain your abstraction, be consistent, and if you think of man and nature as non-existent (XI) think of yourself too as non-existent, for you are also man and nature. Do not think, do not ask me any questions, for as soon as you think and ask questions your *abstraction* from the existence of nature and man becomes meaningless. Or are you such an egoist that you conceive everything as non-existence and yet want to exist yourself?

You may reply: I do not want to conceive the nothingness of nature, etc.; I only ask you about the act of its creation, just as I ask the anatomist about the formation of bones, etc.

Since, however, for socialist man, the *whole of what is called world history* is nothing but the creation of man by human labor, and the emergence of nature for man, he therefore has the evident and irrefutable proof of his *self-creation*, of his own *origins*. Once the essence of man and of nature, man as a natural being and nature as a human reality, has become evident in practical life, in sense experience, the quest for an *alien* being, a being above man and nature (a quest which is an avowal of the unreality of man and nature) becomes impossible in practice. *Atheism*, as a denial of this unreality, is no longer meaningful, for atheism is a *negation of God* and seeks to assert by this negation the *existence of man*. Socialism no longer requires such a roundabout method; it begins from the *theoretical* and *practical sense perception* of man and nature as essential beings. It is positive human *self-consciousness*, no longer a self-consciousness attained through the negation of religion; just as the *real life* of man is positive and no longer attained through the negation of private property, through *communism*. Communism is the phase of negation of the negation and is, consequently, for the next stage of historical development, a real and necessary factor in the emancipation and rehabilitation of man. Communism is the necessary form and the dynamic principle of the immediate future, but communism is not itself the goal of human development – the form of human society.

(Needs, production, and division of labor)

(XIV) (7) We have seen what importance should be attributed, in a socialist perspective, to the *wealth of* human needs, and consequently also to a *new mode of production* and to a new *object* of production. A new manifestation of *human* powers and a new enrichment of the human being. Within the system of private property it has the opposite meaning. Every man speculates upon creating a *new* need in another in order to force him to a new sacrifice, to place him in a new dependence, and to entice him into a new kind of pleasure and thereby into economic ruin. Everyone tries to establish over others an *alien* power in order to find there the satisfaction of his own egoistic need. With the mass of objects, therefore, there also increases the realm of alien entities to which man is subjected. Every new product is a new *potentiality* of mutual deceit and robbery. Man becomes increasingly poor as a man; he has increasing need of *money* in order to take possession of the hostile being. The power of his *money* diminishes directly with the growth of the quantity of production, i.e., his need increases with the increasing *power* of money. The need for money is therefore the real need created by the modern economy, and the only need which it creates. The *quantity* of money becomes increasingly its only important quality. Just as it reduces every entity to its abstraction, so it

reduces itself in its own development to a *quantitative* entity. Excess and immoderation become its true standard. This is shown subjectively, partly in the fact that the expansion of production and of needs becomes an *ingenious* and always *calculating* subservience to inhuman, depraved, unnatural, and *imaginary* appetites. Private property does not know how to change crude need into *human* need; its *idealism* is *fantasy*, *caprice* and *fancy*. No eunuch flatters his tyrant more shamefully or seeks by more infamous means to stimulate his jaded appetite, in order to gain some favor, than does the eunuch of industry, the entrepreneur, in order to acquire a few silver coins or to charm the gold from the purse of his dearly beloved neighbor. (Every product is a bait by means of which the individual tries to entice the essence of the other person, his money. Every real or potential need is a weakness which will draw the bird into the lime. Universal exploitation of human communal life. As every imperfection of man is a bond with heaven, a point from which his heart is accessible to the priest, so every want is an opportunity for approaching one's neighbor, with an air of friendship, and saying, "Dear friend, I will give you what you need, but you know the *conditio sine qua non*. You know what ink you must use in signing yourself over to me. I shall swindle you while providing your enjoyment.") The entrepreneur accedes to the most depraved fancies of his neighbor, plays the role of pander between him and his needs, awakens unhealthy appetites in him, and watches for every weakness in order, later, to claim the remuneration for this labor of love.

This alienation is shown in part by the fact that the refinement of needs and of the means to satisfy them produces as its counterpart a bestial savagery, a complete, primitive and abstract simplicity of needs; or rather, that it simply reproduces itself in its opposite sense. For the worker even the need for fresh air ceases to be a need. Man returns to the cave dwelling again, but it is now poisoned by the pestilential breath of civilization. The worker has only a *precarious* right to inhabit it, for it has become an alien dwelling which may suddenly not be available, or from which he may be evicted if he does not pay the rent. He has to *pay* for this mortuary. The dwelling full of light which Prometheus, in Aeschylus, indicates as one of the great gifts by which he has changed savages into men, ceases to exist for the worker. Light, air, and the simplest *animal* cleanliness cease to be human needs. *Filth*, this corruption and putrefaction which runs in the *sewers* of civilization (this is to be taken literally) becomes the *element in which man lives*. Total and *unnatural* neglect, putrified nature, becomes the *element in which he lives*. None of his senses exist any longer, either in a human form, or even in a *non-human*, animal form. The crudest *methods* (and *instruments*) of human labor reappear; thus the *tread-mill* of the Roman slaves has become the mode of production and mode of existence of many English workers. It is not enough that man should lose his human needs; even animal needs disappear. The Irish no longer have any need but that of *eating – eating potatoes*, and then only the worst kind, *mouldy potatoes*. But France and England already possess in every industrial town a *little* Ireland. Savages and animals have at least the need for hunting, exercise and companionship. But the simplification of machinery and of work is used to make workers out of those who are just growing up, who are still immature, *children*, while the worker himself has become a child deprived of all care. Machinery is adapted to the weakness of the human being, in order to turn the weak human being into a machine.

The fact that the growth of needs and of the means to satisfy them results in a lack of needs and of means is demonstrated in several ways by the economist (and by the capitalist; in fact, it is always *empirical* businessmen we refer to when we speak of economists, who are their *scientific* self-revelation and existence). First, by reducing the needs of the worker to the miserable necessities required for the maintenance of his physical existence, and by reducing his activity to the most abstract mechanical movements, the economist asserts that man has no needs, for activity or enjoyment, beyond that; and yet he declares that this kind of life is a *human* way of life. Secondly, by reckoning as the general standard of life (general because it is applicable to the mass of men) the *most impoverished* life conceivable, he turns the worker into a being who has neither senses nor needs, just as he turns his activity into a pure abstraction from all activity. Thus all working class *luxury* seems to him blameworthy, and everything which goes beyond the most abstract need (whether it be a passive enjoyment or a manifestation of personal activity) is regarded as a *luxury*. Political economy, the science of *wealth*, is therefore, at the same time, the science of renunciation, of privation and of saving, which actually succeeds in depriving man of fresh *air* and of physical *activity*. This science of a marvelous industry is at the same time the science of asceti-

cism. Its true ideal is the *ascetic* but *usurious* miser and the *ascetic* but *productive* slave. Its moral ideal is the *worker* who takes a part of his wages to the savings bank. It has even found a servile art to embody this favorite idea, which has been produced in a sentimental manner on the stage. Thus, despite its worldly and pleasure-seeking appearance, it is a truly moral science, the most moral of all sciences. Its principal thesis is the renunciation of life and of human needs. The less you eat, drink, buy books, go to the theatre or to balls, or to the public house, and the less you think, love, theorize, sing, paint, fence, etc. the more you will be able to save and the *greater* will become your treasure which neither moth nor rust will corrupt – your *capital*. The less you *are*, the less you express your life, the more you *have*, the greater is your *alienated* life and the greater is the saving of your alienated being. Everything which the economist takes from you in the way of life and humanity, he restores to you in the form of *money* and *wealth*. And everything which you are unable to do, your money can do for you; it can eat, drink, go to the ball and to the theatre. It can acquire art, learning, historical treasures, political power; and it can travel. It *can* appropriate all these things for you, can purchase everything; it is the true *opulence*. But although it can do all this, it only *desires* to create itself, and to buy itself, for everything else is subservient to it. When one owns the master, one also owns the servant, and one has no need of the master's servant. Thus all passions and activities must be submerged in *avarice*. The worker must have just what is necessary for him to want to live, and he must want to live only in order to have this.

It is true that some controversy has arisen in the field of political economy. Some economists (Lauderdale, Malthus, etc.) advocate luxury and condemn saving, while others (Ricardo, Say, etc.) advocate saving and condemn luxury. But the former admit that they desire luxury in order to create *work*, i.e., absolute saving, while the latter admit that they advocate saving in order to create *wealth*, i.e., luxury. The former have the romantic notion that avarice alone should not determine the consumption of the rich, and they contradict their own laws when they represent *prodigality* as being a direct means of enrichment; their opponents then demonstrate in detail and with great earnestness that prodigality diminishes rather than augments my *possessions*. The second group are hypocritical in not admitting that it is caprice and fancy which determine production. They forget the "refined needs", and that without consumption there would be no production. They forget that through competition production must become ever more universal and luxurious, that it is use which determines the value of a thing, and that use is determined by fashion. They want production to be limited to "useful things", but they forget that the production of too many useful things results in too many *useless* people. Both sides forget that prodigality and thrift, luxury and abstinence, wealth and poverty are equivalent.

You must not only be abstemious in the satisfaction of your direct senses, such as eating, etc. but also in your participation in general interests, your sympathy, trust, etc. if you wish to be economical and to avoid being ruined by illusions.

Everything which you own must be made *venal*, i.e., useful. Suppose I ask the economist: am I acting in accordance with economic laws if I earn money by the sale of my body, by prostituting it to another person's lust (in France, the factory workers call the prostitution of their wives and daughters the *n*th hour of work, which is literally true); or if I sell my friend to the Moroccans (and the direct sale of men occurs in all civilized countries in the form of trade in conscripts)? He will reply: you are not acting contrary to my laws, but you must take into account what Cousin Morality and Cousin Religion have to say. My *economic* morality and religion have no objection to make, but ... But whom then should we believe, the economist or the moralist? The morality of political economy is *gain*, work, thrift and sobriety – yet political economy promises to satisfy my needs. The political economy of morality is the riches of a good conscience, of virtue, etc., but how can I be virtuous if I am not alive and how can I have a good conscience if I am not aware of anything? The nature of alienation implies that each sphere applies a different and contradictory norm, that morality does not apply the same norm as political economy, etc., because each of them is a particular alienation of man; (XVII) each is concentrated upon a specific area of alienated activity and is itself alienated from the other.

Thus M. Michel Chevalier reproaches Ricardo with leaving morals out of account. But Ricardo lets political economy speak its own language; he is not to blame if this language is not that of morals. M. Chevalier ignores political economy in so far as he concerns himself with morals, but he really and necessarily ignores morals when he is concerned

with political economy; for the bearing of political economy upon morals is either arbitrary and accidental and thus lacking any scientific basis or character, a mere *sham*, or it is *essential* and can then only be a relation between economic laws and morals. If there is no such relation, can Ricardo be held responsible? Moreover, the antithesis between morals and political economy is itself only *apparent*; there is an antithesis and equally no antithesis. Political economy expresses, *in its own fashion*, the moral laws.

The absence of needs, as the principle of political economy, is shown in the most *striking* way in its *theory of population*. There are *too many* men. The very existence of man is a pure luxury, and if the worker is *"moral"* he will be *economical* in procreation. (Mill proposes that public commendation should be given to those who show themselves abstemious in sexual relations, and public condemnation to those who sin against the sterility of marriage. Is this not the moral doctrine of asceticism?) The production of men appears as a public misfortune.

The significance which production has in relation to the wealthy is *revealed* in the significance which it has for the poor. At the top its manifestation is always refined, concealed, ambiguous, an appearance; at the bottom it is rough, straightforward, candid, a reality. The *crude* need of the worker is a much greater source of profit than the *refined* need of the wealthy. The cellar dwellings in London bring their landlords more than do the palaces; i.e., they constitute *greater wealth* as far as the landlord is concerned and thus, in economic terms, greater *social* wealth.

Just as industry speculates upon the refinement of needs so also it speculates upon their *crudeness*, and upon their artificially produced crudeness whose true soul therefore is *self-stupefaction*, the *illusory* satisfaction of needs, a civilization *within* the crude barbarism of need. The English gin-shops are therefore *symbolical* representations of private property. Their *luxury* reveals the real relation of industrial luxury and wealth to man. They are therefore rightly the only Sunday enjoyment of the people, treated mildly at least by the English police.

We have already seen how the economist establishes the unity of labor and capital in various ways: (1) capital is *accumulated* labor; (2) the purpose of capital within production – partly the reproduction of capital with profit, partly capital as raw material (material of labor), partly capital as itself a *working instrument* (the machine is fixed capital which is identical with labor) – is *productive work*; (3) the worker is capital; (4) wages form part of the costs of capital; (5) for the worker, labor is the reproduction of his life-capital; (6) for the capitalist, labor is a factor in the activity of his capital.

Finally (7) the economist postulates the original unity of capital and labor as the unity of capitalist and worker. This is the original paradisaical condition. How these two factors, (XIX) as two persons, spring at each other's throats is for the economist a *fortuitous* occurrence, which therefore requires only to be explained by external circumstances (see Mill).

The nations which are still dazzled by the sensuous glitter of precious metals and who thus remain fetishists of metallic money are not yet fully developed money nations. Contrast between France and England. The extent to which the solution of a theoretical problem is a task of practice, and is accomplished through practice, and the extent to which correct practice is the condition of a true and positive theory is shown, for example, in the case of *fetishism*. The sense perception of a fetishist differs from that of a Greek because his sensuous existence is different. The abstract hostility between sense and spirit is inevitable so long as the human sense for nature, or the human meaning of nature, and consequently the *natural* sense of *man*, has not been produced through man's own labor.

Equality is nothing but the German "Ich = Ich" translated into the French, i.e., political, form. Equality as the *basis* of communism is a *political* foundation and is the same as when the German founds it upon the fact that he conceives man as *universal self-consciousness*. Of course, the transcendence of alienation always proceeds from the form of alienation which is the *dominant* power; in Germany, *self-consciousness*; in France, *equality*, because politics; in England, the real, material, self-sufficient, *practical* need. Proudhon should be appreciated and criticized from this point of view.

If we now characterize *communism* itself (for as negation of the negation, as the appropriation of human existence which mediates itself with itself through the negation of private property, it is not the *true*, self-originating position, but rather one which begins from private property)...[A part of the page is torn away here, and there follow fragments of six lines which are insufficient to recon-

struct the passage. – *Tr. Note*]...the alienation of human life remains and a much greater alienation remains the more one is conscious of it as such) can only be accomplished by the establishment of communism. In order to supersede the *idea* of private property communist *ideas* are sufficient but *genuine* communist activity is necessary in order to supersede *real* private property. History will produce it, and the development which we already recognize in *thought* as self-transcending will in reality involve a severe and protracted process. We must however consider it an advance that we have previously acquired an awareness of the limited nature and the goal of the historical development and can see beyond it.

When communist *artisans* form associations, teaching and propaganda are their first aims. But their association itself creates a new need – the need for society – and what appeared to be a means has become an end. The most striking results of this practical development are to be seen when French socialist workers meet together. Smoking, eating and drinking are no longer simply means of bringing people together. Society, association, entertainment which also has society as its aim, is sufficient for them; the brotherhood of man is no empty phrase but a reality, and the nobility of man shines forth upon us from their toilworn bodies.

(XX) When political economy asserts that supply and demand always balance each other, it forgets at once its own contention (the theory of population) that the supply of *men* always exceeds the demand, and consequently, that the disproportion between supply and demand is most strikingly expressed in the essential end of production – the existence of man.

The extent to which money, which has the appearance of a means, is the real power and the unique *end*, and in general the extent to which *the* means which gives me being and possession of the alien objective being is an *end in itself*, can be seen from the fact that landed property where land is the source of life, and *horse* and *sword* where these are the *real means of life*, are also recognized as the real political powers. In the middle ages an estate becomes emancipated when it has the right to carry the *sword*. Among nomadic peoples it is the *horse* which makes me a free man and a member of the community.

We said above that man is regressing to the *cave dwelling*, but in an alienated, malignant form. The savage in his cave (a natural element which is freely offered for his use and protection) does not feel himself a stranger; on the contrary he feels as much at home as a *fish* in water. But the cellar dwelling of the poor man is a hostile dwelling, "an alien, constricting power which only surrenders itself to him in exchange for blood and sweat". He cannot regard it as his home, as a place where he might at last say, "here I am at home". Instead, he finds himself in *another person's* house, the house of a *stranger* who lies in wait for him every day and evicts him if he does not pay the rent. He is also aware of the contrast between his own dwelling and a human dwelling such as exists in *that other world*, the heaven of wealth.

Alienation is apparent not only in the fact that *my* means of life belong to *someone else*, that *my* desires are the unattainable possession of *someone else*, but that everything is *something different* from itself, that my activity is *something else*, and finally (and this is also the case for the capitalist) that *an inhuman power* rules over everything. There is a kind of wealth which is inactive, prodigal and devoted to pleasure, the beneficiary of which *behaves* as an *ephemeral*, aimlessly active individual who regards the slave labor of others, human *blood and sweat*, as the prey of his cupidity and sees mankind, and himself, as a sacrificial and superfluous being. Thus he acquires a contempt for mankind, expressed in the form of arrogance and the squandering of resources which would support a hundred human lives, and also in the form of the infamous illusion that his unbridled extravagance and endless unproductive consumption is a condition for the *labor* and *subsistence* of others. He regards the realization of the *essential powers* of man only as the realization of his own disorderly life, his whims and his capricious, bizarre ideas. Such wealth, however, which sees wealth merely as a means, as something to be consumed, and which is therefore both master and slave, generous and mean, capricious, presumptuous, conceited, refined, cultured and witty, has not yet discovered *wealth* as a wholly *alien power* but sees in it its own power and enjoyment rather than wealth [...]

62

Manifesto of the Communist Party

A spectre is haunting Europe – the spectre of Communism. All the Powers of old Europe have entered into a holy alliance to exorcize this spectre: Pope and Czar, Metternich and Guizot, French Radicals and German police spies.

Where is the party in opposition that has not been decried as Communistic by its opponents in power? Where the Opposition that has not hurled back the branding reproach of Communism, against the more advanced opposition parties, as well as against its reactionary adversaries?

Two things result from this fact:

i. Communism is already acknowledged by all European Powers to be itself a Power.

ii. It is high time that Communists should openly, in the face of the whole world, publish their views, their aims, their tendencies, and meet this nursery tale of the Spectre of Communism with a Manifesto of the party itself.

To this end, Communists of various nationalities have assembled in London, and sketched the following Manifesto, to be published in the English, French, German, Italian, Flemish and Danish languages.

Bourgeois and Proletarians

The history of all hitherto existing society is the history of class struggles.

Freeman and slave, patrician and plebeian, lord and serf, guild-master and journeyman, in a word,

The Communist Manifesto (with Friedrich Engels) (1847), tr. and ed. David McLellan (Oxford University Press, 1992). Selection: pp. 2–9.

oppressor and oppressed, stood in constant opposition to one another, carried on an uninterrupted, now hidden, now open fight, a fight that each time ended, either in a revolutionary reconstitution of society at large, or in the common ruin of the contending classes.

In the earlier epochs of history, we find almost everywhere a complicated arrangement of society into various orders, a manifold gradation of social rank. In ancient Rome we have patricians, knights, plebeians, slaves; in the Middle Ages, feudal lords, vassals, guild-masters, journeymen, serfs; in almost all of these classes, again, subordinate gradations.

The modern bourgeois society that has sprouted from the ruins of feudal society has not done away with class antagonisms. It has but established new classes, new conditions of oppression, new forms of struggle in place of the old ones.

Our epoch, the epoch of the bourgeoisie, possesses, however, this distinctive feature: it has simplified the class antagonisms. Society as a whole is more and more splitting up into two great hostile camps, into two great classes directly facing each other: Bourgeoisie and Proletariat.

From the serfs of the Middle Ages sprang the chartered burghers of the earliest towns. From these burgesses the first elements of the bourgeoisie were developed.

The discovery of America, the rounding of the Cape, opened up fresh ground for the rising bourgeoisie. The East-Indian and Chinese markets, the colonization of America, trade with the colonies, the increase in the means of exchange and in commodities generally, gave to commerce, to navigation, to industry, an impulse never before known, and thereby, to the revolutionary element in the tottering feudal society, a rapid development.

The previous feudal or guild organization of industry, under which industrial production was monopolized by closed guilds, now no longer sufficed for the growing wants of the new markets. The manufacturing system took its place. The guild-masters were pushed on one side by the manufacturing middle class; division of labour between the different corporate guilds vanished in the face of division of labour in each single workshop.

Meantime the markets kept ever growing, the demand ever rising. Even manufacture no longer sufficed. Thereupon, steam and machinery revolutionized industrial production. The place of manufacture was taken by the giant, Modern Industry, the place of the industrial middle class, by industrial millionaires, the leaders of whole industrial armies, the modern bourgeois.

Large-scale industry has established the world market, for which the discovery of America paved the way. This market has given an immense development to commerce, to navigation, to communication by land. This development has, in its turn, reacted on the extension of industry; and in proportion as industry, commerce, navigation, railways extended, in the same proportion the bourgeoisie developed, increased its capital, and pushed into the background every class handed down from the Middle Ages.

We see, therefore, how the modern bourgeoisie is itself the product of a long course of development, of a series of revolutions in the modes of production and of exchange.

Each step in the development of the bourgeoisie was accompanied by a corresponding political advance. An oppressed class under the sway of the feudal nobility, an armed and self-governing association in the medieval commune; here independent urban republic, there taxable "third estate" of the monarchy, afterwards, in the period of manufacture proper, serving either the estate or the absolute monarchy as a counterpoise against the nobility, and, in fact, corner-stone of the great monarchies in general, the bourgeoisie has at last, since the establishment of Modern Industry and of the world market, conquered for itself, in the modern representative State, exclusive political sway. The executive of the modern State is but a committee for managing the common affairs of the whole bourgeoisie.

The bourgeoisie, historically, has played a most revolutionary part.

The bourgeoisie, wherever it has got the upper hand, has put an end to all feudal, patriarchal, idyllic relations. It has pitilessly torn asunder the motley feudal ties that bound man to his "natural superiors", and has left remaining no other nexus between man and man than naked self-interest, than callous "cash payment". It has drowned the most heavenly ecstasies of religious fervour, of chivalrous enthusiasm, of philistine sentimentalism, in the icy water of egotistical calculation. It has resolved personal worth into exchange value, and in place of the numberless indefeasible chartered freedoms, has set up that single, unconscionable freedom – Free Trade. In one word, for exploitation, veiled by religious and political illusions, it has substituted naked, shameless, direct, brutal exploitation.

The bourgeoisie has stripped of its halo every occupation hitherto honoured and looked up to with reverent awe. It has converted the physician, the lawyer, the priest, the poet, the man of science, into its paid wage-labourers.

The bourgeoisie has torn away from the family its sentimental veil, and has reduced the family relation to a mere money relation.

The bourgeoisie has disclosed how it came to pass that the brutal display of vigour in the Middle Ages, which Reactionists so much admire, found its fitting complement in the most slothful indolence. It has been the first to show what man's activity can bring about. It has accomplished wonders far surpassing Egyptian pyramids, Roman aqueducts, and Gothic cathedrals; it has conducted expeditions that put in the shade all former Exoduses of nations and crusades.

The bourgeoisie cannot exist without constantly revolutionizing the instruments of production, and thereby the relations of production, and with them the whole relations of society. Conservation of the old modes of production in unaltered form, was, on the contrary, the first condition of existence for all earlier industrial classes. Constant revolutionizing of production, uninterrupted disturbance of all social conditions, everlasting uncertainty and agitation distinguish the bourgeois epoch from all earlier ones. All fixed, fast-frozen relations, with their train of ancient and venerable prejudices and opinions are swept away, all new-formed ones become antiquated before they can ossify. All that is solid melts into air, all that is holy is profaned, and man is at last compelled to face with sober senses, his real conditions of life, and his relations with his kind.

The need of a constantly expanding market for its products chases the bourgeoisie over the whole surface of the globe. It must nestle everywhere, settle everywhere, establish connexions everywhere.

The bourgeoisie has through its exploitation of the world market given a cosmopolitan character to production and consumption in every country. To the great chagrin of Reactionists, it has drawn from under the feet of industry the national ground on which it stood. All old-established national industries have been destroyed or are daily being destroyed. They are dislodged by new industries, whose introduction becomes a life and death question for all civilized nations, by industries that no longer work up indigenous raw material, but raw material drawn from the remotest zones; industries whose products are consumed, not only at home, but in every quarter of the globe. In place of the old wants, satisfied by the productions of the country, we find new wants, requiring for their satisfaction the products of distant lands and climes. In place of the old local and national seclusion and self-sufficiency, we have intercourse in every direction, universal inter-dependence of nations. And as in material, so also in intellectual production. The intellectual creations of individual nations become common property. National one-sidedness and narrow-mindedness become more and more impossible, and from the numerous national and local literatures, there arises a world literature.

The bourgeoisie, by the rapid improvement of all instruments of production, by the immensely facilitated means of communication, draws all, even the most barbarian, nations into civilization. The cheap prices of its commodities are the heavy artillery with which it batters down all Chinese walls, with which it forces the barbarians' intensely obstinate hatred of foreigners to capitulate. It compels all nations, on pain of extinction, to adopt the bourgeois mode of production; it compels them to introduce what it calls civilization into their midst, i.e., to become bourgeois themselves. In one word, it creates a world after its own image.

The bourgeoisie has subjected the country to the rule of the towns. It has created enormous cities, has greatly increased the urban population as compared with the rural, and has thus rescued a considerable part of the population from the idiocy of rural life. Just as it has made the country de-

pendent on the towns, so it has made barbarian and semi-barbarian countries dependent on the civilized ones, nations of peasants on nations of bourgeois, the East on the West.

The bourgeoisie keeps more and more doing away with the scattered state of the population, of the means of production, and of property. It has agglomerated population, centralized means of production, and has concentrated property in a few hands. The necessary consequence of this was political centralization. Independent, or but loosely connected, provinces with separate interests, laws, governments and systems of taxation, became lumped together into one nation, with one government, one code of laws, one national class-interest, one frontier and one customs-tariff.

The bourgeoisie, during its rule of scarce one hundred years, has created more massive and more colossal productive forces than have all preceding generations together. Subjection of Nature's forces to man, machinery, application of chemistry to industry and agriculture, steam-navigation, railways, electric telegraphs, clearing of whole continents for cultivation, canalization of rivers, whole populations conjured out of the ground – what earlier century had even a presentiment that such productive forces slumbered in the lap of social labour?

We see then: the means of production and of exchange, on whose foundation the bourgeoisie built itself up, were generated in feudal society. At a certain stage in the development of these means of production and of exchange, the conditions under which feudal society produced and exchanged, the feudal organization of agriculture and manufacturing industry, in one word, the feudal relations of property became no longer compatible with the already developed productive forces; they hindered production rather than advancing it; they became so many fetters. They had to be burst asunder; they were burst asunder.

Into their place stepped free competition, accompanied by a social and political constitution adapted to it, and by the economical and political sway of the bourgeois class.

A similar movement is going on before our own eyes. Modern bourgeois society with its relations of production, of exchange and of property, a society that has conjured up such gigantic means of production and of exchange, is like the sorcerer, who is no longer able to control the powers of the nether world whom he has called up by his spells. For many a decade past the history of industry and commerce is but the history of the revolt of modern productive forces against modern conditions of production, against the property relations that are the conditions for the existence of the bourgeoisie and of its rule. It is enough to mention the commercial crises that by their periodical return put on its trial, each time more threateningly, the existence of the entire bourgeois society. In these crises a great part not only of the existing products, but also of the previously created productive forces, are periodically destroyed. In these crises there breaks out a social epidemic that, in all earlier epochs, would have seemed an absurdity – the epidemic of over-production. Society suddenly finds itself put back into a state of momentary barbarism; it appears as if a famine, a universal war of devastation had cut off the supply of every means of subsistence; industry and commerce seem to be destroyed; and why? Because there is too much civilization, too much means of subsistence, too much industry, too much commerce.

The productive forces at the disposal of society no longer tend to further the development of bourgeois civilization and the conditions of bourgeois property; on the contrary, they have become too powerful for these conditions, by which they are fettered, and so soon as they overcome these fetters, they bring disorder into the whole of bourgeois society, endanger the existence of bourgeois property. The conditions of bourgeois society are too narrow to comprise the wealth created by them. And how does the bourgeoisie get over these crises? On the one hand by enforced destruction of a mass of productive forces; on the other, by the conquest of new markets, and by the more thorough exploitation of the old ones. That is to say, by paving the way for more extensive and more destructive crises, and by diminishing the means whereby crises are prevented.

The weapons with which the bourgeoisie felled feudalism to the ground are now turned against the bourgeoisie itself. [...]

63

Capital: A Critique of Political Economy

Section 4: The Fetishism of Commodities and the Secret Thereof

A commodity appears, at first sight, a very trivial thing, and easily understood. Its analysis shows that it is, in reality, a very queer thing, abounding in metaphysical subtleties and theological niceties. So far as it is a value in use, there is nothing mysterious about it, whether we consider it from the point of view that by its properties it is capable of satisfying human wants, or from the point that those properties are the product of human labour. It is as clear as noon-day, that man, by his industry, changes the forms of the materials furnished by Nature, in such a way as to make them useful to him. The form of wood, for instance, is altered, by making a table out of it. Yet, for all that, the table continues to be that common, every-day thing, wood. But, so soon as it steps forth as a commodity, it is changed into something transcendent. It not only stands with its feet on the ground, but, in relation to all other commodities, it stands on its head, and evolves out of its wooden brain grotesque ideas, far more wonderful than "table-turning" ever was.

The mystical character of commodities does not originate, therefore, in their use-value. Just as little does it proceed from the nature of the determining factors of value. For, in the first place, however varied the useful kinds of labour, or productive activities, may be, it is a physiological fact, that

Capital: A Critique of Political Economy, vol. 1 (1867), tr. Samuel Moore and Edward Aveling (New York: International Publishers, 1967). Selection: sect. 4, pp. 71–83.

they are functions of the human organism, and that each such function, whatever may be its nature or form, is essentially the expenditure of human brain, nerves, muscles, &c. Secondly, with regard to that which forms the ground-work for the quantitative determination of value, namely, the duration of that expenditure, or the quantity of labour, it is quite clear that there is a palpable difference between its quantity and quality. In all states of society, the labour-time that it costs to produce the means of subsistence, must necessarily be an object of interest to mankind, though not of equal interest in different stages of development.[1] And lastly, from the moment that men in any way work for one another, their labour assumes a social form.

Whence, then, arises the enigmatical character of the product of labour, so soon as it assumes the form of commodities? Clearly from this form itself. The equality of all sorts of human labour is expressed objectively by their products all being equally values; the measure of the expenditure of labour-power by the duration of that expenditure, takes the form of the quantity of value of the products of labour; and finally, the mutual relations of the producers, within which the social character of their labour affirms itself, take the form of a social relation between the products.

A commodity is therefore a mysterious thing, simply because in it the social character of men's labour appears to them as an objective character stamped upon the product of that labour: because the relation of the producers to the sum total of their own labour is presented to them as a social relation, existing not between themselves, but between the products of their labour. This is the reason why the products of labour become commodities, social things whose qualities are at the same time perceptible and imperceptible by the senses. In the same way the light from an object is perceived by us not as the subjective excitation of our optic nerve, but as the objective form of something outside the eye itself. But, in the act of seeing, there is at all events, an actual passage of light from one thing to another, from the external object to the eye. There is a physical relation between physical things. But it is different with commodities. There, the existence of the things *quâ* commodities, and the value-relation between the products of labour which stamps them as commodities, have absolutely no connexion with their physical properties and with the material relations arising therefrom. There it is a definite social relation between men, that assumes, in their eyes, the fantastic form of a relation between things. In order, therefore, to find an analogy, we must have recourse to the mist-enveloped regions of the religious world. In that world the productions of the human brain appear as independent beings endowed with life, and entering into relation both with one another and the human race. So it is in the world of commodities with the products of men's hands. This I call the Fetishism which attaches itself to the products of labour, so soon as they are produced as commodities, and which is therefore inseparable from the production of commodities.

This Fetishism of commodities has its origin, as the foregoing analysis has already shown, in the peculiar social character of the labour that produces them.

As a general rule, articles of utility become commodities, only because they are products of the labour of private individuals or groups of individuals who carry on their work independently of each other. The sum total of the labour of all these private individuals forms the aggregate labour of society. Since the producers do not come into social contact with each other until they exchange their products, the specific social character of each producer's labour does not show itself except in the act of exchange. In other words, the labour of the individual asserts itself as a part of the labour of society, only by means of the relations which the act of exchange establishes directly between the products, and indirectly, through them, between the producers. To the latter, therefore, the relations connecting the labour of one individual with that of the rest appear, not as direct social relations between individuals at work, but as what they

really are, material relations between persons and social relations between things. It is only by being exchanged that the products of labour acquire, as values, one uniform social status, distinct from their varied forms of existence as objects of utility. This division of a product into a useful thing and a value becomes practically important, only when exchange has acquired such an extension that useful articles are produced for the purpose of being exchanged, and their character as values has therefore to be taken into account, beforehand, during production. From this moment the labour of the individual producer acquires socially a two-fold character. On the one hand, it must, as a definite useful kind of labour, satisfy a definite social want, and thus hold its place as part and parcel of the collective labour of all, as a branch of a social division of labour that has sprung up spontaneously. On the other hand, it can satisfy the manifold wants of the individual producer himself, only in so far as the mutual exchangeability of all kinds of useful private labour is an established social fact, and therefore the private useful labour of each producer ranks on an equality with that of all others. The equalisation of the most different kinds of labour can be the result only of an abstraction from their inequalities, or of reducing them to their common denominator, viz., expenditure of human labour-power or human labour in the abstract. The two-fold social character of the labour of the individual appears to him, when reflected in his brain, only under those forms which are impressed upon that labour in every-day practice by the exchange of products. In this way, the character that his own labour possesses of being socially useful takes the form of the condition, that the product must be not only useful, but useful for others, and the social character that his particular labour has of being the equal of all other particular kinds of labour, takes the form that all the physically different articles that are the products of labour, have one common quality, viz., that of having value.

Hence, when we bring the products of our labour into relation with each other as values, it is not because we see in these articles the material receptacles of homogeneous human labour. Quite the contrary: whenever, by an exchange, we equate as values our different products, by that very act, we also equate, as human labour, the different kinds of labour expended upon them. We are not aware of this, nevertheless we do it.[2] Value, therefore, does not stalk about with a label describing what it is. It is value, rather, that converts every product into a social hieroglyphic. Later on, we try to decipher the hieroglyphic, to get behind the secret of our own social products; for to stamp an object of utility as a value, is just as much a social product as language. The recent scientific discovery, that the products of labour, so far as they are values, are but material expressions of the human labour spent in their production, marks, indeed, an epoch in the history of the development of the human race, but, by no means, dissipates the mist through which the social character of labour appears to us to be an objective character of the products themselves. The fact, that in the particular form of production with which we are dealing, viz., the production of commodities, the specific social character of private labour carried on independently, consists in the equality of every kind of that labour, by virtue of its being human labour, which character, therefore, assumes in the product the form of value – this fact appears to the producers, notwithstanding the discovery above referred to, to be just as real and final, as the fact, that, after the discovery by science of the component gases of air, the atmosphere itself remained unaltered.

What, first of all, practically concerns producers when they make an exchange, is the question, how much of some other product they get for their own? in what proportions the products are exchangeable? When these proportions have, by custom, attained a certain stability, they appear to result from the nature of the products, so that, for instance, one ton of iron and two ounces of gold appear as naturally to be of equal value as a pound of gold and a pound of iron in spite of their different physical and chemical qualities appear to be of equal weight. The character of having value, when once impressed upon products, obtains fixity only by reason of their acting and re-acting upon each other as quantities of value. These quantities vary continually, independently of the will, foresight and action of the producers. To them, their own social action takes the form of the action of objects, which rule the producers instead of being ruled by them. It requires a fully developed production of commodities before, from accumulated experience alone, the scientific conviction springs up, that all the different kinds of private labour, which are carried on independently of each other, and yet as spontaneously developed branches of the social division of labour, are continually being reduced to the quantitative proportions in which society requires them. And why?

Because, in the midst of all the accidental and ever fluctuating exchange-relations between the products, the labour-time socially necessary for their production forcibly asserts itself like an over-riding law of Nature. The law of gravity thus asserts itself when a house falls about our ears.[3] The determination of the magnitude of value by labour-time is therefore a secret, hidden under the apparent fluctuations in the relative values of commodities. Its discovery, while removing all appearance of mere accidentality from the determination of the magnitude of the values of products, yet in no way alters the mode in which that determination takes place.

Man's reflections on the forms of social life, and consequently, also, his scientific analysis of those forms, take a course directly opposite to that of their actual historical development. He begins, post festum, with the results of the process of development ready to hand before him. The characters that stamp products as commodities, and whose establishment is a necessary preliminary to the circulation of commodities, have already acquired the stability of natural, self-understood forms of social life, before man seeks to decipher, not their historical character, for in his eyes they are immutable, but their meaning. Consequently it was the analysis of the prices of commodities that alone led to the determination of the magnitude of value, and it was the common expression of all commodities in money that alone led to the establishment of their characters as values. It is, however, just this ultimate money-form of the world of commodities that actually conceals, instead of disclosing, the social character of private labour, and the social relations between the individual producers. When I state that coats or boots stand in a relation to linen, because it is the universal incarnation of abstract human labour, the absurdity of the statement is self-evident. Nevertheless, when the producers of coats and boots compare those articles with linen, or, what is the same thing, with gold or silver, as the universal equivalent, they express the relation between their own private labour and the collective labour of society in the same absurd form.

The categories of bourgeois economy consist of such like forms. They are forms of thought expressing with social validity the conditions and relations of a definite, historically determined mode of production, viz., the production of commodities. The whole mystery of commodities, all the magic and necromancy that surrounds the products of labour as long as they take the form of commodities, vanishes therefore, so soon as we come to other forms of production.

Since Robinson Crusoe's experiences are a favourite theme with political economists,[4] let us take a look at him on his island. Moderate though he be, yet some few wants he has to satisfy, and must therefore do a little useful work of various sorts, such as making tools and furniture, taming goats, fishing and hunting. Of his prayers and the like we take no account, since they are a source of pleasure to him, and he looks upon them as so much recreation. In spite of the variety of his work, he knows that his labour, whatever its form, is but the activity of one and the same Robinson, and consequently, that it consists of nothing but different modes of human labour. Necessity itself compels him to apportion his time accurately between his different kinds of work. Whether one kind occupies a greater space in his general activity than another, depends on the difficulties, greater or less as the case may be, to be overcome in attaining the useful effect aimed at. This our friend Robinson soon learns by experience, and having rescued a watch, ledger, and pen and ink from the wreck, commences, like a true-born Briton, to keep a set of books. His stock-book contains a list of the objects of utility that belong to him, of the operations necessary for their production; and lastly, of the labour-time that definite quantities of those objects have, on an average, cost him. All the relations between Robinson and the objects that form this wealth of his own creation, are here so simple and clear as to be intelligible without exertion, even to Mr. Sedley Taylor. And yet those relations contain all that is essential to the determination of value.

Let us now transport ourselves from Robinson's island bathed in light to the European middle ages shrouded in darkness. Here, instead of the independent man, we find everyone dependent, serfs and lords, vassals and suzerains, laymen and clergy. Personal dependence here characterises the social relations of production just as much as it does the other spheres of life organised on the basis of that production. But for the very reason that personal dependence forms the ground-work of society, there is no necessity for labour and its products to assume a fantastic form different from their reality. They take the shape, in the transactions of society, of services in kind and payments in kind. Here the particular and natural form of labour, and not, as in a society based on production

of commodities, its general abstract form is the immediate social form of labour. Compulsory labour is just as properly measured by time, as commodity-producing labour; but every serf knows that what he expends in the service of his lord, is a definite quantity of his own personal labour-power. The tithe to be rendered to the priest is more matter of fact than his blessing. No matter, then, what we may think of the parts played by the different classes of people themselves in this society, the social relations between individuals in the performance of their labour, appear at all events as their own mutual personal relations, and are not disguised under the shape of social relations between the products of labour.

For an example of labour in common or directly associated labour, we have no occasion to go back to that spontaneously developed form which we find on the threshold of the history of all civilised races.[5] We have one close at hand in the patriarchal industries of a peasant family, that produces corn, cattle, yarn, linen, and clothing for home use. These different articles are, as regards the family, so many products of its labour, but as between themselves, they are not commodities. The different kinds of labour, such as tillage, cattle tending, spinning, weaving and making clothes, which result in the various products, are in themselves, and such as they are, direct social functions, because functions of the family, which, just as much as a society based on the production of commodities, possesses a spontaneously developed system of division of labour. The distribution of the work within the family, and the regulation of the labour-time of the several members, depend as well upon differences of age and sex as upon natural conditions varying with the seasons. The labour-power of each individual, by its very nature, operates in this case merely as a definite portion of the whole labour-power of the family, and therefore, the measure of the expenditure of individual labour-power by its duration, appears here by its very nature as a social character of their labour.

Let us now picture to ourselves, by way of change, a community of free individuals, carrying on their work with the means of production in common, in which the labour-power of all the different individuals is consciously applied as the combined labour-power of the community. All the characteristics of Robinson's labour are here repeated, but with this difference, that they are social, instead of individual. Everything produced by him was exclusively the result of his own personal labour, and therefore simply an object of use for himself. The total product of our community is a social product. One portion serves as fresh means of production and remains social. But another portion is consumed by the members as means of subsistence. A distribution of this portion amongst them is consequently necessary. The mode of this distribution will vary with the productive organisation of the community, and the degree of historical development attained by the producers. We will assume, but merely for the sake of a parallel with the production of commodities, that the share of each individual producer in the means of subsistence is determined by his labour-time. Labour-time would, in that case, play a double part. Its apportionment in accordance with a definite social plan maintains the proper proportion between the different kinds of work to be done and the various wants of the community. On the other hand, it also serves as a measure of the portion of the common labour borne by each individual, and of his share in the part of the total product destined for individual consumption. The social relations of the individual producers, with regard both to their labour and to its products, are in this case perfectly simple and intelligible, and that with regard not only to production but also to distribution.

The religious world is but the reflex of the real world. And for a society based upon the production of commodities, in which the producers in general enter into social relations with one another by treating their products as commodities and values, whereby they reduce their individual private labour to the standard of homogeneous human labour – for such a society, Christianity with its *cultus* of abstract man, more especially in its bourgeois developments, Protestantism, Deism, &c., is the most fitting form of religion. In the ancient Asiatic and other ancient modes of production, we find that the conversion of products into commodities, and therefore the conversion of men into producers of commodities, holds a subordinate place, which, however, increases in importance as the primitive communities approach nearer and nearer to their dissolution. Trading nations, properly so called, exist in the ancient world only in its interstices, like the gods of Epicurus in the Intermundia, or like Jews in the pores of Polish society. Those ancient social organisms of production are, as compared with bourgeois society, extremely simple and transparent. But they are founded either on the immature development of man individually, who has not yet severed the umbilical cord that unites him with his fellowmen in a primitive tribal community, or upon direct relations of subjection. They can arise and exist only when the development of the productive power of labour has not risen beyond a low stage, and when, therefore, the social relations within the sphere of material life, between man and man, and between man and Nature, are correspondingly narrow. This narrowness is reflected in the ancient worship of Nature, and in the other elements of the popular religions. The religious reflex of the real world can, in any case, only then finally vanish, when the practical relations of every-day life offer to man none but perfectly intelligible and reasonable relations with regard to his fellowmen and to Nature.

The life-process of society, which is based on the process of material production, does not strip off its mystical veil until it is treated as production by freely associated men, and is consciously regulated by them in accordance with a settled plan. This, however, demands for society a certain material ground-work or set of conditions of existence which in their turn are the spontaneous product of a long and painful process of development.

Political Economy has indeed analysed, however incompletely,[6] value and its magnitude, and has discovered what lies beneath these forms. But it has never once asked the question why labour is represented by the value of its product and labour-time by the magnitude of that value.[7] These formulæ, which bear it stamped upon them in unmistakeable letters that they belong to a state of society, in which the process of production has the mastery over man, instead of being controlled by him, such formulæ appear to the bourgeois intellect to be as much a self-evident necessity imposed by Nature as productive labour itself. Hence forms of social production that preceded the bourgeois form, are treated by the bourgeoisie in much the same way as the Fathers of the Church treated pre-Christian religions.[8]

To what extent some economists are misled by the Fetishism inherent in commodities, or by the objective appearance of the social characteristics of labour, is shown, amongst other ways, by the dull and tedious quarrel over the part played by Nature in the formation of exchange-value. Since exchange-value is a definite social manner of expressing the amount of labour bestowed upon an object, Nature has no more to do with it, than it has in fixing the course of exchange.

The mode of production in which the product takes the form of a commodity, or is produced directly for exchange, is the most general and most embryonic form of bourgeois production. It therefore makes its appearance at an early date in history, though not in the same predominating and characteristic manner as now-a-days. Hence its Fetish character is comparatively easy to be seen through. But when we come to more concrete forms, even this appearance of simplicity vanishes. Whence arose the illusions of the monetary system? To it gold and silver, when serving as money, did not represent a social relation between producers, but were natural objects with strange social properties. And modern economy, which looks down with such disdain on the monetary system, does not its superstition come out as clear as noon-day, whenever it treats of capital? How long is it since economy discarded the physiocratic illusion, that rents grow out of the soil and not out of society?

But not to anticipate, we will content ourselves with yet another example relating to the commodity-form. Could commodities themselves speak, they would say: Our use-value may be a thing that interests men. It is no part of us as objects. What, however, does belong to us as objects, is our value. Our natural intercourse as commodities proves it. In the eyes of each other we are nothing but exchange-values. Now listen how those commodities speak through the mouth of the economist. "Value" – (*i.e.*, exchange-value) "is a property of things, riches" – (*i.e.*, use-value) "of man. Value, in this sense, necessarily implies exchanges, riches do not."[9] "Riches" (use-value) "are the attribute of men, value is the attribute of commodities. A man or a community is rich, a pearl or a diamond is valuable ... A pearl or a diamond is valuable" as a pearl or diamond.[10] So far no chemist has ever discovered exchange-value either in a pearl or a diamond. The economic discoverers of this chemical element, who by-the-by lay special claim to critical acumen, find however that the use-value of objects belongs to them independently of their material properties, while their value, on the other hand, forms a part of them as objects. What confirms them in this view, is the peculiar circumstance that the use-value of objects is realised without exchange, by means of a direct relation between the objects and man, while, on the other hand, their value is realised only by exchange, that is, by means of a social process. Who fails here to call to mind our good friend, Dogberry, who informs neighbour Seacoal, that, "To be a well-favoured man is the gift of fortune; but reading and writing comes by Nature."[11]

Notes

1 Among the ancient Germans the unit for measuring land was what could be harvested in a day, and was called Tagwerk, Tagwanne (jurnale, or terra jurnalis, or diornalis), Mannsmaad, &c. (See G. L. von Maurer, "Einleitung zur Geschichte der Mark—, &c. Verfassung," München, 1854, p. 129 sq.)

2 When, therefore, Galiani says: Value is a relation between persons – "La Ricchezza è una ragione tra due persone," – he ought to have added: a relation between persons expressed as a relation between things. (Galiani: Della Moneta, p. 221, V III of Custodi's collection of "Scrittori Classici Italiani di Economia Politica." Parte Moderna, Milano, 1803.)

3 "What are we to think of a law that asserts itself only by periodical revolutions? It is just nothing but a law of Nature, founded on the want of knowledge of those whose action is the subject of it." (Friedrich Engels: "Umrisse zu einer Kritik der Nationalökonomie," in the "Deutsch-Französische Jahrbücher," edited by Arnold Ruge and Karl Marx. Paris, 1844.)

4 Even Ricardo has his stories à la Robinson. "He makes the primitive hunter and the primitive fisher straightway, as owners of commodities, exchange fish and game in the proportion in which labour-time is incorporated in these exchange-values. On this occasion he commits the anachronism of making these men apply to the calculation, so far as their implements have to be taken into account, the annuity tables in current use on the London Exchange in the year 1817. 'The parallelograms of Mr. Owen' appear to be the only form of society, besides the bourgeois form, with which he was acquainted." (Karl Marx: "Zur Kritik der Politischen Oekonomie," Berlin, 1859, pp. 38, 39.)

5 "A ridiculous presumption has latterly got abroad that common property in its primitive form is specifically a Slavonian, or even exclusively Russian form. It is the primitive form that we can prove to have existed amongst Romans, Teutons, and Celts, and even to this day we find numerous examples, ruins though they be, in India. A more exhaustive study of Asiatic, and especially of Indian forms of common property, would show how from the different forms of primitive common property, different forms of its dissolution have been developed. Thus, for instance, the various original types of Roman and Teutonic

private property are deducible from different forms of Indian common property." (Karl Marx, "Zur Kritik, &c.," p. 10.)

6 The insufficiency of Ricardo's analysis of the magnitude of value, and his analysis is by far the best, will appear from the 3rd and 4th books of this work. As regards value in general, it is the weak point of the classical school of Political Economy that it nowhere, expressly and with full consciousness, distinguishes between labour, as it appears in the value of a product and the same labour, as it appears in the use-value of that product. Of course the distinction is practically made, since this school treats labour, at one time under its quantitative aspect, at another under its qualitative aspect. But it has not the least idea, that when the difference between various kinds of labour is treated as purely quantitative, their qualitative unity or equality, and therefore their reduction to abstract human labour, is implied. For instance, Ricardo declares that he agrees with Destutt de Tracy in this proposition: "As it is certain that our physical and moral faculties are alone our original riches, the employment of those faculties, labour of some kind, is our only original treasure, and it is always from this employment that all those things are created, which we call riches. . . . It is certain, too, that all those things only represent the labour which has created them, and if they have a value, or even two distinct values, they can only derive them from that (the value) of the labour from which they emanate." (Ricardo, "The Principles of Pol. Econ.," 3 Ed. Lond. 1821, p. 334.) We would here only point out, that Ricardo puts his own more profound interpretation upon the words of Destutt. What the latter really says is, that on the one hand all things which constitute wealth represent the labour that creates them, but that on the other hand, they acquire their "two different values" (use-value and exchange-value) from "the value of labour." He thus falls into the commonplace error of the vulgar economists, who assume the value of one commodity (in this case labour) in order to determine the values of the rest. But Ricardo reads him as if he had said, that labour (not the value of labour) is embodied both in use-value and exchange-value. Nevertheless, Ricardo himself pays so little attention to the two-fold character of the labour which has a two-fold embodiment, that he devotes the whole of his chapter on "Value and Riches, Their Distinctive Properties," to a laborious examination of the trivialities of a J. B. Say. And at the finish he is quite astonished to find that Destutt on the one hand agrees with him as to labour being the source of value, and on the other hand with J. B. Say as to the notion of value.

7 It is one of the chief failings of classical economy that it has never succeeded, by means of its analysis of commodities, and, in particular, of their value, in discovering that form under which value becomes exchange-value. Even Adam Smith and Ricardo, the best representatives of the school, treat the form of value as a thing of no importance, as having no connexion with the inherent nature of commodities. The reason for this is not solely because their attention is entirely absorbed in the analysis of the magnitude of value. It lies deeper. The value-form of the product of labour is not only the most abstract, but is also the most universal form, taken by the product in bourgeois production, and stamps that production as a particular species of social production, and thereby gives it its special historical character. If then we treat this mode of production as one eternally fixed by Nature for every state of society, we necessarily overlook that which is the differentia specifica of the value-form, and consequently of the commodity-form, and of its further developments, money-form, capital-form, &c. We consequently find that economists, who are thoroughly agreed as to labour-time being the measure of the magnitude of value, have the most strange and contradictory ideas of money, the perfected form of the general equivalent. This is seen in a striking manner when they treat of banking, where the commonplace definitions of money will no longer hold water. This led to the rise of a restored mercantile system (Ganilh, &c.), which sees in value nothing but a social form, or rather the unsubstantial ghost of that form. Once for all I may here state, that by classical Political Economy, I understand that economy which, since the time of W. Petty, has investigated the real relations of production in bourgeois society, in contradistinction to vulgar economy, which deals with appearances only, ruminates without ceasing on the materials long since provided by scientific economy, and there seeks plausible explanations of the most obtrusive phenomena, for bourgeois daily use, but for the rest, confines itself to systematising in a pedantic way, and proclaiming for everlasting truths, the trite ideas held by the self-complacent bourgeoisie with regard to their own world, to them the best of all possible worlds.

8 "Les économistes ont une singulière manière de procéder. Il n'y a pour eux que deux sortes d'institutions, celles de l'art et celles de la nature. Les institutions de la féodalité sont des institutions artificielles, celles de la bourgeoisie sont des institutions naturelles. Ils ressemblent en ceci aux théologiens, qui eux aussi établissent deux sortes de religions. Toute religion qui n'est pas la leur, est une invention des hommes, tandis que leur propre religion est une émanation de Dieu – Ainsi il y a eu de l'histoire, mais il n'y en a plus." (Karl Marx, Misère de la Philosophie. Réponse à la Philosophie de la Misère par M. Proudhon, 1847, p. 113.) Truly comical is M. Bastiat, who imagines that the ancient Greeks and Romans lived by plunder alone. But when people plunder for centuries, there must always be something at hand for them to seize, the objects of plunder must be con-

tinually reproduced. It would thus appear that even Greeks and Romans had some process of production, consequently, an economy, which just as much constituted the material basis of their world, as bourgeois economy constitutes that of our modern world. Or perhaps Bastiat means, that a mode of production based on slavery is based on a system of plunder. In that case he treads on dangerous ground. If a giant thinker like Aristotle erred in his appreciation of slave labour, why should a dwarf economist like Bastiat be right in his appreciation of wage-labour? – I seize this opportunity of shortly answering an objection taken by a German paper in America, to my work, "Zur Kritik der Pol. Oekonomie, 1859." In the estimation of that paper, my view that each special mode of production and the social relations corresponding to it, in short, that the economic structure of society, is the real basis on which the juridical and political superstructure is raised, and to which definite social forms of thought correspond; that the mode of production determines the character of the social, political, and intellectual life generally, all this is very true for our own times, in which material interests preponderate, but not for the middle ages, in which Catholicism, nor for Athens and Rome, where politics, reigned supreme. In the first place it strikes one as an odd thing for any one to suppose that these well-worn phrases about the middle ages and the ancient world are unknown to anyone else. This much, however, is clear, that the middle ages could not live on Catholicism, nor the ancient world on politics. On the contrary, it is the mode in which they gained a livelihood that explains why here politics, and there Catholicism, played the chief part. For the rest, it requires but a slight acquaintance with the history of the Roman republic, for example, to be aware that its secret history is the history of its landed property. On the other hand, Don Quixote long ago paid the penalty for wrongly imagining that knight errantry was compatible with all economic forms of society.

9 "Observations on certain verbal disputes in Pol. Econ., particularly relating to value and to demand and supply." Lond., 1821, p. 16.

10 S. Bailey, "A Critical Dissertation on the Nature, Measures and Causes of Value," London, 1825, p. 165.

11 The author of "Observations" and S. Bailey accuse Ricardo of converting exchange-value from something relative into something absolute. The opposite is the fact. He has explained the apparent relation between objects, such as diamonds and pearls, in which relation they appear as exchange-values, and disclosed the true relation hidden behind the appearances, namely, their relation to each other as mere expressions of human labour. If the followers of Ricardo answer Bailey somewhat rudely, and by no means convincingly, the reason is to be sought in this, that they were unable to find in Ricardo's own works any key to the hidden relations existing between value and its form, exchange-value.

Friedrich Nietzsche (1844–1900)

Introduction

All of the selections in this chapter are from the relatively early writings of Nietzsche. The first is from *Human, All Too Human* (1878), the second from *Daybreak* (1881), and the third from *The Gay Science* (1882–7). While these books are not among Nietzsche's most popular works, they contain some of the clearest statements of his central ideas and are less marred by vitriol and overstatement than later ones. In these selections one sees a Nietzsche intent on exposing the narrowness and rigidity of contemporary thought, but not yet committed to perspectivism. The last remnants of Schopenhauerian idealism are cast out and the full consequences of Schopenhauer's empiricism drawn. Mind, reason, morality, and the quest for truth are located squarely among the instincts. A thorough skepticism pervades the whole, qualified by the discovery of "a conscience behind the conscience" that saves the possibility of science. The philosopher is transformed into "the wanderer," "a subterranean man," a "preparatory human being," one of the "cheerful ones," an "incomprehensible one," and finally made "homeless" by his conscience.

64

Human, All Too Human

Man Alone With Himself

[...] 629

Of conviction and justice. – That a man must, in subsequent cold sobriety, continue to adhere to what he has said, promised, resolved in passion – this demand is among the heaviest of the burdens that oppress mankind. To be obliged to recognize the consequences of anger, of a blazing revengefulness, of an enthusiastic devotion, for all future time – that can engender an animosity towards these sensations made the more bitter by their idolization everywhere and especially by the artists. These latter greatly encourage the *high value accorded the passions* and have always done so; they also, to be sure, glorify the fearful amends one must make for these same passions, the death, maiming and voluntary banishment following on outbursts of revenge, the resignation of the broken heart. In any event, they keep awake our curiosity regarding the passions, as though to say: "experience without passion is nothing at all". – Because we have sworn to be faithful, perhaps even to a purely fictitious being such as a god, because we have surrendered our heart to a prince, to a party, to a woman, to a priestly order, to an artist, to a thinker, in a state of deluded infatuation that made that being seem worthy of every kind of sacrifice and reverence – are we now ineluctably committed? Were we not indeed at that time deceiving ourselves? Was it not a hypothetical prom

Human, All Too Human (1878), tr. R. J. Hollingdale (Cambridge University Press, 1986). Selection: "Man Alone With Himself," pp. 198–204.

ise, made under the admittedly silent condition that the beings to which we consecrated ourselves were in reality what they appeared to us to be? Are we obliged to be faithful to our errors, even when we realize that through this faithfulness we are injuring our higher self? – No, there exists no law, no obligation, of this kind; we *have* to become traitors, be unfaithful, again and again abandon our ideals. We cannot advance from one period of our life into the next without passing through these pains of betrayal and then continuing to suffer them. If we were to avoid these pains, would it not be necessary for us to guard ourselves against these ebullitions of our emotions? Would the world not then become too dreary, too spectral for us? Let us ask ourselves, rather, whether these pains are *necessarily* attendant on a change in our convictions, or whether they do not proceed from an *erroneous* evaluation and point of view. – Why do we admire him who is faithful to his convictions and despise him who changes them? I am afraid the answer must be: because everyone assumes that such a change can be motivated only by considerations of vulgar advantage or personal fear. That is to say, we believe at bottom that no one would change his convictions so long as they are advantageous to him, or at least so long as they do not do him any harm. If this is so, however, it is an ill witness as to the *intellectual* significance of all convictions. Let us for once examine how convictions originate, and let us see whether they are not greatly overestimated: what will emerge too is that a *change* in convictions has also invariably been assessed by a false criterion and that we have hitherto been accustomed to suffer too much when such a change has occurred.

630

Conviction is the belief that on some particular point of knowledge one is in possession of the unqualified truth. This belief thus presupposes that unqualified truths exist; likewise that perfect methods of attaining to them have been discovered; finally, that everyone who possesses convictions avails himself of these perfect methods. All three assertions demonstrate at once that the man of convictions is not the man of scientific thought; he stands before us in the age of theoretical innocence and is a child, however grown up he may be in other respects. But whole millennia have lived in these childish presuppositions and it is from them that mankind's mightiest sources of energy have flowed. Those countless numbers who have sacrificed themselves for their convictions thought they were doing so for unqualified truth. In this they were all wrong: probably a man has never yet sacrificed himself for truth; at least the dogmatic expression of his belief will have been unscientific or half-scientific. In reality one wanted to be in the right because one thought one *had* to be. To allow oneself to be deprived of one's belief perhaps meant calling one's eternal salvation into question. In a matter of such extreme importance as this the "will" was only too audibly the prompter of the intellect. The presupposition of every believer of every kind was that he *could* not be refuted; if the counter-arguments proved very strong it was always left to him to defame reason itself and perhaps even to set up the "*credo quia absurdum est*" ["I believe it because it is absurd"] as the banner of the extremest fanaticism. It is not conflict of opinions that has made history so violent but conflict of belief in opinions, that is to say conflict of convictions. But if all those who have thought so highly of their convictions, brought to them sacrifices of every kind, and have not spared honour, body or life in their service, had devoted only half their energy to investigating with what right they adhered to this or that conviction, by what path they had arrived at it, how peaceable a picture the history of mankind would present! How much more knowledge there would be! We should have been spared all the cruel scenes attending the persecution of heretics of every kind, and for two reasons: firstly because the inquisitors would have conducted their inquisition above all within themselves and emerged out of the presumptuousness of being the defenders of unqualified truth; then because the heretics themselves would, after they had investigated them, have ceased to accord any further credence to such ill-founded propositions as the propositions of all religious sectarians and "right believers" are.

631

From the ages in which men were accustomed to believe in possession of unqualified truth there has come a profound *displeasure* with all sceptical and relativistic positions in regard to any question of knowledge whatever; one usually prefers to surrender unconditionally to a conviction harboured by people in authority (fathers, friends, teachers, princes) and feels a kind of pang of conscience if one fails to do so. This tendency is quite comprehensible, and its consequences give us no right to any violent reproaches against the way human reason has evolved. But gradually the scientific spirit in men has to bring to maturity that virtue of *cautious reserve*, that wise moderation which is more familiar in the domain of the practical life than in the domain of the theoretical life and which, for example, Goethe has depicted in Antonio as an object of animosity for all Tassos, that is to say for unscientific and at the same time inactive natures. The man of conviction has in himself the right to fail to comprehend the man of cautious thinking, the theoretical Antonio; the scientific man, on the other hand, has no right to blame him for that: he makes allowances for him, and knows moreover that in the end the latter will come to cleave to him, as Tasso finally does to Antonio.

632

He who has not passed through different convictions, but remains in the belief in whose net he was first captured, is on account of this unchangeability under all circumstances a representative of *retarded* cultures; in accordance with this lack of cultivation (which always presupposes cultivatability) he is a man hard, uncomprehending, unteachable, ungenerous, everlastingly suspicious and unheeding, who neglects no means of constantly asserting his own point of view because he is quite incapable of grasping that there are bound to be other points of view; on this account he is perhaps a source of strength, and in cultures grown too slack and flabby even salutary, but only because he arouses vigorous opposition: for in being compelled to struggle against him the more fragile structure of the new culture itself grows strong.

633

We are essentially the same men as those of the age of the Reformation: and how could it be otherwise? But that we no longer permit ourselves certain means of assisting our opinion to victory distinguishes us from that age and demonstrates that we belong to a higher culture. He who still, in the manner of the Reformation man, combats and crushes other opinions with defamations and outbursts of rage betrays clearly that he would have burned his opponents if he had lived in another age, and that he would have had recourse to all the methods of the Inquisition if he had been an opponent of the Reformation. This Inquisition was at that time reasonable, for it signified nothing other than the state of siege that had to be decreed for the whole domain of the Church and which, like every state of siege, justified the extremest measures, always under the presupposition (which we now no longer share with the men of those days) that in the Church one *possessed* the truth and was *obliged* to preserve it at the cost of any sacrifice for the salvation of mankind. Nowadays, however, we no longer so easily concede to anyone that he is in possession of the truth: the rigorous procedures of inquiry have propagated distrust and caution, so that anyone who advocates opinions with violent word and deed is felt to be an enemy of our present-day culture, or at least as one retarded. And the pathos of *possessing* truth does now in fact count for very little in comparison with that other, admittedly gentler and less noisy pathos of seeking truth that never wearies of learning and examining anew.

634

The methodical search for truth is, moreover, itself a product of those ages in which convictions were at war with one another. If the individual had not been concerned with *his* "truth", that is to say with his being in the right, there would have been no methods of inquiry at all; but with the claims of different individuals to unqualified truth everlastingly in conflict with one another, men went on step by step to discover incontestable principles by which these claims could be tested and the contest decided. At first they appealed to authorities, later they criticized the ways and means through which the other's supposed truths had been discovered; in between there was a period when they drew the consequences of their opponent's proposition and perhaps found it harmful and productive of unhappiness: from which everyone was supposed to

see that the opponent's conviction contained an error. *The personal strife of thinkers* at last rendered their procedures so acute that truths really could be discovered and the aberrations of earlier procedures exposed for all to see.

635

On the whole, the procedures of science are at least as important a product of inquiry as any other outcome: for the scientific spirit rests upon an insight into the procedures, and if these were lost all the other products of science together would not suffice to prevent a restoration of superstition and folly. There are people of intelligence who can *learn* as many of the facts of science as they like, but from their conversation, and especially from the hypotheses they put forward, you can tell that they lack the spirit of science: they have not that instinctive mistrust of devious thinking which, as a consequence of long practice, has put its roots down in the soul of every scientific man. For them it is enough to have discovered any hypothesis at all concerning any matter, then they are at once on fire for it and believe the whole thing is accomplished. To possess an opinion is to them the same thing as to become a fanatical adherent of it and henceforth to lay it to their heart as a conviction. When something is in need of explanation they grow impassioned for the first idea to enter their head that looks in any way like an explanation of it: a procedure productive of the evilest consequences, especially in the domain of politics. – It is for this reason that everyone now should have acquired a thorough knowledge of at least *one* science: then he would know what is meant by method and procedure and how vital it is to exercise the greatest circumspection. Women are especially in need of this advice: for they are at present the helpless victims of every hypothesis that appears, especially when it produces the impression of being intelligent, thrilling, animating, invigorating. On closer examination, indeed, one sees that by far the greater part of all educated people even now still desire from a thinker convictions and nothing but convictions, and that only a small minority want *certainty*. The former want to be violently carried away, so as themselves to experience an increase in strength; the latter few possess that objective interest that ignores personal advantage, even the increase in strength referred to. The former, vastly preponderant class is what the thinker has in view when he takes himself for a *genius*, and presents himself as a higher being possessing authority. Insofar as genius of every kind maintains the fire of convictions and awakens distrust of the modesty and circumspection of science, it is an enemy of truth, no matter how much it may believe itself to be truth's suitor.

636

There is, to be sure, a quite different species of genius, that of justice; and I cannot in any way persuade myself to regard it as lower than any kind of philosophical, political or artistic genius. It is the way of this kind of genius to avoid with hearty indignation everything that confuses and deceives us in our judgement of things; it is consequently an *opponent of convictions*, for it wants to give to each his own, whether the thing be dead or living, real or imaginary – and to that end it must have a clear knowledge of it; it therefore sets every thing in the best light and observes it carefully from all sides. In the end it will give to its opponent, blind or shortsighted "conviction" (as men call it: – women call it "faith"), what is due to conviction – for the sake of truth.

637

Opinions grow out of *passions*; *inertia of the spirit* lets them stiffen into *convictions*. – He, however, whose spirit is *free* and restlessly alive can prevent this stiffening through continual change, and even if he should be altogether a thinking snowball, he will have in his head, not opinions, but only certainties and precisely calculated probabilities. – But let us, who are compound creatures, now heated up by fire, now cooled down by the spirit, kneel down before justice as the only goddess we recognize over us. *The fire* in us usually makes us unjust and, from the viewpoint of that goddess, impure; in this condition we may never grasp her hand, never will the smile of her pleasure light upon us. We revere her as the veiled Isis of our lives; abashed, we offer up to her our pain as penance and sacrifice whenever the fire seeks to burn and consume us. It is *the spirit* that rescues us, so that we are not wholly reduced to ashes; it tears us away from the sacrificial altar of justice or encloses us in a coat of asbestos. Redeemed from the fire, driven now by the spirit, we advance from

opinion to opinion, through one party after another, as noble *traitors* to all things that can in any way be betrayed – and yet we feel no sense of guilt.

638

The Wanderer. – He who has attained to only some degree of freedom of mind cannot feel other than a wanderer on the earth – though not as a traveller *to* a final destination: for this destination does not exist. But he will watch and observe and keep his eyes open to see what is really going on in the world; for this reason he may not let his heart adhere too firmly to any individual thing; within him too there must be something wandering that takes pleasure in change and transience. Such a man will, to be sure, experience bad nights, when he is tired and finds the gate of the town that should offer him rest closed against him; perhaps in addition the desert will, as in the Orient, reach right up to the gate, beasts of prey howl now farther off, now closer to, a strong wind arise, robbers depart with his beasts of burden. Then dreadful night may sink down upon the desert like a second desert, and his heart grow weary of wandering. When the morning sun then rises, burning like a god of wrath, and the gate of the town opens to him, perhaps he will behold in the faces of those who dwell there even more desert, dirt, deception, insecurity than lie outside the gate – and the day will be almost worse than the night. Thus it may be that the wanderer shall fare; but then, as recompense, there will come the joyful mornings of other days and climes, when he shall see, even before the light has broken, the Muses come dancing by him in the mist of the mountains, when afterwards, if he relaxes quietly beneath the trees in the equanimity of his soul at morning, good and bright things will be thrown down to him from their tops and leafy hiding-places, the gifts of all those free spirits who are at home in mountain, wood and solitude and who, like him, are, in their now joyful, now thoughtful way, wanderers and philosophers. Born out of the mysteries of dawn, they ponder on how, between the tenth and the twelfth stroke of the clock, the day could present a face so pure, so light-filled, so cheerful and transfigured: – they seek the *philosophy of the morning*.

65

Daybreak

Preface

1

In this book you will discover a "subterranean man" at work, one who tunnels and mines and undermines. You will see him – presupposing you have eyes capable of seeing this work in the depths – going forward slowly, cautiously, gently inexorable, without betraying very much of the distress which any protracted deprivation of light and air must entail; you might even call him contented, working there in the dark. Does it not seem as though some faith were leading him on, some consolation offering him compensation? As though he perhaps desires this prolonged obscurity, desires to be incomprehensible, concealed, enigmatic, because he knows what he will thereby also acquire: his own morning, his own redemption, his own *daybreak*? . . . He will return, that is certain: do not ask him what he is looking for down there, he will tell you himself of his own accord, this seeming Trophonius and subterranean, as soon as he has "become a man" again. Being silent is something one completely unlearns if, like him, one has been for so long a solitary mole – – –

2

And indeed, my patient friends, I shall now tell you what I was after down there – here in this late preface which could easily have become a funeral oration: for I have returned and, believe it or not, returned safe and sound. Do not think for a moment that I intend to invite you to the same hazardous enterprise! Or even only to the same solitude! For he who proceeds on his own path in this fashion encounters no one: that is inherent in "proceeding on one's own path". No one comes along to help him: all the perils, accidents, malice and bad weather which assail him he has to tackle by himself. For his path is *his alone* – as is, of course, the bitterness and occasional ill-humour he feels at this "his alone": among which is included, for instance, the knowledge that even his friends are unable to divine where he is or whither he is going, that they will sometimes ask themselves: "what? is he going at all? does he still have – a path?" – At that time I undertook something not everyone may undertake: I descended into the depths, I tunnelled into the foundations, I commenced an investigation and digging out of an ancient *faith*, one upon which we philosophers have for a couple of millennia been accustomed to build as if upon the firmest of all foundations – and have continued to do so even though every building hitherto erected on them has fallen down: I commenced to undermine our *faith in morality*. But you do not understand me?

3

Hitherto, the subject reflected on least adequately has been good and evil: it was too dangerous a subject. Conscience, reputation, Hell, sometimes even the police have permitted and continue to permit no impartiality; in the presence of morality, as in the face of any authority, one is not *allowed* to think, far less to express an opinion: here one has to – *obey*! As long as the world has existed no

Daybreak: Thoughts on the Prejudices of Morality (1881), tr. R. J. Hollingdale (Cambridge University Press, 1982). Selection: Preface, pp. 1–5.

authority has yet been willing to let itself become the object of criticism; and to criticise morality itself, to regard morality as a problem, as problematic: what? has that not been – *is* that not – immoral? – But morality does not merely have at its command every kind of means of frightening off critical hands and torture-instruments: its security reposes far more in a certain art of enchantment it has at its disposal – it knows how to "inspire". With this art it succeeds, often with no more than a single glance, in paralysing the critical will and even in enticing it over to its own side; there are even cases in which morality has been able to turn the critical will against itself, so that, like the scorpion, it drives its sting into its own body. For morality has from of old been master of every diabolical nuance of the art of persuasion: there is no orator, even today, who does not have recourse to its assistance (listen, for example, even to our anarchists: how morally they speak when they want to persuade! In the end they even go so far as to call themselves "the good and the just"). For as long as there has been speech and persuasion on earth, morality has shown itself to be the greatest of all mistresses of seduction – and, so far as we philosophers are concerned, the actual *Circe of the philosophers*. Why is it that from Plato onwards every philosophical architect in Europe has built in vain? That everything they themselves in all sober seriousness regarded as *aere perennius* is threatening to collapse or already lies in ruins? Oh how false is the answer which even today is reserved in readiness for this question: "because they had all neglected the presupposition for such an undertaking, the testing of the foundations, a critique of reason as a whole" – that fateful answer of Kant's which has certainly not lured us modern philosophers on to any firmer or less treacherous ground! (– and, come to think of it, was it not somewhat peculiar to demand of an instrument that it should criticise its own usefulness and suitability? that the intellect itself should "know" its own value, its own capacity, its own limitations? was it not even a little absurd? –). The correct answer would rather have been that all philosophers were building under the seduction of morality, even Kant – that they were apparently aiming at certainty, at "truth", but in reality at *"majestic moral structures"*: to employ once again the innocent language of Kant, who describes his own "not so glittering yet not undeserving" task and labour as "to level and make firm the ground for these majestic moral structures" (*Critique of Pure Reason*

II, p. 257). Alas, we have to admit today that he did not succeed in doing that, quite the contrary! Kant was, with such an enthusiastic intention, the true son of his century, which before any other can be called the century of enthusiasm: as he fortunately remained also in regard to its more valuable aspects (for example in the good portion of sensism he took over into his theory of knowledge). He too had been bitten by the moral tarantula Rousseau, he too harboured in the depths of his soul the idea of that moral fanaticism whose executor another disciple of Rousseau felt and confessed himself to be, namely Robespierre, "*de fonder sur la terre l'empire de la sagesse, de la justice et de la vertu*" (speech of 7 June 1794). On the other hand, with such a French fanaticism in one's heart, one could not have gone to work in a less French fashion, more thoroughly, more in a German fashion – if the word "German" is still permitted today in this sense – than Kant did: to create room for *his* "moral realm" he saw himself obliged to posit an undemonstrable world, a logical "Beyond" – it was for precisely that that he had need of his critique of pure reason! In other words: *he would not have had need of it* if one thing had not been more vital to him than anything else: to render the "moral realm" unassailable, even better incomprehensible to reason – for he felt that a moral order of things was only too assailable by reason! In the face of nature and history, in the face of the thorough *immorality* of nature and history, Kant was, like every good German of the old stamp, a pessimist; he believed in morality, not because it is demonstrated in nature and history, but in spite of the fact that nature and history continually contradict it. To understand this "in spite of", one might perhaps recall something similar in Luther, that other great pessimist who, with all the audacity native to him, once admonished his friends: "if we could grasp by reason how the God who shows so much wrath and malice can be just and merciful, what need would we have of *faith*?" For nothing has from the beginning made a more profound impression on the German soul, nothing has "tempted" it more, than this most perilous of all conclusions, which to every true Roman is a sin against the spirit: *credo quia absurdum est*: – it was with this conclusion that German logic first entered the history of Christian dogma: but even today, a millennium later, we Germans of today, late Germans in every respect, still sense something of truth, of the *possibility* of truth behind the celebrated dialectical principle with which in his day Hegel assisted the German spirit to conquer Europe – "Contradiction moves the world, all things contradict themselves" – : for we are, even in the realm of logic, pessimists.

4

But *logical* evaluations are not the deepest or most fundamental to which our audacious mistrust can descend: faith in reason, with which the validity of these judgments must stand or fall, is, as faith, a *moral* phenomenon . . . Perhaps German pessimism still has one last step to take? Perhaps it has once again to set beside one another in fearful fashion its *credo* and its *absurdum*? And if *this* book is pessimistic even into the realm of morality, even to the point of going beyond faith in morality – should it not for this very reason be a German book? For it does in fact exhibit a contradiction and is not afraid of it: in this book faith in morality is withdrawn – but why? *Out of morality!* Or what else should we call that which informs it – and *us*? for our taste is for more modest expressions. But there is no doubt that a "thou shalt" still speaks to us too, that we too still obey a stern law set over us – and this is the last moral law which can make itself audible even to us, which even we know how to *live*, in this if in anything we too are still *men of conscience*: namely, in that we do not want to return to that which we consider outlived and decayed, to anything "unworthy of belief", be it called God, virtue, truth, justice, charity; that we do not permit ourselves any bridges-of-lies to ancient ideals; that we are hostile from the heart to everything that wants to mediate and mix with us; hostile to every kind of faith and Christianness existing today; hostile to the half-and-halfness of all romanticism and fatherland-worship; hostile, too, towards the pleasure-seeking and lack of conscience of the artists which would like to persuade us to worship where we no longer believe – for we are artists; hostile, in short, to the whole of European *feminism* (or idealism, if you prefer that word), which is for ever "drawing us upward" and precisely thereby for ever "bringing us down": – it is only as men of *this* conscience that we still feel ourselves related to the German integrity and piety of millennia, even if as its most questionable and final descendants, we immoralists, we godless men of today, indeed in a certain sense as its heirs, as the executors of its innermost will – a pessimistic will, as aforesaid, which does not draw back from denying itself because it denies with *joy*! In us there is accomplished – supposing you want a formula – the *self-sublimation of morality*. – –

5

– Finally, however: why should we have to say what we are and what we want and do not want so loudly and with such fervour? Let us view it more coldly, more distantly, more prudently, from a greater height; let us say it, as it is fitting it should be said between ourselves, so secretly that no one hears it, that no one hears *us*! Above all let us say it *slowly* . . . This preface is late but not too late – what, after all, do five or six years matter? A book like this, a problem like this, is in no hurry; we both, I just as much as my book, are friends of *lento*. It is not for nothing that I have been a philologist, perhaps I am a philologist still, that is to say, a teacher of slow reading: – in the end I also write slowly. Nowadays it is not only my habit, it is also to my taste – a malicious taste, perhaps? – no longer to write anything which does not reduce to despair every sort of man who is "in a hurry". For philology is that venerable art which demands of its votaries one thing above all: to go aside, to take time, to become still, to become slow – it is a goldsmith's art and connoisseurship of the *word* which has nothing but delicate, cautious work to do and achieves nothing if it does not achieve it *lento*. But for precisely this reason it is more necessary than ever today, by precisely this means does it entice and enchant us the most, in the midst of an age of "work", that is to say, of hurry, of indecent and perspiring haste, which wants to "get everything done" at once, including every old or new book: – this art does not so easily get anything done, it teaches to read *well*, that is to say, to read slowly, deeply, looking cautiously before and aft, with reservations, with doors left open, with delicate eyes and fingers . . . My patient friends, this book desires for itself only perfect readers and philologists: *learn* to read me well! –

Ruta, near Genoa, in the autumn of 1886

66

The Gay Science

[Book 4]

283

Preparatory human beings. – I welcome all signs that a more virile, warlike age is about to begin, which will restore honor to courage above all. For this age shall prepare the way for one yet higher, and it shall gather the strength that this higher age will require some day – the age that will carry heroism into the search for knowledge and that will *wage wars* for the sake of ideas and their consequences. To this end we now need many preparatory courageous human beings who cannot very well leap out of nothing, any more than out of the sand and slime of present-day civilization and metropolitanism – human beings who know how to be silent, lonely, resolute, and content and constant in invisible activities; human beings who are bent on seeking in all things for what in them must be *overcome*; human beings distinguished as much by cheerfulness, patience, unpretentiousness, and contempt for all great vanities as by magnanimity in victory and forbearance regarding the small vanities of the vanquished; human beings whose judgment concerning all victors and the share of chance in every victory and fame is sharp and free; human beings with their own festivals, their own working days, and their own periods of mourning, accustomed to command with assurance but instantly ready to obey when that is called for –

The Gay Science (1882–7), tr. Walter Kaufmann (New York: Random House, Inc., 1974). Selection: Bk 4, §§ 283–335, pp. 228–66 (excerpts); Bk 5, §§ 343–383, pp. 279–348 (excerpts).

equally proud, equally serving their own cause in both cases; more endangered human beings, more fruitful human beings, happier beings! For believe me: the secret for harvesting from existence the greatest fruitfulness and the greatest enjoyment is – to *live dangerously*! Build your cities on the slopes of Vesuvius! Send your ships into uncharted seas! Live at war with your peers and yourselves! Be robbers and conquerors as long as you cannot be rulers and possessors, you seekers of knowledge! Soon the age will be past when you could be content to live hidden in forests like shy deer. At long last the search for knowledge will reach out for its due; it will want to *rule* and *possess*, and you with it!

284

Faith in oneself. – Few people have faith in themselves. Of these few, some are endowed with it as with a useful blindness or a partial eclipse of their spirit (what would they behold if they could see to the bottom of themselves!), while the rest have to acquire it. Everything good, fine, or great they do is first of all an argument against the skeptic inside them. They have to convince or persuade *him*, and that almost requires genius. These are the great self-dissatisfied people.

285

Excelsior. – "You will never pray again, never adore again, never again rest in endless trust; you do not permit yourself to stop before any ultimate wisdom, ultimate goodness, ultimate power, while unharnessing your thoughts; you have no perpetual guardian and friend for your seven solitudes; you live without a view of mountains with snow on their peaks and fire in their hearts; there is no avenger for you any more nor any final improver; there is no longer any reason in what happens, no love in what will happen to you; no resting place is open any longer to your heart, where it only needs to find and no longer to seek; you resist any ultimate peace; you will the eternal recurrence of war and peace: man of renunciation, all this you wish to renounce? Who will give you the strength for that? Nobody yet has had this strength!"

There is a lake that one day ceased to permit itself to flow off; it formed a dam where it had hitherto flown off; and ever since this lake is rising higher and higher. Perhaps this very renunciation will also lend us the strength needed to bear this renunciation; perhaps man will rise ever higher as soon as he ceases to *flow out* into a god.

286

Interruption. – Here are hopes; but what will you hear and see of them if you have not experienced splendor, ardor, and dawns in your own souls? I can only remind you; more I cannot do. To move stones, to turn animals into men – is that what you want from me? Oh, if you are still stones and animals, then better look for your Orpheus.

287

Delight in blindness. – "My thoughts," said the wanderer to his shadow, "should show me where I stand; but they should not betray to me where I am going. I love my ignorance of the future and do not wish to perish of impatience and of tasting promised things ahead of time."

288

Elevated moods. – It seems to me that most people simply do not believe in elevated moods, unless these last for moments only or at most a quarter of an hour – except for those few who know at firsthand the longer duration of elevated feelings. But to be a human being with one elevated feeling – to be a single great mood incarnate – that

has hitherto been a mere dream and a delightful possibility; as yet history does not offer us any certain examples. Nevertheless history might one day give birth to such people, too – once a great many favorable preconditions have been created and determined that even the dice throws of the luckiest chance could not bring together today. What has so far entered our souls only now and then as an exception that made us shudder, might perhaps be the usual state for these future souls: a perpetual movement between high and low, the feeling of high and low, a continual ascent as on stairs and at the same time a sense of resting on clouds.

289

Embark! – Consider how every individual is affected by an overall philosophical justification of his way of living and thinking: he experiences it as a sun that shines especially for him and bestows warmth, blessings, and fertility on him; it makes him independent of praise and blame, self-sufficient, rich, liberal with happiness and good will; incessantly it refashions evil into good, leads all energies to bloom and ripen, and does not permit the petty weeds of grief and chagrin to come up at all. In the end one exclaims: How I wish that many such new suns were yet to be created! Those who are evil or unhappy and the exceptional human being – all these should also have their philosophy, their good right, their sunshine! What is needful is not pity for them. We must learn to abandon this arrogant fancy, however long humanity has hitherto spent learning and practicing it. What these people need is not confession, conjuring of souls, and forgiveness of sins; what is needful is a new *justice*! And a new watchword. And new philosophers. The moral earth, too, is round. The moral earth, too, has its antipodes. The antipodes, too, have the right to exist. There is yet another world to be discovered – and more than one. Embark, philosophers!

290

One thing is needful. – To "give style" to one's character – a great and rare art! It is practiced by those who survey all the strengths and weaknesses of their nature and then fit them into an artistic plan until every one of them appears as art and reason and even weaknesses delight the eye. Here a large mass of second nature has been added; there a piece of original nature has been removed – both times through long practice and daily work at it. Here the ugly that could not be removed is concealed; there it has been reinterpreted and made sublime. Much that is vague and resisted shaping has been saved and exploited for distant views; it is meant to beckon toward the far and immeasurable. In the end, when the work is finished, it becomes evident how the constraint of a single taste governed and formed everything large and small. Whether this taste was good or bad is less important than one might suppose, if only it was a single taste!

It will be the strong and domineering natures that enjoy their finest gaiety in such constraint and perfection under a law of their own; the passion of their tremendous will relents in the face of all stylized nature, of all conquered and serving nature. Even when they have to build palaces and design gardens they demur at giving nature freedom.

Conversely, it is the weak characters without power over themselves that *hate* the constraint of style. They feel that if this bitter and evil constraint were imposed upon them they would be demeaned; they become slaves as soon as they serve; they hate to serve. Such spirits – and they may be of the first rank – are always out to shape and interpret their environment as *free* nature: wild, arbitrary, fantastic, disorderly, and surprising. And they are well advised because it is only in this way that they can give pleasure to themselves. For one thing is needful: that a human being should *attain* satisfaction with himself, whether it be by means of this or that poetry and art; only then is a human being at all tolerable to behold. Whoever is dissatisfied with himself is continually ready for revenge, and we others will be his victims, if only by having to endure his ugly sight. For the sight of what is ugly makes one bad and gloomy. [...]

333

The meaning of knowing. – *Non ridere, non lugere, neque detestari, sed intelligere!* says Spinoza ["Not to laugh, not to lament, nor to detest, but to understand" (*Tractatus Politicus*, I. § 4) Tr.] as simply and sublimely as is his wont. Yet in the last analysis, what else is this *intelligere* than the form in which we come to feel the other three at

once? One result of the different and mutually opposed desires to laugh, lament, and curse? Before knowledge is possible, each of these instincts must first have presented its onesided view of the thing or event; after this comes the fight of these onesided views, and occasionally this results in a mean, one grows calm, one finds all three sides right, and there is a kind of justice and a contract; for by virtue of justice and a contract all these instincts can maintain their existence and assert their rights against each other. Since only the last scenes of reconciliation and the final accounting at the end of this long process rise to our consciousness, we suppose that *intelligere* must be something conciliatory, just, and good – something that stands essentially opposed to the instincts, while it is actually nothing but a *certain behavior of the instincts toward one another*.

For the longest time, conscious thought was considered thought itself. Only now does the truth dawn on us that by far the greatest part of our spirit's activity remains unconscious and unfelt. But I suppose that these instincts which are here contending against one another understand very well how to make themselves felt by, and how to hurt, *one another*. This may well be the source of that sudden and violent exhaustion that afflicts all thinkers (it is the exhaustion on a battlefield). Indeed, there may be occasions of concealed *heroism* in our warring depths, but certainly nothing divine that eternally rests in itself, as Spinoza supposed. *Conscious* thinking, especially that of the philosopher, is the least vigorous and therefore also the relatively mildest and calmest form of thinking; and thus precisely philosophers are most apt to be led astray about the nature of knowledge.

334

One must learn to love. – This is what happens to us in music: First one has to *learn to hear* a figure and melody at all, to detect and distinguish it, to isolate it and delimit it as a separate life. Then it requires some exertion and good will to *tolerate* it in spite of its strangeness, to be patient with its appearance and expression, and kindhearted about its oddity. Finally there comes a moment when we are *used* to it, when we wait for it, when we sense that we should miss it if it were missing; and now it continues to compel and enchant us relentlessly until we have become its humble and enraptured lovers who desire nothing better from the world than it and only it.

But that is what happens to us not only in music. That is how we have *learned to love* all things that we now love. In the end we are always rewarded for our good will, our patience, fair-mindedness, and gentleness with what is strange; gradually, it sheds its veil and turns out to be a new and indescribable beauty. That is its *thanks* for our hospitality. Even those who love themselves will have learned it in this way; for there is no other way. Love, too, has to be learned.

335

Long live physics! – How many people know how to observe something? Of the few who do, how many observe themselves? "Everybody is farthest away – from himself"; all who try the reins know this to their chagrin, and the maxim "know thyself!" addressed to human beings by a god, is almost malicious. That the case of self-observation is indeed as desperate as that is attested best of all by the manner in which *almost everybody* talks about the essence of moral actions – this quick, eager, convinced, and garrulous manner with its expression, its smile, and its obliging ardor! One seems to have the wish to say to you: "But my dear friend, precisely this is my specialty. You have directed your question to the one person who is entitled to answer you. As it happens, there is nothing about which I am as wise as about this. To come to the point: when a human being judges '*this is right*' and then infers '*therefore it must be done,*' and then proceeds to *do* what he has thus recognized as right and designated as necessary – then the essence of his action is *moral*."

But my friend, you are speaking of three actions instead of one. When you judge "this is right," that is an action, too. Might it not be possible that one could judge in a moral and in an immoral manner? *Why* do you consider this, precisely this, right?

"Because this is what my conscience tells me; and the voice of conscience is never immoral, for it alone determines what is to be moral."

But why do you *listen* to the voice of your conscience? And what gives you the right to consider such a judgment true and infallible? For this *faith* – is there no conscience for that? Have you never heard of an intellectual conscience? A conscience behind your "conscience"? Your judgment "this is right" has a pre-history in your instincts, likes, dislikes, experiences, and lack of experiences. "*How* did it originate there?" you must ask, and then also: "What is it that impels me to listen to it?" You can listen to its commands like a good soldier who hears his officer's command. Or like a woman who loves the man who commands. Or like a flatterer and coward who is afraid of the commander. Or like a dunderhead who obeys because no objection occurs to him. In short, there are a hundred ways in which you can listen to your conscience. But that you take this or that judgment for the voice of conscience – in other words, that you feel something to be right – may be due to the fact that you have never thought much about yourself and simply have accepted blindly that what you had been *told* ever since your childhood was right; or it may be due to the fact that what you call your duty has up to this point brought you sustenance and honors – and you consider it "right" because it appears to you as your own "condition of existence" (and that you have a *right* to existence seems irrefutable to you).

For all that, the *firmness* of your moral judgment could be evidence of your personal abjectness, of impersonality; your "moral strength" might have its source in your stubbornness – or in your inability to envisage new ideals. And, briefly, if you had thought more subtly, observed better, and learned more, you certainly would not go on calling this "duty" of yours and this "conscience" of yours duty and conscience. Your understanding *of the manner in which moral judgments have originated* would spoil these grand words for you, just as other grand words, like "sin" and "salvation of the soul" and "redemption" have been spoiled for you. – And now don't cite the categorical imperative, my friend! This term tickles my ear and makes me laugh despite your serious presence. It makes me think of the old Kant who had obtained the "thing in itself" *by stealth* – another very ridiculous thing! – and was punished for this when the "categorical imperative" crept stealthily into his heart and led him *astray – back* to "God," "soul," "freedom," and "immortality," like a fox who loses his way and goes astray back into his cage. Yet it had been *his* strength and cleverness that had *broken open* the cage!

What? You admire the categorical imperative within you? This "firmness" of your so-called moral judgment? This "unconditional" feeling that "here everyone must judge as I do"? Rather admire your *selfishness* at this point. And the blindness, pettiness, and frugality of your selfishness. For it is selfish to experience one's own judgment as a universal law; and this selfishness is blind, petty, and frugal because it betrays that you have not yet discovered yourself nor created for yourself an ideal of your own, your very own – for that could never be somebody else's and much less that of all, all!

Anyone who still judges "in this case everybody would have to act like this" has not yet taken five steps toward self-knowledge. Otherwise he would know that there neither are nor can be actions that are the same; that every action that has ever been done was done in an altogether unique and irretrievable way, and that this will be equally true of every future action; that all regulations about actions relate only to their coarse exterior (even the most inward and subtle regulations of all moralities so far); that these regulations may lead to some semblance of sameness, *but really only to some semblance*; that as one contemplates or looks back upon *any* action at all, it is and remains impenetrable; that our opinions about "good" and "noble" and "great" can never be *proved true* by our actions because every action is unknowable; that our opinions, valuations, and tables of what is good certainly belong among the most powerful levers in the involved mechanism of our actions, but that in any particular case the law of their mechanism is indemonstrable.

Let us therefore *limit* ourselves to the purification of our opinions and valuations and to the *creation of our own new tables of what is good*, and let us stop brooding about the "moral value of our actions"! Yes, my friends, regarding all the moral chatter of some about others it is time to feel nauseous. Sitting in moral judgment should offend our taste. Let us leave such chatter and such bad taste to those who have nothing else to do but drag the past a few steps further through time and who never live in the present – which is to say the many, the great majority. We, however, *want to become those we are* – human beings who are new, unique, incomparable, who give themselves laws, who create themselves. To that end we must become the best learners and discoverers of everything that is lawful and necessary in the world: we must become *physicists* in order to be able to be *creators* in this sense – while hitherto all valuations and ideals have been based on *ignorance* of physics or were constructed so as to *contradict* it. Therefore: long live physics! And even more so that which *compels* us to turn to physics – our honesty! [...]

[Book 5]

343

The meaning of our cheerfulness. – The greatest recent event – that "God is dead," that the belief in the Christian god has become unbelievable – is already beginning to cast its first shadows over Europe. For the few at least, whose eyes – the *suspicion* in whose eyes is strong and subtle enough for this spectacle, some sun seems to have set and some ancient and profound trust has been turned into doubt; to them our old world must appear daily more like evening, more mistrustful, stranger, "older." But in the main one may say: The event itself is far too great, too distant, too remote from the multitude's capacity for comprehension even for the tidings of it to be thought of as having *arrived* as yet. Much less may one suppose that many people know as yet *what* this event really means – and how much must collapse now that this faith has been undermined because it was built upon this faith, propped up by it, grown into it; for example, the whole of our European morality. This long plenitude and sequence of breakdown, destruction, ruin, and cataclysm that is now impending – who could guess enough of it today to be compelled to play the teacher and advance proclaimer of this monstrous logic of terror, the prophet of a gloom and an eclipse of the sun whose like has probably never yet occurred on earth?

Even we born guessers of riddles who are, as it were, waiting on the mountains, posted between today and tomorrow, stretched in the contradiction between today and tomorrow, we firstlings and premature births of the coming century, to whom the shadows that must soon envelop Europe really *should* have appeared by now – why is it that even we look forward to the approaching gloom without any real sense of involvement and above all without any worry and fear for *ourselves*? Are we perhaps still too much under the impression of the *initial consequences* of this event – and these initial consequences, the consequences for *ourselves*, are quite the opposite of what one might perhaps expect: They are not at all sad and gloomy but rather like a new and scarcely describable kind of light, happiness, relief, exhilaration, encouragement, dawn.

Indeed, we philosophers and "free spirits" feel, when we hear the news that "the old god is dead," as if a new dawn shone on us; our heart overflows with gratitude, amazement, premonitions, expectation. At long last the horizon appears free to us again, even if it should not be bright; at long last our ships may venture out again, venture out to face any danger; all the daring of the lover of knowledge is permitted again; the sea, *our* sea, lies open again; perhaps there has never yet been such an "open sea." –

344

How we, too, are still pious. – In science convictions have no rights of citizenship, as one says with good reason. Only when they decide to descend to the modesty of hypotheses, of a provisional experimental point of view, of a regulative fiction, they may be granted admission and even a certain value in the realm of knowledge – though always with the restriction that they remain under police supervision, under the police of mistrust. – But does this not mean, if you consider it more precisely, that a conviction may obtain admission to science only when it *ceases* to be a conviction? Would it not be the first step in the discipline of the scientific spirit that one would not permit oneself any more convictions?

Probably this is so; only we still have to ask: *To make it possible for this discipline to begin, must there not be some prior conviction* – even one that is so commanding and unconditional that it sacrifices all other convictions to itself? We see that science also rests on a faith; there simply is no science "without presuppositions." The question whether *truth* is needed must not only have been affirmed in advance, but affirmed to such a degree that the principle, the faith, the conviction finds expression: "*Nothing* is needed *more* than truth, and in relation to it everything else has only second-rate value."

This unconditional will to truth – what is it? Is it the will *not to allow oneself to be deceived*? Or is it the will *not to deceive*? For the will to truth could be interpreted in the second way, too – if only the special case "I do not want to deceive myself" is subsumed under the generalization "I do not want to deceive." But why not deceive? But why not allow oneself to be deceived?

Note that the reasons for the former principle belong to an altogether different realm from those for the second. One does not want to allow oneself to be deceived because one assumes that it is harmful, dangerous, calamitous to be deceived. In this sense, science would be a long-range prudence, a caution, a utility; but one could object

in all fairness: How is that? Is wanting not to allow oneself to be deceived really less harmful, less dangerous, less calamitous? What do you know in advance of the character of existence to be able to decide whether the greater advantage is on the side of the unconditionally mistrustful or of the unconditionally trusting? But if both should be required, much trust *as well as* much mistrust, from where would science then be permitted to take its unconditional faith or conviction on which it rests, that truth is more important than any other thing, including every other conviction? Precisely this conviction could never have come into being if both truth and untruth constantly proved to be useful, which is the case. Thus – the faith in science, which after all exists undeniably, cannot owe its origin to such a calculus of utility; it must have originated *in spite of* the fact that the disutility and dangerousness of "the will to truth," of "truth at any price" is proved to it constantly. "At any price": how well we understand these words once we have offered and slaughtered one faith after another on this altar!

Consequently, "will to truth" does *not* mean "I will not allow myself to be deceived" but – there is no alternative – "I will not deceive, not even myself"; *and with that we stand on moral ground.* For you only have to ask yourself carefully, "Why do you not want to deceive?" especially if it should seem – and it does seem! – as if life aimed at semblance, meaning error, deception, simulation, delusion, self-delusion, and when the great sweep of life has actually always shown itself to be on the side of the most unscrupulous *polytropoi.* Charitably interpreted, such a resolve might perhaps be a quixotism, a minor slightly mad enthusiasm; but it might also be something more serious, namely, a principle that is hostile to life and destructive. – "Will to truth" – that might be a concealed will to death.

Thus the question "Why science?" leads back to the moral problem: *Why have morality at all* when life, nature, and history are "not moral"? No doubt, those who are truthful in that audacious and ultimate sense that is presupposed by the faith in science *thus affirm another world* than the world of life, nature, and history; and insofar as they affirm this "other world" – look, must they not by the same token negate its counterpart, this world, *our* world? – But you will have gathered what I am driving at, namely, that it is still a *metaphysical faith* upon which our faith in science rests – that even we seekers after knowledge today, we godless anti-metaphysicians still take our fire, too, from the flame lit by a faith that is thousands of years old, that Christian faith which was also the faith of Plato, that God is the truth, that truth is divine. – But what if this should become more and more incredible, if nothing should prove to be divine any more unless it were error, blindness, the lie – if God himself should prove to be our most enduring lie? –

345

Morality as a problem. – The lack of personality always takes its revenge: A weakened, thin, extinguished personality that denies itself is no longer fit for anything good – least of all for philosophy. "Selflessness" has no value either in heaven or on earth. All great problems demand *great love*, and of that only strong, round, secure spirits who have a firm grip on themselves are capable. It makes the most telling difference whether a thinker has a personal relationship to his problems and finds in them his destiny, his distress, and his greatest happiness, or an "impersonal" one, meaning that he can do no better than to touch them and grasp them with the antennae of cold, curious thought. In the latter case nothing will come of it; that much one can promise in advance, for even if great problems should allow themselves to be *grasped* by them they would not permit frogs and weaklings to *hold on* to them; such has been their taste from time immemorial – a taste, incidentally, that they share with all redoubtable females.

Why is it then that I have never yet encountered anybody, not even in books, who approached morality in this personal way and who knew morality as a problem, and this problem as his own personal distress, torment, voluptuousness, and passion? It is evident that up to now morality was no problem at all but, on the contrary, precisely that on which after all mistrust, discord, and contradiction one could agree – the hallowed place of peace where our thinkers took a rest even from themselves, took a deep breath, and felt revived. I see nobody who ventured a *critique* of moral valuations; I miss even the slightest attempts of scientific curiosity, of the refined, experimental imagination of psychologists and historians that readily anticipates a problem and catches it in flight without quite knowing what it has caught. I have scarcely detected a few meager preliminary efforts to explore the *history of the origins* of these feelings and valuations (which is

something quite different from a critique and again different from a history of ethical systems). In one particular case I have done everything to encourage a sympathy and talent for this kind of history – in vain, as it seems to me today.

These historians of morality (mostly Englishmen) do not amount to much. Usually they themselves are still quite unsuspectingly obedient to one particular morality and, without knowing it, serve that as shield-bearers and followers – for example, by sharing that popular superstition of Christian Europe which people keep mouthing so guilelessly to this day, that what is characteristic of moral actions is selflessness, self-sacrifice, or sympathy and pity. Their usual mistaken premise is that they affirm some consensus of the nations, at least of tame nations, concerning certain principles of morals, and then they infer from this that these principles must be unconditionally binding also for you and me; or, conversely, they see the truth that among different nations moral valuations are *necessarily* different and then infer from this that *no* morality is at all binding. Both procedures are equally childish.

The mistake made by the more refined among them is that they uncover and criticize the perhaps foolish opinions of a people about their morality, or of humanity about all human morality – opinions about its origin, religious sanction, the superstition of free will, and things of that sort – and then suppose that they have criticized the morality itself. But the value of a command "thou shalt" is still fundamentally different from and independent of such opinions about it and the weeds of error that may have overgrown it – just as certainly as the value of a medication for a sick person is completely independent of whether he thinks about medicine scientifically or the way old women do. Even if a morality has grown out of an error, the realization of this fact would not as much as touch the problem of its value.

Thus nobody up to now has examined the *value* of that most famous of all medicines which is called morality; and the first step would be – for once to *question* it. Well then, precisely this is our task. – [...]

354

On the "genius of the species." – The problem of consciousness (more precisely, of becoming conscious of something) confronts us only when we begin to comprehend how we could dispense with it; and now physiology and the history of animals place us at the beginning of such comprehension (it took them two centuries to catch up with *Leibniz's* suspicion which soared ahead). For we could think, feel, will, and remember, and we could also "act" in every sense of that word, and yet none of all this would have to "enter our consciousness" (as one says metaphorically). The whole of life would be possible without, as it were, seeing itself in a mirror. Even now, for that matter, by far the greatest portion of our life actually takes place without this mirror effect; and this is true even of our thinking, feeling, and willing life, however offensive this may sound to older philosophers. *For what purpose*, then, any consciousness at all when it is in the main *superfluous*?

Now, if you are willing to listen to my answer and the perhaps extravagant surmise that it involves, it seems to me as if the subtlety and strength of consciousness always were proportionate to a man's (or animal's) *capacity for communication*, and as if this capacity in turn were proportionate to the *need for communication*. But this last point is not to be understood as if the individual human being who happens to be a master in communicating and making understandable his needs must also be most dependent on others in his needs. But it does seem to me as if it were that way when we consider whole races and chains of generations: Where need and distress have forced men for a long time to communicate and to understand each other quickly and subtly, the ultimate result is an excess of this strength and art of communication – as it were, a capacity that has gradually been accumulated and now waits for an heir who might squander it. (Those who are called artists are these heirs; so are orators, preachers, writers – all of them people who always come at the end of a long chain, "late born" every one of them in the best sense of that word and, as I have said, by their nature squanderers.)

Supposing that this observation is correct, I may now proceed to the surmise that *consciousness has developed only under the pressure of the need for communication*; that from the start it was needed and useful only between human beings (particularly between those who commanded and those who obeyed); and that it also developed only in proportion to the degree of this utility. Consciousness is really only a net of communication between human beings; it is only as such that it had to develop; a solitary human being who lived like a beast of prey would not have needed it. That our actions, thoughts, feelings, and movements enter our own consciousness – at least a part of them – that is the result of a "must" that for a terribly long time lorded it over man. As the most endangered animal, he *needed* help and protection, he needed his peers, he had to learn to express his distress and to make himself understood; and for all of this he needed "consciousness" first of all, he needed to "know" himself what distressed him, he needed to "know" how he felt, he needed to "know" what he thought. For, to say it once more: Man, like every living being, thinks continually without knowing it; the thinking that rises to *consciousness* is only the smallest part of all this – the most superficial and worst part – for only this conscious thinking *takes the form of words, which is to say signs of communication*, and this fact uncovers the origin of consciousness.

In brief, the development of language and the development of consciousness (*not* of reason but merely of the way reason enters consciousness) go hand in hand. Add to this that not only language serves as a bridge between human beings but also a mien, a pressure, a gesture. The emergence of our sense impressions into our own consciousness, the ability to fix them and, as it were, exhibit them externally, increased proportionately with the need to communicate them to *others* by means of signs. The human being inventing signs is at the same time the human being who becomes ever more keenly conscious of himself. It was only as a social animal that man acquired self-consciousness – which he is still in the process of doing, more and more.

My idea is, as you see, that consciousness does not really belong to man's individual existence but rather to his social or herd nature; that, as follows from this, it has developed subtlety only insofar as this is required by social or herd utility. Consequently, given the best will in the world to understand ourselves as individually as possible, "to know ourselves," each of us will always succeed in becoming conscious only of what is not individual but "average." Our thoughts themselves are continually governed by the character of consciousness – by the "genius of the species" that commands it – and translated back into the perspective of the herd. Fundamentally, all our actions are altogether incomparably personal, unique, and infinitely individual; there is no doubt of that. But as soon as we translate them into consciousness *they no longer seem to be.*

This is the essence of phenomenalism and per-spectivism as *I* understand them: Owing to the nature of *animal consciousness*, the world of which we can become conscious is only a surface- and sign-world, a world that is made common and meaner; whatever becomes conscious *becomes* by the same token shallow, thin, relatively stupid, general, sign, herd signal; all becoming conscious involves a great and thorough corruption, falsification, reduction to superficialities, and generalization. Ultimately, the growth of consciousness becomes a danger; and anyone who lives among the most conscious Euro-peans even knows that it is a disease.

You will guess that it is not the opposition of subject and object that concerns me here: This distinction I leave to the epistemologists who have become entangled in the snares of grammar (the metaphysics of the people). It is even less the opposition of "thing-in-itself" and appearance; for we do not "know" nearly enough to be entitled to any such distinction. We simply lack any organ for knowledge, for "truth": we "know" (or believe or imagine) just as much as may be *useful* in the interests of the human herd, the species; and even what is here called "utility" is ultimately also a mere belief, something imaginary, and per-haps precisely that most calamitous stupidity of which we shall perish some day.

355

The origin of our concept of "knowledge." – I take this explanation from the street. I heard one of the common people say, "he knew me right away." Then I asked myself: What is it that the common people take for knowledge? What do they want when they want "knowledge"? Nothing more than this: Something strange is to be reduced to something *familiar*. And we philosophers – have we really meant *more* than this when we have spoken of knowledge? What is familiar means what we are used to so that we no longer marvel at it, our everyday, some rule in which we are stuck, anything at all in which we feel at home. Look, isn't our need for knowledge precisely this need for the familiar, the will to uncover under everything strange, unusual, and questionable something that no longer disturbs us? Is it not the *instinct of fear* that bids us to know? And is the jubilation of those who attain knowledge not the jubilation over the restoration of a sense of security?

Here is a philosopher who fancied that the world was "known" when he had reduced it to the "idea." Was it not because the "idea" was so familiar to him and he was so well used to it – because he hardly was afraid of the "idea" any more?

How easily these men of knowledge are satis-fied! Just have a look at their principles and their solutions of the world riddle with this in mind! When they find something in things – under them, or behind them – that is unfortunately quite famil-iar to us, such as our multiplication tables or our logic, or our willing and desiring – how happy they are right away! For "what is familiar is known": on this they are agreed. Even the most cautious among them suppose that what is familiar is at least *more easily knowable* than what is strange, and that, for example, sound method demands that we start from the "inner world," from the "facts of consciousness," because this world is *more familiar to us*. Error of errors! What is familiar is what we are used to; and what we are used to is most difficult to "know" – that is, to see as a problem; that is, to see as strange, as distant, as "outside us."

The great certainty of the natural sciences in comparison with psychology and the critique of the elements of consciousness – one might almost say, with the *unnatural* sciences – is due precisely to the fact that they choose for their object what is *strange*, while it is almost contradictory and absurd to even *try* to choose for an object what is not-strange.

356

How things will become ever more "artistic" in Europe. – Even today, in our time of transition when so many factors cease to compel men, the care to make a living still compels almost all male Europeans to adopt a particular *role*, their so-called occupation. A few retain the freedom, a merely apparent freedom, to choose this role for them-selves; for most men it is chosen. The result is rather strange. As they attain a more advanced age, almost all Europeans confound themselves with their role; they become the victims of their own "good performance"; they themselves have forgot-ten how much accidents, moods, and caprice disposed of them when the question of their "vocation" was decided – and how many other roles they might perhaps have been *able* to play;

for now it is too late. Considered more deeply, the role has actually *become* character; and art, nature.

There have been ages when men believed with rigid confidence, even with piety, in their predestination for precisely this occupation, precisely this way of earning a living, and simply refused to acknowledge the element of accident, [mood], and caprice. With the help of this faith, classes, guilds, and hereditary trade privileges managed to erect those monsters of social pyramids that distinguish the Middle Ages and to whose credit one can adduce at least one thing: durability (and duration is a first-rate value on earth). But there are opposite ages, really democratic, where people give up this faith, and a certain cocky faith and opposite point of view advance more and more into the foreground – the Athenian faith that first becomes noticeable in the Periclean age, the faith of the Americans today that is more and more becoming the European faith as well: The individual becomes convinced that he can do just about everything and *can manage almost any role*, and everybody experiments with himself, improvises, makes new experiments, enjoys his experiments; and all nature ceases and becomes art.

After accepting this *role faith* – an artist's faith, if you will – the Greeks, as is well known, went step for step through a rather odd metamorphosis that does not merit imitation in all respects: *They really became actors.* As such they enchanted and overcame all the world and finally even "the power that had overcome the world" (for the *Graeculus histrio* vanquished Rome, and *not*, as innocents usually say, Greek culture). But what I fear, what is so palpable that today one could grasp it with one's hands, if one felt like grasping it, is that we modern men are even now pretty far along on the same road; and whenever a human being begins to discover how he is playing a role and how he *can* be an actor, he *becomes* an actor.

With this a new human flora and fauna emerge that could never have grown in more solid and limited ages; or at least they would be left there "below" under the ban and suspicion of lacking honor. It is thus that the maddest and most interesting ages of history always emerge, when the "actors," *all* kinds of actors, become the real masters. As this happens, another human type is disadvantaged more and more and finally made impossible; above all, the great "architects": The strength to build becomes paralyzed; the courage to make plans that encompass the distant future is discouraged; those with a genius for organization become scarce: who would still dare to undertake projects that would require thousands of years for their completion? For what is dying out is the fundamental faith that would enable us to calculate, to promise, to anticipate the future in plans of such scope, and to sacrifice the future to them – namely, the faith that man has value and meaning only insofar as he is *a stone in a great edifice*; and to that end he must be *solid* first of all, a "stone" – and above all not an actor!

To say it briefly (for a long time people will still keep silent about it): What will not be built any more henceforth, and *cannot* be built any more, is – a society in the old sense of that word; to build that, everything is lacking, above all the material. *All of us are no longer material for a society*; this is a truth for which the time has come. It is a matter of indifference to me that at present the most myopic, perhaps most honest, but at any rate noisiest human type that we have today, our good socialists, believe, hope, dream, and above all shout and write almost the opposite. Even now one reads their slogan for the future "free society" on all tables and walls. Free society? Yes, yes! But surely you know, gentlemen, what is required for building that? Wooden iron! The well-known wooden iron. And it must not even be wooden. [...]

370

What is romanticism? – It may perhaps be recalled, at least among my friends, that initially I approached the modern world with a few crude errors and overestimations and, in any case, hopefully. Who knows on the basis of what personal experiences, I understood the philosophical pessimism of the nineteenth century as if it were a symptom of a superior force of thought, of more audacious courage, and of more triumphant *fullness* of life than had characterized the eighteenth century, the age of Hume, Kant, Condillac, and the sensualists. Thus tragic insight appeared to me as the distinctive *luxury* of our culture, as its most precious, noblest, and most dangerous squandering, but, in view of its over-richness, as a *permissible* luxury. In the same way, I reinterpreted German music for myself as if it signified a Dionysian power of the German soul: I believed that I heard in it the earthquake through which some primeval force that had been dammed up for ages finally liberated itself – indifferent whether everything else that one calls culture might begin to tremble. You see, what I failed to recognize at that time both in philosophical pessimism and in German music was what is really their distinctive character – their *romanticism*.

What is romanticism? – Every art, every philosophy may be viewed as a remedy and an aid in the service of growing and struggling life; they always presuppose suffering and sufferers. But there are two kinds of sufferers: first, those who suffer from the *over-fullness of life* – they want a Dionysian art and likewise a tragic view of life, a tragic insight – and then those who suffer from the *impoverishment of life* and seek rest, stillness, calm seas, redemption from themselves through art and knowledge, or intoxication, convulsions, anaesthesia, and madness. All romanticism in art and insight corresponds to the dual needs of the latter type, and that included (and includes) Schopenhauer as well as Richard Wagner, to name the two most famous and pronounced romantics whom I *misunderstood* at that time – *not*, incidentally, to their disadvantage, as one need not hesitate in all fairness to admit. He that is richest in the fullness of life, the Dionysian god and man, cannot only afford the sight of the terrible and questionable but even the terrible deed and any luxury of destruction, decomposition, and negation. In his case, what is evil, absurd, and ugly seems, as it were, permissible, owing to an excess of procreating, fertilizing energies that can still turn any desert into lush farmland. Conversely, those who suffer most and are poorest in life would need above all mildness, peacefulness, and goodness in thought as well as deed – if possible, also a god who would be truly a god for the sick, a healer and savior; also logic, the conceptual understandability of existence – for logic calms and gives confidence – in short, a certain warm narrowness that keeps away fear and encloses one in optimistic horizons.

Thus I gradually learned to understand Epicurus, the opposite of a Dionysian pessimist; also the "Christian" who is actually only a kind of Epicurean – both are essentially romantics – and my eye grew ever sharper for that most difficult and captious form of *backward inference* in which the most mistakes are made: the backward inference from the work to the maker, from the deed to the doer, from the ideal to those who *need it*, from every way of thinking and valuing to the commanding need behind it.

Regarding all aesthetic values I now avail myself of this main distinction: I ask in every instance, "is it hunger or superabundance that has here become creative?" At first glance, another distinction may seem preferable – it is far more obvious – namely the question whether the desire to fix, to immortalize, the desire for *being* prompted creation, or the desire for destruction, for change, for future, for *becoming*. But both of these kinds of desire are seen to be ambiguous when one considers them more closely; they can be interpreted in accordance with the first scheme that is, as it seems to me, preferable. The desire for *destruction*, change, and becoming can be an expression of an overflowing energy that is pregnant with future (my term for this is, as is known, "Dionysian"); but it can also be the hatred of the ill-constituted, disinherited, and underprivileged, who destroy, *must* destroy, because what exists, indeed all existence, all being, outrages and provokes them. To understand this feeling, consider our anarchists closely.

The will to *immortalize* also requires a dual interpretation. It can be prompted, first, by gratitude and love; art with this origin will always be an art of apotheoses, perhaps dithyrambic like Rubens, or blissfully mocking like Hafiz, or bright and gracious like Goethe, spreading a Homeric light and glory over all things. But it can also be the tyrannic will of one who suffers deeply, who struggles, is tormented, and would like to turn what is most personal, singular, and narrow, the real idiosyncrasy of his suffering, into a binding law and compulsion – one who, as it were, revenges himself on all things by forcing his own image, the image of his torture, on them, branding them with it. This last version is *romantic pessimism* in its most expressive form, whether it be Schopenhauer's philosophy of will or Wagner's music – romantic pessimism, the last *great* event in the fate of our culture.

(That there still *could* be an altogether different kind of pessimism, a classical type – this premonition and vision belongs to me as inseparable from me, as my *proprium* and *ipsissimum*; only the word "classical" offends my ears, it is far too trite and has become round and indistinct. I call this pessimism of the future – for it comes! I see it coming! – *Dionysian* pessimism.)

371

We incomprehensible ones. – Have we ever complained because we are misunderstood, misjudged, misidentified, slandered, misheard, and not heard?

Precisely this is our fate – oh, for a long time yet! let us say, to be modest, until 1901 – it is also our distinction; we should not honor ourselves sufficiently if we wished that it were otherwise. We are misidentified – because we ourselves keep growing, keep changing, we shed our old bark, we shed our skins every spring, we keep becoming younger, fuller of future, taller, stronger, we push our roots ever more powerfully into the depths – into evil – while at the same time we embrace the heavens ever more lovingly, more broadly, imbibing their light ever more thirstily with all our twigs and leaves. Like trees we grow – this is hard to understand, as is all of life – not in one place only but everywhere, not in one direction but equally upward and outward and inward and downward; our energy is at work simultaneously in the trunk, branches, and roots; we are no longer free to do only one particular thing, to *be* only one particular thing.

This is our fate, as I have said; we grow in *height*; and even if this should be our fatality – for we dwell ever closer to the lightning – well, we do not on that account honor it less; it remains that which we do not wish to share, to make public – the fatality of the heights, *our* fatality.

372

Why we are no idealists. – Formerly philosophers were afraid of the senses. Have we perhaps unlearned this fear too much? Today all of us are believers in the senses, we philosophers of the present and the future, *not* in theory but in praxis, in practice.

They, however, thought that the senses might lure them away from their own world, from the cold realm of "ideas," to some dangerous southern island where they feared that their philosopher's virtues might melt away like snow in the sun. Having "wax in one's ears" was then almost a condition of philosophizing; a real philosopher no longer listened to life insofar as life is music; he *denied* the music of life – it is an ancient philosopher's superstition that all music is sirens' music.

We today are inclined to make the opposite judgment (which actually could be equally wrong), namely that *ideas* are worse seductresses than our senses, for all their cold and anemic appearance, and not even in spite of this appearance: they have always lived on the "blood" of the philosopher, they always consumed his senses and even, if you will believe us, his "heart." These old

philosophers were heartless; philosophizing was always a kind of vampirism. Looking at these figures, even Spinoza, don't you have a sense of something profoundly enigmatic and uncanny? Don't you notice the spectacle that unrolls before you, how they *become ever paler* – how desensualization is interpreted more and more ideally? Don't you sense a long concealed vampire in the background who begins with the senses and in the end is left with, and leaves, mere bones, mere clatter? I mean categories, formulas, *words* (for, forgive me, what was left of Spinoza, *amor intellectualis dei* ["intellectual love of God" (*Ethics* V.33ff.) Tr.], is mere clatter and no more than that: What is *amor*, what *deus*, if there is not a drop of blood in them?).

In sum: All philosophical idealism to date was something like a disease, unless it was, as it was in Plato's case, the caution of an over-rich and dangerous health, the fear of *over-powerful* senses, the prudence of a prudent Socratic. – Perhaps we moderns are merely not healthy enough *to be in need of* Plato's idealism? And we are not afraid of the senses because –

373

"Science" as a prejudice. – It follows from the laws of the order of rank that scholars, insofar as they belong to the spiritual middle class, can never catch sight of the really great problems and question marks; moreover, their courage and their eyes simply do not reach that far – and above all, their needs which led them to become scholars in the first place, their inmost assumptions and desires that things might be such and such, their fears and hopes all come to rest and are satisfied too soon. Take, for example, that pedantic Englishman, Herbert Spencer. What makes him "enthuse" in his way and then leads him to draw a line of hope, a horizon of desirability – that eventual reconciliation of "egoism and altruism" about which he raves – almost nauseates the likes of us; a human race that adopted such Spencerian perspectives as its ultimate perspectives would seem to us worthy of contempt, of annihilation! But the mere fact that he had to experience as his highest hope something that to others appears and may appear only as a disgusting possibility poses a question mark that Spencer would have been incapable of foreseeing.

It is no different with the faith with which so many materialistic natural scientists rest content nowadays, the faith in a world that is supposed to have its equivalent and its measure in human thought and human valuations – a "world of truth" that can be mastered completely and forever with the aid of our square little reason. What? Do we really want to permit existence to be degraded for us like this – reduced to a mere exercise for a calculator and an indoor diversion for mathematicians? Above all, one should not wish to divest existence of its *rich ambiguity*: that is a dictate of good taste, gentlemen, the taste of reverence for everything that lies beyond your horizon. That the only justifiable interpretation of the world should be one in which *you* are justified because one can continue to work and do research scientifically in *your* sense (you really mean, mechanistically?) – an interpretation that permits counting, calculating, weighing, seeing, and touching, and nothing more – that is a crudity and naiveté, assuming that it is not a mental illness, an idiocy.

Would it not be rather probable that, conversely, precisely the most superficial and external aspect of existence – what is most apparent, its skin and sensualization – would be grasped first – and might even be the only thing that allowed itself to be grasped? A "scientific" interpretation of the world, as you understand it, might therefore still be one of the *most stupid* of all possible interpretations of the world, meaning that it would be one of the poorest in meaning. This thought is intended for the ears and consciences of our mechanists who nowadays like to pass as philosophers and insist that mechanics is the doctrine of the first and last laws on which all existence must be based as on a ground floor. But an essentially mechanical world would be an essentially *meaningless* world. Assuming that one estimated the *value* of a piece of music according to how much of it could be counted, calculated, and expressed in formulas: how absurd would such a "scientific" estimation of music be! What would one have comprehended, understood, grasped of it? Nothing, really nothing of what is "music" in it!

374

Our new "infinite." – How far the perspective character of existence extends or indeed whether existence has any other character than this; whether existence without interpretation, without "sense," does not become "nonsense"; whether, on the other hand, all existence is not essentially actively engaged in *interpretation* – that cannot be decided even by the most industrious and most scrupulously conscientious analysis and self-examination of the intellect; for in the course of this analysis the human intellect cannot avoid seeing itself in its own perspectives, and *only* in these. We cannot look around our own corner: it is a hopeless curiosity that wants to know what other kinds of intellects and perspectives there *might* be; for example, whether some beings might be able to experience time backward, or alternately forward and backward (which would involve another direction of life and another concept of cause and effect). But I should think that today we are at least far from the ridiculous immodesty that would be involved in decreeing from our corner that perspectives are permitted only from this corner. Rather has the world become "infinite" for us all over again, inasmuch as we cannot reject the possibility that *it may include infinite interpretations*. Once more we are seized by a great shudder; but who would feel inclined immediately to deify again after the old manner this monster of an unknown world? And to worship the unknown henceforth as "the Unknown One"? Alas, too many *ungodly* possibilities of interpretation are included in the unknown, too much devilry, stupidity, and foolishness of interpretation – even our own human, all too human folly, which we know.

375

Why we look like Epicureans. – We are cautious, we modern men, about ultimate convictions. Our mistrust lies in wait for the enchantments and deceptions of the conscience that are involved in every strong faith, every unconditional Yes and No. How is this to be explained? Perhaps what is to be found here is largely the care of the "burned child," of the disappointed idealist; but there is also another, superior component: the jubilant curiosity of one who formerly stood in his corner and was driven to despair by his corner, and now delights and luxuriates in the opposite of a corner, in the boundless, in what is "free as such." Thus an almost Epicurean bent for knowledge develops that will not easily let go of the questionable character of things; also an aversion to big moral words and gestures; a taste that rejects all crude, foursquare opposites and is proudly conscious of its practice in having reservations. For this constitutes our pride, this slight tightening of the reins as our urge for certainty races ahead, this self-control of the rider during his wildest rides; for we still ride mad and fiery horses, and when we hesitate it is least of all danger that makes us hesitate.

376

Our slow periods. – This is how all artists and people of "works" feel, the motherly human type: at every division of their lives, which are always divided by a work, they believe that they have reached their goal; they would always patiently accept death with the feeling, "now we are ripe for it." This is not the expression of weariness – rather of a certain autumnal sunniness and mildness that the work itself, the fact that the work has become ripe, always leaves behind in the author. Then the tempo of life slows down and becomes thick like honey – even to the point of long *fermata*, of the faith in long *fermata* [a prolongation at the performer's discretion of a musical note, chord, or rest beyond its given time value: Tr.].

377

We who are homeless. – Among Europeans today there is no lack of those who are entitled to call themselves homeless in a distinctive and honorable sense: it is to them that I especially commend my secret wisdom and *gaya scienza*. For their fate is hard, their hopes are uncertain; it is quite a feat to devise some comfort for them – but what avail? We children of the future, how *could* we be at home in this today? We feel disfavor for all ideas that might lead one to feel at home even in this fragile, broken time of transition; as for its "realities," we do not believe that they will *last*. The ice that still supports people today has become very thin; the wind that brings the thaw is blowing; we ourselves who are homeless constitute a force that breaks open ice and other all too thin "realities."

We "conserve" nothing; neither do we want to return to any past periods; we are not by any means "liberal"; we do not work for "progress"; we do not need to plug up our ears against the sirens who in the market place sing of the future: their song about "equal rights," "a free society," "no more masters and no servants" has no allure for us. We simply do not consider it desirable that a realm of justice and concord should be established on earth (because it would certainly be the realm of the deepest leveling and *chinoiserie*); we are delighted with all who love, as we do, danger, war, and adventures, who refuse to compromise, to be captured, reconciled, and castrated; we count ourselves among conquerors; we think about the necessity for new orders, also for a new slavery – for every strengthening and enhancement of the human type also involves a new kind of enslavement. Is it not clear that with all this we are bound to feel ill at ease in an age that likes to claim the distinction of being the most humane, the mildest, and the most righteous age that the sun has ever seen? It is bad enough that precisely when we hear these beautiful words we have the ugliest suspicions. What we find in them is merely an expression – and a masquerade – of a profound weakening, of weariness, of old age, of declining energies. What can it matter to us what tinsel the sick may use to cover up their weakness? Let them parade it as their *virtue*; after all, there is no doubt that weakness makes one mild, oh so mild, so righteous, so inoffensive, so "humane"!

The "religion of pity" to which one would like to convert us – oh, we know the hysterical little males and females well enough who today need precisely this religion as a veil and make-up. We are no humanitarians; we should never dare to permit ourselves to speak of our "love of humanity"; our kind is not actor enough for that. Or not Saint-Simonist enough, not French enough. One really has to be afflicted with a *Gallic* excess of erotic irritability and enamored impatience to approach in all honesty the whole of humanity with one's lust!

Humanity! Has there ever been a more hideous old woman among all old women – (unless it were "truth": a question for philosophers)? No, we do not love humanity; but on the other hand we are not nearly "German" enough, in the sense in which the word "German" is constantly being used nowadays, to advocate nationalism and race hatred and to be able to take pleasure in the national scabies of the heart and blood poisoning that now leads the nations of Europe to delimit and barricade themselves against each other as if it were a matter of quarantine. For that we are too openminded, too malicious, too spoiled, also too well informed, too "traveled": we far prefer to live on mountains, apart, "untimely," in past or future centuries, merely in order to keep ourselves from experiencing the silent rage to which we know we should be condemned as eyewitnesses of politics that are desolating the German spirit by making it vain and that is, moreover, *petty* politics: to keep its own creation from immediately falling apart again, is it not finding it necessary to plant it between two deadly hatreds? *must* it not desire the eternalization of the European system of a lot of petty states?

We who are homeless are too manifold and mixed racially and in our descent, being "modern men," and consequently do not feel tempted to participate in the mendacious racial self-admiration and racial indecency that parades in Germany today as a sign of a German way of thinking and that is doubly false and obscene among the people of the "historical sense." We are, in one word – and let this be our word of honor – *good Europeans*, the heirs of Europe, the rich, oversupplied, but also overly obligated heirs of thousands of years of European spirit. As such, we have also outgrown Christianity and are averse to it – precisely because we have grown out of it, because our ancestors were Christians who in their Christianity were uncompromisingly upright: for their faith they willingly sacrificed possessions and position, blood and fatherland. We – do the same. For what? For our unbelief? For every kind of unbelief? No, you know better than that, friends! The hidden Yes in you is stronger than all Nos and Maybes that afflict you and your age like a disease; and when you have to embark on the sea, you emigrants, you, too, are compelled to this by – a *faith*! [...]

382

The great health. – Being new, nameless, hard to understand, we premature births of an as yet un-proven future need for a new goal also a new means – namely, a new health, stronger, more seasoned, tougher, more audacious, and gayer than any previous health. Whoever has a soul that craves to have experienced the whole range of values and desiderata to date, and to have sailed around all the coasts of this ideal "mediterranean"; whoever wants to know from the adventures of his own most authentic experience how a discoverer and conqueror of the ideal feels, and also an artist, a saint, a legislator, a sage, a scholar, a pious man, a soothsayer, and one who stands divinely apart in the old style – needs one thing above everything else: the *great health* – that one does not merely

have but also acquires continually, and must acquire because one gives it up again and again, and must give it up.

And now, after we have long been on our way in this manner, we argonauts of the ideal, with more daring perhaps than is prudent, and have suffered shipwreck and damage often enough, but are, to repeat it, healthier than one likes to permit us, dangerously healthy, ever again healthy – it will seem to us as if, as a reward, we now confronted an as yet undiscovered country whose boundaries nobody has surveyed yet, something beyond all the lands and nooks of the ideal so far, a world so overrich in what is beautiful, strange, questionable, terrible, and divine that our curiosity as well as our craving to possess it has got beside itself – alas, now nothing will sate us any more!

After such vistas and with such a burning hunger in our conscience and science, how could we still be satisfied with *present-day man*? It may be too bad but it is inevitable that we find it difficult to remain serious when we look at his worthiest goals and hopes, and perhaps we do not even bother to look any more.

Another ideal runs ahead of us, a strange, tempting, dangerous ideal to which we should not wish to persuade anybody because we do not readily concede *the right to it* to anyone: the ideal of a spirit who plays naively – that is, not deliberately but from overflowing power and abundance – with all that was hitherto called holy, good, untouchable, divine; for whom those supreme things that the people naturally accept as their value standards, signify danger, decay, debasement, or at least recreation, blindness, and temporary self-oblivion; the ideal of a human, superhuman well-being and benevolence that will often appear *inhuman* – for example, when it confronts all earthly seriousness so far, all solemnity in gesture, word, tone, eye, morality, and task so far, as if it were their most incarnate and involuntary parody – and in spite of all of this, it is perhaps only with him that *great seriousness* really begins, that the real question mark is posed for the first time, that the destiny of the soul changes, the hand moves forward, the tragedy *begins*.

383

Epilogue. – But as I slowly, slowly paint this gloomy question mark at the end and am still willing to remind my readers of the virtues of the right reader – what forgotten and unknown virtues they are! – it happens that I hear all around me the most malicious, cheerful, and koboldish laughter: the spirits of my own book are attacking me, pull my ears, and call me back to order. "We can no longer stand it," they shout at me; "away, away with this raven-black music! Are we not surrounded by bright morning? And by soft green grass and grounds, the kingdom of the dance? Has there ever been a better hour for gaiety? Who will sing a song for us, a morning song, so sunny, so light, so fledged that it will *not* chase away the blues but invite them instead to join in the singing and dancing? And even simple, rustic bagpipes would be better than such mysterious sounds, such swampy croaking, voices from the grave and marmot whistles as you have employed so far to regale us in your wilderness, Mr. Hermit and Musician of the Future! No! Not such tones! Let us strike up more agreeable, more joyous tones!"

Is that your pleasure, my impatient friends? Well then, who would not like to please you? My bagpipes are waiting, and so is my throat – which may sound a bit rough; but put up with it, after all we are in the mountains. At least what you are about to hear is new; and if you do not understand it, if you misunderstand the *singer*, what does it matter? That happens to be "the singer's curse." His music and manner you will be able to hear that much better, and to his pipes – dance that much better. Is that your *will*?

Select Bibliography of Recent Literature

The following list represents some of the best single-author studies that have been published or reissued since 1990.

Adorno, Theodor. *Hegel: Three Studies*. Cambridge, MA: MIT Press, 1994.

Ariew, Roger. *Descartes and the Last Scholastics*. Ithaca: Cornell University Press, 1999.

Atherton, Margaret. *Berkeley's Revolution in Vision*. Ithaca: Cornell University Press, 1991.

Ayers, Michael. *Locke*. 2 vols. London: Routledge, 1991.

Berman, David. *George Berkeley: Idealism and the Man*. Oxford: Oxford University Press, 1996.

Blondel, Eric. *Nietzsche: The Body and Culture*. Stanford, CA: Stanford University Press, 1991.

Carver, Terrell. *The Postmodern Marx*. University Park: Pennsylvania State University Press, 1999.

Cohen, G. A. *Karl Marx's Theory of History: A Defense*. First expanded edn. Oxford: Oxford University Press, 2001.

Cranston, Maurice. *Jean-Jacques: The Early Life of Jean-Jacques Rousseau, 1712–1754*. Chicago: University of Chicago Press, 1991.

Cranston, Maurice. *The Noble Savage: Jean-Jacques Rousseau 1754–1762*. Chicago: University of Chicago Press, 1999.

Cranston, Maurice. *Solitary Self: Jean-Jacques Rousseau in Exile and Adversity*. Chicago: University of Chicago Press, 1999.

Donner, Wendy. *The Liberal Self: John Stuart Mill's Moral and Political Philosophy*. Ithaca: Cornell University Press, 1992.

Forster, M. *Hegel's Idea of a Phenomenology of Spirit*. Chicago: University of Chicago Press, 1998.

Friedman, Michael. *Kant and the Exact Sciences*. Cambridge, MA: Harvard University Press, 1992.

Garber, Daniel. *Descartes' Metaphysical Physics*. Chicago: University of Chicago Press, 1992.

Garff, Joakim. *Søren Kierkegaard*. Princeton, NJ: Princeton University Press, 2001.

Gaukroger, Stephen. *Descartes: An Intellectual Biography*. Oxford: Oxford University Press, 1995.

Guyer, Paul. *Kant and the Experience of Freedom*. Cambridge: Cambridge University Press, 1993.

Hannay, Alastair. *Kierkegaard: A Biography*. Cambridge: Cambridge University Press, 2001.

Harris, H. S. *Hegel's Ladder*. 2 vols. Indianapolis: Hackett Publishing Co., 1997.

Harris, Ian. *The Mind of John Locke: A Study of Political Theory in Its Intellectual Setting*. Cambridge: Cambridge University Press, 1998.

Harrison, Ross. *Bentham*. London: Routledge, 1999.

Hollingdale, R. J. *Nietzsche: The Man and His Philosophy*. 2nd rev. edn. Cambridge: Cambridge University Press, 2001.

Janaway, Christopher. *Self and World in Schopenhauer's Philosophy*. Oxford: Oxford University Press, 1999.

Janaway, Christopher. *Willing and Nothingness: Schopenhauer as Nietzsche's Educator*. Oxford: Clarendon Press, 1998.

Jolley, Nicholas. *Locke: His Philosophical Thought*. Oxford: Oxford University Press, 1999.

Jolley, Nicholas. *The Light of the Soul: Theories of Ideas in Leibniz, Malebranche, and Descartes*. Oxford: Clarendon Press, 1998.

Kirmmse, Bruce H. *Kierkegaard in Golden Age Denmark*. Bloomington: Indiana University Press, 1990.

Kitcher, Patricia. *Kant's Transcendental Psychology*. Oxford: Oxford University Press, 1990.

Kraynak, Robert P. *History and Modernity in the Thought of Thomas Hobbes*. Ithaca: Cornell University Press, 1990.

Kuehn, Manfred. *Kant: A Biography*. Cambridge: Cambridge University Press, 2001.

Lehrer, Keith. *Thomas Reid*. London: Routledge, 1999.

Magee, Bryan. *The Philosophy of Schopenhauer*. Rev. edn. Oxford: Oxford University Press, 1997.

Manuel, Frank E. *A Requiem for Karl Marx*. Cambridge, MA: Harvard University Press, 1997.

Martinich, A. P. *Hobbes: A Biography*. Cambridge: Cambridge University Press, 1999.

Martinich, A. P. *The Two Gods of Leviathan: Thomas Hobbes on Religion and Politics*. Cambridge: Cambridge University Press, 1992.

Mason, Richard. *The God of Spinoza: A Philosophical Study*. Cambridge: Cambridge University Press, 1999.

Mercer, Christia. *Leibniz's Metaphysics: Its Origins and Development*. Cambridge: Cambridge University Press, 2001.

Mossner, Ernest Campbell. *The Life of David Hume*. Oxford: Clarendon Press, 2001.

Nadler, Steven. *Spinoza: A Life*. Cambridge: Cambridge University Press, 1999.

Nadler, Steven. *Malebranche and Ideas*. Oxford: Oxford University Press, 1992.

Pappas, George. *Berkeley's Thought*. Ithaca: Cornell University Press, 2000.

Pinkard, Terry P. *Hegel: A Biography*. Cambridge: Cambridge University Press, 2000.

Rockmore, T. *Before and After Hegel: A Historical Introduction to Hegel's Thought*. Berkeley: University of California Press, 1993.

Rowe, William L. *Thomas Reid on Freedom and Morality*. Ithaca: Cornell University Press, 1991.

Rutherford, Donald. *Leibniz and the Rational Order of Nature*. Cambridge: Cambridge University Press, 1997.

Safranski, Rüdiger. *Schopenhauer and the Wild Years of Philosophy*. Cambridge, MA: Harvard University Press, 1991.

Safranski, Rüdiger. *Nietzsche: A Philosophical Biography*. New York: W. W. Norton & Co., 2001.

Schouls, Peter A. *Reasoned Freedom: John Locke and Enlightenment*. Ithaca: Cornell University Press, 1992.

Semple, Janet. *Bentham's Prison: A Study of the Panopticon Penitentiary*. Oxford: Clarendon Press, 1993.

Skorupski, John. *John Stuart Mill*. London: Routledge, 1999.

Sleigh, R. C. *Leibniz and Arnauld*. New Haven, CT: Yale University Press, 1990.

Tuck, Richard. *Hobbes*. Oxford: Oxford University Press, 1991.

Wheen, Francis. *Karl Marx: A Life*. New York: W. W. Norton & Co., 2000.

Yirmiyahu, Yovel. *Spinoza and Other Heretics*. 2 vols. Princeton, NJ: Princeton University Press, 1992.

Index

Index

Index

Index compiled by Indexing Specialists